A QUIET WILL

THE LIFE OF CLARA BARTON

BY

WILLIAM E. BARTON

1922

Discover more lost history from BIG BYTE BOOKS

Contents

INTRODUCTION

The life of Clara Barton is a story of unique and permanent interest; but it is more than an interesting story. It is an important chapter in the history of our country, and in that of the progress of philanthropy in this country and the world. Without that chapter, some events of large importance can never be adequately understood.

Hers was a long life. She lived to enter her tenth decade, and when she died was still so normal in the soundness of her bodily organs and in the clarity of her mind and memory that it seemed she might easily have lived to see her hundredth birthday. Hers was a life spent largely in the Nation's capital. She knew personally every president from Lincoln to Roosevelt, and was acquainted with nearly every man of prominence in our national life. When she went abroad, her associates were people of high rank and wide influence in their respective countries. No American woman received more honor while she lived, either at home or abroad, and how worthily she bore these honors those know best who knew her best.

The time has come for the publication of a definitive biography of Clara Barton. Such a book could not earlier have been prepared. The "Life of Clara Barton," by Percy H. Epler, published in 1915, was issued to meet the demand which rose immediately after her death for a comprehensive biography, and it was published with the full approval of Miss Barton's relatives and of her literary executors, including the author of the present work. But,

by agreement, the two large vaults containing some tons of manuscripts which Miss Barton left, were not opened until after the publication of Mr. Epler's book. It was the judgment of her literary executors, concurred in by Mr. Epler, that this mine of information could not be adequately explored within any period consistent with the publication of a biography such as he contemplated. For this reason, the two vaults remained unopened until his book was on the market. The contents of these vaults, containing more than forty closely packed boxes, is the chief source of the present volume, and this abundant material has been supplemented by letters and personal reminiscences from Clara Barton's relatives and intimate friends.

Clara Barton considered often the question of writing her own biography. A friend urged this duty upon her in the spring of 1876, and she promised to consider the matter. But the incessant demands made upon her time by duties that grew more steadily imperative prevented her doing this.

In 1906 the request came to her from a number of school-children that she would tell about her childhood; and she wrote a little volume of one hundred and twenty-five pages, published in 1907 by Baker and Taylor, entitled, *The Story of my Childhood*. She was gratified by the reception of this little book, and seriously considered using it as the corner stone of her long contemplated autobiography. She wrote a second section of about fifteen thousand words, covering her girlhood and her experiences as a teacher at home and in Borden town, New Jersey. This was never published, and has been utilized in this present biography.

Beside these two formal and valuable contributions toward her biography, she left journals covering most of the years from her girlhood until her death, besides vast quantities of letters received by her and copies of her replies. Her personal letters to her intimate friends were not copied, as a rule, but it has been possible to gather some, hundreds of these. Letter-books, scrap-books, newspaper clippings, magazine articles, records of the American Red Cross, and papers, official and personal, swell the volume of material for this book to proportions not simply embarrassing, but almost overwhelming.

She appears never to have destroyed anything. Her temperament and the habits of a lifetime impelled her to save every scrap of material bearing upon her work and the subjects in which she was interested. She gathered, and with her own hand labeled, and neatly tied up her documents, and preserved them against the day when she should be able to sift and classify them and prepare them for such use as might ultimately be made of them. It troubled her that she was leaving these in such great bulk, and she hoped vainly for the time when she could go through them, box by box, and put them into shape. But they accumulated far more rapidly than she could have assorted them, and so they were left until her death, and still remained untouched, until December, 1915, when the vaults were opened and the heavy task began of examining this material, selecting from it the papers that tell the whole story of her life, and preparing the present volumes. If this book is large, it is because the material compelled it to be so. It could easily have been ten times as thick.

The will of Clara Barton named as her executor her beloved and trusted nephew, Stephen E. Barton. It also named a committee of literary executors, to whom she entrusted the use of her manuscripts for such purpose, biographical or otherwise, as they should deem best. The author of these volumes was named by her as a member of that committee. The committee elected him as its chairman, and requested him to undertake the preparation of the biography. This task was undertaken gladly, for the writer knew and loved his kinswoman and held her in honor and affection; but he knew too well the magnitude of the task ahead of him to be altogether eager to accept it. The burden, however, has been measurably lightened by the assistance of Miss Saidee F. Riccius, a grand-niece of Miss Barton, who, under the instruction of the literary executors, and the immediate direction of Stephen E. Barton and the author, has rendered invaluable service, without which the author could not have undertaken this work.

In her will, written a few days before her death, Miss Barton virtually apologized to the committee and to her biographer for the heavy task which she bequeathed to them. She said:

"I regret exceedingly that such a labor should devolve upon my friends as the overlooking of the letters of a lifetime, which should properly be done by me, and shall be, if I am so fortunate as to regain a sufficient amount of strength to enable me to do it. I have never destroyed my letters, regarding them as the surest chronological testimony of my life, whenever I could find the time to attempt to write it. That time has never come to me, and the letters still wait my call."

They still were there, undisturbed, thousands of them, when the vaults were opened, and none of them have been destroyed or mutilated. They are of every sort, personal and official; and they bear their consistent and cumulative testimony to her indefatigability, her patience, her heroic resolution, and most of all to her greatness of heart and integrity of soul.

Interesting and valuable in their record of every period and almost every day and hour of her long and eventful life, they are the indisputable record of the birth and development of the organization which almost single-handed she created, the American Red Cross.

Among those who suggested to Miss Barton the desirability of her writing the story of her own life, was Mr. Houghton, senior partner in the firm of Houghton, Mifflin and Company. He had one or more personal conferences with her relating to this matter. Had she been able to write the story of her own life, she would have expected it to be published by that firm. It is to the author a gratifying circumstance that this work, which must take the place of her autobiography, is published by the firm with whose senior member she first discussed the preparation of such a work.

The author of this biography was a relative and friend of Clara Barton, and knew her intimately. By her request he conducted her funeral services, and spoke the last words at her grave. His own knowledge of her has been supplemented and greatly enlarged by the personal reminiscences of her nearer relatives and of the friends who lived under her roof, and those who accompanied her on her many missions of mercy.

In a work where so much compression was inevitable, some incidents may well have received scant mention which deserved fuller treatment. The question of proportion is never an easy one to settle in a work of this character. If she had given any direction, it would have been that little be said about her, and much about the work she loved. That work, the founding of the American Red Cross, must receive marked emphasis in a Life of Clara Barton: for she was its mother. She conceived the American Red Cross, carried it under her heart for years before it could be brought forth, nurtured it in its cradle, and left it to her country and the world, an organization whose record in the great World War shines bright against that black cloud of horror, as the emblem of mercy and of hope.

Wherever, in America or in lands beyond, the flag of the Red Cross flies beside the Stars and Stripes, there the soul of Clara Barton marches on.

First Church Study Oak Park, July 16, 1921

ATTEMPT AT AUTOBIOGRAPHY

Though she had often been importuned to furnish to the public some account of her life and work, Clara Barton's first autobiographical outline was not written until September, 1876, when Susan B. Anthony requested her to prepare a sketch of her life for an encyclopedia of noted women of America. Miss Barton labored long over her reply. She knew that the story must be short, and that she must clip conjunctions and prepositions and omit "all the sweetest and best things." When she had finished the sketch, she was appalled at its length, and still was unwilling that anyone else should make it shorter; so she sent it with stamps for its return in case it should prove too long. "It has not an adjective in it," she said.

Her original draft is still preserved, and reads as follows:

For Susan B. Anthony Sketch for Cyclopedia

September, 1876

Barton, Clara; her father, Capt. Stephen Barton, a non-commissioned officer under "Mad Anthony Wayne," was a farmer in Oxford, Mass. Clara, youngest child, finished her education at Clinton, N.Y. Teacher, popularized free schools in New Jersey.

First woman appointed to an independent clerkship by Government at Washington.

On outbreak of Civil War, went to aid suffering soldiers. Labored in advance and independent of commissions. Never in hospitals; selecting as scene of operations the battle-field from its earliest moment, 'till the wounded and dead were removed or cared for; carrying her own supplies by Government transportation.

At the battles of Cedar Mountain, Second Bull Run, Chantilly, South Mountain, Falmouth and "Old Fredericksburg," Siege of Charleston, Morris Island, Wagner, Wilderness, Fredericksburg, The Mine, Deep Bottom, through sieges of Petersburg and Richmond under Butler and Grant.

At Annapolis on arrival of prisoners.

Established search for missing soldiers, and, aided by Dorence Atwater, enclosed cemetery, identified and marked the graves of Andersonville.

Lectured on Incidents of the War in 1866-67. In 1869 went to Europe for health. In Switzerland on outbreak of Franco-Prussian War; tendered services. Was invited by Grand Duchess of Baden, daughter of Emperor William, to aid in establishing her hospitals. On fall of Strassburg entered with German Army, remained eight months, instituted work for women which held twelve hundred persons from beggary and clothed thirty thousand.

Entered Metz on its fall. Entered Paris the day succeeding the fall of Commune; remained two months, distributing money and clothing which she carried. Met the poor of every besieged city of France, giving help.

Is representative of the "Comité International of the Red Cross" of Geneva. Honorary and only woman member of Comite de Strasbourgoes. Was decorated with the Gold Cross of Remembrance by the Grand Duke and

Duchess of Baden and with the "Iron Cross" by the Emperor and Empress of Germany.

Miss Anthony regarded the sketch with the horror of offended modesty.

"For Heaven's sake, Clara," she wrote, "put some flesh and clothes on this skeleton!"

Thus admonished, Miss Barton set to work to drape the bones of her first attempt, and was in need of some assistance from Miss Anthony and others. The work as completed was not wholly her own. The adjectives, which had been conspicuously absent from the first draft together with some characterizations of Miss Barton and her work, were supplied by Miss Anthony and her editors. It need not here be reprinted in its final form; for it is accessible in Miss Anthony's book. As it finally appeared, it is several times as long as when Clara Barton wrote it, and is more Miss Anthony's than Miss Barton's.

In the foregoing account, mention is made of her being an official member of the International Committee of the Red Cross. In that capacity she did not at that time represent any American organization known as the Red Cross, for there was no such body. Although such an organization had been in existence in Europe from the time of our Civil War, and the Reverend Dr. Henry W. Bellows, late of the Christian Commission, had most earnestly endeavored to organize a branch of it in this country, and to secure official representation from America in the international body, the proposal had been met not merely by indifference, but by hostility.

Clara Barton wrote her autobiographical sketch from a sanitarium. She had not yet recovered from the strain of her service in the Franco-Prussian War. One reason why she did not recover more rapidly was that she was bearing on her heart the burden of this as yet unborn organization, and as yet had found no friends of sufficient influence and faith to afford to America a share in the honor of belonging to the sisterhood of nations that marched under that banner.

The outbreak of the World War found America unprepared save only in her wealth of material resources, her high moral purpose, and her ability to adapt her forms of organized life to changed and unwelcome conditions. The rapidity with which she increased her army and her navy to a strength that made it possible for her to turn the scale, where the fate of the world hung trembling in the balance, was not more remarkable than her skill in adapting her institutions of peace to the exigencies of war. Most of the agencies, which, under the direction of civilians, ministered to men in arms had either to be created out of hand or adapted from institutions formed in time of peace and for other objects. But the American Red Cross was already organized and in active service. It was a factor in the fight from the first day of the world's agony, through the invasion of Belgium, and the three years of our professed neutrality; and by the time of America's own entrance into the war it had assumed such proportions that everywhere the Red Cross was seen floating beside the Stars and Stripes. everyone knew what it stood for. It was the emblem of mercy, even as the flag of our Nation was the symbol of liberty and the hope of the world.

The history of the American Red Cross cannot be written apart from the story of its founder, Clara Barton.

For years before it came into being, her voice almost alone pleaded for it, and to her persistent and almost sole endeavor it came at length to be established in America. For other years she was its animating spirit, its voice, its soul. Had she lived to see its work in the great World War, she would have been humbly and unselfishly grateful for her part in its beginnings, and overjoyed that it had outgrown them. The story of the founding and of the early history of the American Red Cross is the story of Clara Barton.

THE BIRTH OF CLARA BARTON

Clara Barton was a Christmas gift to the world. She was born December 25, 1821. Her parents named her Clarissa Harlowe. It was a name with interesting literary associations.

Novels now grow overnight and are forgotten in a day. The paper mills are glutted with the waste of yesterday's popular works of fiction; and the perishability of paper is all that prevents the stopping of all the wheels of progress with the accumulation of obsolete "best-sellers." But it was not so in 1821. The novels of Samuel Richardson, issued in the middle of the previous century, were still popular. He wrote "Pamela; or, Virtue Rewarded," a novel named for its heroine, a pure and simple-minded country girl, who repelled the dishonorable proposals of her employer until he came to respect her, and married her, and they lived happily ever after. The plot of this story lives again in a thousand moving-picture dramas, in which the heroine is a shop girl or an art student; but Richardson required two volumes to tell the story, and it ran through five editions in a year. He also wrote "Sir Charles Grandison," and it required six volumes to portray that hero's smug priggishness; but the Reverend Dr. Finney, president of Oberlin College, who was also the foremost evangelist of his time, and whose system of theology wrought in its day a revolution, was not the only distinguished man who bore the name of Charles Grandison.

But Richardson's greatest literary triumph was "Clarissa Harlowe." Lady Mary Wortley Montagu was not far wrong when she declared that the chambermaids of all nations wept over Pamela, and that all the ladies of quality were on their knees to Richardson imploring him to spare Clarissa. Clarissa was not a servant like Pamela: she was a lady of quality, and she had a lover socially her equal, but morally on a par with a considerable number of the gentry of his day. His name, Lovelace, became the popular designation of the gentleman profligate. Clarissa's sorrows at his hands ran through eight volumes, and, as the lachrymose sentiment ran out to volume after volume, the gentlewomen of the English-reading world wept tears that might have made another flood.

Samuel Richardson wrote the story of "Clarissa Harlowe" in 1748, but the story still was read, and the name of the heroine was loved, in 1821.

But Clarissa Harlowe Barton did not permanently bear the incubus of so long a name. Among her friends she was always Clara, and though for years she signed her name "Clara H. Barton," the convenience and rhythm of the shorter name won over the time-honored sentiment attached to the title of the novel, and the world knows her simply as Clara Barton.

He who rides on the electric cars from Worcester to Webster will pass Bartlett's Upper Mills, where a weather-beaten sign at the crossroads points the way "To Clara Barton's Birthplace." About a mile from the main street, on the summit of a rounded hill, the visitor will find the house where she was bom. It stands with its side to the road, a hall dividing it through the middle. It is an unpretentious home, but comfortable, one story high at the eaves, but rising with the rafters to afford elevation for chambers upstairs. In the rear room, on the left side, on the ground floor, the children of the Barton family were born. Clara was the fifth and youngest child, ten years younger than her sister next older. The eldest child, Dorothy, was born October 2, 1804, and died April 19, 1846. The next two children were sons, Stephen, the third to bear the name, born March 29, 1806, and David, born August 15, 1808. Then came another daughter, Sarah, born March 20, 1811. These four children followed each other at intervals of a little more than two years; but Clara had between her and the other children the wide gap of more than a decade. Her brothers were fifteen and thirteen, respectively, and her sister was "going on eleven" when she arrived. She came into a world that was already well grown up and fully occupied with concerns of its own. Had there been between her and the other children an ascending series of four or five graduated steps of heads, the first a little taller than her own, and the others rising in orderly sequence, the rest of the universe would not have been quite so formidable; but she was the sole representative of babyhood in the home at the time of her arrival. So she began her somewhat solitary pilgrimage, from a cradle fringed about with interested and affectionate observers, all of whom had been babies a good while before, but had forgotten about it, into that vast and vague domain inhabited by the adult portion of the human race; and while she was not unattended, her journey had its elements of solitude.

PARENTAGE AND INFANCY

Captain Stephen Barton won his military title by that system of post-bellum promotion familiar in all American communities. He was a non-commissioned officer in the wars against the Indians. He was nineteen when he enlisted, and marched on foot with his troop from Boston to Philadelphia, which at that time was the Nation's capital. The main army was then at Detroit under command of General Wayne, whom the soldiers lovingly knew as "Mad Anthony." William Henry Harrison and Richard M. Johnson, later President and Vice-President of the United States, were then lieutenants, and Stephen Barton fought side by side with them. He was present when Tecumseh was slain, and at the signing of the treaty of peace which followed. His military service extended over three years. At the close of the war he marched home on foot through northern Ohio and central New York. He and the other officers were greatly charmed by the Genesee and Mohawk valleys, and he purchased land somewhere in the vicinity of Rochester. He had some thought of establishing a home in that remote region, but it was so far distant from civilization that he sold his New York land and made his home in Oxford.

In 1796, Stephen Barton returned from the Indian War. He was then twenty-two years of age. Eight years later he married Sarah Stone, who was only seventeen. They established their home west of Oxford, near Chariton, and later removed to the farm where Clara Barton was born.

It was a modest home, and Stephen Barton was a hardworking man, though a man of influence in the community. He served often as moderator of town meetings and as selectman for the town. He served also as a member of the Legislature. But he wrought with his own hands in the tillage of his farm, and in the construction of most of the articles of furniture in his home, including the cradle in which his children were rocked.

Stephen Barton combined a military spirit with a gentle disposition and a broad spirit of philanthropy. Sarah Stone was a woman of great decision of character, and a quick temper. She was a housewife of the good old New England sort, looking well to the ways of her household and eating not the bread of idleness. From her father Clara Barton inherited those humanitarian tendencies which became notably characteristic, and from her mother she derived a strong will which achieved results almost regardless of opposition. Her mother's hot temper found its restraint in her through the inherited influence of her father's poise and benignity. Of him she wrote:

His military habits and tastes never left him. Those were also strong political days—Andrew Jackson Days—and very naturally my father became my instructor in military and political lore. I listened breathlessly to his war stories. Illustrations were called for and we made battles and fought them. Every shade of military etiquette was regarded. Colonels, captains, and sergeants were given their proper place and rank. So with the political world; the President, Cabinet, and leading officers of the government were learned by heart, and nothing gratified the keen humor of my father more than the parrot-like readiness with which I lisped these difficult names. I thought the President might be as large as the meetinghouse, and the Vice-President perhaps the size of the school-house. And yet, when later I, like all the rest of our country's people, was suddenly thrust into the mysteries of war, and had to find and take my place and part in it, I found myself far less a stranger to the conditions than most women, or even ordinary men for that matter. I never addressed a colonel as captain, got my cavalry on foot, or mounted my infantry!

When a little child upon his knee he told me that, as he lay helpless in the tangled marshes of Michigan the muddy water oozed up from the track of an officer's horse and saved him from death by thirst. And that a mouthful of a lean dog that had followed the march saved him from starvation. When he told me how the feathered arrow quivered in the flesh and the tomahawk swung over the white man's head, he told me also, with tears of honest pride, of the great and beautiful country that had sprung up from those wild scenes of suffering and danger! How he loved these new States for which he gave the strength of his youth!

Two sons and two daughters were born to Stephen and Sarah Barton in their early married life. Then for ten years no other children were born to them. On Christmas, 1821, their eldest daughter, Dorothy, was as old as her mother had been at the time of their marriage. Their eldest son, Stephen, was fifteen, the younger son, David, was thirteen, and the daughter, Sally, was ten. The family had long considered itself complete, when the household received Clara as a Christmas present. Her brothers and sisters were too old to be her playmates. They were her protectors, but not her companions. She was a little child in the midst of a household of grown-up people, as they seemed to her. In her little book entitled *The Story of my Childhood*, she thus describes her brothers and sisters:

I became the seventh member of a household consisting of the father and mother, two sisters and two brothers, each of whom for his and her intrinsic merits and special characteristics deserves an individual history, which it shall be my conscientious duty to portray as far as possible as these pages progress. For the present it is enough to say that each one manifested an increasing personal interest in the newcomer, and, as soon as developments permitted, set about instructing her in the various directions most in accord with the tastes and pursuits of each.

Of the two sisters, the elder was already a teacher. The younger followed soon, and naturally my book education became their first care, and under these conditions it is little to say, that I have no knowledge of ever learning to read, or of a time that I did not do my own story reading. The other studies followed very early.

My elder brother, Stephen, was a noted mathematician. He inducted me into the mystery of figures. Multiplication, division, subtraction, halves, quarters, and wholes, soon ceased to be a mystery, and no toy equaled my little slate. But the younger brother had entirely other tastes, and would have none of these things. My father was a lover of horses, and one of the first in the vicinity to introduce blooded stock. He had large lands, for New England. He raised his own colts; and Highlanders, Virginians, and Morgans pranced the fields in idle contempt of the solid old farm-horses.

Of my brother, David, to say that he was fond of horses describes nothing; one could almost add that he was fond of nothing else. He was the Buffalo Bill of the surrounding country, and here commences his part of my education. It was his delight to take me, a little girl of five years old, to the field, seize a couple of those beautiful young creatures, broken only to the halter and bit, and gathering the reins of both bridles firmly in hand, throw me upon the back of one colt, spring upon the other himself, and catching me by one foot, and bidding me "cling fast to the mane," gallop away over field and fen, in and out among the other colts in wild glee like ourselves. They were merry rides we took. This was my riding-school. I never had any other, but it served me well. To this day my seat on a saddle or on the back of a horse is as secure and tireless as in a rocking-chair, and far more pleasurable. Sometimes, in later years, when I found myself suddenly on a strange horse in a trooper's saddle, flying for life or liberty in front of pursuit, I blessed the baby lessons of the wild gallops among the beautiful colts.

One of the bravest of women, Clara Barton was a child of unusual timidity. Looking back upon her earliest recollections she said, "I remember nothing but fear." Her earliest memory was of her grief in failing to catch "a pretty bird" when she was two and a half years old. She cried in disappointment, and her mother ran to learn what was the trouble. On hearing her complaint, that "Baby" had lost a pretty bird which she had almost caught, her mother asked, "Where did it go, Baby?" "Baby" indicated a small round hole under the doorstep, and her mother gave a terrified scream. That scream awoke terror in the mind of the little girl, and she never quite recovered from it. The "bird" she had almost caught was a snake.

Her next memory also was one of fear. The family had gone to a funeral, leaving her in the care of her brother David. She told of it afterward as follows:

I can picture the large family sitting-room with its four open windows, which room I was not to leave, and my guardian was to remain near me. Some outside duty called him from the house and I was left to my own observations. A sudden thunder-shower came up; massive rifts of clouds rolled up in the east, and the lightning

16

darted among them like blazing fires. The thunder gave them language and my terrified imagination endowed them with life.

Among the animals of the farm was a huge old ram, that doubtless upon some occasion had taught me to respect him, and of which I had a mortal fear. My terrors transformed those rising, rolling clouds into a whole heaven full of angry rams, marching down upon me. Again my screams alarmed, and the poor brother, conscience-stricken that he had left his charge, rushed breathless in, to find me on the floor in hysterics, a condition of things he had never seen; and neither memory nor history relates how either of us got out of it.

In these later years I have observed that writers of sketches, in a friendly desire to compliment me, have been wont to dwell upon my courage, representing me as personally devoid of fear, not even knowing the feeling. However correct that may have become, it is evident I was not constructed that way, as in the earlier years of my life I remember nothing but fear.

SCHOOLS AND TEACHERS

Clara Barton's education began at her cradle. She was not able to remember when she learned to read. When three years old she had acquired the art of reading, and her lessons in spelling, arithmetic, and geography began in her infancy. Both of her sisters and her eldest brother were school-teachers. Recalling their efforts, she said: "I had no playmates, but in effect six fathers and mothers. They were a family of school-teachers. All took charge of me, all educated me, each according to personal taste. My two sisters were scholars and artistic, and strove in that direction. My brothers were strong, ruddy, daring young men, full of life and business."

Before she was four years old she entered school. By that time she was able to read easily, and could spell words of three syllables. She told the story of her first schooling in an account which must not be abridged:

My home instruction was by no means permitted to stand in the way of the "regular school," which consisted of two terms each year, of three months each. The winter term included not only the large boys and girls, but in reality the young men and young women of the neighborhood. An exceptionally fine teacher often drew the daily attendance of advanced scholars for several miles. Our district had this good fortune. I introduce with pleasure and with reverence the name of Richard Stone; a firmly set, handsome young man of twenty-six or seven, of commanding figure and presence, combining all the elements of a teacher with a discipline never questioned.

His glance of disapproval was a reprimand, his frown something he never needed to go beyond. The love and respect of his pupils exceeded even their fear. It was no uncommon thing for summer teachers to come twenty miles to avail themselves of the winter term of "Colonel" Stone, for he was a high militia officer, and at that young age was a settled man with a family of four little children. He had married at eighteen.

I am thus particular in my description of him, both because of my childish worship of him, and because I shall have occasion to refer to him later. The opening of his first term was a signal for the Barton family, and seated on the strong shoulders of my stalwart brother Stephen, I was taken a mile through the tall drifts to school. I have often questioned if in this movement there might not have been a touch of mischievous curiosity on the part of these not at all dull youngsters, to see what my performance at school might be.

I was, of course, the baby of the school. I recall no introduction to the teacher, but was set down among the many pupils in the by no means spacious room, with my spelling book and the traditional slate, from which nothing could separate me. I was seated on one of the low benches and sat very still. At length the majestic schoolmaster seated himself, and taking a primer, called the class of little ones to him. He pointed the letters to each. I named them all, and was asked to spell some little words, "dog," "cat," etc., whereupon I hesitatingly informed him that I did "not spell there." "Where do you spell?" "I spell in 'Artichoke,'" that being the leading word in the three syllable column in my speller. He good naturedly conformed to my suggestion, and I was put into the "artichoke" class to bear my part for the winter, and read and "spell for the head." When, after a few weeks, my brother Stephen was declared by the committee to be too advanced for a common school, and was placed in charge of an important school himself, my unique transportation devolved upon the other brother, David.

No colts now, but solid wading through the high New England drifts.

The Reverend Mr. Menseur of the Episcopal church of Leicester, Massachusetts, if I recollect aright, wisely comprehending the grievous inadaptability of the schoolbooks of that time, had compiled a small geography and atlas suited to young children, known as Menseur's Geography. It was a novelty, as well as a beneficence; nothing of its kind having occurred to makers of the schoolbooks of that day. They seemed not to have recognized the existence of a state of childhood in the intellectual creation. During the winter I had become the happy possessor of a Menseur's Geography and Atlas. It is questionable if my satisfaction was fully shared by others of the household. I required a great deal of

19

assistance in the study of my maps, and became so interested that I could not sleep, and was not willing that others should, but persisted in waking my poor drowsy sister in the cold winter mornings to sit up in bed and by the light of a tallow candle, help me to find mountains, rivers, counties, oceans, lakes, islands, isthmuses, channels, cities, towns, and capitals.

The next May the summer school opened, taught by Miss Susan Torrey. Again, I write the name reverently, as gracing one of the most perfect of personalities. I was not alone in my childish admiration, for her memory remained a living reality in the town long years after the gentle spirit fled. My sisters were both teaching other schools, and I must make my own way, which I did, walking a mile with my one precious little schoolmate, Nancy Fitts. Nancy Fitts! The playmate of my childhood; the "chum" of laughing girlhood; the faithful, trusted companion of young womanhood, and the beloved life friend that the relentless grasp of time has neither changed, nor taken from me.

On entering the wide-open door of the inviting school-house, armed with some most unsuitable reader, a spelling book, geography, atlas, and slate, I was seized with an intense fear at finding myself with no member of the family near, and my trepidation became so visible that the gentle teacher, relieving me of my burden of books, took me tenderly on her lap and did her best to reassure and calm me. At length I was given my seat, with a desk in front for my atlas and slate, my toes at least a foot from the floor, and that became my daily, happy home for the next three months.

All the members of Clara Barton's household became her teachers, except her mother, who looked with interest, and not always with approval, on the methods of instruction practiced by the others. Captain Barton was teaching her military tactics, David was teaching her to ride horseback, Sally, and later Dorothy, established a kind of school at home and practiced on their younger sister, and Stephen contributed his share in characteristic fashion. Sarah Stone alone attempted nothing until the little daughter should be old enough to learn to do housework.

"My mother, like the sensible woman that she was, seemed to conclude that there were plenty of instructors without her," said Miss Barton. "She attempted very little, but rather regarded the whole thing as a sort of mental conglomeration, and looked on with a kind of amused curiosity to see what they would make of it. Indeed, I heard her remark many years after that I came out of it with a more level head than she would have thought possible."

Clara Barton's first piece of personal property was a sprightly, medium-sized white dog, with silky ears and a short tail. His name was Button. Her affection for Button continued throughout her life. Of him she said;

My first individual ownership was "Button." In personality (if the term be admissible), Button represented a sprightly, medium-sized, very white dog, with silky ears, sparkling black eyes and a very short tail. His bark spoke for itself. Button belonged to me. No other claim was instituted, or ever had been. It was said that on my entrance into the family, Button constituted himself my guardian. He watched my first steps and tried to pick me up when I fell down. One was never seen without the other. He proved an apt and obedient pupil, obeying me precept upon precept, if not line upon line. He stood on two feet to ask for his food, and made a bow on receiving it, walked on three legs when very lame, and so on, after the manner of his crude instruction; went everywhere with me through the day, waited patiently while I said my prayers and continued his guard on the foot of the bed at night. Button shared my board as well as my bed.

After her first year's instruction at the hands of Colonel Stone, that gentleman ceased his connection with the common schools, and established what was known as the Oxford High School, an institution of great repute in its day. This left the district school to be taught by the members of the Barton household. For the next three years Clara's sisters were her public school-teachers in the autumn and spring, and her brother Stephen had charge of the school in the winter terms. Two things she remembered about those years. One was her preternatural shyness. She was sensitive and retiring to a degree that seemed to forbid all hope of her making much progress in study with other children. The other was that she had a fondness for writing verses, some of which her brothers and sisters preserved and used to tease her with in later years. One thing she learned outside the schoolroom, and she never forgot it. That was how to handle a horse. She inherited her mother's sidesaddle, and though she protested against having to use it, she learned at an early age to lift and buckle it, and to ride her father's horses.

Meantime her brothers grew to be men and bought out her father's two large farms. Her father purchased another farm of three hundred acres nearer the center of the town, a farm having upon it one of the forts used for security against the Indians by the original Huguenot settlers. She now became interested in history, and added that to her previous accomplishments.

At the age of eight, Clara Barton entered what was called high school, which involved boarding away from home. The arrangement met with only partial success on account of her extreme timidity:

During the preceding winter I began to hear talk of my going away to school, and it was decided that I be sent to Colonel Stone's High School, to board in his family and go home occasionally. This arrangement, I learned in later years, had a double object. I was what is known as a bashful child, timid in the presence of other persons, a condition of things found impossible to correct at home. In the hope of overcoming this undesirable *mauvais honte*, it was decided to throw me among strangers.

How well I remember my advent. My father took me in his carriage with a little dressing-case which I dignified with the appellation of "trunk"—something I had never owned. It was April— cold and bare. The house and schoolrooms adjoined, and seemed enormously large. The household was also large. The long family table with the dignified preceptor, my loved and feared teacher of three years, at its head, seemed to me something formidable. There were probably one hundred and fifty pupils daily in the ample schoolrooms, of which I was perhaps the youngest, except the colonel's own children.

My studies were chosen with great care. I remember among them, ancient history with charts. The lessons were learned, to repeat by rote. I found difficulty both in learning the proper names and in pronouncing them, as I had not quite outgrown my lisp. One day I had studied very hard on the Ancient Kings of Egypt, and thought I had everything perfect, and when the pupil above me failed to give the name of a reigning king, I answered very promptly that it was "Potlomy." The colonel checked with a glance the rising laugh of the older members of the class, and told me, very gently, that the P was silent in that word. I had, however, seen it all, and was so overcome by mortification for my mistake, and gratitude for the kindness of my teacher, that I burst into tears and was permitted to leave the room.

I am not sure that I was really homesick, but the days seemed very long, especially Sundays. I was in constant dread of doing something wrong, and one Sunday afternoon I was sure I had found my occasion. It was early spring. The tender leaves had put out and with them the buds and half-open blossoms of the little cinnamon roses, an unfailing ornamentation of a well-kept New England home of that day. The children of the family had gathered in the front yard, admiring the roses and daring to pick each a little bouquet. As I stood holding mine, the heavy door at my back swung open, and there was the colonel, in his long, light dressing-gown and slippers, direct from his study. A kindly spoken, "Come with me, Clara," nearly took my last breath. I followed his strides through all the house, up the long flights of stairs, through the halls of the schoolrooms, silently wondering what I had done more than the others. I knew he was by no means wont to spare his own children.

I had my handful of roses—so had they. I knew it was very wrong to have picked them, but why more wrong for me than for the others? At length, and it seemed to me an hour, we reached the colonel's study, and there, advancing to meet us, was the Reverend Mr. Chandler, the pastor of our Universalist Church, whom I knew well. He greeted me very politely and kindly, and handed the large, open school reader which he held, to the colonel, who put it into my hands, placed me a little in front of them, and pointing to a column of blank verse, very gently directed me to read it. It was an extract from Campbell's "Pleasures of Hope," commencing, "Unfading hope, when life's last embers burn." I read it to the end, a page or two. When finished, the good pastor came quickly and relieved me of the heavy book, and I wondered why there were tears in his eyes. The colonel drew me to him, gently stroked my short cropped hair, went with me down the long steps, and told me I could "go back to the children and play." I went, much more easy in mind than I came, but it was years before I comprehended anything about it.

My studies gave me no trouble, but I grew very tired, felt hungry all the time, but dared not eat, grew thin and pale. The colonel noticed it, and watching me at table found that I was eating little or nothing, refusing everything that was offered me. Mistrusting that it was from timidity, he had food laid on my plate, but I dared not eat it, and finally at the end of the term a consultation was held between the colonel, my father, and our beloved family physician, Dr. Delano Pierce, who lived within a few doors of the school, and it was decided to take me home until a little older, and wiser, I could hope. My timid sensitiveness must have given great annoyance to my friends. If I ever could have gotten entirely over it, it would have given far less annoyance and trouble to myself all through life.

To this day, I would rather stand behind the lines of artillery at Antietam, or cross the pontoon bridge under fire at Fredericksburg, than to be expected to preside at a public meeting.

Again Clara's instruction fell to her brothers and sisters. Stephen taught her mathematics, her sisters increased her knowledge of the common branches, and David continued to give her lessons in horsemanship. Stephen Barton, her father, was the owner of a fine black stallion, whose race of colts improved the blooded stock of Oxford and vicinity. When she was ten years old she received a present of a Morgan horse named Billy. Mounted on the back of this fine animal, she ranged the hills of Oxford completely free from that fear with which she was possessed in the schoolroom.

When she was thirteen years of age, her education took a new start under the instruction of Lucian Burleigh, who taught her grammar, composition, English literature, and history. A year later Jonathan

Dana became her instructor, and taught her philosophy, chemistry, and writing. These two teachers she remembered with unfaltering affection.

While Clara Barton's brother Stephen taught school, his younger brother, David, gave himself to business. He, no less than Stephen, was remembered affectionately as having had an important share in her education. He had taught her to ride, and she had become his nurse. When he grew well and strong, he took the little girl under his instruction, and taught her how to do things directly and with expedition. If she started anywhere impulsively, and turned back, he reproved her. She was not to start until she knew where she was going, and why, and having started, she was to go ahead and accomplish what she had undertaken. She was to learn the effective way of attaining results, and having learned it was to follow the method which promoted efficiency. He taught her to despise false motions, and to avoid awkward and ineffective attempts to accomplish results. He showed her how to drive a nail without splitting a board, and she never forgot how to handle the hammer and the saw. He taught her how to start a screw so it would drive straight. He taught her not to throw like a girl, but to hurl a ball or a stone with an under swing like a boy, and to hit what she threw at. He taught her to avoid "granny-knots' and how to tie square knots. All this practical instruction she learned to value as among the best features of her education.

One of her earliest experiences, in accomplishing a memorable piece of work with her own hands, came to her after her father had sold the two hill farms to his sons and removed to the farm on the highway nearer the village. It gave her her opportunity to learn the art of painting. This was more than the ability to dip a brush in a prepared mixture and spread the liquid evenly over a plane surface; it involved some knowledge of the art of preparing and mixing paints. She found joy in it at the time, and it quickened within her an aspiration to be an artist. In later years and as part of her education, she learned to draw and paint, and was able to give instruction in water-color and oil painting. It is interesting to read her own account of her first adventure into the field of art:

The hill farms—for there were two—were sold to my brothers, who, entering into partnership, constituted the well-known firm of S. & D. Barton, continuing mainly through their lives. Thus I became the occupant of two homes, my sisters remaining with my brothers, none of whom were married.

The removal to the second home was a great novelty to me. I became observant of all changes made. One of the first things found necessary, on entering a house of such ancient date, was a rather extensive renovation, for those days, of painting and papering. The leading artisan in that line in the town was Mr. Sylvanus Harris, a courteous man of fine manners, good scholarly acquirements, and who, for nearly half a lifetime, filled the office of town clerk. The records of Oxford will bear his name and his beautiful handwriting as long as its records exist.

Mr. Harris was engaged to make the necessary improvements. Painting included more then than in these later days of prepared material. The painter brought his massive white marble slab, ground his own paints, mixed his colors, boiled his oil, calcined his plaster, made his putty, and did scores of things that a painter of to-day would not only never think of doing, but would often scarcely know how to do.

Coming from the newly built house where I was born, I had seen nothing of this kind done, and was intensely interested. I must have persisted in making myself very numerous, for I was constantly reminded not to "get in the gentleman's way." But I was not to be set aside. My combined interest and curiosity for once overcame my timidity, and, encouraged by the mild, genial face of Mr. Harris, I gathered the courage to walk up in front and address him: "Will you teach me to paint, sir?" "With pleasure, little lady; if mamma is willing, I should very much like your assistance." The consent was forthcoming, and so was a gown suited to my new work, and I reported for duty. I question if any ordinary apprentice was ever more faithfully and intelligently instructed in his first month's apprenticeship. I was taught how to hold my brushes, to take care of them, allowed to help grind my paints, shown how to mix and blend them, how to make putty and use it, to prepare oils and dryings, and learned from experience that boiling oil was a great deal hotter than boiling water, was taught to trim paper neatly, to match and help to hang it, to make the most approved paste, and even varnished the kitchen chairs to the entire satisfaction of my mother, which was triumph enough for one little girl. So interested was I, that I never wearied of my work for a day, and at the end of a month looked on sadly as the utensils, brushes, buckets and great marble slabs were taken away. There was not a room that I had not helped to make better; there were no longer mysteries in paint and paper. I knew them all, and that work would bring calluses even on little hands.

When the work was finished and everything gone, I went to my room, lonesome in spite of myself. I found on my candle stand a box containing a pretty little locket, neatly inscribed, "To a faithful worker." No one seemed to have any knowledge of it, and I never gained any.

One other memory of these early days must be recorded as having an immediate effect upon her, and a permanent influence upon her life. While she was still a little girl, she witnessed the killing of an ox, and it seemed so terrible a thing to her that it had much to do with her lifelong temperance in the matter of eating meat. She never became an absolute vegetarian. When she sat at a table where meat was served, and where a refusal to eat would have called for explanation, and perhaps would have embarrassed the family, she ate what was set before her as the Apostle Paul commanded, but she ate very sparingly of all animal food, and, when she was able to control her own diet, lived almost entirely on vegetables. Things that grew out of the ground, she said, were good enough for her:

A small herd of twenty-five fine milch cows came faithfully home each day with the lowering of the sun, for the milking and extra supper which they knew awaited them. With the customary greed of childhood, I had laid claim to three or four of the handsomest and tamest of them, and believing myself to be their real owner, I went faithfully every evening to the yards to receive and look after them. My little milk pail went as well, and I became proficient in an art never forgotten.

One afternoon, on going to the barn as usual, I found no cows there; all had been driven somewhere else. As I stood in the corner of the great yard alone, I saw three or four men—the farm hands—with one stranger among them wearing a long, loose shirt or gown. They were all trying to get a large red ox onto the barn floor, to which he went very reluctantly. At length they succeeded. One of the men carried an axe, and, stepping a little to the side and back, raised it high in the air and brought it down with a terrible blow. The ox fell, I fell too; and the next I knew I was in the house on a bed, and all the family about me, with the traditional camphor bottle, bathing my head to my great discomfort. As I regained consciousness, they asked me what made me fall? I said, "someone struck me." "Oh, no," they said, "no one struck you." But I was not to be convinced, and proceeded to argue the case with an impatient putting away of the hurting hands, "Then what makes my head so sore?" Happy ignorance! I had not then learned the mystery of nerves.

I have, however, a very clear recollection of the indignation of my father (my mother had already expressed herself on the subject), on his return from town and hearing what had taken place. The hired men were lined up and arraigned for "cruel carelessness." They had "the consideration to keep the cattle away," he said, "but allowed that little girl to stand in full view." Of course, each protested he had not seen me. I was altogether too friendly with the farm hands to hear them blamed, especially on my account, and came promptly to their side, assuring my father that they had not seen me, and that it was "no matter," I was "all well now." But, singularly, I lost all desire for meat, if I had ever had it—and all through life, to the present, have only eaten it when I must for the sake of appearance, or as circumstances seemed to make it the more proper thing to do. The bountiful ground has always yielded enough for all my needs and wants.

DAYS OF YOUTH

So large a part of the schooling of Clara Barton was passed under the instruction of her own sisters and her brother Stephen that she ceased to feel in school the diffidence which elsewhere characterized her, and which she never fully overcame. Not all of her education, however, was accomplished in the schoolroom. While her mother refrained from giving to her actual instruction as she received from her father and brothers and sisters, her knowledge of domestic arts was not wholly neglected. When the family removed to the new home, her two brothers remained upon the more distant farm, and the older sisters kept house for them. Into the new home came the widow of her father's nephew, Jeremiah Lamed, with her four children, whose ages varied from six to thirteen years. She now had playmates in her own household, with frequent visits to the old home where her two brothers and two sisters, none of them married, kept house together. Although her mother still had older kitchen help, she taught Clara some of the mysteries of cooking. Her mother complained somewhat that she never really had a fair chance at Clara's instruction as a housekeeper, but Clara believed that no instruction of her youth was more lasting or valuable than that which enabled her, on the battle-field or elsewhere, to make a pie, "crinkly around the edges, with marks of fingerprints," to remind a soldier of home.

Two notable interruptions of her schooling occurred.

The first was caused by an alarming illness when she was five years of age. Dysentery and convulsions came very near to robbing Captain and Mrs. Barton of their baby. Of this almost mortal illness, she preserved only one memory, that of the first meal which she ate when her convalescence set in. She was propped up in a huge cradle that had been constructed for an adult invalid, with a little low table at the side. The meal consisted of a piece of brown bread crust about two inches square, a tiny glass of homemade blackberry cordial, and a wee bit of her mother's well-cured cheese. She dropped asleep from exhaustion as she finished this first meal, and the memory of it made her mouth water as long as she lived.

The other interruption occurred when she was eleven. Her brother David, who was a dare-devil rider and fearless climber, ascended to the ridge-pole on the occasion of a barn-raising. A board broke under his feet, and he fell to the ground. He fell upon solid timbers and sustained a serious injury, especially by a blow on the head. For two years he was an invalid. For a time he hung between life and death, and then was "a sleepless, nervous, cold dyspeptic, and a mere wreck of his former self." After two years of suffering, he completely recovered under a new system of steam baths; but those two years did not find Clara in the schoolroom. She nursed her brother with such assiduity as almost permanently to injure her own health. In his nervous condition he clung to her, and she acquired something of that skill in the care of the sick which remained with her through life.

Clara Barton was growing normally in her twelfth year when she became her brother's nurse. Not until that long vigil was completed was it discovered that she had ceased to grow. Her height in her shoes, with moderately high heels, was five feet and three inches, and was never increased. In later life people who met her gave widely divergent reports of her stature. She was described as "of medium height," and now and then she was declared to be tall. She had a remarkable way of appearing taller than she was. As a matter of fact in her later years, her height shrank a little, and she measured in her stocking-feet exactly sixty inches.

Clara was an ambitious child. Her two brothers owned a cloth-mill where they wove satinet. She was ambitious to learn the art of weaving. Her mother at first objected, but her brother Stephen pleaded for her, and she was permitted to enter the mill. She was not tall enough to tend the loom, so a raised platform was arranged for her between a pair of looms and she learned to manage the shuttle. To her great disappointment, the mill burned down when she had been at work only two weeks; but this brief vacational experience served as a basis of a pretty piece of fiction at which she always smiled, but which annoyed her somewhat—that she had entered a factory and earned money to pay off a mortgage on her father's farm. The length of her service in the mill would not have paid a very large mortgage, but fortunately there was no mortgage to pay off. Her father was a prosperous man for his time, and the family was well to do, possessing not only broad acres, but adding to the family income by manufacture and trade. They were among the most enterprising, prosperous, and respected families in a thrifty and self-respecting community.

One of the enterprises on the Barton farm afforded her great joy. The narrow French River ran through her father's farm. In places it could be crossed by a foot-log, and there were few days when she did not cross and recross it for the sheer joy of finding herself on a trembling log suspended over a deep stream. This river ran the only sawmill in the neighborhood. Here she delighted to ride the carriage which conveyed the logs to the old-fashioned up-and-down saw. The carriage moved very slowly when it was going forward and the saw was eating its laborious way through the log, but it came back with violent rapidity, and the little girl, who remembered nothing but fear of her earliest childhood, was happy when she flaunted her courage in the face of her natural timidity and rode the sawmill carriage as she rode her high-stepping blooded Billy.

She went to church every Sunday, and churches in that day had no fires. Her people had been brought up in the orthodox church, but, revolting at the harsh dogmatism of the orthodox theology of that day, they withdrew and became founders of the first Universalist Church in America. The meeting-house at Oxford, built for the Universalist Society, is the oldest building in existence erected for this communion. Hosea Ballou was the first minister—a brave, strong, resolute man. Though the family liberalized their creed, they did not greatly modify the austerity of their Puritan living. They kept the Sabbath about as strictly as they had been accustomed to do before their break with the Puritan church.

Once in her childhood Clara broke the Sabbath, and it brought a painful memory:

One clear, cold, starlight Sunday morning, I heard a low whistle under my open chamber window. I realized that the boys were out for a skate and wanted to communicate with me. On going to the window, they informed me that they had an extra pair of skates and if I could come out they would put them on me and "learn" me how to skate. It was Sunday morning; no one would be up till late, and the ice was so smooth and "glare." The stars were bright; the temptation was too great. I was in my dress in a moment and out. The skates were fastened on firmly, one of the boy's wool neck "comforters" tied about my waist, to be held by the boy in front. The other two were to stand on either side, and at a signal the cavalcade started. Swifter and swifter we went, until at length we reached a spot where the ice had been cracked and was full of sharp edges. These threw me, and the speed with which we were progressing, and the distance before we could quite come to a stop, gave terrific opportunity for cuts and wounded knees. The opportunity was not lost. There was more blood flowing than any of us had ever seen. Something must be done. Now all of the wool neck comforters came into requisition; my wounds were bound up, and I was helped into the house, with one knee of ordinary respectable cuts and bruises; the other frightful. Then the enormity of the transaction and its attendant difficulties began to present themselves, and how to surround (for there was no possibility of overcoming) them was the question.

The most feasible way seemed to be to say nothing about it, and we decided to all keep silent; but how to conceal the limp? I must have no limp, but walk well. I managed breakfast without notice. Dinner not quite so well, and I had to acknowledge that I had slipped down and hurt my knee a little. This gave my limp more latitude, but the next day it was so decided, that I was held up and searched. It happened that the best knee was inspected; the stiff wool comforter soaked off, and a suitable dressing given it. This was a great relief, as it afforded pretext for my limp, no one observing that I limped with the wrong knee.

But the other knee was not a wound to heal by first intention, especially under its peculiar dressing, and finally had to be revealed. The result was a surgical dressing and my foot held up in a chair for three weeks, during which time I read the Arabian Nights from end to end. As the first dressing was finished, I heard the surgeon say to my father: "That was a hard case, Captain, but she stood it like a

32

soldier." But when I saw how genuinely they all pitied, and how tenderly they nursed me, even walking lightly about the house not to jar my swollen and fevered limbs, in spite of my disobedience and detestable deception (and persevered in at that), my Sabbath-breaking and unbecoming conduct, and all the trouble I had caused, conscience revived, and my mental suffering far exceeded my physical. The Arabian Nights were none too powerful a soporific to hold me in reasonable bounds. I despised myself, and failed to sleep or eat.

My mother, perceiving my remorseful condition, came to the rescue, telling me soothingly, that she did not think it the worst thing that could have been done, that other little girls had probably done as badly, and strengthened her conclusions by telling me how she once persisted in riding a high-mettled, unbroken horse in opposition to her father's commands, and was thrown. My supposition is that she had been a worthy mother of her equestrian son.

The lesson was not lost on any of the group. It is very certain that none of us, boys or girls, indulged in further smart tricks. Twenty-five years later, when on a visit to the old home, long left, I saw my father, then a gray-haired grandsire, out on the same little pond, fitting the skates carefully to the feet of his little twin granddaughters, holding them up to make their first start in safety, I remembered my wounded knees, and blessed the great

Father that progress and change were among the possibilities of His people,

I never learned to skate. When it became fashionable I had neither time nor opportunity.

Another disappointment of her childhood remained with her. She wanted to learn to dance, and was not permitted to do so. It was not because her parents were wholly opposed to dancing, but chiefly because the dancing-school was organized while a revival of religion was in progress in the village, and her parents felt that her attendance at dancing-school at such a time would be unseemly. Of this she wrote:

I recall another disappointment which, though not vital, was still indicative of the times. During the following winter a dancing-school was opened in the hall of the one hotel on Oxford Plain, some three miles from us. It was taught by a personal friend of my father, a polished gentleman, resident of a neighboring town, and teacher of English schools. By some chance I got a glimpse of the dancing-school at the opening, and was seized with a most intense desire to go and learn to dance. With my peculiar characteristics it was necessary for me to want a thing very much before mentioning it; but this overcame me, especially as the cordial teacher took tea with us one evening before going to his school, and spoke very interestingly of his classes. I even went so far as to beg permission to go. The dance was in my very feet. The violin haunted me. "Ladies change" and "All hands round" sounded in my ears and woke me from my sleep at night.

The matter was taken up in family council. I was thought to be very young to be allowed to go to a dancing-school in a hotel. Dancing at that time was at a very low ebb in good New England society, and, besides, there was an active revival taking place in both of the orthodox churches (or, rather, one a church and the other a society without a church), and it might not be a wise, nor even a courteous, thing to allow. Not that our family, with its well-known liberal proclivities, could have the slightest objection on that score; still, like Saint Paul, if meat were harmful to their brethren, they would not eat it, and thus it was decided that I could not go. The decision was perfectly conscientious, kindness itself, and probably wise; but I have wondered, if they could have known (as they never did) how severe the disappointment was, the tears it cost me in my little bed in the dark, the music and the master's voice still sounding in my ears, if this knowledge would have weighed in the decision.

I have listened to a great deal of music since then, interspersed with very positive orders, and which generally called for "All hands round," but the dulcet notes of the violin and the "Ladies change" were missing. Neither did I ever learn to dance.

As she looked back over her childhood, she was unable to recall many social events which could have been characterized as thrilling.

34

By invitation she once wrote out for a gathering of women her recollection of a party which she attended on election day just after she was ten years old. It is worth reading, and may well remind us that happy childhood memories do not always gather about events which seem to be intrinsically great:

It is the "reminiscence of a happy moment" which my beloved friends of the Legion of Loyal Women ask of me—some moment or event so happy as to be worth the telling. That may not be an easy thing in a life like mine, but there are few things the "Legion" could ask of me that I would not at least try to do. But, dear sisters, I fear I must ask of you patiently to travel far back with me to the little childhood days which knew no care. Patiently, I say, for that was long ago.

I lived in the country, a mile or more from the village. Olivia Bruce, my favorite friend, lived in the village.

Olivia had "made a party," and invited twelve little girls, schoolmates and playmates, herself making the thirteenth (we had never learned that there could be bad luck in numbers).

It was May, and the party was to be held on "Old Election Day." Care and thought were given to the occasion.

Each guest was to learn a little poem to recite for the first time, as a surprise to the others.

There was some effort at costume. We were all to wear aprons alike, from the village store—white, with a pretty vine, and cozy, little, brown birds in the corners. Embroidered? Oh, no! just stamped; but what embroidery has since ever borne comparison with that?

Our ages must conform—no one under ten, or over twelve. How glad I was that I had been ten the Christmas before!

At length arrangements were completed, and nothing to be wished for but a pleasant day.

The morning came, heavy and dark. The thunder rolled, the clouds gathered and broke, and the lightning as if in cruel mockery darted in and out among them, lighting up their ragged edges, or enveloping the whole mass in quivering flame. The rain came down in torrents, and I fear there were torrents of tears as well. Who could give comfort in a disappointment and grief like that? Who, but old Morgan, the gardener, with his poetic prophecy—

"Rain before seven, be clear before 'leven."

I watched the clouds, I watched the clock, but most of all I watched the hopeful face of old Morgan. How long and how dark the morning was! At length, as the clock pointed half-past ten, the clouds broke again, but this time with the bright, clear sun behind them, and the high arching rainbow resting on the tree-tops of the western woods.

It was long to wait, even for dinner, and the proper time to go. Finally, all traces of tears were washed away, the toilet made even to the apron and hat, the mother's kiss given upon the cheek of her restless child with the gentle admonition "Be a good girl!" and, as I sprang from the doorstep striving hard to keep at least one foot on the ground, who shall say that the happiness and joy of that little bit of humanity was not as complete as ever falls to the lot of humanity to be?

The party was a success. The thirteen little girls were there; each wore her pretty apron and the knot of ribbon in her hair; each recited her little poem unknown to the others.

We danced—played ring plays.

"The needle's eye that can supply
The thread that runs so truly."
"For no man knows
Where oats, peas, beans, or barley grows."

We "chased the squirrel," "hunted the slipper," trimmed our hats with wild flowers and stood in awe before the great waterwheel of the busy mill.

At five o'clock a pretty tea was served for us, and dark-eyed Olivia presided with the grace and gravity of a matron; and, as the sun was sinking behind the western hills, we bade good-bye, and each sped away to the home awaiting her, I to be met by a mother's approving kiss, for I had been "a good girl," and gladly sought the little bed, and the long night of unbroken sleep that only a child may know.

Long, long years ago the watchful mother went to that other world; one after another the guests of the little party followed her—some in girlhood, some in young womanhood, some in weary widowhood. One by one,

I believe, she has met and welcomed them—welcomed each of the twelve, and waits

Clara Barton

Another formative influence which must not be overlooked was that of phrenology. This now discredited science had great influence in the early part of the nineteenth century. Certain men, among whom the Fowler brothers were most conspicuous, professed to be able to read character and to portray mental aptitude by a tactual examination of the head. The perceptive faculties, according to this theory, were located in the front part of the brain, the moral faculties in the top of it, and the faculties that governed the animal nature in the back. They professed to be able by feeling over the "bumps" or "organs of the brain," to discover what vocation a person was good for and what undesirable tendencies he ought to guard against. The mother of Clara Barton was greatly troubled by the abnormal sensitiveness of this little child. She asked L. W. Fowler, who was then staying at the Barton home, what this little girl ought to do in life. Mr. Fowler answered: "The sensitive nature will always remain. She will never assert herself for herself; she will suffer wrong first. But for others she will be perfectly fearless. Throw responsibility upon her."

He advised that she should become a school-teacher. School-teaching scarcely seemed a suitable vocation for a child of so shrinking a nature. Clara was fifteen at the time, and still diffident. She was lying in bed with the mumps, and overheard her mother's question and the answer. Her mother was impressed by it, and so was Clara. Years afterward she looked back upon that experience as the turning-point in her life. Long after she had ceased to have very much faith in phrenology, she blessed the day that sent a phrenologist into her home. When asked in later years what book had influenced her most, she wrote the following reply:

THE BOOK WHICH HAS MOST INFLUENCED ME

Superlatives are difficult to deal with, the comparative is always so near.

That which interests most, may influence little. Most books interest in a greater or less degree, and possibly have a temporary influence. The yellow-covered literature which the boy from twelve to sixteen reads, surely interests him, and only too often creates an involuntary influence, the results of which mark his entire life. He adopts methods and follows courses which he otherwise would not have done, and reaps misfortune for a harvest.

And so with the girl of like age who pores and weeps over some tender, unwholesome, love-lorn picture of impossible personages, until they become real to her, and, while she can never personate them, they stand in the way of so much which she really does need, it may well be said that the results influence her entire life.

Not alone the character of what is read, but the period in life of the reader, may and will have much to do with the potency of results. The little girl who is so fortunate as to clasp her child fingers around a copy of "Little Women," or "Little Men" (Bless the memory of my friend and co-worker Louisa M. Alcott!), is in small danger from the effects of the literature she may afterwards meet. Her tastes are formed for wholesome food.

And the boy! Ah, well; it will require a great deal of prodding to curb and root the wild grass out of his nature! But what a splendid growth he makes, once it is done!

All of these conditions of character, circumstances, and time may be said to have found place in the solution of the little problem now before me; viz: "What book most influenced me?" If it had read "interested" rather than "influenced," I should have made a wide range—"The Fables of Aesop," "Pilgrim's Progress," "Arabian Nights," "The Ballads of Scott," "The Benign Old Vicar," "The Citizens of the World," and mainly the mass of choice old English classics—for who can select?—The glorious "Idylls of the King." In fancy I should have sat at the round table with Arthur's knights, searched for the Holy Grail with Sir Galahad, roamed Africa with Livingstone and Stanley, breakfasted with the Autocrat, and dropped the gathering tear for the loved Quaker poet, so dear to us all.

How grateful I am for all this; and to these writers immortal! How they have sweetened life! But they really changed no course, formed no character, opened no doors, "influenced" nothing.

In a little children's booklet I have explained my own nature—timid, sensitive, bashful to awkwardness—and that at this period of a dozen years or so I chanced to make the acquaintance of L. W. Fowler, of the "Fowler Brothers," the earliest, and then only, exponents of Phrenology in the country.

I had at that time read much of the literatures above cited which then existed. Mr. Fowler placed in my hands their well-written book and brochures on Phrenology, "The Science of the Mind." This carried me to another class of writers, Spurzheim, and Combe—"The Constitution of Man." These became my exemplars and "Know thyself" became my text and my study. A long life has passed, and so have they, but their influence has remained. In every walk of life it has gone with me. It has enabled me to better comprehend the seeming mysteries about me; the course of those with whom I had to deal, or come in contact; not by the studying of their thoughts, or intentions, for I abhor the practice of reading one's friends; but to enable me to excuse, without offense, many acts which I could in no other way have accounted for. It has enabled me to see, not only that, but why it was their nature, and could not be changed. They "could no other, so help them God." It has enriched my field of charitable judgment; enlarged my powers of forgiveness, made those things plain that would have been obscure to me, easy, that would have been hard, and sometimes made possible to endure, without complaint, that which might otherwise have proved unendurable. "Know thyself" has taught me in any great crisis to put myself under my own feet; bury enmity, cast ambition to the winds, ignore complaint, despise retaliation, and stand erect in the consciousness of those higher qualities that made for the good of human kind, even though we may not clearly see the way.

"I know not where His Islands lift Their fronded palms in air;

I only know I cannot drift Beyond His love and care."

Even though phrenology be now regarded as a scientific error, it must not be supposed that all the men who practiced it were conscious charletans, or that all who believed in it were ignorant dupes. It was in its day what popularized psychology has become in the present day. Apart from the exploded idea that the brain contains separate "organs" which act more or less independently in the development and manifestation of character, it dealt with the study of the human mind in more nearly practical fashion than anything which up to that time had become popularly available. The phrenologist would now be called a psychologist, and would make no pretense of reading character by manipulating the skull. But some of those men taught people to consider their own mental possibilities, and to determine to realize all that was potentially best within them. This was the effect of phrenology upon Clara Barton.

A TEACHER

The avenues which open into life are many now, and the feet of young people who leave home or school are set at the intersection of many highways. But it was not so in the early part of the nineteenth century. For those who had aspirations for something else than the farm or shop, the most common and convenient path to larger knowledge and a professional career lay through the teaching of the district school. When Mr. Fowler advised that responsibility be laid upon Clara to develop her self-reliance and overcome her shyness, there were not many kinds of work which could easily have been recommended. School-teaching followed almost inevitably, and as something foreordained. She belonged to a generation of teachers, and to a family which was quite at home in the schoolroom. Her elder sister Dorothy developed symptoms of invalidism, never married, and in time had to give up teaching, and her younger sister Sally married and became Mrs. Vassall. Her brother Stephen had graduated from the work of teaching, and he and David were associated in farm, gristmill, sawmill, cloth-mill, and other enterprises. There was no difficulty in securing for Clara the opportunity to teach in the district where her married sister lived. Bearing in mind the advice of Mr. Fowler, she did up her hair, lengthened her skirts, and prepared for her first work as a teacher.

At the close of the second term of school, the advice was acted upon, and it was arranged that I teach the school in District No. 9. My sister resided within the district. How well I remember the preparations—the efforts to look larger and older, the examination by the learned committee of one clergyman, one lawyer, and one justice of the peace; the certificate with "excellent" added at the close; the bright May morning over the dewy, grassy road to the schoolhouse, neither large nor new, and not a pupil in sight.

On entering, I found my little school of forty pupils all seated according to their own selection, quietly waiting with folded hands. Bright, rosy-cheeked boys and girls from four to thirteen, with the exception of four lads, as tall and nearly as old as myself. These four boys naturally looked a little curiously at me, as if forming an opinion of how best to dispose of me, as rumor had it that on the preceding summer, not being en rapport with the young lady teacher, they had excluded her from the building and taken possession themselves. All arose as I entered, and remained standing until requested to sit. Never having observed how schools were opened, I was compelled, as one would say, to "blaze my own way." I was too timid to address them, but holding my Bible, I said they might take their Testaments and turn to the Sermon on the Mount. All who could read, read a verse each, I reading with them in turn. This opened the way for remarks upon the meaning of what they had read. I found them more ready to express themselves than I had expected, which was helpful to me as well. I asked them what they supposed the Saviour meant by saying that they must love their enemies and do good to them that hated and misused them? This was a hard question, and they hesitated, until at length a little bright-eyed girl with great earnestness replied: "I think He meant that you must be good to everybody, and mustn't quarrel or make nobody feel bad, and I'm going to try." An ominous smile crept over the rather hard faces of my four lads, but my response was so prompt, and my approval so hearty, that it disappeared and they listened attentively, but ventured no remarks. With this moderate beginning the day progressed, and night found us social, friendly, and classed for a school. Country schools did not admit of home dinners. I also remained. On the second or third day an accident on their outside field of rough play called me to them. They had been playing unfairly and dangerously and needed teaching, even to play well. I must have thought they required object lessons, for almost imperceptibly, either to them or to myself, I joined in the game and was playing with them.

My four lads soon perceived that I was no stranger to their sports or their tricks; that my early education had not been neglected, and that they were not the first boys I had seen. When they found that I was as agile and as strong as themselves, that my throw was as sure and as straight as theirs, and that if they won a game it was because I permitted it, their respect knew no bounds. No courtesy within their knowledge was neglected. Their example was sufficient for the entire school. I have seen no finer type of boys. They were faithful to me in their boyhood, and in their manhood faithful to their country. Their blood crimsoned its hardest fields, and the little bright-eyed girl with the good resolve has made her whole life a blessing to others, and still lives to follow the teaching given her. Little Emily has "made nobody feel bad."

My school was continued beyond the customary length of time, and its only hard feature was our parting. In memory I see that pitiful group of children sobbing their way down the hill after the last good-bye was said, and I was little better. We had all been children together, and when, in accordance with the then custom at town meetings, the grades of the schools were named and No. 9 stood first for discipline, I thought it the greatest injustice, and remonstrated, affirming that there had been no discipline, that not one scholar had ever been disciplined.

Child that I was, I did not know that the surest test of discipline is its absence.

Clara Barton was now embarked upon what seemed likely to be a life vocation. Her success in teaching was marked, and her reputation increased year by year. For twenty years the schoolroom was her home. She taught in district schools near Oxford, and established a school of her own, which she conducted for ten years. Then she stopped teaching for a time, in order to complete her own education, as completion then was accepted and understood. She did a memorable piece of school work in Bordentown, New Jersey, and, but for the failure of her voice, might have continued a teacher to the end of her life.

Her experiences during the years when she was teaching and pursuing further studies were recorded by her in 1908, in a manuscript which has never been published. She had already written and printed a little book entitled "The Story of my Childhood," which was well received and brought her many expressions of pleasure from its readers. She thought of continuing her autobiography in sections, and publishing these separately. She hoped then to revise and unify them, supplement them with adequate references to her record, and make a complete biography.

But she got no farther than the second installment, which must appear as a chapter in this present work.

Before turning to this narrative which marks the beginning of her life away from the parental roof, we may listen to the story of her first journey away from home. It occurred at the end of her first term of school, when her brother David set out on a journey to the State of Maine to bring home his bride, and asked her to accompany him.

One day, early in September, my brother David, now one of the active, popular business men of the town, nearly took my breath away by inviting me to accompany him on a journey to the State of Maine, to be present at his wedding and with him bring back the wife who was to grace his home and share his future life.

There was now more lengthening of skirts, and a rush of dressmaking such as I had never known before; and when, two weeks later, I found myself with my brother and a rather gay party of ladies and gentlemen, friends of his, at one of the most elegant hotels in Boston (where I had never been), waiting the arrival of a delayed steamer, I was so overcome by the dread of committing some impropriety or indiscretion which might embarrass my brother that I begged him to permit me to go back home. I was not distressed about what might be thought of me. I did not seem to care much about that; but how it might reflect upon my brother, and the mortification that my awkwardness could not fail to inflict on him.

I had never set foot on a vessel or seagoing craft of any kind, and when, in the glitter of that finely equipped steamer, I really crossed over a corner of the great Atlantic Ocean, the very waves of which touched other continents as well, I felt that my world was miraculously widening.

It was another merry party, and magnificent spans of horses that met and galloped away with us over the country to our destination.

But the crowning astonishment came when I was informed that it was the desire and decision of all parties, that I act as bridesmaid; that I assist in introducing the younger of the guests, and stand beside the tall, handsome young bride who was to be my sister, while she pledged her troth to the brother dearer to me than my own life.

This responsibility seemed to throw the whole world wide open to me. How well I remember the tearful resolution with which I pledged myself to try to overcome my troublesome propensities and to strive only for the courage of the right, and for the fearlessness of true womanhood so much needed and earnestly desired, and so painfully lacking.

November found us home again. Under the circumstances, there must naturally be a share of social gayeties during the winter, and some preparations for my new school duties; and I waited with more or less apprehension for what would be my first life among strangers, and the coming of my anticipated "First of May." With slight variation I could have joined truthfully in the dear old child refrain:

> "Then wake and call me early,
> Call me early, mother dear,"
> For that will be the veriest day
> "Of all the glad New Year."

LEAVES FROM HER UNPUBLISHED AUTOBIOGRAPHY

When Clara Barton began to teach school, she was only a little girl. To her family, she seemed even younger and more tiny than she was. But she had taken the words of Dr. Fowler to heart, and she determined to teach and to teach successfully. Mrs. Stafford, formerly Mamie Barton, remembers hearing her mother tell how seriously Clara took the edict of the phrenologist. To her it was nothing less than predestination and prophecy. In her own mind she was already a teacher, but she realized that in the mind of her household she was still a child. She stood beside the large stone fireplace, looking very slender and very small, and with dignity asked, "But what am I to do with only two little old waifish dresses?"

Julia, David Barton's young bride, was first to discern the pertinence of the question. If Clara was to teach school, she must have apparel suitable for her vocation. The "two little old waifish dresses," which had been deemed adequate for her home and school life, were replaced by new frocks that fell below her shoe-tops, and Clara Barton began her work.

She was a quick-tempered little teacher, dignified and self-possessed. Little and young though she was, she was not to be trifled with. She flogged, and on occasion expelled, but she won respect at the outset and very soon affection. Then floggings ceased almost altogether.

At first she was teacher only of the spring and autumn school nearest her home; then she taught in districts in Oxford farther away; then came the incontrovertible certificate of success in her invitation to teach the winter school, which according to predecent must be managed by a man capable of whipping the entire group of big boys. And in all this experience of teaching she succeeded.

In 1908 she wrote the second installment of her autobiography, and in that she related how she finished her teaching in Oxford and went for further education to Clinton Institute:

Hard, tiresome years were these, with no advancement for me. Some, I hoped, for others. Little children grew to be large, and mainly "well behaved." Boys grew to manhood, and continued faithfully in their work, or went out and entered into business, seeking other vocations. A few girls became teachers, but more continued at their looms or set up housekeeping for themselves, but whatever sphere opened to them, they were all mine, second only to the claims and interests of the real mother. And so they have remained. Scattered over the world, some near, some far, I have been their confidant, standing at their nuptials if possible, lent my name to their babies, followed their fortunes to war's gory fields, staunched their blood, dressed their wounds, and closed their Northern eyes on the hard-fought fields of the Southland; and yet, all this I count as little in comparison with the faithful, grateful love I hold to-day of the few survivors of my Oxford schools.

I shall have neglected a great, I could almost say a holy, duty, if I fail to mention the name, and connect the presence, of the Reverend Horatio Bardwell with this school. Reverend Dr. Bardwell, an early India missionary, and for over twenty years pastor of the Congregational Church of Oxford, where his memory lovingly lingers to-day, as if he had passed from them but yesterday, or indeed had not passed at all.

Dr. Bardwell was continuously on the School Board of the town, and his custom was to drop in upon a school, familiarly, at a most unexpected moment. I recall the amusing scenes, when, by some unusual sound behind me, my attention would be called from the class I had before me, to see my entire school, which had risen unbidden, standing with hands resting on the desk before them, heads reverently bent, and Dr. Bardwell midway of the open door, with hands upraised in mute wonder and admiration. At length he would find voice, with, "What a sight, what a multitude!" The school reseated itself when bidden and prepared for the visit of a half-hour of pleasant conversation, anecdotes, and advice that even the smallest would not willingly have missed. It was the self-reliant, self-possessed, and unbidden courtesy of these promiscuous children that won the Doctor's admiration. He saw in these something for a future to build upon.

47

It is to be remembered that I am not writing romance, nor yet ancient history, where I can create or vary my models to suit myself. It is, in fact, semi-present history, with most notable characters still existing, who can, at any moment, rise up and call me to order. To avoid such a contingency, I may sometimes be more explicit than I otherwise would be at the risk of prolixity. This possibility leads me to state that a few times in the years I was borrowed, for a part of a winter term, by some neighboring town, where it would be said there was trouble, and some school was "not getting on well." I usually found that report to have been largely illusive, for they got on very well with me. Probably it was the old adage of a "new broom," for I did nothing but teach them. I recall one of these experiences as transpiring in Millbury, the grand old town where the lamented and honored mother of our President-elect Judge Taft has just passed to a better land. That early and undeserved reputation for "discipline" always clung to me.

Most of this transpired during years in which I should have been in school myself, using time and opportunities for my own advancement which could not be replaced. This thought grew irresistibly upon me, until I decided that I must withdraw and find a school, the object of which should be to teach me something. The number of educational institutions for women was one to a thousand as compared with to-day. I knew I must place myself so far away that a "run of bad luck" in the home school could not persuade me to return—it would be sure to have one.

Religiously, I had been educated in the liberal thought of my family, and preferring to remain in that atmosphere, I decided upon the "Liberal Institute," of Clinton, New York.

I recall with pain even now the regret with which my family, especially my brothers, heard my announcement. I had become literally a part, if not a partner, of them in school and office. My brother Stephen was school superintendent, thus there was no necessity for making my intentions public, and I would spare both my school and myself the pain of parting. I closed my autumn term, as usual, on Friday night. On Monday night the jingling cutter of my brothers (for it was early sleighing), took me to the station for New

48

York. This was in reality going away from home. I had left the smothered sighs, the blessings, and the memories of a little life behind me. My journey was made in silence and safety, and the third day found me installed as a guest in the "Clinton House" of Clinton, Oneida County, New York—a typical old-time tavern. My hosts were Mr. and Mrs. Samuel Bertram—and again the hand rests, and memory pauses, to pay its tribute of grateful, loving respect to such as I shall never know again this side the Gates Eternal.

It was holiday season. The Institute was undergoing a transfer from old to new buildings. These changes caused a delay of some weeks, while I became a part and parcel of the family I had so incidentally and fortunately fallen among.

Clinton was also the seat of Hamilton College. The sisters and relatives of the students of Hamilton contributed largely to the personnel of the Institute. Reverend Dr. Sawyer presided over Hamilton, and Miss Louise Barker with a competent corps of assistants presided over the Institute.

It was a cold, blustering winter day that assembled us in the almost as cold schoolrooms of the newly finished and sparsely furnished building. Even its clean new brick walls on its stately eminence looked cold, and the two-plank walk with a two-foot space between, leading up from town, was not suggestive of the warmest degree of sociability, to say the least of it. My introduction to our Preceptress, or President, Miss Barker, was both a pleasure and a surprise to me. I found an unlooked-for activity, a cordiality, and an irresistible charm of manner that none could have foreseen—a winning, indescribable grace which I have met in only a few persons in a whole lifetime. Those who remember the eminent Dr. Lucy Hall Brown, of Brooklyn, who only a year ago passed out through California's "Golden Gate," will be able to catch something of what I mean, but cannot describe. Neither could they. To no one had I mentioned anything of myself, or my past. No "certificate of character" had been mentioned, and no recommendation from my "last place" been required of me. There was no reason why I should volunteer my history, or step in among that crowd of eager pupils as a "school-marm," expected to know everything.

The easiest way for me was to keep silent, as I did, and so well kept that I left that Institute at the close without a mistrust on the part of any one that I had ever taught school a day.

The difficulty to be met lay mainly in the assignment of studies. The prescribed number was a cruel limit. I was there for study. I required no rudiments, and wanted no allowance for waste time; I would use it all; and diffidently I made this fact known at the head, asking one more and one more study until the limit was stretched out of all reasonable proportions. I recall, with amusement, the last evening when I entered with my request. The teachers were assembled in the parlor and, divining my errand, as I had never any other, Miss Barker broke into a merry laugh—with "Miss Barton, we have a few studies left; you had better take what there are, and we will say nothing about it." This broke the ice, and the line. I could only join in the laugh, and after this studied what I would, and "nothing was said."

I would by no means be understood as crediting myself with superior scholarship. There were doubtless far more advanced scholars there than I, but I had a drilled rudimentary knowledge which they had never had, and I had the habit of study, with a burning anxiety to make the most of lost time. So true it is that we value our privileges only when we have lost them.

Miss Barton spent her vacations at the Institute. A few teachers were there, and a small group of students; and she pursued her studies and gave her reading wider range. She wanted to go home, but the distance seemed great, and she was there to learn.

Her mother died while she was at Clinton. Her death occurred in July, but before the term had ended. Clara could not reach home in time for the funeral and her family knew it and sent her word not to undertake the journey.

She finished her school year and her course, made a visit to her home, and then journeyed to Bordentown,

New Jersey, to visit her friends, the Norton family. There the opportunity came to her of teaching the winter term of the Bordentown school.

"Public schools of that day," she wrote, "ceased with the southern boundary of New England and New York. Each pupil was assessed a certain fee, the aggregate of which formed the teacher's salary."

She undertook the school on the fee basis, but in a short time changed it to a public school, open to all the children of school age in Bordentown. It was that town's first free school. The School Board agreed to give her the opportunity to try the experiment. She tells how it came about. She looked over the little group who attended her subscription school, and then saw the much larger number outside, and she was not happy:

But the boys! I found them on all sides of me. Every street corner had little knots of them idle, listless, as if to say, what shall one do, when one has nothing to do? I sought every inconspicuous occasion to stop and talk with them. I saw nothing unusual in them. Much like other boys I had known, unusually courteous, showing special instruction in that line, and frequently of unusual intelligence. They spoke of their banishment or absence from school with far less of bravado or boasting than would have been expected, under the circumstances, and often with regret. "Lady, there is no school for us," answered a bright-faced lad of fourteen, as he rested his foot on the edge of a little park fountain where I had accosted him. "We would be glad to go if there was one." I had listened to such as this long enough, and, without returning to my hotel, I sought Mr. Suydam, as chairman of the School Committee, and asked for an interview.

By this time, in his capacity of postmaster, we had formed a tolerable acquaintance. Now, for the first time,

I made known my desire to open a public school in Bordentown, teaching it myself.

Surprise, discouragement, resistance, and sympathy were all pictured on his manly face. He was troubled for terms in which to express the mental conflict, but in snatches something like this.

These boys were renegades, many of them more fit for the penitentiary than school—a woman could do nothing with them. They wouldn't go to school if they had the chance, and the parents

51

would never send them to a "pauper school." I would have the respectable sentiment of the entire community against me; I could never endure the obloquy, not to call it disgrace that I should meet; and to crown all, I should have the bitter opposition of all the present teachers, many of whom were ladies of influence in society and would contend vigorously for their rights. A strong man would quail and give way under what he would be compelled to meet, and what could a woman—a young woman, and a stranger—do?

He spoke very kindly and appreciatingly of the intention, acknowledging the necessity, and commending the nature of the effort, but it was ill-timed, and had best be at once abandoned as impracticable.

With this honest effort, and, wiping the perspiration from his forehead, he rested. After a moment's quiet and seeing that he did not resume, I said with a respect, which I most sincerely felt, "Thank you, Mr. Suydam, shall I speak?" "Certainly, Miss Barton," and with a little appreciative laugh, "I will try to be as good a listener as you have been."

I thanked him again for the evident sincerity of his objections, assuring him that I believed them drawn entirely in my interest, and his earnest desire to save me from what seemed to him an impossible undertaking, with only failure and humiliation as sure and logical results. A few of these I would like to answer, and throwing off the mask I had worn since Clinton, told him plainly that I was, and had been for years, a teacher of the public schools of New England. That was my profession, and that, if entered in the long and honored competitive list of such, I did not suppose that in either capacity, experience, or success I should stand at the foot. I had studied the character of these boys, and had intense pity for, but no fear of, them. As for exclusion from society, I had not sought society, and could easily dispense with it, if they so willed; I was not here for that. As for reputation, I had brought with me all I needed, and that of a character that a bit of village gossip could not affect. With all respect for the prejudices of the people, I should try not to increase them. My only desire was to open and teach a school in Bordentown, to which its outcast children could go and be taught;

and I would emphasize that desire by adding that I wished no salary. I would open and teach such a school without remuneration, but my effort must have the majesty of the law, and the power vested in its offices behind it or it could not stand. If I secured a building and proceeded to open a school, it would be only one more private school like the score they already had; that the School Board, as officers of the law, with accepted rights and duties, must so far connect themselves with the effort as to provide quarters, the necessary furnishings, and to give due and respectable notice of the same among the people. In fact, it must stand as by their order, leaving the work and results to me.

I was not there for necessity. Fortunately I needed nothing of them—neither as an adventuress. I had no personal ambitions to serve, but as an observer of unwelcome conditions, and, as I thought, harmful as well, to try, so far as possible, the power of a good, wise, beneficent, and established state law, as against the force of ignorance, blind prejudice, and the tyranny of an obsolete, outlived public opinion. I desired to see them both fairly placed upon their merits before an intelligent community, leaving the results to the winner. If the law, after trial, were not acceptable, or of use to the people serving their best interest, abolish or change it—if it were, enforce and sustain it.

My reply was much longer than the remarks that had called for it, but the pledge of good listening was faithfully kept.

When he spoke again, it was to ask if I desired my proposition to be laid before the School Board? I surely did. He would speak with the gentlemen this evening, and call a meeting for to-morrow. Our interview had consumed two hours, and we parted better friends than we commenced.

The following afternoon, to my surprise, I was most courteously invited to sit with the School Board in its deliberations, and I made the acquaintance of two more, plain, honest-minded gentlemen. The subject was fairly discussed, but with great misgivings, a kind of tender sympathy running through it all. At length Mr. Suydam arose, and, addressing his colleagues, said, "Gentlemen, we feel alike, I am sure, regarding the hazardous nature of this experiment and its probable results, but situated as we are, officers of a law which we are sworn to obey and enforce, can we legally decline to accede to this proposition, which is in every respect within the law. From your expressed opinions of last evening I believe we agree on this point, and I put the vote."

It was a unanimous yea, with the decision that the old closed schoolhouse be refitted, and a school commenced.

The school speedily outgrew its quarters, and Clara sent word to Oxford that she must have an assistant. Her brother Stephen secured the services of Miss Frances Childs, who subsequently became Mrs. Bernard Barton Vassall. Frances had just finished her first term as teacher of a school in Oxford, and she proved a very capable assistant. Letters from, and personal interviews with, her have brought vividly before me the conditions of Clara's work in Bordentown.

She thus writes me of her happy memories:

When Clara's school in Bordentown had become so pronounced a success that she could not manage it alone, she sent for me. I had a separate schoolroom, the upstairs room over a tailor shop. I had about sixty pupils. Clara and I boarded and roomed together. The editor of the Bordentown "Gazette" roomed at the same place. He frequently commented on the fact that when Clara and I were in our room together, we were always talking and laughing. It was a constant wonder to him. He could not understand how we found so much to laugh at.

Clara was so sensitive, she felt it keenly when any pupil had to be punished, or any parent was disappointed, but she did not indulge very long in mourning or self-reproach, she knew she had done her best and she laughed and made the best of it. Clara had an unfailing sense of humor. She said to me once that of all the qualities she possessed, that for which she felt most thankful was her sense of humor. She said it helped her over many hard places.

Clara had quick wit, and was very ready with repartee and apt reply. I remember an evening when she brought to a close a rather lengthy discussion by a quick reply that set us all to laughing. We spent an evening at the home of the Episcopalian minister, who was one of the School Committee. The discussion turned to phrenology. Clara had great faith in it. The minister did not believe in it at all. They had quite an argument about it. He told Clara of a man who had suffered an injury to the brain which had resulted in the removal of a considerable part of it. He argued that if there was anything in phrenology, that man would have been deprived of a certain group of mental capabilities, but that he got on very well with only a part of a brain. Clara replied quickly, "Then there's hope for me." So the discussion ended in a hearty laugh.

As a school-teacher, Clara Barton was a pronounced success. We are not dependent wholly upon her own account of her years as a teacher. From many and distant places her pupils rose up and called her blessed. Nothing pleased her more than the letters which she received from time to time, in after years, from men and women who had been pupils of hers and who wrote to tell her with what satisfaction and gratitude they remembered her instruction. Some of these letters were received by her as early as 1851, when she was at Clinton Institute. Her answers were long, appreciative, and painstaking. In those days Clara Barton was something of an artist, and had taught drawing and painting. One or two of her letters of this period have ornamented letterheads with birds and other scroll work. Her letters always abounded in good cheer, and often contained wholesome advice, though she did not preach to her pupils. Some of these letters from former pupils continued to reach her after she had become well-known. Men in business and in political life wrote reminding her that they had been bad boys in her school, and telling of her patience, her tact, and the inspiration of her ideals.

Her home letters in the years before the war are the letters of a dutiful daughter and affectionate sister. She wrote to her father, her brothers, and especially to Julia, the wife of David Barton, who was perhaps the best correspondent in the family. She bore on her heart all the family anxieties. If any member of the family was sick, the matter was constantly on her mind. She wanted to know every detail, in what room were they keeping him? Was the parlor chimney drawing well? And was every possible provision made for comfort? She made many suggestions as to simple remedies, and more as to nursing, hygiene, and general comfort. Always when there was sickness she wished that she were there. She wanted to assist in the nursing. She sent frequent messages to her brothers and sisters, nieces and nephews. The messages were always considerate, affectionate, and unselfish. She was not often homesick; in general she made the best of her absences from home, and busied herself with the day's task. But whenever there was anything at home which suggested an occasion for anxiety or an opportunity for service, then she wished herself home. She visualized the home at such times, and carried a mental picture of the house, the room, the bedside of the patient. One of these letters, written from Washington to Julia Barton, when her father was dangerously ill, may here be inserted as an illustration of her devotion to her parents and to all members of her family:

Washington, D.C., 29th Dec., 1860

Dear Sister:

I don't know what to say or how to write you, I am so uncertain of the scenes you may be passing through. In thought and spirit I am in the room with you every moment—that it is sad and painful, or sad and desolate I know. I can almost see, and almost hear, and almost know, how it all is—between us seems to be only the "veil so thin so strong," there are moments when I think I can brush it away with my hand and look upon that dear treasured form and face, the earliest loved and latest mourned of all my life. Sometimes I am certain I hear the patient's feeble moan, and at others above me the clouds seem to divide, and, in the opening up among the blue and golden, that loved face, smiling and pleasant, looks calmly down upon me; then I think it is all past, and my poor father is at rest. Aye! more that he has learned the password to the Mystic Lodge of God and entered in: that the Providences and mysteries he has loved so much to contemplate are being made plain to him; that the inquiries of his intelligent soul are to be satisfied and that the God he has always worshiped he may now adore.

And in spite of all the grief, the agony of parting, there is pleasure in these reflections, and consolation in the thought that while we may have one the less tie upon earth, we shall have one more treasure in Heaven.

And yet again, when I look into my own heart, there is underlying the whole a little of the old-time hope—hope that he may yet be spared to us a

56

little longer; that a few more months or years may be given us in which to prove the love and devotion of our hearts; that we may again listen to his wise counsels and kind admonitions, and hourly I pray Heaven that, if it be consistent with Divine arrangement, the cup may pass from him. But God's will, not mine, be done.

If my father still lives and realizes, will you tell him how much I love him and regret his sufferings, and how much rather I would endure them myself if he could be saved from them?

With love and sympathy to all,
I am, your affectionate sister

Clara

Her letters to members of her family are seldom of great importance. They concern themselves with the trivial details of her and their daily life; thoughtful answers to all their inquiries, and expressions of affection and interest in all their concerns. In some respects the letters are more interesting which she wrote when she was temporarily in Oxford. One of these was addressed to her brother David, who had gone South to visit Stephen, then a resident of North Carolina. It was written at the time when she had been removed from her position in the Patent Office, and for a while was at home. David had written Julia in some concern lest he should not have provided in advance for her every possible want before his leaving her to go South. Clara replied to this letter, making merry over the "destitute" condition in which David had left his wife, and giving details about business affairs and home life. It is a thoroughly characteristic letter, full of fun and detail and neighborhood gossip and sisterly good-will. If her brothers were to stay in the South in hot weather, she wanted to be with them. She had already proposed to Stephen that he let her go South and look after him, and Stephen had sought to dissuade her, telling her that the conditions of life were uncomfortable, and that she would be shocked by seeing the almost nude condition of the negro laborers. None of these things frightened her. The only things she was afraid of were things about which she had told David, and we cannot help wishing we knew what they were. It is good to know that by this time the objects of her fear made rather a short list, for she was by nature timid and easily terrified, but had become self-reliant and strong.

Dear Brother:

This is an excessively warm day, and Julia scarcely thinks she can get her courage up to the sticking point to sit down to letter-writing, but I will try it, for the weather is all alike to me, only just comfortably warm, and I can as well scribble letters as anything. We are rejoiced to hear such good reports from Stephen. It cannot be, however, that he was ready to return with you? For his sake I hope he could, but should be frightened if I knew he attempted it. We are all well; received your short letter in due time. Julia has discoursed considerably upon the propriety of that word "destitute" which you made use of. She says you left her with a barrel and a half of flour, a barrel and a half of crackers, a good new milch cow, fish, ham, dried beef, a barrel of pork, four good hogs in the pen, a field of early potatoes just coming on, a good garden, plenty of fowls, a good grain crop in and a man to take care of them, a good team, thirty cords of wood at the door and a horse and chaise to ride where she pleased. This she thinks is one of the last specimens of destitution. Can scarcely sleep at night through fear of immediate want—and beside we have not mentioned the crab apples. I shouldn't wonder if we have fifty bushels of them; this only depends upon the size they attain, there are certainly enough in number. The hoeing is all done once, and the piece out by Mr. Baker's gone over the second time. Uncle Joe helped. The taxes are paid, yours, Colonel Davis's, and Brine's. The two latter I have charged to them and pasted the receipts in the books. I have put down Brine's* time for last week and made out a new time page for July. Brine has gone to Worcester with old Eb to-day, and I have put that down and carried his account to a new page.

*Brine Murphy, a hired man.

Whitlock has not paid yet, but the 2'-40" man on the hill has paid .75. Old Mrs. Collier is going to pay before she gets herself a new pair of shoes, and Sam avers that she is not only in need of shoes, but stockings, to which fact he is a living eye-witness. Johnson "hasn't a cent—will pay next week—"This, I believe, finishes up the schedule of money matters until we report next time. Mr. Samuel Smith is dead. Was buried Thursday, I think. I have just written to the Colonel at Boston and to Cousin Ira the intelligence from Stephen when we first learned that he was really better, and had hardly sent the letters away before the Judge came in. He was anxious to hear from us and also to attend the funeral, so took the morning train and came out, took dinner, and then he and father took Dick and the chaise and went to the funeral, came back, stayed to supper, and I went and carried him to the depot. We had a most delightful visit from him. Every time I see Cousin

Ira, I think he is a better and better cousin. It is hardly possible for us to esteem him enough. I forgot to tell you about the garden. Julia has hoed it all over, set out the cabbage plants, waters them almost every day; they are looking finely. She has weeded all the beds, and Sam says he will help her some about the garden. Brine doesn't seem to take an interest in the fine arts. Julia says she hopes you will not take a moment's trouble about us, for we are getting on finely and shall do so, but you must take care of yourself. We—i.e. Julia and I—shall ride down to the Colonel's this evening after sundown. I should like to see him and know he would like to hear from you again. I have not heard where Stephen is or how since you wrote, but trust he is no worse, and I also hope you may be able to favor and counsel him so as to keep him up when he gets back. I feel as much solicitude on your account as his, for I know how liable you are to get out of fix. I wish every day that I was there to see that both of you had what you needed to take and to be done for you. I was earnest in what I wished you to say to Stephen, that I was ready to go to Carolina or anywhere else if I could serve him; not that I want a job, as I should insist on putting my labor against my board, but earnestly if you are both going to try to summer there and Stephen so feeble as he is, I shall be glad to be with you. Still, if not proper or acceptable, I, of course, shall not urge myself or feel slighted, but I feel afraid to have you both there by yourselves; while you go away on business, he will be obliged to do something at home to get sick, and maybe I could do it for him if I were there, or at least take care of him in time. I am not afraid of naked negroes or rough houses, and you know the only things in all the world I should fear, for I told you—nothing else aside from these. I have no precaution or care for anything there could be there, but I have said enough and too much. Stephen may think I am willing to make myself more plenty than welcome, but I have obeyed the dictates of my feelings and judgment and can do no more, and I could not have done it and done less, so I leave it. If I can serve you, tell me. I have seen neither of the Washington tourists yet, and I went to the depot this morning to meet Irving I if he was there, but he did not come. Please tell me if Mr. Vassall talks of going to Carolina this summer, or will he come North? I have offered Julia this space to fill up, but she says I have told all the news and declines, and it is almost time to get ready to ride; so good-bye, and write a word or two often. Don't trouble to send long letters, it is hot work to write. Sleep all you can, don't drink ice water, be careful about grease, don't expose yourself to damp evenings or mornings if too misty, or you will get the chills. Love to Stephen. Will he ever write me, I wonder?

From your affectionate sister

Great as was Clara Barton's success in Bordentown, she did not move forward without opposition. Although she had built up the public school to a degree of efficiency which it had not before known, she met the resolute her nephew. opposition of those who objected to a woman's control of a school as important as this had now grown to be. It was rather pathetic that her very success should have been used as an occasion of opposition. The school was alleged to be too large for a woman to manage. A woman had made it large and had managed it while it was in process of becoming large, and was continuing to manage it very well. However, the demand for a male principal grew very strong, and, against the wishes of a large majority of the pupils, a male principal was chosen. Clara Barton would not remain and occupy a second place. Moreover, it was time for her to leave the schoolroom. For almost twenty years she had been constantly teaching, and her work at Bordentown, never easy, had ended in a record of success which brought its own reaction and disappointment. Suddenly she realized that her energy was exhausted. Her voice completely failed. A nervous collapse, such as came to her a number of times later in life, laid her prostrate. She left her great work at Bordentown and went to Washington to recuperate. She did not know it, but she was leaving the schoolroom behind her forever.

In those days Clara Barton was much given to writing verse. She never entirely gave it up. The most of her poetical writing during this period is of no especial interest, but consists of verses for autograph albums, and other ephemeral writing. Once, while she was at Bordentown, she tried a rhymed advertisement. At least twice while she was teaching in that village, she made a round trip to Philadelphia on the steamboat John Stevens. On the second occasion the steamboat had been redecorated, and she scribbled a jingle concerning its attractions in the back of her diary. She may have had some idea that her Pegasus could be profitably harnessed to the chariot of commerce, and it is possible that she offered this little jingle to the proprietors of the boat or to the editor of the Bordentown "Gazette," who roomed at the house where she boarded. The files of that enterprising publication have not been searched, but they probably would show that now and then Clara Barton handed to the editor some poetical comment on passing events. So far as is known, however, these lines about the beauty of the rejuvenated John Stevens have not appeared in print before, and it is now too late for them to be of value in increasing the business of her owners. It is pleasant, however, to have this reminder of her occasional outings while she was teaching school, and to know that she enjoyed them as she did her river journey to Philadelphia and back:

ADVERTISEMENT

Written on board the John Stevens between Bordentown and Philadelphia March 12, 1853

You've not seen the John Stevens since her new dress she donned?
Why, you'd think she'd been touched by a fairy's wand! Such carpets, such curtains, just sprang into light,
Such mirrors bewildering the overcharged sight.
Such velvets, such cushions, such sofas and all,
Then the polish that gleams on her glittering wall.
Now if it be true that you've not seen her yet,
We ask you, nay! urge you, implore and beset,
That you will no longer your interests forget,
But at once take a ticket as we have to-day,
And our word as a warrant—
You'll find it will pay.

THE HEART OF CLARA BARTON

When Clara Barton left the schoolroom for the life of a clerk in Washington, she was well past thirty years of age. When the war broke out, and she left the Patent Office for the battle-field, she was forty. Why was not she already married? Her mother married at seventeen; her sister married early: why was she single and teaching school at thirty, or available for hospital service at forty? And why did she not marry some soldier whom she tended? Did any romance lie behind her devotion to what became her life-work? Had she suffered any disappointment in love before she entered upon her career?

The question whether Clara Barton was ever in love has been asked by everyone who has attempted anything approaching a sketch of her career. Mr. Epler's biography contained a chapter on this subject, but later it was found so incomplete and unsatisfactory it was thought best to omit it and to await the opening of her personal and official papers. These now are available, as well as the personal recollections of those of her relatives whose knowledge of her life includes any possibility of affairs of the heart.

On the subject of her personal affections, Clara Barton was very reticent. To the present writer she said that she chose, somewhat early in life, the course which seemed to her more fruitful of good for her than matrimony. In her girlhood she was shy, and, when she found her life vocation, as she then esteemed it, as a teacher, she was so much interested in her school that she gave little thought to matrimony, and was satisfied that on the whole it would be better in her case if she lived unmarried. She had little patience, however, with women who affect to despise men. Always loyal to her own sex, and proud of every woman who accomplished anything notable, she was no man-hater, but, on the contrary, enjoyed the society of men, trusted their judgment, and liked their companionship.

Her nephew, Stephen E. Barton, furnishes me this paragraph:

My aunt said to me at one time that I must not think she had never known any experience of love. She said that she had had her romances and love affairs like other girls; but that in her young womanhood, though she thought of different men as possible lovers, no one of them measured up to her ideal of a husband. She said to me that she could think of herself with satisfaction as a wife and mother, but that on the whole she felt that she had been more useful to the world by being free from matrimonial ties.

So far as her diaries and letters show, she remained heart-whole through the entire period of her girlhood in Oxford. There was, however, a young man of about her own age, born in Oxford, and a very distant relative between whom and herself there existed something approaching affection. The families were long-time friends, and the young people had interests in common. A lady who remembers him well says: "She was fond of him and he of her. He was a handsome young fellow, and Clara once said to me that she should not want the man to have all the good looks in the family."

This friendship continued for many years, and developed on the part of the young man a very deep affection, and on Clara's part sincere respect. He visited her when she was a student in Clinton Institute, and was of real service to her there, making fine proof of his faithful friendship, but she could not be sure that she loved him.

She had another ardent admirer in Oxford, who followed her to Bordentown and there pressed his suit. Clara had long corresponded with him, and for a time was uncertain how much she cared for him. This young man had come to know her while she was a teacher in Oxford and she was boarding in the family where he lived. In 1849 he went to California in search of gold, and on his return was eager to take her out of the schoolroom and establish her in a home. For this purpose he visited her in Bordentown. She welcomed him, and sincerely wished that she could love him, but, while she held him in thorough respect, she did not see in him the possibilities of a husband, such as she would have chosen. He pressed his suit, and she sorrowfully declined. They remained firm friends as long as he lived.

A third young man is known to have made love to her while she was at Clinton Institute. He was the brother of one of the young women in the school whom she cherished as a dear friend. He was a young man of fine character, but her heart did not respond to him.

Two or more of these affairs lay heavy on her heart and conscience about the time of her leaving Clinton Institute and of her teaching in Bordentown. She was then in correspondence with three young men who loved her, and in a state of some mental uncertainty. If letters were delayed she missed them, and recorded in her diary:

Rather melancholy. Don't know why. I received no intelligence from certain quarters.

In the spring of 1852 she had a brief period of depression, growing, in part at least, out of her uncertainty in these matters. On Tuesday, March 2, 1852, she wrote in her diary:

Morning cold and icy. Walked to school. Dull day and unpleasant, cheerless indoors and out. Cannot see much in these days worth living for; cannot but think it will be a quiet resting-place when all these cares and vexations and anxieties are over, and I no longer give or take offense. I am badly organized to live in the world, or among society; I have participated in too many of its unpleasant scenes; have always looked on its most unhappy features and have grown weary of life at an age when other people are enjoying it most.

On Thursday, March 13, she wrote:

I have found it extremely hard to restrain the tears today, and would have given almost anything to have been alone and undisturbed. I have seldom felt more friendless, and I believe I ever feel enough so. I see less and less in the world to live for, and in spite of all my resolution and reason and moral courage and everything else, I grow weary and impatient. I know it is wicked and perhaps foolish, but I cannot help it. There is not a living thing but would be just as well off without me. I contribute to the happiness of not a single object; and often to the unhappiness of many and always of my own, for I am never happy. True, I laugh and joke, but could weep that very moment, and be the happier for it.

"There's many a grief lies hid, not lost,
And smiles the least befit who wear them most."

How long I can endure such a life I do not know, but often wish that more of its future path lay on the other side of the present. I am grateful when so many of the days pass away. But this repining is of no use, and I would not say or write it for any ear or eye but my own. I cannot help thinking it, and it is a relief to say it to myself; but I will indulge in such useless complaints no more, but commence once more my allotted task.

The mood did not last long. Its immediate occasion had been a not very cheerful letter from friends in Oxford, and a discussion with the mother of a dull pupil who was troubled because her daughter was not learning faster. Three days later she was seeking to account for her depression by some possible telepathic influence from home; for she had word of the burning of Stephen's factory. Far from being the more depressed by this really bad news, she was much relieved to know that he had not rushed into the burning building, as would have been just like him, and have been killed or injured in trying to save the property or to help someone else.

On Friday night she had finished a reasonably good week, and had a longer letter than usual from the lover whom she had known longest. It "of course pleased me in proportion to its length." She adds, "I am puzzled to know how I can manage one affair, and fear I cannot do it properly."

The reader of these yellow pages, after seventy years and more, knows better than she knew then what was troubling her most, and can smile at what caused her so much concern.

By the following Tuesday she resolved to "begin to think earnestly of immediate future. Have not made any definite plans."

This necessity of planning for the immediate future brought back her bad feelings. She wrote on Wednesday, March 24:

Think I shall not write as much in future. Grow dull and I fear selfish in my feelings and care less what is going on. Not that I think less of others, but less of myself, and am more and more certain every day that there is no such thing as true friendship, at least for me; and I will not dupe and fool myself with the idle, vain hobby any longer. It is all false; in fact, the whole world is false. This brings me to my old inquiry again, what is the use of living in it? I can see no possible satisfaction or benefit arising from my life; others may from theirs.

A week later she wrote that she had no letters, but had "grown indifferent and did not care either to write or to receive letters."

She had resolved not to write so much, but she went on:

I am thinking to-night of the future, and what my next move must be. Wish I had someone to advise me, or that I could speak to someone of it. Had ever one poor girl so many strange, wild thoughts, and no one to listen or share one of them, or even to realize that my head contains one idea beyond the present foolish moment?

But she resolves to stop this vain and moody introspection:

I will not allow myself anymore such grumbling! I know it is wicked. But how can I make myself happy and contented under such circumstances as I am ever placed in?

Her diary then grew irregular, with no entries between April 20 and May 25. Within that time she solved a part of her love-problem:

Have kept no journal for a month or more. Had nothing to note, but some things are registered where they will never be effaced in my lifetime.

But she finished her school successfully; went to Trenton and bought a silk dress. She filled the back of this book with a list of the English poets with the dates of their birth and death, and a sentence or two descriptive of each of the more prominent. She had this habit of writing, in the back of her journal, things that belonged to no one day. The volume previous contained a sentimental poem of a tragic parting of lovers, and a lachrymose effusion entitled "A Prayer for Death."

These entries and incidents are cited because they are wholly exceptional. While she was ever morbidly sensitive, to the day of her death, and under strain of criticism or lack of appreciation given to great and wholly disproportionate depression of spirits, these entries, made when she had no less than three possible matrimonial entanglements in prospect, and was not sure whether she wanted any, must be the sole documentary evidence of a strain from which both she and the men concerned wholly recovered. All of the men are known by name, and they married and left families, and were little if any the worse, and quite possibly were the better, for having loved Clara Barton. Nor, though the perplexities of having too many lovers, mingled as these perplexities were with the daily problems of the schoolroom and a long absence from home, during which her home letters made her homesick, did the experience do her any permanent harm. Not long did she wish to die.

Indeed, her mood was soon a very different one. The entries that have been cited were made at Hightstown.

Next year she was at Bordentown, and there she throve so well she had to send back to her home town for an assistant. She still had one love affair, already referred to, but it had ceased to depress her seriously.

A young woman of thirty is not to be blamed for stopping to consider that she may not always be bothered by three simultaneous offers of marriage. On the other hand, while all of these were worthy men, there was not one of them so manifestly stronger than she that she felt she was safe in giving her heart to him. The vexations of the schoolroom suggested the quiet of a home as a pleasant contrast, but which should she choose, and were there any of the men to whom she could forever look up with affection and sustained regard?

For each one of these three young men she appears to have had a genuine regard. She liked them, all of them, and it was not easy for her to see them go out of her life. The time came when each of them demanded to know where he stood in her affections; and each time this occurred she had a period of heart-searching, and thought herself the most miserable young woman alive. In each case, however, she came to the sane and commendable decision, not to bestow her hand where her heart could not go utterly.

From one who knew her intimately in those days I have this statement:

Clara Barton had many admirers, and they were all men whom she admired and some whom she almost loved. More men were interested in her than she was ever interested in; some of them certainly interested her, yet not profoundly. I do not think she ever had a love affair that stirred the depths of her being. The truth is, Clara Barton was herself so much stronger a character than any of the men who made love to her that I do not think she was ever seriously tempted to marry any of them. She was so pronounced in her opinions that a man who wanted a submissive wife would have stood somewhat in awe of her. However good a wife she might have made to a man whom she knew to be her equal, and for whom she felt real admiration, she would not have been an ideal wife for a man to whom she could not look up, not only in regard to moral character, which in every case was above reproach, but also as to intellect, education, and ambition.

Clara Barton's diaries did not ordinarily indulge in self-analysis. She recorded the events of the day briefly, methodically, and without much comment. She indicated by initials the young men to whom she wrote and from whom she received letters, relatives being spoken of by their first names. The passages quoted from her diaries are exceptional. While she was highly sensitive, and morbidly conscientious, her usual moods were those of quiet and sensible performance of her day's work.

For ten years after she began to teach, she was shut out from any real opportunity for love. Her elevation to the teacher's platform, while still a child, shut out her normal opportunity for innocent flirtation. Love hardly peeped in at her during her teens, or in her early twenties. By the time it came to her, other interests had gained a long start. She was ambitious, she was determined to find out what she was good for, and to do something worthwhile in life. Had some young man come into her life as worthy as those who made love to her, and who was her equal or superior in ability and education, she might have learned to love him. As it was, she decided wisely both for herself and for the men who sought her hand.

Having thus chosen, she did not mourn her fate. She enjoyed her friendships with men and with women, and lived her busy, successful, and happy life. She did not talk of these affairs, nor did she write of them. She retained the personal friendship of the men whom she refused; and two of them, who lived not far from her in New England, made their friendship manifest in later years. Few people knew that they had ever been rejected lovers of hers; they were esteemed and lifelong friends.

There were times when her heart cried out for something more than this. From the day of her birth she was too isolated. Her public career began before her shy childhood had ended. She was too solitary; she had "strange, wild thoughts," and no one to whom to confide them. She could have welcomed the love of a strong, true man. She was always over-sensitive. She was cut to the very heart by experiences which she ought to have treated as almost negligible. She met opposition, criticism, injustice with calm demeanor, but she bled within her armor, and covered herself with undeserved reproaches and unhappy reflections that she seemed doomed to give and to suffer pain. In some respects she was peculiarly unfitted to meet the world alone. But she met it and conquered it. She turned her loneliness into a rich companionship of friendships; she forgot her solitude in unselfish ministry. Spite of her shrinking nature, her natural timidity, her over-sensitiveness, she lived a full and happy life. Those who knew her remember few laments and fewer tears, but many a constant smile, a quick and unfailing sense of humor, a healthy and hearty laugh, a ready sympathy and a generous spirit. The love which she was forbidden to bestow upon any one man, she gave to the world at large, and the world loved her in return.

The most direct reference to affairs of the heart which Clara Barton appears to have made in her letters is in a letter written by her to her cousin, Judge Robert Hale, on August 16, 1876.

When Clara Barton went abroad in search of health in 1869, she hardly expected to return. She took two thousand dollars' worth of bonds which belonged to her and deposited them with a friend, with instructions that if she died, the money was to be used for the improvement of the Barton lot in the Oxford cemetery. It was a large lot on the brow of a hill, and had been heavily washed by the rains. She wished it properly graded and cared for, and this was likely to be, and proved to be, an expensive undertaking.

This friend did not keep the bonds separate from his own property, and in time of financial stress he sold them and applied the money to his own needs. When she returned and learned of this, she was displeased. To her it seemed hardly less than a criminal action. She had no purpose of prosecuting him, but, on the other hand, she wished him to realize that this was something more than an ordinary debt. She put the matter in the hands of her cousin, Judge Hale, who accepted a note in lieu of the bonds. This did not please her, and she wrote her cousin a letter which caused him to chide her as being a rather importunate creditor.

She replied that this was not true, but that she herself had kept all her money for French relief separate from her own money, and she always kept trust funds separate from her own money, and she expected people dealing with her to do the same. She said:

I am not, as I seem to you, a "relentless creditor." On the contrary, I would give him that debt rather than break him down in his business, or if the gift would keep him from going down. I am less grieved about the loss than I am about the manner of his treating my trust. I was his teacher and he was one of my boys. I have always dealt straight and plain with my boys. I am not a lawyeress, nor a diplomat, only a woman artless to simplicity; but I am as square as a brick, and I expect my boys to be square.

In some way Judge Hale had gotten the idea that this former pupil of hers had been a youthful lover, and that that fact had influenced her in the loan of the money. It is in reply to this suggestion that she said:

It seems very ludicrous to me, the idea which has fastened itself upon you, relative to my supposed love affair. I, poor I, who never had a love affair in all my born days, and really don't much expect one after this date! My dear cousin, I trust this letter will show you clearly that my pecuniary affairs and my heart affairs are not at all mixed; and I beg you to believe that, if in the future I should be

70

stricken by the tender malady, I shall never attempt to facilitate or perpetuate the matter by the loaning of money. My observation has not been favorable to such a course of procedure.

Whether she ultimately recovered the two thousand dollars or not, her biographer does not know, but she lived to put the cemetery lot in good order, and in her will she left a fund of sixteen hundred dollars for its perpetual maintenance. She also kept her financial transactions free from any heart complications. Her letter is a pretty certain indication that no love affair had ever taken very strong hold of her in the first fifty years of her life.

The war might easily have brought to Clara Barton a husband if she had inclined toward one, but she found other interests, and was happy in them. Later in life she had on more than one occasion to consider the possibility of a home; and we shall have occasion to make brief mention of one or two of these incidents. What is essential now is to know that Clara Barton did not enter upon her life-work by reason of a broken heart. Her relations with men were wholesome and enjoyable, but none of them brought her such complete assurance of a happy home as to win her from what she came to feel was her life-work. Some possibilities of matrimony gave her deep concern at the time; but she was able to tell Judge Hale in 1876, when she was fifty-five years of age, that she had never had a love affair, and did not expect to have one; but that if she had, she would keep it wholly separate from her financial interests; which was a very sensible resolution, and one to which she lived up faithfully.

FROM SCHOOLROOM TO PATENT OFFICE

Clara Barton's work in Bordentown was a marked success. But it involved strenuous labor and not a little mental strain. When it was over, she found her reserve force exhausted. In the latter part of 1854 her voice gave out, and she gave up teaching, for a time as she supposed, and went to Washington.

She did not know it, but she was leaving the schoolroom forever. Yet she continued to think of herself as a teacher, and to consider her other work as of a more or less temporary character. Twenty years later, she still reminded herself and others that "fully one fifth of my life has been passed as a teacher of schools." The schoolroom had become temporarily impracticable, and she wanted to see Washington and to spend time enough in the capital of the Nation to know something about it. Washington became her home and the center of her life plans for the next sixty years.

Clara Barton did not long remain idle in Washington. At the request of Colonel Alexander De Witt, the representative in Congress from her home district, she received an appointment as clerk in the Patent Office at a salary of $1400 a year. She was one of the first, and believed herself to have been the very first, of women appointed to a regular position in one of the departments, with work and wages equal to that of a man. Her appointment was made under President Pierce, in 1854. The records when searched in later years were found to be imperfect, but the following letter from the Honorable Alexander DeWitt to the Honorable Robert McClelland, Secretary of the Interior, shows clearly her status at the time of its date, September 22, 1855:

Having understood the Department had decided to remove the ladies in the Patent Office on the first of October, I have taken the liberty to address a line on behalf of Miss Clara Barton, a native of my town and district, who has been employed in the past year in the Patent Office, and I trust to the entire satisfaction of the Commissioner.

She had, indeed, performed her work to the entire satisfaction of the Commissioner. There had been serious leaks in the Patent Office, some dishonest clerks selling secrets to their own financial advantage and to the scandal of the department and injury of owners of patents. She became confidential clerk to the Honorable Charles Mason—"Judge Mason" he was called—the Superintendent of Patents. That official himself had a hard time under the Secretary of the Interior, Robert McClelland.

At different periods in her life, Clara Barton had several different styles of handwriting. There is a marked contrast between the clear, strong penmanship which she used when she left the schoolroom and the badly deteriorated form which she employed after her more serious nervous breakdowns. When she was lecturing, she wrote a very large hand, easy to read from manuscript, and that affected her correspondence. Some of her lectures are written in characters nearly a half-inch in height. Then she reverted to the "copperplate" style of her young womanhood, and in that clear, fine, strong penmanship she wrote till the end of her life.

Handwriting such as hers was a joy to the head of the Patent Department. It was clear, regular, easily read, and accurate. The characters were well formed, and the page, when she had done with it, was clean and clear as that of an old missal.

She was not long in rousing the jealousy of men in the department who loafed and smoked and drew their pay. Some of them were anything but polite to her. They blew smoke in her face, and otherwise affronted her. But she attended strictly to her business. She was removed, but Judge Mason gave her a "temporary appointment," and she worked, sometimes in the office, and sometimes, when political affairs were such that her presence there gave rise to criticism, at home. She waded through great volumes and filled other great volumes. A letter to her brother Stephen in the autumn of 1856 gives some idea of what was happening in Washington:

Monday Morning, Sept. 28, 1856

Dear Brother:

I don't know why I have not written you before, only I suppose I thought you had enough to occupy your attention without my uninteresting scrawls. I have been hearing of late that you were better than when you first came home, but I have not heard a word when you expect to return.

We are having a remarkably fine fall, cool and clean, and I have not seen more than a dozen mosquitoes this summer.

The city has just been somewhat disturbed, i.e., the official portions of it (and this is the greater portion at this particular time), in consequence of the resignation of Judge Mason, which was tendered to the President some eight days ago, and no notice whatever taken of it until day before yesterday morning, the Judge in the meantime drawing his business to a close, packing his library, and Mrs. Mason packing their wardrobes, and on Friday evening, when I called on them, they were all ready to leave for Iowa next Tuesday at three o'clock. They both explained particularly the nature of the circumstances which induced them to leave. You have known before that Congress guaranteed to the Commissioner of Patents the exclusive right of making all temporary appointments in his department, and that Secretary McClelland had previously interfered in and claimed the same. He commenced upon the most vulnerable points, something like a year ago, when he removed us ladies, and, partially succeeding in his attempts, has been enlarging his grasp ever since, and a few weeks ago sent a note to Judge Mason forbidding him to appoint any temporary clerk unless subject to his decision and concurrence, giving to the Judge the right to nominate, reserving to himself the privilege of appointing. Then Congress having voted some $70,000 to be used by the Commissioner of Patents in procuring sugar-cane slips (if so they might be termed) from South America for the purpose of restoring the tone of the sugar growth in the South, which is becoming exhausted, and the Commissioner having procured his agent to go for them, the Secretary interfered, said it was all useless to send an agent, the military could attend to it; he had the agent discharged, and delayed the matter until it was too late to obtain the cuttings this year, and the Commissioner, being thus deprived of the privilege of complying with the directions received from Congress, and thereby unable to acquit himself creditably, resigned, but at the last moment the President came to his room, and invested him with power to act as he pleased in all matters over which the law gave him jurisdiction, and he promised to remain until the Secretary should return from Michigan, and see how he behaved then. The Secretary is making himself extremely odious; he may have, and doubtless has, friends and admirers, but I never met with one of them.

Fannie writes me that little Mary has burned her arm; is it badly burned? Does father still think of coming South this winter? Hobart was a slippery stick, wasn't he, and what did he mean? How do you arrange with Fisher? Some way I hope that will last so that he can't slip his halter and leave poor Dave to chase after him, with a measure of oats in one hand and a cudgel in the other, as he has all summer. You will come to Washington, I am sure, on your way to Carolina; it is best that you should—I want so much to see you. I want to talk a good long talk with you that I cannot write. I have so many things to say, all very important, of course. But write me soon and tell me when you will return. I must go over to the city and look what I can do to make ready for the comers.

Please give my love to all inquiring friends; write and come and see us.

Your affectionate sister

Clara

How stand politics, and who is going to be President? The Democrats are looking pale in this quarter.

Buchanan was elected, and Clara Barton continued in the Patent Office for a time unmolested. But the election lost her one of her best friends in Washington, Colonel De Witt, a resident of Oxford, and representative from her home district, through whom her first appointment had come, and who had been her constant friend. Just before the inauguration of President Buchanan, she wrote her home letter to Julia, and sent it by the hand of the retiring representative, who volunteered to take her letter to her home:

Washington, D.C., Mar. 3rd, 1857

Dear Sister Julia:

Our good friend Colonel De Witt has kindly offered to become the bearer and deliverer of any despatches which I may wish to send to Yankee Land, and knowing from good authority that a call upon you might not be a hard medicine for him to take, I avail myself of the opportunity to tell you that we are all engaged in making a president; intend, if no bad luck follow, to finish him off and send him home to-morrow. I hope he may finally give satisfaction, for there has been a great deal of pains taken in fitting and making him up, but there are so many in the family to wear him that it is scarcely possible that he should be an exact fit for them all. ...

We are at our same old tricks yet here in the capitol, i.e., killing off everybody who doesn't just happen to suit us or our peculiar humor at the moment; we have indeed some shocking occurrences at times. You have probably seen some account of the homicide which took place in the Pension Office the other day; if not I think the Colonel will be so kind as to give you some of the first points and relieve me from the disagreeable task of reciting so abrupt and melancholy a matter. My opinion of the matter is that the man who gave the offense, and from whom the apology was due, remained doggedly at his office, armed, and shot down his adversary who came to make the very explanation which the offender should have sought. Colonel Lee (I think), instead of sitting there at his desk hugging a concealed pistol to his unchristian and unmanly breast, should at that very moment have been on his way to Alexandria to apologize to Mr. House for the previous night's offense. The man may perhaps meet the sympathy of the world at large, but at present he has not mine.

And last night a terrible thing occurred within the district. It appears that the almshouse and workhouse are, or rather were, both the same building, very large, new and fine. Last night, curiosity or something else equally powerful caused the keepers of the establishment all to leave the premises and come up to the city, a distance of three miles, I suppose, locking the building very securely, fastening in all the inmates, I have no idea how many, but the house took fire, and burned down, consuming a great portion of its inhabitants, old, lame, and sick men and women and helpless infants. Only such were saved as could force an escape through the barred windows—was not that horrible? Now it would seem to me that in both these cases there was room left for reflection on the part of someone. I think there would be for me if I were in either of their places

I would attempt to tell you something how sorry I am that the Colonel is going home to return to us no more, but if I wrote all night I should not have half expressed it. I am sorry for myself, that I shall have no good friend left to whom I can run with all my annoyances, and find always a sympathizer and benefactor, and especially am I sorry for our (generally) old State. I pity their folly; they have cut off their own hands after having blocked all their wheels; they cannot stir a peg after the Colonel leaves; they have not a man on the board they can move; and who is to blame but their own poor foolish selves? Well, I am sorry, and if crying would do any good I would cry a week, steadily. I don't know but I shall as it is....

Remember me especially to "Grandpa," and tell Dave I like him a leetle particularly since he didn't sign that petition.

From your affectionate sister

Clara

For a time after the election, political matters settled down, and Clara continued her work unmolested. She was home for a time in the spring of 1857, but back in Washington through the summer, and in that time went through huge volumes of technical description and copied the essential parts into record books for the purpose of reference and preservation.

It would make this volume more consecutive in its connections if out of her letters were culled only such items as related to particular topics; but her letters must be read as she wrote them, with news, gossip, inquiry about home matters, answers to questions, and all just as she thought of them and wrote about them. In the early autumn of 1857 she wrote to Julia:

Washington, D.C., Sept. 6th, 1857

Dear Sister Julia:

I dare not ask you to excuse me for neglecting you so badly, but still I have a kind of indefinable hope that you will do so, when you remember how busy I am and that this is summer with its long weary days and short sleepy nights; and then the "skeeters!" Just as soon as you try to write a letter in the evening to anybody, they must come in flocks to "stick their bills." In vain have I placarded myself all over on every side of me, "Stick no bills here"—it doesn't do a bit of good, and but for the gallant defense of a couple of well-fitted nets at my windows, I should long ere this have been pasted, scarred, and battered as the wooden gateway to an old theater, or the brick wall adjacent to an eleven-penny-bit lecture-room. I should, however, have written out of selfishness just to hear from you, only that by some means intelligence gets to us that father is better, and the rest of you well. My health is much better than when I was at home. I have been gaining ever since Miss Haskell came. She relieves me many ways. The yellow has almost gone off of my forehead, else it has grown yellow all alike; but it looks better, let it be which way it may; it isn't so spotted. Bernard has been home and got cured of the chills and fever, and gone back again; expect

Vest, home soon. I am not much better settled than ever; liable to pick up my traps and start any day. I am glad you found my mits, for I began to think I must have had a crazy fit and destroyed my things while I was at home. To pay for losing my parasol, I made myself carry one that cost fifty-six cents! Did you ever hear of such a thing? Well, it is the best I have had all summer, and I walked to church under it to-day; so much to pay for carelessness. I also left a large bottle of some kind of drugs, I guess in your parlor cupboard. Please give it closet room awhile, and I will come sometime between this and the middle of January at farthest and relieve you of it. I may spend Christmas with you, cannot tell yet, but I shall be home while the snow is on the ground if I live, and maybe before it comes, but if I do I shall stay until it is there, for I am determined to have a sleigh-ride with old Dick. Oh, I am so glad every time I think of it, that he beat Dr. Newton, blast his saucy picture! Will try it again when the snow comes.

I have written "a heap" since my return; let me see, seven large volumes, the size of ledgers, I have read all through and collected and transferred something off of every page—3500 pages of dry lawyer writing is something to wade through in three months; and out of them I have filled a great volume almost as heavy as I can lift. My arm is tired, and my poor thumb is all calloused holding my pen. I begin to feel that my Washington life is drawing to a close, and I think of it without regret, not that I have not prized it, not that it has not on the whole been a great blessing to me. I realize all this, but if I could tell you in detail all I have gone through along with it, you would agree with me that it had not been all sunshine. I look back upon it as a weary pilgrimage which it was necessary for me to accomplish. I have nearly done, so it has been a sturdy battle, hard-fought, and I trust well won.

But how do you all do? How are Grandfather and Dave, and the little ones? How I do want to see you all! Has father's leg got so he can use it well again? Does it pain him? Do the children go to school? How are Mary's* congress gaiters?—a perfect fit, I hope. Tell her to be a good girl and learn to read, for I shall want to hear her when I come home. Wash Bubby's eyes in bluing water; it may improve the color. Please give my love to Cousin Vira, Mrs. Abom, and after this according to discretion. Is Martha in New Worcester? I should like to see her. We have had a fine summer thus far—very few hot days.

Please tell father that I was not silent so long because I had forgotten him, but I had scarce time to write, and I get so tired of writing. Please write me soon and tell me all the news. I will bring your jewelry when I come. I feel guilty to have taken it away.

Your sister, most affectionately &c &c &c

Clara

*Mary was Mrs. Mamie Barton Stafford, daughter of David. Bubby was Stephen E. Barton, son of David, Clara's brother.

The Democrats had some reason to look pale, for no one could predict just how well John C. Fremont would run. But he was not elected. The Democrats returned to power, with James Buchanan as their successful candidate. As the election approached, it became evident that this was to be the result, and the Democratic chief clerk of the Pension Office, certain that he was to succeed Judge Mason, desired Clara Barton to be as good a Democrat as possible that she might not fail to be his confidential clerk: but she was already a "Black Republican." Her father had been an old-time Jackson Democrat, and the administration under which she was appointed was Democratic; but she heard Charles Sumner's great speech on the "Crime Against Kansas" and she was convinced. "Freedom is national; slavery is sectional," he said, and she believed him.

She was not yet sure that slavery ought to be interfered with where it was, but she was with the party that opposed its further extension, and this imperiled her future as a clerk if James Buchanan was elected. Just before the November election, she wrote to Julia, David's wife:

Washington, D.C., Nov. 2nd, 1856 Sunday Evening
Dear Sister Julia:
Your looked-for letter came safe to hand; you may well suppose we were anxious to hear from you considering the alarming nature of the one which had preceded it. Stephen must have had a very distressing time, but I am so glad to know that he is relieved and has decided to let someone else be his judge in reference to getting out. I hope he will continue firm in the faith and venture nothing; it is of no use to strive against nature; he must have time to recruit and he has no idea of the time and care it will require to rid his system of the troublesome disease which has fastened upon him. I am glad you have found a physician there who knew how to name his disease. I have known all the time, since the first time he wrote me of his illness in Carolina, what the trouble was, and said when I was at home that he had the dumb chills, but no one would believe an ignoramus like me. I have no doubt but he had had his ague fits regularly since his first attack without ever once mistrusting the real cause of his bad feelings. People say there are two classes of community that the shaking ague never attacks, viz., those who are too lazy to shake and those who will not stop. Stephen belongs to the latter and I to the former, so we must have dumb ague if any. I am glad that father is better, and hope I shall not hear of David's getting

down again this winter; he must keep well enough to come out and see us. We are all very well, only that I have a slight cold, which will wear off, I guess. The weather is delightful, but getting quite cool. We saw a few flakes of snow last Friday, but one would never mistrust it by the Indian summer haze which is spread over the city this evening.

We are all dreading the confusion of day after tomorrow night, when the election returns are made. There will be such an excitement, but the Democrats are the most certain set of men that I ever saw; their confidence of success in the approaching contest is unbounded. Judge Mason has gone to Iowa to vote, and Mr. Stugert (our chief clerk) will leave the city tomorrow night in order to reach Pennsylvania in time the next day. He is one of Mr. Buchanan's most intimate friends. He called to take me to Georgetown one evening last week, and during the evening he conversed respecting the approaching election. His spirits were unbounded, and his confidence in the right results of the election as unbounded. He wished me to say I would be commissioner and chief clerk for him until his return, but I declined the honor, declaring myself a Freemonter [supporter of John C. Fremont, The Pathfinder]. This he would not hear a word of and walked all around the parlors in company with the Reverend Mr. Halmead assuring all the company that I was an "old school Loco," "dyed in the wool," and my father before me was the same, and requested them to place no confidence in anything I might say on the present occasion, as the coffee was exceedingly strong and he passed my cup up five times. I thought this latter three fifths of a mistake, but could not quite tell.

Lo, Bubby [Stephen, her nephew] says he will come to Washington. Well, he must go and ask Colonel De Witt to make him a page, and if the Colonel can do it, Bub can come and stay; he is large enough to carry letters and papers about the House, and do little errands for the Members. I guess he had best ask the Colonel and see what he says about it. Irving is getting ready to take our mail to the office and I must hasten to close my scrawl for the present. I had intended to write to Stephen to-day, but it is rather late; I may get time the first of the week, although I have a heavy week's business in contemplation. How I wish I could drop in and see you all to-night, but that cannot be just yet. Please give my love to "Grandpa" [her father] and then all the others in succession as they come along, down to Dick [the horse]; is he as nice as ever? I want to see him too. Please remember me to Elvira and Mrs. Abom, and write me soon again.

Tell Stephen he is a nice fellow to mind so well, and be must keep doing so. Irving is ready.

80

So good-bye.
Your affectionate sister

Clara

The country was steadily drifting toward war, and Clara Barton felt the danger of it. Although she was convinced that slavery ought not to be extended further, she was not yet an abolitionist, and she felt that violent agitators were taking upon themselves a serious risk in bringing the Nation to the very brink of bloodshed. She did not approve of the John Brown raid, and she was greatly concerned about the meetings that were held that seemed to her calculated to induce riot. She had her convictions, and was never afraid to speak them boldly, but she said, "It will be a strange pass when the Bartons get fanatical, and cannot abide by and support the laws they live under." A neighbor who had been with Stephen in Carolina was driven away on account of utterances that followed the John Brown raid. She wrote to her brother Stephen at this time—the letter is not dated—and gave the fullest account of her own feelings and convictions concerning the issues then before the country, having in special mind the duty of Northern people resident in the South to be considerate of the conditions under which Southern people had to live. It is a very interesting letter, and the author of this volume could wish that it had been in his possession while Clara Barton was living, that he might have asked her to what extent her views changed in the years that followed:

I have not seen Mr. Seaver since his return, and regret exceedingly that there should have been any necessity for such a termination to his residence in the South. I should not have supposed that he would have felt it his duty to uphold such a cause as "Harper's Ferry," and if he did not, it is a pity he had the misfortune to make it appear so. Of course I could not for a moment believe him a dangerous man, hostile to either human life, rights, or interests, or antagonistic to the community among whom he resided, but if they felt him to be so, I do not by any means blame them for the course they took. Situated as they are, they have a right to be cautious, and adopt any measures for safety and quiet which their own judgment may suggest. They have a right even to be afraid, and it is not for the North, who in no way share in the danger, to brand them as cowards; they are the same that people the world over are and would be under the circumstances. Unorganized men everywhere are timid, easy and quick to take alarm. It is only when bodies of men are organized and disciplined, and prepared to defend themselves against expected dangers, that they stand firm and unshrinking, and face death unmoved. Occasionally we hear that you have been or will be requested to leave—this amuses me. It would be singular, indeed, if in all this time your Southern friends had not learned you well enough to tolerate you. It will be a strange pass when the Bartons get fanatical, and cannot abide by and support the laws they live under, and mind their own business closely enough to remain anywhere they may chance to be. I am grieved and ashamed of the course which our Northern people have taken relative to the John Brown affair. Of their relief societies, and mass meetings and sympathetic gatherings, I can say nothing, for I have never witnessed one, and never shall. From the first they seemed to me to be wrong and ill-advised, and had a strained and forced appearance; and the longer they are persisted in, and the greater extent to which they are carried, the more ridiculous they become in my sight. If they represented the true sentiments and feeling of the majority of candid thinking men at the North, it would savor more of justice, but this I believe to be very far from the facts. Their gatherings and speechifyings serve the purpose of a few loud-mouthed, foaming, eloquent fanatics, who would be just as ready in any other cause as this. They preach for notoriety and oratorical praise, fearlessly and injudiciously, with characters long stamped and nothing to lose. It matters little to them that every rounded sentence which falls from their chiseled lips, every burst of eloquence which "brings down the house," drives home one more rivet in slavery's chain; if slavery be an evil, they are but helping it on; it is only human nature that it should be so, and so plain a fact "that the wayfaring man cannot err therein." Nature, and cause and effect, are, I suppose, much the same the world over, and if our Southern neighbors clasp their rights all the firmer, when assailed, and plant the foot of resistance toe to toe with the foot of aggression, it is not for us to complain of it; what differently should we ourselves do? That slavery be an evil I am neither going to affirm nor deny; let those pass judgment whom greater experience and observation have made capable of judging; but allowing the affirmative in its most exaggerated form, could it possibly be equal to the pitiful scene of confusion, distrust, and national paralysis before and around us at the present hour, with the prospect of all the impending danger threatening our vast Republic? Men talk flippantly of dissolving the Union. This may happen, but in my humble opinion never till our very horses gallop in human blood.

But I must hold or I shall get to writing politics to you, and you might tell me, as old Mr. Perry of New Jersey did Elder Lampson when he advised him to leave off drinking whiskey and join the Temperance Society. After listening long and patiently until the Elder had finished his remarks, he looked up very, very benignly with, "Well, Elder, your opinions are very good, and probably worth as much to yourself as anybody."

Lincoln was elected and duly inaugurated. Clara heard the inauguration address and liked it. She witnessed nothing in the ceremony of inauguration which seemed immediately threatening. So far as she could discover, no one present had any objection to permitting the new President to live. There were rumors that Eli Thayer, of Worcester, who had done more than any other man to make Kansas a free State, was to be Commissioner of Patents. That was delightful news for her. It meant not only an assured position, but an opportunity of service undisturbed by needless annoyances. She had an invitation to the inauguration ball, but had to decline that dreary function on account of a cold. On the day following the inauguration, she wrote to Annie Childs, sister of Frances, her account of the day's events:

Washington City, March 5th, 1861

My Dear Annie:

I have just a few minutes before dinner for which I have no positive call, and I am going to inflict them on you. Of course you will not expect an elaborate letter, for I by no means feel competent to the task to-day if I had the time.

The 4th of March has come and gone, and we have a live Republican President, and, what is perhaps singular, during the whole day we saw no one who appeared to manifest the least dislike to his living. We had a crowd, of course, but not so utterly overwhelming as had been anticipated; everywhere seemed to be just full, and no more, which was a very pleasant state of affairs. The ceremony was performed upon the East Capitol steps facing Capitol Hill, you remember. The inaugural address was first delivered in a loud, fine voice, which was audible to many, or a majority of the assemblage. Only a very few of the United States troops were brought to the Capitol at all, but were in readiness at their quarters and other parts of the city; they were probably not brought out, lest it look like menace. Great pains appeared to be taken to avoid all such appearances, and indeed a more orderly crowd I think I never saw and general satisfaction expressed at the trend and spirit of the Address. Of course, it will not suit your latitude quite as well, but I hope they may find it endurable.

It is said that the Cabinet is formed and has been or will be officially announced to-day. And there is some prospect of the Honorable Eli Thayer being appointed Commissioner of Patents. Only think of it! Isn't it nice if it is true? Mr. Suydam has been spending the week with us; left this morning. Mrs. Suydam is better, he says. Mr. Starr is here.

We have had the most splendid spring weather you ever saw for two weeks past, no rain, but bright sunshine; it has been frightfully dusty some of the time and this day is one apparently borrowed from Arabia, by the clouds of sand.

I hear from you sister sometimes, but not until I have almost lost trace of her each time, but I am, of course, most to blame. I hope your business has revived with the approach of spring, as it doubtless has. You will not be surprised if I tell you that I am in a hopeless state of semi-nudity, just clear the law and nothing more. Sally told me on her return that you would have come out and stayed with us some this winter if you had thought it could have been made to pay, but as usual I knew nothing of this until it was too near spring to think of your leaving your business. How glad I should have been to have had you here a month or two, and I think I could have relieved you of the most of expense to say the least of it, if you were not doing much at home, and what a comfort it would have been to me to get right in the clothing line. Will there ever be another time that you would think you could leave, and come to Washington if I should remain?

Where is Fannie? Is she having a vacation now? Please give my love to her, and all inquiring friends, reserving a large share for yourself, and believe me,

As ever, your loving friend

P.S. Everybody would send love if they knew I were writing. I cannot report the Inauguration Ball personally, as I was not present; after a delightful invitation could not go. I have been having a very bad cold for a few days and a worse cough than I ever had, but I hope to get over it soon. I did not attend the last Levee.

THE BATTLE CRY OF FREEDOM

The unit of Massachusetts history is eighty-six years. As a considerable part of American history relates to Massachusetts, or traces its origin from there, the same unit measures much of the life of the Nation itself. It begins in the year 1603 when Queen Elizabeth died, and King James came to the throne, and the season was the spring. It was King James who determined to make the Puritans conform or to harry them out of his kingdom. He did not succeed in making them conform, but he harried the Pilgrims into Holland whence they came to Plymouth Rock. For eighty-six years Massachusetts was managed under a colonial government, whose last days were those of a province with a royal governor in control. It was on the 19th of April, 1689, that this royal governor, whose name was Andros, looked out through the porthole of the ship on which he was a prisoner, and saw the sun rise over Boston Harbor prior to his enforced return to England. That was the end of provincial governors in New England, and the beginning of the assertion of the doctrine of independence. Eighty-six years later to a day, a little band of Massachusetts soldiers stood in a line on the green at Lexington, and on the same day a larger company mustered by the bridge in Concord, and the Revolutionary War began. Eighty-six years later to a day, the Sixth Massachusetts Regiment, hastening through Baltimore in response to President Lincoln's call for troops, was fired upon, and the first blood was shed in a long and cruel war which did not end until it was decided that the house which was divided against itself was no longer to be divided; that this was to be one nation and that nation a free nation.

Fort Sumter had been fired upon on April 12, 1861 while Union troops were attempting to resupply it.—Ed.

If one had been privileged to visit the Senate Chamber of the United States in three days after the assault upon the Massachusetts troops, he might have beheld an interesting sight. Behind the desk of the President of the Senate stood a little woman reading to the Massachusetts soldiers who were quartered there from their home paper, the Worcester "Spy." Washington had need of these troops.

Had they and their comrades in arms arrived a few days later, the capital would have been in the hands of the Confederates. They came none too soon; Washington had no place to put them, nor was the War Department adequately equipped with tents or other supplies. The Capitol building itself became the domicile of some of the first regiments, and the Senate Chamber was the habitation of the boys from Worcester County. A few of the boys Clara Barton knew personally.

Already the war had become a reality to these Yankee lads. Lincoln's call for men was issued on April 15, 1861. Massachusetts had four regiments ready. The first of these reached Baltimore four days after the President's Proclamation. Three men were killed by a mob, and thirty were injured as they marched through Baltimore. The regiment fought its way to the' station, regained possession of their locomotive and train, and moved on to Washington.

Clara Barton's first service to the soldiers was only incidentally to the wounded. There were only thirty of them, and they were adequately cared for. But she, in company with other women, visited the regiment at the Capitol, and she performed her first service to the armies of her country by reading to the homesick boys as they gathered in the Senate Chamber, and she stood in the place that was ordinarily occupied by the Vice-President of the United States. Her own account of this proceeding is contained in a letter to her friend, B. W. Childs:

Washington, April 25th, 1861

My Dear Will:

As you will perceive, I wrote you on the 19th, but have not found it perfectly *convenient* to send it until now, but we trust that "navigation is open now" for a little. As yet we have had no cause for alarm, if indeed we were disposed to feel any. The city is filling up with troops. The Massachusetts regiment is quartered in the Capitol and the 7th arrived to-day at noon. Almost a week in getting from New York here; they looked tired and warm, but sturdy and brave. Oh! but you should hear them praise the Massachusetts troops who were with them, "Butler's Brigade." They say the "Massachusetts Boys" are equal to anything they undertake—that they have constructed a railroad, laid the track, and built an engine since they entered Maryland. The wounded at the Infirmary are all improving—some of them recovered and joined the regiment. We visited the regiment yesterday at the Capitol; found some old friends and acquaintances from Worcester; their baggage was all seized and they have *nothing* but their heavy woolen clothes—not a, cotton shirt—and many of them not even a pocket handkerchief. We, of course, emptied our pockets and came home to tear up old sheets for towels and handkerchiefs, and have filled a large box with all manner of serving utensils, thread, needles, thimbles, scissors, pins, buttons, strings, salves, tallow, etc., etc., have filled the largest market basket In the house and it will go to them in the next hour.

But don't tell us they are not determined—just fighting mad; they had just one Worcester *Spy* of the 22d, and all were so anxious to know the contents that they begged me to read it aloud to them, which I did. You would have smiled to see me and my audience in the Senate Chamber of the United States. Oh! but it was better attention than I have been accustomed to see there in the old time. "Ber" writes his mother that Oxford is raising a company. God bless her, and the noble fellows who may leave their quiet, happy homes to come at the call of their country! So far as our poor efforts can reach, they shall never lack a kindly hand or a sister's sympathy if they come. In my opinion this city will be attacked within the next sixty days. If it must be, let it come; and when there is no longer a soldier's arm to raise the Stars and Stripes above our Capitol, may God give strength to mine.

Write us and tell our friends to write and I will answer when I can. Love to all.

C. H. Barton

Several things are of interest in this letter. One is the place where her work for the soldiers began. It was the Government's poverty in the matter of tents and barracks which caused the soldiers to be quartered in the Capitol, but it was certainly an interesting and significant thing that her great work had its beginning there. Washington was still expecting to be attacked; she believed that the attack would occur shortly. It was rather a fine sentence with which her letter closed—"If it must be, let it come; and when there is no longer a soldier's arm to raise the Stars and Stripes above our Capitol, may God give strength to mine."

She was still signing her formal letters Clara H. Barton. She was no longer Clarissa, and before very long she dropped the middle name and letter entirely, and, from the Civil War on, was simply Clara Barton.

This letter which deals entirely with her military experiences is the first of many of this general character. To a large extent personal matters from this time on dropped out of sight. It will be of interest to go back a few weeks and quote one of her letters to her brother David, in which there is no mention of political or military matters. It is a letter of no great importance in itself, but shows her concern for her father, who had partially recovered from his serious illness, for her niece Ida, her nephew Bub, as she still called Stephen E., though he was now a lad of some size, and for home affairs generally. For her father she had adopted the name given him by her nephews and nieces, and called him "Grandpa":

Feb. 2nd, 1861

Dear Brother:

I enclose in this a draft for twelve dollars, and will send you another for the remaining fifteen on the first of next month, i.e., provided Uncle Sam is not bankrupt, which he nearly is now and his payments have been very irregular. I have only received a part of my salary for this month—but all right in the end. I have been very sorry that I took the money of you lest you might have wanted it when I might just as well have drawn upon myself, only for the trouble of getting at the Colonel. Another time I should do so, however, for I believe I am the poorest hand in all the world to owe anything. I never rest a moment until all is square. And now, if you have the least need of the remaining fifteen dollars just say so to the Colonel and he will honor your draft so quick you will never know you made it. You may want it for something about the house, or to make out a payment, and if so don't wait, I pray you, but just call over when you get your draft changed and get the remainder of the Colonel, and tell him in that case he will hear from me very soon. Perhaps Julia or the children have wanted something, and if I have been keeping them out of any comfort I am wry sorry.

As it is my intention to keep a strict account with myself of all my expenditures and profits from this time henceforth, you may, if you please, sign the receipt at the top of this sheet, and hand it to Sally to bring to me.

I had thought I should get a line, or some kind of word from you, perhaps, but I suppose you are too busy. Well, this is a very busy world. You will be glad to know that I am very happily situated here; the winter is certainly passing very pleasantly. I find all my old friends so numerous, and so kind, and, unless they falsify grossly, so glad to have me back among them again; I could not have believed that there was half so much kind feeling stored away for me here in this big city of comers and goers. The office and my business relations are all right, and they say I am all right too. The remainder of the winter will be very gay, and I must confers that I fear I am getting a little dissipated, not that I drink champagne and play cards—oh, no—but I do go to levees and theaters. I don't know that I should own up so frankly, only that I am afraid "Mr. Grover" will show me up if I try to keep still and dark. Now, if he does, just tell him that it gets no better, but rather worse if anything, and that he ought to have stayed to attend Mr. Buchanan's big party. It was splendid—General Scott and the military; in fact, we are getting decidedly military in this region. But we have no winter. Mr. J. S. Brown, of Worcester, came to us in the theater last night at eleven and said a dispatch from Worcester declared the snow to be six feet deep in Massachusetts. We decided to put it down at a foot and a half, and didn't know but that was big! We couldn't realize even that, for we have only now and then a little spot of snow, and this morning a monster fog has come and settled down on that, and in two hours we shall forget how snow looks, and in two days, if it doesn't rain, the dust will blow; but no fears but that it will rain, though.

But I haven't said a word about Grandpa. I am so glad to know that he is better and even gets into the kitchen; that is splendid, and besides he has had company as well as you all. Ah, ha, I found it out, if none of you told me! Ben Porter came at last!! Please give my congratulations to Grandpa, and you too Julia, for I am writing to you just as much as to Dave, only I don't know as I said so before. I forgot to tell you—and now if you don't write me how Adeline and Viola are, I will do some awful thing to come up to you. I don't justly know what, for if Frank wrote a week he never would tell me. Oh, I had a letter from him last night; said he was over his boots in snow, was going "down east" to Bangor, Dr. Porter's, etc.

I am afraid my trunk and other things are in your way, and I would ask Sally to take the trunk, only that it seems to me that I had best wait until I see what the 4th of March brings about, and find where I am in the new administration, or at least if we have one. If we are to have a war, I have plenty of traps and trunks in this region, and if all comes right and I remain, it may be that someone will be coming South pretty soon without much baggage who would take something for me.

How are all the children? I must write to somebody soon; I guess it will be Bub, but Ida isn't forgotten. She was a faithful little correspondent to tell me how Grandpa was. I shall not forget it of Ida. Can she skate yet? Now, aren't you going to write me and tell me all the news? And you must remember me to Mrs. Wadding-ton, Mrs. Abom, and family, and, Jule, you must give my regards to Silas and Mr. Smith, for I don't wish to be lost sight of by my old-time friends, among all the new ones here. And don't forget to give my love to Mrs. Kidder and tell me how she is. You had best clap your hands for joy that I have no more room, only to say I am Your affectionate sister

Clara

I forgot to cut my draft loose until I had written on the back of it, and then I cut it loose without thinking that I had written; so much for doing things in a hurry, and I can't stop to rewrite a single word to anybody, so patch up and read if you can.

The Sixth Massachusetts left Washington and moved farther south. She tells of her feelings with regard to these men in a letter written May 19, 1861, to Annie Childs., The letter to which she referred as having been written on the same day to Frances Childs, and containing war news, has not been found:

Washington, D.C., May 19, 1861

My dear Annie:

I am very sorry that it will be in my power to write you so little and no more, but these are the busy days which know no rest, and there are at this moment thirty unanswered letters lying by my side—besides a perfect rush of ordinary *business*, and liable to be interrupted by soldier calls any moment. I wish I could tell you something of the appearance of our city, grand, noble, true, and brave. I wish you could see it just as it is, and if it were not that at this season of the year I had no thought that you could leave your business, I would say to you come—and indeed I will say this much, hopeless as I deem it, aye, *know* it to be—but this—if you have the least curiosity to witness the events of our city as they are transpiring or enough so that you could come, you shall be doubly welcome, have a quiet nook to stay in, and I will find you all you want to do while you will stay, longer or shorter, and pay you all you ask for your services. If it were winter I should hope you would think well enough of it to come, but at this season of the year, I dare not, but rest assured nothing would please me as much, and Sally too. We often wish you would come, and I am in a most destitute condition. I cannot get a moment to sew in and can trust no one here. I know I must not urge you, but only add that I mean just what I say. If you care to come, you shall not lose your time, although I feel it to be preposterous in me to say such a thing at this time of the year, but I have said it at a venture and cannot retract. I saw your friend Mr. Parker before he left the city for the Relay House, and we had a long talk about you. I had never met him before, but was much pleased with his easy, pleasant manners and cordial ways. Allow me to congratulate you upon the possession of such friends.

For war news I must refer you to a letter I have written *your sister* to-day; she will show it to you.

I was sorry when the Sixth Regiment left us, but nothing could have delighted them more than the thought of nearing Baltimore again, and how successfully they have done it. I wept for joy when I heard of it all, and they so richly deserved the honor which is meted out to them—*noble old regiment they*; everyone admires, and no one envies; there seems to be no jealousy towards them, all yield the precedence without a word, and their governor! I have no words good enough to talk about him with. Will this little scrap be better than nothing from your

Loving Coz

Clara

I have not forgotten my debt, but have nothing small enough to enclose. I will pay it.

How deeply stirred Clara Barton was by the events, which now were happening thick and fast, is shown by a portion of a letter in which she describes the funeral of Colonel Elmer Ellsworth. The death of this young man affected the Nation as that of no other who perished in the early days of the war. When Alexandria, which was practically a suburb of Washington, was occupied by the Federal troops, this young soldier was in command. After the troops had taken possession of the town, the Confederate flag was still flying from the roof of the hotel. Ellsworth ascended the stairs, tore down the flag, and was descending with it when he was shot by the proprietor of the hotel. Elmer Ellsworth was a fine and lovable man, and had been an intimate friend of President Lincoln in whose house he lived for a time [and studied law in Lincoln's office]. His theory of military organization was that a small body of men thoroughly disciplined was more effective than a large body without discipline. The Zouaves were largely recruited from volunteer fire companies. They were soldiers expert in climbing ladders and in performing hazardous deeds. Their picturesque uniform and their relatively high degree of discipline, as well as the death of their first commander, attracted great attention to them. Just after the funeral of Colonel Ellsworth, whose death Lincoln mourned as he would have mourned for a son, Clara Barton wrote a letter containing this description of his funeral:

Our sympathies are more enlisted for the poor bereaved *Zouaves* than aught else. They who of all men in the land most *needed* a leader and *had* the best—to lose him now in the very beginning; if they commit excesses upon their enemies, only their enemies are to blame, for they have killed the only man who ever *thought* to govern them, and now, when I read of one of them breaking over and committing some trespass and is called to account and punished for it, my blood rises in an instant. I would not have them punished. I know I am wrong in my conclusions, and do not desire to be justified, but I am not accountable for my feelings. The funeral of the lamented Ellsworth was one of the most imposing and touching sights I ever witnessed or perhaps ever shall. First those broad sidewalks from the President's to the Capitol, two impossible lines of living beings, then company after company and whole regiments of sturdy soldiers with arms reversed, drums muffled, banners furled and draped, following each other in slow, solemn procession, the four white horses and the gallant dead, with his Country's flag for a pall; the six bearers beside the hearse, and then the little band of Zouaves (for only a part could be spared from duty even to bury their leader), clad in their plain loose uniform, entirely weaponless, heads bowed in grief, eyes fixed on the coffin before them, and the great tears rolling down their swarthy cheeks, told us only too plainly of the smothered grief that would one day burst into rage and wreak itself in vengeance on every seeming foe; the riderless horse, and the rent and blood-stained Secession flag brought up the rear of the little band of personal mourners; then followed an official "train" led by the President and Cabinet—all of whom looked small to us that day; they were no longer dignitaries, but mourners with the throng. I stood at the Treasury, and with my eye glanced down the Avenue to the Capitol gate, and not one inch of earth or space could I see, only one dense living, swaying, moving mass of humanity. Surely it was great love and respect to be meted out to the memory of one so young and from the common ranks of life. I thought of it long that day and wondered if he had not sold himself at his highest price for his Country's good—if the inspiration of "*Ellsworth dead*" were not worth more to our cause than the life of any man could be. I could not tell, but He who knows all things and ruleth all in wisdom hath done all things well.

How deeply she felt the sorrow of the soldier, and the anxiety of his loved ones at home, is shown in a letter which she wrote in June before there had been a decisive battle, but while the boys were rallying to the flag, "Shouting the Battle Cry of Freedom." The most of her letters of this period are descriptive of events which she witnessed, but this one is a meditation on a Sunday afternoon while the Nation was waiting for a great battle which everyone felt was impending:

Washington, June 9th, 1861
Sunday afternoon

My dear Cousin Vira:

We have one more peaceful Sabbath, one more of God's chosen days, with the sun shining calmly and brightly over the green, quiet earth as it has always looked to us; the same green fields, and limpid waters; and but that the long lines of snow-white tents flashed back the rays I might forget, on such an hour as this, the strange confusion and unrest that heaves us like a mighty billow, and the broad, dark, sweeping wing of war hovering over our heads, whose flap and crash is so soon to blacken our fair land, desolate our hearths, crush our mothers' sacrificing hearts, drape our sisters in black, still the gleesome laugh of childhood, and bring down the doting father's gray hair with sorrow to the grave. For however cheerfully and bravely he has given up his sons and sent them out to die on the altar of Liberty, however nobly and martyr-like he may have responded, they are no longer "*mine*" when their Country calls. Still has he given them up in hope—and somewhat of trust—that one day his dim eyes shall again rest on that loved form, his trembling voice be raised and his hand rest in blessing on the head of his darling soldier boy returned from the wars; and when he shall have sat and waited day by day, and trained his time-worn ear to catch the faintest, earliest lisp of tidings, and strained his failing eye, and cleared away the mist to read over day by day "the last letter," until its successor shall have been placed in his trembling hands to be read and blotted in its turn; and finally there shall come a long silence, and then another letter in a strange handwriting—then, and not till then, shall the

94

old patriot know how much of the great soul strength, that enabled him to bear his cherished offering to the altar, was loyalty, patriotism, and principle, and how much of it was hope.

The battle of Bull Run was fought on Sunday, July 21, 1861. Clara Barton witnessed the preparations for it, and saw its results. The boys marched so bravely, so confidently, and they came back in terror leaving 481 killed, 1011 wounded, and 1460 missing. The next night she began a letter to her father, but stopped at the end of the first page, and waited until near the end of the week before resuming. Unfortunately, the latter part of this letter is lost. She undertook to give somewhat in detail a description of the battle, and what she saw before it and after. That part of the letter which has been preserved is as follows:

Washington, D.C., July 22nd, 1861
Monday evening, 6 o'clock, p.m.

My dear Father:

It becomes my painful duty to write you of the disaster of yesterday. Our army has been unfortunate. That the results amount to a defeat we are not willing to admit, but we have been severely repulsed, and our troops returned in part to their former quarters in and around the city. This has been a hard day to witness, sad, painful, and mortifying, but whether in the aggregate it shall sum up a defeat, or a victory, depends (in my poor judgment) entirely upon circumstances; viz. the tone and spirit in which it leaves our men; if sad and disheartened, we are defeated, the worst and sorest of defeats; if roused to madness, and revenge, it will yet prove victory. But no mortal could look in upon this scene to-night and judge of effects. How gladly would I close my eyes to it if I could. I am not fit to write you now, I shall do you more harm than good.

July 26th, Friday noon

You will think it strange that I commenced so timely a letter to you and stopped so suddenly. But I did so upon more mature reflection. You could not fail to know all that I could have told you so soon as I could have got letters through to you, and everything was so unreliable, vague, uncertain, and I confidently hoped exaggerated, that I deemed it the part of prudence to wait, and even now, after all this interval of time, I cannot tell you with certainty and accuracy the things I would like to. It is certain that we have at length had the "Forward Movement" which has been so loudly clamored for, and I am a living witness of a corresponding Backward one. I know that our troops continued to go over into Virginia from Wednesday until Saturday, noble, gallant, handsome fellows, armed to the teeth, apparently lacking nothing. Waving banners and plumes and bristling bayonets, gallant steeds and stately riders, the roll of the drum, and the notes of the bugle, the farewell shout and martial tread of armed men, filled our streets, and saluted our ears through all those days. These were all noble sights, but to me never pleasant; where I fain would- have given them a smile and cheer, the hitter tears would come; for well I knew that, though the proudest of victories perch upon our banner, many a brave boy marched down to die; that, reach it when, and as they would, the Valley of Manassas was the Valley of Death.

Friday brought the particulars of Thursday's encounter. We deplored it, but hoped for more care, and shrewder judgment next time. Saturday brought rumors of intended battle, and most conflicting accounts of the enemy's strength; the evening and Sunday morning papers told us reliably that he had eighty thousand men, and constantly reenforced. My blood ran cold as I read it, lest our army be deceived; but then they knew it, the news came from them; surely they would never have the madness to attack, from open field, an enemy of three times their number behind entrenchments fortified by batteries, and masked at that. No, this could not be; then we breathed freer, and thought of all the humane consideration and wisdom of our time-honored, brave commanding general, that he had never needlessly sacrificed a man.

Clara Barton went immediately to the Washington hospitals to render assistance after the battle of Bull Run. But it did not require all the women in Washington to minister to a thousand wounded men. Those of the wounded who got to Washington were fairly well cared for; but two things appalled her, the stories she heard of suffering on the part of the wounded before they could be conveyed to the hospitals, and the almost total lack of facilities for the care of the wounded. She thought of the good clean cloth in New England homes that might be used for bandages; of the fruits and jellies in Northern farm homes which the soldiers would enjoy. She began advertising in the Worcester *Spy* for provisions for the wounded. She had immediate responses, and soon had established a distributing agency.

I am very glad to have first-hand testimony as to the establishment which she now set up. Mrs. Vassall, who, as Miss Frances Maria

Childs, had been her assistant teacher in Bordentown, has described the home of Clara Barton during the Civil War. She said:

The rooms she took were in a business block. It was not an ideal place for a home-loving woman. Originally there had been one large room, but she had a wooden partition put through, and she made it convenient and serviceable. She occupied one room and had her stores in the other. It was a kind of tent life, but she was happy in it and made it a center from which she brought cheer to others.

Before the end of 1861 the Worcester women had begun to inquire whether there was any further need of their sending supplies to her. They had sent so much, they thought the whole army was provided for, and for the period of the war. We have her letter in reply:

Washington, D.C., December 16, 1861

Mrs. Miller, Sec.,
Ladies' Relief Committee,
Worcester, Mass.
Dear Madam:
Your letter, mailed to me on the 11th, came duly to hand at a moment when I was *more* than busy, and, as I had just written Mrs. Dickensen (of whom I received the articles) a detailed account of their history and final destination, I have ventured with much regret to allow your letter to remain unanswered for a day, that I might find time to write you at greater length. You must before this have learned from my letter to Mrs. D. the occasion of the delay (viz., uncertain orders, rainy weather, and Maryland roads), and decided with me that the (anxious) package has long before this accomplished its mission of charity and love. The bundles were all packed together in a stout box, securely nailed, and given to the sutler of the 15th Regiment, who promised to deliver them safely at Headquarters. I have no doubt but it has all been properly done. A box for the 25th I had delivered to Captain Atwood's Company, and heard with much satisfaction the gratification it afforded the various recipients. The men were looking splendidly, and I need not tell you that the 25th is a "live" regiment from its Colonel and Chaplain down. Worcester County has just cause for pride.

I come now to the expressions in your excellent letter which I had all along feared—"Are our labors needed, are we doing any good, shall we work, or shall we forbear?" From the first I have dreaded lest a sense of vague uncertainty in regard to matters here should discourage the efforts of our patriotic ladies at home; it was this fear and only this which even gave me courage to assemble the worthy ladies of your Committee (so vastly my superiors) to confer upon a matter with which they seemed perfectly familiar, while I knew so little. And even now I scarce know how to reply. It is *said*, upon proper authority, that "our army is supplied." Well, this may be so, it is not for me to gainsay, and so far as our *New England* troops are concerned, it may be that in these days of quiet idleness they have really no pressing wants, but in the event of a battle who can tell what their necessities might grow to in a single day? They would want *then* faster than you could make. But only a small portion of our army, comparatively speaking, are *New England* troops—New York, Pennsylvania, Ohio, Indiana, and Missouri have sent their hundreds of thousands, and I greatly fear that those States lack somewhat the active, industrious, intelligent organizations at home which are so characteristic of our New England circles. I think I discern traces of this in this camp. I feel, while passing through them, that they could be better supplied without danger of enervation from luxuries. Still it is said that "our army is supplied." It is said also, upon the same authority, that we "need no nurses," either male or female, and none are admitted.

I wished an hour ago that you had been with me. In compliance with a request of my sister in this city I went to her house and found there a young Englishman, a brother of one of their domestics who had enlisted during the summer in a regiment of Pennsylvania Cavalry. They are stationed at Camp Pierpont; the sister heard that her brother was sick, and with the energetic habit of a true Englishwoman crossed the country on foot nine miles out to his camp and back the same day, found him in an almost dying condition and begged that he be sent to her. He was taken shortly after in an ambulance, and upon his arrival his condition was found to be most deplorable; he had been attacked with ordinary fever six weeks before, and had lain unmoved until the flesh upon all parts of the body which rested hard upon whatever was under him had decayed, grown perfectly black, and was falling out; his heels had assumed the same appearance; his stockings had never been removed during all his illness and his toes were matted and grown together and are now *dropping off at the joint*; the cavities in his back are absolutely frightful. When intelligent medical attendance was summoned from the city, the verdict rendered upon examination was that his extremities were perishing for want of nourishment. He had been neglected until he was literally starving; too little nourishment had been taken into the system during his illness to preserve life in the extremities. This conclusion seems all the more reliable from the famished appearance which he presents. I am accustomed to see people *hungry* when recovering from a fever, but I find that hunger and starvation are two distinct conditions. He can lie only on his face with his insteps propped up with hair pillows to prevent his toes from touching the bed (for with the life engendered by food and care, sensation is returning to them), and asks only for "something to eat." Food is placed by him at night, and with the earliest dawn of day commence his bowls of broths and soups and a little meat, and he eats and begs for "more," and sleeps and eats and begs. Three of his toes are to be amputated today. The surgeon of the regiment comes to see him, but had no idea of his condition; said that their assistant surgeon was killed and that it "was true that the men had not received proper care; he was very sorry." With the attention which this young man is now receiving, he will probably recover, but had it been otherwise? Only thus, that not far from this time the city papers under caption of "Death of Soldiers" would have contained the paragraph— "Benjamin (or Berry) Pollard, *private*, Camp Pierpont," and this would have been the end. Whoever could have mistrusted that this soldier had *starved to death* through lack of proper attendance? Ah, me, all of our poor boys have not a sister within nine miles of them. And still it is said, upon authority, "we have no need of nurses" and "our army is supplied." How this can be so I fail to see; still again it is not for me to gainsay. We are loyal and our authority must be respected, though our men perish. I only mention such facts as come under my own observation, and only a fraction of those. This is not by any means in accordance with our home style of judging. If we New England people saw men lying in camp uncared for until their toes rotted from their feet, with not persons enough about them to take care of them, we should think they needed *more* nurses; if with plenty of persons about who failed to care for them we should think they needed *better*. I can only repeat that I fail to see clear. I greatly fear that the few privileged, elegantly dressed ladies who ride over and sit in their carriages to witness "splendid services" and "inspect the Army of the Potomac" and come away "delighted," learn very little of what lies there under canvas.

Since receiving your letter I have taken occasion to converse with a number of the most intelligent and competent ladies who are or have been connected with the hospitals in this city, and all agree upon one point, viz., that *our army cannot afford* that our ladies lay down their needles and fold their hands; if their contributions are not needed just to-day, they may be to-morrow, and *somewhere* they are needed to-day. And again all agree in advising that whatever be sent be gotten as nearly direct as possible from the hands of the donors to the very spot for which it is designed, not to pass through too general distribution, strengthening their advice by many reasons and circumstances which I do not feel at liberty to lay before you. No one can fail to perceive that a house of general receipts and distribution of stores of all descriptions from the whole United States must be a mammoth concern, abounding in confusion which always involves loss and destruction of property. I am confident that this idea cannot be incorrect, and therefore I will not hesitate to advance it upon my own responsibility, viz., that every State should have, in the vicinity of her greatest body of troops, a depot of her own where all her contributions should be sent and dispersed; if her own soldiers need it all, to them; if not, then let her share generously and intelligently with those who do need; but know what she has and what she gives. We shall never have any other precise method of discovering the real wants of our soldiers. When the storehouse of any State should be found empty, it would be safe to conclude that her troops are in need; then let the full garners render the required assistance. This would systematize the whole matter, and do away with all necessary confusion, doubt, and uncertainty; it would preclude all possibility of loss, as it would be the business of each house to look to its own property. There is some truth in the old maxim that "what is everybody's business is nobody's business." I believe that as long ago as the early settlement of our country it was found that the plan, general labor, general storehouse, and general distribution, proved ineffective and reduced our own little colony to a state of confusion and almost ruin; there were one hundred persons then, one hundred thousand now. If, pecuniarily I were able, Massachusetts should have her depot in this city and I should have no fear of unreliability; this to me would be no experiment, for however dimly and slowly I discern *other* points, *this* has been clear to me from the first, strengthened by eight months' daily observation.

While I write another idea occurs to me—has it been thought of to provide each of our regiments that are to accompany the next expedition with some strong, well-filled boxes of useful articles and stores, which are not to be opened until some battle, or other strong necessity renders supplies necessary. These necessities are sure to follow, and, unless anticipated and guarded against, no activity on the part of friends at home can prevent the suffering which their absence will create. With regard to our 23d, 25th, and 27th Regiments, I cannot speak, but our 21st I *know* have no such provisions, and will not have unless thought of at home, and the consequence of neglect will be that by and by our very hearts will be wrung by accounts of our best officers and dearest friends having their limbs amputated by the light of two inches of tallow candle in the midst of a battle, and pitchy darkness close down upon men bleeding to death, or since essaying to stanch their wounds with husks and straw.

A note just now informs me that our four companies of surgeons from Fort Independence, now stationed at the arsenal in this city (some two miles from me), in waiting for their supplies from Boston, were compelled to sleep in low, damp places with a single blanket and are taking severe colds and coughing fearfully. My ingenuity points no way of relief but to buy sacking, run up many ticks to be filled with hay to raise them from the drafts a little, and to this the remainder of my day must be devoted; they are far more exposed than they would be on the ground under a good tent. I almost envy you ladies where so many of you can work together and accomplish so much, while my poor labors are so single-handed. The future often looks dark to me, and it seems sometimes that the smiles of Heaven are almost with- drawn from our poor, rent, and distracted country; and yet there is everything to be grateful for, and by no means the least is this strangely mild winter.

But I must desist and crave pardon for my (perhaps unpardonably) long letter, for if you have followed me thus far, and especially at comparatively as rapid a rate as I have written, you must be weary. I did not intend to say so much, but let my interest be my apology. And with one more final word in answer to your rational question I have done. Ladies, remember that the call for your organized efforts in behalf of our army was not from any commission or committee, but from Abraham Lincoln and Simon Cameron, and when they no longer need your labors they will tell you.

But all this preliminary work bore in upon the mind of Clara Barton two important truths. The first was a necessity for organization. People were ready to give if they knew where to give and how their gifts would be made effective. The problem was one of publicity, and then of effective organization for distribution. But the other matter troubled her yet more. Supplies distributed from Washington and relief given to men there reached the wounded many hours or even days after the beginning of their needs. What was required was not simply good nurses in hospitals and adequate food and medicine for the soldiers who were conveyed thither, but some sort of provision on the battle-field itself. In later years she described her own misgivings as she considered the kind of service that ought to be rendered, and of the difficulties, including those of social duties, which might stand in the way:

I was strong and thought I might go to the rescue of the men who fell. The first regiment of troops, the old 6th

Massachusetts that fought its way through Baltimore brought my playmates and neighbors, the partakers of my childhood; the brigades of New Jersey brought scores of my brave boys, the same solid phalanx; and the strongest legions from old Herkimer, brought the associates of my seminary days. They formed and crowded around me. What could I do but go with them, or work for them and my country? The patriot blood of my father was S warm in my veins. The country which he had fought for,

I might at least work for, and I had offered my service to the Government in the capacity of a double clerkship at twice $1600 a year, upon discharge of two disloyal clerks from its employ—the salary never to be given to me, but to be turned back into the United States Treasury, then poor to beggary, with no currency, no credit. But there was no law for this, and it could not be done, and I would not draw salary from our Government in such peril, so I resigned and went into direct service of the sick and wounded troops wherever found.

But I struggled long and hard with my sense of propriety—with the appalling fact that I was only a woman whispering in one ear, and thundering in the other, the groans of suffering men dying like dogs, unfed and unsheltered, for the life of every institution which had protected and educated me!

I said that I struggled with my sense of propriety and I say it with humiliation and shame. I am ashamed that I thought of such a thing.

The thing that became increasingly plain to Clara Barton was that every hour that elapsed after a man was wounded before relief reached him was an hour on which might easily hang the issues of life and death. Somehow she must get relief to men on the battle-field itself.

In later years people used sometimes to address her in terms which implied that she had nursed with her own hands more soldiers than any other American woman who labored in military hospitals; that her hands had bound up more wounds than those of other nurses and sanitary leaders. She always tried to make it plain that she put forth no such claim for herself. Her distinctive contribution to the problem was one of organization and distribution, and especially of the prompt conveyance of relief to the places of greatest need and of greatest danger. In this she was soon to organize a system, and, indeed, had already effected the beginning of an organization which was to constitute her distinctive work in the Civil War and to lay the foundation for her great contribution to humanity, the American Red Cross.

HOME AND COUNTRY

The family and home life of Clara Barton occupy of necessity a smaller place in this narrative than they rightfully deserve. Reference has been made in the early pages of this work to Clara Barton's advent into a home which for several years had believed itself complete. It must not be inferred on that account that the little late arrival was other than heartily welcome. Nor must the fact that her more than normal shyness and introspection during her childhood made her a problem be understood as indicating any lack of sympathy between her and any member of her household. On the contrary, her childhood memories were happy ones, and her affection for every member of the household was sincere and almost -unbounded. Nor yet again must it be supposed that her long absences from home weaned her heart away from those who were entitled to her love. Love of family and pride of family and sincere affection for every member of the home group were manifest in all her correspondence. She left her home and went out into the world while she was still a child in her own thought and in the thought of her family. She became a teacher while she was still wearing the "little waifish" dresses of her childhood. She had to do a large part of her thinking and planning apart from the companionship of those she loved best. But she loved them deeply and sincerely. The members of her family receive only incidental mention in this narrative, and, with her advent into wider fields of service, they must drop increasingly into the background and out of view. In order, however, that we may have in mind their incidental mention, let us here record the condition of her immediate family at the time of the outbreak of the Civil War.

Her eldest sister Dorothy, born October 2, 1804, became an invalid and died unmarried April 19, 1846, aged forty-one. Her brother Stephen, born March 20, 1806, married November 24, 1833, Elizabeth Rich, and died in Washington, March 10, 1865, aged fifty-nine years. At the outbreak of the Civil War he was living in Hertford County, North Carolina, wither he had gone in 1854. He had established a large sawmill there, and gathered about it a group of industries which by 1861 had become the most important concern in the village. Indeed, the village itself had grown up about his enterprise, and took its name, Bartonville, from him. When the war broke out, he was past the age for military service. At the beginning of the struggle, however, he had no mind to leave the South. While he was a Union man, and everyone knew it, he had been long enough in the South to appreciate the position of the Southern people and had no mind needlessly to wound their feelings. His mill, his store, his blacksmith shop, his lands, his grain, his cattle, had been accumulated by him through years of toil, and he desired to stay where he was and protect his property. He did not believe—no one believed—that the war was going to last so long. There was no service which at the beginning he could render to the Northern cause. So he remained. As the war went on, his situation grew less and less tenable, and, in time, dangerous. He sent his helpers North, some twenty of them. They made their way amid perils and hardship, reached Washington where Clara Barton rendered them assistance, and ultimately the most of them entered the Union army. But earlier than this, in 1861 and at the beginning of 1862, his family was growing increasingly anxious about him, and very desirous, if possible, that he should get away. He was warned and threatened; at one time he suffered a night assault by a mob. Bruised and battered though he was, he fought them off single-handed and remained in the South.

Her younger brother David, born August 15, 1808, married, September 30, 1829, Julia Ann Maria Porter, lived to the age of eighty, and died March 12, 1888. At the outbreak of the war David and Julia Barton had four children—their twin daughters Ada and Ida, born January 18, 1847, the one son, Stephen Emery, born December 24, 1848, and in 1861 a lad of twelve, and the daughter Mary, born December Ii, 1851.

With her brother David, his wife Julia and his four children, Clara was in continuous correspondence. His family lived in the old home, and she kept in constant touch with them. Her sister-in-law Julia was very dear to her, and perhaps the best correspondent in the family.

Her sister Sarah, born March 20, 1811, married, April 17, 1834, Vester Vassall, and died in May, 1874. At the outbreak of the war both the children of this marriage were living. The younger son Irving, died April 9, 1865. The elder son, Bernard Barton Vassall, born October 10, 1835, married, October 26, 1863, Frances Maria Childs, and died March 23, 1894. Mrs. Vassall is still living.

With this family Clara's relations were those of peculiar intimacy. Her sister and her sister's children were very dear to her. Irving was a young man of fine Christian character, not physically strong enough to bear arms, and was in Washington in the service of the Government during the war. Bernard married Clara's dear friend and assistant at Bordentown. He was a soldier and during the war his wife Fannie lived for a considerable time in Washington.

Clara Barton's mother, Sarah or Sally Stone, born November 13, 1783, died July 10, 1851, aged sixty-eight. Her death occurred while Clara was studying at Clinton, and the expressions of solitude in Clara's diary at the time of her perplexities over her love affairs, were induced in part, though perhaps unconsciously, by her loneliness after her mother's death.

Clara's relations to her father were always those of peculiar nearness and sympathy. In her childhood he was more constantly her companion than her mother ever was. When Clara was away from home, nothing more surely gave her concern than news from her brother or sister that "father," or from her nieces and nephews that "grandpa," was not as well as usual. Her diaries and her letters are burdened with her solicitude for him. In the latter part of 1861 his health gave occasion for some concern, but he seemed to recover. She made a journey to Worcester and Oxford in December, but returned to Washington before Christmas, taking with her boxes and trunks of provisions for the soldiers which she wished to deliver if possible at Arlington, so as to be closer to the place of actual need. Her nephew, Irving Vassall, was with her on the return journey. The letter which preserves the account of this expedition is interesting as recording her account of a Sunday spent with the army. What took her there was her determination to deliver her goods to the place of need before she returned to her home in Washington. She was still learning military manners and the ways of camp life, and was giving herself unsparingly to the collection of supplies. She was assisting in hospital work in Washington, and definitely planning to have a hospital there assigned to herself. As yet, apparently, she had no definite plan to go herself directly to the battle-field.

November and the early part of December were mild. Day by day she thanked God for every ray of sunshine, and night by night she lifted up her heart in thanksgiving that the boys, who were sleeping on the bare ground with only single threads of white canvas above them, were not compelled to suffer from the rigors of cold. On December 9, 1861, she wrote the following which was a kind of prayer of thanksgiving for mild weather:

December 9, 1861

The streets are thronged with men bright with tinsel, and the clattering hoofs of galloping horses sound continually in our ears. The weather is bright and warm as May, for which blessing I feel hourly to thank the great Giver of all good gifts, that upon this vast army lying like so many thousand herds of cattle on every side of our bright, beleaguered city, with only the soil, for which they peril life, beneath, and the single threads of white canvas above, watching like so many faithful dogs, held by bonds stronger than death, yet patient and uncomplaining. A merciful God holds the warring, pitiless elements in his firm, benignant grasp, withholds the rigors of early winter, and showers down upon their heads the genial rays of untimely warmth changing the rough winds of December to the balmy breezes of April. Well may we hold thanksgiving and our army unite in prayer and songs of praise to God.

Her diary at this period is irregular, and I have not yet discovered a definite record of her journey from Washington and back, except in her letter to the wife of an army surgeon, which she wrote on the day before Christmas, 1861:

Washington, D.C., December 24th, 1861

My darling Cousin:

How naughtily I have neglected your cheering little letter, but it has been all my hands and none my heart which have done the naughty thing. I have wanted so to write you all the time, and intruders would come between us and would have all my time. It was not always people. Oh, no—work and care, and an o'ergrown correspondence intruded upon me, but I always solace myself with the thought that, if my friends will only have a little patience with me, it will all come right, and their turn will come at last, and after a time the best of them learn me, and then in my easy, hurrying, slipshod way we come to be correspondents for ayc. In the course of a year I say a great deal of nonsense to my correspondents, but I cannot always say it when my head and heart are the fullest of it. But first let me hasten to tell you what cannot fail of being exceedingly gratifying to you, viz., that I am in a "habit" of receiving daily visits from your husband. But I was a long time in getting about it, however. I sent twice to his hotel, the great Pandemonium wherein he is incarcerated, before Sunday, but could get no tidings all the time. I was fearful he was here and I missing him, and then I was almost certain that he was not able to be here; but at length I could risk it no longer and wrote a hurried little note and dropped in the office for him, and sure enough It brought him. I was so glad to see him and so much better too, It is splendid; but then he had been trying to find me, and I in the meantime had, along with all Washington, removed! Just think of it, but I removed out of a burden of care to perfect ease and yet can command just as much room as I desire in case I need, and if I have no need of it am not troubled with it—only that I have the trouble of furnishing, at which Doctor may inform you I am making very slow progress. I have so many things in Massachusetts now that I want; my walls are perfectly bare, not a picture, and I have plenty to furnish them. It is vexatious that I didn't "know to take them" when I was there. I fear to allow others to pack them.

I suspect that, after the daily letter of your husband, inimitable correspondent and conversationist that he is, there is nothing left for me to relate of our big city, grown up so strangely like a gourd all in a night; places which never before dreamed of being honored by an inhabitant save dogs, cats, and rats, are converted into "elegantly furnished rooms for rent," and people actually live in them with all the city airs of people really living in respectable houses, and I suspect many of them do not know that they are positively living in sheds, but we, who have become familiar with every old roof years agone, know perfectly well what shelters them. Well, the present aspect of our capital is a wide, fruitful field for description, and I will leave it for the Doctor; he will clothe it in a far richer dress than I could do.

Perhaps you wish to know somewhat about my journey with my big trunks. Well, it was perfectly quiet; nothing like an adventure to enliven until we reached Baltimore, to which I had checked my baggage as the nearest point to Annapolis, for which place I could not get checks, but to which I had determined to go before proceeding to Washington. I delivered my checks to the expressman, took receipts, and gave every conductor on the train to understand that my baggage was to be taken through the city in the same train with myself (for we disconnect and come through Baltimore in horse-cars); but just imagine my vexation when, as our train commenced to move off, I saw my baggage just moving by slow teams up the street in the direction of our train. It had no checks, and I must not become long separated from it; the train was in motion and I could not leave it. I had no idea what would be done with it, whether retained in Baltimore, sent to Annapolis junction, or forwarded to Washington. I had to think fast, and you remember it was Saturday night. Relay House was the nearest station. I left the train there (Irving went on to Washington), and proceeded directly to the telegraph office and telegraphed back to Baltimore describing the baggage and directing it to come on the next train one hour later. They had just time to get it aboard, and on the arrival of the train I found it in the baggage car, took that train, and proceeded "nine miles to the junction," stopped too late for Annapolis that night, chartered the parlor and sofa—every room in the house filled with officers—and as good luck would have it a train (special) ran down from Annapolis the next day about eleven, for a regiment of Zouaves, and I claimed my seat, and went, too, and the first anyone knew I presented myself at the Headquarters of the 21st. You will have to imagine the cordial, affable Colonel springing from his seat with both hands extended, the extremely polite Lieutenant-Colonel Maggie, always in full dress with the constantly worn sword, with eyes and hair so much blacker than night, going through a succession of bows and formalities, which I, a simple, home-bred, unsophisticated Yankee didn't know what upon earth to do with, completely confounded!— till the clear, appreciative, knowing twinkle of our "cute" Major Clark's eyes set things right again; and almost the last, our honest, modest "Cousin" Fletcher coming up away round on the other side for his word, and not one among them all to whom I could extend a more cordial greeting. Please tell Grandma that he hasn't broken a limb; his horse fell with him and hurt his shoulder, but it is nearly well now. I was just in time for a seat between the Colonel and Lieutenant-Colonel at dinner, and accompanying them to the Chapel to listen to the opening discourse of their newly arrived chaplain, Rev. Mr. Ball, Unitarian. He addressed the men with great kindness of manner, beseeching them to come near to him with all their trials, burdens, and temptations, and let him help to bear them. He was strong to bear, patient to hear, and willing to do, and his arm, and his ear, and his heart were theirs for all good purposes. There was many a glistening eye among that thousand waiting men, still as the night of death; for a regiment of soldiers can be the stillest living thing I ever looked at. The 21st are in the main good, true men, and I was glad that a man of gentle speech and kind and loving heart had come among them.

Next morning brought some of our good Worcester ladies from the 25th to our Camp, among whom was the daughter-in-law of your neighbor Mr. Denny. A beautiful coach and span of horses were found, and a cozy, but rather gay, party of us started for the Camp of the 25th, and here we found your excellent pastor, Mr. James, the best specimen of a true soldier that I ever saw; nothing too vast for his mind to grasp, nothing too trivial (if needful) to interest him, cheerful, brave, and tireless, watching like a faithful sentry the wants of every soldier, and apparently more than equal to every emergency. What a small army of such men were sufficient to overcome all our present difficulties! You should see his tent; it was a cold, raw day, more so than any which has followed it, but the moment I was inside I found myself so warm and my feet grew warm as if I were standing over a register, and I could not see where the heat came from; but my curiosity was irrepressible, and I had to ask an explanation of the mystery—when Mr. James raised a little square iron lid, like the door of a stove (which I believe it was), almost hidden in the ground, in among the dried grass, and to my astonishment revealed a miniature volcano blazing beneath our very feet. The whole ground beneath his tent seemed to be on fire, with currents of air passing through which fed the flame, and took away the smoke. There was, of course, no dampness in the tent, and I could see no reason why it should be less healthy, or comfortable indeed (excepting small space), than any house, and such piles of letters and books and Neddy's picture over the table, and the quiet little boy, following close and looking up in his master's face, like any pet, all presented a scene which I wished his intelligent and appreciative wife, at least, could have looked in upon. Oh, yes, I must not "forget" to mention the conspicuous position which Grandma's mittens occupied upon the table. Mr. James put them on to show what a nice fit they were and wondered what "Grandma" would say if she were to look in upon him in his tent.

Clara Barton was still in Washington through January and apparently through February, 1862. Not always was she able to include pleasant weather among the occasions of her thanksgiving. Every now and again a pitiless storm beat down upon the soldiers, who were poorly provided with tents and blankets. Frequently she met among the soldiers in Washington some of her old pupils. She was never able to look upon armies as mere masses of troops; she had to remember that they were individual men, each capable of

111

suffering pain in his own person, and each of them carrying with him to the front the anxious thought of loved ones at home. This was the burden of a letter which she wrote on January 9, 1862:

Washington, D.C., Jan'y 9th, 1862
Thursday morning

My darling Sis Fannie:

In spite of everything, I shall this moment commence this note to you, and I shall finish it as soon as I can, and when it is finished, I shall send it. In these days of "Proclamations," this is mine.

I am truly thankful for the institution of ghosts, and that mine haunted you until you felt constrained to cry out for "relief"—not that I would have invoked discomfort upon you, or welcomed it when it should come, but your letter was so welcome, how could I in mortal weakness be so unselfish as not to hail with joy any "provoking cause"? You perceive that my idea of ghosts is not limited to graveyards and tombs, or the tenants thereof; indeed, so far from it, the most troublesome I have ever known were at times the inmates of living and moving bodies habiting among other people, coming out only occasionally like owls and bats to frighten the weak and discourage the weary. I am rejoiced to know that you are comfortable and happy, and that your school is not wearing you—you are perfectly right, never let another school be a burden of care upon you; you will do all your duty without any such soul-vexing labors. I envy you and Miss Bliss your long social intellectual evenings; please play I am there sometimes. I will be so quiet, and never disturb a bit, but, dear me, I am in rougher scenes, if in scenes at all. My head is just this moment full to aching, bursting with all the thoughts and doings of our pet expedition. A half-hour ago came to my room the last messenger from them, the last I shall have in all probability until the enemy's galling shot shall have raked through the ranks of my dear boys, and strewn them here and there, bleeding, crippled, and dying. Only think of it! the same fair faces that only a few years ago came every morning, newly washed, hair nicely combed, bright and cheerful, and took their places quietly and happily among my scholars—the same fair heads (perhaps now a few shades darker) that I have smoothed and patted in fond approval of some good deed or well-learned task, so soon to lie low in the Southern sands, blood-matted and tangled, trampled underfoot of man and horse, buried in a common trench "unwept, uncoffined, and unknown." For the last two weeks my very heart has been crushed by the sad thoughts and little touching scenes which have come in my way. It tires me most when one would get a few hours' leave from his regiment at Annapolis, and come to me with some little sealed package, and perhaps his "warrant" as a non-commissioned officer, and ask me to keep it for him, either until he returns for it, or—*when I should read his name in the "Black List," send it home.* And by the time his errand were well done, his little hour would be up and, with a hearty grasp of the hand, an earnest, deep-toned "good-bye," he stepped from my presence, marching cheerfully, bravely out—"To die," I said to myself, as my soul sunk within me, and the struggling breath would choke and stop, until the welcome shower of tears came to my relief. Oh, the hours I have wept alone over scenes like these, no mortal knows! To any other friend than you, I should not feel like speaking so freely of such things, but you, who know how foolishly tender my friendships are, and how I loved "my boys," will pardon me, and not think me strange or egotistical. But I must forget myself, and tell you what the messenger said. It was simply that they were all on board; that, when he left, the harbor was full, literally crammed with boats and vessels, covered with men, shouting from every deck. At every breeze that lifted the drooping flag aloft, a shout went up that deafened and drowned every other sound, save the roar of the cannon, following instantly, drowning them in return. The...

Well, just as I knew it would be when I commenced twenty days ago to write you, someone interrupted me, and then came the returning hours of tedious labor, and a thrice-told quantity has held me fast until now. I have been a great deal more than busy for the past three weeks, owing to some new arrangements in the office, mostly, by which I lead the Record, and hurry up the others who lag.

Our city has known very little change, since I commenced my first sheet, although everybody but the wise people have looked intently for something new, and desperately dreadful, some "forward movement" or backward advance, but nothing of the kind has happened, doubtless much to our credit and comfort. No private returns from the "expedition" yet, but the Commandant of the Post at Annapolis, who just left me a moment ago, says that the Baltic will leave there this p.m. to join them in their landing wherever it may be.

Colonel Allen's death was a most sad affair: his regiment was the first to embark at Annapolis, a splendid regiment 1200 strong. But a truce to wars, so here's my white flag, only I suppose you "don't see it," do you? By this time you are reveling in the February number of the "Atlantic." So am I. I have just laid down "A. C." after a hurried perusal; not equal to "Love and Skates," though; what a capital thing that is! But the "Yankee Idyll" caps all that has yet been done or said. I cannot lay that down, and keep it there; it will come up again, the thoughts to my mind, and the pages to my hand.

113

"Old Uncle S—says he, I guess,
God's price is high, says he."

From James Russell Lowell's second series of "Biglow Papers," *then appearing in the* Atlantic.—Ed.

Who ever heard so much, so simply and so quaintly expressed?—there are at least ten volumes of good sound Orthodoxy embodied just there in that single stanza. But "Port Royal" mustn't be eclipsed. The glories of that had been radiating through my mind, however, since its first appearance in the *Tribune* (if that were the first; it was the first I saw of it), and I thought it so beautiful that I shouldn't be able to relish another poem for at least six weeks, and here it is, so soon bedimmed by a *rival*. Oh, the fickleness of human nature, and human loves, a beautiful pair they are, surmounted by the Godlike "Battle Hymn"* tossing over all. What did our poets do for subjects before the war? It's a Godsend to them, I am certain, and they equally so to us; sometimes I think them the only bright spot in the whole drama.

*A reference to Julia Ward Howe's "Battle Hymn of the Republic," then new.—Ed.

Well, here I am at war again. I knew 'twould be so when I signed that treaty on the previous page. I'm as bad as England; the fight is in me, and I will find a pretext.

I have not seen our North Oxford "Regulars" for some time owing to the fact that a sea of mud has lain between me and them for the last three weeks, utterly impassable. A few weeks ago Cousin Leander called me to see a member of his "mess" who was just attacked with pleuritic fever. I went, and found him in hospital. He was cheerful (a fine young man) and thought he should be out soon. Work and storm kept me from him three days, and the fourth we bought him a grave in the Congressional Burying Ground. Poor fellow, and there he lies all alone. A soldier's grave, a sapling at the head, a rough slab at the foot, nine shots between, and all is over. He waits God's bugle to summon him to a reenlistment in the Legion of Angels.

Well, it's no use, I've broken the peace again, and I can't keep it. I hope you live in a more peaceful community than I do, and are consequently more manageable and less belligerent....

Clara

The foregoing letter dealt almost wholly with national affairs. Family matters were giving her little concern during the twenty days in which this unfinished missive lay on her desk. But scarcely had she mailed it when she received this letter concerning her father:

North Oxford, Mass., January 13, 1862

My dear Clara:

I sat up with Grandpa last night and he requested me to write to you and tell how he was. someone has to sit up with him to keep his fire regulated. He takes no medicine, and says he shall take no more. He is quite low-spirited at times, and last night very much so. Complains of pains in his back and bowels; said he should not stop long with us, and should like to see you once more before he died. He spoke in high terms of Julie and of the excellent care she had taken of him, but said after all there was no one like you. I think he fails slowly and is gradually wearing out. A week ago he was quite low; so feeble that he was unable to raise himself in bed; now he is more comfortable and walks out into the sitting-room most every day. He cannot be prevailed upon to go to bed, but sits in his great chair and sleeps on the lounge. When he was the sickest I notified Dr. Darling of his situation and he called. Grandpa told him his medicine did not help or hurt him. Doctor left him some drops, but said he had no confidence in his medicine and he did not think it would help him. His appetite is tolerably good for all kinds of food, and what he wants he will have. I hardly know what to write about him. I do not wish to cause unnecessary alarm, and at the same time I want you to fully understand his case. As I said before, he gets low-spirited and disconsolate, but I think he may stand by us some months longer, and yet, he may be taken away at any moment. Of course every new attack leaves him feebler and more childish. He wants to see you again and seems quite anxious about it, but whether about anything in particular he did not say...

Sam Barton

Thus, at the beginning of February, 1862, she was called back to Oxford. Her father, who had several times seemed near to death, but who had recovered again and again, was now manifestly nearing the end. She was with him more than a month before he died. His mind was clear, and they were able to converse about all the great matters which concerned them and their home and country. He made his final business arrangements; he talked with the children who were there, and about the children who were away. He was greatly concerned for Stephen, at that time shut in by the Confederate army. Even if the Northern armies could reach him, as they seemed likely to do before long, neither Clara nor her father felt sure that he would leave. There was an element of stubbornness in the Barton family, and Stephen was disposed to stand his ground against all threats and all entreaties. Clara and her father felt that the situation was certainly more serious than even Stephen could realize. To invite him to return to Oxford and sit down in idleness was worse than useless, and he could not render any military service. Not only was he too old, but he had a hernia. But she felt sure that if he were in Washington there would be something that he could do; and, as was subsequently proved, she was right about it. There were no mails between Massachusetts or Washington and the place of his residence, but Clara had opportunity to send a letter which she hoped would reach him. She wrote guardedly, for it was not certain into whose hands the letter might fall. Sitting by her father's bedside she wrote the following long epistle;

North Oxford, March 1st, 1862
My dear Exiled Brother:
I trust that at length I have an opportunity of speaking to you without reserve. I only wish I might talk with you face to face, for in all the shades of war which have passed over us, we must have taken in many different views. I would like to compare them, but as this cannot be, I must tell you mine, and in doing so I shall endeavor to give such opinions and facts as would be fully endorsed by every friend and person here whose opinions you would ever have valued. I would sooner sever the hand that pens this than mislead you, and you may *depend* upon the *strict fact* of everything I shall say, remembering that I shall overcolor nothing.

In the first place, let me remove the one great error, prevalent among all (Union) people at the South, I presume viz., that this is a war of "Abolitionism" or abolitionists. This is not so; our Government has for its object the restoration of the Union as it was, and will do so, unless the resistance of the South prove so obstinate and prolonged that the abolition or overthrow of slavery follow as a *consequence*—never an object. Again, the idea of "*subjugation.*" This application never originated with the North, nor is it tolerated there, for an instant; desired by no one unless, like the first instance, it follows as a necessity incident upon a course of protracted warfare. Both these ideas are used as stimulants by the Southern (mis)

116

leaders, and without them they could never hold their army together a month. The North are fighting for the maintenance of the Constitutional Government of the United States and the defense and honor of their country's flag. This accomplished, the army are ready to lay down their arms and return to their homes and peaceable pursuits, and our leaders are willing to disband them. Until such time, there will be found no willingness on the part of either. We have now in the field between 500,000 and 600,000 soldiers; more cavalry and artillery than we can use to advantage, our navy growing to a formidable size, and all this vast body of men, clothed, fed, and paid, as was never an army on the face of the earth before, perfectly uniformed, and hospital stores and clothing lying idly by waiting to be used; we feel no scarcity of money. I am not saying that we are not getting a large national debt, but I mean to say that our people are not feeling the pinchings of "war-time." The people of the North are as comfortable as you used to see them. You should be set down in the streets of Boston, Worcester, New York, or Philadelphia to-day, and only by a profusion of United States flags and occasionally a soldier home on a furlough would you ever mistrust that we were *at war*. Let the fire bells ring in any of those cities, and you will never miss a man from the crowds you have ordinarily seen gather on such occasions. We can raise another army like the one we have in the field (only better men as a *mass*), arm and equip them for service, and still have men and means enough left at home for all practical purposes. Our troops are just beginning to be effective, only just properly drilled, and are now ready to commence work in earnest or just as ready to lay down their arms when the South are ready to return to the Union, as "loyal and obedient States"; not obedient to the *North*, but obedient to the laws of the whole country. Our relations with foreign countries are amicable, and our late recent victories must for a long time set at rest all hope or fears of foreign interference, and even were such an event probable, the Federal Government would not be dismayed. We are doubtless in better condition to meet a foreign foe, along with all our home difficulties to-day, than we should have been all together one year ago to-day. Foreign powers stand off and look with wonder to see what the Americans have accomplished in ten months; they will be wary how they wage war with "Yankees" after this. I must caution here, lest you think there is in all I say something of the spirit of "brag." There is not a vestige of it. I am only stating plain facts, and not the hundredth part of them. I do not feel exultant, but humble and grateful that under the blessing of God, my country and my people have accomplished what they have; and even *were* I exulting, it would be *for* you, and not over, or against you, for "according to the straightest of your sect," have you lived a "Yankee." And this brings me to the point of my subject; here comes my request, my prayer, supplication, entreaty, command—call it what you will, only *heed* it, at once. Come home, not home to Massachusetts, but home to *my* home; I want you in Washington. I could cover pages, fill volumes, in telling you all the anxiety that has been felt for you, all the hours of anxious solicitude that I have known in the last ten months, wondering where you were, or if you were at all, and planning ways of getting to you, or getting you to me, but never until now has any safe or suitable method presented itself, and now that the expedition has opened a means of escape, I am tortured with the fear that, under the recent call of the State, you may have been drafted into the enemy's service. If you are still at your place and this letter reaches you, I desire, and most sincerely advise, you to make ready, and, when the opportunity shall present (which surely will), place yourself, with such transportable things as you may desire to take, on board one of our boats, under protection of our officers, and be taken to the landing at Roanoke, and from thence by some of our transports up to Annapolis, where either myself or friends will be waiting for you, then go with me to Washington and call your days of trial over;—for so it can be done. If we could have known when General Burnside's expedition left, that it was destined for your place, Sam would have accompanied them, and made his way to you on the first boat up your river; as it is, he is coming now, hoping that he may be in time to reach you, and have your company back. I want in some way that this and other letters reach you before he does, that you may make such preparations as will be necessary, and be ready, whenever he shall appear, to step on board and set your face toward a more peaceful quarter. You will meet a welcome from our officers such as you little dream of, unless perchance you have already met them. If you have, you have found them gentlemen and friends; you will find scores of old friends in that expedition, all anxious to see you, would do anything to serve you if you were with them, but don't know where to find you. There are some down on the Island, among General Burnside's men, who have your address, but they would scarcely be on our gunboats. There are plenty of men there who have not only your name in their pockets, but your memory in their hearts, and would hail you with a brother's welcome. General Butler came in at Hatteras with a long letter in his possession relating to you, and if he had advanced so far, he would have claimed you. I don't know how many of our prominent Worcester men have come or sent to me for your address, to make it known among our troops if ever they reached you, that they might offer you any aid in their power. No one can bear the idea of our forces going near you without knowing all about you, and claiming and treating you as a brother; you were never as near and dear to the people of

Worcester County as you are to-day. I have seen the tears roll over more than one man's face when told that Sam was going to see and take something to you, and bring you away if you would come. "God grant he may" is the hearty ejaculation which follows. I want to tell you who you will find among the officers and men composing the Expedition near you; Massachusetts has five regiments—21st, 23rd, 24th, 25th, 27th; the 21st and 25th were raised in Worcester, the former under Colonel Augustus Morse, of Leominster, formerly Major-General Morse, of the 3rd Division, State Militia: he is detached from the regiment and is commandant (or second in command now) of the post at Annapolis. It is he who will send Sam free of cost to you. He is a good, true friend of mine, and tells me to send Sam to him, and he will put him on the track to you. He will also interest both General Burnside and Commander Goldsburgh in both of you and leave nothing undone for your comfort and interest. In the meantime he is waiting to grasp your hand, and share his table and blanket with you at Annapolis. So much for him; the other officers of the regiment are Lieutenant-Colonel Maggi, Major Clark (of Amherst College, Professor of Chemistry), Dr. Calvin Cutter as surgeon (you remember Cutter's Physiology), Adjutant Stearns, Chaplain Ball, etc. etc. all of whom know me, are my friends, and will be yours in an instant; among the men are scores of boys whom you know. You can't enter *that* regiment without a shout of welcome, unless you do it *very slyly*. Then for the 25th, Colonel Upton, of Fitchburg, Lieutenant-Colonel Sprague, of Worcester, Major Caffidy, of W., Chaplain Reverend Horace James, of the Old South, Cousin Ira's old minister, one of the bravest men in the regiment, one of my best friends, and yours too; Captain I. Waldo Denny, son of Denny the insurance agent. The Captain has been talking about you for the last six months, and if he once gets hold of you will be slow to release you unless you set your face for me; the old gentleman (his father) has been very earnest in devising plans all through the difficulties to reach, aid, or get you away as might be best. He came to me in Washington for your address and all particulars long months ago, hoping that he could reach you through just some such opening as the present. I state all this because it is due you that you should know the state of feeling held towards you by your old friends and acquaintances whether you choose to come among them or not. Even old Brine was in here a few minutes ago, and is trying to have Sam take a hundred dollars of *his* money out to you, lest you should need it and cannot get it there; the old fellow urged it upon me with the tears running down his cheeks. There is no bitterness here, even towards the Southerners themselves, and men would give their lives to save the Union men of the South. The North feel it to be a necessity to put down a rebellion, and there the animosity ends. Now, my advice to you would be this; if you do not see fit to follow it, you will promise not to take offense or think me conceited in *presuming* to advise you; under ordinary circumstances I would not think of the thing, as you very well know. I get my privilege merely from the different standpoint I occupy. No word or expression has ever come from you, and you are regarded as a Union man closed in and unable to leave, standing by your property to guard it. This expedition is supposed to have opened the way for your safe exit or escape to your native land, friends, and loyal Government, and if now you should take the first opportunity to leave and report yourself at your own Government you would find yourself a hundred times more warmly received than if you had been here naturally, all the time. So far as lay in the power of our troops your property would be sacredly protected, far more so than if you remained on it in a manner a little hostile or doubtful. I am not certain but the best thing for Mr. Riddick would be for you to leave just in this way, and surely I would have his property harmed no more than yours. I have understood Mr. Riddick to be a Union man at heart like hundreds of other men whom our Government desires to protect from all harm and secure against all loss. This being the case, the best course for both of you which could be adopted, in my judgment, is for you to leave with our troops. This will secure the property against them; they would never harm a hair of it intentionally knowing it to belong to you, a Union man who had come away with them, and you could so represent the case of Mr. Riddick that his rights and property would be respected by them. *He would be infinitely more secure for such a move on your part*, while his connection with you would, I trust, be sufficient to secure your property from molestation by his neighbors, who would be slow to offend or injure him. If you leave and your property be *un*officially injured by our troops, the Federal Government must be held responsible for it, and if, after matters are settled, and business revives, you should find your attachment to your home so strong as to desire to return, I trust you could do so, as I would by no means have you do anything to weaken the goodly feeling between you and your friend, Mr. Riddick, for whom we have all learned to feel the utmost degree of grateful respect, and I cannot for a moment think that he would seriously disagree with my conclusions or advice. At all events, I am willing he should know them, or see or hear any portions of this letter which might be desired. I deal perfectly fairly and honestly with all, and I have written or said nothing that I am or shall be unwilling to have read by either side. I am a plain Northern Union woman, honest in my feelings and counsels, desiring only the good of all, disguising nothing, covering nothing, and so far my opinions are entitled to respect, and will, I trust, be received with confidence. If you will do this as I suggest and come at once to me at Washington, you need have no fears of remaining idle. This Sam will tell you of when you see him, better than for me to write so much. Washington had never so many people and so much business as now. Some of it would be for you at once.

You must not for a moment suppose that you would be offered any position which would interfere with any oath you may have given, for all know that you must have done something of this nature to have remained in that country through such times, unharmed, and all know you too well to approach you with any such request, as that you shall forfeit your word. Now, what more can I say, only to repeat my advice, and desire you to consult Mr. Riddick in relation to the matter (if you think best) and leave the result with you, and you with the good God, whom I daily desire and implore to sustain, guide, keep, and protect you in the midst of all your trials and isolation.

I sent a short letter to you some weeks ago, which I rather suppose must have reached you, in which I told you of the failing condition of our dear old father. He is still failing and rapidly; he cannot remain with us many days, I think (this calls me home); his appetite has entirely failed; he eats nothing and can scarcely bear his weight, growing weaker every hour. He has talked a *hundred volumes* about you; wishes he could see you, knows he cannot, but hopes you will come away with Sam until the trials are ended which distress our beloved country. Samuel will tell you more than I can write.

Hoping to see you soon I remain
Ever your affectionate sister

Clara

It was beside her father's death-bed that Clara Barton consecrated herself to work at the battle-front. She talked the whole problem over with him. She told him what she had seen in the hospitals at Washington, and that was none too encouraging. But the thing that distressed her most of all was the shocking loss of life and increase of suffering due to the transportation of soldiers from the battle-field to the base hospitals in Washington. She saw more of this later, but she had seen enough of it already to be appalled by the conditions that existed. After Fredericksburg she wrote about it in these terms:

I went to the 1st Division, 9th Corps Hospital; found eight officers of the 57th lying on the floor with a blanket under them, none over; had had some crackers once that day. About two hundred left of the regiment. Went to the Old National Hotel, found some hundreds (perhaps four hundred) Western men sadly wounded, all on the floors; had nothing to eat. I carried a basket of crackers, and gave two apiece as far as they went and some pails of coffee; they had had no food that day and there was none for them. I saw them again at ten o'clock at night; they had had nothing to eat; a great number of them were to undergo amputation sometime, but no surgeons yet; they had not dippers for one in ten. I saw no straw in any hospital, and no mattresses, and the men lay so thick that gangrene was setting in, and in nearly every hospital there has been set apart an erysipelas ward.

There is not room in the city to receive the wounded, and those that arrived yesterday mostly were left lying in the wagons all night at the mercy of the drivers. It rained very hard, many died in the wagons, and their companions, where they had sufficient strength, had raised up and thrown them out into the street. I saw them lying there early this morning; they had been wounded two and three days previous, had been brought from the front, and after all this lay still another night without care, or food, or shelter, many doubtless famished after arriving in Fredericksburg. The city is full of houses, and this morning broad parlors were thrown open and displayed to the view of the rebel occupants the bodies of the dead Union soldiers lying beside the wagons in which they perished. Only those most slightly wounded have been taken on to Washington; the roads are fearful and it is worth the life of a wounded man to move him over them. A common ambulance is scarce sufficient to get through. We passed them this morning four miles out of town, full of wounded, with the tongue broken or wheels crushed in the middle of a hill, in mud from one to two feet deep; what was to be done with the moaning, suffering occupants God only knew.

Dr. Hitchcock most strongly and earnestly and indignantly remonstrates against anymore removals of broken or amputated limbs. He declares it little better than murder, and says the greater

122

proportion of them will die if not better fed and afforded more room and better air. The surgeons do all they can, but no provision had been made for such a wholesale slaughter on the part of any one, and I believe it would be impossible to comprehend the magnitude of the necessity without witnessing it.

Clara Barton knew these matters better in 1863 than she did at the beginning of 1862, but she knew something about them when she reached her father's bedside, and he entered intelligently and with sympathy into the recital of her story. He had been a soldier and he understood exactly the conditions which she described. Her old friend Colonel De Witt, formerly a member of Congress from her home district, also appreciated what she had to say. On a day when her father was able to be left, she went with Colonel De Witt to Boston to call on Governor John A. Andrew. She had much to tell him about conditions and life in the hospitals, and also something concerning leaks which she knew to be occurring in Washington and vicinity, and of treasonable organizations operating close to the capital, in constant communication with the enemy. A few days after this call the Washington papers contained an account of the arrest of twenty-five or thirty Secessionists at Alexandria, and the disclosure of just such a "leak" and plot as she had related to Governor Andrew:

Sunday Chronicle, March 2nd, 1862

Important Arrests at Alexandria.—Quite a sensation was produced in Alexandria on last Thursday evening by the arrest of some twenty-five or thirty alleged secessionists, who are charged with being concerned in a secret association for the purpose of giving aid and comfort to the rebels. The conspiracy, it seems, was organized under the pretended forms of a relief association, and comprised all the treasonable objects of affording relief to the enemy. It is further stated that a fund was obtained from rebel sympathizers for the purpose of supporting the families of soldiers in the service of the "Confederate States," on the identical plan of the noble Relief Commission of Philadelphia, established with such different motives. It has also been engaged in the manufacture of rebel uniforms, which were distributed among the subordinate female associations. The purpose of the plotters was also to furnish arms and munitions of war. A considerable quantity has been discovered packed for shipment, consisting of knapsacks and weapons. Letters were found acknowledging the receipt through the agency of the association of rifles and pistols in Richmond. ...

Among the papers secured are many letters implicating persons heretofore unsuspected.

The parties were brought to this city on Friday, and lodged in the old Capital prison. As they passed along the avenue, under the guard of soldiers, they appeared to be quite indifferent as to their fate and the enormity and baseness of the crime with which they are charged. The majority of them presented a very respectable appearance, and were followed to jail by an anxious crowd of men and boys.

Clara Barton asked her father his opinion of the feasibility of her getting to the front. He did not discourage the idea. He knew his daughter and believed her capable of accomplishing what she set out to do. Moreover, he knew the American soldier. He felt sure that Clara would be protected from insult, and that her presence would be welcome to the soldiers.

Having thus been favorably introduced to Governor Andrew, and her story of the secret operations of Secessionists near Washington having been confirmed, she felt that she could write the Governor and ask him for permission to go to the very seat of war. She had been sending supplies to Roanoke, and Newbern, North Carolina, and she wished very much that, as soon as her father should have passed away, she might be permitted to go with her supplies and perform her own work of distribution. From her father's bedside she wrote the following letter to Governor Andrew:

North Oxford, Mar. 20, 1862

To His Excellency John A. Andrew,
Governor of the Commonwealth of Massachusetts.
Governor Andrew will perhaps recollect the writer as the lady who waited upon him in company with Hon. Alexander De Witt, to mention the existence of certain petitions from the officers of the Massachusetts Regiments of Volunteers, relating to the establishment of an agency in the City of Washington.

With the promise of Your Excellency to "look after the leak" came a "lessening of my fears," and the immediate discovery of the truly magnificent rebel organization in Alexandria, and the arrest of twenty-five of the principal actors, including the purchasing committee, brought with it not only entire satisfaction, but a joy I had scarce known in months. Since September I had been fully conscious in my own mind of the existence of something of this kind, and in October attempted to warn our Relief Societies, but, in the absence of all proof, I must perforce say very little. I should never have brought the subject before you again, only that I incidentally learned that our excellent Dr. Hitchcock has taken back from Roanoke other papers relating to the same subject, which will doubtless be laid before you, and, as I have an entirely different boon to crave, I find it necessary to speak.

I desire Your Excellency's permission to go to Roanoke. I should have proffered my request weeks earlier, but I am called home to witness the last hours of my old soldier father, who is wearing out the remnant of an oak and iron constitution, seasoned and tempered in the wild wars of "Mad Anthony." His last tale of the Red Man is told; a few more suns, and the old soldier's weary march is ended, -—honorably discharged, he is journeying home.

With this, my highest duties close, and I would fain be allowed to go and administer comfort to our brave men, who peril life and limb in defense of the priceless boon the fathers so dearly won.

If I know my own heart, I have none but right motives. I ask neither pay nor praises, simply a soldier's fare and the sanction of Your Excellency to go and do with my might, whatever my hands find to do.

In General Burnside's noble command are upwards of forty young men who in former days were my pupils. I am glad to know that somewhere they have learned their duty to their country, and have come up neither cowards nor traitors. I think I am safe in saying that I possess the entire confidence and respect of every one of them. For the officers, their signatures are before you.

If my request appear unreasonable, and must be denied, I shall submit, patiently, though sorrowfully, but trusting, hoping better things. I beg to submit myself

With the highest respect,
Yours truly

Clara H. Barton

John A. Andrew was one of the great war governors. Massachusetts is one of the States that can always be proud of the record of its chief executive during the dark days of the Civil War. He responded promptly to Clara Barton's appeal. On the day of her father's funeral she received the following letter from Governor Andrew:

Commonwealth of Massachusetts Executive Department Boston,
March 24th, 1862

Miss Clara H. Barton,
North Oxford, Mass.

I beg to assure you, Miss Barton, of my cordial sympathy with your most worthy sentiments and wishes; and that if I have any power to promote your design in aid of our soldiers I will surely use it. Whenever you may be ready to visit General Burnside's division I will cheerfully give you a letter of introduction, with my hearty approval of your visit and my testimony to the value of the service to our sick and wounded it will be in your power to render.

With high respect I am,
Your ob. servant

John A. Andrew

This letter seemed a practical assurance that Clara Barton was to be permitted to go to the front. She had the Governor's virtual promise, conditioned, of course, upon recommendations from proper authorities, and she thought she had sufficient influence with the surgeon, Dr. Hitchcock, to secure the required recommendation. Through an official friend she took up the matter with Dr. Hitchcock, but in a few days his letter to the Doctor came back to Clara by way of the Governor. Dr. Hitchcock did not believe that the battle-field was a suitable place for women. Among Clara Barton's papers the letter to Dr. Hitchcock is found bearing his comment and the Governor's brief reference with which the letter was forwarded to Clara Barton. This closed, for the time being, her prospect of getting to the front:

Boston, March 22, 1862

Dr. Hitchcock,
Dear Sir:

A friend of mine, Miss Clara H. Barton, is very desirous of doing what she can to aid our sick and wounded men at Roanoke, or Newbern, and I to-day presented a letter from her to Governor Andrew asking that she might be sent there by the State. Governor Andrew said he would confer with you relative to the matter. I presume Miss Barton will write to you. She has been a resident of Washington and the petitions you brought for me to present to the Governor were for her appointment as an agent at Washington. She now desires to go to the Burnside expedition.

I need not say that she would render efficient service to our sick and wounded and would not be an encumbrance to the service.

Truly yours

J. W. Fletcher

This letter bears written on its back these endorsements by Dr. Alfred Hitchcock and Governor Andrew:

I do not think at the present time Miss Barton had better undertake to go to Burnside's Division to act as a nurse.

Alfred Hitchcock
March 25th, 1862.

Respectfully referred for the information of Miss Barton.

J. A. Andrew

March 25, 62.

Old Captain Stephen Barton died at last, aged almost eighty-eight. The entries in Clara Barton's diary on these days are brief and interesting:

Thursday, March 20, 1862. Wrote Governor Andrew, and watched by poor, suffering Grandpa. Sent a letter to Irving by the morning mail.

Friday, March 21, 1862. At 10.16 at night, my poor father breathed his last. By him were Misses Grover, Hollendrake, Mrs. Vial, David, Julia, and I.

Saturday, March 22, 1862. David and Julia went to Worcester. Mrs. Rich here. Sent letters to Irving, Judge, Mary, Dr. Darling.

Sunday, March 23, 1862. Call from Deacon Smith.

Monday, March 24, 1862. Mrs. Rich went to Worcester for me. Left a note for Arba Pierce to make a wreath for poor Grandpa's coffin.

Tuesday, March 25, 1862. At two p.m., commenced the services of the burial, Rev. Mr. Holmes of Charlton officiating. House and grounds crowded. Ceremony solemn and impressive. At evening Cousin Jerry Stone came and brought me a letter from Governor J. A. Andrew.

This was all she found time to write in the diary. Of the letters she wrote to her cousin, Corporal Leander A. Poor, relating to her father's death, one has been recovered:

North Oxford, March 27th, 1862
Thursday Afternoon

My dear Cousin Leander:

Your welcome second letter came to me this noon—-doubtless before this you have learned the answer to your kind inquiry, "How is Grandsire?" But if not, and the sentinel post is mine, I must answer, "All is well." Down under the little pines, beside my mother, he rests quietly, sleeps peacefully, dreams happily. The old soldier's heavy march is ended, for him the last tattoo has sounded, and, resting upon the unfailing arms of truth, hope, and faith, he awaits the "reveille of the eternal morning."

"Grandsire" had been steadily failing since I came home. For more than thirty days he did not taste a morsel of food, and could retain nothing stronger or more nourishing than a little milk and water—for over ten of the last days not that, simply a little cold water, which he dared not swallow. And still he lived and moved himself and talked strongly and sensibly and wisely as you had always heard him. Who ever heard of such constitutional strength?

You will be gratified to know that he arranged all his business to his entire satisfaction some days previous to his death. After being raised up and writing his name, he said to me, "This is the last day I shall ever do any business; my work in this world is done."

He remained until Friday, the 21st [of March], sixteen minutes past ten o'clock at night. He spoke for the last time about five o'clock, but made us understand by signs until the very last, when he straightened himself in bed, closed his mouth firmly, gave one hand to Julia, and the other to me, and left us.

Clara Barton's hopes of going to the front received a severe disappointment when Governor Andrew returned Dr. Hitchcock's communication with the refusal to endorse her application. But she was nothing if not persistent. Almost immediately after her receipt of the Governor's letter, she began again seeking to bring influence to bear on a Massachusetts captain (Denney), whose wife she had come to know. In this she gives more detail of the so-called "leak" in stores, which had been sent more or less recklessly for the benefit of troops, and without the prepaying of express charges. An organization of Confederate sympathizers had been formed to purchase these goods from the express company, and slip them through the lines. In some way she had found this out, and so as to be morally certain of it before the exposure and arrest of the conspirators, she had relied upon advance information that she possessed of this system to commend her to Governor Andrew, and he was, evidently, favorably impressed. But she encountered the red tape of the surgeons who were not willing that she should go to the battle-field.

No immediate results came from her continued efforts to secure permission to go to the front. She still remained in New England through the month of May, but in June returned to Washington and remained there until the 18th of July.

She had already been receiving supplies from her friends in New Jersey as well as from Massachusetts. She now went to Bordentown and from there to New York, Boston, Worcester, and Oxford. This journey was made for the purpose of ensuring a larger and continuous supply of provisions, for she had now obtained what she long had coveted, her permission to go to the front. Authority, when it finally came, was direct from the Surgeon-General's office, and it gave her as large liberty as she could well have asked. The following passes and authorizations were all issued within twenty-four hours. Just how she obtained them, we do not know. In some way her persistence triumphed over all official red tape, and when she secured her passes they were practically unlimited either as to time or destination. The following are from the official records:

Surgeon-General's Office July 11, 1862

129

Miss C. H. Barton has permission to go upon the sick transports in any direction—for the purpose of distributing comforts for the sick and wounded—and nursing them, always subject to the direction of the surgeon in charge.

William A. Hammond
Surgeon-General, U.S.A.

———

Surgeon-General's Office
Washington City, July 11, 1862

Sir:

At the request of the Surgeon-General I have to request that you give every facility to Miss Barton for the transportation of supplies for the comfort of the sick. I refer you to the accompanying letter.

Very respectfully
R. C. Wood, A.S. Gen'l.

Major D. H. Rucker, A.Q.M.
Washington, D.C.

———

Office of Depot Quartermaster
Washington, July 11, 1862

Respectfully referred to General Wadsworth, with the request that permission be given this lady and friend to pass to and from Acquia Creek on Government transports at all times when she may wish to visit the sick and hospitals, etc., with such stores as she may wish to take for the comfort of the sick and wounded.

D. H. Rucker, Quartermaster and Col.

———

H'd Qrs. Mr. Div. of Va.
Washington, D.C., July 11, 1862

The within mentioned lady (Miss Barton) and friend have permission to pass to and from Fredericksburg by Government boat and railroad at all times to visit sick and wounded and to take with her all such stores as she may wish to take for the sick, and to pass anywhere within the lines of the United States forces (excepting to the Army of the Potomac), and to travel on any military railroad or

Government boat to such points as she may desire to visit and take such stores as she may wish by such means of transportation.

By order of Brig.-Gen'l Wadsworth, Mil. Gov. D.C.
T. E. Ellsworth, Capt. and A.D.C.

———

Inspector-General's Office, Army of Virginia
Washington, D.C., August 12, 1862

No. 83

To Whom it may Concern:

Know ye, that the bearers, Miss Barton and two friends, have permission to pass within the lines of this army for the purpose of supplying the sick and wounded. Transportation will be furnished by Government boat and rail.

By command of Major-General Pope
R. Jones, Asst. Inspector-General

It is said that when Clara Barton finally succeeded in getting permission to go to the front, she broke down and burst into tears. That is possible, but her diary shows no sign of her emotion. Nor is it true, as has been affirmed, that, as soon as she received her passes, she rushed immediately to the front. Her self-possession and deliberate action at this moment of triumph are thoroughly characteristic of her. Instead of going to the front, she went to New Jersey and New England, as has already been intimated. She had no intention of going to the front until she had assurance of supplies which she could take with her and could continue to receive. She was no love-lorn, sentimental maiden, going with unreckoning and hysterical ardor into conditions which she did not understand. She was forty years old, and she knew what hospitals were. She also knew a good deal about official red tape and the reasonable unwillingness of surgeons to have anyone around the hospital unless she could earn her keep. With a pocket full of passes which she now possessed, she could go almost anywhere. To be sure, it was necessary to get special passes for particular objects, but in general all she had to do was to present these blanket credentials, and particular permission for a specific journey was promptly forthcoming. Indeed, she seldom needed that when her lines of operation were definitely established, but at the beginning she took no chances. Among the other friends whom she gained while she was procuring these certificates was Assistant Quartermaster-General D. H. Rucker. He proved an unfailing friend. Never thereafter did she go to him in vain with any request for transportation for herself or her goods.

Her first notable expedition in supplies started from Washington on Sunday, August 3, 1862, just as the people were going to church. Frequent mention has been made of the fact that this occurred on Sunday, and some incorrect inferences have been drawn from it. Clara Barton had two large a conception of the sacredness of her task to have waited until Monday for a thing that needed to be done on Sunday. On the other hand, she had too much religion of her own, and too much regard for other people's religion, to have chosen deliberately the day and hour when people were going to church as that on which she would mount a loaded truck and conspicuously take her journey to the boat. She began her arrangements to go to Fredericksburg on Wednesday, July 30th, as her diary shows. But it was Friday afternoon before her arrangements were complete, including the special passes which she had to procure from General Polk's headquarters. Saturday she started, but the boat was withdrawn, and it was due to this delay that she rode on top of her load on Sunday morning. She was taking no chances concerning her load of provisions; she knew that her welcome at the front and her efficiency there depended upon her getting her supplies there as well as herself. So she climbed over the wheel and sat beside the mule-driver as he carted her provisions to the dock. The boat conveyed her to Acquia Creek where she stayed all night, being courteously treated by the quartermaster. On Monday she went on to Fredericksburg, where she visited the general hospital, located in a woolen factory. There she witnessed her first amputation. The next day she visited the camp of the 21st Massachusetts. She distributed her supplies, and found where more were needed. Returning, she reached Washington at six o'clock Tuesday night. The next few days she had conferences with the Sanitary Commission, and suggested some improvement in the methods of supplying the hospitals.

She found the Sanitary Commission quite ready to cooperate with her, and obtained from them without difficulty some stores for the 8th and 11th Connecticut Regiments. She took time to write the story of her visit to Fredericksburg, and to secure its full value in additional supplies.

This was the way she spent her time for a full month after she secured her passes. She visited the friends who were to supply her with the articles she was to need; she visited the front and personally oversaw the method of distributing supplies; she placed herself in sympathetic relationship with the Sanitary Commission, whose work was next of kin to her own, and she wrote letters that were to bring her a still larger volume of resources for her great work. A more businesslike, methodical, or sensible method of procedure could not be imagined than that which her diary and letters disclose.

How she felt about going to the front at this time is finely set forth in a letter to her cousin, Corporal Leander A. Poor, who was sick in a hospital at Point Lookout, Maryland, and whom she succeeded in getting transferred to a hospital in Washington. She did not expect to be there when he arrived, for she was committed to her plan of getting to the front. Not that she expected to stay continuously; it was her purpose to come and go; to get relief directly where it was needed, and to keep her lines of communication open. This letter shows that she labored under no delusion concerning the difficulties of transportation. She was going in with her eyes open.

Washington, D.C., Aug. 2, 1862
Saturday p.m.

Oh, MY DEAREST COUZ:

Can you believe it! that this afternoon's mail takes an order from the Surgeon-General for you to report in Washington (provided the state of your health will permit)? I have just seen the order written.

You are to report to Dr. Campbell, Medical Director, and he is to assign you to some hospital. Now I want you assigned near me, but am not certain that I can influence it in the least—but I'll try! I can tell you the ropes and you can help pull them when you go to report.

At the Medical Director's, I have an especial friend in the person of Dr. Sheldon, one of the *chargés des affaires* of the Institution. I will acquaint him with the facts before your arrival either by a personal interview or a note, and then, when you go to report to Dr. Campbell, see first, if possible, Dr. Sheldon, and ask him if he can assist you in getting assigned to some hospital near me (7th Street) or in the vicinity of the Post-Office, he knows my residence, having called upon me.

My choice would be the "Armory Square," a new hospital on 7th Street a few rods the other side of the Avenue from me, on the way to the Arsenal, you will recollect, just opposite the Smithsonian Institute, on the east side of 7th. This is designed as a model hospital, but perhaps one difficulty will be that it is intended more exclusively for extreme cases, or desperately wounded who can be conveyed but little distance from the boat. There are in it *now*, however, some very slight cases, some whom I visit every day. The chaplain, E. W. Jackson, is from Maine, near Portland—and I would not be surprised if more Maine men were in charge there, too.

After this I have not much choice in any of the hospitals near me. E Street Church is near, and so many of the churches, and perhaps being less in magnitude they are less strict. I don't even know if you will be allowed to see me before making your report to the Medical Director, and there is one bare possibility that I may be out on a scout when you arrive. Lord knows the condition of our poor wretched soldiers down in the army; all communication cut off to and from, they must be dying from want of care, and I am promised to go to them the first moment access can be had, but this would not discourage you, for I should come home again when the poor fellows were a little comfortable.

I am not certain when you can come, probably not until some Government boat comes up; one went down yesterday, and if I had had your order then, I should have come for you, but to start in one now after this I might miss you, as they only go some once a week or so.

All sorts of rumors in town—that we are whipping the rebels, they are whipping us, Jackson defeated, Pope defeated. But one thing I do suppose to be true, viz., that our army is isolated, cut off from supplies of food, and that we cannot reach them with more until they fight their way out. This is not generally believed or understood, but your cousin both understands and believes it. People talk like children about "*transporting supplies*" as if it were the easiest thing imaginable to transport supplies by wagon thirty miles across a country scouted by guerrilla bands. Our men *must* be on part rations, tired and hungry, fighting like tigers, and dying like dogs. There! Doesn't that sound impatient. I won't speak again.

Of course you will write me instantly and tell me if you are able to come, and when as nearly as possible, etc., etc.

I will enclose $5.00 lest you may need and not have.
Your affectionate Cousin

Clara H. Barton

Washington, D.C.

Thus did Clara Barton at her father's death-bed consecrate herself to a work more difficult than any woman had at that time undertaken for the relief of suffering caused by the war. Other women were equally brave; others, equally tender in their personal ministrations; but Clara Barton knew the difficulties of transportation and the awful agonies and loss of life endured by men through neglect and delay and the distance of the hospital from the battle-field. She was ready to carry relief right behind the battle lines. She had not long to wait for her opportunity.

TO THE FRONT

When the author of this volume was a schoolboy, the advanced readers in the public schools partook largely of a patriotic character, and the rhetorical exercises of Friday afternoons contained recitations and declamations inspired by the great Civil War. The author remembers a Friday when he came upon the platform with his left arm withdrawn from his coat-sleeve and concealed inside the coat, while he recited a poem of which he still remembers certain lines:

> My arm? I lost it at Cedar Mountain;
> Ah, little one, that was a dreadful fight;
> For brave blood flowed like a summer fountain,
> And the cannon roared till the fall of night.
>
> Nay, nay! Your question has done me no harm, dear,
> Though it woke for the moment a thrill of pain;
> For whenever I look at my stump of an arm here,
> I seem to be living that day again.

The poem went on to relate the scenes of the battle, the desperate charge, the wound, the amputation, and now the necessity of earning a livelihood by the peddling of needles, pins, and other inexpensive household necessities. It was a poem with rather large dramatic possibilities, and the author utilized them according to the best of his then ability. Since that Friday afternoon in his early boyhood he has always thought of Cedar Mountain as a battle in which he had something of a share.

If he had really been there and had lost an arm in the manner which the poem described, one of the things he would have been almost certain to remember would have been the presence there of Clara Barton. She afterward told of it in this simple fashion:

When our armies fought on Cedar Mountain, I broke the shackles and went to the field. Five days and nights with three hours' sleep—a narrow escape from capture—and some days of getting the wounded into hospitals at Washington brought Saturday, August 30. And if you chance to feel that the positions I occupied were rough and unseemly for a woman—I can only reply that they were rough and unseemly for men. But under all, lay the life of the Nation. I had inherited the rich blessing of health and strength of constitution— such as are seldom given to woman—and I felt that some return was due from me and that I ought to be there.

The battle of Cedar Mountain, also called Cedar Run and Culpeper, was fought on Saturday, August 9, 1862. Stonewall Jackson, as directed by General Lee, moved to attack Pope before McClellan could reenforce him. The corps attack was under command of General Banks, and the Confederates were successful. The Federal losses were 314 killed, 1465 wounded, and 622 missing. News of the battle reached Washington on Monday. Clara Barton's entry for that day contains no suggestion of the heroic; no appearance of consciousness that she was beginning for herself and her country, and the civilized world, a new epoch in the history of woman's ministration to men wounded on the battle-field:

Monday, August 11, 1862. Battle at Culpeper reached us. Went to Sanitary Commission. Concluded to go to Culpeper. Packed goods.

The next day she went to General Pope's headquarters and got her pass, General Rucker accompanying her. The remainder of the day she spent in completing her arrangements and in conference with Gardiner Tufts, of Massachusetts, an agent sent by the State to look after Massachusetts wounded. That night she went to Alexandria, which was as far as she could get, and the next morning she resumed her journey and arrived at Culpeper at half-past three in the afternoon.

The next days were busy days. It is interesting to find in her diary that she ministered not only to the Union, but also to the Confederate wounded. For several days she had little rest. When she returned to Washington later in the month, she was not permitted to remain. She learned that her cousin, Corporal Poor, had been brought to a hospital in the city, but she was unable to visit him, being called to minister to the wounded who were being brought to Alexandria as the result of the fighting that followed Cedar Mountain. Her hastily written note is not dated, but the time is in the latter part of August, 1862:

My own darling Cousin:

I was almost (all-but) ready to come to you, and then came this bloody fight at Culpeper and the State agent for Massachusetts comes and claims me to go to Alexandria where 600 wounded are to be brought in to-day, and I may have to go on further. I hope to be back yet in time to come to you this week; if not I will write you.

I am distressed that I cannot come to you to-morrow as I had intended.

I hope you are as well as when I last heard. I should have written, but I thought to come so soon.

I must leave now. My wagon waits for me.

God bless you, my poor dear Cousin, and I will see you if the rebels don't catch me.

Good-bye,
Your affec. cousin

Clara

Whether she was able to visit her cousin or not on her return from Alexandria, we do not know. Her diary for the latter part of the year 1862 ceases to be consecutive. It contains not the record of her own comings and goings, but names of wounded soldiers, memoranda of letters to write for men who had died, and other data of this character. Her entry for Saturday, August 30, 1862, is significant. It reads:

Visited Armory Hospital. Took comb to Sergeant Field, of Massachusetts 21st. On my way saw everybody going to wharf. I went.

That was her last record for more than a week. We know what was taking the people to the wharf. We know what sad sights awaited those who made their way to the Potomac. We know the sad procession that came over the long bridge; the second battle of Bull Run had been fought. After the first battle of Bull Run there was nothing she could do but stay in Washington and write her father such distracting news that she had to stop. The situation was different now; Clara Barton knew where she was needed, and she had authority to go. No time was wasted now in special passes. She had proved the value of her worth at Cedar Mountain.

That very night she was in a box car on her way to the battle-field.

Shortly after the second battle of Bull Run, Clara Barton wrote the following account to a friend, and later revised it as a part of one of her war lectures. It is, in some respects, the most vivid of all her recitals of experiences on battle-fields:

Our coaches were not elegant or commodious; they had no windows, no seats, no platforms, no steps, a slide door on the side was the only entrance, and this higher than my head. For my manner of attaining my elevated position, I must beg of you to draw on your own imaginations and spare me the labor of reproducing the boxes, barrels, boards, and rails, which, in those days, seemed to help me up and on in the world. We did not criticize the unsightly helpers and were only too thankful that the stiff springs did not quite jostle us out. This description need not be limited to this particular trip or train, but will suffice for all that I have known in army life. This is the kind of conveyance by which your tons of generous gifts have reached the field with the precious freights. These trains, through day and night, sunshine and rain, heat and cold, have thundered over heights, across plains, through ravines, and over hastily built army bridges ninety feet across the rocky stream beneath.

At ten o'clock Sunday (August 31) our train drew up at Fairfax Station. The ground, for acres, was a thinly wooded slope—and among the trees, on the leaves and grass, were laid the wounded who were pouring in by scores of wagonloads, as picked up on the field under the flag of truce. All day they came, and the whole hillside was covered. Bales of hay were broken open and scattered over the ground like littering for cattle, and the sore, famishing men were laid upon it.

And when the night shut in, in the mist and darkness about us, we knew that, standing apart from the world of anxious hearts, throbbing over the whole country, we were a little band of almost empty-handed workers literally by ourselves in the wild woods of Virginia, with three thousand suffering men crowded upon the few acres within our reach.

After gathering up every available implement or convenience for our work, our domestic inventory stood, two water buckets, five tin cups, one camp kettle, one stewpan, two lanterns, four bread knives, three plates, and a two-quart tin dish, and three thousand guests to serve.

You will perceive, by this, that I had not yet learned to equip myself, for I was no Pallas, ready armed, but grew into my work by hard thinking and sad experience. It may serve to relieve your apprehension for the future of my labors if I assure you that I was never caught so again.

You have read of adverse winds. To realize this in its full sense you have only to build a camp-fire and attempt to cook something on it.

There is not a soldier within the sound of my voice but will sustain me in the assertion that, go whichsoever side of it you will, wind will blow the smoke and flame directly in your face. Notwithstanding these difficulties, within fifteen minutes from the time of our arrival we were preparing food and dressing wounds. You wonder what, and how prepared, and how administered without dishes.

You generous thoughtful mothers and wives have not forgotten the tons of preserves and fruits with which you filled our hands. Huge boxes of these stood beside that railway track. Every can, jar, bucket, bowl, cup or tumbler, when emptied, that instant became a vehicle of mercy to convey some preparation of mingled bread and wine or soup or coffee to some helpless, famishing sufferer, who partook of it with the tears rolling down his bronzed cheeks and divided his blessings between the hands that fed him and his God. I never realized until that day how little a human being could be grateful for, and that day's experience also taught me the utter worthlessness of that which could not be made to contribute directly to our necessities. The bit of bread which would rest on the surface of a gold eagle was worth more than the coin itself.

But the most fearful scene was reserved for the night. I have said that the ground was littered with dry hay and that we had only two lanterns, but there were plenty of candles. The wounded were laid so close that it was impossible to move about in the dark. The slightest misstep brought a torrent of groans from some poor mangled fellow in your path.

Consequently here were seen persons of all grades, from the careful man of God who walked with a prayer upon his lips to the careless driver hunting for his lost whip—each wandering about among this hay with an open flaming candle in his hand.

The slightest accident, the mere dropping of a light could have enveloped in flames this whole mass of helpless men.

How we watched and pleaded and cautioned as we worked and wept that night! How we put socks and slippers upon their cold damp feet, wrapped your blankets and quilts about them, and when we had no longer these to give, how we covered them in the hay and left them to their rest!

On Monday (September 1) the enemy's cavalry appeared in the wood opposite and a raid was hourly expected. In the afternoon all the wounded men were sent off and the danger became so imminent that Mrs. Fales thought best to leave, although she only went for stores. I begged to be excused from accompanying her, as the ambulances were up to the fields for more, and I knew I should never leave a wounded man there if I were taken prisoner forty times. At six o'clock it commenced to thunder and lighten and all at once the artillery began to play, joined by the musketry about two miles distant. We sat down in our tent and waited to see them break in, but Reno's forces held them back. The old 21st Massachusetts lay between us and the enemy and they could not pass. God only knows who was lost, I do not, for the next day all fell back. Poor Kearny, Stephen, and Webster were brought in, and in the afternoon Kearny's and Heintzelman's divisions fell back through our camp on their way to Alexandria. We knew this was the last. We put the thousand wounded men we then had into the train. I took one carload of them and Mrs. M. another. The men took to the horses. We steamed off, and two hours later there was no Fairfax Station. We reached Alexandria at ten o'clock at night, and, oh, the repast which met those poor men at the train. The people of the island are the most noble I ever saw or heard of. I stood in my car and fed the men till they could eat no more. Then the people would take us home and feed us, and after that we came home. I had slept one and one half hours since Saturday night and I am well and strong and wait to go again if I have need.

Immediately after the second Bull Run, or Manassas, followed the battle of Chantilly. It was a woeful battle for the Federal cause. The Confederates were completely successful. Pope's army retreated to Washington in almost as great a state of panic as had characterized the army of McDowell in the previous year. Nothing saved Washington from capture but the fact that the Confederate forces had been so reduced by continuous fighting that they were unable to take advantage of their success. But they had captured the Federal wagon trains; had inflicted far greater losses than they had themselves endured, and were in so confident a frame of mind that Lee immediately prepared to cross the Potomac, invade the North, and bring the war, as he hoped, to a speedy end. It was under these conditions that Clara Barton continued her education at the battle-front.

Among many other experiences on the field of Chantilly, Miss Barton recalled these incidents:

The slight, naked chest of a fair-haired lad caught my eye, and dropping down beside him, I bent low to draw the remnant of his torn blouse about him, when with a quick cry he threw his left arm across my neck and, burying his face in the folds of my dress, wept like a child at his mother's knee. I took his head in my hands and held it until his great burst of grief passed away. "And do you know me?" he asked at length; "I am Charley Hamilton who used to carry your satchel home from school!" My faithful pupil, poor Charley. That mangled right arm would never carry a satchel again.

About three o'clock in the morning I observed a surgeon with his little flickering candle in hand approaching me with cautious step far up in the wood. "Lady," he said as he drew near, "will you go with me? Out on the hills is a poor distressed lad, mortally wounded and dying. His piteous cries for his sister have touched all our hearts and none of us can relieve him, but rather seem to distress him by our presence."

142

By this time I was following him back over the bloody track, with great beseeching eyes of anguish on every side looking up into our faces saying so plainly, "Don't step on us."

"He can't last half an hour longer," said the surgeon as we toiled on. "He is already quite cold, shot through the abdomen, a terrible wound." By this time the cries became plainly audible to me.

"Mary, Mary, sister Mary, come—oh, come, I am wounded, Mary! I am shot. I am dying—oh, come to me—I have called you so long and my strength is almost gone—Don't let me die here alone. Oh, Mary, Mary, come!"

Of all the tones of entreaty to which I have listened—and certainly I have had some experience of sorrow—I think these, sounding through that dismal night, the most heart-rending. As we drew near, some twenty persons, attracted by his cries, had gathered around and stood with moistened eyes and helpless hands waiting the change which would relieve them all. And in the midst, stretched upon the ground, lay, scarcely full grown, a young man with a graceful head of hair, tangled and matted, thrown back from a forehead and a face of livid whiteness. His throat was bare. His hands, bloody, clasped his breast, his large, bewildered eyes turning anxiously in every direction. And ever from between his ashen lips pealed that piteous cry of "Mary! Mary! Come."

I approached him unobserved, and, motioning the lights away, I knelt by him alone in the darkness. Shall I confess that I intended if possible to cheat him out of his terrible death agony? But my lips were truer than my heart, and would not speak the word "Brother," I had willed them to do. So I placed my hands upon his neck, kissed his cold forehead, and laid my cheek against his.

The illusion was complete; the act had done the falsehood my lips refused to speak. I can never forget that cry of joy. "Oh, Mary! Mary! You have come? I knew you would come if I called you and I have called you so long. I could not die without you, Mary. Don't cry, Darling, I am not afraid to die now that you have come to me. Oh, bless you. Bless you, Mary." And he ran his cold, blood-wet hands about my neck, passed them over my face, and twined them in my hair, which by this time had freed itself from fastenings and was hanging damp and heavy upon my shoulders. He gathered the loose locks in his stiffened fingers and holding them to his lips continued to whisper through them, "Bless you, bless you, Mary!" And I felt the hot tears of joy trickling from the eyes I had thought stony in death. This encouraged me, and, wrapping his feet closely in blankets and giving him such stimulants as he could take, I seated myself on the ground and lifted him on my lap, and drawing the shawl on my own shoulders also about his I bade him rest.

I listened till his blessings grew fainter, and in ten minutes with them on his lips he fell asleep. So the gray morning found us; my precious charge had grown warm, and was comfortable.

Of course the morning light would reveal his mistake. But he had grown calm and was refreshed and able to endure it, and when finally he woke, he seemed puzzled for a moment, but then he smiled and said: "I knew before I opened my eyes that this couldn't be Mary. I know now that she couldn't get here, but it is almost as good. You've made me so happy. Who is it?"

I said it was simply a lady who, hearing that he was wounded, had come to care for him. He wanted the name, and with childlike simplicity he spelled it letter by letter to know if he were right. "In my pocket," he said, "you will find mother's last letter; please get it and write your name upon it, for I want both names by me when I die."

"Will they take away the wounded?" he asked. "Yes," I replied, "the first train for Washington is nearly ready now." "I must go," he said quickly. "Are you able?" I asked. "I must go if I die on the way. I'll tell you why; I am poor mother's only son, and when she consented that I go to the war, I promised her faithfully that if I were not killed outright, but wounded, I would try every means in my power to be taken home to her dead or alive. If I die on the train, they will not throw me off, and if I were buried in Washington, she can get me. But out here in the Virginia woods in the hands of the enemy, never. I must go!"

I sent for the surgeon in charge of the train and requested that my boy be taken.

"Oh, impossible, madam, he is mortally wounded and will never reach the hospital! We must take those who have a hope of life." "But you must take him." "I cannot"—"Can you, Doctor, guarantee the lives of all you have on that train?" "I wish I could," said he sadly. "They are the worst cases; nearly fifty per cent must die eventually of their wounds and hardships."

"Then give this lad a chance with them. He can only die, and he has given good and sufficient reasons why he must go—and a woman's word for it, Doctor. You take him. Send your men for him." Whether yielding to argument or entreaty, I neither knew nor cared so long as he did yield nobly and kindly. And they gathered up the fragments of the poor, torn boy and laid him carefully on a blanket on the crowded train and with stimulants and food and a kind-hearted attendant, pledged to take him alive or dead to Armory Square Hospital and tell them he was Hugh Johnson, of New York, and to mark his grave.

Although three hours of my time had been devoted to one sufferer among thousands, it must not be inferred that our general work had been suspended or that my assistants had been equally inefficient. They had seen how I was engaged and nobly redoubled their exertions to make amends for my deficiencies.

Probably not a man was laid upon those cars who did not receive some personal attention at their hands, some little kindness, if it were only to help lift him more tenderly.

This finds us shortly after daylight Monday morning. Train after train of cars was rushing on for the wounded, and hundreds of wagons were bringing them in from the field still held by the enemy, where some poor sufferers had lain three days with no visible means of sustenance. If immediately placed upon the trains and not detained, at least twenty-four hours must elapse before they could be in the hospital and properly nourished. They were famishing, weak and sinking from loss of blood, and they could ill afford a further fast of twenty-four hours. I felt confident that,

145

unless nourished at once, all the weaker portion must be past recovery before reaching the hospitals of Washington. If once taken from the wagons and laid with those already cared for, they would be overlooked and perish on the way. Something must be done to meet this fearful emergency. I sought the various officers on the grounds, explained the case to them, and asked permission to feed all the men as they arrived before they should be taken from the wagons. It was well for the poor sufferers of that field that it was controlled by noble-hearted, generous officers, quick to feel and prompt to act.

They at once saw the propriety of my request and gave orders that all wagons should be stayed at a certain point and only moved on when everyone had been seen and fed. This point secured, I commenced my day's work of climbing from the wheel to the brake of every wagon and speaking to and feeding with my own hands each soldier until he expressed himself satisfied.

Still there were bright spots along the darkened lines. Early in the morning the Provost Marshal came to ask me if I could use fifty men. He had that number, who for some slight breach of military discipline were under guard and useless, unless I could use them. I only regretted there were not five hundred. They came—strong, willing men—and these, added to our original force and what we had gained incidentally, made our number something over eighty, and, believe me, eighty men and three women, acting with well-directed purpose, will accomplish a good deal in a day. Our fifty prisoners dug graves and gathered and buried the dead, bore mangled men over the rough ground in their arms, loaded cars, built fires, made soup, and administered it. And I failed to discern that their services were less valuable than those of the other men. I had long suspected, and have been since convinced, that a private soldier may be placed under guard, court-martialed, and even be imprisoned without forfeiting his honor or manliness; that the real dishonor is often upon the gold lace rather than the army blue.

At three o'clock the last train of wounded left. All day we had known that the enemy hung upon the hills and were waiting to break in upon us...

At four o'clock the clouds gathered black and murky, and the low growl of distant thunders was heard while lightning continually illuminated the horizon. The still air grew thick and stifled, and the very branches appeared to droop and bow as if in grief at the memory of the terrible scenes so lately enacted and the gallant lives so nobly yielded up beneath their shelter.

This was the afternoon of Monday. Since Saturday noon I had not thought of tasting food, and we had just drawn around a box for that purpose, when, of a sudden, air and earth and all about us shook with one mingled crash of God's and man's artillery. The lightning played and the thunder rolled incessantly and the cannon roared louder and nearer each minute. Chantilly with all its darkness and horrors had opened in the rear.

The description of this battle I leave to those who saw and moved in it, as it is my purpose to speak only of events in which I was a witness or actor. Although two miles distant, we knew the battle was intended for us, and watched the firing as it neared and receded and waited minute by minute for the rest.

With what desperation our men fought hour after hour in the rain and darkness! How they were overborne and rallied, how they suffered from mistaken orders, and blundered, and lost themselves in the strange mysterious wood. And how, after all, with giant strength and veteran bravery, they checked the foe and held him at bay, is an all-proud record of history.

And the courage of the soldier who braved death in the darkness of Chantilly let no man question.

The rain continued to pour in torrents, and the darkness became impenetrable save from the lightning leaping above our heads and the fitful flash of the guns, as volley after volley rang through the stifled air and lighted up the gnarled trunks and dripping branches among which we ever waited and listened.

In the midst of this, and how guided no man knows, came still another train of wounded men, and a waiting train of cars upon the track received them. This time nearly alone, for my worn-out assistants could work no longer, I continued to administer such food as I had left.

Do you begin to wonder what it could be? Army crackers put into knapsacks and haversacks and beaten to crumbs between stones, and stirred into a mixture of wine, whiskey, and water, and sweetened with coarse brown sugar.

Not very inviting you will think, but I assure you it was always acceptable. But whether it should have been classed as food, or, like the Widow Bedott's cabbage, as a delightful beverage, it would puzzle an epicure to determine. No matter, so it imparted strength and comfort.

The departure of this train cleared the grounds of wounded for the night, and as the line of fire from its plunging engines died out in the darkness, a strange sensation of weakness and weariness fell upon me, almost defying my utmost exertion to move one foot before the other.

A little Sibley tent had been hastily pitched for me in a slight hollow upon the hillside. Your imaginations will not fail to picture its condition. Rivulets of water had rushed through it during the last three hours. Still I attempted to reach it, as its white surface, in the darkness, was a protection from the wheels of wagons and trampling of beasts.

Perhaps I shall never forget the painful effort which the making of those few rods and the gaining of the tent cost me. How many times I fell, from sheer exhaustion, in the darkness and mud of that slippery hillside, I have no knowledge, but at last I grasped the welcome canvas, and a well-established brook, which washed in on the upper side at the opening that served as door, met me on my entrance. My entire floor was covered with water, not an inch of dry, solid ground.

One of my lady assistants had previously taken train for Washington and the other, worn out by faithful labors, was crouched upon the top of some boxes in one corner fast asleep. No such convenience remained for me, and I had no strength to arrange one. I sought the highest side of my tent which I remembered was

148

grass-grown, and, ascertaining that the water was not very deep, I sank down. It was no laughing matter then. But the recollection of my position has since afforded me amusement.

I remember myself sitting on the ground, upheld by my left arm, my head resting on my hand, impelled by an almost uncontrollable desire to lie completely down, and prevented by the certain conviction that if I did, water would flow into my ears.

How long I balanced between my desires and cautions, I have no positive knowledge, but it is very certain that the former carried the point by the position from which I was aroused at twelve o'clock by the rumbling of more wagons of wounded men. I slept two hours, and oh, what strength I had gained! I may never know two other hours of equal worth. I sprang to my feet dripping wet, covered with ridges of dead grass and leaves, wrung the water from my hair and skirts, and went forth again to my work.

When I stood again under the sky, the rain had ceased, the clouds were sullenly retiring, and the lightning, as if deserted by its boisterous companions, had withdrawn to a distant corner and was playing quietly by itself. For the great volleying thunders of heaven and earth had settled down on the fields. Silent? I said so. And it was, save the ceaseless rumbling of the never-ending train of army wagons which brought alike the wounded, the dying, and the dead.

And thus the morning of the third day broke upon us, drenched, weary, hungry, sore-footed, sad-hearted, discouraged, and under orders to retreat.

A little later, the plaintive wail of a single fife, the slow beat of a muffled drum, the steady tramp, tramp, tramp of heavy feet, the gleam of ten thousand bayonets on the hills, and with bowed heads and speechless lips, poor Kearny's leaderless men came marching through

This was the signal for retreat. All day they came, tired, hungry, ragged, defeated, retreating, they knew not wither—they cared not wither.

The enemy's cavalry, skirting the hills, admonished us each moment that we must soon decide to go from them or with them. But our work must be accomplished, and no wounded men once given into our hands must be left. And with the spirit of desperation, we struggled on.

At three o'clock an officer galloped up to me, with "Miss Barton, can you ride?" "Yes, sir," I replied.

"But you have no lady's saddle—could you ride mine?"

"Yes, sir, or without it, if you have blanket and surcingle."

"Then you can risk another hour," he exclaimed, and galloped off.

At four he returned at a break-neck speed, and, leaping from his horse, said, "Now is your time. The enemy is already breaking over the hills; try the train. It will go through, unless they have flanked, and cut the bridge a mile above us. In that case I've a reserve horse for you, and you must take your chances to escape across the country."

In two minutes I was on the train. The last wounded man at the station was also on. The conductor stood with a torch which he applied to a pile of combustible material beside the track. And we rounded the curve which took us from view and we saw the station ablaze, and a troop of cavalry dashing down the hill. The bridge was uncut and midnight found us at Washington.

You have the full record of my sleep—from Friday night till Wednesday morning—two hours. You will not wonder that I slept during the next twenty-four.

On Friday (the following), I repaired to Armory Square Hospital to learn who, of all the hundreds sent, had reached that point.

I traced the chaplain's record, and there upon the last page freshly written stood the name of Hugh Johnson

Turning to Chaplain Jackson, I asked—"Did that man live until to-day?"

"He died during the latter part of last night," he replied. "His friends reached him some two days ago, and they are now taking his body from the ward to be conveyed to the depot."

I looked in the direction his hand indicated, and there, beside a coffin, about to be lifted into a wagon, stood a gentleman, the mother, and Sister Mary!

"Had he his reason?" I asked.

"Oh, perfectly."

"And his mother and sister were with him two days."

"Yes."

There was no need of me. He had given his own messages; I could add nothing to their knowledge of him, and would fain be spared the scene of thanks. Poor Hugh, thy piteous prayers reached and were answered, and with eyes and heart full, I turned away, and never saw Sister Mary.

These were days of darkness—a darkness that might be felt.

The shattered bands of Pope and Banks! Burnside's weary legions! Reenforcements from West Virginia—and all that now remained of the once glorious Army of the Peninsula had gathered for shelter beneath the redoubts and guns that girdled Washington.

How the soldiers remembered these ministrations is shown in letters such as this:

Charles E. Simmons, Secretary, 21st Regt. Mass. Vol.
Charles E. Frye, President
7 Jaques Avenue, Worcester, Mass.
September 13th, 1911

To Clara Barton

The survivors of the Veteran 21st Massachusetts Regiment, assembled in "Odd Fellows Temple in the City of Worcester," wish to put on record the day of your coming to us at Bull Run and Chantilly, when we were in our deepest bereavement and loss; how your presence and deeds brought assurance and comfort; and how you assisted us up the hot and rugged sides of South Mountain by your ministry forty-nine years ago to-day, at and over the "Burnside Bridge" at Antietam, then through Pleasant Valley,

151

to Falmouth, and in course of time were across the Rappahannock and storming the heights of Fredericksburg; were with us, indeed, when we recrossed the river and found shelter in our tents—broken, bruised, and sheared. With us evermore in body and spirit, lo, these fifty years. The prayer of the 21st Regiment is, God bless our old and tried friend. It was also voted that we present to Clara Barton a bouquet of flowers.

Charles E. Simmons, Secretary

HARPER'S FERRY TO ANTIETAM

Clara Barton had now definitely settled the method of her operations. She had demonstrated the practicability of getting to the front early, and had begun to learn what equipment was necessary if she were to perform her work successfully. Washington was still to be her headquarters, her base of supplies, but from Washington as a center she would radiate in any direction where the need was, going by the most direct route and arriving on the scene of conflict as soon as possible after authentic news of the battle. This was in contravention of all established custom, which was for women, if they assisted at all, to remain far in the rear until wounded soldiers were conveyed to them, or until the retreat of the opposing army made it safe for them to come upon the field where the conflict had been. It disheartened her to have to remain in Washington where there was no lack of willing assistance, and wait till it was safe to stir.

Moreover, she did not find her service in the Washington hospitals wholly cheerful. It depressed her to move among the wounded and witness the after effects of the battle, the gangrene, the infection of wounds, and the slow fevers, and to think how much of this might have been avoided if the men could have had relief earlier. An extract from a letter to her sister-in-law, written in the summer of 1862, indicates something of her feeling at this time:

Washington, D.C., June 26th, 1862

My dear Sister Julia:

I cannot make a pleasant letter of this; everything is sad; the very pain which is breathed out in the atmosphere of this city is enough to sadden any human heart. Five thousand suffering men, and room preparing for eight thousand more—poor, fevered, cut-up wretches, it agonizes me to think of it. I go when I can; to-day am having a visit from a little Massachusetts (Lowell) boy, seventeen, his widowed mother's only child, whom I found recovering from fever in Mount Pleasant Hospital. It had left him with rheumatism. He was tender, and, when I asked him "what he wanted," burst in tears and said, "I want to see my mother. She didn't know when I left." I appealed to the chief surgeon and applied for his discharge as a native of Massachusetts. It was promised me, and, when the astonished little fellow heard it, he threw himself across the back of his chair and sobbed so he could scarcely get his breath. He had been ordered to another hospital next day; the order was checked; this was a week ago, and yesterday he came to me discharged, and with forty-three dollars and some new clothes. I send him on to-night to his mother as a Sunday present. She knows nothing of it, only that he is suffering in hospital. I am ungrateful to be heavy-hearted when I have been able to do only that little. His name is William Diggles, nephew of Jonas Diggles, tailor of New Sharon, Maine.

Authentic news of battles reached Washington slowly. At first there was no certainty whether a battle was a battle or only a skirmish. Then, when it became certain that a battle had been fought, the first news was almost always unreliable. It would have been a great advantage if Clara Barton could have known where a battle was to be fought. Manifestly, she could not always know.

The generals in command did not always know. But there were times when official Washington had premonitory information. She sought to establish relationship with sufficiently high authority to enable her to know in advance where such battles were to be fought as were brought on by a Union offensive. On Saturday night, September 13, 1862, she had secret information that a great battle was about to be fought. A small battle had been fought the day before and it had been disastrous. There had been an engagement at Harper's Ferry in which the Union army had 44 killed, 173 wounded, and the amazing number of 12,520 missing or captured. She already suspected, and a little later she knew, that that long list of men missing and captured, was more ominous than an added number killed or wounded:

"Our army was weary," she said, "and lacked not only physical strength, but confidence and spirit. And why should they not? Always defeated! Always on the retreat! I was almost demoralized myself! And I had just commenced."

She "had just commenced"; that was characteristic of her. She had been ministering to the soldiers ever since the day when the first blood was shed on the 19th of April, 1861, and had been at it without rest or stint ever since. But she had just commenced; she had just learned how to do it in the way that was hereafter to characterize her methods.

The defeat at Harper's Ferry threw Washington into a panic. But it moved McClellan to a long-deferred engagement with the Union forces in the offensive.

154

The long maneuvering and skirmishing [she wrote], had yielded no fruit. Pope had been sacrificed and all the blood shed from Yorktown to Malvern Hill seemed to have been utterly in vain. But the minor keys, upon which I played my infinitesimal note in the great anthem of war and victory which rang through the land when these two fearful forces met and closed, with gun-lock kissing gun-lock across the rocky bed of Antietam, are yet known only to a few. Washington was filled with dismay, and all the North was moved as a tempest stirs a forest.

Maryland lay temptingly in view, and Lee and Jack-son with the flower of the rebel army marched for its ripening fields. Who it was that whispered hastily on Saturday night, September 13—"Harper's Ferry, not a moment to be lost"—I have never dared to name.

In thirty minutes I was waiting the always kindly spoken "Come in," of my patron saint, Major, now Quartermaster-General, Rucker.

"Major," I said—"I want to go to Harper's Ferry; can I go?"

"Perhaps so," he replied, with genial but doubtful expression. "Perhaps so; do you want a conveyance?"

"Yes," I said.

"But an army wagon is the only vehicle that will reach there with any burden in safety. I can send you one of these to-morrow morning."

I said, "I will be ready."

But here was to begin a new experience for me. I was to ride eighty miles in an army wagon, and straight into battle and danger at that.

I could take no female companion, no friend, but the stout working-men I had use for.

You, who are accustomed to see a coach and a pair of fine horses with a well-dressed, gentlemanly driver draw up to your door, will scarcely appreciate the sensation with which I watched the approach of the long and high, white-covered, tortoise-motioned vehicle, with its string of little, frisky, long-eared animals, with the broad- shouldered driver astride, and the eternal jerk of the single rein by which he navigated his craft up to my door.

The time, you will remember, was Sunday; the place, 7th Street, just off Pennsylvania Avenue, Washington City.

155

Then and there, my vehicle was loaded, with boxes, bags, and parcels, and, last of all, I found a place for myself and the four men who were to go with me.

I took no Saratoga trunk, but remembered, at the last moment, to tie up a few articles in my handkerchief.

Thus equipped, and seated, my chain of little uneasy animals commenced to straighten itself, and soon brought us into the center of Pennsylvania Avenue, in full gaze of the whole city in its best attire, and on its way to church.

Thus all day we rattled on over the stones and dikes, and up and down the hills of Maryland.

At nightfall we turned into an open field, and, dismounting, built a camp-fire, prepared supper, and retired, I to my work in my wagon, the men wrapped in their blankets, camping about me.

All night an indistinct roar of artillery sounded upon our ears, and waking or sleeping, we were conscious of trouble ahead; but it was well for our rest that no messenger came to tell us how death reveled among our brave troops that night.

Before daybreak, we had breakfasted, and were on our way. You will not infer that, because by ourselves, we were alone upon the road. We were directly in the midst of a train of army wagons, at least ten miles in length, moving in solid column—the Government supplies and ammunition, food, and medicine for an army in battle.

Weary and sick from their late exposures and hardships, the men were falling by the wayside, faint, pale, and often dying.

I busied myself as I rode on hour by hour in cutting loaves of bread in slices and passing them to the pale, haggard wrecks as they sat by the roadside, or staggered on to avoid capture, and at each little village we entered, I purchased all the bread its inhabitants would sell.

Horses as well as men had suffered and their dead bodies strewed the wayside.

My poor words can never describe to you the consternation and horror with which we descended from our wagon, and trod, there in the mountain pass, that field of death.

There, where we now walked with peaceful feet, twelve hours before the ground had rocked with carnage. There in the darkness God's angels of wrath and death had swept and, foe facing foe, the souls of men went out. And there, side by side, stark and cold in death mingled the Northern Blue and the Southern Gray.

To such of you as have stood in the midst or followed in the track of armies and witnessed the strange and dreadful confusion of recent battle-grounds, I need not describe this field. And to you who have not, no description would ever avail.

The giant rocks, hanging above our heads, seemed to frown upon the scene, and the sighing trees which hung lovingly upon their rugged edge drooped low and wept their pitying dews upon the livid brows and ghastly wounds beneath.

Climbing hills and clambering over ledges we sought in vain for some poor wretch in whom life had still left the power to suffer. Not one remained, and, grateful for this, but shocked and sick of heart, we returned to our waiting conveyance.

So far as Harper's Ferry was concerned, her advance information appeared to have come too late to be of any value. The number of wounded was not large, and these had all been taken to Frederick, Maryland. Only the day before, Stonewall Jackson and his men had passed through, and Barbara Frietchie had refused to haul down her flag. There had not been many wounded, anyway; the Federal army simply had failed to fight at Harper's Ferry. The word "morale" was not then in common use, but that was what the Union army had lost. On Monday, September 15, 1862, was fought the battle of South Mountain, Maryland. There Hooker and Franklin and Reno were defeated with a loss of 325 men killed, 1403 wounded, and 85 prisoners. There were few prisoners as compared with Harper's Ferry, but that was partly because the mountainous country gave the defeated Union soldiers a better chance to escape. The defeat was beyond question, and General Reno was killed. While Clara Barton was driving from Harper's Ferry where she had expected to find a battle, she came suddenly upon a battle-field, that of South Mountain. There she did her ministering work. But Harper's Ferry and South Mountain were both preliminary to the real battle of which she had had her Washington warning. And now she made a discovery. If she was ever to get to the front in time to be of the greatest possible service, she must short-circuit the ordinary military method which would have put her and her equipment among the baggage-wagons. For her the motto from this time on was, "Follow the cannon." This gave her something approaching an open road, and afforded her the opportunity which she was just learning how to utilize with greatest efficiency.

The increase of stragglers along the road [Barton recalled] was alarming, showing that our army was weary, and lacked not only physical strength, but confidence and spirit.

And why should they not? Always defeated! Always on the retreat! I was almost demoralized myself! And I had just commenced.

I have already spoken of the great length of the army train, and that we could no more change our position than one of the planets. Unless we should wait and fall in the rear, we could not advance a single wagon.

And for the benefit of those who may not understand, I may say that the order of the train was, first, ammunition; next, food and clothing for well troops; and finally, the hospital supplies. Thus, in case of the battle the needed stores for the army, according to the slow, cautious movement of such bodies, must be from two to three days in coming up.

Meanwhile, as usual, our men must languish and die. Something must be done to gain time. And I resorted to strategy. We found an early resting-place, supped by our camp-fire, and slept again among the dews and damps.

At one o'clock, when everything was still, we arose, breakfasted, harnessed, and moved on past the whole train, which like ourselves had camped for the night. At daylight we had gained ten miles and were up with the artillery and in advance even of the ammunition.

All that weary, dusty day I followed the cannon, and nightfall brought us up with the great Army of the Potomac, 80,000 men resting upon their arms in the face of a foe equal in number, sullen, straitened, and desperate.

Closely following the guns we drew up where they did, among the smoke of the thousand camp-fires, men hastening to and fro, and the atmosphere loaded with noxious vapors, till it seemed the very breath of pestilence. We were upon the left wing of the army, and this was the last evening's rest of Burnside's men. To how many hundred it proved the last rest upon the earth, the next day's record shows.

In all this vast assemblage I saw no other trace of womankind. I was faint, but could not eat; weary, but could not sleep; depressed, but could not weep.

So I climbed into my wagon, tied down the cover, dropped down in the little nook I had occupied so long, and prayed God with all the earnestness of my soul to stay the morrow's strife or send us victory. And for my poor self, that He impart somewhat of wisdom and strength to my heart, nerve to my arm, speed to my feet, and fill my hands for the terrible duties of the coming day. Heavy and sad I awaited its approach.

The battle of Antietam occurred on September 16 and 17, 1862. It was the first battle in the East that roused to any considerable degree the forlorn hope of the friends of the Union. It was the first real Eastern victory for the Union army. It was not as decided a victory as it ought to have been, but it was a victory. It put heart into Abraham Lincoln and certified to his conscience that the time had come to redeem the promise he had made to God—that if He would give victory to the Union arms Lincoln would free the slaves. McClellan did not follow up his advantage as he should have done and make that victory triumphant. But he did something other than delay and retreat, and he put some heart into the Union army when it discovered that it need not forever be on the defensive, nor always suffer defeat. In this great, and, in spite of its limitations, victorious, battle, Clara Barton was on the ground before the first gun was fired, and she did not leave the field until the last wounded man had been cared for. At the outset she watched the battle, but almost immediately she laid down her field-glasses, went to the place where the wounded were being brought in, and was able to perform her work of ministration without a single hour's delay,

She told her story of the conflict as she saw it:

The battle commenced on the right and already with the aid of field-glasses we saw our own forces, led by "Fighting Joe" [Hooker], overborne and falling back.

Burnside commenced to send cavalry and artillery to his aid, and, thinking our place might be there, we followed them around eight miles, turning into a cornfield near a house and barn, and stopping in the rear of the last gun, which completed the terrible line of

159

artillery which ranged diagonally in the rear of Hooker's army. That day a garden wall only separated us. The infantry were already driven back two miles, and stood under cover of the guns. The fighting had been fearful. We had met wounded men, walking or borne to the rear for the last two miles. But around the old barn there lay, too badly wounded to admit of removal, some three hundred thus early in the day, for it was scarce ten o'clock.

We loosened our mules and commenced our work. The corn was so high as to conceal the house, which stood some distance to the right, but, judging that a path which I observed must lead to it, and also that surgeons must be operating there, I took my arms full of stimulants and bandages and followed the opening.

Arriving at a little wicker gate, I found the dooryard of a small house, and myself face to face with one of the kindest and noblest surgeons I have ever met, Dr. Dunn, of Conneautville, Pennsylvania.

Speechless both, for an instant, he at length threw up his hands with "God has indeed remembered us! How did you get from Virginia here so soon? And again to supply our necessities! And they are terrible. We have nothing but our instruments and the little chloroform we brought in our pockets. We have torn up the last sheets we could find in this house. We have not a bandage, rag, lint, or string, and all these shell-wounded men bleeding to death."

Upon the porch stood four tables, with an etherized patient upon each, a surgeon standing over him with his box of instruments, and a bunch of green com leaves beside him.

With what joy I laid my precious burden down among them, and thought that never before had linen looked so white, or wine so red. Oh! be grateful, ladies, that God put it in your hearts to perform the work you did in those days. How doubly sanctified was the sacred old household linen woven by the hands of the sainted mother long gone to her reward. For you arose the tender blessings of those grateful men, which linger in my memory as faithfully to-night as do the bugle notes which called them to their doom.

Thrice that day was the ground in front of us contested, lost, and won, and twice our men were driven back under cover of that fearful range of guns, and each time brought its hundreds of wounded to our crowded ground.

A little after noon, the enemy made a desperate attempt to regain what had been lost; Hooker, Sedgwick, Dana, Richardson, Hartsuff, and Mansfield had been borne wounded from the field and the command of the right wing devolved upon General Howard.

The smoke became so dense as to obscure our sight, and the hot, sulphurous breath of battle dried our tongues and parched our lips to bleeding.

We were in a slight hollow, and all shell which did not break over our guns in front came directly among or over us, bursting above our heads or burying themselves in the hills beyond.

A man lying upon the ground asked for a drink; I stopped to give it, and, having raised him with my right hand, was holding him.

Just at this moment a bullet sped its free and easy way between us, tearing a hole in my sleeve and found its way into his body. He fell back dead. There was no more to be done for him and I left him to his rest. I have never mended that hole in my sleeve. I wonder if a soldier ever does mend a bullet hole in his coat?

The patient endurance of these men was most astonishing. As many as could be were carried into the barn, as a slight protection against random shot. Just outside the door lay a man wounded in the face, the ball having entered the lower maxillary on the left side and lodged among the bones of the right cheek. His imploring look drew me to him, when, placing his finger upon the sharp protuberance, he said, "Lady, will you tell me what this is that burns so?" I replied that it must be the ball which had been too far spent to cut its way entirely through.

"It is terribly painful," he said. "Won't you take it out?"

I said I would go to the tables for a surgeon. "No! No!" he said, catching my dress. "They cannot come to me. I must wait my turn, for this is a little wound. You can get the ball. There is a knife in your pocket. Please take the ball out for me."

This was a new call. I had never severed the nerves and fibers of human flesh, and I said I could not hurt him so much. He looked up, with as nearly a smile as such a mangled face could assume, saying, "You cannot hurt me, dear lady, I can endure any pain that your hands can create. Please do it. It will relieve me so much."

I could not withstand his entreaty and, opening the best blade of my pocket-knife, prepared for the operation. Just at his head lay a stalwart orderly sergeant from Illinois, with a face beaming with intelligence and kindness, and who had a bullet directly through the fleshy part of both thighs. He had been watching the scene with great interest and, when he saw me commence to raise the poor fellow's head, and no one to support it, with a desperate effort he succeeded in raising himself to a sitting posture, exclaiming as he did so, "I will help do that." Shoving himself along the ground he took the wounded head in his hands and held it while I extracted the ball and washed and bandaged the face.

I do not think a surgeon would have pronounced it a scientific operation, but that it was successful I dared to hope from the gratitude of the patient.

I assisted the sergeant to lie down again, brave and cheerful as he had risen, and passed on to others.

Returning in half an hour, I found him weeping, the great tears rolling diligently down his manly cheeks. I thought his effort had been too great for his strength and expressed my fears. "Oh! No! No! Madam," he replied. "It is not for myself. I am very well, but," pointing to another just brought in, he said, "this is my comrade, and he tells me that our regiment is all cut to pieces, that my captain was the last officer left, and he is dead."

Oh, God! what a costly war! This man could laugh at pain, face death without a tremor, and yet weep like a child over the loss of his comrades and his captain.

At two o'clock my men came to tell me that the last loaf of bread had been cut and the last cracker pounded. We had three boxes of wine still unopened. What should they do?

"Open the wine and give that," I said, "and God help us."

The next instant an ejaculation from Sergeant Field, who had opened the first box, drew my attention, and, to my astonished gaze, the wine had been packed in nicely sifted Indian meal.

If it had been gold dust it would have seemed poor in comparison. I had no words. No one spoke. In silence the men wiped their eyes and resumed their work.

Of twelve boxes of wine which we carried, the first nine, when opened, were found packed in sawdust, the last three, when all else was gone, in Indian meal.

A woman would not hesitate long under circumstances like these.

This was an old farmhouse. Six large kettles were picked up and set over fires, almost as quickly as I can tell it, and I was mixing water and meal for gruel.

It occurred to us to explore the cellar. The chimney rested on an arch, and, forcing the door, we discovered three barrels and a bag. "They are full," said the sergeant, and, rolling one into the light, found that it bore the mark of Jackson's army. These three barrels of flour and a bag of salt had been stored there by the rebel army during its upward march.

I shall never experience such a sensation of wealth and competency again, from utter poverty to such riches.

All that night my thirty men (for my corps of workers had increased to that number during the day) carried buckets of hot gruel for miles down the line to the wounded and dying where they fell.

This time, profiting by experience, we had lanterns to hang in and around the barn, and, having directed it to be done, I went to the house and found the surgeon in charge, sitting alone, beside a table, upon which he rested his elbow, apparently meditating upon a bit of tallow candle which flickered in the center.

Approaching carefully, I said, "You are tired, Doctor." He started up with a look almost savage, "Tired! Yes, I am tired, tired of such heartlessness, such carelessness!" Turning full upon me, he continued: "Think of the condition of things. Here are at least one thousand wounded men, terribly wounded, five hundred of whom cannot live till daylight, without attention. That two inches of candle is all I have or can get. What can I do? How can I endure it?"

I took him by the arm, and, leading him to the door, pointed in the direction of the barn where the lanterns glistened like stars among the waving com.

"What is that?" he exclaimed.

"The barn is lighted," I said, "and the house will be directly."

"Who did it?"

"I, Doctor."

"Where did you get them?"

"Brought them with me."

"How many have you?"

"All you want—four boxes."

He looked at me a moment, as if waking from a dream, turned away without a word, and never alluded to the circumstances, but the deference which he paid me was almost painful.

During a lecture in the West, Miss Barton related this incident, and as she closed a gentleman sprang upon the stage, and, addressing the audience, exclaimed: "Ladies and gentlemen, if I never have acknowledged that favor, I will do it now. I am that surgeon."

Darkness [Barton continues] brought silence and peace, and respite and rest to our gallant men. As they had risen, regiment by regiment, from their grassy beds in the morning, so at night the fainting remnant again sank down on the trampled blood-stained earth, the weary to sleep, and the wounded to die.

Through the long starlit night we wrought and hoped and prayed. But it was only when in the hush of the following day, as we glanced

164

over that vast Aceldama, that we learned at what a fearful cost the gallant Union army had won the battle of Antietam.

Antietam! With its eight miles of camping armies, face to face; 160,000 men to spring up at dawn like the old Scot from the heather! Its miles of artillery shaking the earth like a chain of Ætnas! Its ten hours of uninterrupted battle! Its thunder and its fire! The sharp, unflinching order—"Hold the Bridge, boys—always the Bridge." At length, the quiet! The pale moonlight on its cooling guns! The weary men, the dying and the dead! The flag of truce that buried our enemies slain, and Antietam was fought, and won, and the foe turned back!

Clara Barton remained on the battle-field of Antietam until her supplies were exhausted and she was completely worn out. Not only fatigue but fever came upon her, and she was carried back to Washington apparently sick. But the call of duty gave her fresh strength, and she was soon wondering where the next battle was to be and planning to be on the field. Almost the only entry in her diary in the autumn of 1862, aside from memoranda of wounded men and similar entries relating to people other than herself, is one of October 23, which she began in some detail, but broke off abruptly. She records that she "left Washington for Harper's Ferry expecting to meet a battle there. Have taken four teams of Colonel Rucker loaded at his office, traveled and camped as usual, reaching Harper's Ferry the third day. At the first end of the pontoon bridge one of Peter's mules ran off and we delayed the progress of the army for twenty minutes to be extricated."

The rest of the entry contains the names of her drivers, details of the overturned wagon, and other memoranda. Two things are of interest in this fragmentary record. One is the definiteness of the method which she now had adopted of going where she "expected to meet a battle." The other is the fact that a delay of twenty minutes, caused by an accident to one of her wagons on the pontoon bridge, illustrates a reason why, in general, armies cannot permit even so necessary things as supplies for the wounded to get in the way of the free movement of troops. However, this delay was quite exceptional. She did not usually cause any inconvenience of this sort, nor did it in this instance result in any serious harm. On this occasion she was provided with an ambulance for her own use. That thoughtful provision for her convenience and means of conserving her energy, was provided for her by Quartermaster-General Rucker.

On this journey the question was decided who was really in command of her part of the expedition. In one of her lectures she described her associates on this and subsequent expeditions:

There may be those present who are curious to know how eight or ten rough, stout men, who knew nothing of me, received the fact that they were to drive their teams under the charge of a lady.

This question has been so often asked in private that I deem it proper to answer it publicly.

Well, the various expressions of their faces afforded a study. They were not soldiers, but civilians in Government employ. Drovers, butchers, hucksters, mule-breakers, probably not one of them had ever passed an hour in what could be termed "ladies' society," in his life. But every man had driven through the whole peninsular campaign. Every one of them had taken his team unharmed out of that retreat, and had sworn an oath never to drive another step in Virginia.

They were brave and skillful, understood their business to perfection, but had no art. They said and looked what they thought; and I understood them at a glance.

These teamsters proposed to go into camp at four o'clock in the afternoon, and start when they got ready in the morning, but she first established her authority over them, and then cooked them a hot supper, the first and last she ever cooked for army teamsters, and they came to her later in the evening, apologized for their obstinacy, and were ready to drive her anywhere.

"We come to tell you we are ashamed of ourselves" [their leader said].

I thought honest confession good for the soul, and did not interrupt him.

"The truth is," he continued, "in the first place we didn't want to come. There's fighting ahead and we've seen enough of that for men who don't carry muskets, only whips; and then we never seen a train under charge of a woman before and we couldn't understand it, and we didn't like it, and we thought we'd break it up, and we've been mean and contrary all day, and said a good many hard things and you've treated us like gentlemen. We hadn't no right to expect that supper from you, a better meal than we've had in two years. And you've been as polite to us as if we'd been the General and his staff, and it makes us ashamed. And we've come to ask your forgiveness. We shan't trouble you no more."

My forgiveness was easily obtained. I reminded them that as men it was their duty to go where the country had need of them. As for my being a woman, they would get accustomed to that. And I assured them that, as long as I had any food, I would share it with them. That, when they were hungry and supperless, I should be; that if harm befell them, I should care for them; if sick, I should nurse them; and that, under all circumstances, I should treat them like gentlemen.

They listened silently, and, when I saw the rough, woolen coat-sleeves drawing across their faces, it was one of the best moments of my life.

Bidding me "good-night" they withdrew, excepting the leader, who went to my ambulance, hung a lighted lantern in the top, arranged the few quilts inside for my bed, assisted me up the steps, buckled the canvas down snugly outside, covered the fire safely for morning, wrapped his blanket around him, and lay down a few feet from me on the ground.

At daylight I became conscious of low voices and stifled sounds, and soon discovered that these men were endeavoring to speak low and feed and harness their teams quietly, not to disturb me.

On the other side I heard the crackling of blazing chestnut rails and the rattling of dishes, and George came with a bucket of fresh water, to undo my buckle door latches, and announce that breakfast was nearly ready.

I had cooked my last meal for my drivers. These men remained with me six months through frost and snow and march and camp and battle; and nursed the sick, dressed the wounded, soothed the dying, and buried the dead; and if possible grew kinder and gentler every day.

There was one serious difficulty about following advance information and attempting to be on the battlefield when the battle occurred. The battle does not always occur at the time and place expected. The battle at Harper's Ferry in October, 1862, did not take place as planned. General Lee "may have received the same advance information which was conveyed to Clara Barton. At all events, he was not among those present when the battle was scheduled to take place. He withdrew his army and waited until he was ready to fight. McClellan decided to follow Lee, and Clara Barton moved with the army. As she moved, she cared for the sick, supplying them from her own stores, returning to Washington with a body of sick men about the first of December. She was suffering from a felon on her hand from the first of November until near the end of that month. Her hand was lanced in the open field, and she suffered from the cold, but did not complain.

She did not remain long in Washington, but returned by way of Acquia Creek and met the army at Falmouth. From Falmouth she wrote a letter to some of the women who had been assisting her, and sent it by the hand of the Reverend C. M. Wells, one of her reliable associates. It contains references to her sore finger and to the nature of accommodations:

Camp near Falmouth, Va.
Headquarters General Sturgis, 2nd Division
December 8th, 1862

Messrs. Brown & Co.

Dear Friends:

Mr. Wells returns to-morrow and I improve the opportunity to send a line by him to you, not feeling quite certain if posted matter reaches directly when sent from the army.

We reached Acquia Creek safely in the time anticipated, and to my great joy learned immediately that our old friend Captain (Major) Hall (of the 21st) was Quartermaster. As soon as the boat was unloaded, he came on board and spent the remainder of the evening with me.—We had a home chat, I assure you. Remained till the next day, sent a barrel of apples, etc., up to the Captain's quarters, and proceeded with the remainder of our luggage, for which it is needless to say ready transportation was found, and the Captain chided me for having left anything behind at the depot, as I told him I had done. On reaching Falmouth Station we found another old friend, Captain Bailey, in charge, who instituted himself as watch over the goods until he sent them all up to Headquarters. My ambulance came through that p.m., but for fear it might not, General Sturgis had his taken down for me, and had supper arranged and a splendid serenade. I don't know how we could have had a warmer "welcome home," as the officers termed it.

Headquarters are in the dooryard of a farmhouse, one room of which is occupied by Miss G. and myself. My wagons are a little way from me, out of sight, and I am wishing for a tent and stove to pitch and live near them. The weather is cold, and the ground covered with snow, but I could make me comfortable with a good tent, floor, and stove, and should prefer it to a room in a rebel house and one so generally occupied.

The 21st are a few rods from me; many of the officers call to see me every day. Colonel Clark is very neighborly; he is looking finely now; he was in this p.m., and was going in search of Colonel Morse whom he thought to be a mile or two distant. I learned to-night that the 15th are only some three miles away; the 36th I cannot find yet. I have searched hard for them and shall get on their track soon, I trust.

Of army movements nothing can be said with certainty; no two persons, not even the generals, agree in reference to the future programme. The snow appears to have deranged the plans very seriously. I have received calls from two generals to-day, and in the course of conversation I discovered that their views were entirely different. General Burnside stood a long time in front of my door to-day, but to my astonishment *he did not express his opinion*—strange!

I have not suffered for want of the boots yet, but should find them convenient, I presume, and shall be glad to see them. The sore finger is much the same; not very troublesome, although somewhat so. If you desire to reach this point, I think you would find no difficulty after getting past the guard at Washington—at Acquia you would find all right I am sure.

I can think of a host of things I wish you could take out to me.

In spite of her wish that she might have had a tent, and so have avoided living in a captured house, her residence was the Lacy house on the shore of the Rappahannock and close to Fredericksburg. There was nothing uncertain about her information this time. She knew when the battle was to occur, and at two o'clock in the morning she wrote a letter to her cousin, Vira Stone, just before the storm of battle broke:

Headquarters 2nd Division
Army of the Potomac
Camp near Falmouth, Va.
December 12, 1862, 2 o'clock A.M.

Dear Cousin Vira:

Five minutes' time with you, and God only knows what that five minutes might be worth to the—may be—doomed thousands sleeping around me. It is the night before a "battle." The enemy, Fredericksburg, and its mighty entrenchments lie before us—the river between. At to-morrow's dawn our troops will essay to cross and the guns of the enemy will sweep their frail bridges at every breath. The moon is shining through the soft haze with a brightness almost prophetic; for the last half-hour I have stood alone in the awful stillness of its glimmering light gazing upon the strange, sad scene around me striving to say, "Thy will, O God, be done." The camp-fires blaze with unwonted brightness, the sentry's tread is still but quick, the scores of little shelter tents are dark and still as death; no wonder, for, as I gazed sorrowfully upon them, I thought I could almost hear the slow flap of the grim messenger's wings as one by one he sought and selected his victims for the morning's sacrifice.

Sleep, weary ones, sleep and rest for to-morrow's toil! Oh, sleep and visit in dreams once more the loved ones nestling at home! They may yet live to dream of you, cold, lifeless, and bloody; but this dream, soldier, is thy last; paint it brightly, dream it well. Oh, Northern mothers, wives, and sisters, all unconscious of the peril of the hour, would to Heaven that I could bear for you the concentrated woe which is so soon to follow; would that Christ would teach my soul a prayer that would plead to the Father for grace sufficient for you all! God pity and strengthen you everyone.

Mine are not the only waking hours; the light yet bums brightly in our kind-hearted General's tent, where he pens what may be a last farewell to his wife and children, and thinks sadly of his fated men. Already the roll of the moving artillery is sounding in my ears. The battle draws near and I must catch one hour's sleep for to-day's labor.

Good-night, and Heaven grant you strength for your more peaceful and terrible, but not less weary, days than mine.

Clara

All her apprehensions were less than the truth. It was a terrible battle, and a disheartening disaster. The Union army lost 1284 in killed, 9600 wounded, and 1769 missing. The memories of Fredericksburg remained with her distinct and terrible to the day of her death. She described the battle and the events which followed it in her war lectures:

We found ourselves beside a broad, muddy river, and a little canvas city grew up in a night upon its banks. And there we sat and waited "while the world wondered." Ay, it did more than wonder! It murmured, it grumbled, it cried shame, to sit there and shiver under the canvas. "Cross over the river and occupy those brick houses on the other shore!" The murmurs grew to a clamor!

Our gallant leader heard them and his gentle heart grew sore as he looked upon his army that he loved as it loved him and looked upon those fearful sights beyond. Carelessness or incapacity at the capital had baffled his best-laid plans till time had made his foes a wall of adamant. Still the country murmured. You, friends, have not forgotten how, for these were the dark days of old Fredericksburg, and our little canvas city was Falmouth.

Finally, one soft, hazy winter's day the army prepared for an attack; but there was neither boat nor bridge, and the sluggish tide rolled dark between.

The men of Hooker and Franklin were right and left, but here in the center came the brave men of the silvery-haired Sumner.

Drawn up in line they wait in the beautiful grounds of the stately mansion whose owner, Lacy, had long sought the other side, and stood that day aiming engines of destruction at the home of his youth and the graves of his household.

There on the second portico I stood and watched the engineers as they moved forward to construct a pontoon bridge. It will be remembered that the rebel army occupying the heights of

Fredericksburg previous to the attack was very cautious about revealing the position of its guns.

A few boats were fastened and the men marched quickly on with timbers and planks. For a few rods it proved a success, and scarcely could the impatient troops be restrained from rending the air with shouts of triumph.

On marches the little band with brace and plank, but never to be laid by them. A rain of musket balls has swept their ranks and the brave fellows lie level with the bridge or float down the stream.

No living thing stirs on the opposite bank. No enemy is in sight. Whence comes this rain of death?

Maddened by the fate of their comrades, others seize the work and march onward to their doom. For now, the balls are hurling thick and fast, not only at the bridge, but over and beyond to the limit of their range—crashing through the trees, the windows and doors of the Lacy house. And ever here and there a man drops in the waiting ranks, silently as a snowflake. And his comrades bear him in for help, or back for a grave.

There on the lower bank under a slouched hat stands the man of honest heart and genial face that a soldier could love and honor even through defeat. The ever-trusted, gallant Burnside. Hark—that deep-toned order rising above the heads of his men: "Bring the guns to bear and shell them out."

Then rolled the thunder and the fire. For two long hours the shot and shell hurled through the roofs and leveled the spires of Fredericksburg. Then the little band of engineers resumed its work, but ere ten spaces of the bridge were gained, they fell like grass before the scythe.

For an instant all stand aghast; then ran the murmurs: "The cellars are filled with sharp-shooters and our shell will never reach them."

But once more over the heads of his men rose that deep-toned order: "Man the boats."

Into the boats like tigers then spring the 7th Michigan.

"Row!! Row!! Ply for your lives, boys." And they do. But mark! They fall, some into the boats, some out. Other hands seize the oars and strain and tug with might and main. Oh, how slow the seconds drag! How long we have held our breath.

Almost across—under the bluffs—and out of range! Thank God— they'll land!

Ah, yes; but not all. Mark the windows and doors of those houses above them. See the men swarming from them armed to the teeth and rushing to the river.

They've reached the bluffs above the boats. Down point the muskets. Ah, that rain of shot and shell and flame!

Out of the boats waist-deep in the water; straight through the fire. Up, up the bank the boys in blue! Grimly above, that line of gray!

Down pours the shot. Up, up the blue, till hand to hand like fighting demons they wrestle on the edge.

Can we breathe yet? No! Still they struggle. Ah, yes, they break, they fly, up through the street and out of sight, pursuer and pursued.

It were long to tell of that night crossing and the next terrible day of fire and blood. And when the battle broke o'er field and grove, like a resistless flood daylight exposed Fredericksburg with its fourth-day flag of truce, its dead, starving, and wounded, frozen to the ground. The wounded were brought to me, frozen, for days after, and our commissions and their supplies at Washington with no effective organization or power to go beyond! The many wounded lay, uncared for, on the cold snow.

Although the Lacy house was exposed to fire she was not permitted to remain within the shelter of its walls. While the fight was at its hottest, she crossed the river under fire for a place of greater danger and of greater need:

At ten o'clock of the battle day when the rebel fire was hottest, the shell rolling down every street, and the bridge under the heavy cannonade, a courier dashed over and, rushing up the steps of the

Lacy house, placed in my hand a crumpled, bloody slip of paper, a request from the lion-hearted old surgeon on the opposite shore, establishing his hospitals in the very jaws of death.

The uncouth penciling said: "Come to me. Your place is here."

The faces of the rough men working at my side, which eight weeks ago had flushed with indignation at the very thought of being controlled by a woman, grew ashy white as they guessed the nature of the summons, and the lips which had cursed and pouted in disgust trembled as they begged me to send them, but save myself. I could only permit them to go with me if they chose, and in twenty minutes we were rocking across the swaying bridge, the water hissing with shot on either side.

Over into that city of death, its roofs riddled by shell, its very church a crowded hospital, every street a battle line, every hill a rampart, every rock a fortress, and every stone wall a blazing line of forts!

Oh, what a day's work was that! How those long lines of blue, rank upon rank, charged over the open acres, up to the very mouths of those blazing guns, and how like grain before the sickle they fell and melted away.

An officer stepped to my side to assist me over the debris at the end of the bridge. While our hands were raised in the act of stepping down, a piece of an exploding shell hissed through between us, just below our arms, carrying away a portion of both the skirts of his coat and my dress, rolling along the ground a few rods from us like a harmless pebble into the water.

The next instant a solid shot thundered over our heads, a noble steed bounded in the air, and, with his gallant rider, rolled in the dirt, not thirty feet in the rear! Leaving the kind-hearted officer, I passed on alone to the hospital. In less than a half-hour he was brought to me—dead.

I mention these circumstances not as specimens of my own bravery. Oh, no! I beg you will not place that construction upon them, for I never professed anything beyond ordinary courage, and a thousand times preferred safety to danger.

But I mention them that those of you, who have never seen a battle, may the better realize the perils through which these brave men passed, who for four long years bore their country's bloody banner in the face of death, and stood, a living wall of flesh and blood, between the invading traitor and your peaceful homes.

In the afternoon of Sunday an officer came hurriedly to tell me that in a church across the way lay one of his men shot in the face the day before. His wounds were bleeding slowly and, the blood drying and hardening about his nose and mouth, he was in immediate danger of suffocation.

(Friends, this may seem to you repulsive, but I assure you that many a brave and beautiful soldier has died of this alone.)

Seizing a basin of water and a sponge, I ran to the church, to find the report only too true. Among hundreds of comrades lay my patient. For any human appearance above his head and shoulders, it might as well have been anything but a man.

I knelt by him and commenced with fear and trembling lest some unlucky movement close the last aperture for breath. After some hours' labor, I began to recognize features. They seemed familiar. With what impatience I wrought. Finally my hand wiped away the last obstruction. An eye opened, and there to my gaze was the sexton of my old home church!

I have remarked that every house was a hospital. Passing from one to another during the tumult of Saturday, I waited for a regiment of infantry to sweep on its way to the heights. Being alone, and the only woman visible among that moving sea of men, I naturally attracted the attention of the old veteran, Provost Marshal General Patrick, who, mistaking me for a resident of the city who had remained in her home until the crashing shot had driven her into the street, dashed through the waiting ranks to my side, and, bending down from his saddle, said in his kindliest tones, "You are alone and in great danger, Madam. Do you want protection?"

Amused at his gallant mistake, I humored it by thanking him, as I turned to the ranks, adding that I believed myself the best protected woman in the United States.

The soldiers near me caught my words, and responding with "That's so! That's so!" set up a cheer. This in turn was caught by the next line and so on, line after line, till the whole army joined in the shout, no one knowing what he was cheering at, but never doubting there was a victory somewhere. The gallant old General, taking in the situation, bowed low his bared head, saying, as he galloped away, "I believe you are right, Madam."

It would be difficult for persons in ordinary life to realize the troubles arising from want of space merely for wounded men to occupy when gathered together for surgical treatment and care. You may suggest that "all out-of-doors" ought to be large, and so it would seem, but the fact did not always prove so. Civilized men seek shelter in sickness, and of this there was ever a scarcity.

Twelve hundred men were crowded into the Lacy house, which contained but twelve rooms. They covered every foot of the floors and porticoes, and even lay on the stair landings! A man who could find opportunity to lie between the legs of a table thought himself lucky: he was not likely to be stepped on. In a common cupboard, with four shelves, five men lay, and were fed and attended. Three lived to be removed, and two died of their wounds.

Think of trying to lie still and die quietly, lest you fall out of a bed six feet high!

Among the wounded of the 7th Michigan was one Faulkner, of Ashtabula County, Ohio, a mere lad, shot through the lungs and, to all appearances, dying. When brought in, he could swallow nothing, breathed painfully, and it was with great difficulty that he gave me his name and residence. He could not lie down, but sat leaning against the wall in the comer of the room.

I observed him carefully as I hurried past from one room to another, and finally thought he had ceased to breathe. At this moment another man with a similar wound was taken in on a stretcher by his comrades, who sought in vain for a spot large enough to lay him down, and appealed to me. I could only tell them that when that poor boy in the comer was removed, they could set him down in his place. They went to remove him, but, to the astonishment of all, he objected, opened his eyes, and persisted in retaining his comer, which he did for some two weeks, when, finally, a mere bundle of skin and bones, for he gave small evidence of either flesh or blood, he was wrapped in a blanket and taken away in an ambulance to Washington, with a bottle of milk punch in his blouse, the only nourishment he could take.

On my return to Washington, three months later, a messenger came from Lincoln Hospital to say that the men of Ward 17 wanted to see me. I returned with him, and as I entered the ward seventy men saluted me, standing, such as could, others rising feebly in their beds, and falling back—exhausted with the effort.

Every man had left his blood in Fredericksburg—everyone was from the Lacy house. My hand had dressed every wound—many of them in the first terrible moments of agony. I had prepared their food in the snow and winds of December and fed them like children.

How dear they had grown to me in their sufferings, and the three great cheers that greeted my entrance into that hospital ward were dearer than the applause. I would not exchange their memory for the wildest hurrahs that ever greeted the ear of conqueror or king. When the first greetings were over and the agitation had subsided somewhat, a young man walked up to me with no apparent wound, with bright complexion, and in good flesh. There was certainly something familiar in his face, but I could not recall him, until, extending his hand with a smile, he said, "I am Riley Faulkner, of the 7th Michigan. I didn't die, and the milk punch lasted all the way to Washington!"

The author once inquired of Miss Barton how she dressed for these expeditions. She dressed simply, she said, so that she could get about easily, but her costume did not greatly differ from that of the ordinary woman of the period. She added humorously that her wardrobe was not wholly a matter of choice. Her clothes underwent such hard usage that nothing lasted very long, and she was glad to wear almost anything she could get.

This was not wholly satisfactory, for those were the days of hoop-skirts and other articles of feminine attire which had no possible place in her work. From Mrs. Vassall the author obtained somewhat more explicit information. She said:

When Clara went to the front, she dressed in a plain black print skirt with a jacket. She wished to dress so that she could easily get about and not consume much time in dressing. Her clothing received hard usage, and when she returned from any campaign to Washington, she was in need of a new outfit. At one time the women of Oxford sent her a box for her own personal use. Friends in Oxford furnished the material, and Annie Childs made the dresses. The box was delivered at her room during her absence, and she returned from the field, weary and wet, her hair soaked and falling down her back, and entered her cold and not very cheerful room. There she found this box with its complete outfit, and kneeling beside it she burst into happy tears.

The author counts it especially fortunate that he has been able to find a letter from Clara relating to this very experience, which was on the occasion of her return from the battle of Fredericksburg. It was addressed to Annie Childs, and dated four months later:

Port Royal, May 28th, 1863

My dear Annie:

I remember, four long months ago, one cold, dreary, windy day, I dragged me out from a chilly street-car that had found me ankle-deep in the mud of the 6th Street wharf, and up the slippery street and my long flights of stairs into a room, cheerless, in confusion, and alone, looking in most respects as I had left it some months before, with the exception of a mysterious box which stood unopened in the middle of the floor. All things looked strange to me, for in that few months I had taken in so much that yet I had no clear views. The great artist had been at work upon my brain and sketched it all over with life scenes, and death scenes, never to be erased. The fires of Fredericksburg still blazed before my eyes, and her cannon still thundered at my ear, while away down in the depths of my heart I was smothering the groans and treasuring the prayers of her dead and dying heroes; worn, weak, and heartsick, I was home from Fredericksburg; and when, there, for the first time I looked at myself, shoeless, gloveless, ragged, and bloodstained, a new sense of desolation and pity and sympathy and weariness, all blended, swept over me with irresistible force, and, perfectly overpowered, I sank down upon the strange box, unquestioning its presence or import, and wept as I had never done since the soft, hazy, winter night that saw our attacking guns silently stealing their approach to the river, ready at the dawn to ring out the shout of death to the waiting thousands at their wheels.

I said I wept, and so I did, and gathered strength and calmness and consciousness—and finally the strange box, which had afforded me my first rest, began to claim my attention; it was clearly and handsomely marked to myself at Washington, and came by express—so much for the outside; and a few pries with a hatchet, to hands as well accustomed as mine, soon made the inside as visible, only for the neat paper which covered all. It was doubtless something sent to some soldier; pity I had not had it earlier—it might be too late now; he might be past his wants or the kind remembrances of the loved ones at home. The while I was busy in removing the careful paper wrappings a letter, addressed to me, opened—"From friends in Oxford and Worcester"—no signature. Mechanically I commenced lifting up, one after another, hoods, shoes, boots, gloves, skirts, handkerchiefs, collars, linen—and that beautiful dress! look at it, all made—who—! Ah, there is no mistaking the workmanship—Annie's scissors shaped and her skillful fingers fitted that. Now, I begin to comprehend; while I had been away in the snows and frosts and rains and mud of Falmouth, forgetting my friends, myself, to eat or sleep or rest, forgetting everything but my God and the poor suffering victims around me, these dear, kind friends, undismayed and not disheartened by the great national calamity which had overtaken them, mourning, perhaps, the loss of their own, had remembered me, and with open hearts and willing hands had prepared this noble, thoughtful gift for me at my return. It was too much, and this time, burying my face in the dear tokens around me, I wept again as heartily as before, but with very different sensations; a new chord was struck; my labors, slight and imperfect as they had been, had been appreciated; I was not alone; and then and there again I re-dedicated myself to my little work of humanity, pledging before God all that I have, all that I am, all that I can, and all that I hope to be, to the cause of Justice and Mercy and Patriotism, my Country, and my God. And cheered and sustained as I have been by the kind remembrances of old friends, the cordial greeting of new ones, and the tearful, grateful blessings of the thousands of noble martyrs to whose relief or comfort it has been my blessed privilege to add my mite, I feel that my cup of happiness is more than full. It is an untold privilege to have lived in this day when there is work to be done, and, still more, to possess health and strength to do it, and most of all to feel that I bear with me the kindly feelings and perhaps prayers of the noble mothers and sisters who have sent sons and brothers to fight the battles of the world in the armies of Freedom. Annie, if it is not asking too much, now that I have gathered up resolution enough to speak of the subject at all (for I have never been able to before), I would like to know to whom besides yourself I am indebted for these beautiful and valuable gifts. It is too tame and too little to say that I am thankful for them. You did not want that, but I will say that, God willing, I will yet wear them where none of the noble donors would be ashamed to have them seen. Some of those gifts shall yet see service if Heaven spare my life. With thanks I am the friend of my "Friends in Oxford and Worcester."

Clara Barton

CHANGE OF BASE SPRING OF 1863

The events we have been describing bring Miss Barton to the end of 1862. The greater part of the year 1863 was spent by her in entirely different surroundings. Believing that the most significant military events of that year would be found in connection with a campaign against Charleston, South Carolina, and that the Army of the Potomac, which she had thus far accompanied, was reasonably well cared for in provisions which were in large degree the result of her establishment, she began to consider the advisability of going farther south.

Her reasons for this were partly military and partly personal. The military aspect of the situation was that she learned in Washington that the region about Charleston was likely to be the place of largest service during the year 1863. On the personal side was first her great desire to establish communication with her brother Stephen, who still was in North Carolina. When Charleston was captured, the army could move on into the interior. If she were somewhere near, she could have a part in the rescue of her brother, and she had reason to believe that he might have need of her service after his long residence within the bounds of the Confederacy. Her brother David received a commission in the Quartermaster's Department, and he was sent to Hilton Head in the vicinity of Charleston. Her cousin, Corporal Leander T. Poor, in the Engineers' Department, was assigned there, partly through her influence. It seemed as though that field promised to her every possible opportunity for public and private usefulness. There she could most largely serve her country; there she could have the companionship of her brother David and her cousin, Leander Poor; there she could most probably establish communications with Stephen, who might be in great need of her assistance. It is difficult to see how in the circumstances she could have planned with greater apparent wisdom. If in any respect the outcome failed to justify her expectations, it was because she was no wiser with respect to the military developments of the year 1863 than were the highest officials in Washington. Her request for permission to go to Port Royal was written early in 1863, and was addressed to the Assistant Secretary of War.

This request was promptly granted, and she was soon planning for a change of scene. The first three months of 1863, however, were spent in Washington, and we have few glimpses of her activities. In the middle of January she rejoined the army, acting on information which led her to believe that a battle was impending.

It should be stated that Clara Barton's diaries are most fragmentary where there is most to record. She was much given to writing, and, when she had time, enjoyed recording in detail almost everything that happened. She was accustomed to record the names of her callers, and the persons from whom she received, and those to whom she sent, letters; her purchases with the cost of each; her receipts and expenditures; her repairs to her wardrobe, and innumerable other little items; but a large proportion of the most significant events in her public life are not recorded in her diaries, or, if recorded at all, are merely set down in catchwords, and the details are given, if at all, in her letters. Of this expedition in the winter of 1863 we have no word either in her diary, which she probably left in Washington, or in her letters which she may have been too busy to write, or which, if written, have not been preserved. Our knowledge of her departure upon this expedition is contained in a letter from her nephew Samuel Barton:

Surgeon-General's Office
Washington City, D.C., January 18th, 1863

My dear Cousin Mary:

Your very acceptable letter, with Ada's and Ida's, was received last Thursday evening. I could not answer sooner, for I have been quite busy evenings ever since it was received. Aunt Clara left the city this morning for the army. Her friend, Colonel Rucker, the Assistant Quartermaster-General, told her last Thursday that the army were about to move and they were expecting a fight and wanted her to go if she felt able, so this morning she, Mr. Welles, who always goes with her to the battles, and Mr. Doe, a Massachusetts man, took the steamboat for Acquia Creek, where they will take the cars for Falmouth and there join the army. Colonel Rucker gave her two new tents, and bread, flour, meal, and a new stove, and requested her to telegraph to him for anything she wanted and he would send it to her. Aunt Sally left for Massachusetts last Thursday evening....

Sam Barton

In the State House in Boston is the battle-flag of the 21st Massachusetts, stained with the blood of Sergeant Thomas Plunkett. Both his arms were shot away in the battle of Fredericksburg, but he planted the flagstaff between his feet and upheld the flag with his two shattered stumps of arms. Massachusetts has few relics so precious as this flag. Clara Barton was with him at Fredericksburg and ministered to him there, and remained his lifelong friend. In many ways she manifested her interest in him, rendering her aid in a popular movement which secured him a purse of $4000. Sergeant Plunkett was in need of a pension, and Clara Barton addressed to the Senate's Committee on Military Affairs a memorial on his behalf. It was written on Washington's Birthday, after her return from the field:

Washington, D.C., Feb. 22nd,'63

To the Members of the
Military Committee, U.S. Senate.
Senators:
Nothing less than a strong conviction of duty owed to one of the brave defenders of our Nation's honor could induce me to intrude for a moment upon the already burdened, and limited term of action yet remaining to your honorable body.

During the late Battle of Fredericksburg, the 21st Massachusetts Regiment of Volunteers were ordered to charge upon a battery across an open field; in the terrible fire which assailed them, the colors were three times in quick succession bereft of their support; the third time they were seized by Sergeant Thomas Plunkett, of Company E, and borne over some three hundred yards of open space, when a shell from the enemy's battery in its murderous course killed three men of the regiment and shattered both arms of the Sergeant. He could no longer support the colors upright, but, planting his foot against the staff, he endeavored to hold them up, while he strove by his shouts amid the confusion to attract attention to their condition; for some minutes he sustained them against his right arm torn and shattered just below the shoulder, while the blood poured over and among the sacred folds, literally obliterating the stripes, leaving as fit emblem of such heroic sacrifice only the crimson and the stars. Thus

183

drenched in blood, and rent by the fury of eight battles, the noble standard could be no longer borne, and, while its gallant defender lay suffering in field hospital from amputation of both arms, it was reverently wrapped by Colonel Clark and returned to the State House in Boston, with the request that others might be sent them; the 21st had never lost their colors, but they had worn them out.

The old flag and its brave bearer are alike past their usefulness save as examples for emulation and titles of glory for some bright page of our Nation's history, and, while the one is carefully treasured in the sacred archives of the State, need I more than ask of this noble body to put forth its protecting arm to shelter, cherish, and sustain the other? If guaranty were needful for the private character of so true a soldier, it would have been found in the touching address of his eloquent Colonel (Clark) delivered on Christmas beside the stretcher waiting at the train at Falmouth to convey its helpless burden to the car, wither he had been escorted not only by his regiment, but his General. The tears which rolled over the veteran cheeks around him were ample testimony of the love and respect he had won from them, and to-day his heart's deepest affections twine round his gallant regiment as the defenders of their country.

A moment's reflection will obviate the necessity of any suggestions in reference to the provisions needful for his future support; it is only to be remembered that he can nevermore be unattended, a common doorknob is henceforth as formidable to him as a prison bolt. His little pension as a Sergeant would not remunerate an attendant for placing his food in his mouth, to say nothing of how it shall be obtained for both of them.

For the sake of formality merely, for to you gentlemen I know the appeal is needless, I will close by praying your honorable body to grant to Sergeant Plunkett such pension as shall in your noble wisdom be ample for his future necessities and a fitting tribute to his patriotic sacrifice.

C. B.

The assignment of her brother David to duty in the vicinity of Charleston was the event which decided her to ask for a transfer to that field, or rather for permission to go there with supplies.

It must be remembered that Miss Barton's service was a voluntary service. She was not an army nurse, and had no intention of becoming one. The system of army nurses was under the direct supervision of Dorothea Lynde Dix, a woman from her own county, and one for whom she cherished feelings of the highest regard, but under whom she had no intention of working. Indeed, it is one of the fine manifestations of good sense on the part of Clara Barton that she never at any time attempted what might have seemed an interference with Miss Dix, but found for herself a field of service, and developed it according to a method of her own. It will be well at this time to give some account of Miss Dix, and a little outline of her great work in its relation to that of Clara Barton.

*One story of Dorothea Dix was related by a veteran of the 13th New Hampshire Volunteer Regiment who was hospitalized. Dix had ordered that the women nurses should report to work in dresses of muted colors, wearing no jewelry or makeup. The nurses all reported in their best and brightest dresses, wearing what jewelry they owned. The patients cheered; Dix did not press the issue.—Ed.

Dorothea Lynde Dix was born April 4, 1802, and died July 17, 1887. She was twenty-nine years older than Clara Barton, and their lives had many interesting parallels. Until the publication of her biography by Francis Tiffany in 1890, it was commonly supposed that she was born in Worcester County, Massachusetts, where she spent her childhood. But her birth occurred in Maine. Unlike Clara Barton she had no happy home memories. Her father was an unstable, visionary man, and it was on one of his frequent and futile migrations that she was born. Her biographer states that her childhood memories were so painful that "in no hour of the most confidential intimacy could she be induced to unlock the silence which, to the very end of life, she maintained as to all the incidents of her early days." She had no happy memories of association with school or church, or sympathetic friends. The background of her childhood memory was of poverty with a lack of public respect for a father who, though of good family, led an aimless, shiftless, wandering life. Unhappily, he was a religious fanatic, associated with no church, but issuing tracts which he paid for with money that should have been used for his children, and, to save expense, required her to paste or stitch. She hated the employment and the type of religion which it represented. She broke away from it almost violently and went to live with her grandmother in Boston.

There she fell under the influence of William Ellery Channing, and was born again. To her through his ministry came the spirit that quickened and gave life to her dawning hope and aspiration.

How she got her education we hardly know, but she began teaching, as Clara Barton did, when she was fifteen years of age. And like Clara Barton she became a pioneer in certain forms of educational work. Dorothea Dix opened a school "for charitable and religious uses," above her grandmother's barn, and in time she inherited property which made her independent, so that she was able to devote herself to a life of philanthropy.

In 1837, being then thirty-five years of age, and encouraged by her pastor, Dr. Channing, in whose home she spent much of her time, she launched forth upon her career of devotion to the amelioration of the condition of convicts, lunatics, and paupers. In her work for the insane she was especially effective. She traveled in nearly all of the States of the Union, pleading for effective legislation to promote the establishment of asylums for the insane. Like Clara Barton she found an especially fruitful field of service in New Jersey; the Trenton Asylum was in a very real sense her creation. The pauper, the prisoner, and especially the insane of our whole land owe her memory a debt of lasting gratitude.

By 1861 her reputation was well established. She was then almost sixty years of age and had gained the well-merited confidence of the medical profession. She was on her way from Boston to Washington, and was spending a few days at the Trenton Asylum, when the Sixth Massachusetts was fired upon in Baltimore on April 19, 1861. Like Clara Barton she hastened immediately to the place of service. On the very next day she wrote to a friend: "I think my duty lies near military hospitals for the present. This need not be announced. I have reported myself and some nurses for free service at the War Department, and to the Surgeon-General." Her offer was accepted with great heartiness and with ill-considered promptness. She was appointed "Superintendent of Female Nurses." She was authorized "to select and assign female nurses to general or permanent military hospitals; they not to be employed without her sanction and approval except in case of urgent need." Whether the United States contained any woman better qualified to undertake such a task as this than Dorothea Dix may be questioned. Certainly none could have been found with more of experience or with a higher consecration. It was an impossible task for any one, and, while Miss Dix was possessed of some of the essential qualities, she did not possess them all. Her biographer very justly says:

The literal meaning, however, of such a commission as had thus been hastily bestowed on Miss Dix—applying, as it did to the women nurses of the military hospitals of the whole United States not in actual rebellion—was one which, in those early days of the war, no one so much as began to take in...Such a commission—as the march of events was before long to prove—involved a sheer, practical impossibility. It implied, not a single-handed woman, nearly sixty and shattered in health, but immense organized departments at twenty different centers." 1

The War Department acted upon what must have appeared a wise impulse in turning this whole matter of women nurses over to the authority of a woman known in all the States—as Miss Dix was known—and possessing the confidence of the people of the whole country. But she was not only sixty years of age and predisposed to consumption, and at that time suffering from other ailments, but she had never learned to delegate responsibility to her subordinates. It had been well for Clara Barton if she had known better how to set others to work, but she knew how better than Dorothea Dix and was twenty years younger. Indeed, Clara Barton was younger at eighty than Dorothea Dix was at sixty, but she herself suffered somewhat from this same limitation. Dorothea Dix could not be everywhere, and with her system she needed to be everywhere, just as Clara Barton under her system had to be at the very front in direct management of her own line of activities. But Dorothea Dix, besides needing to be simultaneously on twenty battle-fields, had to be where she could examine and sift out and prepare for service the chosen from among a great many thousand women applying for the privilege of nursing wounded soldiers, and ranging all the way from sentimental school-girls to sickly and decrepit grandmothers. Again, Mr. Tiffany says:

Women nurses were volunteering by the thousands, the majority of them without the experience or health to fit them for such arduous service. Who should pass on their qualifications, who station, superintend, and train them? Now, under the Atlas weight of care and responsibilities so suddenly thrust on Miss Dix, the very qualifications which had so preeminently fitted her for the sphere in which she had wrought such miracles of success began to tell against her. She was nearly sixty years old, and with a constitution sapped by malaria, overwork, and pulmonary weakness. She had for years been a lonely and single-handed worker, planning her own projects, keeping her own counsel, and pressing on, unhampered by the need of consulting others, toward her self-chosen goal. The lone worker could not change her nature. She tried to do everything herself, and the feat before long became an impossibility. At length she came to recognize this, again and again exclaiming in her distress, "This is not the work I would have my life judged by."

By that, however, in part her life-work must be judged, and, in the main, greatly to her advantage and wholly to her honor. We can see, however, the inevitable limitations of her work. Up to that time, she had dealt with small groups of subordinates from whom she could demand and secure some approach to perfection of organization and discipline. This she could not possibly secure in her present situation. Again we quote the discriminating words of her biographer:

But in war—especially in a war precipitately entered into by a raw and inexperienced people.—all such perfection of organization and discipline is out of the question. If a good field hospital is not to be had, the best must be made of a bad one. If a skillful surgeon is not at hand, then an incompetent one must hack away after his own butcher fashion. If selfish and greedy attendants eat up and drink up the supplies of delicacies and wines for the sick, then enough more must be supplied to give the sick the fag end of a chance. It is useless to try to idealize war.... All this, however, Miss Dix could not bring herself to endure. Ready to live on a crust, and to sacrifice herself without stint, her whole soul was on fire at the spectacles of incompetence and callow indifference she was doomed daily to witness. She became overwrought, and lost the requisite self-control. ... Inevitably she became involved in sharp altercations with prominent medical officials and with regimental surgeons.

It is necessary to recall this in order to understand Clara Barton's attitude toward the established military hospitals. She was not, in any narrow or technical term, a hospital nurse. She stood ready to assist the humblest soldier in any possible need, and to work in any hospital at any task howsoever humble, if that was where she could work to advantage. But she knew the hospitals in and about Washington too well not to appreciate these infelicities. She had no intention whatever of becoming a cog in that great and unmanageable machine.

Clara Barton held Dorothea Dix in the very highest regard. In all her diaries and letters and in her memoranda of conversations which her diaries sometimes contain, there is no word concerning Dorothea Dix that is not appreciative. In 1910 the New York *World* wired her a request that she telegraph to that newspaper, at its expense, a list of eight names of women whom she would nominate for a Woman's Hall of Fame. The eight names which she sent in reply to this request were Abigail Adams, Lucretia Mott, Lucy Stone Blackwell, Harriet Beecher Stowe, Frances Dana Gage, Maria Mitchell, Dorothea Dix, and Mary A. Bickerdyke*. It was a fine indication of her broad-mindedness that she should have named two women, Dorothea Dix and Mother Bickerdyke, who should have won distinction in her own field and might have been deemed her rivals for popular affection. If Clara Barton was capable of any kind of jealousy, it was not a jealousy that would have thought ever to undermine or belittle a woman like Dorothea Dix. Few women understood so well as Clara Barton what Dorothea Dix had to contend with. Her contemporary references show how fully she honored this noble elder sister, and how loyally she supported her.

*Known to the boys as "Mother Bickerdyke," it's written that William Tecumseh Sherman once responded to a complaint about Bickerdyke's circumvention of army protocol by saying, "There is nothing I can do. She ranks me."—Ed.

At the same time, Clara Barton kept herself well out from under the administration and control of Miss Dix. In some respects the two women were too much alike in their temperament for either one to have worked well under the other. For that matter, neither one of them greatly enjoyed working under anybody. It is at once to the credit of Clara Barton's loyalty and good sense that she went as an independent worker.

But the hospitals in and about Washington were approaching more and more nearly something that might be called system, and that system was the system of Dorothea Dix. Clara Barton had all the room she wanted on the battle-field. There was no great crowd of women clamoring to go with her when under fire she crossed the bridge at Fredericksburg. But by the spring of 1863 it began to be less certain that there was going to be as much fighting as there had been in the immediate vicinity of Washington. There was a possibility that actual field service with the Army of the Potomac was going to be less, and that the base hospitals with their organized system would be able to care more adequately for the wounded than would the hospitals farther south where the next great crisis seemed to be impending.

These were among the considerations in the mind of Clara Barton when she left the Army of the Potomac—"my own army," as she lovingly called it—and secured her transfer to Hilton Head, near Charleston.

THE ATTEMPT TO RECAPTURE FORT SUMTER

"I am confounded! Literally speechless with amazement! When I left Washington everyone said it boded no peace; it was a bad omen for me to start; I never missed finding the trouble I went to find, and was never late. I thought little of it. This p.m. we neared the dock at Hilton Head and the boat came alongside and boarded us instantly. The first word was, "The first gun is to be fired upon Charleston this p.m. at three o'clock." We drew out watches, and the hands pointed three to the minute. I felt as if I should sink through the deck. I am no fatalist, but it is so singular."

Thus wrote Clara Barton in her journal on Tuesday night, April 7, 1863, the night of her arrival at Port Royal. She had become so expert in learning where there was to be a battle that her friends looked upon her as a kind of stormy petrel and expected trouble as soon as she arrived. She had come to Hilton Head in order to be on hand when the bombardment of Charleston should occur, and the opening guns of the bombardment were her salute as her boat, the *Arogo*, warped up to the dock. Everything seemed to indicate that she had come at the very moment when she was needed.

But the following Saturday the transports which had loaded recruits at Hilton Head, ready to land and capture Charleston as soon as the guns had done their work, returned to Hilton Head and brought the soldiers back. Her diary that morning recorded that the *Arogo* returning would stop off at Charleston for dispatches, but her entry that night said:

In the P.M., much to the consternation of everybody, the transports laden with troops all hove in sight. Soon the harbor was literally filled with ships and boats, the wharf crowded with disembarking troops with the camp equipage they had taken with them. What had they returned for? was the question hanging on every lip. Conjecture was rife; all sorts of rumors were afloat; but the one general idea seemed to prevail that the expedition "had fizzled," if anyone knows the precise meaning and import of that term. Troops landed all the evening and perhaps all night, and returned to the old camping grounds. The place is alive with soldiers. No one knows why he is here, or why he is not there; all seem disappointed and chagrined, but no one is to blame. For my part, I am rather pleased at the turn it has taken, as I thought from the first that we had "too few troops to fight and too many to be killed." I have seen worse retreats if this be one.

"Fizzled" appears to have been a new word, but the country had abundant opportunity to learn its essential meaning. The expedition against Charleston was one of several that met this inglorious end, and the flag was not raised over Sumter until 1865.

Now followed an interesting chapter in Clara Barton's career, but one quite different from anything she had expected when she came to Hilton Head. After the "fizzle" in early April, the army settled down to general inactivity. Charleston must be attacked simultaneously by land and sea and reduced by heavy artillery fire before the infantry could do anything. There was nothing for Clara Barton to do but to wait for the battle which had been postponed, but was surely coming. She distributed her perishable supplies where they would do the most good, and looked after the comfort of such soldiers as needed her immediate ministration. But the wounded were few in number and the sick were in well-established hospitals where she had no occasion to offer her services.

Moreover, she found the situation here very different from what she had seen only a few miles from Washington. There were no muddy roads between Hilton Head and New York Harbor. The *Arogo* was a shuttle moving back and forward every few days, and in time another boat was added. There was a regular mail service between New York and Hilton Head, and every boat took officers and soldiers going upon, or returning from, furloughs, and the boats from New York brought nurses and supplies. The Sanitary Commission had its own depot of supplies and a liberal fund of money from which purchases could be made of fruits and such other local delicacies as were procurable. It is true, as Miss Barton was afterward to learn, that the hospital management left something to be desired, and that fewer delicacies were purchased than could have been. But that was distinctly not her responsibility, nor did she for one moment assume it to be such. She came into conflict with official red tape quite soon enough in her own department, without intruding where she did not belong. She settled down to await the time when she should be needed for the special work that had brought her to Hilton Head. That time came, but it did not come soon, and its delay was the occasion of very mixed emotions on her part.

Clara Barton came to Hilton Head with a reputation already established. She no longer needed to be introduced, nor was there any difficulty in her procuring passes to go where she pleased, excepting as she was sometimes refused out of consideration for her own personal safety. But not once while she was in Carolina was she asked to show her passes. When she landed, she found provision made for her at regimental headquarters. Colonel J. G. Elwell, of Cleveland, to whom she reported, was laid up at this time with a broken leg. She had him for a patient and his gratitude continued through all the subsequent years. Her journal described him as a noble, Christian gentleman, and she found abundant occasion to admire his manliness, his Christian character, his affection for his wife and children, his courtesy to her, and later, his heroism as she witnessed it upon the battle-field. The custody of her supplies brought her into constant relations with the Chief Quartermaster, Captain Samuel T. Lamb, for whom she cherished a regard almost if not quite as high as that she felt for Colonel, afterward General, Elwell. Her room was at headquarters, under the same roof with these and other brave officers, who vied with each other in bestowing honors and kindnesses upon her. As Colonel Elwell was incapacitated for service, she saw him daily, and the care of her supplies gave her scarcely less constant association with Captain Lamb. General Hunter called upon her, paid her high compliments, issued her passes and permits, and offered her every possible courtesy. Her request that her cousin, Corporal Leander Poor, be transferred to the department over which her brother David presided, met an immediate response. The nurses from the hospital paid her an official call, and apparently spoke very gracious words to her, for she indicates that she was pleased with something they said or did. Different officers sent her bouquets; her table and her window must have been rather constantly filled with flowers. More than once the band serenaded her, and between the musical numbers there was a complimentary address which embarrassed, even more than it pleased her, in which a high tribute was paid "To Clara Barton, the Florence Nightingale of America."

The officers at headquarters had good saddle horses, and invited her to ride with them. If there was any form of exercise which she thoroughly enjoyed, it was horseback riding. She procured a riding-skirt and sent for her sidesaddle, which the *Arogo* in due time brought to her. So far nothing could have been more delightful. The very satisfaction of it made her uncomfortable. She hoped that God would not hold her accountable for misspent time, and said so in her diary.

Lest she should waste her time, she began teaching some negro boys to read, and sought out homesick soldiers who needed comfort. Whenever she heard of any danger or any likelihood of a battle anywhere within reach, she conferred with Colonel Elwell about going there. He was a religious man, and she discussed with him the interposition of Divine Providence, and the apparent indication that she was following a Divine call in coming to Hilton Head exactly when she did. But no field opened immediately which called for her ministrations. She felt sometimes that it would be a terrible mistake if she had come so far away from what really was her duty, when she wrote: "God is great and fearfully just. Truly it is a fearful thing to fall into His hands; His ways are past finding out." Still she could not feel responsible for the fact that no great battle had occurred in her immediate vicinity. Each time the *Arogo* dropped anchor, she wondered if she ought to return on her; but each time it seemed certain that it was not going to be very long until there was a battle. So she left the matter in God's hands. She wrote: "It will be wisely ordered, and I shall do all for the best in the end. God's will, not mine, be done. I am content. How I wish I could always keep in full view the fact and feeling that God orders all things precisely as they should be; all is best as it is."

On Sunday she read Beecher's sermons and sometimes copied religious poetry for Colonel Elwell, who, in addition to his own disability, had tender memories of the death of his little children, and many solicitous thoughts for his wife.

In some respects she was having the time of her life. A little group of women, wives of the officers, gathered at the headquarters, and there grew up a kind of social usage. One evening when a group of officers and officers' wives were gathered together, one of the ladies read a poem in honor of Clara Barton. One day, at General Hunter's headquarters and in his presence, Colonel Elwell presented her with a beautiful pocket Bible on behalf of the officers. If she needed anything to increase her fame, that need was supplied when Mr. Page, correspondent of the New York "Tribune," whom she remembered to have met at the Lacy house during the battle of Fredericksburg, arrived at Hilton Head, and he, who had seen every battle of the Army of the Potomac except Chancellorsville, told the officers how he had heard General Patrick, at the battle of Fredericksburg, remonstrate with Miss Barton on account of her exposing herself to danger, saying afterward that he expected to see her shot every minute. The band of a neighboring regiment came over and serenaded her. Her windows were filled with roses and orange blossoms, and she wrote in her diary: "I do not deserve such friends as I find, and how can I deserve them? I fear that in these later years our Heavenly Father is too merciful to me."

It would have been delightful if she could only have been sure that she was doing her duty. Surrounded by appreciative friends, bedecked with flowers, serenaded and sung to, and with a saddled horse at her door almost every morning and at least one officer if not a dozen eager for the joy and honor of a ride with her, only two things disturbed her. The first was that she still had no word from Stephen, and the other was the feeling that, unless the Lord ordained a battle in her vicinity before long, she ought to be back with what she called "my own army."

Clara Barton's diary displays utter freedom from cant. She was not given to putting her religious feelings and emotions down on paper. But in this period she gave much larger space to her own reflections than was her custom when more fully occupied. She was feeling in a marked degree the providential aspects of her own life; she was discussing with Christian officers their plans for what Colonel Elwell called his "soldier's church." Her religious nature found expression in her diary more adequately than she had usually had time to express.

Toward the end of her period of what since has been termed her watchful waiting, she received a letter from a friend, an editor, who felt that the war had gone on quite long enough, and who wished her to use her influence in favor of an immediate peace. Few people wanted peace more than Clara Barton, but her letter in answer to this request shows an insight into the national situation which at that time could hardly have been expected:

Hilton Head, S.C., June 24th, 1863
T. W. Meighan, Esq.,
My kind friend, your welcome letter of the 6th has been some days in hand. I did not get "frightened." I am a U. S. soldier, you know, and therefore not supposed to be susceptible to fear, and, as I am merely a soldier, and not a statesman, I shall make no attempt at discussing political points with you. You have spoken openly and frankly, and I have perused your letter and considered your sentiments with interest, and, I believe, with sincerity and candor, and, while I observe with pain the wide difference of opinion existing between us, I cannot find it in my heart to believe it more than a matter of opinion. I shall not take to myself more of honesty of purpose, faithfulness of zeal, or patriotism, than I award to you. I have not, aye! never shall forget where I first found you. The soldier who has stood in the ranks of my country's armies, and toiled and marched and fought, and fallen and struggled and risen, but to fall again more worn and exhausted than before, until my weak arm had greater strength than his, and could aid him, and yet made no complaint, and only left the ranks of death when he had no longer strength to stand up in them—is it for me to rise up in judgment and accuse this man of a want of patriotism? True, he does not see as I see, and works in a channel in which I have no confidence, with which I have no sympathy, and through which I could not go; still, I must believe that in the end the same results which would gladden my heart would rejoice his.

Where you in prospective see peace, glorious, coveted peace, and rest for our tired armies, and home and happiness and firesides and friends for our war-worn heroes, I see only the beginning of war. If we should make overtures for "peace upon any terms," then, I fear, would follow a code of

196

terms to which no civilized nation could submit and present even an honorable existence among nations. God forbid that I should ask the useless exposure of the life of one man, the desolation of one more home; I never for a moment lose sight of the mothers and sisters, and white-haired fathers, and children moving quietly about, and dropping the unseen, silent tear in those far-away saddened homes, and I have too often wiped the gathering damp from pale, anxious brows, and caught from ashy, quivering lips the last faint whispers of home, not to realize the terrible cost of these separations; nor has morbid sympathy been all—out amid the smoke and fire and thunder of our guns, with only the murky canopy above, and the bloody ground beneath, I have wrought day after day and night after night, my heart well-nigh to bursting with conflicting emotions, so sorry for the necessity, so glad for the opportunity of ministering with my own hands and strength to the dying wants of the patriot martyrs who fell for their country and mine. If my poor life could have purchased theirs, how cheerfully and quickly would the exchange have been made; more than this I could not do, deeper than this I could not feel, and yet among it all it has never once been in my heart, or on my lips, to sue to our enemies for peace. First, they broke it without cause; last, they will not restore it without shame. True, we may never find peace by fighting, certainly we never shall by asking. "Independence?" They always had their independence till they madly threw it away; if there be a chain on them to-day it is of their own riveting. I grant that our Government has made mistakes, sore ones, too, in some instances, but ours is a human government, and like all human operations liable to mistakes; only the machinery and plans of Heaven move unerringly and we short-sighted mortals are, half our time, fain to complain of these. I would that so much of wisdom and foresight and strength and power fall to our rulers as would show them to-morrow the path to victory and peace, but we shall never strengthen their hands or incite their patriotism by deserting and upbraiding them. To my unsophisticated mind, the Government of my country is my country, and the people of my country, the Government of my country as nearly as a representative system will allow. I have taught me to look upon our "Government" as the band which the people bind around the bundle of sticks to hold it firm, where every patriot hand must grasp the knot the tighter, and our "Constitution" as a symmetrical framework unsheltered and unprotected, around which the people must rally, and brace and stay themselves among its inner timbers, and lash and bind and nail and rivet themselves to its outer posts, till in its sheltered strength it bids defiance to every elemental jar—till the winds cannot rack, the sunshine warp, or the rains rot, and I would to Heaven that so we rallied and stood to-day. If our

Government is "too weak" to act vigorously and energetically, strengthen it till it can. Then comes the peace we all wait for as kings and prophets waited—and without which, like them, we seek and never find.

Pardon me, my good friend, I had never thought to speak at this length, or, indeed, any length upon this strangely knotted subject, so entirely out of my line. My business is stanching blood and feeding fainting men; my post the open field between the bullet and the hospital. I sometimes discuss the application of a compress or a wisp of hay under a broken limb, but not the bearing and merits of a political movement. I make gruel—not speeches; I write letters home for wounded soldiers, not political addresses—and again I ask you to pardon, not so much what I have said, as the fact of my having said anything in relation to a subject of which, upon the very nature of things, I am supposed to be profoundly ignorant.

With thanks for favors, and hoping to hear from you and yours as usual,

I remain as ever
Yours truly

Clara Barton

I am glad to hear from your wife and mother, and I am most thankful for your cordial invitation to visit you, which I shall (if I have not forfeited your friendship by my plainness of speech, which I pray I may not) accept most joyously, and I am even now rejoicing in prospect over my anticipated visit. We are not suffering from heat yet, and I am enjoying such horseback rides as seldom fall to the lot of ladies, I believe. I don't know but I should dare ride with a cavalry rider by and by, if I continue to practice. I could at least take lessons. I have a fine new English leaping saddle on the way to me. I hope you will endeavor to see to it that the rebel privateers shall not get hold of it. I could not sustain both the loss and disappointment, I fear.

Love to all. Yours

C. B.

While Miss Barton was engaged in these less strenuous occupations she issued a requisition upon her brother in the Quartermaster's Department for a flatiron. She said: "My clothes are as well washed as at home, and I have a house to iron in if I had the iron. I could be as clean and as sleek as a kitten. Don't you want a smooth sister enough to send her a flatiron?"

In midsummer, hostilities began in earnest. On July 11 an assault on Fort Wagner was begun from Morris Island, and was followed by a bombardment, Admiral Dahlgren firing shells from his gunboats, and General Gillmore opening with his land batteries. Then followed the charge of the black troops under Colonel R. G. Shaw, and the long siege in which the "swamp angel," a two-hundred-pounder Parrott, opened fire on Charleston. It was then that Clara Barton found what providential leading had brought her to this place. Not from a sheltered retreat, but under actual fire of the guns she ministered to the wounded and the dying. All day long under a hot sun she boiled water to wash their wounds, and by night she ministered to them, too ardent to remember her need of sleep. The hot winds drove the sand into her eyes, and weariness and danger were ever present. But she did her work unterrified. She saw Colonel Elwell leading the charge, and he believed that not only himself, but General Voris and Leggett would have died but for her ministrations.

Follow me, if you will, through these eight months [Miss Barton said shortly afterward]. I remember eight months of weary siege—scorched by the sun, chilled by the waves, rocked by the tempest, buried in the shifting sands, toiling day after day in the trenches, with the angry fire of five forts hissing through their ranks during every day of those weary months.

This was when your brave old regiments stood thundering at the gate of proud rebellious Charleston.

There, frowning defiance, with Moultrie on her left, Johnson on her right, and Wagner in front, she stood hurling fierce death and destruction full in the faces of the brave band who beleaguered her walls.

Sumter, the watch-dog, that stood before her door, lay maimed and bleeding at her feet, pierced with shot and torn with shell, the tidal waves lapping his wounds.

Still there was danger in his growl and death in his bite.

Fort Sumter, fiercely bombarded July 24, repulsed an assault against it on September 8, and was not completely silenced until October 26.

One summer afternoon our brave little army was drawn up among the island sands and formed in line of march. For hours we watched. Dim twilight came, then the darkness for which they had waited, while the gloom and stillness of death settled down on the gathered forces of Morris Island. Then we pressed forward and watched again. A long line of phosphorescent light streamed and shot along the waves ever surging on our right.

I remember so well these islands, when the guns and the gunners, the muskets and musketeers, struggled for place and foothold among the shifting sands. I remember the first swarthy regiments with their unsoldierly tread, and the soldierly bearing and noble brows of the patient philanthropists who volunteered to lead them. I can see again the scarlet flow of blood as it rolled over the black limbs beneath my hands and the great heave of the heart before it grew still. And I remember Wagner and its six hundred dead, and the great-souled martyr that lay there with them when the charge was ended and the guns were cold.

Vividly she went on to describe the siege of Fort Wagner from Morris Island, thus:

I saw the bayonets glisten. The "swamp angel" threw her bursting bombs, the fleet thundered its cannonade, and the dark line of blue trailed its way in the dark line of belching walls of Wagner. I saw them on, up, and over the parapets into the jaws of death, and heard the clang of the death-dealing sabers as they grappled with the foe. I saw the ambulances laden down with agony, and the wounded, slowly crawling to me down the tide-washed beach, Voris and Cumminger gasping in their blood. And I heard the deafening clatter of the hoofs of "Old Sam" as Elwell madly galloped up under the walls of the fort for orders. I heard the tender, wailing fife, the muffled drum and the last shots as the pitiful little graves grew thick in the shifting sands.

Of this experience General Elwell afterward wrote:

I was shot with an Enfield cartridge within one hundred and fifty yards of the fort and so disabled that I could not go forward. I was in an awful predicament, perfectly exposed to canister from Wagner and shell from Gregg and Sumter in front, and the enfilade from James Island. I tried to dig a trench in the sand with my saber, into which I might crawl, but the dry sand would fall back in place about as fast as I could scrape it out with my narrow implement. Failing in this, on all fours I crawled toward the lee of the beach, which was but a few yards off. A charge of canister all around me aroused my reverie to thoughts of action. I abandoned the idea of taking the fort and ordered a retreat of myself, which I undertook to execute in a most unmartial manner on my hands and knees spread out like a turtle.

After working my way for a half-hour and making perhaps two hundred yards, two boys of the 62d Ohio found me and carried me to our first parallel, where had been arranged an extempore hospital. After resting awhile I was put on the horse of my lieutenant-colonel, from which he had been shot that night, and started for the lower end of the island one and a half miles off, where better hospital arrangements had been prepared. Oh, what an awful ride that was! But I got there at last, by midnight. I had been on duty for forty-two hours without sleep under the most trying circumstances and my soul longed for sleep, which I got in this wise: an army blanket was doubled and laid on the soft side of a plank with an overcoat for a pillow, on which I laid my worn-out body.

And such a sleep! I dreamed that I heard the shouts of my boys in victory, that the rebellion was broken, that the Union was saved, and that I was at my old home and that my dear wife was trying to soothe my pain...

My sleepy emotions awoke me and a dear, blessed woman was bathing my temples and fanning my fevered face. Clara Barton was there, an angel of mercy doing all in mortal power to assuage the miseries of the unfortunate soldiers.

While she was still under fire, but after the stress of the first assault, she found time to send a little note which enables us to identify with certainty her headquarters. Her work was not done in the shelter of any of the base hospitals in the general region of Charleston, it was with the advance hospital and under fire.

The midsummer campaign left Clara Barton desperately sick. She came very near to laying down her life with the brave men for whose sake she had freely risked it. What with her own sickness and the strenuous nature of her service, there is only a single line in her diary (on Thanksgiving Day) between July 23 and December 1. On July 22 she personally assisted at two terrible surgical operations as the men were brought directly in from the field. The soldiers were so badly wounded she wanted to see them die before the surgeon touched them. But the surgeons did their work well, and, though it was raining and cold, she covered them with rubber blankets and was astonished to find how comfortable they came to be. She returned to see them in the evening and they were both sleeping soundly. On the following day, the day of her last entry for the summer, she reported the wounded under her care as doing well; also, that she had now a man detailed to assume some of the responsibility for the food of the wounded. Fresh green corn was available, and she was having hominy cooked for men who had had quite too much of salt pork. She was arranging the meals, but had other people to serve them.

Then Clara Barton dropped; her strength gave out. Overcome with fatigue and sick with fever, she lay for several weeks and wrote neither letters nor in her journal.

By October she was ready to answer Annie Childs's thoughtful inquiry about her wardrobe. There were two successive letters two weeks apart that consisted almost wholly of the answers she made to the question wherewithal she should be clothed. Lest we should suppose Clara Barton to be an institution and not a wholly feminine woman, it is interesting to notice her concern that these dresses be of proper material and suitably made.

The dresses arrived with rather surprising promptness, and they fitted with only minor alterations which she described in detail to Annie. Toward the end of October she had occasion to write again to Annie thanking the friends who had remembered her so kindly, and expressing in her letter the feeling, which she so often recorded in her diary, that she was not doing as much as she ought to merit the kindness of her friends. In another letter a few days later, she told of one use she was making of her riding-skirt; she was furnishing a hospital at Fort Mitchell, seven miles away, and her ride to that hospital combined both business and pleasure.

About this time she gathered some trophies and sent to Worcester for the fair. They were exhibited and sold to add to the resources of the good people who were providing in various ways for the comfort of the soldiers. At this time she wrote to other organizations who had sent her supplies, telling of the good they had done.

But again she fell upon a time of relative inactivity. There were no more battles to be fought immediately. She again wondered if she had any right to stay in a place where everything was so comfortable, especially as Annie Childs had written to her that the Worcester and Oxford women would not permit her to bear any part of the expense for the new clothes that had been made for her.

About this time her brother David received a letter from Stephen which showed that it was useless for her to stay where she was with any present expectation of securing his relief. He was still remaining with his property unmolested by both sides, and thought it better to continue there than run what seemed to him the larger risks of leaving.

One of the most interesting and in its way pathetic entries in her diary at this season is a long one on December 5, 1863. Miss Barton had collided with official arrogance, and had unhappy memories of it. She probably would have said nothing about it had she not been appealed to by one of the women at the headquarters to do something to improve conditions at the regular hospital. And that was something which Clara Barton simply could not do. She knew better than almost anyone else how much those hospitals lacked of perfection. She herself did not visit them, excepting as she went there to return official calls. She had made it plain to those in charge that she had not come to interfere with any form of established work, but to do a work of her own in complete sympathy and cooperation with theirs. She knew that Dorothea Dix had undertaken an impossible task. She saw some nurses near to where she was who were much more fond of spending pleasant evenings at headquarters than they were of doing the work for which they were supposed to have come down. But she also knew that even such work as she was doing was looked upon by some of them with feelings of jealousy, as work outside of the general organization, yet receiving from the public a confidence and recognition not always accorded their own. One night, after one of the officer's wives had poured out her soul to Clara Barton, she poured out her soul to her diary. It is a very long entry, but it treats of some highly important subjects:

"I moved along to the farther end of the piazza and found Mrs. D., who soon made known to me the subject of her desires. As I suspected, the matter was hospitals. She has been visiting the hospital at this place and has become not only interested, but excited upon the subject; the clothing department she finds satisfactory, but the storeroom appears empty and a sameness prevailing through food as provided which seems to her appalling for a diet for sick men. She states that they have no delicacies such as the country at the North are flooding hospitals with; that the food is all badly cooked, served cold, and always the same thing—dip toast, meat cooked dry, and tea without milk, perhaps once a week a potato for each man, or a baked apple. She proposed to establish a kitchen department for the serving of proper food to these men, irrespective of the pleasure of the "Powers that Be." She expects opposition from the surgeons in charge and Mrs. Russell, the matron appointed and stationed by Miss Dix, but thinks to commence by littles and work herself in in spite of opposition, or make report direct to Washington through Judge Holt, and other influential friends and obtain a carte blanche from Secretary Stanton to act independently of all parties. She wished to know if I thought it would be possible to procure supplies sufficient to carry on such a plan, and people to cook and serve if it were once established and directed properly. She had just mailed a letter to Miss Dame calling upon her to stir people at the North and make a move if possible in the right direction. She said General Gillmore took tea with her the evening previous and inquired with much feeling, "How are my poor boys?" She desired me to attend church at the hospital to-morrow (Sunday) morning; not with her, but go, pass through, and judge for myself. In the meantime the Major came in and the subject was discussed generally. I listened attentively, gave it as my opinion that there would be no difficulty in obtaining supplies and means of paying for the preparation of them, but of the manner and feasibility of delivering and distributing them among the patients I said nothing. I had nothing to say. I partly promised to attend church the next morning, and retired having said very little. What I have thought is quite another thing. I have no doubt but the patients lack many luxuries which the country at large endeavors to supply them with, and supposes they have, no doubt; but men suffer and die for the lack of the nursing and provisions of the loved ones at home. No doubt but the stately, stupendous, and magnificent indolence of the "officers in charge" embitters the days of the poor sufferers who have become mere machines in the hands of the Government to be ruled and oppressed by puffed-up, conceited, and self-sufficient superiors in position. No doubt but a good, well-regulated kitchen, presided over with a little good common sense and womanly care, would change the whole aspect of things and lengthen the days of some, and brighten the last days of others of the poor sufferers within the thin walls of this hospital. I wish it might be, but what can I do? First it is not my province; I should be out of place there; next, Miss Dix is supreme, and her appointed nurse is matron; next, the surgeons will not brook any interference, and will, in my opinion, resent and resist the smallest effort to break over their own arrangements. What others may be able to do I am unable to conjecture, but I feel that my guns are effectually silenced. My sympathy is not destroyed, by any means, but my confidence in my ability to accomplish anything of an alleviating character in this department is completely annihilated. I went with all I had, to work where I thought I saw greatest need. A man can have no greater need than to be saved from death, and after six weeks of unremitting toil I was driven from my own tents by the selfish cupidity or stupidity of a pompous staff surgeon with a little accidental temporary authority, and I by the means thrown upon a couch of sickness, from which I barely escaped with my life. After four weeks of suffering most intense, I rose in my weakness and repaired again to my post, and scarcely were my labors recommenced when, through the same influence or no influence brought to bear upon the

General Commanding, I was made the subject of a general order, and commanded to leave the island, giving me three hours in which to pack, remove, and ship four tons of supplies with no assistance that they knew of but one old female negro cook. I complied, but was remanded to Beaufort to labor in the hospitals there. With this portion of the "order" I failed to comply, and went home to Hilton Head and wrote the Commanding General a full explanation of my position, intention, proposed labors, etc., etc., which brought a rather sharp response, calling my humanity to account for not being willing to comply with his specified request, viz. to labor in Beaufort hospitals; insisting upon the plan as gravely as if it had been a possibility to be accomplished. But for the extreme ludicrousness of the thing I should have felt hurt at the bare thought of such a charge against me and from such a quarter. The hospitals were supplied by the Sanitary Commission, Miss Dix holding supremacy over all female attendants by authority from Washington, Mrs. Lander claiming, and endeavoring to enforce the same, and scandalizing through the Press—each hospital labeled, No Admittance, and its surgeons bristling like porcupines at the bare sight of a proposed visitor. How in reason's name was I "to labor there"? Should I prepare my food and thrust it against the outer walls, in the hope it might strengthen the patients inside? Should I tie up my bundle of clothing and creep up and deposit it on the doorstep and slink away like a guilty mother, and watch afar off to see if the master of the mansion would accept or reject the "foundling"? If the Commanding General in his wisdom, when he assumed the direction of my affairs, and commanded me where to labor, had opened the doors for me to enter, the idea would have seemed more practical. It did not occur to me at the moment how I was to effect an entrance to these hospitals, but I have since thought that I might have been expected to watch my opportunity some dark night, and storm them, although it must be confessed that the popularity of this mode of attack was rather on the decline in this department at that time, having reached its height very soon after the middle of July."

One other uncomfortable experience Clara Barton had at this time. When she first began her work for the relief of the soldiers, she went forth from Washington as a center and still kept up her work in the

Patent Office. When she found that this work was to take all her time, she approached the Commissioner of Patents and asked to have her place kept for her, but without salary. He refused this proposal, and said her salary should continue to be paid. The other clerks, also, were in hearty accord with this proposal, and offered to distribute her work among them. But as the months went by, this grew to be a somewhat laborious undertaking. The number of women clerks in the Patent Office had increased as so many of the men were in the army. There were twenty of these women clerks, some of whom had never known Clara Barton, and they did not see any reason why she should be drawing a salary and winning fame for work which they were expected to do. Moreover, the report became current that she was drawing a large salary for her war work in addition. The women in the Patent Office drew up a "round robin" demanding that her salary cease. This news, with the report that the Commissioner had acted upon the request, came to her while she had other things to trouble her. Had the salary ceased because she was no longer doing the work, it would have been no more than she had herself proposed. But when her associates, having volunteered to do the work for her that her place might be kept and her support continued, became the agents for the dissemination of a false report, she was hurt and indignant.

To the honor of Judge Holloway and his associates in the Patent Office, be it recorded that she received a letter from Judge Holloway that she had been misinformed about the termination of her salary; there had, indeed, been such a rumor and request, but he would not have acted on it without learning the truth, and did not credit it. Her desk would await her return if he continued as Commissioner.

A few days before Christmas another pleasant event occurred. Her nephew Stephen, whom she had continued to call "Bub," arrived in uniform. Though hardly fifteen, he had enlisted in the telegraph corps, and was sent to be with her. He became her closest friend in an intimacy of relation that did not cease until her eyes closed in death; and then, in her perfect confidence in him, she appointed him her executor.

A letter in this month reviews the experiences of her sojourn at Hilton Head:

Hilton Head, S.C.
Wednesday, December 9th, 1863

Mr. Parker,
My dear kind Friend:

It would be impossible for me to tell how many times I have commenced to write you. Sometimes I have put my letter by because we were doing so little there was nothing of interest to communicate; at other times, because there was so much I had not time to tell it, until some greater necessity drew me away, and my half-written letter became "rubbish" and was destroyed. And now I have but one topic which is of decided interest to me, and that is so peculiarly so that I will hasten to speak of it at once. After almost a year's absence, I am beginning to think about once more coming home, once more meeting the scores of kind friends I have been from so long; and the nearer I bring this object to my view, the brighter it appears. The nearer I fancy the meeting, the dearer the faces and the kinder the smiles appear to me and the sweeter the welcome voices that fall upon my ear. Not that I have not found good friends here. None could have been kinder. I came with one brother, loving, kind, and considerate; I have met others here scarcely less so, and those, too, with whom rested the power to make me comfortable and happy, and I have yet to recall the first instance in which they have failed to use their utmost endeavor to render me so, and while a tear of joy glistens in my eye at the thought of the kind friends I hope so soon to meet, there will still linger one of regret for the many of those I leave.

Eight months and two days ago we landed at the dock in this harbor. When nations move as rapidly as ours moves at present, that is a long time, and in it as a nation we have done much, gained much, and suffered much. Still much more remains to be done, much more acquired, and I fear much more suffered. Our brave and noble old Army of Virginia still marches and fights and the glorious armies of the West still fight and conquer; our soldiers still die upon the battle-field, pine in hospitals, and languish in prison; the wives and sisters and mothers still wait, and weep and hope and toil and pray, and the little child, fretting at the long-drawn days, asks in tearful impatience, "When will my papa come?"

The first sound which fell upon my ear in this Department was the thunder of our guns in Charleston Harbor, and still the proud city sits like a queen and dictates terms to our army and navy. Sumter, the watch-dog that lay before her door, fell, maimed and bleeding, it is true; still there is defiance in his growl, and death in his bite, and pierced and prostrate as he lies with the tidal waves lapping his wounds, it were worth our lives, and more than his, to go and take him.

We have captured one fort—Gregg—and one charnel house—Wagner—and we have built one cemetery, Morris Island. The thousand little sand-hills that glitter in the pale moonlight are a thousand headstones, and the restless ocean waves that roll and break upon the whitened beach sing an eternal requiem to the toil-worn, gallant dead who sleep beside.

As the year drew to a close, the conviction grew stronger that her work in this field was done. Charleston still resisted attempts to recapture it. Sumter, though demolished, was in the hands of the Confederates. There was no prospect of immediate battle, and unless there was fresh bloodshed there was no imperative call for her. Moreover, little jealousies and petty factions grew up around the hospitals and headquarters, where there were few women and many men, and there were rumors of mismanagement which she must hear, but not reply to. She had many happy experiences to remember, and she left a record of much good done. But her work was finished at that place. In her last entries in her diary she is disposing of her remaining stores, packing her trunk, and when, after a rather long interval, we hear from her again, she is in Washington.

THE WILDERNESS TO THE JAMES IN 1864

Clara Barton returned from Port Royal and Hilton Head sometime in January, 1864. On January 28 she was in Worcester, whence she addressed a letter to Colonel Clark in regard to the forthcoming reunion of veterans in Worcester. She did not expect to be present, as her stay in Massachusetts was to be brief.

On Sunday, February 14, she was in Brooklyn, and, as usual, went to hear Henry Ward Beecher. He preached on "Unwritten Heroism," and related some heroic incidents in the life of an Irish servant girl who, all unknown to fame, was still a heroine. Clara meditated on the sermon and regretted that she herself was not more heroic.

Before many days she was in Washington. It was rainy and cold. She found very little that was inspiring. Her room was cheerless, though she does not say so, but the little touches which she gave to it, as recorded, show how bare and comfortless it must have been. Her salary at the Patent Office continued, but it now becomes apparent that the arrangement whereby the other women in the Patent Office were to do her work had not continued indefinitely. She was hiring a partially disabled man to do her writing and was dividing her salary with him. Out of the balance she paid the rent of her room, eighty-four dollars a year, payable a year in advance. It was not exorbitant rent considering the demand for space in Washington. But it was a cheerless place, and she did not occupy it much. Principally, it was a storehouse for her supplies, with a place partitioned off for her own bedroom. She had many callers, however, Senator Wilson coming to see her frequently, and aiding her in every possible way. More than once she gave him information which he, as chairman of the Committee on Military Affairs of the United States Senate, utilized with far-reaching results. Sometimes she told him in the most uncompromising manner of what she regarded as abuses which she had witnessed. There were times when men seemed to her very cowardly, and the Government machinery very clumsy and ineffective. On the evening of April 13, 1864, she was fairly well disgusted with all mankind. She thus wrote her opinion of the human race, referring particularly to the masculine part of it:

I am thinking very busily about the result of the investigation into the Florida matter. Is General Seymour to be sacrificed when so many hundred people and the men know it to be all based on falsehood and wrong? Is there no manly justice in the world? Is there not one among them all that dares risk the little of military station he may possess to come out and speak the truth, and do the right? Oh, pity! O Lord, what is man that thou art mindful of him!

The next day was not a cheerful day for her. She was still brooding on some of these same matters. She tried in those days to escape from these unhappy reflections by going where she would be compelled to think of something else. But not even in church could she always keep her mind off of them. She wrote at length in her diary on the morning of the 14th, and that evening, when

Senator Wilson called, she told him what she thought of the United States Army, the United States Senate, and of people and things in general:

Thursday, April 14th, 1864. This was one of the most down-spirited days that ever came to me. All the world appeared selfish and treacherous. I can get no hold on a good noble sentiment anywhere. I have scanned over and over the whole moral horizon and it is all dark, the night clouds seem to have shut down, so stagnant, so dead, so selfish, so calculating. Is there no right? Are there no consequences attending wrong? How shall the world move on in all this weight of dead, morbid meanness? Shall lies prevail forevermore? Look at the state of things, both civil and military, that curse our Government. The pompous air with which little dishonest pimps lord it over their betters. Contractors ruining the Nation, and oppressing the poor, and no one rebukes them. See a monkey-faced official, not twenty rods from me, oppressing and degrading poor women who come up to his stall to feed their children, that he may steal with better grace and show to the Government how much his economy saves it each month. Poor blind Government never feels inside his pockets, pouching with ill-gotten gain, heavy with sin. His whole department know it, but it might not be quite wise for them to speak—they will tell it freely enough, but will not, dare not affirm it—cowards! Congress knows it, but no one can see that it will make votes for him at home by meddling with it, so it is winked at. The Cabinet know it, but people that live in glass houses must not throw stones. So it rests, and the women live lighter and sink lower, God help them. And next an ambitious, dishonest General lays a political plot to be executed with human life. He is to create a Senator, some memberships, a Governor, commissions, and all the various offices of a state, and the grateful recipients are to repay the favor by gaining for him his confirmation as Major-General. So the poor rank and file are marched out to do the job, a leader is selected known to be brave to rashness if need be, and given the command in the dark, that he may never be able to claim any portion of the glory—so that he cannot say did it. Doomed, and he knows it, he is sent on, remonstrates, comes back and explains, is left alone with the responsibility on his shoulders, forces divided, animals starving, men suffering, enemy massing in front, and still there he is. Suddenly he is attacked, defeated as he expected he must be, and the world is shocked by the tales of his rashness and procedure contrary to orders. He cannot speak; he is a subordinate officer and must remain silent; the thousands with him know it, but they must not speak; Congress does not know it, and refuses to be informed; and the doomed one is condemned and the guilty one asks for his reward, and the admiring world claims it for him. He has had a battle and only lost two thousand men and gained nothing. Surely, this deserved something. And still the world moves on. No wonder it looks dark, though, to those who do not wear the tinsel. And so my day has been weary with these thoughts, and my heart heavy and I cannot raise it—I doubt the justice of almost all I see.

Evening. At eight Mr. Wilson called. I asked him if the investigation was closed. He replied yes, and that General Seymour would leave the Department in disgrace. This was too much for my fretted soul, and I poured out the vials of my indignation in no stinted measure. I told him the facts, and what I thought of a Committee that was too imbecile to listen to the truth when it was presented to them; that they had made themselves a laughing-stock for even the privates in the service by their stupendous inactivity and gullibility; that they were all a set of dupes, not to say knaves, for I knew Gray of New York had been on using all his blarney with them that was possible to wipe over them. When I had freed my mind, and it was some time, he looked amazed and called for a written statement. I promised it. He left. I was anxious to possess myself of the most reliable facts in existence and decide to go to New York and see Colonel Hall and Dr. Marsh again; make my toilet ready, write some letters, and at three o'clock retired.

From all of this it will appear that Clara Barton had a rather gloomy time of it after her return to Washington. Old friends called on her and she was amid pleasant surroundings, but she was ill at ease. The Army of the Potomac had failed to hold its old position north of the Rappahannock. She anticipated the same old round which she had witnessed, marching and counter-marching with ineffective fighting, great suffering, and no permanent results. Nor did she see how she was henceforth to be of much assistance. The Sanitary and Christian Commissions were doing increasingly effective work in the gathering and distribution of supplies. The hospitals were approaching what ought to have been a state of efficiency. There seemed little place for her. She went to the War Department to obtain blanket passes, permitting herself and friend to go wherever she might deem it wise to go, and to have transportation for their supplies. She could hardly ask for anything less if she were to ask for anything, but it was a larger request than Secretary Stanton was at that time ready to grant. Her attempts to secure what she deemed necessary through the Medical Department were unavailing. The Medical Department thought itself competent to manage its own affairs. But she knew that there was desperate need of the kind of service which she could render.

For a time she questioned seriously whether she should not give up the whole attempt to return to the front. She even considered the possibility of asking for her old desk at the Patent Office, and letting the doctors and nurses take care of the wounded in the way they thought best.

The national conventions were approaching. A woman in Ohio who had worked with her on the battle-field wrote asking Miss

Barton for whom she intended to vote. She replied at considerable length. She intended to vote for the Republican candidate whoever he might be, because in so doing she would vote for the Union. She would not vote for McClellan nor for any other candidate nominated by his party. For three years she had been voting for Abraham Lincoln. She thought she still would vote for him; she trusted him and believed in him. But still if the Republicans should nominate Fremont, she would not withhold her approval. There was in Washington and in the army so much incompetence, so much rascality, it was possible that another President—especially one with military experience—would push the war to a speedier finish, and rout out some of the rascality she saw in Washington. She thought that Fremont might possibly have some advantage over Lincoln in this respect. But she rather hoped Lincoln would be renominated. He was so worthy, so honest, so kind, and the people could trust him. Though the abuses which had grown up under his administration were great, they were mostly inevitable. And so she rather thought she would vote for Lincoln, even in preference to the very popular hero, Fremont. Fremont had, indeed, seen, sooner than Lincoln, the necessity of abolition, and she thought would have a stronger grip on military affairs. But her heart was with Lincoln.

While she was waiting for a new call to service and was busy every day with a multitude of cares, she heard a lecture by the Reverend George Thompson, which is of interest because it enables us to discover how she now had come to feel about "Old John Brown." It will be remembered that she had not wholly approved the John Brown raid, nor shared in the public demonstrations that followed his execution. She had come, however, to a very different feeling with regard to him. On April 6, 1864, George Thompson, the abolitionist, gave an address in Washington. The address was delivered in the hall of the House of Representatives, and the President and Cabinet were among those who attended. Clara Barton was present, and close beside her in the gallery sat John Brown's brother.

For a few days previous she had been reading *No Name*, by Wilkie Collins. She compared his style to that of Dickens with some discriminating comments on the literary work of each. But she discontinued *No Name* when near the end of it, in order to read in preparation for the lecture by George Thompson. It will be well to quote her entry in her diary for the 5th and 6th of April:

Washington, April 5th, 1864, Tuesday. Rained all day just as if it had not rained every other day for almost two weeks, and I read as steadily indoors as it rained out; am nearly through with "No Name." Until 4 o'clock p.m. I had no disturbance, and then a most pleasant one. Mr. Brown came in to bring me letters from Mary Norton and Julia, and next to ask me to mend a little clothing, and next to present me a beautiful scrapbook designed for my own articles. It is a very beautiful article and I prize it much. Then my friend, Mr. Parker, called for a chat, and I read to him some two hours, in order to prepare his mind for George Thompson's lecture which is to occur to-morrow night. Then a call from Senator W., and next Dr. Elliott which lasted till just now, and it is almost eleven o'clock, and I have set my fire out and apparently passed the day to little purpose; still, I think it has glided away very innocently, and with a few minutes' preparation I shall retire with a grateful heart for the even, pleasant days which run so smoothly in my course.

Washington, April 6th, 1864, Wednesday. There are signs of clear weather, although it is by no means an established fact yet. I laid my reading aside, and took up my pen to address a letter to Mr. Wilson. I wrote at greater length than I had expected and occupied quite a portion of the day. The subject woke up the recollection of a train of ills and wrongs submitted to and borne so long that I suffered intensely in the reproduction of them, but I did reproduce, whether to any purpose or not time will reveal. It is not to be supposed that any decided revolution is to follow, as this is never to be looked for in my case. I have done expecting it, and done, I trust, with my efforts in behalf of others. I must take the little remnant of life that may remain to me as my own special property, and appropriate it accordingly. I had asked an appointment, as before referred to. I find I cannot make the use of it I had desired, and I have asked to recall the application. I have said I could not afford to make it. This was the day preceding the night of Mr. George Thompson's lecture in the Hall of Representatives. I went early with Mr. Brown. We went into the gallery and took a front seat in a side gallery. The House commenced to fill very rapidly with one of the finest-looking audiences that could be gathered in Washington. Conspicuous among them were Mr. Chase, Governor Sprague, Senator Wilson, Governor Boutwell and lady, Speaker Colfax, Thad. Stevens, and, to cap all, the brother of "Old John Brown" came and sat with us. At eight the orator of the evening entered the Hall in the same group with President Lincoln, Vice-President Hamlin, Rev. Mr. Pierpont, and others whom I did not recognize. Preliminary remarks were made by Mr. Pierpont. Next followed Mr. Hamlin, who introduced Mr. Thompson, who arose under so severe emotions that he could scarce utter a word. It seemed for a time that he would fall before the audience he had come to address. The contrast was evidently too great to be contemplated with composure; his sensitive mind reverted doubtless to his previous visits to this country, when he had seen himself hung and burnt in effigy, been mobbed, stoned, and assailed with "filthy missiles," and now he stood, almost deafened with applause, in the Hall of Representatives of America, America "free" from the shackles of slavery, and to address the President, and great political heads of the Nation. No wonder he was overcome, no wonder that the air felt thick, and his words came feebly, and his body bent beneath the weight of the contrast, the glorious consummation of all he had so earnestly labored and so devoutly prayed for. But by degrees his strength returned, and the rich melody of his voice filled every inch of the vast hall, and delighted every loyal, truth-loving ear. It would be useless for me to attempt a description of his address—it is so far immortal as to be always found, I trust, among the records of the glorious doings and sayings of our country's supporters. His endorsement of the President was one of the most touching and sublime things I have ever heard uttered, and the messages from England to him breathed a spirit of friendship which I was not prepared to listen to. Surely we are not to growl at and complain of England as jealous and hostile when her working-people, deprived of their daily labor and the support of their families through our difficulties, bid us Godspeed, and never to yield till our purpose has been accomplished, and congratulate us upon having achieved our independence in the War of the Revolution, and ask us now to go on and achieve a still greater independence, which shall embrace the whole civilized world. Surely these words show a nobler spirit in England than we had any reason or real right to expect. His remarks touching John Brown were strong, and, sitting as I was, watching the immediate effect upon the brother at my side, and when in a few minutes the band struck up the familiar air dedicated to him the world over, I truly felt that John Brown's Soul was marching on, and that the mouldering in the grave was of little account; the brother evidently felt the same. There was a glistening of the eye and a compression of the lip which spoke it all and more; he was evidently proud of the gallows rope that hung Old John Brown, "Old Hero Brown!"

On leaving the Hall, Mr. Parker joined us, and we all took a cream at Simmod's and returned, and I made good my escape to my room.

Since her return from Hilton Head, she had been furnished no passes. Official Washington had forgotten her in her year of absence. But there came a day when Clara Barton had no difficulty in obtaining passes, and when all Washington was willing enough to have her go to the front. That was when the battle of Spotsylvania occurred, May 8, 1864. It took Washington a day or two to realize the gravity of the situation; and Clara Barton was begging and imploring the opportunity to hasten at the sound of the first gun. There was refusal and delay; then, when it was realized that more than 2700 men had been killed and more than 13,000 wounded, her passes came. General Rucker, who had been endeavoring to secure them for her, obtained them, and sent them in haste by special messenger; and Clara Barton was back on the boat, landing, as so often before, at Acquia Creek, and wading through the red mud to where the wounded were.

They were everywhere; and most of all they were in wagons sunk to the hub in mud, and stalled where they could not get out, while men groaned and died and maggots crawled in their wounds. Bitterly she lamented the lost hours while she had been clamoring for passes; but now she set herself to work with such facilities as she could command, first for the relief of the wounded men in wagons:

The terrible slaughter of the Wilderness and Spotsylvania turned all pitying hearts and helping hands once more to Fredericksburg [she wrote afterward]. And no one who reached it by way of Belle Plain, while this latter constituted the base of supplies for General Grant's army, can have forgotten the peculiar geographical location, and the consequent fearful condition of the country immediately about the landing, which consisted of a narrow ridge of high land on the left bank of the river. Along the right extended the river itself. On the left, the hills towered up almost to a mountain height. The same ridge of high land was in front at a quarter of a mile distant, through which a narrow defile formed the road leading out, and on to Fredericksburg, ten miles away, thus leaving a level space or basin of an area of a fourth of a mile, directly in front of the landing.

Across this small plain all transportation to and from the army must necessarily pass. The soil was red clay. The ten thousand wheels and hoofs had ground it to a powder, and a sudden rain upon the surrounding hills had converted the entire basin into one vast mortar-bed, smooth and glassy as a lake, and much the color of light brick dust.

The poor, mutilated, starving sufferers of the Wilderness were pouring into Fredericksburg by thousands—all to be taken away in army wagons across ten miles of alternate hills, and hollows, stumps, roots, and mud!

The boats from Washington to Belle Plain were loaded down with fresh troops, while the wagons from Fredericksburg to Belle Plain were loaded with wounded men and went back with supplies. The exchange was transacted on this narrow ridge, called the landing.

I arrived from Washington with such supplies as I could take. It was still raining. Some members of the Christian Commission had reached an earlier boat, and, being unable to obtain transportation to Fredericksburg, had erected a tent or two on the ridge and were evidently considering what to do next.

To nearly or quite all of them the experience and scene were entirely new. Most of them were clergymen, who had left at a day's notice, by request of the distracted fathers and mothers who could not go to the relief of the dear ones stricken down by thousands, and thus begged those in whom they had the most confidence to go for them. They went willingly, but it was no easy task they had undertaken. It was hard enough for old workers who commenced early and were inured to the life and its work.

I shall never forget the scene which met my eye as I stepped from the boat to the top of the ridge. Standing in this plain of mortar-mud were at least two hundred six-mule army wagons, crowded full of wounded men waiting to be taken upon the boats for Washington. They had driven from Fredericksburg that morning. Each driver had gotten his wagon as far as he could, for those in front of and about him had stopped.

Of the depth of the mud, the best judgment was formed from the fact that no entire hub of a wheel was in sight, and you saw nothing of any animal below its knees and the mass of mud all settled into place perfectly smooth and glassy.

As I contemplated the scene, a young, intelligent, delicate gentleman, evidently a clergyman, approached me, and said anxiously, but almost timidly: "Madam, do you think those wagons are filled with wounded men?"

I replied that they undoubtedly were, and waiting to be placed on the boats then unloading.

"How long must they wait?" he asked.

I said that, judging from the capacity of the boats, I thought they could not be ready to leave much before night.

"What can we do for them?" he asked, still more anxiously.

"They are hungry and must be fed," I replied.

For a moment his countenance brightened, then fell again as he exclaimed: "What a pity; we have a great deal of clothing and reading matter, but no food in any quantity, excepting crackers."

I told him that I had coffee and that between us I thought we could arrange to give them all hot coffee and crackers.

"But where shall we make our coffee?" he inquired, gazing wistfully about the bare wet hillside.

I pointed to a little hollow beside a stump. "There is a good place for a fire," I explained, "and any of this loose brush will do."

"Just here?" he asked.

"Just here, sir."

He gathered the brush manfully and very soon we had some fire and a great deal of smoke, two crotched sticks and a crane, if you please, and presently a dozen camp-kettles of steaming hot coffee. My helper's pale face grew almost as bright as the flames and the smutty brands looked blacker than ever in his slim white fingers.

Suddenly a new difficulty met him. "Our crackers are in barrels, and we have neither basket nor box. How can we carry them?"

I suggested that aprons would be better than either, and, getting something as near the size and shape of a common tablecloth as I could find, tied one about him and one about me, fastened all four of the corners to the waist, and pinned the sides, thus leaving one hand for a kettle of coffee and one free, to administer it.

Thus equipped we moved down the slope. Twenty steps brought us to the abrupt edge which joined the mud, much as the bank of a canal does the black line of water beside it.

But here came the crowning obstacle of all. So completely had the man been engrossed in his work, so delighted as one difficulty after another vanished and success became more and more apparent, that he entirely lost sight of the distance and difficulties between himself and the objects to be served.

If you could have seen the expression of consternation and dismay depicted in every feature of his fine face, as he imploringly exclaimed, "How are we to get to them?"

"There is no way but to walk," I answered.

He gave me one more look as much as to say, "Are you going to step in there?" I allowed no time for the question, but, in spite of all the solemnity of the occasion, and the terribleness of the scene before me, I found myself striving hard to keep the muscles of my face all straight. As it was, the comers of my mouth would draw into wickedness, as with a backward glance I saw the good man tighten his grasp upon his apron and take his first step into military life.

But thank God, it was not his last.

I believe it is recorded in heaven—the faithful work performed by that Christian Commission minister through long weary months of rain and dust and summer suns and winter snows. The sick soldier blessed and the dying prayed for him, as through many a dreadful day he stood fearless and firm among fire and smoke (not made of brush), and walked calmly and unquestioningly through something redder and thicker than the mud of Belle Plain.

No one has forgotten the heart-sickness which spread over the entire country as the busy wires flashed the dire tidings of the terrible destitution and suffering of the wounded of the Wilderness whom I attended as they lay in Fredericksburg. But you may never have known how many hundredfold of these ills were augmented by the conduct of improper, heartless, unfaithful officers in the immediate command of the city and upon whose actions and indecisions depended entirely the care, food, shelter, comfort, and lives of that whole city of wounded men. One of the highest officers there has since been convicted a traitor. And another, a little dapper captain quartered with the owners of one of the finest mansions in the town, boasted that he had changed his opinion since entering the city the day before; that it was in fact a pretty hard thing for refined people like the people of Fredericksburg to be compelled to open their homes and admit "these dirty, lousy, common soldiers," and that he was not going to compel it.

This I heard him say, and waited until I saw him make his words good, till I saw, crowded into one old sunken hotel, lying helpless upon its bare, wet, bloody floors, five hundred fainting men hold up their cold, bloodless, dingy hands, as I passed, and beg me in Heaven's name for a cracker to keep them from starving (and I had none); or to give them a cup that they might have something to drink water from, if they could get it (and I had no cup and could get none); till I saw two hundred six-mule army wagons in a line,

221

ranged down the street to headquarters, and reaching so far out on the Wilderness road that I never found the end of it; every wagon crowded with wounded men, stopped, standing in the rain and mud, wrenched back and forth by the restless, hungry animals all night from four o'clock in the afternoon till eight next morning and how much longer I know not. The dark spot in the mud under many a wagon, told only too plainly where some poor fellow's life had dripped out in those dreadful hours.

I remembered one man who would set it right, if he knew it, who possessed the power and who would believe me if I told him [says Miss Barton in describing this experience]. I commanded immediate conveyance back to Belle Plain. With difficulty I obtained it, and four stout horses with a light army wagon took me ten miles at an unbroken gallop, through field and swamp and stumps and mud to Belle Plain and a steam tug at once to Washington. Landing at dusk I sent for Henry Wilson, chairman of the Military Committee of the Senate. A messenger brought him at eight, saddened and appalled like every other patriot in that fearful hour, at the weight of woe under which the Nation staggered, groaned, and wept.

He listened to the story of suffering and faithlessness, and hurried from my presence, with lips compressed and face like ashes. At ten he stood in the War Department. They could not credit his report. He must have been deceived by some frightened villain. No official report of unusual suffering had reached them. Nothing had been called for by the military authorities commanding Fredericksburg.

Mr. Wilson assured them that the officers in trust there were not to be relied upon. They were faithless, overcome by the blandishments of the wily inhabitants. Still the Department doubted. It was then that he proved that my confidence in his firmness was not misplaced, as, facing his doubters he replies: "One of two things will have to be done—either you will send someone to-night with the power to investigate and correct the abuses of our wounded men at Fredericksburg, or the' Senate will send someone to-morrow."

This threat recalled their scattered senses.

At two o'clock in the morning the Quartermaster-General and staff galloped to the 6th Street wharf under orders; at ten they were in Fredericksburg. At noon the wounded men were fed from the food of the city and the houses were opened to the "dirty, lousy soldiers" of the Union Army.

Both railroad and canal were opened. In three days I returned with carloads of supplies.

No more jolting in army wagons! And every man who left Fredericksburg by boat or by car owes it to the firm decision of one man that his grating bones were not dragged ten miles across the country or left to bleach in the sands of that city.

Yes, they owed it all to Senator Wilson. And he owed it to Clara Barton.

Why was there such neglect, and why did no one else report it?

The surgeons on the front were busy, and they did not see it. The surgeons and nurses in the base hospitals were busy, and they knew nothing of it. Military commanders only knew that the roads were bad, and that it was difficult to move troops to the front or wounded men back to the rear, but supposed that the best was being made of a bad matter. But Clara Barton knew that, if someone in authority could realize that thousands of men were suffering needless agony and hundreds were dying who might be saved, something would be done.

Something was done; and many a soldier who lived and regained his health had reason, without knowing it, to bless the name of Clara Barton.

At the close of the Wilderness campaign, Clara Barton found time to answer some letters and acknowledge some remittances. In one of these letters she answered the question why, being as she was in close touch and entire sympathy with the work of the Sanitary and Christian Commissions, she still continued to do her work independently. It is a thoroughly characteristic letter:

May 30, 1864

223

... The question would naturally arise with strangers, why I, feeling so in unison with the Commission and among whose members I number my best friends, should maintain a separated organization. To those who know me it is obvious. Long before either commission was in the field, or had even an existence, I was laboring by myself for the little I might be able to accomplish and, gathering such helpers about me as I was best able to do, toiled in the front of our armies wherever I could reach, and thus I have labored on up to the present time. Death has sometimes laid his hand upon the active forces of my co-workers and stilled the steps most useful to me, but others have risen up to supply the place, and now it does not seem wise or desirable, after all this time, to change my course. If I have by practice acquired any skill, it belongs to me to use untrammeled, and I might not work as efficiently, or labor as happily, under the direction of those of less experience than myself. It is simply just to all parties that I retain my present position, and through all up to the present time I have been always able to meet my own demands with such little supplies as came voluntarily from my circle of personal friends, which fortunately was not small. But the necessities of the present campaign were well-nigh overwhelming, and my duty required that I gather all I could, even if I shouted aloud to strangers for those who lay fainting and speechless by the wayside or moaning in this wilderness. I did so and such responses as yours have been the reply. Dearly do I think God poured his blessing on my little work, for the friends He has raised up to aid me, for the uninterrupted health and unfailing strength He has given me, and more and more with each day's observation do I stand overawed by the great lessons He is teaching us His children, grand and stern as the earthquake's shock, judgments soft and terrible as the lightning stroke. He is leading us back to a sense of justice and duty and humanity, while our thousand guns flash freedom and our martyrs die. It is a terrible sacrifice which He requires at our hands and in obedience the Nation has builded its altar and uplifted its arm of faith and the knife gleams above the child. He who commands it alone knows when His angel shall call from heaven to stay our hands and bid us no longer slay our own. Then may we find hidden in the peaceful thicket the appropriate sacrifice that in blessing He may bless us, that our young men return together, that our seed shall possess the gates of our enemies, and that all the nations of the earth be blessed..

TO THE END OF THE WAR

At the end of May, 1864, Clara Barton was in Washington. She wrote to her brother David informing him of her return to the city on the night of May 24. There had been, she told him, a series of terrible battles; she doubted if history had ever known men to be mowed down in regiments as in these battles. Victory had been won, but it was incomplete, and the cost had been terrible. She had seen nine thousand Confederate prisoners.

As to her future plans, she thought she would not go out from Washington a great deal during the excessively hot weather. She remembered her sickness of the previous summer, and did not wish to repeat it. But as for keeping her away in case there should be a battle, she would not count a kindness on anybody's part to attempt that. She said: "I suppose I should feel about as much benefited as my goldfish would if some kind-hearted person should take him out of his vase where he looked so wet and cold, and wrap him up in warm, dry flannel. We can't live out of our natural element, can we? I'll keep quiet when the war is over."

She was not permitted to stay in Washington and guard her health. She was appointed Superintendent of the Department of Nurses for the Army of the James. She was under the authority of Surgeon McCormack, Chief Medical Director. The army was commanded by General B. F. Butler. She entered this new field of service June 18, 1864. We have a letter which she wrote concerning a celebration, such as it was, of the 4th of July.

Point of Rocks, Va., July 5, 1864
General Butler's Department

My Most Esteemed and Dear Friend:

Here in the sunshine and dust and toil and confusion of camp life, the mercury above a hundred, the atmosphere and everything about black with flies, the dust rolling away in clouds as far as the eye can penetrate, the ashy ground covered with scores of hospital tents shielding nearly all conceivable maladies that soldier "flesh" is heir to, and stretching on beyond the miles of bristling fortifications, entrenchments, and batteries encircling Petersburg—all ready to blaze—just here in the midst of all this your refreshing letter dropped in upon me.

New York! It seemed to me that in the very postmark I could see pictured nice Venetian blinds, darkened rooms where never a fly dared enter, shady yards with cool fountains throwing their spray almost in at the open windows, watered streets flecked with the changing shadows of waving trees, bubbling soda fountains and water ices and grottoes and pony gallops in Central Park and cool drives at evening, and much more I have not time to enumerate, and for an instant I fear human selfishness triumphed, and, before I was aware, the mind had instinctively drawn a contrast, and the sun's rays glowed hotter and fiercer, and the dust rolled heavier, and my wayward heart complained to me that I was ever in the sun or dust or mud or frost, and impatiently asked if all the years of my life should pass and I never know again a season of quiet rest; and I confess it with shame. I trust that the suddenness with which it was rebuked may atone for its wickedness in some degree, and when I remembered the thousands who would so gladly come and share the toils with us, if only they could be free to do so, I gave thanks anew for my great privileges, and broke the seal of the welcome missive.

And you find hot weather even there, and have time among all the business of that driving city to remember the worn-out sufferers who are lying so helpless about us, many of whom have fought the last fight, kept the last watch, and, standing at the outer post, only wait to be relieved. The march has been toilsome, but the relief comes speedily at last—sometimes almost before we are aware. Yesterday in passing through a ward (if wards they might be termed) filled mostly from the U.S. Colored Regiments I stopped beside a sergeant who had appeared weak all day, but made no complaint, and asked how he was feeling then. Looking up in my face, he replied, "Thank you, Miss, a little better, I hope." "Can I do anything for you?" I asked. "A little water, if you please." I turned to get it, and that instant he gasped and was gone. Men frequently reach us at noon and have passed away before night. For such we can only grieve, for there is little opportunity to labor in their cases. I find a large number of colored people, mostly women and children, left in this vicinity, the stronger having been taken by their owners "up country." In all cases they are destitute, having stood the sack of two opposing armies—what one army left them, the other has taken.

On the plantation which forms the site of this hospital is a colored woman, the house servant of the former owner, with thirteen children, eight with her and five of her oldest taken away. The rebel troops had taken her bedding and clothing and ours had taken her money, forty dollars in gold, which she had saved, she said, and I do not doubt her statement in the least. I gave her all the food I had that was suitable for her and her children and shall try to find employment for her.

For the last few days we have been constantly meeting and caring for the wounded and broken-down from Wilson's cavalry raid; they have endured more than could be expected of men, and are still brave and cheerful under their sufferings.

I hope I shall not surprise you by the information that we celebrated the Fourth (yesterday) by giving an extra dinner. We invited in the lame, the halt, and the blind to the number of some two hundred or more to partake of roast beef, new potatoes, squash, blancmange, cake, etc., etc. We had music, not by the band, but from the vicinity of Petersburg, and, if not so sweet and perfectly timed as that discoursed by some of your excellent city bands, it must be acknowledged as both startling and thrilling, and was received with repeated "bursts."

I thank you much for your kind solicitude for my health. I beg to assure you that I am perfectly well at present and, with the blessing of Heaven, I hope to remain so.

Of the length of the campaign I have no adequate idea, and can form none. I should be happy to write you pages of events as they transpire every day, but duty must not be neglected for mere gratification.

Thus far I have remained at the Corps (which is, in this instance, only an overburdened and well-conducted field) hospital. This point, from its peculiar location, is peculiarly adapted to this double duty service, situated as it is at one terminus of the line of entrenchments.

This part of Clara Barton's war experience is least known of all that she performed. Her diaries were unkept and as her war lectures were mostly occupied with her earlier service in the field, they make almost no reference to this important part of her work. It is through her letters that we know something of what she experienced and accomplished in the closing months of 1864, and the early months of 1865. There is less material here of the kind that makes good newspaper copy or lecture material than was afforded by her earlier work in the open field, and it is probably on this account that this period has fallen so much into the shadow of forgetfulness that it has sometimes been said that Clara Barton retired from active service after the Wilderness campaign. Two letters, one to Frances Childs Vassall, and the other to Annie Childs, give somewhat intimate pictures of her life in this period, and may be selected out of her correspondence for that purpose.

Tenth Army Corps Hospital
September 3rd, 1864

My darling Sis Fannie:

It is almost midnight, and I ought to go to bed this minute, and I want to speak to you first, and I am going to indulge my inclination just a little minute till this page is down, if no more; but it will be all egotism, so be prepared, and don't blame me. I know you are doing well and living just as quietly and happily as you deserve to do. I hear from no one, and indeed I scarce write at all; and no one would wonder if they could look in upon my family and know besides that we had moved this week—yes, moved a family of fifteen hundred sick men, and had to keep our housekeeping up all the time; and no one to be ready at hand and ask us to take tea the first night either.

I have never told you how I returned—well, safely, and got off from City Point and my goods off its dock just in time to avoid that terrible catastrophe. I was not blown to atoms, but might have been and no one the wiser. I found my "sick family" somewhat magnified on my return, and soon the Corps (10th) was ordered to cross the James, and make a feint while the Weldon Railroad was captured, and this move threw all the sick in Regimental Hospital into our hospital, five hundred in one night. Only think of such an addition to a family between supper and breakfast and no preparation; and just that morning our old cook John and his assistant Peter both came down sick, one with inflammation of the lungs and the other with fever. It was all the surgeons, stewards, and clerks could do to keep the names straight and manage the official portion of the reception; and, would you believe it, I stepped into the gap and assumed the responsibility of the kitchen and feeding of our twelve hundred, and I held it and kept it straight till I selected a new boss cook and got him regularly installed and then helped him all the time up to the present day. I wish I had some of my bills of fare preserved as they read for the day. The variety is by no means so striking as the quantity. Say for breakfast seven hundred loaves of bread, one hundred and seventy gallons of hot coffee, two large wash-boilers full of tea, one barrel of apple sauce, one barrel of sliced boiled pork, or thirty hams, one half barrel of corn-starch blancmange, five hundred slices of butter toast, one hundred slices of broiled steak, and one hundred and fifty patients, to be served with chicken gruel, boiled eggs, etc. For dinner we have over two hundred gallons of soup, or boiled dinner of three barrels of potatoes, two barrels of turnips, two barrels of onions, two

228

barrels of squash, one hundred gallons of minute pudding, one wash-boiler full of whiskey sauce for it, or a large washtub full of codfish nicely picked, and stirred in a batter to make one hundred and fifty gallons of nice home codfish, and the Yankee soldiers cry when they taste it (I prepared it just the old home way, and so I have everything cooked), and the same toasts and corn starch as for breakfast. And then for supper two hundred gallons of rice, and twenty gallons of sauce for it, two hundred gallons of tea, toast for a thousand, and some days I have made with my own hands ninety apple pies. This would make a pie for some six hundred poor fellows who had not tasted pie for months, it might be years, sick and could not eat much. I save all the broken loaves of bread from transportation and make bread puddings in large milk pans; about forty at once will do. The patients asked for gingerbread, and I got extra flour and molasses and make it by the score. I have all the grease preserved and clarified, and to-morrow, if our new milk comes, we are to commence to make doughnuts. I have a barrel of nice lard ready (they had always burned it before to get it out of the way).

Last Saturday night we learned that we were to change with the Eighteenth Corps, and go up in front of Petersburg, and their first loads of sick came with the order. At dark I commenced to cook puddings and gingerbread, as I could carry them best. At two o'clock a.m. I had as many of these as I could carry in an ambulance, and packed my own things in an hour, and at three a.m. in the dark, started over the pontoon bridge across the Appomattox to our new base, about four miles. Got there a little before day, and got some breakfast ready about 8.30 for four hundred men that had crossed the night previous, nearly one hundred officers. The balance followed, and in eighteen hours from the receipt of the order we were all moved—but a poor change for us. Since dark forty wounded men have been brought in, many of which will prove mortal, one with the shoulder gone, a number of legs off, one with both arms gone, some blown up with shells and terribly burned, some in the breast. By request of the surgeons, I made a pail full of nice thick eggnog (eggs beaten separately and seasoned with brandy), and carried all among them, to sleep on, and chicken broth, and I have left them all falling asleep, and I have stolen away to my tent, which is as bare as a cuckoo's nest—dirt floor, just like the street, a narrow bed of straw, and a three-legged stand made of old cracker boxes, and a wash dish. A hospital tent without any fly constitutes my apartment and furnishing. And here it is one o'clock, damp and cold, one little fellow from the 11th Maine dying, whose groans have echoed through the camp for hours. Another noble Swiss boy, I fear mortally wounded, who thinks he shall not live till morning, and has gained a promise from me that I will see him and be with him when he dies (I have still hopes of his recovery). Oh, what a volume it would make if I could only write you what I have seen, known, heard, and done since I first came to this department, June 18th. The most surprising of all of which is (tell Sally) that I should have turned cook. Who would have "thunk it"?

I am writing on bits of paper for want of whole sheets. I am entirely out. My dresses are equal to the occasion; the skirt is finished, but not worn yet. I am choice of it. The striped print gets soiled and washes nicely, all just right, and I have plenty, and I bless you every day for it. I want so to write Annie a good long letter, but how can I get time? Please give her from this, if you please, an idea of what I am doing, and she will not blame me so much.

Tell Sally that our purchases of tinware were just the thing, and but for them this hospital could not be kept comfortable a single day, not a meal. I wish I had as much more, and a nice stove of my own, with suitable stove furniture besides. And I think I could do as much good with it as some missionaries are supposed to do. Our spices and flavorings were Godsends when I got them here. I wish I had boxes of them. I need to use so much in my big cooking. There, I said it would be all egotism, but I am too stupid to think of anybody but myself, so forgive me. Give my love to all and write your loving Sis,

Clara

From letters such as this we are able to rescue from oblivion a full year of war service of Clara Barton. Contrary to all her previous intent, she was a head-nurse, in charge of the hospitals of an entire army corps. Not only so, but she was on occasion chief cook and purveyor of pie and gingerbread, and picked codfish and New England boiled dinners so like what the soldiers loved at home that they sometimes cried for joy. But she did not relinquish her purpose to be at the front. The front was very near to her. Another of her letters must be quoted:

Base Hospital, 10th Army Corps Broadway Landing, Va.

Sept. 14th, 1864

My dear Sis Annie:

Your excellent and comforting letter reached me some time ago, and, like its one or two abused predecessors, has vainly waited a reply. I cannot tell how badly I have wanted to write you, how impossible I found it to get the time. But often enough an attack of illness has brought me a leisure hour, and I am almost glad that I can make it seem right for me to sit down in daylight and pen a letter.

For once in my life I am at a loss where to commence. I have been your debtor so long, and am so full of unsaid things, that I don't know which idea to let loose first. Perhaps I might as well speak of the weather. Well, it rains, and that is good for my conscience again, for I couldn't get out in that if I were well enough. Rain here means mud, you must understand, but I am sheltered. Why, I have a whole house of my own, first and second floors, two rooms and a flight of stairs, and a great big fireplace, a bright fire burning, a west window below, a south one above, an east door, with a soldier-built frame arbor of cedar, twelve feet in front of it and all around it, so close and green that a cat couldn't look in, unless at my side opening. It was the negro house for the plantation, and was dirty, of course, but ten men with brooms and fifty barrels of water made it all right, and they moved me into it one night when I was sick, and here I have lain and the winds have blown and the rains descended and beat upon my house, and it fell not, and for hours in the dark night I have listened to the guy ropes snapping and the tent flies flapping in the wind and rain, and thunder and lightning. All about me are the frail habitations of my less fortunate neighbors. One night I remembered a darling little Massachusetts boy, sick of fever and chronic diarrhoea, a mere skeleton, and I knew he was lying at the very edge of his ward, tents, of course—delicate little fellow, about fifteen—and I couldn't withstand the desire to shield him, and sent through the storm and had him brought, bed and all, and stored in my lower room, and there he lay like a little kitten, so happy, till about noon the next day, when his father, one of the wealthy merchants of Suffolk, came for him. He had just heard of his illness, had searched through the damp tents for him and finally traced him to me. The unexpected sight of his little boy, sheltered, warm, and fed, nearly deprived him of speech, but when those pale lips said, "Auntie—father—this is my Auntie; doesn't she look like mother?" It was too much. Women's and children's tears amount to little, but the convulsive sobs of a strong man are not forgotten in an hour.

Well, I have made a queer beginning of this letter. One would have supposed I should have made it my first duty to speak of the nice box that came to me, from you, by Mrs. Rich, and how choice I was of it, and did not take it with me the first time I went for fear I might not find the most profitable spot to use it in just then till I had found my field. As good luck would have it, it did not take long to find my field of operations; and

nothing but want of time to write has prevented me from acknowledging the box many times, and expressing the desire that others might follow it. I can form no estimate of what I would and should have made use of during the campaign thus far, if I had had it to use. I doubt if you at home could realize the necessities if I could describe everyone accurately, and now the cold weather approaches, they will increase in some respects. The army is filling up with new troops to a great degree and the nights are getting cold..
..

I was rejoiced to hear from Lieutenant Hitchcock and that he is doing well. You are favored in so pleasant a correspondent as I know he must be, and what a comfort to his wife to have him home so soon. I hope his wound will not disable him very much. Please give my love and congratulations to them when you write. Poor fellows! how sorry I was to see them lying there under the trees, so cut and mangled. Poor Captain Clark! Do you know if he is alive? the surgeons told me he couldn't survive. I went up again to see them, a day or two after they all left. Colonel Gould had gone the day before. Yes! I lost one friend. Poor Gardner! He fought bravely and died well, they said, and laid his mangled body at the feet of his foe. I feel sad when I think of it all. "Tired a little"—not tired of the war, but tired of our sacrifices.

I passed a most pleasant hour with Lieutenant Hitchcock. It seemed so comfortable and withal so quaint and strange to sit down under the sighing pines of Virginia away out in the woods in the war of the guns and talk of you. I have asked a great many times for Mr. Chamberlain and only heard twice—he was well each time, but this was not lately. I shall surely go to him if I get near the dear old regiment (21st regiment)—that is more than I ever said of any other regiment in the service. I am a stranger to them now, I know, after all their changes; few of them ever heard of me, and yet the very mention of the number calls up all the old-time love and pride I ever had. I would divide the last half of my last loaf with any soldier in that regiment, though I had never seen him. I honor him for joining it, be he who he may; for he knew well if he marched and fought with that regiment he had undertaken no child's play, and those who measured steel with them knew it as well.

The Oxford ladies at work for me again!! I am very glad if they have the confidence to do so. I had thought, perhaps, my style of labor was not approved by them; but I could not help it. I knew it was rough, but I thought it none the less necessary. If they do so far approve as to send me the proceeds of some of their valuable labors, it will be an additional stimulant to me to persevere.

Do you know I am thinking seriously of remaining "out" the winter unless the campaign should come to a sudden and decisive stand, and nothing be done and no one exposed.

You know that my range here is very extended; this department is large, and I am invited by General Butler to visit every part of it, and all medical and other officers within the department are directed to afford me every facility in their power. But so little inclination do they display to thwart me that I have never shown my "pass and order" to an officer since I have been in the department. I have had but one trouble since I came, and that has been to extend my labor without having the point that I leave miss me.

We have now in the 10th Corps two main hospitals and no regimental hospital; the "base," where I am at present, about four miles from the extreme front, and the "Flying" Hospital three miles farther up—in the rear of the front line of works. The most skillful operators are always here, and all the surgeons at that post are my old-time personal friends. Dr. Barlow I worked with at Cedar Mountain and through Pope's retreat, and again on Morris Island; and he says, if I am going to desert my old friends now, just say so, that's all. And I have stood by Dr. Porter all summer, and Porter says he will share me some with the upper hospital, but I must not leave the Corps on any condition whatever. And yet the surgeon in charge of one of the largest corps in General Grant's army at City Point came for me one day last week and would hardly be denied; wanted me to help him "run" his hospital—"not to touch a bit of the work." I begin to think I can "keep a hotel," but I didn't think so a year ago. Well, I have told you all this to show you how probable it is that I shall find it difficult to get off the field this fall or even winter.

And thank you many times for your sisterly invitation to spend some portion of the winter with you. I should be most happy to do so, but it is a little doubtful if I get north of Washington this winter, unless the war ends suddenly, and I am beginning to study my duty closely. I can go to the Flying Hospital, and be just along with the active army; and then, if I had a sufficient quantity of good suitable supplies, I could keep the needy portion of a whole corps comfortably supplied; and being connected with the hospital and convalescent camp, conversant with the men, surgeons, and nurses, I could meet their wants more timely and surely than any stranger or outside organization of men could do. And ladies, most of the summer workers, will draw off, with the cool nights; men who have been accustomed to feather beds, will seek them if they can when the frost comes. Nevertheless the troops will need the same care—good warm shirts, socks, drawers, and mittens, and the sick will need the same good, well-cooked diet that they did in summer; and yet it would try me dreadfully to be among them in the cold and nothing comfortable to give them. And this corps especially never passed a winter north of South Carolina and they will nearly freeze, I fear. I have scraped together and given already the last warm article I have just for the few frosty nights we have had. I haven't a pair of socks or shirts or drawers for a soldier in my possession. I shall look with great anxiety now for anything to reach me, for I shall require it both on account of the increased severity of the weather and my proposed extended field of labor. I have the 4th Massachusetts Cavalry on hand, and they have a hospital of their own and a good many sick. I gave them, one day last week, the last delicacy I possessed; it was but little—some New York and New Jersey fruits; nothing from Massachusetts for them. I was sorry; I wish I had. If I go to the Flying Hospital it will be entirely destitute of all but soldier's blankets and rations, not a bedsack or pillow, sheet or pillowcase, or stove or tin dishes, except cups and plates. Now, I should want some of all these things, and if I go I must write to some of the friends of the soldiers the wants I see, and if they are disposed they can place it in my power to make them comfortable, independent of army regulations. You know this front hospital is for operations in time of battle, and subject to move at an hour's notice, or when the shot might reach it, or the enemy press too near, and must not be encumbered with baggage. Ask Lieutenant Hitchcock to explain it to you, and he will also tell you how useful a private supply connected with it might be, what comfort there would be in it, and how I could distribute from such a point to the troops along the front. Now, with my best regards to the good ladies of Oxford, I am done about soldiers and hospitals.

Oh, if I had time to write! I have material enough, "dear knows," but I cannot get time to half acknowledge favors received. If someone would come and act as scribe for me, I might be the means of relating some interesting incidents; but I have not even a cook or orderly, not to say a clerk. I do not mean that I cannot have the two former, but I do not use them myself at all when I hold them in detail. I immediately get them at work for someone who I think needs them more. I am glad you see my Worcester friends. You visited at Mr. Newton's, I suppose. I hope they are well. Please give my love to them

We are firing a salute for something at this minute, don't yet know what. We fired one over the fall of Atlanta; solid shot and shell with the guns pointed toward Petersburg. Funny salutes we get up here. Yesterday morn we had terrible firing along the whole line, but it amounted to only an artillery duel. Yet it brought us fourteen wounded, three or four mortally.

What a long letter I have written you and I am not going to apologize and I know you are not tired even if it is long, you are glad of it, and so am I, although it is not very interesting.

Please give my kindly and high regards to Miss Sanford and Mrs. Burleigh, Colonel De Witt, also, and all inquiring-friends and write soon to your affectionate

Sis

Clara

This letter was copied by Annie Childs, and bears this note in the handwriting of Annie Childs:

I have my friend Clara's permission to show any portion of her "poor scrawls" that I think would interest the excellent ladies who are laboring so faithfully for the good and comfort of the soldiers, and trust to their charity to overlook imperfections. Many portions of the above are copied for the benefit of persons in Worcester and other places, as I could not get time to write many copies like this, which is three fourths of my letter from her.

Annie E. Childs

It must have been something of a relief to Clara Barton to be working in a definite sphere under military authority, and not as a volunteer worker. Not that she regretted for a moment the method of her previous activity. She would never have worked cheerfully as a part of the organization commanded by Miss Dix. She had too clear ideas of her own, and saw the possibilities of too large a work for her to be content with any sort of long-range supervision. All the women who really achieved large success at the front were individualists. "Mother" Bickerdyke, for instance, took no orders from anyone. General Sherman was accustomed to say of her that she ranked him. But Miss Barton's field for volunteer service was now limited. The war was closing in, and nearing its end. Clara Barton wisely accepted a definite appointment and took up her work with the army of General Butler. How highly he esteemed her service is shown by his lifelong friendship for her, and his appointment of her to be matron of the Massachusetts Reformatory for Women.

Clara Barton knew, before she went to the Army of the James, how impossible it was to obtain ideal conditions in a military hospital. She must have been very glad that she had refused to criticize the hospitals at Hilton Head, even when she knew that things were going wrong. She had her own experience with headstrong surgeons and incompetent nurses. But on the whole her experience in the closing days of the war was satisfactory.

One incident which she had looked forward to with eager longing, and had almost given up, occurred while she was with the Army of the James. Her brother Stephen was rescued.

It was a pathetic rescue. He was captured by the Union army, and robbed of a considerable sum of money which had been in his possession. When he was brought within the Union lines, he was sick, and he suffered ill treatment after his capture. The date of his capture was September 25, 1864. It was some days before Miss Barton learned about it. She then reported the matter to General Butler, and it was at once ordered that Stephen be brought to his headquarters with all papers and other property in his possession at the time of his capture. The prisoner was sent and such papers as had been preserved, but the money was not recovered. Two long letters, written by Stephen Barton from the hospital, tell the story of his life within the Confederate lines, and it is a pathetic story.

Stephen Barton was treated with great kindness while he remained in the hospital at Point of Rock. He was there during the assault on Petersburg, and well toward the end of the campaign against Richmond. Then he was removed to Washington, where, on March 10, 1865, he died. Miss Barton had the satisfaction of ministering to him during those painful days, and she afterward wrote down her recollection of a prayer he offered one night after a battle in front of Richmond:

An hour with my dear noble brother Stephen, during a night after a battle in front of Richmond.

Clara. Barton

My brother Stephen, when with me in front of Richmond

Hearing a voice I crept softly down my little confiscated stairway and waited in the shadows near his bedside. He had turned his face partly into his pillow and, resting it upon his hands, was at prayer. The first words which my ear caught distinctly were, "O God, whose children we all are, look down with thine eye of justice and mercy upon this terrible conflict, and weaken the wrong and strengthen the right till this unequal contest close. O God, save my Country. Bless Abraham Lincoln and his armies." A sob from me revealed my presence. He started, and, raising his giant skeleton form until he rested upon his elbow, he said, "I thought I was alone." Then, turning upon me a look of mingled anxiety, pity, and horror, which I can never describe, he asked hastily, "Sister, what are those incessant sounds I hear? The whole atmosphere is filled with them; they seem like the mingled groans of human agony. I have not heard them before. Tell me what it is." I could not speak the words that would so shock his sensitive nature, but could only stand before him humbled and penitent as if I had something to do with it all, and feel the tears roll over my face. My silence confirmed his secret suspicions, and raising himself still higher, and every previous expression of his face intensifying tenfold, he exclaimed, "Are these the groans of wounded men? Are they so many that my senses cannot take them in?—that my ear cannot distinguish them?" And raising himself fully upright and clasping his bony hands, he broke forth in tones that will never leave me. "O our God, in mercy to the poor creatures thou hast called into existence, send down thine angels either in love or wrath to stay this strife and bid it cease. Count the least of these cries as priceless jewels, each drop of blood as ruby gems, and let them buy the Freedom of the world. Clothe the feet of thy messengers with the speed of the lightning and bid them proclaim, through the sacrifices of a people, a people's freedom, and, through the sufferings of a nation, a nation's peace." And there, under the guns of Richmond, amid the groans of the dying, in the darkling shadows of the smoky rafters of an old negro hut by the rude chimney where the dusky form of the bondman had crouched for years, on the ground trodden hard by the foot of the slave, I knelt beside that rough couch of boards and sobbed "Amen" to the patriot prayer that rose above me.

The stolen money was never restored. Stephen struggled on a few weeks longer, alternating, hoping, and despairing, suffering from the physical abuse he had received, crushed in spirit, battling with disease and weakness as only a brave man can, worrying over his unprotected property and his debts in the old home he never reached, watching the war, and praying for the success of the Union armies, and died without knowing—and God be praised for this—that the reckless torches of that same Union army would lay in ashes and ruins the result of the hard labor of his own worn-out life and wreck the fortunes of his only child.

Although doubting and fearing, we had never despaired of his recovery, until the morning when he commenced to sink and we saw him rapidly passing away. He was at once aware of his condition and spoke of his business, desiring that, first of all, when his property could be reached, his debts should be faithfully paid. A few little minutes more and there lay before us, still and pitiful, all that remained to tell of that hard life's struggle and battle, which had failed most of all through a greathearted love for humanity, his faithfulness to what he conceived to be his duty, and his readiness to do more for mankind than it was willing to do for itself.

Clara Barton did not long continue in hospital service after the immediate need was passed. With the firing of the last gun she returned to Washington. One chapter in her career was closed. Another and important work was about to open, and she already had it in mind. But the work she had done was memorable, and its essential character must not be forgotten.

Clara Barton was more and other than a hospital nurse. She was not simply one of a large number of women who nursed sick soldiers. She did that, hastening to assist them at the news of the very first bloodshed, and continuing until Richmond had fallen. Hers was the distinction of doing her work upon the actual field of battle; of following the cannon so as to be on the ground when the need began; of not waiting for the wounded soldier to be brought to the hospital, but of conveying the hospital to the wounded soldier. Others followed her in this good work; others accompanied her and were her faithful associates, but she was, in a very real sense, the soul and inspiration of the movement which carried comfort to wounded men while the battle was still in progress. She was not, in any narrow sense, a hospital nurse; she was, as she has justly been called, "the angel of the battlefield."

One characteristic of Clara Barton during these four years deserves mention and emphasis because her independent position might have made it easy for her to assume a critical attitude toward those who worked under the regular organization or through different channels. In all her letters, in all the entries in her diaries, there is found no hint of jealousy toward any of the women who worked as nurses in the hospitals, or under the Sanitary or Christian Commission.

ANDERSONVILLE AND AFTER

Clara Barton's name continued on the roll of clerks in the Patent Office until August, 1865. She drew her salary as a clerk throughout the period of the Civil War, and it was the only salary that she drew during that time. Out of it she paid the clerk who took her place during the latter months of her employment, and also the rent of the room in Washington, where she stored her supplies and now and then slept. When she was at the front, she shared the rations of the army. Most of the time her food was the food of the officers of the division where she was at work. Much of the time it was the humble fare of the common soldier. Mouldy and even wormy hardtack grew to be quite familiar to her, and was eaten without complaint.

As the end of the war drew near, she discovered a field of service in which her aid was greatly needed. Every battle in the Civil War had, in addition to its list of known dead and wounded, a list of "missing." Some of these missing soldiers were killed and their bodies not found or identified. Of the 315,555 graves of Northern troops, only 172,400 were identified. Almost half of the soldiers buried in graves known to the quartermaster of the Federal army were unidentified; 143, 155 were buried in graves known to be the graves of soldiers, but with no soldier's name to mark them. Besides these there were 43,973 recorded deaths over and above the number of graves. The total of deaths recorded was 359,528, while the number of graves, as already stated, was 315,555. As a mere matter of statistics, this may not seem to mean very much, but it actually means that nearly two hundred thousand homes received tidings of the death of a father, son, or brother, and did not know where that loved one was buried. This added to grief the element of uncertainty, and in many cases of futile hope.

In the twenty-first century, it's accepted that approximately 620,000 soldiers died on both sides from combat, accident, starvation, and disease during the Civil War. This number comes from an 1889 study of the war performed by William F. Fox and Thomas Leonard Livermore. Other estimates have been higher. Over 3.1 million men served.—Ed.

Moreover, there were many other thousands of men reported missing of whom no certain knowledge could be obtained at the close of the Civil War. Some were deserters, some were bounty-jumpers, some were prisoners, some were dead. Clara Barton received countless letters of inquiry. From all over the country letters came asking whether in any hospital she had seen such and such a soldier.

Clearly foreseeing that the end of the war was in sight, Clara Barton, who had gone from City Point, where she was serving with General Butler's army, to Washington, where she witnessed the death of her brother Stephen, brought to the attention of President Lincoln the necessity of instituting some agency for the finding of missing soldiers. She knew what her own family had suffered in the anxious months when Stephen was immured within the Confederate lines, and his relatives did not know whether he was living or dead. President Lincoln at once approved her plan, and issued a letter advising the friends of missing soldiers to communicate with Miss Barton at Annapolis, where she established her headquarters. President Lincoln's letter was dated March 11, 1865, the day following the death of her brother Stephen. This was followed, March 25, by a letter from General Hitchcock;

Washington, D.C., March 25, 1865
For the Commanding Officer at Annapolis, Md.
Sir:
The notice, which you have doubtless seen, over the name of Miss Barton, of Massachusetts, proffering her services in answering inquiries with respect to Union officers and soldiers who have been prisoners of war (or who remain so) was made by my authority under the written sanction of His Excellency the President.

The purpose is so humane and so interesting in itself that I beg to recommend Miss Barton to your kind civilities, and to say that any facilities which you may have it in your power to extend to her would be properly bestowed, and duly appreciated, not only by the lady herself, but by the whole country which is interested in her self-appointed mission.

With great resp. your obt. servant
(Signed) E. A. Hitchcock Maj. Gen'l. Vols.

Although she was backed by the authority of the President, it took the War Department two months to establish Clara Barton in her work at Annapolis with the title "General Correspondent for the Friends of Paroled Prisoners." A tent was assigned her, with furniture, stationery, clerks, and a modest fund for postage. By the time she was established at Annapolis, she found bushels of mail awaiting her, and letters of inquiry came in at the rate of a hundred a day. To bring order out of this chaos, and establish a system by which missing soldiers and their relatives could be brought into communication with each other, called for swift action and no little organizing skill. For a time difficulties seemed to increase. Discharged prisoners returned from the South by thousands. In some cases there was no record, in others the record was defective. Inquiries came in much faster than information in response to them.

Notwithstanding all the difficulties, Clara Barton had a long list of missing men ready for publication by the end of May. Then the question rose how she was to get it published. It was not wholly a matter of expense, though this was an important item. There was only one printing office in Washington which had type enough, and especially capitals enough, to set up such a roll as at that time she had ready. In this emergency she appealed directly to the President of the United States, asking that the roll be printed at the Government Printing Office. Her original letter to President Johnson is in existence, together with a series of endorsements, the last of them by Andrew Johnson himself. General Rucker was the first official to endorse it, Major-General Hitchcock added his commendation, General Hoffman followed, then came General Grant, and last of all the President:

Abraham Lincoln was assassinated on April 14, 1865. This letter is to his successor, Andrew Johnson.—Ed.

Washington, D.C., May 31st, 1865

His Excellency
President of the United States
Sir:
May I venture to enclose for perusal the within circular in the hope that it may to a certain extent explain the object of the work in which I am engaged. The undertaking having at its first inception received the cordial

and written sanction of our late beloved President, I would most respectfully ask for it the favor of his honored successor.

The work is indeed a large one; but I have a settled confidence that I shall be able to accomplish it. The fate of the unfortunate men failing to appear under the search which I shall institute is likely to remain forever unrevealed.

My rolls are now ready for the press; but their size exceeds the capacity of any private establishment in this city, no printer in Washington having forms of sufficient size or a sufficient number of capitals to print so many names.

It will be both inconvenient and expensive to go with my rolls to some distant city each time they are to be revised. In view of this fact I am constrained to ask our honored President, when he shall approve my work, as I must believe he will, to direct that the printing may be done at the Government Printing Office.

I may be permitted to say in this connection that the enclosed printed circular appealing for pecuniary aid did not originate in any suggestion of mine, but in the solicitude of personal friends, and that thus far, in whatever I may have done, I have received no assistance either from the Government or from individuals. A time may come when it will be necessary for me to appeal directly to the American People for help, and in that event, such appeal will be made with infinitely greater confidence and effect, if my undertaking shall receive the approval and patronage of Your Excellency.

I have the honor to be, Sir
Most respectfully
Your obedient servant

Clara Barton

Official endorsements on back of her letter

Chief Quartermaster's Office Depot of Washington

June 2, 1865
I most heartily concur in the recommendations on this paper. I have known Miss Barton for a long time and it gives me great pleasure to aid her in her good works.

F. H. Rucker Brig. Gen'l & Chf. Q.M.

The undersigned, with a full understanding of the benevolent purpose of Miss Barton and of its deep interest for the public, most cordially commends it to the approval of the President of the United States.

E. A. Hitchcock Maj. Gen. Vol.

June 2, 1865

I most heartily concur in the foregoing recommendations.

W. Hoffman Com. Gen'l Pris.

Respectfully recommended that the printing asked for be authorized at the Government Printing Office. The object being a charitable one, to look up and ascertain the fate of officers and soldiers who have fallen into the hands of the enemy and have never been restored to their families and friends, is one which Government can well aid.

U. S. Grant
L.G.

June 2d, 1865.

June 3d, 1865

Let this printing be done as speedily as possible consistently with the public interest.

Andrew Johnson
Prest. U.S.

To Mr. Defrees Supt. Pub. Printing

On the same date, June 2, 1865, Miss Barton received a pass from General Grant commending her to the kind consideration of all officers and instructing them to give her all facilities that might be necessary in the prosecution of her mission. By General Grant's order, there was also issued to her transportation for herself and two assistants on all Government railroads and transports:

Headquarters Armies of the United States

Washington, D.C., June 2d, 1865

The bearer hereof, Miss Clara Barton, who is engaged in making inquiries concerning the fate of soldiers reported as missing in action, is commended to the kind consideration of all officers of the military service, and she will be afforded by commanders and others such facilities in the prosecution of her charitable mission as can properly be extended to her.

U. S. Grant
Lieut. General Comdg.

———

Headquarters Armies of the United States

Washington, D.C., June 2nd, 1865 Miss Clara Barton, engaged in making inquiries for soldiers reported as missing in action, will be allowed, until further orders, with her assistants, not to exceed two in number, free transportation on all Government railroads and transports.

By Command of Lieut.-General Grant

T. S. Breck Asst. Adjt. Genl.

Clara Barton had learned the value of publicity. She knew that the Press could be counted upon to assist an undertaking so near to the hearts of all readers of the papers. She therefore arranged her lists by States, and sent the list of each State to every newspaper in the State with the request for its free publication. Before long she had established definite connections with scores of newspapers which responded favorably to her request. No one read these lists more eagerly than recently discharged men, including prisoners and men released from hospitals. In innumerable instances these men wrote to her to give information of the death or survival, with location, of some comrade whose name had been published in one of her lists.

Sometimes she succeeded not only beyond her own expectation, but beyond the desire of the man who was sought. Occasionally a soldier who went into voluntary obscurity at the end of the war found himself unable to remain in as modest a situation as he had chosen for himself. A few letters are found of men who indignantly remonstrated against being discovered by their relatives. One such case will serve as an illustration. The first of the following letters is from the sister of a missing soldier. The second, six months later, is a protest from the no longer missing man, and the third is Clara's indignant reply to him:

Lockport, N.Y., April 17th, 1865

Miss Clara Barton Dear Madam:

Seeing a notice in one of our village papers stating that you can give information concerning soldiers in the army or navy, you will sincerely oblige me if you can give any intelligence of my brother, Joseph H. H—, who was engaged in the 2nd Maryland Regiment under General Goldsborough, and from whom we have not heard in nearly two years. His mother died last winter, to whom his silent absence was, I assure you, a great grief, and to whom I promised to make all inquiries in my power, so that I might if possible learn my brother's fate. I would most willingly remunerate you for all trouble.

Yours respectfully

E— H—

___

Springfield, Ills., Oct. 16, 1865

Miss Clara Barton,
Washington, D.C.
Madam:

I have seen my name on a sheet of paper somewhat to my mortification, for I would like to know what I have done, so that I am worthy to have my name blazoned all over the country. If my friends in New York wish to know where I am, let them wait until I see fit to write them. As you are anxious of my welfare, I would say that I am just from New Orleans, discharged, on my way North, but unluckily taken with chills and fever and could proceed no farther for some time at least. I shall remain here for a month.

Respectfully, your obt. servt.

J.H. H—

___

Mr. J.H. H—
Sir:—

I enclose copies of two letters in my possession. The writer of the first I suppose to be your sister. The lady for whose death the letter was draped in mourning I suppose to have been your mother. Can it be possible that you were aware of that fact when you wrote that letter? Could you have spoken thus, knowing all?

The cause of your name having been "blazoned all over the country" was your unnatural concealment from your nearest relatives, and the great distress it caused them. "What you have done" to render this necessary I certainly do not know. It seems to have been the misfortune of your family to think more of you than you did of them, and probably more than you deserve from the manner in which you treat them. They had already waited until a son and brother possessing common humanity would have "seen fit" to write them. Your mother died waiting, and the result of your sister's faithful efforts to comply with her dying request "mortify" you. I cannot apologize for the part I have taken. You are mistaken in supposing that I am "anxious for your welfare." I assure you I have no interest in it, but your

246

accomplished sister, for whom I entertain the deepest respect and sympathy, I shall inform of your existence lest you should not "see fit" to do so yourself.

I have the honor to be, sir

Clara Barton

Such letters as the foregoing remind us that not all the cases of missing soldiers were purely accidental. There were instances where men went to war vowing loyalty to the girls they left behind them, and who formed other ties. There were cases where men formed wholly new associations and deliberately chose to begin anew and let the past be buried. But there were thousands of instances in which the work of Clara Barton brought her enduring gratitude. In very large proportion these missing men were dead. The testimony of a comrade who had witnessed the death on the battle-field or in prison set at rest any suspicion of desertion or any other form of dishonor. In other cases, where the soldier was alive, but had grown careless about writing, her timely reminder secured a prompt reunion and saved a long period of anxiety. Letters like the following came to her to the end of her life:

Greenfield, Mass., Sept. 25, 1911

Miss Clara Barton Oxford, Mass.

My dear Miss Barton:

I am a stranger to you, but you are far from being a stranger to me. As a member of the old Vermont Brigade through the entire struggle, I was familiar with your unselfish work at the front through those years when we were trying to restore a broken Union, and being a prisoner of war at Andersonville at its close, my mother, not knowing whether I was alive, appealed to you for information.

Two letters bearing your signature (from Annapolis, Maryland) are in my possession, the pathos of one bearing no tidings, and the glad report of my arrival about the middle of May, 1865.

The thankful heart that received them has long been stilled, but the letters have been preserved as sacred relics.

I also have a very vivid recollection of your earnest appeal to us to notify our friends of our arrival by first mail for their sake.

If to enjoy the gratitude of a single heart be a pleasure, to enjoy the benediction of a grateful world must be sweet to one's declining years. To have earned it makes it sublime.

I have also another tie which makes Oxford seem near to me. An old tent-mate, a member of our regimental quartette, a superb soldier and a very warm friend, lies mouldering there these many years. He survived, I think, more than thirty battles only to die of consumption in January, 1870. Whenever I can I run down from Worcester to lay a flower on George H. Amidon's grave.

I write not to tax you with a reply, but simply to wish for you all manner of blessings.

Yours truly

F. J. Hosmer Co. I, 4th Vt.

Her headquarters at this time was theoretically at Arlington where she had a tent. Arlington was the headquarters receiving and discharging returned prisoners. But much of her work was in Washington, and the constant journeys back and forth caused her to ask for a conveyance. She made her application to General William Hoffman, Commissary-General of prisoners, on June 16, 1865. Her request went the official rounds, and by the 25th of October a horse was promised as soon as a suitable one could be found. It is to be hoped that within a year or two a horse either with side-saddle or attached to a wheeled conveyance was found tethered in front of her bare lodging on the third floor of No. 488-1/2 7th Street, between D and E:

Washington, D.C., June 16th, 1865

Brig.-Gen'l. Wm. Hoffman
Commsy. Gen'l of Prisoners General:

It would not appear so necessary to explain to you the nature of my wants, as to apologize for imposing them upon you, but your great kindness to me has taught me not to fear the abuse of it in any request which seems needful.

If I say that in my present undertaking I find the duties of each day quite equal to my strength, and often of a character which some suitable mode of conveyance at my own command like the daily use of a Government wagon would materially lighten, I feel confident that you would both comprehend and believe me, but if I were to desire you to represent my wishes to the

248

proper authorities and aid in obtaining such a facility for me, I may have carried my request to a troublesome length and could only beg your kind pardon for the liberty taken which I would most humbly and cheerfully do.

With grateful respect,
I am, General Very truly yours

Clara Barton

———

Headquarters Military District of Washington
Washington, D.C., October 25, 1865
Miss Clara Barton:
I have conferred with General Wadsworth on the subject of obtaining a horse for your use, and he has directed that I place a horse at your disposal as soon as a suitable one can be found.

Very respectfully
Yr. Obt. Svt.

John P. Sherburne
Asst. Adjt. Gen'l,

For four years Clara Barton carried on this important work for missing soldiers. She spared neither her time nor her purse. At the outset there was no appropriation that covered the necessary expenses of such a quest, and the work was of a character that would not wait. From the beginning of the year 1865 to the end of 1868 she sent out 63, 182 letters of inquiry. She mailed printed circulars of advice in reply to correspondents to 58,693 persons. She wrote or caused to be written 41,855 personal letters. She distributed to be posted on bulletin boards and in public places 99,057 slips containing printed rolls. According to her estimate at the end of this heavy task, she succeeded in bringing information, not otherwise obtainable, to not less than 22,000 families of soldiers.

How valuable this work was then believed to be is shown in the fact that Congress, after an investigation by a committee which examined in detail her method and its results and the vouchers she had preserved of her expenses, appropriated to reimburse her the sum of 15,000.

It soon became evident that one of the most important fields for investigation was such record as could be found of the Southern prisons, especially Andersonville. To Andersonville her attention was directed through a discharged prisoner, Dorence Atwater, of Connecticut. He was in the first detachment transferred, the latter part of February, 1864, to the then new prison of Andersonville, and because of his skillful penmanship was detailed to keep a register of deaths of the prisoners. He occupied a desk next to that of General Wirz, the Confederate officer commanding the prison. Here, at the beginning of 1865, he made up a list of nearly thirteen thousand Union prisoners who died in that year, giving the full name, company and regiment, date and cause of death. Besides the official list he made another and duplicate list, which he secreted in the lining of his coat, and was able to take with him on his discharge.

At the close of the war he returned to his home in Terryville, Connecticut, where he was immediately stricken with diphtheria. Weakened and emaciated by his imprisonment, he nearly died of this acute attack. Before he was fully recovered, he was summoned to Washington, and his rolls were demanded by the Government. He gave them up and they were copied in Washington, but were not published. He wrote to Clara Barton informing her of these rolls and affirmed that by means of them he could identify almost every grave in Andersonville Prison. Clara Barton was greatly interested, and proposed to Secretary Stanton that she be sent to Andersonville and that Dorence Atwater accompany her. She proposed that there should go with them a number of men equipped with material for enclosing the cemetery with a fence, and for the marking of each grave with a suitable headboard.

Secretary Stanton received this suggestion not only with approval, but with enthusiasm. Miss Barton wrote the account of her interview with him on some loose sheets for her diary. The sheets were at least three in number, and only the second sheet is preserved. This sheet, however, covers the personal interview with Secretary Stanton. It was written at the time, and manifests his keen interest in her enterprise and desire to carry it through promptly and effectively:

On entering General Hardy's room, he asked my business. I said, "I didn't know, sir. I supposed I had some, as the Secretary sent for me." "Oh," he said, "you are Miss Barton. The Secretary is very anxious to see you," and sent a messenger to announce me. Mr. Stanton met me halfway across the room with extended hand, and said he had taken the liberty to send for me to thank me for what I had done both in the past, and in my present work; that he greatly regretted that he had not known of me earlier, as from all he now learned he feared I had done many hard things which a little aid from him would have rendered comparatively easy, but that especially now he desired to thank me for helping him to think; that it was not possible for him to think of everything which was for the general good, and no one knew how grateful he was to the person who put forth, among all the impracticable, interested, wild, and selfish schemes which were continually crowded upon him, one good, sensible, practical, unselfish idea that he could take up and act upon with safety and credit. You may believe that by this time my astonishment had not decreased. In the course of the next twenty minutes he informed me that he had decided to invite me (for he could not order me) to accompany Captain Moore, with Atwater and his register, to Andersonville, and see my suggestions carried out to my entire satisfaction; that unlimited powers as quartermaster would be given Captain Moore to draw upon all officers of the Government in that vicinity for whatever would be desired; that a special boat would be sent with ourselves and corps of workmen, and to return only when the work was satisfactorily accomplished. To call the next day and consult with him farther in...

If Miss Barton's horse, which she had asked for in June, had gotten to her door more promptly than is customary in such matters of official routine, he might have grown hungry waiting for her return. As we have already noticed, permission to have the horse assigned was granted in October, which left the summer free for the Andersonville expedition. Fortunately, no long interval elapsed after Secretary Stanton's approval of the plan before the starting of the expedition. On July 8 the propeller Virginia, having on board headboards, fencing material, clerks, painters, letterers, and a force of forty workmen, under command of Captain James M. Moore, Quartermaster, left Washington for Andersonville, by way of Savannah. On board also were Dorence Atwater and Clara Barton.

They reached Savannah on July 12, and remained there seven days, arriving at Andersonville on July 25.

Her first impressions were wholly favorable. The cemetery was in much better; condition than she had been led to fear. As the bodies had been buried in regular order, and Dorence Atwater's lists were minute as to date and serial number, the task of erecting a headboard giving each soldier's name, state, company, regiment, and date of death, appeared not very difficult. On the second night of her stay in Andersonville she wrote to Secretary Stanton of the success of the undertaking and suggested that the grounds be made a national cemetery. She assured him that for his prompt and humane action in ordering the marking of these graves the American people would bless him through long years to come. She was correct in her prediction. But for her proposal and Mr. Stanton's prompt cooperation and Dorence Atwater's presence with the list, hundreds if not thousands of graves now certainly are identified at Andersonville which would have needed to be marked "Unknown":

Hon. E. M. Stanton
Sec'y. of War, United States
Sir:
It affords me great pleasure to be able to report to you that we reached Andersonville safely at 1 o'clock p.m. yesterday, 25th inst. Found the grounds undisturbed, the stockade and hospital quarters standing protected by order of General Wilson.

We have encountered no serious obstacle, met with no accident, our entire party is well, and commenced work this morning. Any misgivings which might have been experienced are happily at an end; the original plan for identifying the graves is capable of being carried out to the letter. We can accomplish fully all that we came to accomplish, and the field is wide and ample for much more in the future. If desirable, the grounds of Andersonville can be made a National Cemetery of great beauty and interest. Be assured, Mr. Stanton, that for this prompt and humane action of yours, the American people will bless you long after your willing hands and mind have ceased to toil for them.

With great respect,
I have the honor to be, Sir
Your very obedient servant

Andersonville, Ga.
July 26th, 1865

The remaining period of her work in Andersonville was fruitful in the accomplishment of all the essential results for which she had undertaken the expedition, but it resulted in strained relations between one of the officers of the expedition and Dorence Atwater, and Clara Barton came to the defense of Atwater. During her absence at Andersonville, two letters were published in a Washington paper, over her signature, alleged to have been written by her to her Uncle James. She had no Uncle James, and wrote no such letters; and she attributed the forgery, correctly or incorrectly, to this officer. Her official report to the Secretary of War contains a severe arraignment of that officer, whom she never regarded with any favor.

This is all that need be recorded of Clara Barton's great work at Andersonville, of which a volume might easily be made. She saw the Union graves marked. Out of the almost thirteen thousand graves of Union soldiers at Andersonville four hundred and forty were marked "Unknown" when she finished her work, and they were unknown only because the Confederate records were incomplete. She saw the grounds enclosed and protected, and with her own hands she raised the United States flag for the first time since their death above these men who. had died for it.

But this expedition involved trouble for Atwater. When he handed over his rolls to the Government it was with the earnest request that steps be taken immediately to mark these graves. His request and the rolls had been pigeonholed. Then he had learned of Clara Barton's great work for missing soldiers and wrote her telling her that the list he had made surreptitiously and preserved with such care was gathering dust, while thirteen thousand graves were fast becoming unidentifiable. She brought this knowledge to Secretary Stanton as has already been set forth, and Stanton ordered the rolls to be produced and sent on this expedition for Atwater's use in identification.

Dorence Atwater had enlisted at the age of sixteen in the year 1862. He was now under twenty, but he was resolute in his determination that the lists which he had now recovered should not again be taken from him. On his return from Andersonville the rolls which he had made containing the names of missing soldiers disappeared. He was arrested and questioned, and replied that the rolls were his own property. He was sent to prison in the Old Capital, was tried by a court-martial, adjudged guilty of larceny, and sentenced to be confined for eighteen months at hard labor in the State Prison at Auburn, New York, fined three hundred dollars, and ordered to stand committed until the rolls were returned.

Atwater made no defense, but issued a statement which Clara Barton probably prepared for him:

"I am charged with and convicted of theft, and sentenced to eighteen months' imprisonment, and after that time until I shall have paid my Government three hundred dollars. I have called no witnesses, made no appeal, adduced no evidence. A soldier, a prisoner, an orphan, and a minor, I have little with which to employ counsel to oppose the Government of the United States.

"Whatever I may have been convicted of, I deny the charge of theft. I took my rolls home with me that they might be preserved; I considered them mine; it had never been told or even hinted to me that they were not my own rightful, lawful property. I never denied having them, and I was not arrested for stealing my rolls, but for having declared my intention of appealing to higher authority for justice. I supposed this to be one of the privileges of an American citizen, one of the great principles of the Government for which we had fought and suffered; but I forgot that the soldier who sacrificed his comforts and risked his life to maintain these liberties was the only man in the country who would not be allowed to claim their protection.

"My offense consists in an attempt to make known to the relatives and friends the fate of the unfortunate men who died in Andersonville Prison, and if this be a crime I am guilty to the fullest extent of the law, for to accomplish it I have risked my life among my enemies and my liberty among my friends.

"Since my arrest I have seen it twice publicly announced that the record of the dead of Andersonville would be published very soon; one announcement apparently by the Government, and one by Captain James M. Moore, A.G.M. No such intimation was ever given until after my arrest, and if it prove that my imprisonment accomplishes that which my liberty could not, I ought, perhaps, to be satisfied. If this serves to bring out the information so long and so cruelly withheld from the people, I will not complain of my confinement, but when accomplished, I would earnestly plead for that liberty so dear to all, and to which I have been so long a stranger.

"I make this statement, which I would confirm by my oath if I were at liberty, not as appealing to public sympathy for relief, but for the sake of my name, my family, and my friends. I wish it to be known that I am not sentenced to a penitentiary as a common thief, but for attempting to appeal from the trickery of a clique of petty officers.

Dorence Atwater"

On September 25, 1865, just one month from the day when he returned from Andersonville from the marking of the soldiers' graves, Dorence Atwater, as Clara Barton records, "was heavily ironed, and under escort of a soldier and captain as guard, in open daylight, and in the face of his acquaintances, taken through the streets of Washington to the Baltimore depot, and placed upon the cars, a convict bound to Auburn State Prison."

Clara Barton had moved heaven and earth to save Dorence from imprisonment; had done everything excepting to advise him to give up the rolls. She knew so well what the publication of those names meant to thirteen thousand anxious homes, she was willing to see Dorence go to prison rather than that should fail. Secretary Stanton was out of Washington when Dorence was arrested. She followed him to West Point and had a personal interview, which she supplemented by a letter:

Roe's Hotel, West Point,
September 5th, 1865

Hon. E. M. Stanton
Sec'y. of War, U.S.A.
My Honored Friend:

Please permit me before leaving to reply to the one kind interrogatory made by you this morning, viz: "What do you desire me to do in the case?" Simply this, sir—do nothing, believe nothing, sanction nothing in this present procedure against Dorence Atwater until all the facts with their antecedents and bearings shall have been placed before you, and this upon your return (if no one more worthy offer) I promise to do, with all the fairness, truthfulness, and judgment that in me lie.

There is a noticeable haste manifested to dispose of the case in your absence which leads me to fear that there are those who, to gratify a jealous whim, or serve a personal ambition, would give little heed to the dangers of unmerited public criticism they might thus draw upon you, while young Atwater, honest and simple-hearted, both loving and trusting you, has more need of your protection than your censure.

With the highest esteem, and unspeakable gratitude,
I am, sir

Clara Barton

Failing to secure the release of Dorence by appeal to Secretary Stanton, who was not given to interference with military courts, Clara Barton tried the effect of public opinion and also sought to arouse the military authority of the State of Connecticut. Two letters of hers are preserved addressed to friends in the newspaper world, but they did not immediately accomplish the release of Dorence.

Clara Barton was not a woman to desist in an effort of this kind. She had set about to procure the release of Dorence Atwater; she had the support of Senator Henry Wilson and of General B. F. Butler, and she labored day and night to enlarge the list of influential friends who should finally secure his freedom. She surely would have succeeded. While the Government saw no convenient way of issuing him a pardon until he returned the missing rolls, public sentiment in his favor grew steadily under her insistent propaganda. At the end of two months' imprisonment, he was released under a general order which discharged from prison all soldiers sentenced there by court-martial for crimes less than murder. Even after the issue of the President's general order,

Atwater was detained for a little time until Clara Barton made a personal visit to Secretary Stanton and informed him that Dorence was still in prison and secured the record of his trial for future use.

Then she set herself to work to secure the publication of his rolls. He must copy them and rearrange them by States and in alphabetical order, a task of no light weight, and must then arrange with some responsible newspaper to undertake to secure their publication. Moreover, this must be done quickly and quietly, for she believed that Dorence still had an enemy who would thwart the effort if known.

The large task of copying the rolls and rearranging the names required some weeks. When it was finished, Clara Barton, who had previously thought of the New York "Times" as a possible medium of publicity on account of an expression of interest which it had published, and even had considered the unpractical idea of simultaneous publication in a number of papers, turned instead to Horace Greeley. She wrote to him in January, 1866, and then went to New York and conferred with him.

Greeley told her that the list was quite too long for publication in the columns of any newspaper. The proper thing to do, as he assured her, was to bring it out in pamphlet form at a low price, and, on the day of publication, to exploit it as widely as possible through the columns of the "Tribune." To get the list in type, read the proof, print the edition, and have it ready for delivery required some days if not weeks. Valentine's Day was fixed as that upon which the list was to appear. On February 14, 1866, the publication occurred.

Horace Greeley was a good advertiser. All through the advertising pages of the *Tribune* on that day appeared the word "Andersonville" in a single line of capitals, varied here and there by "Andersonville; See Advertisement on 8th page." No one who read that day's *Tribune* could escape the word "Andersonville." The editorial page contained the following paragraph:

We have just issued a carefully compiled List of the Union Soldiers Buried at Andersonville—arranged alphabetically under the names of their respective States, and containing every name that has been or can be recovered. Aside from the general and mournful interest felt in these martyrs personally, this list will be of great importance hereafter in the settlement of estates, etc. A copy should be preserved for reference in every library, however limited. It constitutes a roll of honor wherein our children's children will point with pride to the names of their relatives who died that their country might live. See advertisement.

The eighth page contained a half-page article by Clara Barton, telling in full of the marking of the Andersonville graves. This article was hailed with nation-wide interest, and the pamphlet had an enormous circulation, bringing comfort to thousands of grief-stricken homes.

Dorence Atwater never recovered from his treatment at the hands of the United States Government. For many years the record of the court-martial stood against him, and his status was that of a released prisoner still unpardoned. His spirit became embittered, and he said that the word "soldier" made him angry, and the sight of a uniform caused him to froth at the mouth. The Government gave him a consulship in the remote Seychelles Islands, and later transferred him to the Society Islands in the South Pacific. He died in November, 1910, and his monument is erected near Papeete on the Island of Tahiti.

ON THE LECTURE PLATFORM

At the close of the Civil War, Clara Barton wanted to write a book. Other women who had engaged in war work were writing books, and the books were being well received. She had as much to tell as any other one woman, and she thought she would like to tell it.

In this respect she was entirely different from Miss Dorothea Dix. She met Miss Dix now and then during the war, and made note of the fact in her diary, but either because these meetings occurred in periods when she was too busy to make full record, or because nothing of large importance transpired between them, she gives no extended account of them. Miss Dix was superintendent of female nurses, and Miss Barton was doing an independent work, so there was little occasion for them to meet. But all her references to Miss Dix which show any indication of her feeling manifest a spirit of very cordial appreciation of Dorothea Dix's work. Miss Dix managed her work in her own line, insisting that nurses whom she appointed should be neither young nor good-looking, and fighting her valiant battles with quite as much success as in general could have been expected. But Dorothea Dix had no desire for publicity. She shrank from giving to the world any details of her own life, partly because of her unhappy childhood memories, and partly because she did not believe in upholding in the mind of young women the successful career of an unmarried woman. Accepting as she did her own lonely career, and making it a great blessing to others, she did not desire that young women should emulate it or consider it the ideal life. She wished instead that they should find lovers, establish homes, and become wives and mothers.

Clara Barton, too, had very high regard for the home, and she saw quite enough of the folly of sentimental young women who were eager to rush to the hospitals and nurse soldiers, but she did not share Miss Dix's fear of an attractive face, and she knew rather better than Miss Dix the value of publicity. Timid as she was by nature, she had discovered the power of the Press. She had succeeded in keeping up her supply of comforts for wounded soldiers largely by the letters which she wrote to personal friends and to local organizations of women in the North. She made limited but effective use of the newspaper for like purposes. At first she did not fully realize her own gift as a writer. Once or twice she bemoaned in her diary the feebleness of her descriptive effort. If she could only make people see what she had actually seen, she could move their hearts, and the supply of bandages and delicacies for her wounded men would be unfailing.

Her search for missing soldiers led her to a larger utilization of the Press, and gave her added confidence in her own descriptive powers. Her name was becoming more and more widely known, and she thought a book by her, if she could procure means to publish it, would afford her opportunity for self-expression and quite possibly be financially profitable.

On this subject she wrote two letters to Senator Henry Wilson. They are undated, and it is probable that she never sent either of them, but they show what was in her heart. One of these reads as follows:

My always good Friend:
Among all the little trials, necessities, and wants, real or imaginary, that I have from time to time brought and laid down at your feet, or even upon your shoulders, your patience has never once broken, or if it did your broad charity concealed the rent from me, and I come now in the hope that this may not prove to be the last feather. It is not so much that I want you to do anything as to listen and advise, and it may be all the more trying as I desire the advice to be plain, candid, and honest even at the risk of wounding my pride.

Perhaps no previous proposition of mine, however wild, has ever so completely astonished you as the present is liable to do. Well, to end suspense. I am desirous of writing a book. You will very naturally ask two questions—what for and what of. In reply to the first. The position which I have assumed before the public renders some general exposition necessary. They require to be made acquainted with me, or perhaps I might say they should either be made to know more of me or less. As it is, everyone knows my name and something of what I am or have been doing, but not one in a thousand has any idea of the manner in which I propose to serve them. Out of six thousand letters lying by me, probably not two hundred show any tolerably clear idea of the writer as to what use I am to make of that very letter. People tell me the color of the hair and eyes of the friends they have lost, as if I were expected to go about the country and search them. They ask me to send them full lists of the lost men of the army; they tell me that they have looked all through my list of missing men and the name of their son or husband or somebody's else is not on it, and desire to be informed why he is made an exception. They suppose me a part of the Government and it is my duty to do these things, or that I am carrying on the "business" as a means of revenue and ask my price, as if I hunted men at so much per head. But all suppose me either well paid or abundantly able to dispense with it; and these are only a few of the vague ideas which present themselves in my daily mail. A fair history of what I have done and desire to do, and a plain description of the practical working of my system, would convince people that I am neither sorceress nor spiritualist and would appall me with less of feverish hope and more of quiet, potent faith in the final result.

Then there is all of Andersonville of which I have never written a word. I have not even contradicted the base forgeries which were perpetrated upon me in my absence. I need not tell you how foully I am being dealt by in this whole matter and the crime which has grown out of the wickedness which overshadows me. I need to tell some plain truths in a most inexpensive manner, that the whole country shall not be always duped and honest people sacrificed that the ambition of one man be gratified. I do not propose controversy, but I have a truth to speak; it belongs to the people of our country and I desire to offer it to them.

And lastly, if a suitable work were completed and found salable and any share of proceeds fell to me, I need it in the prosecution of the work before me.

Next—What of? The above explanation must have partially answered that I would give the eight months' history of my present work, and I think I might be permitted by the writers to insert occasionally a letter sent me by some noble wife or mother, and there are no better or more touching letters written.

I would show how the expedition to Andersonville grew out of this very work; how inseparably connected the two were; and how Dorence Atwater's roll led directly to the whole work of identifying the graves of the thirteen thousand sleeping in that city of the dead.

I would endeavor to insert my report of the expedition now with the Secretary. I have some materials from which engravings could be made, I think, of the most interesting features of Andersonville, and my experiences with the colored people while there I believe to have been of exceeding interest. I would like to relate this. You recollect I have told you that they came from twenty miles around to see me to know if Abraham Lincoln was dead and if they were free. This, if well told, is a little book of itself. And if still I lack material I might go back a little and perhaps a few incidents might be gleaned from my last few years' life which would not be entirely without interest. I think I could glean enough from this ground to eke out my work, which I would dedicate to the survivors of Andersonville and the friends of the missing men of the United States Army. I don't know what title I would give it.

Now, first, I want your yes or no. If the former, I want your advice still further. Who can help me do all this? I have sounded among my friends, and all are occupied; numbers can write well, but have no knowledge of book-making which I suppose to be a trade in itself and one of which I am entirely ignorant. I never attempted any such thing myself and have no conceit of my own ability as a writer. I don't think I can write, but I would try to do something at it; might do more if there were time, but this requires to be done at once. I want a truthful, easy, and I suppose touching rather than logical book, which it appears to me would sell among the class of persons to whom I should dedicate it, and their name is legion. Now, it is no wonder that I have found no one ready to take hold and help me carry this on when it is remembered that I have not ten thousand dollars to offer them in advance, but must ask that my helper wait and share his remuneration out of the profits. If he knew me, he would know that I would not be illiberal, especially as pecuniary profit is but a secondary consideration.

It is of greater importance to me that I bring before the country and establish the facts that I desire than that I make a few thousand dollars out of it, but I would like to do both if I could, but the first if not the last. But I want to stand as the author and it must be my book, and it should be in very truth if I had the time to write it. I want no person to reap a laurel off it (dear knows I have had enough of that of late), but the man or woman who could and would take hold and work side by side with me in this matter, making it a heart interest, and having my interest at heart, be unselfish and noble with me as I think I would be with them, should reap pecuniary profit if there were any to reap. An experienced bookmaker or publisher would understand if such a work would sell—it seems to me that it would.

Now, can you point me to any person who could either help me do this or be so kind as to inform me that I must not attempt it?

It will be noted that in this letter she indicates her present lack of means to publish such a book as she had in mind. She had not always lacked means for such an object. While her salary as a teacher had never been large, she had always saved money out of it. The habit of New England thrift was strong upon her, and her investments were carefully made so that her little fund continually augmented. Her salary in the Patent Office was fourteen hundred dollars, and for a time sixteen hundred dollars, and though she paid a part of it to her substitute during the latter portion of the war, she was able to keep up the rental of her lodging and meet her very modest personal expenses without drawing upon her savings. The death of her father brought to her a share in his estate, and this was invested in Oxford, conservatively and profitably. When she began her search for missing soldiers, therefore, she had quite a little money of her own. She began that work of volunteer service, expecting it to be supported as her work in the field had been supported, by the free gifts of those who believed in the work. When a soldier or a soldier's mother or widow sent her a dollar, she invariably returned it.

As the work proceeded, she was led to believe that Congress would make an appropriation to reimburse her for her past expenditures, and add a sufficient appropriation for the continuance of the work. She had two influential friends at court, Senator Henry Wilson, her intimate and trusted friend, Chairman of the Committee on Military Affairs of the Senate, and General Benjamin F. Butler, with whose army she had last served in the field.

She knew very well how laws were passed and official endorsements secured. She frequently interceded with her friends in high places on behalf of people or causes in whom she believed. She, in common with Miss Dix, had altercations with army surgeons, yet her diary shows her working hard to secure for them additional recognition and remuneration. On Sunday, January 29, 1865, she attempted to attend the third anniversary of the Christian Commission, but the House of Representatives was packed; thousands, she says, were turned away. That afternoon or evening Senator Wilson called on her and she talked with him concerning army surgeons: "I spoke at length with Mr. Wilson on the subject of army surgeons. I think their rank will be raised. I believe I will see Dr. Crane in the morning and make an effort to bring Dr. Buzzell here to help frame the bill."

She did exactly what she believed she would do; saw Dr. Crane, got her recommendation that Dr. Buzzell be allowed to come, and then went to the Senate. The thing she labored for was accomplished, though it called for considerable added effort.

About this same time she had a visit from a woman who was seeking to obtain the passage of a special act for her own benefit. She shared Clara Barton's bed and board, with introduction to Senator Wilson and other influential people, until the bill passed both houses, and still as Miss Barton's guest continued in almost frantic uncertainty, awaiting the President's signature. It happened at the very time Clara Barton was very desirous of getting her work for missing soldiers under way. The idea came to her in the night of February 19, 1865:

Thought much during the night, and decided to invite Mr. Brown to accompany me to Annapolis and to offer my services to take charge of the correspondence between the country and the Government officials and prisoners at that point while they continued to arrive.

Mr. Brown called upon her that very day and they agreed to go to Annapolis the next day, which they did. She nursed her brother Stephen, accomplished a large day's work, did her personal washing at nine o'clock at night, and the next day went to Annapolis. There she met Dorothea Dix; found a captain who deserved promotion, and resolved to get it for him; assisted in welcoming four boatloads of returned prisoners, and defined more clearly in her own mind the kind of work that needed to be done.

The next Sunday Senator Wilson called on her again, and she told him she had offered her services for this work, and wanted the President's endorsement in order that she might not be interfered with. Senator Wilson offered to go with her to see President Lincoln, and they went next day, but did not succeed in seeing him. She went again next day, this time without Senator Wilson, for he was busy working on the bill for the lady who was her guest, so she sought to obtain her interview with President Lincoln through the Honorable E. B. Washburne, of Illinois. Mr. Washburne agreed to meet her at the White House, and did so, but the President was in a conference preceding a Cabinet meeting, and the Cabinet meeting, which was to begin at noon, was likely to last the rest of the day, so Mr. Washburne took her paper and said he would see the President and obtain his endorsement. She saw Senator Wilson that afternoon, and reported that her papers were still unendorsed, and General Hitchcock was advising her to go on without any formal authority. She was not disposed to do it, for she felt sure that she would no sooner get established than Secretary Stanton would interfere. The difficulty was to get at the President in those crowded days just before his second inaugural, when events both in Washington and in the field were crowding tremendously.

Senator Wilson was still interested in what she wanted to do, but was preoccupied. "He had labored all night on Miss B.'s bill." In fact Clara Barton read the probable fate of her own endeavor. Senator Wilson had given himself with such ardor to the cause of her guest that he had no time to help her. She had borrowed a set of furs to wear when she went to the President. She took them back that afternoon and wrote in her diary: "Very tired; could not reconcile my poor success; I find that some hand above mine rules and restrains my progress; I cannot understand, but try to be patient, but still it is hard. I was never more tempted to break down with disappointment."

On Thursday, March 2, two days before the inauguration, she went again to see the President. Just as she reached the White House in the rain, she saw Secretary Stanton go in. She waited until 5.15, and Stanton did not come out. She returned home "still more and more discouraged." Her guest, also, had been out in the rain, but was overjoyed. Her bill had passed the Senate without opposition, and would go to the House next day, if not that very night. Miss Barton wrote in her diary: "I do not tell her how much I am inconvenienced

265

by her using all my power. I have no helper left, and I am discouraged. I could not restrain the tears, and gave up to it."

It is hardly to be wondered that she almost repented of her generosity in loaning Senator Wilson to her friend when she herself had so much need of him. Nor need she be blamed for lying awake and crying while her guest slept happily on the pillow beside her. She did not often cry.

Just at this time she was doubly anxious, for Stephen, her brother, was nearing his end, and Irving Vassall, her nephew, was having hemorrhages and not long for this world, and her day's journal shows a multiplicity of cares crowding each day.

Stephen died Friday, March 10. She was with him when he died and mourned for her "dear, noble brother." She believed he had gone to meet the loved ones on the other side, and she wondered whether her mother was not the first to welcome him. His body was embalmed, and a service was held in Washington, and another in Oxford. Between the time of Stephen's death and her departure with his body, she received her papers with the President's endorsement. General Hitchcock presented them to her. She wrote:

We had a most delightful interview. He aided me in drawing up a proper article to be published; said it would be hard, but I should be sustained through such a work, he felt, and that no person in the United States would oppose me in my work; he would stand between me and all harm. The President was there, too. I told him I could not commence just yet, and why, and he said, "Go bury your dead, and then care for others." How kind he was!

President Johnson later endorsed the work and authorized the printing of whatever matter she required at the Government Printing Office. Her postage was largely provided by the franking privilege. Her work was a great success and the time came in the following October, when it seemed certain her department was to have official status with the payment of all its necessary expenses by the Government. On Wednesday, October 4, she wrote:

Of all my days, this, I suspect, has been my greatest, and I hope my best. About six p.m. General Butler came quickly into my room to tell me that my business had been presented to both the President and Secretary of War, and fully approved by both; that it was to be made a part of the Adjutant-General's department with its own clerks and expenses, and that I was to be at the head of it, exclusively myself; that he made that a sine qua non, on the ground that it was proper for parents to bring up their own children; that he wished me to make out my own programme of what would be required; and on his return he would overlook it and I could enter at once upon my labor. Who ever heard of anything like this—who but General Butler? He left at 7.30 for home. I don't know how to comport me.

On that same night she had a very different call, and the only one which the author has found referred to in all her diaries where any man approached her with an improper suggestion. Mingling as she did with men on the battle-field, living alone in a room that was open to constant calls from both men and women, she seems to have passed through the years with very little reason to think ill of the attitude of men toward a self-respecting and unprotected woman. That evening she had an unwelcome call, but she promptly turned her visitor out, went straight to two friends and told them what had been said to her, and wrote it down in her diary as a wholly exceptional incident, and with this brief comment, "Oh, what a wicked man!"

The plan to make her department an independent bureau seemed humanly certain to succeed. When, a few days later, General Butler left Washington without calling to see her, she was surprised, but thought it explained, a few days later, when the Boston "Journal" published an editorial saying that General Butler was to be given a seat in the Cabinet and to make his home in Washington.

But General Butler's plans failed. He fell into disfavor, and all that he had recommended and was still pending became anathema to the War Department. The bureau was not created, and Clara Barton's official appointment did not come.

During all this time she had been supporting her work of correspondence out of her own pocket. The time came when she invested in it the very last dollar of her quick assets. Her old friend

Colonel De Witt, through whom she had obtained her first Government appointment, had invested her Oxford money. At her request he sent her the last of it, a check for $228. She wrote in her diary: "This is the last of my invested money, but it is not the first time in my life that I have gone to the bottom of my bag. I guess I shall die a pauper, but I haven't been either stingy or lazy, and if I starve I shall not be alone; others have. Went to Mechanics' Bank and got my check cashed."

She certainly had not been lazy, and she never was stingy with anyone but herself. Keeping her own expenses at the minimum and living so frugally that she was sometimes thought parsimonious, she saw her last dollar of invested money disappear, and recorded a grim little joke about her poverty and the possibility of starvation. But she shed no tears. In the few times when she broke down and wept, the occasion was not her own privation or personal disappointment, but the failure of some plan through which she sought to be of service to others.

This is a rather long retrospect, but it explains why Clara Barton, when she wanted to publish a book, contemplated the cost of it as an item beyond her personal means. She could have published the book at her own expense had it not been for the money she had spent for others.

Congress did not permit her to lose the money which she had expended. In all her diary and correspondence no expression of fear has been found as to her own remuneration. She thought it altogether likely she could get her money back, but there is no hint that she would have mourned, much less regretted what she had done, if she had never seen her money again.

Sad days came for Clara Barton when she found that General Butler was worse than powerless to aid her work. Heartily desirous of assisting her as he was, his name was enough to kill any measure which he sponsored. When Senator Wilson came to see her, just before Christmas, and told her that the plan was hopeless, she was already prepared for it. He suspected that she was nearly out of money, and tried to make her a Christmas gift of twenty dollars, but she declined. She wakened, on these mornings, "with the deepest feeling of depression and despair that I remember to have known." But this feeling gave place to another. Waking in the night and thinking clearly, she was able to outline the programme of the next day's task so distinctly and unerringly that she began to wonder whether the spirit of her noble brother Stephen was not guiding her. She did not think she was a Spiritualist, but it seemed to her that some influence which he was bringing to her from her mother helped to shape her days aright. It was such a night's meditation that made plain to her that Dorence Atwater, released but not pardoned, must get his list published immediately, and that he must do it without a cent of compensation so that no one should ever be able to say that he had stolen the list in order to profit by it. She found that she did not need many hours' sleep. If she could rest with an untroubled mind, she could waken and think clearly.

Gradually, her plan to publish a book changed. Instead she would write a lecture. She went to hear different women speakers, and was gratified whenever she found a woman who could speak in public effectively. A woman preacher came to Washington, and she listened to her. Even in the pulpit a woman could speak acceptably. When she traveled on the train, she was surprised and gratified to find how many people knew her, and she came to believe that the lecture platform offered her a better opportunity than the book.

There was one other consideration—a book would cost money for its publication and the getting of it back was a matter of uncertainty. But the lecture platform promised to be immediately remunerative.

She conferred with John B. Gough. She read to him a lecture which she prepared. Said he, "I never heard anything more touching, more thrilling, in my life." He encouraged her to proceed.

Thus encouraged, Clara Barton laid out her itinerary, and prepared for three hundred nights upon the platform. Her rates were one hundred dollars per night, excepting where she spoke under the auspices of the Grand Army Post, when her charge was seventy-five.

She took Dorence Atwater with her to look after her baggage and see to her comfort, and exhibit a box of relics which he had brought from Andersonville. She paid his expenses and a salary besides. Sometimes she thought he earned it, and sometimes she doubted it, for he was still a boy and exhibited a boy's limitations. But she cherished a very sincere affection for him and to the end of her life counted him as one of her own kin.

During this period she had abundant time to write in her diary; for, while there were long journeys, the ordinary distance from one engagement to another was not great. She lectured in the East in various New England cities, in Cooper Institute in New York, and in cities and moderate-sized towns through Indiana, Ohio, Illinois, Iowa, Kansas, and Nebraska. She had time to record and did record all the little incidents of her journey, together with the exact sum she received for each lecture, with every dime which she expended for travel, hotel accommodation, and incidental expenses. It was a hard but varied and remunerative tour. It netted her some twelve thousand dollars after deducting all expenses.

A soldier of the Legion lay dying in Algiers;
There was lack of woman's nursing, there was dearth of woman's tears;
But a comrade stood beside him, as the life-blood ebbed away,
And bent with pitying glances to hear what he might say;
The dying soldier faltered—as he took that comrade's hand—
And said, "I never more shall see my own—my native land.
Take a message and a token to some distant friend of mine,
For I was born at Bingen, fair Bingen on the Rhine."

With this quotation from the familiar but effective poem of Mrs. Norton, Clara Barton opened her first public lecture, which she delivered at Poughkeepsie, on Thursday evening, October 25, 1866. The lecture was an hour and a quarter in length as she read it aloud in her room, but required about an hour and a half as she delivered it before a public audience. It was, as she recorded in her diary, "my first lecture," and "the beginning of remunerative labor" after a long period in which she had been without salary. She knew that it was her first lecture, but the audience did not. She returned from it to the house of Mr. John Mathews, where she was entertained, ate an ice-cream, went to bed and slept well. She received her first fee of one hundred dollars. On Saturday night she spoke in Schenectady, where she received fifty dollars, and found, what many a lecturer has learned, that it was not profitable to cut prices. A diminished fee means less local advertising. The audience was smaller and less appreciative. On Monday evening she spoke in Brooklyn. Theodore Tilton presided and introduced her. There she had an ovation. Mr. Tilton accompanied her to her hotel after the lecture, and she told him that she was just beginning, and asked for his criticism. He told her the lecture contained no flaw for him to mend. She went back to Washington enthusiastic over the success of her new venture. She had spoken three times, and two of the lectures had been a pronounced success. Her expenses had been less than fifty dollars, and she was two hundred dollars to the good.

She found awaiting her in Washington a large number of requests to lecture in different places, and she arranged a New England tour. She began with Worcester and Oxford. She did this with many misgivings, not forgetting the lack of honor for a prophet in his own country. She spoke in Mechanic's Hall in Worcester, before a full house. She got her hundred dollars, but was not happy over the lecture. In Oxford, however, things went differently. She had a good house, and "the pleasantest lecture I shall ever deliver. Raced home all happy and at rest. My best visit at home." Here she refused to receive any fee, placing the proceeds of the lecture in the hands of the overseers of the poor.

She lectured at Salem, at Marlborough, and then at Newark, and again returned to Washington convinced that her plan was a success.

Her next tour took her to Geneva and Lockport, New York, Cleveland and Toledo, Ohio, Ypsilanti and Detroit, Michigan, and on the return trip to Ashtabula, Ohio, Rochester and Dansville, New York. Her fee was a hundred dollars in every place excepting Dansville, but her lecture at this last place proved to be of importance. There she learned about the water cure, which later was to have an important influence upon her life. All these lectures on her third trip left a pleasant memory, except the one at Ashtabula, which for some reason did not go well.

She now arranged for a much longer trip. She bought her ticket for Chicago, stopping to lecture at Laporte, Indiana. She reshaped her lecture somewhat for this trip, telling how her father had fought near that town under "Mad" Anthony Wayne. She lectured in Milwaukee, Evanston, Kalamazoo, Detroit, Flint, Galesburg, Des Moines, Rock Island, Muscatine, Washington, Iowa, Dixon, Illinois, Decatur, and Jacksonville. On her way north from Jacksonville, she was in a train wreck in which several people were injured. She also had an experience in an attempt to rob her, and she resolved never to travel by sleeper again when she had to go alone. She was very nearly as good as her word. Very rarely did she make use of a sleeping-car; she traveled by day when she could, and, when unable to do so, sat up in a corner of the seat and rested as best she could.

She lectured at Mount Vernon, Aurora, Belvidere, Rockford, and other Illinois cities, and at Clinton, Iowa.

In most of these cities she was entertained in the homes of distinguished people, Dorence Atwater sometimes staying at the hotel.

In Chicago she had good visits with John B. Gough and Theodore Tilton, both of whom were on the lecture platform, and she herself lectured in the Chicago Opera House.

Other lectures followed in Illinois, Michigan, Indiana, Ohio, New York, and so on back to Washington. Then she took another tour through New England. She lectured in New Haven and found the people unresponsive, but she had a good time at Terryville, Connecticut. There Dorence Atwater was at home. It was characteristic of Clara Barton that at this lecture she insisted that Dorence should preside; not only so, but she called it his lecture and gave him the entire proceeds of that and the lecture at New Haven. It was a proud night for this young man, released from his two imprisonments, and she records that he presided well. She lectured again in Worcester and with better results than before, then extended her tour all over New England.

After this she made other long tours through Ohio, Indiana, Illinois, and States farther west. Now and then she records a disappointing experience, but in the main the results were favorable. She had no difficulty in making a return engagement; everywhere she was hailed as the Florence Nightingale of America. The press comments were enthusiastic; her bank account grew larger than it had ever been.

Clara Barton was now forty-seven years old. For eight years, beginning with the outbreak of the Civil War, she had lived in rooms on the third floor of a business block. The two flights of stairs and the unpretentiousness of the surroundings had not kept her friends away. Her daily list of callers was a long one, and her evenings brought her so many friends that she spoke humorously of her "levees." But she had begun to long for a home of her own, which she now was well able to afford. Since the appropriation of Congress of fifteen thousand dollars and her earnings from her lectures, all of which she had carefully invested, she possessed not less than thirty thousand dollars in good interest-bearing securities. She had brought from Andersonville a colored woman, Rosa, who now presided over her domestic affairs. She spent a rather cheerless Christmas on her forty-seventh birthday in her old room on 7th Street, and determined not to delay longer. She bought a house. On the outside it looked old and shabby, but inside it was comfortable. On Tuesday, December 29, 1868, she packed her belongings. Next day she records:

December 30, 1868, Wednesday. Moved. Mr. Budd came early with five men. Mr. Vassall, Sally, and myself all worked, and in the midst of a fearful snowstorm and a good deal of confusion, I broke away from my old rooking of eight years and launched out into the world all by myself. Took my first supper in my own whole house at the corner of Pennsylvania Avenue and Capitol Hill.

She had engaged her movers at a stipulated price of six dollars, but she was so happy with the result that she paid them ten dollars, which for a woman of Clara Barton's careful habits indicated a very large degree of satisfaction.

The next day, assisted by her colored woman Rosa and her negro man Uncle Jarret, and with some help from two kindly neighbors, she set things to rights. It was a stormy day and she was tired, but happy to be in her home. She wrote in her diary: "This is the last day

273

of the year, and I sometimes think it may be my last year. I am not strong, but God is good and kind."

It is pathetic that the joy of her occupancy of her new home should have been clouded by any forebodings of this character. Her premonition that it might be her last year came very near to being true. Heavy had been the strain upon her from the day when the war began, and the events of the succeeding years had all drawn upon her vitality. What occurred at the height of her success in Bordentown came again to her at the height of her career upon the lecture platform. She rode one night to address a crowded house, and she stood before them speechless. Her voice utterly failed. Her physicians pronounced it nervous prostration, prescribed three years of complete rest, and ordered her to go to Europe.

END OF VOLUME I

HER FIRST KNOWLEDGE OF THE RED CROSS

When in 1869 Clara Barton went to Europe in quest of health, she had never so much as heard of the Red Cross. That organization had been -in existence in Europe for more than five years, but the number of people in America who knew anything about it was exceedingly small. The United States was not then a member of the international organization which recognized the Red Cross, nor did it become a member for many years thereafter. This was not because the United States Government did not know about it, but because this country had no purpose or desire to join in an organization established in Europe for purposes in which it was generally believed this country had no occasion to participate. •

It is necessary to be explicit on this subject. The meeting which gave the Red Cross to the world took place at Geneva, Switzerland, on February 29, 1863. At the call of a committee, which already had behind it the formal endorsement of eleven national governments, the international organization was formed in Geneva on August 22, 1864. At this meeting the cross of red upon a white ground was adopted as the insignia of the convention. Twenty-two governments promptly gave their adherence to this convention. The United States was not among them, although it had been formally invited to be present.

The Red Cross did not lack for an advocate in America in that early day. The Reverend Henry W. Bellows, D.D., chairman of the Sanitary Commission of the United States, earnestly desired that America should have been among the original nations adhering to the treaty; but his pleadings were met with indifference and with pronounced opposition. Mr. George P. Fogg, United States Minister to Switzerland, and Mr. Charles S. P. Bowles, European Agent of the Sanitary Commission, were informally present at the Geneva Convention. The Secretary of State authorized Mr. Fogg "to attend the meeting in an informal manner, for the purpose of giving or receiving such suggestions as you may think likely to promote the humane ends which have prompted it." He added that Mr. Fogg was not to attend if any emissary of the Confederate Government was allowed to be there.

It is interesting and gratifying to know that Mr. Bowles was able to report to the convention concerning the important work done in America by the Sanitary Commission. But neither Mr. Fogg nor Mr. Bowles could give any assurance that the United States would do anything toward the formal endorsement of the Red Cross, or become a member of the convention.

Dr. Bellows exhausted all his efforts to secure some recognition of the movement in America, and finally gave it up in despair. From February 9, 1863, when the movement began in Geneva, until May 20, 1881, when James G. Blaine wrote to Clara Barton that President

Garfield would recommend to Congress the adoption of the international treaty, was a period of eighteen years, during which time the United States of America turned a deaf ear to every entreaty to participate in the work of the Red Cross. That the United States even at that late date came to be a participant in the results of the Geneva Convention was due to the untiring faith, devotion, and perseverance of Clara Barton.

She was not one among many good women working for this common end. She was not a member of a committee or other organization beginning feebly, but gradually gaining strength until the object was accomplished. Alone she learned of the Red Cross; alone she brought tidings of it back to her own country; alone she wrote of it, talked of it, brought it to the attention of distinguished men, carried her faith in it from desk to desk in Washington, and cherished the hope of it through long years, until just before the assassination of President Garfield, she received from him, through his Secretary of State, the assurance that the United States would accept the treaty which thirty-one national governments had previously adopted.

In September, 1869, Clara Barton went abroad in quest of health. For several months following the loss of her voice on the platform she had been fighting nervous prostration in America, and had found that she must turn her back on everything that suggested work. Acting under medical advice, she sailed in September, and, after a, short sojourn in Scotland with no more than a look at London and Paris, she came to Geneva in Switzerland, bearing letters of introduction from the Swiss Minister in Washington, the Honorable John Hitz, to the American Consul and the American Ambassador. It was there Clara Barton learned of the Red Cross.

Had she but known it, a Red Cross Society had actually been formed in the United States in 1866, but had died without securing national recognition or attracting public attention. Of that organization we shall have occasion to speak hereafter. It was called "The American Association for the Relief of the Misery of Battlefields." Information concerning it is preserved in a letter of the Reverend Henry W. Bellows, D.D., President, to Monsieur J. Henri Dunant, Secretaire du "Comite International de Secours aux Militaires Blesses." The few people who knew of this organization in 1866 had very nearly forgotten about it by 1869, and its great-hearted organizer, Dr. Bellows, had become completely discouraged with respect to any recognition of the movement in America. How Clara Barton came into touch with this organization as it existed abroad she told in a lecture which she prepared and delivered in a number of places on her return from Europe at the close of the Franco-Prussian War. As during this period her health was so poor that her diary was kept with great irregularity, this lecture gives us our best account of her journey and succeeding events:

"Most of you, I presume, know of me only as connected with our own war, and probably little of that, and, unless I give a word of explanation, it will remain a mystery to you how I ever came near a war in another country, and, in military parlance, we must connect the two by a "pontoon bridge," and get ourselves across on it.

"Our war closed in the spring of '65. Almost four years longer I worked among the debris, gathering up the wrecks, and sometimes, during the lecture season, telling a few simple war-stories to the people over the country, in their halls and churches.

"One early winter evening in '68 I stood on the platform of one of the finest new opera houses in the East, filled to repletion, it seemed to me, with the most charming audience I had ever beheld—plumed and jeweled ladies, stalwart youths, reverend white-haired men. Gradually, and to my horror, I felt my voice giving out, leaving me; the next moment I opened my mouth, but no sound followed. Again, and again, and again I attempted it, with no result. It was finished! Nervous prostration had declared itself. I went to my home in Washington, lay helpless all winter. Finally, by my physicians I was ordered to Europe, and in early September, '69, I was able to go.

"I came in time to Geneva, when, while we were waiting, anticipating and settling ourselves, one day there was announced a visit from a body of Geneva gentlemen, having some business with me.

"They introduced themselves as the officers of a society known as the International Convention of Geneva—more familiarly, the Red Cross—having for its object the amelioration of the sufferings of war, the succor and nursing of the wounded and sick in battle, the relief of prisoners, the guarding against famine and pestilence, and whatever may befall a people, under the scourge of war.

"And this, in its international character, extends not alone to its own, but to all nations within the compact.

"This society had been formed in 1865, at the instance of Dr. Louis Appia—there present—a noted surgeon in the Italian wars of Napoleon III, who had at that date called a convention composed of delegates from the civilized nations of the whole world, formed their laws for international neutral action in all wars extending to all peoples, framed their treaty and presented it for signature, through the delegates present, to the nations which they respectively represented. In less than two years this compact had been signed and entered into by twenty-five distinct governments comprising all the civilized and some semi-civilized nations of the globe.

"With your kind permission, I will depart for a few moments from my narrative and speak of the nature of the international compact, which may not be familiar to you.

"This treaty, consisting of ten articles, and making material changes in the articles of war governing the medical and hospital departments of all armies, provided among other things for entire neutrality concerning all hospitals for the care of sick and wounded men; that they should not be subject to capture; that not only the rick and wounded themselves, but the persons in attendance upon them, as surgeons, hospital stewards, and nurses should be held neutral, and free from capture; that surgeons, chaplains, and nurses, in attendance upon the wounded of a battle-field at the time of its surrender, should be regarded as non-combatants, not subject to capture, and left unmolested to care for the wounded so long as any remained upon the field, and, when no longer needed for this, be safely escorted to their own lines, and given up; that soldiers too badly wounded to be capable of again bearing arms should not be carried away as prisoners, but offered to their own army if in retreat it could take them. They must be placed in hospitals and cared for, side by side with the wounded of the enemy; that all convoys of wounded or evacuations of posts should be protected by absolute neutrality; that all supplies designed for the use of the sick or wounded should be held as neutral and entirely exempt from capture by either belligerent army; that it should be the duty of both generals in command to apprise the inhabitants, in the vicinity of a battle about to take place, of the fact that any house which should take in and entertain the wounded of either side would be placed under military protection, and remain so as long as any wounded remained therein, and that they would be also exempt from the quartering of troops and ordinary contributions of war, thus literally converting every house in the vicinity of a battle into a furnished hospital and making nurses of its inmates.

"In order to carry into effect these great changes, it would be needful to have someone distinctive sign, a badge by which all these neutral peoples and stores could be designated. There must be but one hospital flag among all nations within the treaty, and this same sign must mark all persons and things belonging to it. The convention studied diligently for this sign; at length it got so far as to decide that a cross would be acceptable to nearly all peoples. They next said, 'We represent here the great war-making monarchy of the world.'

"This little Republic of Switzerland, so small that one of us could crush her between our thumb and finger, has had the courage to invite us here to consider our cruelties and call upon us for some better system of kindness and humanity than we have heretofore practiced. For this brave lesson she deserves something of us. We cannot take her flag; she has fought a thousand years for that, and will not give it up; but if she permits, we will reverse its colors—a white cross upon a red ground—and make a red cross on a white ground the one distinctive sign of humanity in war, the world over. The consent was given and this committee of gentlemen who had called the convention, with Monsieur Gustave Moynier as its president, was reelected by all the nations as the international medium and head of war relief throughout the civilized world. To anticipate a little, I would say here that our adhesion to this treaty in 1882 has changed our articles of war; our military hospital flag. We have no longer the old faded yellow flag, but a bright red cross at every post, and the same sign to be worn by all military surgeons and attendants, if the orders of the War Department have as yet reached them, for we are to-day, you will be glad to know, not only in full accord with this International Treaty of Geneva, but are considered one of the strongest pledged nations within it.

"There were at this time thirty-one nations in this great compact, comprising all the civilized and even some of the semi-civilized nations of the globe, all with one great and incomprehensible exception, the United States of America.

"It had been three times presented to our Government; once at its formation during our war and twice since, without success, and without any reason, which, to the members of the convention, seemed sufficient or intelligent.

"And it was to ask of me the real nature of the grounds of this declination that the interview had been sought.

"If there were something objectionable in their articles, they might be modified to meet our laws, or even our prejudices—that some clue might be gained, which they could understand. They had thought of everything. If it had originated in a monarchical government, they could see some justifiable caution, but a sister

280

Republic older than our own—and yet all monarchies had signed it. In their perplexity they had come to me for a solution of the problem. What could I say? What could each or any of you have said, if confronted with this question?

"Simply that you did not know anything about it and you were sure the American people did not know anything about it or ever had heard of it. That the Government, or rather some officer of the Government, to whom the matter had been assigned, had decided upon and declined it individually, and it had never been considered in the national councils nor in any way made known to the people.

"I knew it must be so; that it had simply gone by default with no real objection; that our Government was too rushing to attend to details outside of political influence.

"I could only answer these gentlemen that I feared the matter was not sufficiently understood, being in a foreign language, and I hoped it could be better presented at some future time. I need not say that this committee of seven members and myself became friends.

"I read their Articles of Convention, their published bulletins and all reports, and, as we progress, we shall see if, in the dark days that followed, I found reason to respect the cause and appreciate the work of the work of the Geneva Convention."

On Miss Barton's arrival in Switzerland she made her home with the Golay family, father and mother of Jules Golay whom she had befriended in America, and who extended to her every possible courtesy while she was in their home and in their country.

Switzerland is beautiful in summer and early autumn, but in winter it is no improvement on New England. The beginning of cold weather found Miss Barton in discomfort. She celebrated Thanksgiving, and soon afterward left Switzerland for a milder climate.

She had a cordial invitation to spend the winter in London, but declined the opportunity. London fogs are inhospitable even to Londoners, and, to anyone in Clara Barton's condition of health, they are most depressing. She determined instead to go to the Island of Corsica.

Corsica did not agree with Clara Barton. The mild weather was favorable, but she found that she needed as much quinine there as she had required in the South. In the spring she returned to Switzerland, where her home was at the United States Consulate with Mr. and Mrs. Upton, and where she resided from March until the 26th Of May. Then she went to Berne for the sake of some baths which had been highly recommended to her. While there, an event occurred which caused her to forget that she was an invalid in search of health.

THE FRANCO-PRUSSIAN WAR

While Miss Barton was at Berne, in the villa of a friend, the Franco-Prussian War broke suddenly upon Europe. Nothing that happens in France or Germany fails to register influence at once on Switzerland. While she was there she received a call from Louise, the Grand Duchess of Baden, who, having learned of the presence there of an American woman so distinguished in war relief, invited her to go to Strassburg, which was in a state of siege, and prepare for the relief which already had become necessary and soon would be urgent. The baths were not so complete a tonic as this call to service. Yet it did not seem to her that she was strong enough to undertake this work.

Only a little later she had another invitation from Dr. Louis Appia, who had been one of the movers in the Geneva Convention. This was her opportunity to witness the actual work of the organization of which she had heard:

On the 15th of July, 1870, France declared war against Prussia. Within three days a band of agents from the International Committee of Geneva, headed by Dr. Louis Appia (one of the prime movers of the convention), equipped for work and en route for the seat of war, stood at the door of my villa inviting me to go with them and take such part as I had taken in our own war. I had not strength to trust for that, and declined with thanks, promising to follow in my own time and way, and I did follow within a week. No shot had been fired—no man had fallen. Yet this organized, powerful commission was on its way, with its skilled agents, ready to receive, direct, and dispense the charities and accumulations which the generous sympathies of twenty-two nations, if applied to, might place at its disposal. These men had treaty power to go directly on to any field, and work unmolested in full cooperation with the military and commanders-in-chief; their supplies held sacred and their efforts recognized and seconded in every direction by either belligerent army. Not a man could lie uncared for nor unfed. I thought of the Peninsula in McClellan's campaign, of Pittsburg Landing, Cedar Mountain, and second Bull Run, Antietam, Old Fredericksburg, with its acres of snow-covered and gun-covered glacée, and its fourth-day flag of truce; of its dead, and starving wounded, frozen to the ground, and our commission and their supplies in Washington, with no effective organization to get beyond; of the Petersburg mine, with its four thousand dead and wounded and no flag of truce, the wounded broiling in a July sun, dying and rotting where they fell. I remembered our prisons, crowded with starving men whom all the powers and pities of the world could not reach even with a bit of bread. I thought of the widows' weeds still fresh and dark through all the land, north and south, from the pine to the palm; the shadows on the hearths and hearts over all my country. Sore, broken hearts, ruined, desolate homes! Was this a people to decline a humanity in war? Was this a country to reject a treaty for the help of wounded soldiers? Were these the women and men to stand aloof and consider? I believed, if these people knew that the last cloud of war had forever passed from their horizon, the tender, painful, deathless memories of what had been would bring them in with a force no power could resist. They needed only to know.

Soon Clara Barton was on her way to the front. She went, not to Strassburg, but to Basle, where she witnessed with great satisfaction the efficiency of the Red Cross system. Basle is in Switzerland, just at the German border, but there representatives of both belligerent nations had their headquarters for purposes of relief of suffering. The Red Cross, protected by international agreement, had its base of supplies in neutral territory, and the agents of both armies organized their relief forces without molestation from each other. Wherever a battle occurred, relief could be and was provided in many cases before the first drop of blood was shed. Miss Barton's admiration for the work of this society grew as she contrasted its efficiency with the unpreparedness and deadly delay which she had known all too well through the Civil War:

As I journeyed on and saw the work of these Red Cross societies in the field, accomplishing in four months under their systematic organization what we failed to accomplish in four years without it— no mistakes, no needless suffering, no starving, no lack of care, no waste, no confusion, but order, plenty, cleanliness, and comfort wherever that little flag made its way, a whole continent marshaled under the banner of the Red Cross—as I saw all this, and joined and worked in it, you will not wonder that I said to myself, "If I live to return to my country, I will try to make my people understand the Red Cross and that treaty." But I did more than resolve, I promised other nations I would do it, and other reasons pressed me to remember my promise. The Franco-Prussian War and the war of the Commune were both enormous in the extent of their operations and in the suffering of individuals. This great modem international impulse of charity went out everywhere to meet and alleviate its miseries. The small, poor countries gave of their poverty and the rich nations poured out abundantly of their vast resources. The contributions of those under the Red Cross went quietly, promptly through international responsible channels, were thoughtfully and carefully distributed through well-known agents; returns, accurate to a franc, were made and duly published to the credit of the contributing nations, and the object aimed at was accomplished.

France, Germany, and Switzerland had been in the international compact for years past, all organized, every town and city with its Red Cross Relief Committee, its well-filled workrooms like our relief societies in our war, but all prepared in times of peace and plenty, awaiting the emergency.

The Swiss headquarters were at Basle, bordering on both France and Germany; and there all the supplies were to be sent and held on call from the hundreds of workers at the fields, for the use of the sick and wounded of either side indiscriminately wherever the need was found greatest. The belligerent nations had each its own headquarters; that of Germany at Berlin, with the Empress Augusta at its head; that of France, at Paris, under the auspices of its lovely Empress.

But you will understand that the international feature of this requires that all contributions from other nations be sent through the international headquarters; hence, no people within the compact, except the belligerents, could send direct to either France or Germany, but must correspond with the Central Committee at Geneva, and learn from it the place of greatest need and the proper agents on the spot to whom the consignment should be made. This wise provision both marked and sustained their neutrality.

Up to this moment, no point beyond Basle had been reached. This was, then, the great central depot of the International Red Cross, and it was worth something to have seen it as I saw it in less than two weeks after the sudden declaration, a declaration as unexpected as if some nation should declare war against us to-morrow.

My first steps were to the storehouses, and to my amazement I found there a larger supply than I had ever seen at any one time in readiness for the field at our own Sanitary Commission rooms in Washington, even in the fourth year of the war; and the trains were loaded with boxes and barrels pouring in from every city, town, and hamlet in Switzerland, even from Austria and northern Italy, and the trained, educated nurses stood awaiting their appointments, each with this badge upon the arm or breast, and every box, package, or barrel with a broad bright scarlet cross, which rendered it as safe and sacred from molestation (one might almost say) as the bread and wine before the altar.

You will conclude that quiet old historic Basle was, by this time, a busy city. It was frightened out of its senses. Bordering on both France and Germany, it lay directly on the possible march of either army on its way to the other; and the moment Switzerland shall allow this crossing, her neutrality will be declared broken, and not only Basle, but all Switzerland, will be held in a state of actual war and become common battle ground for both.

I passed a week in that city among this work, to learn it more thoroughly, to be able to judge it in its practical bearings, its merits and demerits, so far as I could, before giving my qualifications and endorsement. You will not wonder that Basle felt her responsibility and trembled for both her own safety and the safety of the State!

Not very long did she remain in Basle. Soon a dispatch was received from Mülhausen, and Clara Barton, no longer an invalid, set out again for the front. She was not alone; accompanying her was a young woman who thenceforth became her companion, and who some years later followed her to America, Miss Antoinette Margot.

Accompanied by this devoted girl, she set forth as she had done nine years before, for the relief of suffering on the battle-field. She told the story of it in an address which she gave afterward, which was little more than a transcript of her diary:

A mile from Basle, we met the pickets, but passed without serious interruption for the first six miles, when the detentions became longer, and the road lined with fugitives fleeing to Switzerland, entire families, carrying such articles as were possible: the better classes in family and public carriages; the next, in farmer and peasant wagons, drawn by horses, oxen, cows, and often the animals of the family accompanying the wagon which contained the most useful articles for an emergency—kettles, beds, and clothing.

Those who could not afford this style of removal were wearily but hastily trudging along on foot, carrying in their arms such as their strength would allow, and the tired children plodding along on behind, or drawn in little carts, with bundles of clothing and bits of bread.

Sometimes a family was fortunate to have a cow or a goat with them when they had no wagon. Sometimes, after the Bernese custom, a large dog drew the wagon of luggage. But in some manner all were making on, often in tears, and always with grief in their faces. All day we saw but two carriages going in our direction. But all whom we met looked at us in astonishment. "The Prussians are coming," or, "There has been a terrible battle and everybody is being killed. Turn back, turn back!"

Sometimes one would be so earnest as to come to the heads of our horses, to urge us to return, and it was not always easy to keep our driver in heart.

At — we were met and stopped by a large body of people, the mayor at the head, and our destination inquired, and at the same time informed that it was exceedingly hazardous to proceed, as great battles were going on at a short distance from Mülhausen, and that the Prussians were crossing the Rhine in great force. But when to all this we replied that we were aware of the state of things, and that was the reason of our going, that we went to care for the wounded of the battles, they all cried with one voice, "Mon Dieu—God bless you," and the old white-haired mayor led the way to the side of our carriage, to take our hands, exclaiming, "God preserve and be with you, my children, and He is with you, or you would not be here on this mission." And the crowd that jostled in the street, one after another, followed his example, with the tears falling over their faces, even to the little children to whom we reached down our hands to reach theirs, or to touch them as they were held up to us.

No wonder they wept! Their fathers, sons, and brothers would be in the bloody carnage so soon to follow. Already they had bade to God only knows how many the last farewell.

At length they let go our bridles and we passed on, and, with such scenes every moment in some form occurring, we performed the remainder of our journey to Mülhausen.

We made our way directly to the President of the International Committee of the Red Cross of Mülhausen. Monsieur August Dolfus.

A dispatch had just been received from the International Committee of the Red Cross at Mülhausen, France, inviting me to come there. Dr. Appia and his noble band of pioneers had evidently passed that way. This would be in a direct line to Strassburg, and the field of Weissenburg, and I decided to leave by the earliest train next morning.

As good fortune would have it, there came to me at this moment a kind-featured, gentle-toned, intelligent Swiss girl, who had left the *canter de vaud* to go alone to care for the wounded. The society introduced her to me.

Perhaps it would be well to anticipate so far as to speak of this young lady more fully, for all through you will know her as my faithful Antoinette—Antoinette Margot, Swiss by birth, French by cultivation, education, and habit. The two national characteristics met and joined in her. The enthusiasm of the one, the fidelity of the other, were so perfectly blended and balanced in her, that one could never determine which prevailed. No matter, as both were unquenchable, unconquerable. She was raised in the city of Lyons, France, an only daughter, and at that age an artist of great note, even in the schools of artistic France. Fair-haired, playful, bright, and confiding, she spoke English as learned from books, and selected her forms of expression by inference. One day she made the remark that something was "unpretty." Observing a smile on my face, she asked if that were not correct. I replied that we do not say "unpretty" in English. "No. But you say unwise, unselfish, unkind, and ungrateful—why not unpretty?" "I do not know," I answered. I didn't either.

There was something in that face to be drawn to "at sight," and to her astonishment and delight I told her she might accompany me.

Scarce was this arrangement completed when breathless messengers rushed to tell us that the French still fled before the troops of the Prince Royal, that the Prussians were marching direct upon the Rhine, if indeed it were not already crossed, and that the French had destroyed their railroad to Strassburg, that the rolling-stock of the road had been run off to save it, and that even the station was closed.

This was after dark—the news was not of a nature to favor delay. Instead of five o'clock by train next morning, I would start at daybreak by private carriage.

At length a *cochére* was found who would undertake the journey—the task of driving to Mülhausen for a consideration which, under the circumstances, it was quite possible for him to obtain. At the appointed hour, with some small satchels, the requisite supply of shawls and waterproofs, with my quiet, sensible young companion, I set off once more, shall I say—for "the front"? That expression was very strange after a lapse of five years, and I had thought never to hear it again in connection with myself.

Arriving at Mülhausen, Miss Barton found there was no present need of her services. She determined to set forth for Strassburg. With great difficulty she made her way thither. Through rain and mud, with conveyance almost impossible to obtain, she finally arrived, distance of seventy-two miles, which journey she completed in a single day.

She was received with honor at Strassburg. The United States Consul and Vice-Consul were both Germans, but both had fought in the Civil War on the side of the Union, and they both knew of Clara Barton. The Consul had been a surgeon and the Vice-Consul a chaplain. Both welcomed her to the Consulate and to their homes.

But Strassburg was about to undergo bombardment. The city was then under French rule, but its population was mixed. It contained besides its own proper inhabitants many German-Americans just then eager to get out of Alsace. The Consul got an omnibus full of them, with Clara Barton in the van, and set out to place them inside the German lines. He took them as far as he was allowed to go, and turned back on horseback. Clara Barton and her omnibus full of people moved on. They carried the American flag. Part of the way it served to enable them to pass the sentries. But when they reached the German outposts, it ceased to afford them safe passage:

We had the United States flag at our front, and the first sentry halted us to learn what it was. When informed, he promptly disputed it. He had been in Mexico, and Guatemala and Australia and the Sandwich Islands, and it was not the American flag at all. Reference to a chart of flags convinced him, and we passed. But this made us aware of a great mistake we had committed.

In our hurry of getting off in the rain and darkness of the early morning, we had forgotten our International Red Cross Flag, and all our insignia. There was no return—as well seek to go back through the gates of death. We must trust to luck.

At the demand for the Red Cross insignia by the keen, acute sentry, Miss Barton retired, seized the bow of red ribbon, without which color she was seldom seen, and twisted it into a red cross which, with the thread and needle taken from her pocket, she sewed upon her arm.

The next sentinel, about a league from Strassburg, recognized our flag, saluted it, and did not even halt us.

These were the conditions under which, for the first time, Clara Barton wore the insignia which, in America, was destined to be forever associated with her name.

The outer German sentinels were now safely passed; but before she was permitted to enter the lines of the German army she was informed that if she entered she must remain. She might return if she wished within the French lines, or she might make her way again into Switzerland, but if she entered the German lines she must be willing to remain there until the termination of the war. She had no desire to go back to Strassburg and submit to the bombardment. She did not now desire to return to neutral territory. She entered the German lines and made her way to Carlsruhe, where she was a guest in the home of the Duke of Baden. She and the Grand Duchess Louise became devoted friends. The last letter Clara Barton wrote before her death, and with the knowledge that she had but a few hours to live, was written to the Grand Duchess Louise. Among the tributes that lay upon the grave of Clara Barton when the earth closed over her was 'a beautiful laurel wreath from the Grand Duchess Louise.

It was an accident that put Clara Barton inside the German lines. She had planned it otherwise when she went to Strassburg. She had rather expected that her work would be to the wounded French, but the fortunes of war put her within the opposing lines, and to her it mattered little. Her interests were not those of a belligerent. She was ready to minister to the suffering of either army.

Again Clara Barton was on the battle-field. From Carlsruhe she visited in succession several of the bloody fields. But when Strassburg fell, as it did September 28, 1870, she turned her back upon the comforts of the grand ducal palace, and entered the city where a few weeks before she had been the honored guest of the United States Consul. Thousands of its inhabitants were homeless and in danger of starvation. She organized a workroom where she set two hundred and fifty poor women to work. For forty days she and Antoinette Margot did their work amid the ruins of this distressed city. At first there was nothing to do but to give relief on application. There lie before the writer some of the original meal tickets which were issued at this time. But before long she saw that this plan if continued, would pauperize the women. She devised the plan by which they were to work and be paid for it whenever they were able to work. She wrote a letter to Count Bismarck, being introduced to him by the Grand Duchess Louise, and which obtained official recognition for her type of work:

Strassburg, Dec. 9th, 1870

Count Bismarck
Governor-General of Alsace
Honored Count:
Through the politeness of your adjutant and his amiable lady, I learn that Your highness will kindly permit me to communicate with you in reference to the work I am endeavoring to perform among the destitute people who are so fortunate as to fall under your protecting care. But speaking no German, lacking confidence to attempt a conversation in French, and fearing that English may not be familiar to you, I decide to write, subject to translation, the little explanation I would make of my work, its origin, progress, and design.

I entered Strassburg the second day after its fall, and, observing both the distress of its inhabitants and their bitterness toward their captors, who must always remain their neighbors, I deemed it wise, while they should receive the charity so much needed, that something of it be presented by German hands. In this view I was most cordially met by that noblest of ladies, the Grand Duchess of Baden, to whom I am also indebted for this introduction to you, and immediately, under her generous patronage, I returned with an assistant to do what we could in the name of Germany. At first, we could only give indiscriminately to the hundreds who thronged our doors. But, directly, I perceived that a prolonged continuance of this system would be productive of greater disaster to the moral condition of the people than the bombardment had been to their physical; that in a city, comprising less than eighty thousand inhabitants, there would shortly be twenty thousand confirmed beggars. Only a small proportion of these families had been accustomed to receive charity, but one winter of common beggary would reduce the larger part to a state of careless degradation from which they would scarcely again emerge. It seemed morally indispensable that remunerative employment in some form should be given them. Again I consulted Her Royal highness, who kindly approved, generously making the first contribution of materials, and we opened our present "Workrooms for Women" in the month of October. To say that the results have surpassed my most sanguine expectation is little, the facts are much more; but a stranger both to people and language, it is not singular that my work, which depends entirely upon public patronage, has often lacked the necessary means to attain the full measure of success.

My original design was to aid not only the inhabitants of Strassburg, but those in other portions of Alsace who are equally destitute. I thought that to be just to all and produce the best moral influence, the employment, and the payment, should be given to Strassburg, thus making of the inhabitants workers, instead of beggars, but that the warm garments made by them should be sent to the half-naked peasants of the villages, and little country homes where the harvest has been lost, and neither money nor clothing comes within reach. And to the extent of my means I have done this. The peasants have heard of the rooms, and often walk two and three leagues to ask for garments, and the clergymen from around the old battle-fields, and from Bitch, are making appeals in behalf of their half-naked and shivering people. Both my sympathy and my judgment would favor the hearing of these appeals so far as possible. This population must always be the neighbors, if not a part, of the German people; it will be most desirable that they should be also friends; they are in distress—their hearts can never be better reached than now; the little seed sown to-day may have in it the germs of future peace or war.

But pardon my boldness, Honored Count; I am neither a diplomatist nor political counselor; I am only a maker of garments for the poor.

I have objected to the purchasing of materials for my work from magazines, believing that, if the attention of some large manufacturers of stuffs were called to the subject, material could be supplied in a much better manner.

Other noble societies, I rejoice to say, have sprung up later, all of which I believe will confine their praiseworthy efforts to the city of Strassburg, and in every respect but that of affording employment will, I trust, prove sufficient for the necessities. My little work has been the pioneer, that ploughed through the earliest and deepest drifts, and which, though often weary and disheartened, still seeks to push beyond the beaten track, over the fields, and along the hillsides, and gather the sufferers out of the storm.

After this, I fear too lengthy, explanation, will Your highness kindly permit me, for the sake of perspicuity, to arrange under two or three distinct heads the prominent features of my work.

1st, I desire to give employment, and payment therefor at the usual rates, to some portion of the destitute families of Strassburg.

2d, To distribute the garments made by them among the people of the surrounding districts which have been reduced by the calamities of the war.

3d, That, beyond this, I design to make no appropriations of charities, but to refer all such applicants residing within the city to the various societies and committees of the same.

4th, To attain this object and carry on the work is required, material, in warm stuffs of both wool and cotton, suitable for clothing for working-men, women, and children.

5th, Money to pay the workers—sufficient for the number employed.

Miss Barton also sent an appeal to America for assistance in the purchase of material. Her letter to the New York *Tribune* brought her prompt response, and she was not without means for the support of her work. She used the money which was sent to her in such fashion as to make it do double duty. She bought material and had it made into garments largely by the women who needed those garments for themselves or their families. She paid them for their work in vouchers—two francs a day, which was good pay; and she sold them the products of their work at low prices. They received good wages for their labor and good value for their wages, but, wherever they were able, they had to work for the vouchers they got, and pay for the clothing they obtained.

I have some of the odd little two-franc vouchers which she required the women to give. She was not held to any system of accounting, and when there was need she spent money without vouchers; but wherever it was

23 feasible, she did her business in a business-like way, and she taught the women to be business-like. In her final accounting, only a surprisingly small fraction of her money had been expended without vouchers.

On Christmas Day of 1870, her forty-ninth birthday, she wrote to Mrs. Frances Childs Vassall a letter in which she gave an account of her own work and also passed a distinctly unfavorable judgment upon the French as they appeared to her at that time:

"Women's Workroom" Strassburg, Alsace,
Dec. 25, 1870

My Dear Fannie:

With your usual sagacity you timed your letter just to the moment. It was Christmas Eve, five o'clock, cold as Greenland. I had sent my assistants

294

home the day before to enjoy a few days of leisure with their friends. I sat writing at the farthest end of my large room, from which only a range of white curtains separated and enclosed me in my little "counting-room." The postman's rap at the door caused me to look up, and through the curtains I could discern a singular glimmer of lights like stars, but moving from point to point, as if the firmament were not satisfied with the arrangement of its luminaries, and sought the opportunity to rearrange. Startled at first, I rose from my seat to rush out, but suddenly remembering the evening and the occasion it occurred to me that my presence at that especial instant might not be desirable and I reseated. After a minute more of shifting and fluttering, my little domestic Emily appeared between the curtains, "Here are two letters, and will you please to walk out." The letters were from you and Fannie Atwater, and the walking out revealed a Christmas tree in full blaze all for myself. It had been arranged and left by my good ladies before they had departed, with instructions to the domestics to produce and light it at five o'clock in the evening. It abounded in fruit and flowers and mosses, and some little nice things which their good hearts had dictated for my comfort. And so, in the delicate shadows falling like tracery upon the snow which spread beneath its branches, I sat me down and read your dear, welcome letter. Although you did not intend a word of sentiment in it, nor a touching sentence, I could not truly say that my hand did not sometimes brush across my eyes as I read; it was so like old times to receive a whole letter from you, all from you, and all for me. I knew I did not deserve it. I have been so remiss in writing, and I don't know how it happens. I can only account for it on your own grounds, that when we are occupied and feel that there is something to say there is no time to say it, and when unoccupied we become listless and there seems to be nothing to say. I am always disgusted at this state of things in the human economy, but I can neither reconstruct nor mend it. It is a little more than a week since I posted a long letter to Sally all about myself, selfish as could be, and I must not inflict a similar chapter on you, as you will be compelled to go over that when it arrives. I am rejoiced to hear from yourself that you are better than when I left.

The greatest obstacle I meet in the way of a full restoration of strength is the utter inability to get sleep enough; an average of five hours is the maximum. If I by chance succeed in getting a half-hour beyond this one night, I have it "docked off" the next. When I was stronger this would do me; I could run my machine at full speed all day upon this power, and did it for years; but now the belts are slack and the wheels slip and I lose so much power that my pond is all drawn off. I should be so glad if I could adopt your plan of a nap in the afternoon, but I cannot get it unless by mere accident once in a great while. But I, too, am so much better than when we last saw each other that I feel I should never mention the subject of health and strength again while they are as good as at present.

I thank you for mentioning to me Mrs. Livermore's lectures. I know she was a favorite in Worcester; you know she was always a favorite with me, although I never met her. Madame de Gasparin's appeal for peace has found a warm and strong advocate in Mrs. Howe. I hope some good may come of it. All that you say upon the subject is true, and it is no small amount of "picking up" that women have to do in consequence of these reckless fellows; from boyhood to manhood and from manhood to age, it is all the same. I can never see a poor mutilated wreck blown to pieces with powder and lead without wondering if visions of such an end ever flitted before his mother's mind when she washed and dressed her fair-skinned baby. Woman should certainly have some voice in the matter of war, either affirmative or negative, and the fact that she has not this should not be made the ground on which to deprive her of other privileges. She shan't say there will be no war, and she shan't take any part in it when there is one, and because she doesn't take part in war she mustn't vote, and because she can't vote she has no voice in her government, and because she has no voice in her government she isn't a citizen, and because she isn't a citizen she has no rights, and because she has no rights she must submit to wrongs, and because she submits to wrongs she isn't anybody. What does she know about war? Because she doesn't know anything about it, she mustn't say or do anything about it. 11 Three blind mice—cut off their heads with a carving knife—three blind mice." I pray for peace, and all that may promote it, and if there be a power on earth which can right the wrongs for which nations go to war, I pray that it may be made manifest, but when I think I fear. How supreme an international court must it have been to be able to induce the Southerners to liberate their slaves or to convince them that the "mudsills" and "greasy mechanics" and "homed Yankees" were a people entitled to sufficient respect to be treated on fair international ground! And how much legislation would it have taken to convince the world what a worthless bubble of assumption was France, so utterly unworthy the leadership she assumed, and to have laid her in all respects so open before the world that it should with one voice repudiate her leadership and refuse to follow her as heretofore in frivolity, immorality, folly, fashion, vice, and crime! She seems to me to have been only one great balloon, and now that the bayonets and bombs have pierced it full of holes it sends out tens of thousands of little balloons in its collapse.

It is bad for France, but I am not certain but the lesson will be beneficial to the rest of the world. I don't know if we may always trust councils—we had one at Rome not half a year ago that voted a dogma which turned backward the progress of enlightened thought two centuries, and how great a power of legislation would have been required to overthrow that decision! But I suspect the fear of Victor Emmanuel's bayonets have seriously interfered with it. Oh, I don't know; it is such a mystery, and mankind the greatest mystery of all! I shall never get it right in this world, what- ever may happen in the one that sets this right. But how prosy I am—and it all comes of that five hours' sleep. You know Beecher says, "If the preacher doesn't sleep, his hearers will." I hope you reserved the reading of this till you were ready for your nap.

Soon after the fall of Paris, Miss Barton determined to make her way thither, but before leaving Strassburg she placed before the authorities of that city her views of the kind of organization which should be permanently established there for the relief of those who were suffering by reason of the war. That letter shows how thoroughly she understood the problem of administering relief without pauperizing the beneficiaries:

Strassburg, January 3d, 1871

Monsieur Bergmann
Membre du Comité de Secours Strasbourgeois
Monsieur:
Your very courteous request, that I would present something of my ideas in reference to the subject of employment for the poor of your stricken city, demands, perhaps, that I explain, first, the reason and origin of my own presence here. A long and familiar acquaintance with the calamities of war led me to direct my steps to the gates of your besieged city the first day that it was possible to enter, viz., September 29th. Not as a matter of curiosity, for bombarded cities had long ceased to possess any novelty for me, but to ascertain if there were any service I could render.

My earliest visit was to your civil hospital, and its wards of wounded women, which were indeed a novelty in the history of the world. Seeing no better way of serving them, I took a written account of each woman at her bedside, what she had suffered, and what she had lost, and, carrying the sad record, placed it personally in the hand of Her Royal highness, the Grand Duchess of Baden, which, I trust, contributed a little toward directing to your afflicted city the immediate and active sympathy of that Court and Capital.

This accomplished, I returned with my present excellent and efficient assistant, Miss Zimmermann, to learn what further could be done. A few days' observation convinced me that, in the majority of instances, the actual loss of property which had been sustained by the class of persons who came to demand charity was of less real importance to them than the total loss of their customary remunerative occupation; that while the first merely reduced them to want, the latter would make of them permanent beggars and vagrants, thus doing for their moral, all that the bombardment had done for their physical, condition.

With the somewhat forlorn hope of being able to arrest in a few individual instances these disastrous consequences, I at once commenced the system of work-giving, in which occupation you have found me, and concerning which you have done me the honor to ask some opinions and recommendations.

If I might be so bold as to make a single recommendation, in reference to this unhappy population under their present calamitous circumstances, it would be that of the most immediate promotion of honest industry; that at the earliest moment labor be made to walk hand in hand, and step by step with charity, and, wherever it is possible, to precede the charity that gives without return; to open every possible avenue of employment to all classes of individuals, especially the women and children, in view of the peculiar nature of the calamities of the present hour which have left so large a proportion of them without the husband and father of the family upon whose labor they must have been more or less accustomed to depend in former times.

A first step would certainly be the making of garments with which to keep themselves comfortable and wholesome, and, if I might be permitted to make a suggestion, it would be that strong, but cheap, colored material, either of wool or cotton, suitable for dresses, skirts, and sacques for women and girls, and pantaloons and blouses for men and boys, be purchased either from manufacturers or merchants (all of whom are suffering from the effects of the war) and, carefully fitted and arranged, be given to women to make up in their homes, after the manner which we have pursued with the thirty or more who are at present employed from these rooms.

True, every woman will not sew well at first, but we have found that nearly everyone will learn, and have now no trouble with our workers, and the garments made by them are good enough to be placed in any ordinary clothing bazaar for sale.

The immediate disposition to be made of this clothing when finished is still an important question. For the moral effect upon those who are to receive it, I would recommend that it be not given outright and entire, as this course still has the tendency to foster habits of beggary and vagrancy which it is so desirable to discourage. Receipt without return is ever demoralizing, and for this, it were better that the poor, even, pay something for what they receive, if it be only a small proportion of the original cost, and with this view, I would recommend the placing of the articles in a kind of bazaar connected with and forming a part of the present noble establishment of the "Comité" of which you are a member, and a price, more or less real, and more or less nominal, be placed upon them, such a price as will bring them within the reach of all excepting the most abject, who are forever, perhaps, to be treated after the ordinary modes of wholesale charity; but the effort should be always to reduce this class as much as possible, by lifting up out of it every family and individual that kindly encouragement, paid labor, and reasonable prices can elevate above it. One would soon find that a small sale room of this kind would not necessarily be confined to the few varieties which I have named, but shoes, stockings, and many articles of ordinary apparel, and perhaps, also, many articles useful in the family household would find their way into it, and thus, through the generous and protecting hands of the Comitg, substantial aid and a first impetus be given to many a small but worthy and unfortunate artisan of your city who now finds no purchasers for his products, or no material to commence his work, and to the smaller merchants who find now no purchasers for their goods.

I would not have it supposed that I present this little idea as a permanent cure for existing ills, but as a momentary help in time of trouble until the hard season passes, and business has time to resume a little its ordinary course.

Care would have to be taken to guard against imposition, to see that persons did not buy to sell again. The same vigilance which is now exercised in regard to those demanding charity would be necessary here. One may fog] to sell, as well as buy to sell. But it should not discourage the work that it is liable to abuse. God's best gifts to man are hourly abused; shall we expect more for ours?

All articles would not find purchasers, it may be said. True, but what remains in hand will constitute the supply to be given in direct charity, and it is presumed that there will always remain a demand in this quarter equal to the supply, even under the best systems of distributive and protected labor.

It may be asked if this system will not operate against the merchants who deal in ready-made clothing. It should not in the least, as these people could never purchase a garment at full price and consequently could not become their customers.

In order that my suggestions should not seem merely theoretical, permit me to turn for a moment to the more practical details. It may be asked if garments can be made to fit women and girls without actual measurement? I would reply that, with a graduated scale of five or six sizes, we have found no more difficulty in fitting women than the tailor finds in fitting men and boys without actual measurement.

Again, will there not be much waste of material in cutting quantities of garments? Very little; literally none; in the graduated sizes, one garment cuts from the form left by the other, down to the smallest size, and of the pieces too small for these we have the custom of making caps for boys and mittens for the hands, so that no piece larger than the size of a child's hand need be left unused.

It would be proper to mention among materials to be purchased the small articles necessary in the making-up of garments, such as thread, laces, buttons, agraffes, tapes, etc., etc., the sale of which would still benefit another class of small merchants.

I may have dwelt too strongly and too long upon the subject of putting a price upon charities, but if so, I can only ask to be excused upon the ground of the moral elevation I so ardently desire for the unhappy people of your city, and remind you that it is a simple thing to leave this idea untouched, as the giving of work by no means depends upon it, and this course alone pursued after the ordinary methods of charity will of itself place the name of the "Comité of Strassburg" high upon the roll of the active charitable institutions of the world.

With sentiments of the highest consideration both for yourself and your Honorable Comité, I remain, dear sir,
Very truly yours

Clara Barton

By this time there were organized American agencies for the relief of suffering caused by the war. Clara Barton endeavored to establish relationships with one of these at Brussels or Antwerp, but without conspicuous success, as shown by her letter to General Burnside:

General Burnside

My Esteemed General:

I am sure that a word will suffice to remind you of our interview at Geneva, and its object; and perhaps you will recollect that I craved the privilege of personal introduction from you to the American Legation at Brussels where it seemed proper to locate the headquarters of the American organization for the relief of the French peasantry which I had then traveled half the length of Germany and the width of Switzerland in the rain and snows to effect. I saw then so clearly all which has since transpired that I could not repress the conscientious demand of duty to use every effort within my power to prepare for the safe receipt and faithful and wise distribution of the forthcoming gifts of our countrymen, although at that moment no societies assisted and no monies had been raised in America to my knowledge except by the French and Germans residing there. I had, like yourself, come fresh from the scenes of strife, want, and desolation, and was chilled and bewildered by the cool indifference of the Americans residing here to whom I referred in such warmth of confidence. Only yourself, of all I met, gave a word of hearty approval. You will remember as I was surrounded that I could not tell you this at that moment; neither had I words to tell you how grateful I was for your commendation of my plans. Even the names of those who knew me well were withheld from me, as it seemed to me to be exceedingly moderate and modest, proper, hesitating and haggling until after you had given yours; then they came, so much weak men need a leader. Then I hurried back to my post of duty at Strassburg, and on to Brussels, still in the rain, to be there on the "fifth day," hoping to find and through you gain the more willing aid of the American representation there, and found something like American headquarters either there or at Antwerp; but to my excessive regret you had already passed out of town as I came in, and I stood alone in that strange city with my heavy, unfinished task. I called upon General Shetland, who very properly recommended me to his superior. I called upon him. He met me sharply and unkindly; informed me in a needlessly rude manner that he never heard of me before, and couldn't understand what I wanted; that he saw no names on my paper which justified him in placing his there, and he should not do it. Of course I left his presence without a word. Genial General Shetland was hurt and offered his name "if it would do any good," but I could not suffer him to place himself in unpleasant relations with his superior and declined it.

Still in the storm and mud, defeated and discouraged, sore and weak, I left Brussels and made Metz, which had that day opened its hungry gates. After a few hard days' work among its famishing, fevered population I came once more to my work in Strassburg. I now saw clearly that I could effect nothing in the way of an organization to aid the work of our countrymen when they should see fit to commence it. I was grieved for the loss, through this account, to the suffering French and the loss of satisfaction to our countrymen eventually when the wiser ones should come to realize that they had not done their own work in their own name and manner, and with the best results. But I was only one woman alone, and had no power to move to action full-fed, sleek-coated, ease-loving, pleasure-seeking, well-paid, and well-placed countrymen in this war-trampled, dead, old land, each one afraid that he should be called upon to do something.

On June I Miss Barton left her well-organized work in Strassburg and hastened to Paris, where she spent about six weeks in the relief of suffering and distress. From there she went to Lyons, where she established another workroom such as she had had in Strassburg. Something of the detail of her work in Paris is afforded us in a brief letter to a gentleman in London, acknowledging a gift of five hundred pounds sterling for her work. We see something of the grim situation which she confronted in that city. A much more cheerful letter is one which she wrote to Annie Childs just as she was about to leave Lyons at the end of August. Annie had been her dressmaker for many years. This letter, informing Annie that she was now the head of a dressmaking establishment of her own, shows how fully at this time she seemed to have recovered her old vivacity, and to be, amidst the desolation of a conquered country, her own wholesome, self-reliant self:

Lyons, Francs, August 20, 1871

My dear Annie:

If I were to make an apology as long as my offense, I could write nothing else, but I don't like apologies; you don't either, do you? Then let me hasten to proclaim myself an idle, lazy, procrastinating, miserable do-nothing and good-for-nothing; if that isn't enough, I leave the sentence open for you to finish and I sign it squarely when you have done and call it "quits." But really it *has* been too bad. I have neglected everybody in general, not you in particular. I thought I was too busy to write. I don't suppose I was, only that I did not employ my time well. I *know* this is often so and perhaps always. I wish I had been better educated in this regard as well as every other. If you are ever married, as you doubtless will be, and have a family of eight or ten children, I beg you will make it a specialty in their several educations that they be taught to do things in the proper time. You will do

302

me a favor to remember this as one of "my efforts for the good of humanity."

I wanted all last winter to tell you about my "dressmaking" and describe to you my "shop." I knew it would interest you if no one else. Now, wasn't that the last thing you would have thought of, that *I* should come to Europe and set up *dressmaking*, and *French* dressmaking at that? I knew the fact would be a little surprise to most of my old friends who knew me best, but to you I imagine it a matter of bewildering letter astonishment. Well, you should have seen the patterns! "Did I have patterns?" Didn't I? And didn't I cut them myself? And didn't I direct all the making until I had imparted my wonderful art to others? And *you* think my garments were fearfully and wonderfully made! Well, that opinion comes of your being an old maid and so particular. I assure you, Miss Annie Childs, that they were nice garments and prettily cut and well-made, and I found them in excellent demand; everyone wanted them and never a word of *complaint of the price*; everybody seemed to be perfectly convinced that they were cheap enough at my first offer. I had ten young girls (like yours) dressmakers, and from one to three men "tailors" who worked twelve hours a day, but only with the shears, never an hour's sewing; and no one sewed at my "shop"; only those who must be taught to take something out and do it over. And we made dresses and sacques and petticoats and chemises and aprons and hoods and mittens and pantaloons, vests, blouses, shirts, socks, of all kinds of material and all sizes that ever the tiniest baby grew to. Oh, yes, and such lots of things for babies—little dresses, little bonnets, cloaks, blankets, two thousand garments every week. I don't think they were gored and flounced and frilled as much as yours, Miss Annie Childs, but they were strong and warm and handsome. It is true all my seamstresses had not such nimble, delicate fingers as one might desire for the finest work; they wore very large thimbles sometimes; but there were plenty of small fingers in the family. They came very gladly twice a week to see me and showed me with great pride their successful efforts; always the work came home in the market basket, and always I knew that that same basket would load the other way with bread and a little meat if it were possible, but this was not always. But it was such a comfort to see them, week by week, grow better clothed themselves and the children, till by and by a woman and her baby came to look only like a big and a little bundle of the same clothing she carried in her basket. And all the working-people of the city came to look like walking bundles of the same clothing. To be sure, it took away something from the picturesque style of the city as I first saw it when at least ten thousand human beings were perfectly arranged for models for

303

the painter and the sculptor. I admit that it was highly artistic, but I thought it a *"peu trop"* for the season, considering that the earliest snows had commenced to fall. Oh, but don't you wish now that you had come and worked at the head of my "shop"—didn't I wish it? More than once I sighed in my inmost soul for you. How rich I should have been, with you at my side! Just think of it! I shall write to Fannie sometime when I hain't told all the news to you—please hand her this if she looks patient and strong enough to stand it.

How much I wonder what you are all doing at home! I seem entirely to have lost the thread, and from the stray little thrums which I get hold of I cannot pick it up. I am just now in despair about Sally. someone writes me that they suppose I know all about her and Vester's *sickness!* Imagine the effect of this piece of intelligence. Another says, it was fortunate they were with Ber and Fannie, as they were sure of good care!!! This is consoling. What did they have, and how did they get it, and how was it, and when was it, and how is it now? Do pray you write and tell me. I am distressed and can't at all help myself. I do hope they have not had a serious illness, but I keep feeling all the time that somebody will be sick. I keep writing Sally at Washington, but have no idea where she is and where you are this hot summer, and Fannie, poor, dear, neglected Fannie. She ought to cross me off her books, and I guess she has before this time. I know there has never been a day since I left that the entire troop of you all has not passed in panorama before me, and I have attempted to place you all as I thought it most likely to be, but I suppose I have been wide of the mark.

For me, as you must have known a hundred times when I left Strassburg, I went to Paris, and, after six weeks there distributing clothing and money, I left and came to Lyons to visit a family of one of the younger ladies who had aided me twice since the war commenced, and I have remained here about as long as I was in Paris, but am ready to leave, and shall again this week go to Paris for a day or two to meet some parties of Americans who will be there on their way home, and from there I am to go, as I have been once, into the central eastern portion of France to see the places and peoples who have been much destroyed by the war and the sieges. I have no idea how much time I shall consume here. I must judge this by the condition I find the people in. I am almost tired of France and long for Germany or something which is solid and Saxon. There is no truth, no fixedness of purpose, nothing reliable, nothing sensible in France, and it only disgusts me that they have always claimed the leadership of the world and that so stupidly it has been conceded to them. I do hope the German bayonets have punched a hole in that bubble large enough to burst it. It is certainly time. If they were even neat, I would not complain so much of them, but they are such a dirty race of people, dirty but fashionable. One gets tired of this. Now, you will see from this that it is a real merit in me to work for the French. I do it out of pity and charity toward suffering humanity, because they need, and not because I gratify my love or my taste by it. I do neither. I think it right to do or I would not touch it, I do assure you.

Now, there are so many people whom you see every day that I would be so glad to see that it makes me almost homesick to write you. Does Willis still remain in Oxford, and Uncle John and Nancy; how are they? And Mrs. Hannah Sanford and Mrs. Sigourney, and all my cousins in Worcester; do you see them? Cousin Lydia Grout, do you see her ever? The Bacons and Starrs and Cousin Maria? I am told that Cousin Ned is to be married, and then my Cousin Jerry, what of him, and the Dennys and Dr. Snow? If you see him, please remember me most kindly. And the Towers and Mr. and Mrs. T. W. Hammond. Don't you see I am homesick to see all these people even if they have forgotten me? I cannot help it. I am sure you will write me a long letter full of news, just as is your specialty, for, Annie Childs, you know, you do know, how to write a letter, and I shall wait for it now till it comes. You will address me as usual care of American Legation, Berne, Switzerland.

How does Ber behave? Does he boss his wife any? If he does, you pull his ears for me, and oblige

Yoors trooly, and believe me, your lovingest Sis

Clara Barton

———

Benjamin Moran, Esq.

Chargé d'Affaires, London Esteemed Sir:

While I acknowledge the receipt of your favor and enclosed cheque for five hundred pounds, permit me, in the name of the suffering of France, to thank you and your Committee most earnestly for the same. Your generous gift will enable me to send comfort into hundreds of desolate and more distraught families, whom I have hitherto been unable to reach. I beg you will permit me to explain that my attempts to clothe the people of France have not been the result of a desire to improve the personal appearance, but to aid in ridding them a little, if possible, from the scourge of pestilence and vermin which the war has so terribly spread among them.

It is to be hoped that few will die of outright hunger during the next six months, but thousands must fall pitiful victims to disease lurking in the only old rags, in which months ago they escaped from fire and destruction. Disease is spread from one family to another, until thousands who are well to-day will rot with smallpox and be devoured by body lice before the end of August. Against the progress of these two scourges there is, I believe, no check but the destruction of all infected garments; hence the imperative necessity for something to take their place. Excuse, sir, I pray you, the plain, ugly terms which I have employed to express myself; the facts are plain and ugly.

How industrious she was in Paris and how bravely and cheerfully she did her work is shown by two home letters which she sent out simultaneously in September, one to her sister Sally and the other to Mrs. Bernard Vassall, her long-time friend, Fannie Childs Vassall:

Paris, Sept. 18, 1871

My dear Fannie:

I have forgotten if I really did send a line in Annie's letter or not. I know I wanted to, but since that I have received that precious "gingerbread" letter from all the family, and I have read and re-read, and spied into little comers to see some other welcome face peeping out. It was so good of Willis and Ber to set their hands and seals. Yes, I know all about receiving letters that call directly upon my heart, and my desire to answer that hour, and a thousand times I have said that those were the very letters which were to lie longest in neglect and likely enough never get answered at all. The fact is I am over-anxious about them, and wait for a few moments of better opportunity, feeling that I have much to say, and so I wait and wait, and these letters are the sore spot, the worrying sin of my existence, that little package which I cannot put by, but which lies around, and looks me in the face on the most impossible of occasions, and reproaches in silence, and comes late at night and early in the morning to haunt, it may be to taunt, me a little; that little package is the plague of my life, and yet I prize it most of all and couldn't have done without it, but I can never quite dispose of it. Oh, yes, yes, I do understand all you try so patiently to explain to me, only that I don't think my poor scrap could ever have been one of the class of letter which burden me, for I have no recollection whatever of it, and seriously suspect it was only a little pile of trash. It has been brave of you not to get sick in all summer with all your work, and company and sickness besides, but I am so glad that Sally was with you, and I suppose Vester was also, but it is not mentioned where he was during his illness.

I am spending some fine days in Paris, just what I most desired. I wanted to see some American people; it had been so long since I had seen them—and indeed there is no lack of them here. All Paris swarms with them, as I suppose it always does, and all grades. Some I am proud of, and some I am ashamed of; some speak remarkably well, and some cannot utter a proper sentence. Generally they are "well dressed," as the world goes, but to my eye "over-rigged," as a sailor would say, but always much better than the English, who are the most fearful dressers in all Christendom. English women are solid and sensible, learned and self-possessed, and all the world respects them; but the art of selecting and putting clothes onto themselves is something quite beyond their line of vision. Not that they do not wear enough—oh, Heavens, no, not that—there is always enough and to spare, but there is no calculation what portion or member of the body corporate it will be found dangling from, and Joseph's coat bore no comparison. Still they are splendid women, and handsome, fifty per cent more beautiful than the French. The French declare that the Germans cannot dress in decent manner, but I have seen much good, comfortable-looking dressing in Germany, and I rather liked it. I don't know what has induced me to write so much upon the silly matter of dress, unless that some of my "sisterin" abroad annoy me a little with theirs.

I can see how busy Ber must be with his large family and congratulate both him and his children upon the relationship. I imagine him to be the most sensible and paternal of parents. I shall be only too glad when you can really take your legitimate place in the work. I can see an equal call for your services. Go and look after the little girls. They may not like to tell all their troubles to their State Papa, but would rejoice to reveal some things to a mamma. Go with Ber. I think that is one of your "rights"—it is at least your privilege, and you know it is very well said that "until women get their rights, they must keep their privileges." I also have something of a family in Europe, some hundreds of state children, but of my own immediate family I have two delightful girls. They are as fully grown and developed as my two boys in America were, rather more, and about as near alike, but charming girls, both good as they can be, and be human, live girls. One is all gentleness, the other all strength, but both are so loving, so obedient, so true. The elder is Miss Antoinette Margot. She is a thorough artist, and is with me at present, painting and visiting the Louvre and the Luxembourg and comparing notes with the Parisian painters. She is at this moment painting an American flag, and looking back over her shoulder to ask me, "How many of the red stripes must commence at the field?" and ends with *"Mais il est très joli."* Miss Anna Zimmermann is at her home in Carlsruhe looking after the thousand wants of a clergyman's house, keeping the big brothers in order for the Universities they are plodding through; obeying her papa and mamma, who tell her she is too "independent and ambitious," writing at odd moments as she can pick them, reading Carlyle, Dickens, Goethe, Schiller, as she can steal the minutes, pining that she must be held in just such bondage of body and soul, praying for the day when she may come and live with me a little more, and beginning a long, strong, logical letter once in a while with "To the Devil with the housework! Why must I fritter away all the best years of my own life and starve my brain to cram my brothers who already have been taught twenty times more than they can apply?" And she is right.

But my sheet will be full and I shall have said nothing at all.

I have just written your "Marm" and I think, perhaps, that will find its way to you, and you must just have had a surfeit through Annie. I am glad she went for a vacation. I wonder what they do at Falmouth. When I am home, can't we go? I am not at all certain where I shall pass the winter; it may be I shall think I must work in France. I cannot tell how they will present themselves by winter, or I may think it well to quarter myself here in Paris and wait; and I have half a mind to go to Spain. This is perhaps the most sensible use I could make of the time. I must wait a little the turning of events. I can tell better after a month more in the east of France. I am glad you have had a visit from Georgie. It was nice of her to send me a line. Is not Alice with you now? Has she turned to ashes?—very possible—human nature can as well as wood or coal. Write me when you have time and don't let Ber abuse you.

Yours Clara

To Ber—
I am first-rate, how are you?
For particulars see within.

Clara

After the terror and bloodshed of the Paris Commune, Miss Barton spent some time in northern France, laboring as she had labored in Paris and in Lyons; at Belfort, where she finished her work on October 27, and went for a little time of rest to Carlsruhe, where she was the guest of the Reverend Mr. Zimmermann, whose daughter had labored with her at Strassburg. Antoinette Margot was there also, glad to turn from scenes of desolation to her work of painting.

The middle of December she went forth again in bitter cold weather, accompanied by Antoinette Margot, distributing relief to the poor at Mülhausen, Belfort, and Montbéliard. She spent Christmas at Strassburg, where she served a great Christmas dinner to some five hundred of her old acquaintances, and then returned to Carlsruhe.

Activity agreed with Clara Barton. She rose to meet great emergencies. When the crisis was passed, she felt the effect of so long a strain. Again and again during her lifetime she carried an enterprise completely through to the triumphant close, and when it was done collapsed from nervous overstrain. Twice in America that collapse had been indicated by the total failure of her voice. At the close of the Franco-Prussian War she collapsed again. This time it was not her voice, but her eyesight. Her eyes were inflamed by the strain and smoke of the battle-fields. The nervous tension aggravated the discomfort of which the inflamed eyes were, after all, only a symptom. For several months in the winter and spring of 1872 she was at Carlsruhe in a state of semi-blindness.

We have a little sidelight on Clara Barton's work among the French women in an undated letter from Belfort, almost certainly by Antoinette Margot. An American woman in Paris had evidently asked her for some account of the work of Clara Barton, and she had promised to write it. The letter gives some intimate glimpses into the character of her work:

[October, 1871]

Dear Madam:
Faithful to the promise made to you one bright day in Paris more than two months ago, I write. You remember that it was a kind of clandestine pledge, made in low tones, that I would one time tell you something of the doings of your compatriot, who has the "singular habit, for a woman," as the world would say, of doing something and saying nothing.

From much observation, I am convinced that Clara Barton never makes the least report of what she does, unless, for some cause, she considers it to be absolutely indispensable, and then, in a form so plain and business-like that one would read, and turn the paper, little dreaming of all the sentiment, strength, heart, poetry, and labor that lay hidden beneath that unpretending exterior.

309

It were too long to tell you of the few weeks in Paris, following your departure. What, between the sympathies for the families of the wretched prisoners of Versailles, and the outpouring Alsatians who refuse to remain German, there was little rest for body or soul. Some entire families had even followed from Strassburg, knowing that Miss Barton went from there to Paris, and certain of relief if they should find her there. They did find her, and now occupy good positions. One is even placed for life in the civil service of the French Government (if the Government shall last so long). But these things, done through rain and storm, cost strength, and I was near to report to you a sick list.

Happily, that is past, and my present hour must be applied to telling you of Miss Barton's work in a third general point of desolate France, viz., the brave little town of Belfort, which has rendered its name illustrious by the heroism of its defense. Here we are, facing the high citadel and the famous cannon "Catharine" that twenty-five thousand German bombs could not silence, and here day after day works your countrywoman trying to overcome the greatest amount of misery possible among so many.

The room in which she received her people has been tendered by Monsieur l'Administrateur of the town, and is in his own mansion, and himself and family are proving at every moment to your noble sister how proud they are of having obtained this favor.

It is in this room that she stands from morning till night, smiling and graceful as always, receiving family after family, and endeavoring to learn by herself what are their circumstances, how deeply they have suffered, to express to them her sympathy, and assist them with some money. It is probable that many of these poor people in this land of aristocracies have never listened to words so respectfully spoken, and are often so overcome by this added kindness of manner extended to them that the first answer which comes is a sob—often no words can come—and trembling, blessing hands held out to her are all that can speak. But oh! how eloquently they speak!

They are very poor, these relics of an eight months' siege.

Some, of course, have lost nothing in material by the war, having nothing to lose but time and labor, but the larger portion have lost all or nearly all they possessed, the fruit of forty or fifty years of hard work, and remain homeless, hopeless, old, broken, dispirited, sick since they have lived in cellars, and without the smallest prospect of regaining their lost property. Do wars in Republics leave the people as badly off, I wonder?

It is not a rare thing to see a-poor woman come in with her garland of six, seven, or eight handsome young children which she presents with both pride and distress. One had even thirteen, and when asked if all of them were still in her charge, she exclaimed, with the most charming simplicity, "Oh! no. madame, two are abroad; I have only eleven to work for." To-day, a tall, thinly clad woman entered, and presented her billet, bearing the stamp of the mayor. "Have you children?" asked Miss Barton kindly, as she took it. "Have I children?" exclaimed the woman in a tone at once proud and pitiful. "*Dear* child, if I haven't. I have ten." Miss Barton turned away to her table, but a stolen glance at her face a moment after detected something there glistening brighter than the gold she dropped into that hard, dark hand. "Ah," thought I, as I hastened down the name as rapidly as possible—"Ah, if only all the world's work were done with a little of the heart in it how much nearer Heaven would seem!" When it was decided that Miss Barton would accept the labor of herself receiving the crowd of victims of the bombardment, the authorities of the town, fearing for her, from the roughness of these people, who, they said, would rush in all together, by all the doors and windows, placed four policemen around the house to protect her against the crowd. Two of them in turn have for their mission to open the only door by which the solicitors are admitted. But never was I so amused as to see Miss Barton *protecting her policemen*, and preventing these rough men and shrill-toned women from crowding them against the wall. When sometimes they are all in a quarrel, the policemen swearing like two thunders according to the approved French manner of preserving respect, she appears at the door, and in the most charming manner prays them to wait a little and be quiet. Then the most piercing voices become silent, the wildest men are ashamed of their noise. The only visible motions are those nearest trying to hide themselves behind others, and those in the distance raising themselves on tiptoe to see "la bonne dame américaine." As for the policemen, they are perfectly puzzled, and could never have supposed that so gentle a lady, who never scolds or swears, could hold in order so undisciplined a crowd.

Often the work is interrupted for more agreeable reasons. Once it is a deputation of the sisters of the civil hospital, in their snowy bonnets, or some other charitable institutions of the town who want to thank her for the gifts sent to their establishment. Another day it is the mayor of the town, who desires to pay respects; another time all the council, mercifully asking to be allowed to express to her their gratitude in the name of Belfort and the county. All this as a personal matter I hear always steadily repelled, and they are politely requested to bear in mind that it is America and the goodly city of Boston to whom, if to any, all thanks are due. But no one is so mad as to expect to outdo a Frenchman in official politeness, and I observed the president of the council, half bent, hat in hand, replying that their three names would be always so united in their hearts that they should never be able to hear the one without thinking of the others.

This is a region almost exclusively Catholic, and the ignorance of the people is something deplorable. Each recipient is asked for a signature, and the proportion who are able to make something beyond an X is less than one in fifteen. Writing is an accomplishment generally not to be thought of, especially by the women, but when one who has attained so far is asked if she can give her signature, she replies, with the assuming grace of a noble of the blood, "*Certainement, pourquoi pas?*" But the common response is a burst of astonishment at the bare supposition. "I write! Mon Dieu, how should I." A difficulty, by no means the smallest, is to find the kind of money to which these poor people have been accustomed. The immense payments of France to Germany all in silver and gold are fast making coin among the things that were. The bank-notes of France never having been small in value, and used rather as a convenience for business than as a currency for the people, the poor are mostly strangers to it, and when a note was placed in their hands they waited, holding it a long time, and then ventured to inquire timidly, if that was something that they could get some money for, and where they should go to get it changed, and how they should do it? It was useless to tell them its value; they would have preferred ten francs in silver to twenty in paper. And, indeed, as they could not read, it were perhaps better for them, as one saw at once that they would be at the mercy of every swindler they met. This would not do. All notes which had been given were recalled and redeemed in coin, and it is certainly the occupation of one man from morning till night to change paper into coin as fast as it is required for distribution.

But it is impossible; the night is not long enough to tell all that transpires during the day, and one must not attempt it. I only wish, as I always do, that her own people could see their countrywoman at work among European poor, as not one European has done. If they are proud of her for what she has done at home, they would be prouder of her in a tenfold greater degree for what she is doing abroad, never at the best strength, in a strange country of foreign customs and divers tongues.

Pardon, *s'il vous plait*, my miserable English; you knew what it was when you gave me leave to write you, and I can only thank you for the kind indulgence.

Yours in sincerity

A.

Antoinette was not quite correct, however, concerning Clara Barton's reports. She made rather full reports to the organizations that supplied her with funds. To Mr. Edmund Dwight, chairman of the Boston Committee, under whose auspices she labored during the latter part of her time in France, she wrote an extended letter, outlining in full her method of work, and shows how sensibly and wisely she did all her work:

Chateau de Belfort
Belfort, Oct 28, 1871

Dear Mr. Dwight:

Sitting down to write you after one of the hardest day's work one might ever hope to find, you will not wonder if I am not dazzlingly brilliant.

I should not select so inauspicious a moment but that I find your letter has been waiting so long without getting to me, and that I cannot rest until I have at least commenced a reply, even if I am not able to finish it to-night. It had been stayed by my own orders. My letters in France for a time went wrongly and some were lost, both for and from me, for which the postal authorities are now busy searching, and as the losing of letters is one of the things I cannot endure, I ordered mine to be held at all points where they would arrive, until I could arrange some safe place of reception. They have come to me at Belfort, and I find yours which has waited a month.

I should have written upon leaving Paris in July if I had not thought every day that I might get a line from either you or Mr. Moran, telling me of the delivery or receipt of my large package of accounts, from which I might draw some inference if my manner of doing things were an acceptable one. After this, I grew so busy that I think I forgot all but my work, or rather did not realize the length of time, as it passed so quickly.

You ask for my views. They have been so many and so varied that it would be impossible to tell them at one sitting, but I may say that my sympathy and judgment have pointed, and my efforts been directed, to three classes of sufferers, with two of which I have nearly finished, and the third I am at this moment among with heart and hand.

1. These were the families of the prisoners of Versailles, and the ships of the Manche.

313

2. The families of Alsace and Lorraine, who, refusing to become German, are passing over the lines into France by hundreds, even thousands.

3. And thirdly, the region of Belfort.

The first-named of these are no longer confined to Paris, but are scattered now, for some distance around, poor, suffering, frightened, and trebly desolate.

First, they have often lost the family support in the person of the prisoner; next, they wait in suspense worse than actual death for the result of the impending trial, and fearing often to reveal to those about them who they are, and why they are so destitute; and lastly, poor as they are, they know that the Government allows but fifty centimes a day for the use of each prisoner, and provides nothing else, not even a bed, only straw, and whatever more he has (and many are very ill) must be provided by the friends from outside. You will see how the hungry mouths and wretched homes would be robbed by pity and anxiety to supply this necessity.

I have made it a portion of my care to find and supply some of these families; it can only be some, for there cannot be less than twenty thousand of them. There are forty thousand prisoners.

The next in order, and a still more wretched class, if possible, so far as extreme homelessness and nothingness can go, are the outcoming Alsatians. The time has arrived for each to decide individually which to become, and remaining to take the oath of allegiance to Germany. In their ignorance and infatuation, they still believe France to be the greatest nation of the earth, and, in spite of her recent reverses, watch with unflinching faith to see her, at no distant day, rise in all her old-time power and glory, and advance in majesty to take back her lost possessions; and to them the thought is death, that, in that proud day, second only to the Resurrection, they and their sons must bend their necks to the Prussian helmet, and point their guns against the Eagles of France. Impudent expressions touching these points bring them into unpleasant relations with the German soldiery still stationed among them, who probably do not hesitate to mention unwelcome and unpalatable facts. This "last feather" is too much, and, finding the burden too heavy to be borne, the incensed father, or, too often, the widowed mother, gathers up the family of growing children, and, turning the back upon the blackened walls and trampled fields of the old home, makes the nearest point of the French lines and comes out defiant, with never a penny or a morsel. The French are glad to receive them, feel complimented by their loyalty, but are burdened and embarrassed by them. Societies for their relief are formed at many points, but it is only the merest trifle they can do for them, excepting to aid in finding employment. This often takes a long time, and the interim of waiting is something fearful. I found them largely at Lyons, which is one of the points they make on their way to the South of France, and Algiers. Again I found them at Paris, where several thousands have come in, every train bringing them, especially the night trains.

I have put in practice a lesson here which I learned in Germany fourteen months ago, when infuriated France drove all her German families over her lines; viz., to meet and provide for them at the trains. No one can suppose for a moment that leaving Alsace and Lorraine and coming into France is not the most unwise and deplorable step these poor people could take; that they would not be a hundred-fold better off to remain. But I did not understand that your mission was to the wise, but to the unhappy, and I have taken the liberty to give them something.

But while occupied with those and these, I had by no means forgotten Belfort, or the fact that this was to be the great point when the right time should come. After leaving Paris, I met some very intelligent and practical gentlemen from that vicinity and learned of them many facts which have been of use to me, and always a confirmation of what we had both thought, viz., that help would be really more serviceable at the commencement of the cold weather than in mid-summer. Their crops were abundant, especially grass. This set me to confer in Switzerland in reference to cows, and from these inquiries I learned something of a plan most gratifying if it could be realized, and I waited a little to see. This was in August, at which time, as you know, nearly all the cattle are on the mountains. On the 9th of October ("Le jour de la Saint Denis") they are returned to the farms! There are then often too many for the winter and they can be purchased at lower rates. This, then, would be the time to purchase. But the good idea had entered into the minds of the Swiss to make a collection of cattle at that time for all the vicinity of Belfort and Montbéliard, or where the stock had been lost. They could do this without sending money out of Switzerland, which they desired to avoid, having already done so much of it. They carried out their plan, and when the time arrived commenced sending, and are still sending, to this region nearly as much stock as it is thought they can keep through the winter.

When I saw these things likely to succeed, I held a conference with the authorities of Belfort, and asked them to tell me plainly what their people most needed. They replied, "Small sums of money to commence the winter with," and gave this reason; There is just now commencing a money panic in France. The large payments she must make to Germany in gold and silver make these commodities exceedingly scarce, and all who have a little bury it in their pockets and bureaus, and hold it against the time when there will be no more and paper worth little or nothing. The smallest note, as you know, is twenty francs, a sum beyond the reach of a poor family, and thus there is nothing for them in money. This state of things, they assured me, would grow worse and worse, and, as France is only at her second payment (I believe), there was no room to doubt the correctness of their judgment. I asked how they would have it, in a sum to give to the people themselves, or should I give it? Apologizing for the labor they were suggesting to me, they begged that I would do it if I could, not that they were too indolent to do the work (for they are splendid men, and have the welfare of their people at heart), but they explained, that, living among and exercising jurisdiction over these people, who looked to them for impossible things, it was embarrassing to them to make distributions among them personally. The people were ignorant, and all had suffered so much that each one believed his or her case to be the worst in the world. And they would be much better satisfied with something from a stranger, which they would receive as a gift, than with ten times the sum from the municipal authorities, to whom they looked for "indemnity. They seemed almost ashamed to ask of me the labor of distribution, and offered all possible assistance. For the town of Belfort and the nearest villages, the Administrateur has made the same kind of arrangement as the Mayor of Villette, and I am at this writing receiving at this house from fifty to a hundred a day, hearing their story and giving to them the proportion which seems best suited to their condition.

I shall go from point to point seeing and aiding personally all I can or until I am too tired to go farther, and after this, if something remain unfinished, find the proper persons to do what I have not done. Montbéliard. Haute Savoie, and Gex will be remembered as you desired. Indeed, is it necessary for me to say that I shall try by all means in my power to carry out all suggestions which you have made? Time and observation have shown them to have been wise and good. I have found nothing better, and only dare hope I may be able to execute something nearly as well as you designed.

The money from Baring Bros. I have drawn through Paris, as far as I thought well in the present state of things, and indeed more of it than I have found convenient for the manner in which I was desired to distribute it, and some I must take through Switzerland or Germany to get the coin which will be useful to these people. The authorities will aid me in all these things. I have so far rather gained than lost in all exchanges.

I believe I have forgotten to speak of my visit to the Prefect of Doube, which was one of the most pleasant that could have been. I found him to be an excellent man (who desired to be remembered to you with great regard, regretting your illness). He seemed glad and touched that I had found and regarded the families of Alsace and Lorraine, and a little surprised that I should have "comprehended their condition so quickly," as he expressed it, as they are a rather new feature in the chapter of French suffering, and he asked that, in anything I might leave with Besanjon, he be allowed to draw one half of it from the "Comité de Secours" from time to time to aid these families on their distressing arrivals and passages through the town. I thank you very much for this pleasant and useful Introduction.

I am unable, my dear friend, at the present moment to report further, as I am just in the midst of my work; when it is a little over, I will write again, and as soon as possible I will send you all explanations and certificates and signatures which have come into my possession, and tell you as well as I am able what I have done, and how it was done.

With the highest esteem
I am very truly yours

Clara Barton

———

I cannot describe how painful and tiresome I find it to work here, abroad, among these strangers, with every thought and sympathy and energy turning and rushing four thousand miles across the ocean to our own beautiful and ill-fated city, with its hundred thousand homeless heads. At night I can realize this a little; in the morning I think I have dreamed a bad dream. The facts will not remain fixed with me.

A message has been sent from the Court of Baden to say that I am desired there. This is the third time I have been asked in the last two months, but was always too busy to go immediately, but now that I am so near and the message made so I This was written shortly after the disastrous Chicago fire. direct, I must go. If I can finish my work first I will; if not, I must leave it a little and return. I have no idea what is wanted of me. I will send this enclosed to Baring Bros.

Hastily

C. B.

This work continued for some time and there came no definite date which could be accounted its termination. For this reason and because of the condition of her health, the final report was not presented until after her return to America. Then in a letter to Mr. Dwight, the chairman, and Mr. Jackson, the secretary, Miss Barton sent her final accounting, asking for its approval, on receipt of which she proposed to return the balance in her hands. Her letter is as follows:

April 24, 1876

Messrs. Edmund Dwight and P. T. Jackson Boston
Esteemed Friends:
It has long been a subject of deep regret to me that I have been unable to make my report of the expenditure of certain sums of money placed in my hands by you, as agents for the distribution of the "French Relief Fund' sent by the city of Boston to the people of France who had been rendered destitute by the war of 1870-71. My apology for this long delay is physical illness, which overtook me before the work of distribution was completed in 1872, and has, with the exception of a few months, held me prostrate from that time until the present, more than two thirds of the time unable to leave my bed, and one year unable to transact the smallest item of my own business, or even hear of it as done by others.

But all this time it has been a source of pain and unrest to me that I could not close the account and make the proper returns to you; and all the more so, as there is still a portion of the money which I did not expend, and which I desire to return to you; and only He who knows and comprehends all can know with what gratitude I welcome the past few weeks of returning strength, which have enabled me to go over the long undisturbed packages of letters, receipts, and vouchers which have traveled with and remained by me all these weak and weary years, and arrange them to be at last given up to you, who have waited upon my silence with a gentlemanly kindness seldom met in the rough business of life.

Although allowed the largest liberty in regard to the place and manner of the distribution, I knew from you both that your preference lay in the direction of the east of France, and accordingly Belfort, Montbéliard, Besançon, Savoie, and Strassburg became the scenes of my labors: and, as you both know my manner was to give in small sums to the needy in person, it only remains for me to repeat that I met the poor of these districts by call, through the civil authorities presiding over them, listened to each story of want and suffering, and gave such a sum as assured by the authorities would be most serviceable to them, and such as they themselves should have given if left in their hands. I was always cautioned from this

318

quarter against making the sum too large, as the people had only the habit of small sums, and were demoralized by too much at once. This, of course, both increased and prolonged the labor of distribution.

I remember to have written you that among the most necessitous I met were the outcoming Alsatians. An extract from a letter of mine, written at Belfort, October, 1871, and kindly embodied in your report, renders a further description of this class of sufferers unnecessary in mine.

As these self-constituted exiles made their way largely into or through the districts I was serving, the people were keenly alive to the distress they witnessed, and humanely devised plans for relief. The one most practicable to their minds was to form a colony of Alsatians in the South of France and help them on to it. The climate was genial and productive, the country not over-populated, and the mayors and prefects besought me to withhold something for this enterprise and aid them personally in the establishment of their colony. I accordingly held back the money I had not expended, and went to Paris to learn what aid would be rendered by influential persons and the Government. But Paris was not so unsophisticated as the good people of the desolated outskirts. She was wise, polite, and had other aims. She immediately foresaw that these people, once broken up in their homes and family ties, placed on the borders of the sea studded with ships, would not withstand a pressure of poverty; but at the first approach of want would emigrate a second time and to some other country. Thus France would lose her soldiers, and she counted largely on the exasperated Alsatians someday to fight for their homes, take bade their lost possessions, and the Rhine. Hence they not only discouraged but forbade the step, and I had my appropriation left on my hands. I went to Carlsruhe to deliberate and rest, was worn out, and became ill, and from that time have never been able either to apply the funds or (until now) arrange the papers showing how I had disposed of what I had applied.

At the end of a year and a half of illness, I was able to figure up what still is due you, which sum, if satisfactory to you, I shall be happy to send you in a draft on my bankers.

Praying that, if upon examination all is not found to be satisfactory, you will not hesitate to inform me, and thanking you for your kindness and patience, I remain,

With the highest respect
Most truly yours

Clara Barton

New England Village, Mass..

Accompanying this letter was a detailed statement of all moneys received and expended, with vouchers for the disbursements. This account was duly audited, and the committee discovered that Miss Barton had deducted nothing for her own expenses, nor for any disbursements excepting those for which she had sent vouchers. They therefore sent to her the following letter:

My dear Miss Barton:

Mr. Dwight informed me some time since that you have about eleven hundred and thirty dollars, still on hand, of the money sent to you by the Committee of the French Fair of which I was treasurer.

Your account shows that you have made no charge for your expenses, and that you have charged us only with items for which you have vouchers, taking no notice of the sums given where you were unable to take receipts. If the account had been made up with all of these items included, the balance would have been nearly or quite absorbed.

The Committee have, therefore, directed me to say that they consider the account balanced, and request that you will accept this letter as a receipt in full settlement of your account with them.

Thanking you for your services in this work of charity and hoping that your health may soon be restored, I remain with great respect,

Yours very truly

(Signed) P. T. Jackson

Treasurer French Fair

There still remained in the hands of the Boston committee a sum of something more than three thousand dollars. The committee desired to present this to Miss Barton, who had accepted no salary during her period of work, and whose broken health they regarded as in a large measure the result of her arduous efforts for the relief of the stricken people of France. This was not acceptable to Miss Barton; she did not want the money; she wrote that she was almost the last of her family, with no dependents, and had neither use nor desire for money a day beyond her life nor beyond the simple needs for which her present income was sufficient. The committee, therefore, decided to give the money remaining in their hands to the Massachusetts General Hospital in Boston, with a provision that the interest should be paid to Clara Barton during the term of her natural life. The hospital concurred in this arrangement and faithfully carried out the trust. Clara Barton received an annuity semi-annually on $3251, the amount which finally was paid over to that institution. With this action the committee placed upon record their high appreciation of her service in France.

60 State Street, Boston July 1st, 1876

Dear Miss Barton:

You will wonder at my long silence, but, owing to the absence of gentlemen of the committee under whom I act, I have only been able to obtain their signatures to-day.

The money in the hands of Messrs. Brown Brothers, including interest on bonds to May first, is $4521, of which one quarter (or $1130) belongs to Mr. Jackson's fund. Of this I am directed to pay $150 to a distressed family from Massachusetts, now in Boston. The balance (or $3240) to pay to the Massachusetts General Hospital in trust, to pay income arising from this money to you during your life; afterwards to become the property of the Hospital.

In making this arrangement the committee desire to express to you their high appreciation of your intelligence and self-sacrifice in distributing the funds placed in your hands, and their great sympathy with you in your long and painful illness, caused partly by the work which you did in their behalf. They recognize the great accuracy of your accounts, the large numbers of vouchers obtained by much labor, and the scrupulous care with which you have guarded the money entrusted to you, They wish you good health and a long life.

I need not tell you, dear Miss Barton, how cordially I join in all good wishes for your health and happiness. May the Hospital pay your annuity until the next Centennial.

Sincerely yours
(Signed) Edmund Dwight

ILLNESS FOLLOWING THE FRANCO-PRUSSIAN WAR

There are few letters and no diary during the winter of 1871 and 1872. Clara Barton was at Carlsruhe endeavoring to recover from nervous overstrain, and learning to write without much use of her eyes. She supposed that she had finished her work for French relief, but a letter from a Boston committee informed her that they still had funds for this purpose, but were not having good success in the matter of local distribution. They begged her to take charge of what remained of their working fund. Almost blinded though she was, she set out in winter and traversed again a route that had become familiar to her, through Mülhausen, Montbéliard, and Strassburg. Her work for women was still going on, and she gave it substantial encouragement and repeated her Christmas banquet of the preceding year in a New Year's Eve banquet at Strassburg. She arranged for the continuation of the work in a way that did not pauperize the women. Then she returned to Carlsruhe and spent the remainder of the winter. Our chief knowledge of her oversight of these activities, as well as of her living arrangements during this period, is contained in a letter to her sister Sarah. She had been living in a hotel, but had taken lodgings of her own, had a little maid to wait on her, and was able to get a breakfast to her liking, which was beefsteak and baked potato, instead of the Continental breakfast of hard rolls and a gallon of coffee. The beefsteak for breakfast is interesting because Clara Barton ate comparatively little meat. She never, however, became a strict vegetarian. Even in her old age she now and then indulged in the luxury of a good, thick beefsteak; but this was exceptional. Her meals, as a rule, were severely frugal, and mostly vegetable.

Carlsruhe, Last Day of January, 1872

Dear Sister:

I believe I can write you a readable letter without looking on at all. I have used my eyes pretty much of late, and they complain so sadly of my bad treatment, that I have decided to give them a rest, and not write anymore at present, but, as I don't know how long the rest must continue, I don't want you to wait without news of me for an indefinite period. I want to tell you that I did receive your good long letter, and was exceedingly glad of it.

It had been a little age that I had not heard of you. I must write without a reference to your letter, for I could not read it to-day; my poor eyes ache too badly for that. It was long ago that I wrote you, I believe. I don't know if I have written since the 25th of November, when I remember to have done so. If not since, I have never told you anything of my going to Montbéliard to give something to the poor people there who suffered so much by the war. I went from Carlsruhe about the middle of December in the coldest time we have had in all the winter. It was fearfully cold. Miss Margot went with me. It was a day and a half's travel, and some of the way it was so cold in the train I dared not let Miss Margot fall asleep. I knew she was exceedingly cold, and I kept her awake through precaution. We spent the first night at Mülhausen with Mr. and Mrs. Dolphus, French people of literary note, whom I have known during all the war. Next day we went to Belfort and passed the night and Sunday with the Administrator, Monsieur Leblue, and arranged some trunks I had left there in October, and Monday morning we went to Montbéliard and called on the Prefect (a Jew), to whom I had previously made a donation of money, and informed him that I wanted to make the next donation in person. I wished to see, therefore, myself. He was very amiable and would arrange it, and I left him to do so while I went still on to Besançon to see the Prefect of Doubs. Here it was so cold and cheerless I could not sleep at night and returned next day. I was made the guest of the noble families of the town, for Montbéliard was an old Court town, and the grandmother of the Czar of Russia was a Princess of Montbéliard, so they have still relics of royalty there and a pretty old castle. I found excellent arrangements for taking care of the poor, the best I have seen in all France. They have committees of both gentlemen and ladies and the president of the ladies' committee is a Mrs. Morell, a person so much like Mrs. Greffing that I feel as if I had really seen Mrs. Greffing and worked with her a few days this winter. They assembled in their hall and called their poor there, and they came in hundreds, and waited in a long line, or two long lines, reaching from the doors away through the yard and down the snowy street. At the suggestion of Mrs. Morell I gave them orders for wood and rent, so that the husbands could not compel the women to give up the money to them to get drunk on and abuse the family. We wrote hundreds of orders. I signed them, and then we went to the hall and received the women. They were my women then. I admitted them, and gave them the order and took in the next, and so day after day till all was done. The orders were drawn immediately, and when I left just before Christmas all the poor had wood for two months and rent paid until the first of April. They looked so poor, but were so happy at such an unexpected fortune and I was so glad to have been able to do it. It was

323

Boston that did this good little thing—I have written the committee about it, a long letter. I thought they would be glad to know it while the fires were still burning.

Then I came back, and I wanted to go to Strassburg and give something to my old working-women there. They would not be so poor as the women of Montbéliard, for much had been done for them, but I wanted to see and remember them, and so I said I would go. I invited Miss Zimmermann to go with me, as she helped me to organize the Strassburg work last year. I said I would not give anything in charity to these women; I had not permitted them to beg—they had always worked for me and been paid. I would give them a Christmas fête and invite them like other people. So we bought two splendid pine trees fresh from the Black Forest, and I knew all my women, so I had only to count the heads and buy purses. I purchased three hundred good strong morocco purses with steel clasps, prettily lined, and pretty little things for the children, and to ornament the trees many dozens of little wax candles and holders to light the trees. I had stopped at Strassburg on my way back from Montbéliard and hired the best hall in town for Saturday night the 30th December. On Wednesday night we went to Strassburg, had our invitations printed and sent to the women by post; then I ordered at a good bakery twenty cakes, I cannot tell you how large and high. Each cake would cut from twenty to twenty-five slices, big slices; and five hundred rolls, and I took a caterer I knew there to arrange chocolate and coffee. The hall had a fine kitchen and dining-rooms, and I asked the banks to change my money into the last issue of French silver, never used, and they did. The best ladies of the city came to help us, and the trees were set, the purses filled, the hall arranged, the tables spread and set so white and clean, and, oh, the trees were so pretty, on a long platform across all one end of the hall in front of two enormous mirrors and all the floors spread with moss, all scattered full of fine-cut white paper and isinglass, which made perfect snow and ice, and brightened with handfuls of little scarlet berries; and the hall was so brilliant with chandeliers and mirrors that one could read the finest print in its most distant corner. I tell you all this so particularly because I think it was the prettiest thing I ever saw. Don't say it was that that made my eyes sore; it wasn't. The hour was seven; at six-thirty the women began to arrive. Mr. Kruger, Vice-Consul from America, received and seated them in the anteroom till it was time to light the trees. I had not seen them yet, and did not know that so many were there, but someone came to tell us that our little wounded children had come and we went to that room to see and welcome them. When we entered the doorway, all these hundreds of women rose up before us like an army—not a word, still like so many soldiers—and stood for us to pass. At seven, the trees were lighted and the doors opened, and all this regiment of women walked in and took seats. A fine parlor organ stood under the trees, a Christmas hymn was struck, and these poor women in the fullness of their hearts joined in a burst of song such as I never heard before. They sang as if they meant God should know how glad they were and how grateful they were to be there. Then there was prayer, an address of welcome (I wouldn't have them instructed), and then Mr. Kruger and your sister went under the trees upon the platform where all the purses hung. There were elegant ladies to take them down from the trees and hand them to me while Mr. Kruger called each woman's name and she came up and gave her hand to me, and I put in it a purse of silver with her name and a pretty buff card attached to it; then the ladies took her round to see the trees and to sign her name at a table presided over by the Misses Rausche, of Strassburg Boarding School. Afterward they were taken to the refreshment room and the daughters of the clergymen of the city, with Miss Zimmermann at the head, received and served them to chocolate and all the good things; and then they did talk and laugh and cry for joy, and such a time some hundreds of poor women almost beggars I think never had. "It was worth going a mile to see."

All this time Mr. Kruger and I were giving the gifts, but when it was done I went and ate with them; then I came back and gave the gifts to my eleven cutters, ten pretty young girls and one tailor. I gave them workboxes and portfolios, etc., and then the Comité de Secours had arranged a little surprise for me, which the women enjoyed exceedingly. M. Bergmann, my old esteemed friend, the president of the syndicate of Alsace, addressed the women, and they all crowded up around the front of the platform like so many children, to listen to him. He told them, among other things, that Miss Barton had said she wished they would all keep the money in the little purses as a keepsake and make it the beginning of a sum for the savings bank, which would reopen next week. Having told them this, he said to them, so pleasantly and familiarly, "I think we ought to make her this promise, eh?" You should have heard the storm of, "Yes, yes, we will," that filled the room. This finished the evening, only their good-bye to me, which each one insisted on making for herself. This occupied almost an hour, till the last one was gone, and then it was past eleven, almost twelve, and we went home to our hotel and to bed; but all the time I knew I had seen a very pretty thing.

There were about sixty women who did not get their invitations. It was no wonder; they never had a letter before in their lives and the letter carriers never heard of them, and they lived in such old alleys and garrets and cellars they could not be found. But the next day I made a list of all these and put it in all the papers of the city, and it was told to them and they came to our old workrooms a few days afterward and we gave them their purses. When it was all done, we came back to Carlsruhe, one of the first days of January, and I have been here ever since. I had a good deal of writing to do, and I suppose I have used my eyes a little too much. I was going over to London directly after leaving Strassburg to stay with Abby and Joseph Sheldon, who are continually writing for me to come to them. I meant to have been there now, but I received a letter on my return from Strassburg from the head of the Boston Committee saying that they had held a meeting after hearing something from me and decided to ask me to take charge of all their unfinished business in France. They see that it is going wrong and beg me to take it in hand, even if I cannot do anything personally, to take the oversight of it. I replied to them and will wait for their answers. I thought then it would be nonsense to cross the Channel if I must recross to France again in a few weeks, so I decided to remain here until I could finish up on the Continent and go to England free.

I do long to be free of work once more for a little while. I have been rather busy. I have a little home here in Carlsruhe I got tired of the hotel and took some small rooms, a little apartment, and furnished it to suit me (rented) and have a little German girl. She was the private waiting maid of Madame de Mentzinger and I knew her, so I live as independently as I please. I can arrange my living to suit myself better. I can have a beefsteak and baked potato for breakfast and not be driven to a choice between a piece of dry bread and a gallon of coffee, and I can have my dinner at four and not be forced to eat at eight o'clock at night, as is done here.

I am sure you have had a great deal of trouble with my things and so has Lieutenant Westfall; I am sorry but can't help it. I want to write the Lieutenant, but dare not send him one of my blind letters. I must wait till I can use my eyes again. I am glad you went and visited all the world of Massachusetts. I want to see our old brother Dave more than I can tell, and I think I shall sometime. I don't understand if Ida has left the Treasury for all time or on a rest. Is she not well? I am sorry you wandered about waiting for someone to carry you from post to pillar. Wait a little, Sail, and we will have a coach and one and ride when we please. I will have it sent over to you every day to take a ride on condition that you will promise to come and take tea with me every time, and you shan't wait to be carried somewhere—it was all vexatious and heart-aching. I know it all by experience, so old that it seems to me it must have been a part of another existence; but it wasn't; it was only the first end of this old patched and tangled web. What a good soul-stirring time you had at the Convention, didn't you? That was splendid; shall I ever see something like that, I wonder? What a meeting! How I want to see and know Mrs. Livermore. I don't suppose I ever shall, but I knew her so long ago. What beautiful things she wrote when she must have been so young; no wonder she can speak well. I speak very much of these things with the Grand Duchess. She sent for me about a week ago to spend an evening and she spoke of little else than the progress of woman and schools for girls in America. She had evidently been reading something, I presume some German criticism upon the too liberal spirit of America, and wished to compare notes, I think. I told her all as it was, and I said I believed in special training for all kinds of life, but that I thought it possible to train too much till the original spirit was crushed out and ashes left in the place of coals, and there was danger of Germany's doing this with her great respect for discipline; that I thought them too strict, and that they cramped their people by rules and regulations and hurt many good original minds. This was plain speech for a woman in a plain black gown without even a ring on her hands to address to a Princess and Sovereign, but when I am asked I answer, let it be where it will. I guess it didn't offend, for she sent me a very pretty letter next morning.

I can't think what the dress is that you speak of having made up and washed. I can just recall that I sent something by Dorr, but it couldn't have been anything but a piece from my shelves where we cut for the women. I can't think if it was calico or cotton gingham. I know I wanted to send something good, but he was afraid to take it lest he have trouble at the custom house, and they trouble him about his own things for it. I know we packed his boxes in terrible haste one night after midnight and I can't think of anything move about them. This was the day but one before I cleared up in Strassburg and started for Paris. It wasn't a quite sure thing if one would get there very safely, and so difficult was it that it took three days to do the traveling of one day in ordinary times. But it is better now.

This winter is easier than the last was. I have made some friends and I am not a stranger in Europe any longer, and I have warm friends in Strassburg, and, if I do say it, last week Mr. and Mrs. Bergmann came to Carlsruhe to visit us, i.e., Miss Zimmermann and me. I had them to tea with me twice (they were at hotel) in my house, and I arranged a visit for them at Court. This is, I expect, the first social exchange of visits between a leading French officer and a German Court since the war—a gentleman may have visited, but not the ladies, but Mrs. Bergmann and the Grand

Duchess visited, and, better still, the poor women came over to Germany to visit me. I have made some peace between them if they won't fight again and spoil it all. I will enclose in this one of my invitations to the Women's Ffite and Christmas Tree. Your German letter-carrier will read it to you. Now I think, in mercy to your eyes, I must stop. Don't be troubled about me; my eyes will be well soon. I will be very careful. I know you can't read near all of this, but some maybe.

Lovingly

Clara

I thought I couldn't write anymore, but I find it so funny to write with my eyes shut, as if I were playing blindman's buff, that I think I must do another sheet. I was afraid to commence to tell you how nice I thought your picture gallery was; indeed, I think it was splendid. How could you think of it all? How did you get up your ideas? I laughed till I cried again and again; indeed, I am not sure but that hurt my eyes some. I wish you had told me more about it. I wanted all the particulars. I related it one evening at tea at Madame General de Freystadt's, and you should have seen the merriment of those German Court ladies—they have a great deal of fun in their heads. They were especially amused at the old line, as I explained to them our bold President swinging around the circle to gain popularity. Miss Margot has not been initiated into the mystery of your gallery yet, as she is at Lyons with her people, but is expected to return any day now to resume her studies here. I will make her full explanations as soon as she is back. She caricatures me sometimes, to her great amusement. She would not be bad help for you on such an occasion, as she would be in the seventh heaven if she could do it.

No, I didn't think of the 17th of September as being the day of Lake City. How well I remember that day, and how anxious a day it was, but after all, not unhappy. We thought that we had gained so much; our experiment had not failed and it did not fail in the end; it accomplished just what you say it did. Our dear boy lived to feel that he had done his work and was ready to go; a little life it was, but full and had in it much more than many another of fourscore and ten. I had not heard of Lizzie Learned's last affliction. Can this be so? Where did Lizzie get such a complication of maladies, and is there anything in the new remedy? I have heard of it. The Grand Duchess asks me about it. Her first maid of honor, Mademoiselle de Sternberg, of whom you must have heard me make mention, is supposed to be dying of a cancer, but she also seems to have a multitude of illnesses. I called on her a few weeks ago. She was a mere skeleton and is too sick now to see any but her nurses.

Does Nancy do the work at home, and are she and Uncle John all there are? I cannot think how it would seem there without—"Bamma"—poor dear, honest, faithful, Christian, guileless Bamma! who worked faithfully up to the last day without complaint and lay down bravely with the harness of life about her, without a murmur.

Do you have much fruit this year? I am out of patience with Europe. I never find fruit here—it is always a "scarce year," they say. Indeed, there was none in all the Rhine Valley. Little gnarly apples are two and three cents apiece; prunes, which are only the plums which grow here, dried, are fifty cents a pound, and I have searched the town over without success for a little dried apple. All oranges here are always either sour or bitter. I have nearly forgotten, but it seems to me that we had better fruit arrangements at home. You see by this that I am quite hungry, don't you, or I shouldn't write of it. Now I think I have finished for this time. I have let my letter wait two days and my eyes are better.

Ever your Sis

Clara

Returning to Carlsruhe, she continued her oversight of American relief for French destitution by correspondence, though still suffering greatly with her eyes. She passed "some very dull weeks, very green and shady, with exceedingly long nights"; after the acute pain was over, she learned to write with bandaged eyes, and wrote a good deal.

Her friends Mr. and Mrs. Sheldon were in London and were not satisfied to have her in Germany alone. They sent her peremptory orders to be ready to accompany them when they came, as they were presently to come, down the Rhine. She went with them, left Carlsruhe, visited Strassburg on her last tour of inspection, and set out for London by way of Paris. On reaching Paris, they encountered an American family by the name of Taylor, friends of the Sheldons, who had just left London for a tour of Italy and besought Miss Barton to accompany them. Hastily she changed her plans, and, after six weeks' travel in Italy, she came to London. She had dropped her diary altogether, and her correspondence with her relatives had nearly ceased on account of her impaired eyesight, but in London she wrote the story of her wanderings to her sister Mrs. Vassall. The last page is missing and the letter ends abruptly, leaving her in

329

Venice. The Italian tour was finished, however, and in the early summer she arrived in London.

No. 5 Newson Street—Wanrey Street Walworth Road
London, July 5th, 1872

Dearest Sister:

In one way and another I imagine you must have become aware of me in England, although I believe I have never told you so directly. By the presence of a half-finished letter to you, dated March 29th, between Paris and Turin, Italy, I see that I cannot have written you since I left Germany just previous to the above-named date. This has all been very wrong, for I received your good and welcome letter here, via Berne, early in June. You know me as neither abundant nor graceful in apologies, although it never hurts my spirit to ask pardon, and your good intuition will perceive this rather extraordinary sheet of note-paper to signify contrition, confession, and serious effort at amendment. For all the interesting details contained in your letter I thank you very much. They constitute my only landmarks of the old coast for months; my explorers have been very silent and my scouts brought small tidings.

I remember that I wrote you when nearly blind. I had used my eyes too hard, and at night, which I ought to have known I could not do with impunity. I passed some very dull weeks, very green and shady, with exceedingly long nights; although after the greater pain and nervous excitement was over, I wrote a great deal with them closely bandaged. This helped to pass the time, but Mr. and Mrs. Sheldon, who were in London, became altogether dissatisfied with this state of things, and determined to put an end to some of it by coming after me and taking me, willing or not, to London. They had given me a short notice and ordered me to pack my knapsack, while they came down the Rhine. I obeyed, and, after a visit of a couple of days, we set out via Strassburg and Paris. I was infinitely better by this time; still must not put any close strain upon my eyes. I made my "good-byes" in Strassburg, which was not an easy thing for the "soul," and, on reaching Paris, we met a family party of Americans, friends of the Sheldons, that had just left London for a trip of six weeks through Italy. There were four of them, Mr. and Mrs. Holmes and their only daughter and son-in-law, Mr. and Mrs. Taylor. Mr. Holmes was the American Commissioner to the Great International Exhibition in London in 1862 and in Paris in 1867, and with his family has resided in London and Paris since, as American representative of science, skill, invention, etc. They were fine travelers, Italy was a familiar route to them, and it entered their heads to attach me to their party. I felt it to be a great piece of temerity on my part

330

to think of dropping "sans cérémonie" plump into the middle of an elegant family party arranged for a private travel, and I said so, and said all I could, but all was overruled, and even Mrs. Sheldon said "go." It was "too good an opportunity to lose," she said, and added at the end of her advice, "What a fool I am. I always did give up all that I wanted most"; and so we separated in the streets of Paris, March 28th, five o'clock in the afternoon, she for London and I for Italy. I had only a little hand satchel, having stored all my European luggage with my Paris bankers till my return. I have never written up my trip, so I cannot give it you, but if I can recall the days a little in order will try to account for some of them. I will draw hard upon my memory, which will probably help me accurately to whatever she will help me at all, she being, not so generally treacherous as repudiatory. I wonder if that is an English word—it ought to be; if not, I can only plead two years' life in Germany, and surely out of all that I must have earned the right to manufacture one word.

As sightseers, it was not, of course, our policy to travel at night, and we did it only twice, of which the first night was one. The road between Paris and Macon, just above Lyons, being as familiar to each one of us, as that between New York and Washington, we could afford to miss it. Reaching Macon at sunrise, from there to Euloz and, passing the custom house, proving ourselves innocent of liquors and tobacco, we were ushered into Italy through the famous Mont Cenis Tunnel, eight miles under a mountain, which rises almost six thousand feet above the level of the sea. It is a well-laid track in the solid rock, well ventilated and lighted by powerful reflectors each half-mile. You remember that it was over Mont Cenis that Napoleon I constructed a road to march his armies into Italy. At ten o'clock at night we were at Turin. By this time I was conscious of being some tired; altogether I was not very strong, and, just for variety, I had a chill in the night, and, of course, decided to abandon my journey and return. But as Turin was one of the cities to be visited and naturally two or more days were to be given it, I could afford to wait and watch further developments. My chill did not recur, and, although I continued weak for some time, I kept on the journey.

Turin is a charming city, by far the most modern in appearance of anything in Italy, well laid out, fine broad streets, excellent markets, abounding in fruit, clean, and entirely free from beggary. It seems also to have no poor quarter, the general practice being for every wealthy family to take into its service and care one, two, or more entire families, lodging them in tenements fitted in the attic stories of their own residences, rather than below on the streets, thus at the same time holding surveillance and

331

compelling respectability. I liked the plan. I don't know if it is one of Victor Emmanuel's ideas. You know that Turin was always his Capital residence, till a few years ago, when he established himself at Florence, which now is in turn abandoned for Rome. It has over one hundred churches, very rich in jewels and antiquities. I remember in the Metropolitan Church to have seen the marble figure, sitting, lifelike, of Marie Adelaide, the wife of Victor Emmanuel, and mother of Princess Clothilde of France. The private jewels of the church were shown us (for a consideration—everything in Italy is displayed for a consideration), but for no consideration could I undertake to describe them; images of solid silver, men and women, weighing hundreds of pounds and covered with jewels, where sometimes one was of greater value than the massive silver image it adorned. The Royal Palace was most magnificent; the rooms were all shown. Here, in this gilded salon where their busts stand, were married Princess Clothilde, and the Queen of Portugal. The plate-glass mirrors are twenty feet high, and everything accords with them. The armory contains an entire gallery of mounted knights in armor, full dress, horses like life, armed to the teeth, and among them lies the sword that Napoleon used at Marengo. Above the city is a fine old monastery to which we climbed for a view of Mont Blanc, Monte Rosa, and all the chain of southern Alps, snow-white and dazzling, stretching away into the eternal blue.

On the second of April, Tuesday, we took train for Milan, riding for hours in the bright spring sunshine of northern Italy, the Alps behind us, and the Apennines before, the wheat waving in all the freshness of early green, and the vines just bursting into leaf. Here at Milan, we were met by a young lady protégé of Mr. Holmes, a young American girl who is to come out soon as a prima donna. She is finishing her musical studies in Milan, and, while we were installed at an excellent hotel, our dinners were always with Mademoiselle Katrina.

The great sight of Milan is its cathedral, the second in size and magnificence in Europe; this also I could not justly describe. It is built entirely of marble, commenced in the thirteenth or fourteenth century and, like all these old massive structures, never finished. It covers many acres, and seems to be one sea of turrets rising at irregular heights toward the clouds. Although the comparison would be most inelegant, I will say that it reminded me of a shipping-yard, where the marble turrets and statues take the place of thousands of masts; indeed, if my memory serve me well, it has 135 spires, and 1923 statues on the outside from the ground to the top and 700 inside. There is on one of the roofs, which you pass as you ascend (far above to the top), an entire flower garden in marble, hundreds of flowers forming minarets, and no two flowers carved alike or representing the same flower. It eras a long way to the top, which at length was gained after many times of sitting, and (for me) even lying down to rest on the various roofs passed in leading from one flight of stairs to another, roofs of pure white marble polished and glistening in the sunshine like the crust of the snowbanks on the New England hills on bright winter days. (wonder if I ever will see them again.) Here again we saw marvelous jewels, "gold, silver, and precious stones." The tomb of Carlo, who "stayed the plague," is in a chapel beneath; the coffin and even the roof of the chapel are of solid silver; mass is held here each morning, and, on certain days of the year miracles are wrought. There are many sacred relics in the cathedral, as several nails from the Cross, the Virgin's shroud, and a seamless coat of the Lord Jesus Christ, etc., etc. The picture galleries were especially fine, many celebrated originals, among which is Leonardo da Vinci's "Last Supper of the Master and Disciples" in the original fresco. And the celebrated "Ambrosian Library," so old and rare its volumes were indeed a curiosity— illustrated volumes of the fourth century. And the Royal Palace erected on the site of the old palace of the early Dukes of Lombardy, where Attila thundered about in his destruction. Later this Palace, like nearly all in Italy, had been at some time or another occupied by Napoleon I. Here was his bedchamber, unchanged, decorated in scarlet and gold, heavy velvet curtains richly wrought in flowers of pure fine gold thread. Then the celebrated theater "La Scala," the largest in the world, its stage one hundred feet in depth, and wide in proportion, and this, not including the recesses. The pit alone holds eleven hundred people, and there are six rows of galleries; one hundred musicians in the orchestra; the principal boxes are purchased by the nobility for the season, a single box from four hundred to five hundred dollars (the season). I name all these particulars for Vester's benefit; he may be interested in the facts. Our young prima donna stepped upon the stage (as our visit was in the daytime) and sang to us; she had sung there before to an audience of five thousand, but I think she took just as much pains for us, and I am sure we were not less enthusiastic. I expect some day to hear her sing when she is famous, but it will never afford me greater pleasure than when she sang to her audience of five in the great "Scala" of Milan.

One little incident, happening not long before, was so pretty that I am tempted to tell it you. "Katrina" (who is of German parents, but born and always lived in New York) had only been led before the public once—i.e., last winter she was the "leading lady" of the first opera in Turin—and on the evening of the close of the engagement she was "called out" to sing a

333

little national air, in which she had been exceedingly popular. When she stepped before the curtain she found the entire house a blaze of light, which at first nearly "upset" her, but, gathering up, she went through her air, to the last strain, when four men entered and placed at her feet an enormous bouquet of the choicest flowers, nearly four feet across. She managed to accept it, but attached to it was a note which requested her, when it should be faded, before throwing it away to open it with care, and at the end of a week this was done, and hidden among the flowers were found a magnificent gold watch and chain, pins, necklaces of coral, turquoises and pearls, bracelets and rings, which I could not enumerate. It had been ordered and arranged in Geneva, and sent all the way through the mountain passes to her. I thought this was a pretty success for the début of a little American girl, studying in a strange land with little money. As a child she used to sing in New York with Patti.

But you must be tired of Milan, and wish I would hasten on if I am going. Well, I will, and so imagine this to be Saturday the 6th of April, 9 o'clock A.M., and I just taking the train eastward. The day was so lovely, so full of the springtime, the grass and grain so green, the swinging vines swaying over all the fields, the birds literally bursting their little throats, the fields filled with peasants in gay dress working to merry tunes, and when you could draw the eyes away from these near scenes they fell to the northward, first upon a line of dim, hazy blue, but over this, skirting the horizon again, the whole chain, peak after peak, of ranging Alps, such an unbroken line of glittering snow—here on the south only four miles away the field of Solferino where France lost one thousand officers in a day.

At 4 p.m. we were at "Verona" wondering if we should see its "gentlemen" and giving certainly more than our usual interest to this subject, and at five we halted at a singular depot, with no rattle of cabs, or hacks, no tramping of horses, still as death all about us, and as we walked out there lay waiting us hundreds of gondolas, black as a pall, some covered, some open, all drawn up to the side of the Canal to take us weary travelers to our hotels. This was, indeed, novel, but we selected our carriage, stepped in with our luggage, sat down, and, leaning lazily back, left it to our gondolier to pick his way through the watery streets, some wide, some narrow, leading into and out of each other, like veritable city streets and lanes, the ways on each side lined perfectly thick with old palaces and majestic buildings of centuries ago, their fronts to the sea and their magnificent stone steps leading directly into the water, and when one would pay a call, the gondolier had only to bring his boat alongside and you stepped out as from another carriage to the steps of a mansion. We were taken to "Hotel Victoria," made as comfortable as a first-class Italian hotel can make one, and after supper commenced upon the sights. Ah, but there was so much to see, not that it is a city of enterprise, a flourishing mart of trade or business. Oh, no, far from it. Venice only exists upon the record of its former greatness; take all this away and the travelers consequent upon it and I believe twelve months would find a famine there, but there is little danger of this while Byron and Shakespeare remain bright in English literature.

Here, as everywhere in Italy, one must commence with the cathedral, and having gone through this, and some scores of churches, the "Campo Santo" and the Bell Tower, one is at liberty to enter upon the palaces, gardens, and theaters. But Venice offers some deviations from this general rule; most cities have prisons, but they have not all the dungeons of Saint Marc. All have bridges, but all have not a "Rialto" nor a "Bridge of Sighs." I suspect I do not need to remind you of many old or historical facts. You who are always digging into the past will have them all "papered and labeled" and stored away ready for use. But I might mention the seventy-two little islands upon which Venice was built, which were only a part of the Adriatic, and not reckoned as land at all. A set of not warlike people from here and there in the vicinity, having grown weary and afraid of their fighting and troublesome neighbors, mostly from Austria, determined to place themselves in a position more difficult to attack, came far over the sea to these little islands and commenced a city, and gave a general invitation to all war-pestered, peace-loving citizens of the world to come and join them; from time to time they united their islands, built their houses for dwelling and trade upon the streets laid down upon the piles, with one side opening upon the street of earth and the opposite upon the sea, as I have before described. But—*the depravity of human nature!!* No sooner were they a little strong and comfortable themselves than they sent out their ships to prey upon and plunder their neighbors, and well-nigh ravaged the cities of the earth. They decorated their palaces with the spoils of other nations, married the sea, and declared themselves Omnipotent and Divine. Among other things their religion and church must have a Hero, and they sent afar, and got (as they said) the body of Saint Mark, brought it, and great numbers of relics belonging to him, buried it with the divinest honors in their principal church, and named it Saint Mark, or "San Marco." This was as early as the ninth century. It is a large but not handsome edifice, facing a paved court, a "piazza" some six hundred feet in length, surrounded by palaces, now used for public purposes, stores, etc. All the world of Venice walks in the "Piazza of San Mara." The pigeon was esteemed a sacred bird with them, and he is still cherished here and treated with great honor. One of the curiosities to be seen are the "pigeons of San Marco." I cannot at this moment recollect definitely enough to state to you how many hundreds are supposed to reside in the immediate vicinity, but their dinner hour is two o'clock in the afternoon. The great bell of the clock strikes three quarters past one and they commence wheeling and circling into the court, they cover the fronts of all the buildings, sit as thickly as possible upon every window seat, hang in all the cornices, and stand in full platoons in every foot of spare pavement for a number of rods around the especial corner where their dinner is served. A young man (it was formerly a young girl) is appointed by the Government as feeder of the pigeons. It is not necessary to say that he is punctual with his repast—he could not live with his tumultuous boarders if he were not. As the bell strikes two, he pours the grain from—

The rest of this letter is missing, but from this time on her letters became frequent, and we are able to follow her, almost day by day.

Her health by this time was much improved. She established pleasant lodgings in London, where her old friends the Sheldons and her new friends the Taylors were, and followed her lifelong habits by rising at five o'clock in the morning and getting in four and a half hours' activity before anyone else in the house appeared for breakfast. She heard Stanley, who had just returned from Africa, and, in the controversy which ensued between him and the Geographical Society, she became a warm partisan of Stanley. Antoinette Margot joined her. She, too, had lived through the war without breaking down, but, when she had nothing to do but to sit down at Carlsruhe and paint, she gave way to nervous overstrain. Mrs. Taylor found her Italian trip rather too much for her and wanted a quiet place outside of London, so they rented a summer home in the Isle of Wight and there spent some restful and health-giving weeks. For a company of nervous invalids, they appear to have had a very merry time. The following jingle was written in London in 1872 for reading at a social gathering of a few families and America's friends, who met once a week for social intercourse over a cup of tea and light refreshments, enlivened by recitations.

The family names are somewhat significant—Mr. and Mrs. Holmes, Mr. and Mrs. Taylor, Mr. and Mrs. Bacon, Mr. and Mrs. Darling, and Mrs. Cynthia Care, a friend then absent.

RETURNING HOME

It would be pleasant to record that the benefits derived from this happy outing on the Isle of Wight proved permanent, but unfortunately that was not the case. Had Clara returned to America in the autumn, it might have been better, but she went back to London for the winter determined to brave its fogs. She had discovered, with many of her countrymen, that it is a mistake to expect relief from cold weather by going to a warm climate. The people who live in warm climates do not know how to prepare for the cold. In London they knew at least the value of a fire. To London she went, and the results were depressing. Her throat and chest were affected badly by the London fogs. All the gains of previous months seemed to have been lost, and she was as far from well as she was at the end of the Franco-Prussian War. At this time she wrote to Mrs. Vassall, who had returned from Washington and was living in Worcester:

London, July n, 1873 Euston Road

Dearest Fannie:

Your dear good letter and that of your "Bear" came a few days ago. It is funny to be interviewed at that distance, and I am glad that you got no worse reports than you did. I don't think I am so homesick as it would seem, but I am weak, and little things seem such a burden to me that it hinders me from doing many things that would make me more at ease if they could be done. However, one must be patient; it is not a month yet that I was in my bed most of the day, and now I can go about town, and even once have been out of town, but not for a long trip.

It is kind of you all to offer to come to help me, but I believe I shall be able to get over my difficulties without giving so much trouble to anyone. By "getting over them," I mean measurably over them. I cannot say that I even hope to be strong again as I was before this last illness. I cannot tell, but it would be a wonder to me if sufficient nervous strength returns to permit any degree of real usefulness. The greatest trouble I meet now is to bear the little burdens of contact with the persons and things around me, and not show too plainly that I have not strength and composure to bear them calmly; in short, to "hold my horses." You, dear Fannie, will know what that means, and how to the weak the grasshopper becomes a burden. I am glad you have found a physician who has some strength for you, if it is

338

really so; but I must confess that my previously small share of confidence in medical aid and wisdom has not increased by the last year's experience.

I hear of you in the most trying heat at home. It is just warm in England some days, but to-day, for instance, ladies are generally clothed in wool suits and a shawl. I went out just now for a few minutes with Mamie, while our rooms were put in order, and came back because I was too cold, and it is never very bright in London. I suppose this has its due influence on one's nervous system, and I would have been glad at any time within the last month to be made ready and go over to France or Germany. I think it would be better, but I could not get strong enough to get ready and go. You wonder what "getting ready" means. It seems to you that it requires little preparation to put up a bag or small trunk of things and cross the Channel, and so it does, but it is summer, and I have several trunks of mainly woolen things for this cool climate. My little strength since I have been in Europe has made it necessary to have them, of course, unpacked, and in a state of utter confusion, for some trunks I have not had my hand in for months and months, but to others I constantly go, and in haste. The moths in London are like flies in abundance. It wouldn't mend my nerves to know I had gone off traveling and left all I have to be devoured, and I have been made worse several times by simply attempting to get a dress or some little article from a trunk. My weak chest will not admit of the least labor of the arms yet. Let Mamie do it? Mamie is only a weak little girl, and until lately could not have packed her own trunk without harm to herself. So I wait for strength as an army waits for quartermaster and commissary supplies before it can march. I made one little trial or two, to see what I could do. Papa Holmes (with whose family I went to Italy) came one day to ask me if I could go to Liverpool where he was going, and over into Wales, and pass a week. It was about the time Colonel Hinton was going to sail, and I thought, with so many good friends on the road, I might try it. So I went as far as Stratford-on-Avon, but I grew so tired I gave out and let the party go on and I came home. It wasn't much of a journey—only a few hours—but I found it quite sufficient.

It is really quite astonishing what those sleeping fellows tell, and how they look us all through! I don't think I am so homesick, if that is the term they give it, but no one knows—only those who have tried it—what the depressing atmosphere of London may be to one who is not strong, and more especially to one who feels he is never to leave it, as I expected last winter. I think I could have faced the prospect of the dark river with a stouter heart if I had been strengthened by a few glimpses of sunlight sometimes, but I waited such months watching my little window panes for a patch of sky over which one could discover that a cloud moved, but the surface was never light and thin enough for this. It was as immovable as a sheet of zinc; one felt himself already in a metallic coffin, only waiting to be closed in a little snugger, and have the screws turned down. But I have tried to be cheerful and as full of life and fun as I could be, with so little ability to speak as I have had, and it may be that you and your Mamma Sally's sleeping men see deeper and get nearer to the reality than those about me, or than perhaps even I am well aware of. It is possible I have at times succeeded in cheating myself a little; all the better if it is so. I should be glad to be spared the trial of going on to the continent of Europe again. I am so tired of it, I never want to see it again, but it may be best, and then Mamie ought not to leave Europe without going there. I should be sorry to embark her for America having seen only poor smoky old London. If someone of our friends had been coming over, with whom I could have sent her to journey some, I should have been very glad of it. I can perhaps arrange it from here, but up to the present moment I have not been able to find the right opportunity. I thank you very much, dear Fannie, for all your interest and care, and hope I may never find a chance to repay it in the same manner.

Afternoon

Mr. Sheldon has just drawn a letter out of his pocket and, looking very wise, announced to me that he had just commenced a correspondence with a very pleasant lady of Worcester and, showing the envelope, I judged the correspondence had been commenced with the lady's husband. But I read it, and became convinced that it was from the lady herself. He informed me that he had replied at the earliest moment, and it happened to be just when they had succeeded in pushing me off for my trip, so he had an opportunity to talk large, but he had scarce time to answer until I was back, and he waited a day or two to see if he might show your letter to me.

I hope Ber will have had an opportunity to hear direct from me, as I gave his Boston address to Colonel Hinton, who promised to see him if he could find him. I have seen no one who was going to Worcester or I would have sent him to you. As for me, I shall try to go home this autumn, I suppose. America will at all events be as well as here, and has a greater range of climate with easier travel. As for the prospects of a full recovery of my original health (i.e., previous to last winter) I cannot decide yet. I may, when once out of this climate and atmosphere in which I have fallen, recover at once and fully; and I may never be able to throw off the effects of such prolonged prostration. My own opinion inclines strongly to the latter. I do not think anyone need come to see me home; I should be sorry to give that trouble to anyone, and will do my best to get on by myself. And now, with a kiss and great love to all, and the best to your own dear self, I am as ever

Yours

Clara

To Fannie's husband, Bernard Barton Vassall, the "Ber" or "Bear" of her playful letters, she had already written:'

5 Heusen St., Wansey St.
Walworth Road, London, April 8, 1873

My dear Good Boy Ber:

I cannot tell you how good and kind it was of you to hasten to write me as soon as you knew I had need of a word of sympathy; neither can I tell how it did me good and made me better and stronger. I was so weak and ill that day. It came at night with one from your mother, and they were the first words of sympathy that had come to me from the old home. I almost hesitate to tell you how long I held them in my hands. I looked at them till they were damp with fever and perspiration before I opened them and kept saying softly to myself, "There's something good for me in there; there are good kind words and sympathy." I waited still and held them close till I got a little accustomed to them, and then I got raised up a little in my hot bed and read them all through and through, and Mamie read them all to me again. How they helped me on after that worst and weakest and hardest of all the days I have passed in all this illness! It seemed providential that they should come just then. It was not my cough that was holding me so low at that moment. I don't know if in all I have written your mother, I have ever told her how I got a part of my illness. I had two physicians, one daily and one consulting occasionally. He came one day in early March, and recommended me to be taken out of bed and bathed in water each day, put back awhile, then taken up and dressed. I could not stand alone, but this was done two days. I had only my cough then, but the third morning after the bathing and "gaping" I couldn't straighten a limb. It proved to be inflammatory rheumatism from my body to my toes; then in two weeks a relapse and a rheumatic fever set in, which was at its height when your letters arrived. But the port wine broke the fever and I am nearly past the effects of the rheumatism, have little or no pain, and my cough is not dangerous now, I am sure; I sleep pretty well for me, and I eat good substantial food. Now, if I can hold fast to all these improvements, I cannot think it will be necessary for any person to leave home and business to come to me. I could not be come for at present, for I should not dare attempt the voyage yet, and I hope to be able to get along by myself, especially as it is almost summer now. But, dear Ber, I think every moment how good and kind it was of you to say you would come if I needed you, and if I should "go to the bad" again, I fear I shall need you. If such a miserable state of things comes, I will telegraph, and you will all consult, and do what seems best to you to do. You know much better than I what would be well to do, and, if it must be done, you will do it. Doesn't the State want to send you over to make some investigations? In that case it wouldn't seem such waste of ammunition on small game as to come just to look after poor miserable me, who never amount to anything anywhere.

But, Ber, I shall never have done thinking how quick and kind you were in writing me, and what strength and purpose I felt in every line of your letter, and it strengthens me still. You saw so clearly how I needed a strong arm near me; all about me is so weak. I have managed everything since my illness, for myself, and all around me, from my banking business and correspondence to my butcher and grocer, the airing of my linen, and the arranging of the chairs in my room. There is no mind or will or thought that can go one inch beyond me, when I stop. There is no hand that has enough magnetic force to take away one nervous twinge, not a hand that does not take magnetism from me even now, and days when I am weakest, , I cannot let a hand be laid upon me, to rub, or even comb my hair. I feel the loss of strength directly and fall into nervous perspiration. I tell you all this because I read between the lines of your dear letter that you half divined the case, and I may as well confess it. I believe I can bring myself up out of this weakness, and then I will come home to thank you, and be "put in my little bed." Won't you write me again soon, now you know how it does me good?

Dear Fannie offers her "Bear" to me—what a good Bear-ess she is, isn't she? Now, dear Ber, with a great big kiss, and I can't say that there aren't a few other little things dropped along with it, here, my good boy, is my good-bye.

From Your Old Sick Auntie

Clara

Ber, you must hold your good mother steady and not let her get alarmed. It will never do for her to come all this way on such an errand. In any case it would be too hard for her.

Though neither medicine nor the climate availed to help her, she found some measure of relief in a cheerful spirit. Of her system of mental therapeutics she wrote to her niece Mamie Barton, Mrs. John Stafford:

Auntie wants to write Mamie a little letter. She is more sorry than she can tell that she has such a stupid illness that forbids her to be company for anyone.

Auntie does not feel less social for this and, although it is hard and painful, she will not feel despondent a moment, but hopeful and cheerful for the present and future, if the circumstances immediately about her do not combine to depress her to a degree which she cannot control. If she had a headache or a nervous head which a noise would disturb or make ache, there would be some good reason for all about her to keep quiet, and leave her to her rest and reflections; but she has nothing of this, and never has. Her head is strong physically. (She will not refer to its mental qualities.) And as she has nothing to do all night but to rest and reflect, she does not need special opportunity for these during the day. If she were all alone, she would not get lonely or nervous on account of the quiet and silence about her. She has had great experiences in this and is accustomed to it. But when she feels herself imposing a dull dead silence on all persons about her, those whom she loves most dearly and for whose hourly comfort and happiness she would sacrifice anything in reason and see her dear little girls gliding about without speaking a sentence—never sees a laugh or scarce a smile—it makes her feel herself such a restriction, such a detractor from their happiness and leaves her such a prey to sad reflections and makes her feel the misfortune of her illness so deeply that at times it seems impossible to bear it. She grows more and more depressed every minute and the poor strained nerves refuse longer control, and, in spite of all her womanly determination, break into tears and groans. This would make me very ill in time. Mamie doesn't want this of all things, Auntie knows, and she writes this poor little letter to explain to her the causes and the results, and tell her how to avoid the one and improve the other.

Just, then, throw away the old-time, never-to-be-departed-from notion, handed down from nobody knows where, that all or aging persons are to be treated the same, and that mainly like a dead person, surrounded by dumb watchers, and dim tapers, waiting to' be buried, and remember that one whose heart is cheery and one whose mind is active, but whose mouth is closed to speech, might like to borrow the use of the mouths of those around diem—might and must want, most of all, someone to talk for them—to say the nonsense and make the fun they cannot say and make for themselves. And that nothing so much as a good funny time a day would so shorten and deaden the pain that must be borne in either case. Now, if the two dear good little girls could only bring themselves to have the same chatty day that Auntie knows they would have if they were in their own room by themselves, laughing, singing, doing nonsense, and, in short, feeling themselves perfectly free to enjoy themselves as I always know they do when by themselves, Auntie would be more grateful to them than for anything else they could do for her. And she has faith in the good understanding of her dear Mamie, to believe that she still sees the real state of the case as she could not see it before. And she knows that once she sees it, that big lump of Benevolence just on the top of her head, will not permit her to do anything but have a good jolly time in spite of her disagreeable old Auntie who can't just now help a bit to make it, but who needs it more than ever, and most of all.

Mamie needn't work on that old puzzling dress unless she greatly desires to.

Now, with great love, and great hopes, and sincere commiseration, Auntie closes this her first epistle to the daughter of David and waiting to hear her cry out in a "loud voice," she remains as usual

Old Dolorous

The summer, however, did her some good. She was able to get out and do a little sight-seeing, her longest journey being to Stratford-on-Avon. Early in October she sailed for home on the steamship Parthia.

Only a few weeks before she had believed that she had but a short time to live, or that if she lived it must be as a hopeless and permanent invalid; but with even the beginning of a restoration to health she recalled her determination to introduce in America the Red Cross, under whose auspices she had labored on the battle-fields of Europe. She knew that America had no knowledge of, or interest in, the Red Cross. She had good reason to question whether it would be possible for her immediately to stir up any great enthusiasm for it. But she was determined to live and bring this to pass.

As usual on trans-Atlantic voyages, there was a concert in the cabin of the Parthia. Clara Barton, returning to America as the heroine of two wars, was asked to participate. She made her contribution to the evening's entertainment in a poem which she wrote on shipboard, in which she expressed her ardent desire and her solicitude. She was going back to America after a long absence. Was there anything for her to do when she got here? For daily bread she had no concern and no need for concern. Her modest income was adequate for her still more modest needs. Even while traveling abroad she had found no occasion to encroach upon her principal, and her expenses at home were certain to leave her each year a little margin between income and outgo. But there had entered into her soul a vision of the contribution which she might be permitted to make to America and the world by securing America's adhesion to the international treaty which included the recognition of the Red Cross. Would America listen to her when she pleaded for this? Had it room for her and her mission?

THE YEARS OF SICKNESS AND RECOVERY

1873-1880

Clara Barton came back from Europe wearing the jewel of the Red Cross presented to her by Queen Natalie of Serbia. She was the only person in America who then, or for nine years thereafter, wore the Red Cross. She was the sole person in the United States who, by service or any form of official recognition, was entitled to that decoration. She wore also the Iron Cross of Merit, presented to her by the Emperor and Empress of Germany. She wore a Gold Cross of Remembrance, presented to her by the Grand Duke and Duchess of Baden; and from Louise, the Grand Duchess, she wore, and prized beyond all wealth, a magnificent amethyst, said to have been the finest amethyst in this country. From poor, defeated France she wore no official decoration, but she brought the love and gratitude of innumerable people there to whom she had ministered.

On her return to America, she went to her old home in Washington, on Pennsylvania Avenue and Capitol Hill, the home she had purchased before leaving, but occupied so short a time before her nervous breakdown. But she was not permitted to live there very long, because the comer was too noisy. Her physician, Dr. Thompson, commanded her to live elsewhere. The doctor assigned her her limits, "jail-limits" she called them; she might live somewhere between Seventh and Sixteenth Streets, and on the farther side of New York Avenue.

She established herself at the comer of Fourteenth and F. Her letters to her nieces in this period are cheerful, but written under the burden of physical pain and nerve fatigue. ,

On May 23 she received word that her sister Sarah, Mrs. Vester Vassall, was fatally ill. Though far from well, she hastened to Massachusetts, arriving in the evening to find that her sister had died that morning. The shock of her sister's death, coming as it did when her own health was so precarious, brought back her old trouble with full force. For several months she remained in Oxford and Worcester, and then went to North Grafton—New England

346

Village it was called—where her relatives, the Learned family, had a country home. There she took a house, and remained for a considerable time attended by Minnie Kupfer, who had served with her in the Franco-Prussian War, and, like Antoinette Margot, had followed her to this country. Her health varied with the season and with other conditions not all of them easy to determine. There were times when she had hard chills, followed by dripping sweats. There were weeks when she had no strength even to lift her head. There were bright days also, when she moved about with some approach to health.

What was the real nature of Clara Barton's illness during this long period of suffering? Material is not lacking for a fairly accurate diagnosis. Having exhausted the resources of local physicians, she entered into correspondence with a series of doctors, each of whom professed to be able to bring her permanent relief. Some of these called for very little information about her condition. Their remedies were supposed to cure almost anything. But others sent long lists of questions calling for full and minute replies. Copies of these questions and of her answers, she preserved.

From her replies it would appear that there was hardly a bodily function which was not disturbed. She was subject to hard colds, to severe headaches, a weak back, digestive trouble, and to periodic attacks of camp diarrhoea from which so many soldiers suffered for so many years after the war, this .condition alternating with stubborn constipation.

But it is evident, as one reads critically these pathetic catechisms, that she had after all a baas of sound physical health. Her careful answers to these questions do not appear to indicate a single organic disease. She had yet to learn that her back, which she thought so weak, was really remarkably strong, and that her head had little need to ache when her eyes were not overstrained. And her digestion need not be seriously disturbed if her nerves were not worn and shattered.

The most serious symptom that Clara Barton had, through all these years, was a temperament abnormally sensitive. She was capable of enduring almost any possible physical or nervous strain, and of standing up under it well, but when the strain was over and she met some trivial exhibition of ingratitude, some captious and wholly negligible criticism, some petulant and despicable bit of opposition, her nervous energy gave way with a sudden collapse. Her voice failed; her eyes failed; whatever organ was weakest gave way first, and she went to pieces like the deacon's "one-hoss shay."

To one who reads those letters at this distance, it seems a thousand pities that someone, whose scientific judgment she could trust, did not say to her: "You are organically sound. There is no good reason why you should be sick. You are tired, and that is not surprising. And you have magnified innumerable foolish little matters of irritation. Forget them. Believe that you are well. Half your years are yet before you—the better and happier and far the more useful half of your life. Get out in the fresh air. Live simply. Throw medicine away and you can be strong again."

In an undated letter written in the early spring of 1876, she gives to Mr. Dwight an account of her experience since her return to America:

[Undated. 1876, early spring]

Dear Mr. Dwight:

I am at New England Village. Some good angel must have inspired you to write me. I was so anxious to hear of you, and only my physical weakness has kept me from commencing a search for you long ago. I had "somewhat" to say to you, as you know, and as soon as I am strong enough shall find a way to say it. Yes, it is true I am at New England Village and have been since last April.

The "world" has not treated me badly in the last four years; but I could have better borne some bad treatment from others than all I have had to bear from myself. I have been an invalid most of the time. I grew very weak at Carlsruhe directly after Belfort, recovered a little, went to England in the spring of '72, kept about some months, but in October broke down with a cough, became too ill to get off the island, was confined to my bed eight months; in June, '73, was able to get over to Paris and recovered sufficiently to come home in October. My cough had left me, but I was weak, and fearing its return went to Washington as soon as I could for the winter, broke down again with "prostration of the nervous system," if anyone knows what that is, which was deepened and nearly rendered fatal by the illness of my only sister in Worcester, whom I strove for months to reach. Was finally brought to Worcester at the peril of my life on the 23d of May, '74, arriving at 4 p.m. to find that she had died at 6 in the morning. I never saw her dead face even. It was one year from that time before I left the house again, and that to be removed here. I could not tell you the suffering, physical and mental, of that year, and I would not if I could. Only a small portion of the time could I stand alone; averaged less than two hours' sleep in twenty-four for almost a year; could not write my name for over four months, and could not have a letter read to me or see my friends or scarcely my attendants. Little by little I have grown better until now I am about my house (for I always keep house). I have for attendant and nurse and housekeeper Miss Kupfer, of Berne, Suisse, a friend I made there, and who came to me as soon as she heard of my illness here a year or more ago and who never leaves me. I am gaining slowly, though weak still; have had neither physician nor medical treatment for over a year. Nature does her work as best she knows how; what measure of strength she may ever give me back I cannot know, probably not great. I suppose diseased nerve centers and worn-out systems are not likely to mend very firmly. But one day I shall want to see you, and you will let me do so, I think. If I am not able to go to Boston, you will come to see me, I believe, and when I see how it is likely to be with me I shall write and tell you. Meantime, it would interest me just as deeply to know how the world has treated you in these last few years as it does you to hear of me. Can I not know something of you and can I not send my most sincere and respectful regards to Mr. Jackson, whom I hope one day to see?

While Clara Barton was touring New York State on her lecture tours, she spoke at Dansville, New York, and was entertained at the sanitarium, popularly spoken of as the water cure. On March 16, 1876, a lady from Worcester who had been a patient at Dansville called and spent the greater part of a day with her. She told her that Dansville was "the place to go and get well."

Miss Barton had resumed her diary, and she recorded that this Miss Adams seemed to her "not an enthusiast, but a calm, sensible girl; looks at things in the light of reason and common sense; and I feel that I can take her reports without discount, and her opinions on trust."

Before many days she had practically determined to go to Dansville, and that place became her home for about ten years. At first she lived in the sanitarium; then she bought a home of her own. She adopted the simple habits of life which there were inculcated. Little by little her strength returned, until, instead of being an invalid, she was for her years a woman in remarkably good health. With the return of health came back her determination to establish the American Red Cross, and it was in Dansville that the first local organization in America was established under that name. How she secured the organization and official recognition we shall presently learn. From her letters at this time, two may be selected which give some account of the troubled years through which she had passed, and the great hope which she was now ardently cherishing. One of these was addressed to the Public Printer at Washington, whose services she remembered kindly, and with whom she hoped to have dealings. The other was to her cherished friend, the Grand Duchess Louise of Baden.

Dansville, Sept. 8, 1877

John D. De Frieze, Esq.
Public Printer, Washington, D.C.
Dear and Esteemed Sir:

It occurs to me that it may not be entirely necessary to introduce myself to you. Even after a lapse of almost a decade you will not quite have forgotten that there was once a woman by the name of Clara Barton who, in common with the rest of the moving world, gave you more or less trouble. However faint these traces remain in your memory, that cannot dim the brightness which gilds her recollection of the uncounted favors you so kindly and generously meted out to her in the hard, busy days when she tried, with little strength and less power, to carry heavy burdens, and accomplish hard things. Through all these years the grateful memory of these kindnesses has never waned, and it so presses itself upon me that I cannot resist the desire to pick up my pen, far away in this quiet nook of the country, and tell you how glad I am, and have been, to know you are back again at your old post, which you ought never to have left, and how thankful I am to our good President for having recalled you. My first impulse was to thank him directly, but unfortunately he does not know of my existence, and could never have found an excuse for my boldness, but you, my good and honored friend, will excuse it and will not call it even bold that a hard-worked woman has remembered the strong, kind hands that helped her on, and after long years has ventured to speak of it.

Physically these intervening years have not been easy years for me, four of them with broken health and a wanderer in foreign lands, two of them in the Franco-Prussian War and its devastations, four more a helpless invalid in my own country, and this year for the first, once more on my feet walking about like other persons, but up to the present never leaving my home even for a short journey. I think of you all in that busy capital and wonder if it is true that I too was once a part of it, and stood erect amid its jostling and excitement. Thank God He has given you strength to endure to the end!

Lest I give a wrong impression, let me add that it was physically only that I referred to my life as hard. Socially and pecuniarily it is and has been easy and beautiful. I have all the world for friends and no unsatisfied wants, no necessities, no regrets except that I am not strong enough to do the work around me which the world needs to have done. Until now it has not in five long years dared ask of me the smallest service. Lately the European people have laid upon my hands an international matter pertaining to humanity for which it seems proper that I see the President. If I should be able to go to Washington for this purpose after his return, would you think it probable I could see and speak with him?

I hope, Mr. De Freize, my long letter has not been too great a burden to you. If so, let it console you that it is not without its uses, for it is a great relief to me to have said a little of that which I wanted to say so much, and I beg to remain with the highest esteem,

Always gratefully your friend

Clara Barton

———

Dansville, Livingston Co., N.Y.

May 19, 1877
My dear Grand Duchess:
How shall I commence to write you after all these years of silence? Can it ever appear to you inexcusable? Will the generosity of your noble nature make you equal to the overlooking of an act which all the world, less noble and generous than yourself, would condemn as neglectful or forgetful? But, my preciously beloved friend, if these thoughts have ever taken hold upon your mind, and left their unpleasant shadow over the memory of your old-time friendship for me, and led you to feel that not only Republics, but their people as well, are ungrateful, and that you are only too happy in being relieved of such as you have known—if all these dark thoughts and shadows lay there in your memory of me to-day, and I knew it, and knew

351

also that they could only be removed by a full portrayal on my part of all the days and years of weakness, illness, suffering, and affliction which have caused the silence, I should hesitate long before I brought the picture to you; your active life and needed energies are not to be clogged and burdened by woes which do not belong to you, and the tax upon your sympathies is great enough from those who feel that they look rightfully to you for sympathy and help. Then let me say as little as possible of all this, and pass on to other things, and that little is, that during almost two years of the time since I last saw you in London, I have been not only too ill to write you, but too weak to have heard read a letter from you if it had been sent to me. You will understand from theory, and I pray the great and good God that you may never know by experience, what helplessness and suffering may follow in the train of utter "prostration of the nervous system." This was the misfortune that fell upon me directly upon my arrival in this country at the close of the year 1873, hastened and deepened by the death of my only sister whose life had been always dearer to me than my own. It was only last year, 1876, that I was able to leave my bed and learn to walk feebly about my room, sometimes see a friend, write a letter, and read my letters; then I was removed from my home in Massachusetts to this place, the largest and most noted water and rest cure in the country, where I have resided since, gradually regaining my strength, and coming back to life a little, but whether to usefulness remains to be seen. I have done everything to surround myself with healthful and strength-giving influences. The climate is delicious and I nearly live in the open air. Sleep, which in all years has been only a visitor, has come back to abide with me more constantly, and there is no night now in which it quite forsakes me. This was the great necessity, and I feel my strength returning under its blessed influence. My flesh is also returning and I am regaining some power of endurance. So far as any usefulness to others is concerned, I can see in all these years of helplessness only entire loss, but to myself I hope they may not have been without their uses and benefits. Through them I have walked narrower and darker paths than ever before, and stood very close to the dark still river. Aye, I have pitched my tents and rested there, waited calmly and sometimes, I fear, looked longingly over on to its other restful and brighter shore; but its shadows have not alarmed, its waters have not terrified. God has stood very near, my trust in Him has never faltered, and my faith has never wavered nor changed. I have known no fear, and if weakness, suffering, and inaction have made me more tender and thoughtful, it is well; if the silvery hair they have spread over temple and brow are a daily reminder that I have no longer the vigor of young strength, that, too, is well, and I will hope for added wisdom and gentler kindness.

Now, my dear, this is all of me, but how is it with you and yours? For I have heard of you ill and suffering, and dared not ask more. I trust that is all past, and I should see only the bright, happy face that left its lovely picture on my memory. The noble husband, is he well? The beautiful children I can scarcely picture them, for some of them are men and women now, and I never forget to pray God to keep and bless them all for the wife's and mother's sake. You will remember that the first great love in my heart for you carried me at one bound beyond all lines of courtly etiquette, blinded me to the positions and conditions of rank and royalty, and made me stupidly, awkwardly dumb to every titled phrase and courtly sentence; it closed and sealed my senses to all these, but opened them to the loving, tender wife and mother, the noble woman and the priceless friend. I could not have spoken a word of flattery to you sooner than I could have put it in my prayer; it could never have entered my thought to courtesy or bend the knee in your presence, but I should have lain in the dust at your feet without knowing it, if I had felt that it could serve you. A strange, uncourtly friend you have in me, this far-away American woman, my child, but a friend, nevertheless.

And now comes up that dread theme that first brought me to know you—war, dreadful war. My heart has stood still for weeks in anxiety, fear, and dread. Is Germany, dear Germany, to be drawn into that terrible vortex? Are her mothers to give out their sons, and her wives their husbands again so soon? Are the graves to be opened again almost before they are green, and the wounds before they are healed? Are the fair fingers of her maidens again to ply the busy hours with bandages and lint and the trembling grandmothers to labor again with shirts and socks? And you and yours, who hold and guard the weal of all, are you to stand in jeopardy, and watch in agony again so soon? Are these dreadful days I so well remember all to be lived over again? I cannot yet believe it; neither can I yet rid me of the fear which haunts me day and night. Constantly the question rises, What can I do? And my weakness answers back, "Nothing, nothing." If I had the strength of ten years ago, and the war opened upon you, I should prepare myself and go, not single-handed and alone, as I was overtaken in 1870, but I would make my arrangements with my people here for all material to work with, select my assistants from the German and German-speaking populations here, take my surgeons and nurses, and go at once and ask you for a field of labor. Surely you and your good husband and father and mother would assign me one somewhere! But it is all too late for this; at the best I can only use my influence and the little strength I have at home. As a means to this, I have written our good friend, Dr. Appia, of Geneva, to ask if any help from me would be desirable, and to say that if it would be acceptable, I would, upon his writing me to that effect, make the effort to establish an international organization in my own country for the collection and receipt of supplies, which should work under the insignia of the Red Cross, and forward through a headquarters which I would attempt to establish somewhere near or at New York. Thus would I try to bring the early and organized efforts of America into direct communication with the activities of Europe, and try for once to make our charities of some timely and real benefit, which the great distance and want of proper organization has hitherto greatly hindered, or nearly prevented. Our people are generous, tender of heart, and quick in their sympathies, but they [are busy and spread over a quarter of the globe. They do not become aware of the necessities for assistance in other lands till great suffering exists and the general Press brings it to their knowledge. Then they spring with a bound of sympathy and generosity and give without stint, but their stream has no channel prepared for it to flow in and runs over and wastes, so that little, very little, ever reaches the real scene of suffering and want for which it is so generously given. If I can learn that it would be acceptable and that there can be established a direct cooperation between the charitable activities of America and Europe, and that Europe desires it, I shall do all in my power to organize the work early, at once in America. It is for this I have written Dr. Appia to have him send me his request that I would do it, that I may use it as a lever with our Government to gain its sanction, protection, prestige, and cooperation so far as I can. I shall watch with all interest every movement and I would be so grateful for any information that I might gain from European sources regarding the true condition of things. How glad I should be of any published work or matter, if any exists, which explains the working of your remarkable system of, or what we term, "Relief Societies." I do not know where to send for this but to you who were the originator and head. If the condition of Europe renders it desirable, and I am strong enough to organize aid in America, every word of information on these points would be held priceless. I am gleaning all I can from such foreign papers as I can get; both the German and French languages are familiarly used in my house. My amanuensis is Swiss and speaks both natively, of course. The more I read, the more I fear what the next months may bring to you, to dear Germany and to all Europe. And the more I fear, the more anxious I am to help. Let us pray God the storm may pass, but if it must come, give us strength and wisdom to meet it well.

I have long been the debtor of good Madame de Mentzinger, and my next European letter will be to her, who I hope will forgive my delay. I was not able to answer her in time. To our dear Hannah I have not written in years, nor heard. I know the parent family is nearly gone, and that she has one of her own. I shall hope to hear of her someday—the precious child!

And dear Princess Wilhelm, who seems to me always to be a part of yourself, may I dare send my love through you to her? I remember once she graciously told me I might write her. I wonder if the privilege still exists, or has time annulled it? I know she has had her griefs and that her precious mother has gone home.

All that happens to you there in that beloved Court circle is reflected and felt here in my distant home as if it were a part of it. I joy in your prosperity and sorrow for your griefs as if in some way they belonged to me or mine. I could not if I attempted to divest myself of this interest. I even could not help feeling a solicitous interest in all that pertained to Prince Alexis in his recent visit to my country, and rejoiced with a kind of motherly pride in all the good impressions he made, and felt that I ought to see him, because he was of your house, and the home cousin of dear Princess Wilhelm. He, the gallant, princely man, would have laughed at the idea of a plain, unpretending American woman cherishing a family pride in him and keeping a motherly watchfulness for his welfare, but your love and kindness to me when a stranger in your country won my gratitude and love forever for all that pertains to you. I have followed the late journeying and visits of your noble father with wonder and joy for his continued vigor. I so well remember the tender care and love that dwelt in my heart for my honored father when fourscore winters had whitened his locks and bared his brow, yet his firm marching step told not more than fifty summers, and his eye was still clear and his voice strong; but he left me, the brave old soldier.

I always regret that I never saw your honored mother, and it was my purpose not to have left Europe without this distinguished pleasure. But her precious gift, the beautiful cross, is the chiefest among my treasures, lying always beside yours. You cannot conceive, I am sure, how precious those gifts are to me, and do you recollect the sweet picture of yourself you once sent me for a Christmas gift? It has comforted me every day through all these suffering years, always near my bed. It was the first to greet me in the morning, and now, in these days of better strength and activity, it is no less the admiration of my friends than it has been the companion of my weakness.

But I must somewhere make an end to this seemingly endless letter, and with one thought more I will.

May I entreat you that, if disturbances and war come upon you, and there arises any contingency, any want, any point upon which it may seem that I could, being here, be of the smallest or largest use to you, or your people, you will not hesitate a moment in making any use of me that you possibly can; consult with me upon any plan (that it shall be strictly confidential I need not add) and it will be always possible for me to confer directly with the head or heads of our Government, and so far as I can I will influence our people to any charitable activities or movements which might be desired and which you kindly suggest to me. How glad I should be to feel myself once more working with you, that I was perhaps helping you a little, and the American people would be glad, for you are no stranger to them, and I want them to know you better still. I pray you let

Your grateful and loving friend

Clara Barton

What she found at Dansville that restored her health is shown in some of her home letters. She found congenial society, wholesome and simple food, and an atmosphere that believed health to be possible. The world is moderately full of sick and half-sick people who could be well if they knew how, and would believe that they were well.

She grew strong enough for short tours to neighboring cities. She became a star performer in the evening entertainments in the sanitarium, reciting poetry, sometimes, writing a poem for a special occasion, and after a time, giving a short lecture about her experiences abroad. A few of her letters will show her state of health and of mind. There was nothing miraculous or sudden about her recovery. She had periods of depression and times of weakness, but she gained strength and gained it permanently, and was able to take up the greatest work of her life and carry it through triumphantly.

"Our Home on the Hillside" Dansville, Livingston Co., N.Y.
July 15, 1876

Dear Coz:

If Miss Kupfer had not written me that she had written to you since our departure, I should have written earlier, but I knew rite had told you of our safe arrival, and I thought I had then nothing of interest to say until I could tell you how I liked my surroundings. I have now been here seven weeks and find no occasion to regret coming. The place is simply beautiful in its location and surroundings, made up of hills and valleys under a high state of cultivation and taste.

The institution is larger and more flourishing than I had expected, with about three hundred patients, or persons as patients, and I think I never saw together any group of people that combines the degrees of intellect, general intelligence, and culture as is collected here. The speech of every person one meets is kind, charitable, and refined.

The faculty connected with the institution is, I should judge, skillful and competent, but the general means for promoting health through proper food, water, bathing, dress, rest, sunshine, open air, and pleasant surroundings are mainly relied upon; little or no medicines are ever used. I have neither seen nor heard of any being used by any person since I have been here; indeed, the great struggle and effort seems to be to get out of the patients the remnants of the medicines already taken in the past.

We have several excellent lectures in the hall during the week and services on the Sabbath. The Hall is so situated all can attend. No change or addition of dress required, other than to go from one room to another. If one is not able to walk, he is carried if he chooses to be, and if one does not wish to sit up, he lies down and listens, so there is no getting weary, no exhaustion, no getting over-tired. One gets all the good without the bad.

The tables are excellent and most abundantly supplied. Meats plainly but well cooked, the freshest of vegetables from their own gardens, and such abundance of fruit as I never saw, all in its turn. We have passed through the era of strawberries and cherries and currants, and are now in the raspberries, white, red, and black. I believe the blackberries follow next, and so on to the peaches, pears, and apples of autumn, but the astonishing thing after their freshness and perfection is their abundance. They are not served to us in saucers, or on individual plates, but placed in large fruit dishes once in about three feet through all the scores of tables, each one to help himself over and over, the dishes being refilled to the last, and we leaving the tables filled as we find them. The fruit is mainly picked from the gardens that day for dinner, or the evening before for breakfast, from two hundred to four hundred quarts for a meal. Besides this we have always the greatest abundance of "Shaker" dried fruits cooked for those who cannot take the fresh. New milk from their own dairy (they have forty or fifty cows), all one can use at every meal; the freshest of oatmeals and grahams, sweet butter, tapioca, etc. The vegetables are largely cooked in milk, and harmless. With all these fruits and vegetables there is no summer complaint here. I have not heard of a case, and among all these invalid people not a person in bed, except a few rheumatics who were brought here in beds and are not up yet. No fevers, no colics, but all out and about in the sunshine, and on the Hillside's stretchers and hammocks under the trees. One has only to be lazy and jolly and get well if they can.

There are a good many very pretty cottages outside the Main Institute where persons room, but all meet in the same dining-hall, and in the same parlor for prayers and singing after breakfast and the distribution of the mail after dinner. I am in the Institute, or main building. The views from the verandas are as fine as many I have heard extolled in foreign countries. A single glance takes in a stretch of the valley of over ten miles in length, as handsome as a landscape garden. We are so high above the town that we seldom walk, but there are always livery teams waiting orders at the door. One drives or is driven as the choice may be. Dr. Jackson has a stable of about twelve horses for his and family uses and the work. They are handsome enough for a fair, and I occasionally find that they are good roadsters. The village below us is pretty and thriving.

Miss Atwater lives in the village about a mile from me, but comes to lectures. She is well and seems very happy. I have ridden down to see her a few times. Her uncle is still with her. He had worked hard in his hotels for a great many years, been broken of his rest a great deal, and was considerably worn down, and seems to be glad of an opportunity to rest a little outside of a hot city. It makes it pleasant for Fanny till she gets more acquainted, but the people are very kind and social here. There is no stiffness.

There are something like fifty people employed as help to do the work of this Home, but not one servant; the word, nor position is not known here, all are treated equally, all ladylike and gentlemanly, all treated alike. There is an amusement society, and one of its features is a beautiful dance once a week from 5 till 8 P.M. Piano and violin music—no round dances—but cotillions and all dances which are not injurious, and the prettiest and most elegant dancers in the hall are from among the help.

There is a regularly organized fire company on the grounds, and the houses are watched and patrolled all night like a first-class manufactory. No doors are ever locked; all stand open if not too cold. I have never turned a key in the house. Now, I believe I have told you all the most important features of the place I have come to, but I have been very careful not to overdraw it, for I hope some of your journeys may sometime bring you to take a look at it for yourself, and I would not like you to be disappointed.

I hope this severely hot weather has not been too much for you, and that sometime you will find time to drop a line to your

Affectionate Coz
Clara

I neglected to say that I find a good many old friends here.

Our chaplain was a member of the Sanitary Commission in Washington, and the Reverend Dr. Abbott, who is here with his family, was President of the Christian Commission. Love to any who may inquire.

———

Clinton Hotel, Rochester Sunday [1876]

Dearest Mamie:

Does the date take you by surprise? Don't be alarmed, it's all right. I am only on a visit of a few days. Dr. Jackson, Miss Austin, and several other lady friends made a party and came last Friday to stay several days in Rochester, and enjoy the change and rest, and here we are having a glorious time. All but I can go to operas, church, lectures, galleries, etc., etc., and I can stay by and keep guard and direct the servants how to order the rooms, to have all ready and jolly for them when they get back. Mrs. Jones, principal of the Dansville Seminary, and a Miss Reynolds, who is "Thirza Ann" in a Betsey Bobbet Club we have here and a capital dramatist, are my room companions in the hotel. There is no lack of fun with two such fertile brains about. We go home next Tuesday.

Now that I am through with myself, let me turn to you and say how glad I am that you have been to the Centennial and enjoyed it so well, made so much of it, and got home so well. What a beautiful gift that was from Mr. and Mrs. Shrubler, to you, that trip, a hundred-fold more than the beautiful dress which was a thing to be most grateful for, but it will wear out in time, while nothing short of eternity can take from you the knowledge and benefits of that exhibition. It is a thing for a lifetime, not only its pleasure but its profits. Please thank them both for me for this thoughtful courtesy to you and for the good dress also, and indeed for all their kindnesses to my little girl, who I know is grateful for herself, but I am also grateful for her.

Now, you see I have not your letter here and cannot answer it as I ought, for I really do not recollect the questions it asks, neither do I recollect when I wrote you last, or what I told you then, so this letter is liable to be a repetition or an omission, but you will forgive this in either of the circumstances. I had a good letter from Ida just an hour before I started from Dansville and have answered it from there. She is a very easy, natural correspondent and would make a fine writer in some special directions if she could be cultivated. She sends me advertisement of your Papa D.'s farm. I was a little surprised at this, but it shows him in earnest in his assertion that he would like to be rid of it, and I do not wonder that he feels it a burden. It is more so than if it were larger and would afford more and efficient help, and pay for outlays. I consider it one of the most laborious sizes that a farm can have if one intends to use it as a farm, and if not, then it is too large. Four acres of nice buildings would really be worth more in the way of comfort, and these buildings have got to an age which will call for constant repairs, and the house is never convenient nor built for a farmhouse; in fact it was not intended for a farm by Grandpa, and there was no farm till your father made it so by his cultivation, for it was waste land.

Did I tell you that the Taylors had sailed for England? They must be there now. How sweet and beautiful they were when here, and how in the two or three little days they spent here they made themselves felt and beloved. Mrs. Taylor is really one of the sweetest women I have ever known. Fannie is at the Centennial and I have just one line from her. She is almost frantic from the confusion. You know her head gets troubled easily, and she had not got it rested from the journey and the first days of the great show. She will remain long enough to find herself and look dearly and see what she "went for to see," I trust. I am glad you have heard from Etta and glad they are getting on so well. Please give a great deal of love to dear Anna and congratulate her on her Centennial trip which, I trust, she enjoyed to its fullest, and thank Mr. Shrubler for his good gift to my dear old brother. I know it has made a warm spot in his heart for all the time he will live to wear it, and with his poor health and tendency to melancholy his joys are not too many. Mr. Shrubler has given him a great many pleasures, and I thank him most earnestly for them all.

My kitty is charming. She knows almost as much as folks, and has just taken to mousing. She often carries in two and three and sometimes four and five bits of game a day, and all the family have to recognize each one before she will be at all quiet. She is too comical, standing at the door with her nice white face and her mouth full of mouse and grass, calling all the household out to see her.

Yours lovingly

Clara

Miss Barton's views on health, on politics, on society, on idle women, and incidentally, perhaps, her best description of herself, her tastes and habits, is contained in a letter of this period to a learned German professor, who, knowing of her life in Germany, wrote to her, and proposed to visit her. It is interesting to note that in this letter she speaks of her hair as having been dark brown and changed in a few months of illness to a silvery gray. It did not remain gray, but with her return of health resumed its color of brown, though not so dark as before:

Dansville, Livingston Co., N.Y.
April 17, 1877

Esteemed and dear Friend:

I beg you not to be alarmed even if you were correct in your conjecture that illness caused my silence. It is very true, but I am so far recovered now that, although not released from my bed, I have taken up my pen again, and yesterday, before receiving your card, had laid out your last letter as one of the first to be answered. I might, or I might not, have reached it to-day in regular order, but now, I place it first, and commence my morning roll-call with "Prof. Thed. Pfau," and a long, narrow, blue-tinted envelope responds, half wearily, half impatiently, "Here." So "here" we have it.

First, having admitted illness, which I never do if possible to avoid, I must settle your apprehensiveness; it is no new play, or act or scene, simply a calling before the curtain for repetition. I have in these exhausted days only a given amount of strength, and if, by any accident or oversight, I overdraw on my accounts, I am at once bankrupt, and can carry on business no further. Having been in former days accustomed to draw from an unlimited and ever-recruiting stock of strength and health, I find it a difficult problem to solve, how to bring myself down to the necessary economies of my present condition.

I cannot realize that a few hours, a few rods, a few steps even, a little overwork at my desk, the quiet arranging of a simple room, a little overrun of company, may use up all my little capital, and I must wait and compromise with my creditors, start business anew on a smaller scale, and work my way up again to the lost point, probably only to lose it again. A month or six weeks ago I committed someone of these extravagances, and immediately comes a notice from my physical banker shutting off my supply of sleep. He had been allowing me nearly seven hours in the four and twenty, but he cut it down to three, two, one, a few minutes, none at all, and so left me for several days and nights, then let it come back in a similar ratio up to—Oh, well, no matter how much, but not seven hours, no, nor for a long time to come; but I can get up and walk about my room and sit part of the day; and I write, because it is better for me to write chatty letters, with no thought in them, than to relapse into solid thinking as I would in doing nothing. One sometimes needs to be saved from himself.

I do not know if I have ever told you of my illness, or what holds me so weak. It is what is known as "prostration of the nervous system' and very complete at that, I suppose. I am not aware of any decided organic disease, only as all the organs are affected by this great letting down of nerve power and force. Of the class of disease generally denominated "female weaknesses" I know nothing experimentally. Of the lame backs and aching lower spine, that the majority of feeble women suffer torture from, I am ignorant, and can sympathize with them only through observation, but of the hoi sore spot on the spine, high up between the shoulders, leading up to the base of the brain, bursting into flame at every over-taxation of mental energy, I know all. It is the same thing that over-worked public men sink under, in sudden deaths, softening of the brain, paralysis, or something analogous to these. This is the illness that has become my master and will one day prove my conqueror. There is no looking forward to "restored health," soundness and security. The price of not only my liberty, but my life is "eternal vigilance." Now a truce to illness, to which, thank God, you are a comparative stranger, and I pray Him you always may be.

I have received "Puck" since his advent into this warring world, and he is growing to be a fine little fellow, stout and healthy, a jolly little elf, isn't he? His wit will get him some clips over the nose by and by, when it begins to be felt, but this he does not care for, for he means to bite. I laughed heartily at his satire on Stanley two weeks ago, and yet Stanley is a valued friend, and I have fought terrible battles for him on both continents, but the imitation is excellent and full of ingenuity. The cuts are, of course, inimitable. Mr. Kepler's pencil has a master touch, and I wish him long life, abundant success, full pockets, and artistic fame.

The spring is opening well here. We have had a succession of charming days, followed now by a rain which is bringing up the green grass and swelling the buds almost to bursting, but we have no leaves yet. Some wild trees which precede their leaf life by their flowers are out in spring dress; a kind of woods willow, which bedecks itself in deep yellow, is very gaudy just now; the peach trees are pushing out their little soft gray pussy toes all over their red branches, and the horse-chestnuts, with their blunt ends tipped with swollen round buds, look as if they had doubled up their fists for fighting and said to all their more tapering, slender neighbors, Come on, we are ready I We are yet a month too early for the first roses.

Perhaps I told you that I removed to a snug brick city-built house for the winter. I have changed it this spring for a much older and country-like wood house, which has some trees, grass, and shade, a garden, and perhaps some flowers if the sunshine brings them up. I am, of course, all too unpretending and simple in my life to have a gardener, so shall lack the beauties which such assistance would develop. I was once a very tolerable gardener myself among flowers, but I have no longer strength to spend on the strong lap of Mother Earth, much as I love her and her dear little nurslings of cowslip and violets, but good sturdy old dame, she does a great deal without help, and knows very well how to dress herself without the aid of a *fille de chambre.*

But here I am on this fourth large page, and not even yet noted the contents of your letter. The photograph! I am sorry that you withheld it, I should have been very glad to receive it, if you would entrust it to me, and I still hope you will decide to do so. I should prize it, but I cannot say when I should be able to return the favor. I have no photographs either good or bad. I am never able to go to a gallery to sit for one. The last time was in Paris. All I ever had have been picked away long ago. I am the debtor of all my friends for pictures, some of them several times over, but they know how it is, and I hope excuse me. If I should ever again be in condition to sit, and can get a result that my friends will accept, I will take them by the hundred and relieve myself from embarrassment, but you should know that as a picture my photograph is not at all to be coveted. If natural, it must be uncomely. I was never what the world calls even "good-looking," leaving out of the case all such terms as "handsome," and "pretty." My features were strong and square, cheek-bones high, mouth large, complexion dark; my best feature was perhaps a luxuriant growth of glossy dark hair shading to blackness, but that is comparatively thin now, and silver gray, all within the last three years. It changed from its original blackness to its present shade in the first six weeks of this present illness in 1874. I never cared for dress, and have no accomplishments, so you will find me plain and prosy both in representation and reality if ever you should chance to meet either. I beg you to believe this and to remember it to avoid any disappointment which might possibly occur. Not that I think it could change the friendship of a sensible person, but I like people, and especially my friends, to know me as I am, and not hold a false estimate of me.

Of poor Miss R. (Lorraine Raymond) I never hear a word. It is charitable to attribute her silence to want of scholarship, but I am inclined to disbelieve the verity of this. I believe her to be a very fair scholar, and an average (to say the least of it) correspondent; but she seldom writes, I know. She wrote me a few letters from Europe years ago, none of late years. She has a kind heart, and I am so so sorry for her.

I hope the trial of your brother will not result disastrously to him. Perhaps one cannot easily control a dislike, but he has certainly chosen a most powerful foe, and the odds seem unequal. I agree with you in more than word, when you declare the Imperial Family of Germany to be a respectable one; it is all of that, nothing in Europe stands before it, and those of it whom I have known personally are of the highest excellence and purest worth. I am sure the more intimately they are known, the better they must be beloved. The Grand Duchess of Baden is to me the loveliest woman on the earth; in this term I mean to combine all qualities of both mind and body; both nature and culture have made her a Princess. And I cannot see why she is not as good a Republican as if she had been born a peasant, or a Suisse, or American citizen; in no position would she knowingly do a wrong or commit an act of tyranny to the lowest human being whether subject or not. "Tired of Republics," you say. Perhaps if you study your own meaning closely you will find that you are rather tired of politics than Republics. And, my esteemed and valued friend, let me in all childlike simplicity suggest what does not perhaps clearly appear to you, viz., that the standpoint one occupies, the surroundings one has, the outlook one takes, have a great deal to do in forming the opinion and swaying the judgment. I am sorry that you must perforce see our country, its political, moral, and social sides, through the slum, and mire, and haze of a lens like New York City. Out on our millions of acres of hills, valleys, and plains is a better, purer, nobler population, the force of whose earnestness and honesty will save our Nation long ages after the pollution of its cities would have turned it into a Sodom and Gomorrah. There is a true, steady, honest pulse beating in the veins of the yeomanry of this land that never throbbed a second in a city like New York, and never will; but when the trial comes, it is the pulse that will tell. Tweed and his "ring" didn't go to the farmers sweating in their hay-fields with their bargains. They went to the politicians, and burrowed in the cities and made their nests like the bats and owls, under the eaves of churches and in halls and steeples; they can plan, and connive, and twiddle and fiddle with the lines a long time while the farmers work in their fields, but when real danger appears, when the load topples and is likely to upset, stouter hearts than theirs will come to the front, stronger hands than theirs will take the reins, and bring out the load in safety. We are not so near destruction as it would seem from your standpoint, and because a few poor, vain, foolish women, with little money and less brains and shriveled hearts, have betaken themselves to the boardinghouses of New York City, and are living false, empty, silly, idle lives for *show*, it does not make it that this is the character or life of *all* the women of America, nor that well-regulated *homelife* is not the rule of the country, for it is; and I, who am a part of it, and have lived it, and over and among it, all my lifetime, know it well. Shall we judge France and its whole people by the courtesans of Paris, or Germany by Berlin? Oh! my friend and brother, do, I beseech of you, get another standpoint, and a wider outlook and a clearer, purer atmosphere than New York City with its floodtide of immigration before you judge, in final judgment, the whole population, male and female, of this great country.

I thank you very much for the hope expressed that we may meet in Paris in '78, but there is small prospect of this. I shall scarcely cross the ocean again. I have much to do to save my strength with no unnecessary waste, but the hope expressed that we may meet before that time is something nearer home, and more within the range of possibilities. I should never dare by any means to invite you to visit me, and I never go to your part of the country, so the prospect of our meeting is small. Perhaps I ought to explain the above remark, having very incautiously made it, and I will. I am a so much more simple person in my mode of life than you have probably ever seen (except those whom poverty compelled to simplicity) that you would not feel happy or homelike in my house. I am simple in my tastes, and plain, avoiding luxuries from choice and principle, both about my house and in its dress, and my table and its furnishings. My living is simple as a hermit's, heavy meats, and wines, teas, and coffees are unknown at my table, my rooms plain. I have only my housekeeper—no retinue of servants at all, no show, no ornaments, no excuses; but with all this there is great peace and quiet, no worry, no fret, no fears of what the world will think or say, no pressure in any direction, abundant supplies for all necessities, no scandal either spoken or listened to, no backbiting, and no "skeleton in the closet," not even the shadow of one. Now, all this simplicity and plainness, and the absence of excitement and luxurious surroundings and living, must be so different from all that you are accustomed to that you could not be happy or even comfortable among it, so I should never dare invite you to visit me, even if you were journeying near me, and so, when you see that I do not, you will understand the true reason and assign the right motive on my part and not feel piqued or slighted, or that I am cold, or eccentric, or

365

reserved, or in any way unaccountable, or any other thing, but just what I am. a plain woman with enough of common sense to perceive that our modes of life are so different that you could not enjoy visiting me, and fearless candor enough to tell you so.

Your sincere friend

Clara Barton

How Clara Barton was regarded at Dansville is shown in many ways, as in the following cutting from the Dansville "Advertiser" of June 7, 1877, giving account of an exercise on the previous Memorial Day:

Ovation to Miss Clara Barton

Toward noon on Memorial Day the bustle of preparation to go downtown to the procession and oration seemed to arouse a new impulse of gratitude to the soldiers' friend, Miss Clara Barton, which spread rapidly through Our Home, and soon organized itself in a programme of proceedings for the evening, when she should have rested a little from the fatigue of her participation in the public celebration.

By six o'clock a goodly number of men and women and children had gathered in Brightside and on the surrounding lawn. Soon this company, consisting of doctors and other officials, the stronger patients and helpers from the Cute, a few near-by neighbors, and the inmates of Brightside, were marshaled two by two on the walk before the gate. Of the hundred nosegays which the girls had hastily tied up and heaped on a server, none were left when each person had taken one; and these, with numerous "flags a-floating," made the procession gay as it moved on, led by the clergy. The Conesus brass band, taking tea at the seminary, had patriotically agreed to add to the dignity of the enterprise by their numbers and their music. Meanwhile one of the company had casually (apparently) in a neighborly way dropped into Miss Barton's parlor, and lured her on to the front piazza in time to witness the approach as the allies joined their forces. Being entirely taken by surprise, she could only exclaim to her attendant, "What does it all mean? What shall I do?" when she saw the battalion bearing down—rather up—on her castle. Evidently she was completely subjugated without a gun being fired, and looked helplessly and speechlessly around on the lines of exultant faces which, filing right and left, had environed the piazza in a semicircle. It still required some gentle force, however, to seat her on the chair in readiness for her. At this juncture Miss Austin, stepping forward, said:

Miss Barton: After joining our sympathies with our fellow citizens at large in paying a tribute of respect and gratitude to the brave men who fought and suffered and died for their country's salvation, the inmates of Our Home come with gladness to greet a living woman— one who worked and suffered and gave her strength and health in alleviating the pains and sorrows, the homesickness and heart-sickness of our soldiers. And we are thankful that your mission was not alone to our soldiers, but that you represented a vastly broader and nobler sentiment than mere patriotism—that you were actuated by that grand humanity which forbade you even in war-times to know any North or any South; but that every man to whom you could in any way minister was your brother. We rejoice in this, because you then represented the selfsame spirit which must yet bridge over the chasm that has hitherto divided the two sections and make us one united brotherhood—a happy and prosperous country.

But, dear Miss Barton, your life and labors have carried you beyond our country, and through you we hold fraternal bonds to the whole world. In foreign countries and in a foreign war, you spent your sympathies and your efforts, not on the Germans, nor on the French, nor on any nationality; but everywhere, every man, every woman, every little child who needed help or loving succor, received these from you in the full measure of your capacity to bestow.

We come, then, to lay our honors at your feet as a citizen of the world, as a friend to humanity, as a lover of your race; recognizing the work which you have done as a foreshadowing of that time when men shall beat their swords into ploughshares and their spears into pruning hooks, when nations shall not lift up sword against nations, neither shall they learn war anymore.

Miss Austin then introduced Reverend Miss Anna Oliver, of Passaic, New Jersey, who said:

The feeling of enthusiastic admiration with which I have long regarded one whose course has reflected honor upon her country, upon womanhood and humanity, prevent me from making a set speech on this occasion.

Several years ago I had the pleasure, Miss Barton—I may say the sad pleasure—of visiting Andersonville Prison, and the cemetery laid out under your supervision, placing a flower on each of those several thousand graves. During that visit through the South, I frequently heard the name of Miss Barton mentioned with gratitude and love, both by those who had served in the Confederate and in the Union armies.

War is terrible, and we all know, of course, that no such thing as a necessary war ever occurred. But as long as wars are actualities, how blessed is the thought that the barbarities of past ages may be superseded by the gentle Christian ministrations, a representative of which we delight to honor to-day.

To-day we pay our tribute of respect to the names of Florence Nightingale and Clara Barton.

Dr. Jackson then, being called by Miss Barton to her aid, thanked her friends in her behalf and happily expressed what he imagined might be her feelings on the occasion. When he had finished, the "Star-Spangled Banner" was sung by the choir.

Miss Barton now spoke briefly and feelingly of the honor done her and the happy memory to be cherished. Sometime she might express herself better. The most she could do now was simply to offer these friends a hand-grasp.

Then each person laid down his offering of flowers till her lap was piled high and her feet were buried deep in a pink-and-white mound, each as he passed claiming the promised hand-shake. While this was going on, the band played an inspiring air and the people of the hillside retired with the pleasant consciousness of having enjoyed a happy half-hour.

Afterward Miss Barton had a personal introduction to each member of the band, who had so kindly assisted in paying honor to one enjoying the reverence and affection of the American people, as of all classes, from the lowest peasantry to the crowned heads in Europe.

THE FORERUNNERS OF THE RED CROSS

When Clara Barton began her ministry in the Civil War, she had practically no knowledge concerning work that had been done in America or elsewhere for the relief of wounded soldiers. She did not remember even to have heard of Florence Nightingale until she was actually engaged in work of a similar character. When, at Port Royal, she was serenaded and hailed as "the Florence Nightingale of America," she knew what it meant, but she had not known very long. She took up the duty just as Dorothea Dix and other brave women did, in an earnest effort to do the thing that needed to be done, and she learned how to do it by doing it. She discovered the defects in other systems then employed, but did not criticize them. She realized the difficulties under which volunteer workers were working, and she carefully refrained from passing any unkind judgments upon organizations that were laboring under almost insuperable difficulties. But she found her own method of work, and she performed it with a success which, without robbing any other brave woman of any portion of her due fame, wrought for Clara Barton a crown of unfading laurel.

Not until she found herself in Switzerland, and was asked by Swiss representatives of the Red Cross why America had refused to join in that movement, had she found occasion to study the history of movements for the relief of wounded on the battle-field.

The sick and wounded in the wars of the Crusades were cared for, inadequately but nobly, by the Knights Hospitallers of St. John of Jerusalem, of Rhodes and of Malta. These Christian knights ministered alike to Christian and Saracen. In some of the subsequent wars of Europe the Sisters of Charity of the Roman Catholic Church rendered such service as they were able.

And yet the history of the care of the wounded in all the wars, from the dawn of history, is one of cruel and, in many respects, of needless suffering.

During the Crimean War Florence Nightingale with thirty-eight nurses went from England to Scutari, across the Bosphorus from

Constantinople, and rendered service which made her name a household word the world around. It was Clara Barton's lifelong regret that she did not meet Florence Nightingale during her long stay in England, but she was sick and so was Miss Nightingale, and neither thought of the other as being within call.

The real beginning of the movement which resulted in the organization of the Red Cross began with Henri Dunant, who was born at Geneva in 1828. When he was thirty-one years of age, in 1859, the forces of Sardinia and of Victor Emmanuel, with the allied army of France under Napoleon III, waged war against Austria for the freedom of northern Italy. At the battle of Solferino, forty thousand soldiers were killed or wounded. The defeated Austrians retreated, and the French and Italians pursued, leaving the wounded almost deserted. Surgeons at that time were not protected from attack, and the surgeons of each army moved on with the army. Dunant gathered women of the neighborhood and gave what relief he could without distinction of nationality.

On his return to Geneva, filled with tragic memories of the scenes of horror he had witnessed, he issued a pamphlet entitled "Souvenir de Solferino." In this he described the scenes which he had witnessed, and propounded this question: "Would it not be possible to found and organize in all civilized countries volunteers which in time of war would render succor to the wounded without distinction of nationality?"

Geneva had an organization for philanthropic and humane work, known as the "Society of Public Utility." Its president was Monsieur Gustave Moynier. He was deeply moved by Dunant's pamphlet, and sent out an invitation for a conference to organize "An International Conference for Investigating Means to Supplement the inadequacy of Medical Services of Armies in Campaigns."

This led to the conference of August, 1864, to which reference has already been made, in which the United States was unofficially represented by Mr. George C. Fogg, American Minister to Switzerland, and Mr. Charles S. P. Bowles, European Agent of the Sanitary Commission.

All this Clara Barton learned as she studied the history which lay behind a movement in which she was to have so important a share. Of movements in the United States she already knew.

The United States Sanitary Commission was organized in New York City on May 18, 1861, with the Reverend Henry W. Bellows, D.D., as president. The good which it did in the Civil War was incalculable. In cooperation with it was the Western Sanitary Commission, organized in St. Louis on September 5, 1861.

The Young Men's Christian Associations of the country led in the organization of the United States Christian Commission, which was formed in New York, November 16, 1861. Besides these were innumerable societies which were formed by women for the furnishing of supplies, the establishment of rest homes, and the distribution of comforts to soldiers.

When, in 1864, the United States was asked to participate in the work of the Red Cross, there was very little inclination on the part of Government officials, to treat this request with anymore courtesy than official etiquette required. The Government did not feel very kindly toward European Governments for their attitude during the war of our rebellion. We had established our own agencies for the relief of suffering, and had no inclination to add another.

When the war was over, however, Dr. Bellows was confident America would join in the International Red Cross. He issued a long letter addressed to Monsieur Henri Dunant, who was acting as "Secrétaire du Comité International de Secours aux Militairet Blessés." This Dr. Bellows did as President of "The American Association for the Relief of Misery of Battle-fields." On its title-page was emblazoned a Red Cross as the insignia of the organization, the first time that symbol was used in America, and, until Clara Barton's day, the last.

In this long and earnest and discriminating letter, intended to arouse public sentiment in America, Dr. Bellows told, with great plainness of speech, of the inadequacy of even those splendid organizations with which he himself had been associated. He said:

Good intentions and humane sentiments are not alone qualifications for this duty.... Volunteer agents are the dearest that can be used.... It is useless to expect correct information on the wants of the soldier from the Government, or the Medical Bureau, or even the General Officers. The last thing to which a Government attends in an active war is the sick and wounded. The Medical is the least interesting bureau to it, and as a rule army surgeons have hard and coarse views of humanity to soldiers. General officers seldom see with their own eyes the details of want and suffering.

He paid a high tribute to the work of the women in the war. He said that virtually the whole womanhood of the Nation was engaged in it. He spoke of the women in hospitals, and said that some of them had done well, but that "detailed men are the appropriate nurses in military hospitals. Women are rarely in place at the front, or even at the base of armies." He said that, of the women who went to the front, "most of them were in the way, with a few rare exceptions, where tact and humanity were united with force and endurance." His letters to Clara Barton leave no doubt as to one whom he considered in the forefront of these exceptions, combining, as she did, tact and humanity with force and endurance.

Dr. Bellows's effort fell completely flat so far as the organization of the society was concerned. He became thoroughly discouraged and gave it up, and years afterward rejoiced when he saw Clara Barton accomplish what he had vainly striven to do.

This was the situation as Clara Barton learned it, when returning health brought back to her the strong purpose of proceeding at once to the organization of an American Red Cross.

THE YEARS OF LONELY STRUGGLE

Fan several years after the Franco-Prussian War, Europe was at peace. But trouble was brewing between Russia and Turkey, and no one knew what the end of it would be. The probability that there would be war in Europe appeared to Clara Barton to indicate a possibly favorable condition of public sentiment in America far the consideration of the Red Cress. If there was to be war in Europe, and we were to be asked to help in the relief of the suffering it would cause, it would seem fitting that there should be some international organization by which relief could be gathered on this side and distributed upon the other. The American public would then see some reason why America should be interested in an organization of this character.

Clara Barton communicated with Dr. Louis Appia, who had called upon her in Switzerland, and with whom she had been associated in the Franco-Prussian War, offering to assist, in such way as she might be able, in effecting a suitable organization.

From Dr. Appia and from President Gustave Moynier, she received prompt letters, and, with these, official appointment to represent in America the International Committee of the Red Crow. This correspondence is lengthy, but of the greatest possible value and must be Included in full;

Dansville, May 17, 1877

Dr. Louis Appia
Member Société Internationale of the Red Cross of Geneva
My Esteemed and dear Friend:
If years have passed since any word from my pen told you of my existence, and if the precious letter from you has lain many months unanswered, it has not been the fault of my memory, nor the loss of friendship, nor interest in you nor in the glorious and holy work which engrosses and fills your noble life. It has been simply that, ill, weak, worn, and suffering, I have been lost to the work of the world, and to the friends I honored and loved. Four long years have found and held me powerless to strike a blow on the great anvil of humanity, or labor one day in its vineyards, and for the most part too weak even to hear of those who did. But the strong brothers and sisters have toiled bravely on while I waited.

The great wheels have slowly turned, until they have ceased to crush me so low, and grind me so small, and once more I begin, under God's Providence, to reach out my hands into the passing atmosphere of life and feel the breezes blow over the seared and fevered palms. Once more I dare turn my eyes toward the labor-fields and their faithful workers; in my land, bright with its western sunbeams, aglow with beauty and abounding in plenty, they sew and glean in peaceful valleys.

But beyond the eastern waves, in that dear old land that four years of life there taught me to love so well, I see again the flash of the bayonet, the march of armies trampling down the harvests; the terror-stricken fly for rescue, and the wounded cry for help. Again the Red Cross, like the bow of promise, rises over the scene, again the shout from its inspired origination rings out amid the din of arms, and its clear, brave tones reach me even here in my quiet chambers, and my heart, with all its old memories stirred to their depths, goes out in response; it bids me seize my pen and say to you that what there is of me is still ready for my work; that like the old war horse that has rested long in quiet pastures, I recognize the bugle-note that calls me to my place, and, though I may not do what I once could, I am come to offer what I may. Then, would I have taken the next steamer, and in two weeks have stood beside you, asking where to go, and what to do, but as that is not for me now, my brain and heart must do what my hands cannot. My plans are made, and, such as they axe, I send them to you for acceptance and cooperation.

First, I cannot quite rid myself of the lingering hope that the terrible vision of war before you will vanish before its full realization, but if not and the nations are drawn into its vortex, God only knows the end. I cannot foresee it, but I can foresee that my country will open its heart and its hand in aid as soon as the cry of want and suffering shall reach it; this never fails. The American nature is free and impulsive, its sympathies are quick and responsive, and it has neither power nor desire to withhold aught from the distressed. But, ready as America will be, she is far away from the scene, can understand but vaguely the steps necessary to the proper gathering, sending, and bestowal of her gifts. So without some definite and well-arranged organization, however large and generous her donations, she will fail of accomplishing any real or perceptible good, as she has always failed before in all similar efforts, at foreign aids. Foreseeing this, I would, if possible, step in to fill this place, and hold back this waste of waters till they can be turned into their proper channels. And for this, my honored friend and brother, I write to you, to ask if I can be of service in this direction. If so, I will do my best to form such an organization in America, if you and your Committee desire it. As it is now, in spite of all efforts which you have so generously made to spread the knowledge of your society and its great objects in this country, it is almost unknown, and the Red Cross, in America, is a Mystery. I am safe in asserting that not one person in a hundred on this side of the Atlantic ever heard of it; not one in five hundred has any clear idea of its uses or design. The Franco-German War failed entirely in introducing it either to the people or the Government, and so will this present war, unless some active hand takes hold of it, to organize the war reliefs under its escutcheon. It is not enough that some good person stands inactively as the representative of the society in this broad country. To be learned it must be brought into active use. It must have a National Headquarters, sanctioned by the Government, where the flag of the beautiful Red Cross floats day and night, in war and in peace. It must have its different State organizations, and its smaller relief societies all working under its insignia.

This accomplished, the charities gathered from the people should be passed to the State and thence to the National Headquarters, and, these being always in communication with you, they would be shipped intelligently and reach at once a field in need of them. My heart aches when I think of all the thousands upon thousands of dollars in goods and grains sent to France in the best of faith by our people in 1871 and wasted; lost, squandered, and sold on its borders, it being impossible to gain transportation or penetrate the army lines; and all for the want of the proper knowledge and organization at home. It will be the same thing again unless some method is taken to centralize, organize, and prevent.

I have only a word more to add, and I feel called to make the suggestion I make by the fact that I am perhaps almost the only American who you can feel has been a co-worker with you, whose manner of work you know something of, and whom you can class as a personal friend and thus address familiarly. And my suggestion is, that if you feel that I can serve your cause, and humanity through it, in the manner I have described, you will let me know your desires at once. If you will write me immediately upon receipt of this, asking in your own name or that of the International Society, that I do all in my power to aid you in the work, and to use my power with my people and my Government, so that it can be seen here that such a want is felt, such a work needed, and that the call is from the highest and original source of international relief in war, investing it with the highest importance, I will have your letter placed before our President and Government and ask their sanction and approval, if not the pecuniary aid; for that I never ask. And if it is inclined to be so gracious, it may perhaps appoint a Head to the work, thus, by its notice, investing it with an importance, and throwing about it a protection, which it could in no other wise secure. This would forever establish the knowledge and the work of the Red Cross for which its noble founders have striven so bravely and faithfully in every mile of American soil. The soldier would learn to trust it, the father would honor and bless it, the mother would bind it over her torn and aching heart as she kissed her soldier boy good-bye, and the little children even in the wilds would come to know and love its beautiful face.

Now, my honored friend, this is not an appeal that you make *me* the head of your noble order in this country, the active working head I mean, for I have little ambition at best and none now, but it is to tell you that such a head must be made before the order here can ever come to be of the smallest possible use to the world. Thus far it has failed, and I see no way to establish it but by a call coming earnestly from you and being actively and unselfishly and powerfully and wisely placed before the moving powers of this Nation and the people. If you have already some person in your mind who will do this, or who you prefer should attempt it, then it is all well, only see that he does his duty and is not asleep at his post. There is no more time for this. But if you have not such a person in mind, and feel that I can serve you acceptably, you have but to let me know and I will do all in my power. Please write me at once. The stronger your appeal to me, the better use I can make of it, and meanwhile I shall not be idle or inactive, but will hope to hear from you within the next six weeks, say by the 1st of July.

Please accept my most grateful thanks for the kind sympathies expressed in your letters of last year which I was too ill to answer, and remember me in great respect to your family and the mutual friends in my home in Geneva.

Perhaps to you, as a physician, it would be proper to state that my long illness has been, as you most likely would suspect, "prostration of the nervous system," and you know how slowly one rallies from this, and with what difficulty the strength is regained. I am now at my best by far since 1873; am about my house and grounds, ride, walk, meet friends, and sleep tolerably well, not as in the old days on the ground without bed or pillow, but comfortably, and am always gaining a little in strength.

I trust this may find you well, and it will carry to you the best wishes and most sincere esteem of

Your friend

Clara Barton

[Translation]

Paris, June 14, 1877

Miss Barton, and Honored Friend:

It is in French that I write to you, for you would laugh at my bad English. I am at present in Paris on a visit at my brother's. I hear that Mr. Moynier has written to you on the same subject which will make the contents of this letter. I expect Mr. Moynier in Paris in a few days, which will give me the opportunity to talk the proposition over with him, which we both wish you to take an interest in.

Mr. Moynier has undoubtedly told you that our Committee has tried for these last ten years to give to an American Committee an active existence, but we failed. In the first years our communications were made through a Mr. Bowles, then residing at Paris, with whom we ceased to correspond, not seeing that we arrived to any certain result by this channel. Later we have been in direct communication with Dr. Henry W. Bellows, President of a phantom Committee in New York, from whom we seldom receive an answer. Having therefore no proof that that committee was active, we ceased to correspond, and we at last learned officially that that committee was officially and entirely dead. From that time, about a year since, we considered the Red Cross as not existing anymore in America. I need not speak here of the disease which has caused that death. You are an American and you know better than we the temperament of your Nation. Our hope to entertain the life has been nourished in us by the reading of the admirable work which America had made for the care of the wounded during the Secession War. We spoke of it at length in the thick volume which Mr. Moynier and myself have published under the title, "The War and Charity," and which obtained the integral prize of the central committee in Berlin. Mr. Moynier has told you, without doubt, how happy we should be to see a work come into life again in your rich and generous America, which had shone with such a bright luster at the epoch when it was stimulated by the mighty auxiliary of the patriotic motive. We know little what America has done for the victims of the Franco-German War, which you have seen and during which we have for some time worked together, and I am not surprised that many generous gifts have been lost for want of a good organization, and especially for want of being able to establish regular communications with the armies by the channel of an American auxiliary committee residing in Europe and which would offer all the security.

If you, my honored friend, could succeed in organizing something durable in America, in relation to the Oriental War which appears only in its beginning, you would have nobly crowned the work of devotedness to which you have consecrated your life. I do not know what means of execution Mr. Moynier proposed. I shall write again upon that subject, when I shall have seen him, so that we agree completely together in what we tell you. Permit me, however, now to communicate to you some ideas. You can without doubt become the soul of this revising work, but you cannot be its body. America is not so different from Europe that my experience cannot profit you for your country. Now, medicine teaches us that a soul without a body has no life at all, at least upon earth. Perhaps even it is better that a woman should be the soul; her moral influence, her earnest entreaties near the Governments and authorities are often better accepted and consequently more efficacious. I do not therefore see any inconvenience that you should be for America the head of the Order, the active working head—why not? If you feel to have the brain power as much as I know you have the moral power, but then create immediately under that head a body, arms to write, to arrange methodically, to publish, to keep the correspondence, either alone or under your dictation, for copying, etc., after that, feet for running, to go, to come, to collect, to buy, to make multitudes of visits and receive visitors, as we were obliged to do in Geneva in 1870, where during two months my ten rooms were never empty all day long, each one containing a secretary, man or woman, to write and to receive a host of visits which would have killed a President, and of which hardly a quarter had really any other practical use than to enlighten the public and to keep up its zeal, not always rational.

Surround yourself at once with a little body of persons full of good-will and capacity, docile to your directions, either women or young men, especially doctors. Amongst the latter choose a secretary who must be entirely at your service and who probably ought to be paid.

1. The first work seems to me to be to awaken the attention, the sympathy, and the confidence of the public. Without the public, no money, and without money no material help. You know as well as myself the means to attain this end is publicity, the power of which is, I believe, greater in America than in any other country.

2. Complete study of the practical and sure means to carry an efficacious relief to the armies in the Orient. To that effect one needs to correspond very often with all the relief committees of Russia, of Rumania, of Serbia, of Montenegro, and even of Constantinople. It is necessary not to conceal to one's self that these intercourses, easy enough on paper, are very difficult

in reality, if one does not want the money or the relief to be lost to the profit of the war, rather than to the profit of the unhappy victims.

In order to obtain this, and our Committee can be of use to you, and between Mr. Moynier and myself we shall do all we can to help to enlighten you. But you must also have direct intercourse with the relief committees of the different countries which are at this moment engaged in the war, although administratively the international communications from neutral countries are made by the International Committee. You know by experience that many letters are in that case lost in the hands of employees, subordinates, or men too much occupied, and that one needs to throw the bait often and on several sides, at the risk of losing much time.

3. You must put yourself in direct communication with your President. I see in it the use, first, to augment your credit in the country; second, especially to obtain that your letters and your sendings be given up by persons in high positions and influential, in particular ambassadors and consuls. You know that question by your experience in the American war better than I do, and I shall not enlarge upon it.

4. You must have money, and you know the means to procure it. The Sanitary Commission has collected sixty millions of francs during your war, especially by immense bazaars. In our country bazaars always succeed, much more so than collections, and produce three to four times as much. They always succeed, while collections oftentimes fail.

5. Once having the necessary money, the question rises, if it would be advisable to choose two commissaries—for example, two young physicians supplied with a recommendation from your President—who should go together to Europe with instructions and *plein-pouvoir* from your new Committee, directed to go first to Geneva to the International Committee and from there to go directly to the Headquarters of the Russian army, in order to make its acquaintance and to obtain from it the authorization to circulate in the army and to gather all the information necessary for your work. It would be desirable that they speak tolerable French, this language being the official one in Europe; if they speak and write only English, they would lose time and would not always be understood. Those two or three commissaries should be posted on the theater seat of the war and should give you all the news by an active correspondence. They ought probably to engage themselves not to write on politics. I never did it in war-time of Italy, Schleswig, and France. Besides these commissaries, you need an office or an agency in Europe to whom all the relief funds must be addressed and who would take the charge of sending them on wherever the

commissaries indicate. I do not know what our International Committee will decide upon this, but I think it will be disposed to be an intermediary between America and the belligerent armies, as it has done during the War of 1870 by the agency residing at Bâle placed there by us. This agency has received five hundred letters, besides other correspondence, every day, either for France or Germany. Notice, however, that our Committee wish to show an absolute neutrality and should certainly refuse to cooperate in anything like a political party. It is, therefore, necessary that your publications speak out your intention to remain neutral and to carry the relief indifferently to all those who suffer. That will not hinder you to correspond more particularly with the Russian army, which for you is more accessible, with whom the communications are easier, and for whom I believe America has more political sympathy; but you must insist on your principle of neutrality in your publications and let this position be known in Constantinople, and especially to the Committee newly formed in that city. Your commissaries, after their arrival at Geneva, might remain there some days in order to study a little our library which contains everything that has appeared since the beginning of our work. It would be desirable, however, that the Committee of the Red Cross in America should buy the principal works, and that there should be a commission of several established persons who would take it upon themselves to study them and to give an account of them; there is a little in every language.

I have sent you a number of our International Bulletins which appear every three months, and in which I have spoken of you. The annual subscription being only six francs, your Committee would take two subscriptions and by it would know all that is done in the different countries. Last year we sent three delegates to Montenegro, an interesting little country, where with material help and money we can do a great deal of good, and where one is received like a Divinity by this enthusiastic population, but which is also jealous and suspicious.

Our old delegates being at Geneva, yours could receive numerous and useful information. Before realizing this ambassador, we had three months' study and treating.

I send you my discourse made in Brussels, which for your case does not contain any immediate application. I might give one to your hypothetical delegates as they pass through Geneva.

As you see, Miss Barton, and honored friend, I began with the idea that the American Society of the Red Cross should revise and assure its stable existence by an immediate employment of its power through a practical application; relief funds to send to the belligerent armies of the Oriental War. Once consecrated by action by the remembrance of what it has done, its basis will be firmer, its credit more assured, and then you will be able to give it a definite form and shape which experience will have shown you to be the most useful.

Not knowing yet what Mr. Moynier has done during my absence, I shall not send you the letter which I wish to address to your President, but shall do it as soon as I shall have seen him, if he has not already done it.

Write to me at any time concerning the affairs of the Red Cross and I shall reply as well as I can, being always in accordance with Mr. Moynier's wishes, who does not know English.

You would do well to have Mr. Moynier's pamphlet translated into English, "What the Red Cross is." My little volume, entitled "The Surgeon at the Ambulance," has been translated into English either in England or in America; perhaps it would be well to have a new edition of it for the circumstance. At last our volume "The War and Charity" has also been translated into English. For all our publications of the International Committee and its members it suffices to address Mr. George, Librarian at Geneva. Perhaps it would be necessary and useful, after you have plenty of money and fellow-laborers, to publish every three months a small bulletin of your work in one of the good American journals.

And now, my dear Miss Barton, I have talked enough to you about the Red Cross. I have given you my ideas provisionally, expecting better ones later. You see, I have spoken to you familiarly and with an entire confidence and fraternal friendship which our intercourse and our common work in Europe has brought forth.

May God sustain you, if you do undertake this new work, and, in entertaining and augmenting your corporal strength and brain power, may He continue to inspire you with that moral irresistible power, that invincible strength, which He alone can give and which the incredulous humanitarian never can give.

Accept, Miss Barton, and honored friend, the assurance of my respectful friendship.

Louis Appia, Dr.

Dansville, July 1st, 1877

Docteur Louis Appia

Membre Comité International de Secours aux Militaires blesses, Geneva
Docteur and Honored Friend:

I cannot find the words to properly express to you my gratitude for the kind and careful manner in which you have treated my letter. But first allow me to thank Madame Appia for her generous part, and all the prompt care she took to place it in the proper hands, and let me thank both for the excellent photograph, so welcome now, and for all the future to be preserved among my choicest and most honored keepsakes.

How kind it was of you, my good friend, to give me so much of your time and labor, embodied in that long letter so filled with valuable suggestions! If nothing more comes of it, it will at least bring us to an understanding in reference to the actual existence and standing of the Order of the Red Cross in America. I was extremely guarded in my letter, not at all knowing how you stood in regard to your selected representative in this country, for I knew you had one, and, if you were satisfied, I did not wish to ripple the calm waters of confidence and security by even one pebble of discontent or doubt. I wrote cautiously like a woman. You have spoken out like a man, and it is well. With the pains your Comité have taken, the Red Cross should have been known and honored in every household in America to-day. It has not died here: it was stillborn; it has never once gasped on our shores; the nurses to whom you delivered it have never even uncovered its face, and America does not know that this holy child was ever an applicant for her adoption. She would have received it with open arms at the close of our war, when her own wounds were unhealed, and her memories fresh and tender. She will be less enthusiastic now at the end of a ten years' peace, and no prospect of war. Still, the understanding and heart of the American people will lead them to examine and promote whatever cause has for its object the benefit of mankind, or the alleviation of human woe. I think I know my people, and although, through want of proper opportunities, or physical strength, or mental capacity, I may not be able to move them in this matter, this fact will in no way affect their general character, and, when all things combine for the proper presentation of this subject to them by whomsoever it may be, it will be received and adopted by them. Your suggestions are excellent and lay out much such a field of labor as I had looked forward to, and all this would be easy of accomplishment in America, if an urgent necessity existed. Until it does, it would be, I suspect, a difficult task to work up sufficient enthusiasm, but it was in anticipation of such a necessity that I was endeavoring to prepare the way. The simple war between Russia and Turkey might not be able to awaken the people, for we have a comparatively small element of either nationality among our populations, but if other European nations engage and Germany, France, and England, or all become involved, the interest in America will be scarcely less than on the other side. Then would be a repetition of the old sad days of the Franco-Prussian War, when every heart was sad and every purse open, they tell me, and half America in mourning.

Now, my idea was, in anticipation of such a state of affairs in Europe as should call for the sympathies and aid of the Americans, to be prepared with an organization, which would be only the body of clay, like the first man Adam, until the breath of life was breathed into its nostrils. This breath would be the necessity and the call for help from the suffering fields and peoples of Europe; then it would be well that the body were created to receive it. The first step, it seems to me, is to find and appoint to the head of the work some person in America who will have the spirit, the interest, the enterprise, the determination to push the work, and bring it before the country and the people, or the honest conscience to resign the position in favor of someone who will, and not hold it for years, as an empty honor, smothering out its life, and leaving the country in ignorance of its existence.

I am very grateful to you for the kindly interest you take in the subject of my health. My sleep, which I know to be the great want, is always gaining, and digestion improving, and these without the slightest artificial aid. I never took a grain of morphia in my life, and probably never in all combined a tablespoonful of medicine to produce sleep, and now I take nothing; for the last three years not one particle of medicine, relying entirely upon my food, rest, and open air for my restoration. All I have gained has been by the aid of nature alone; thus I know the foundation is solid and sure. I allow nothing to trouble me, as indeed I have no cause for trouble. I walk, or work in my garden, or lie on my stretcher like a soldier under the trees several hours every day; and here come around me the memories of the past, the busy present, and the needful future. I wonder what you are all doing over this broad world, and how I can help you. If I find myself able to carry on a work I shall do it; if not, I shall endeavor to inspire those who are.

Your friend

Clara Barton

[Translation]

To Miss Clara Barton

Dansville, Livingston Co., N.Y.
Miss Barton, and Worthy Friend:

According to my promise I write to you after having seen Mr. Moynier, although I have nothing very new to tell you, and have only to confirm what I have written to you in detail. I can therefore be brief this second time. Mr. Moynier and myself are equally sympathetic to your plan, and we shall be happy if you succeed in founding in America a permanent work of the Red Cross. And we shall help you in it with our influence to the extent of our power.

Mr. Moynier has written me that he has already told you so. He has added to his communication a suggestion which indeed is very important, i.e., that you obtain from the Government of the United States the signing of the Convention of Geneva, which has already been done by all other civilized states in Europe and out of Europe. Without this signature, the private work of the Red Cross is paralyzed. Here is an example of what has very recently taken place in Montenegro, of which we have asked the signature before putting ourselves in relation with it, and before sending to it our three delegates with help for their wounded. All succeeded very well, and Montenegro has entered eagerly into the general alliance of the Convention of Geneva. It will be the same with America, we will hope, which has remained back until now. But in order to ensure its success, it will probably be necessary to make a summary communication to the Government what the Convention of Geneva is, its destiny, and what the Red Cross is. You will find all the desirable details upon this point in the pamphlets or works which Monsieur Moynier mentions or sends to you. It will be necessary that some person take cognizance of this work with you, and assist you in it. The Red Cross has existed since 1863. Since then it has given birth to an entire new literature, so as to make by itself a real library.

And now, my worthy friend, go on courageously with faith and hope. The cause is good: let us defend it everywhere and let us be firm in upholding the banner of charity. It will be ever the surest means of combating the principle of war.

Write to me when you have done something, with or without translation. My previous letter will give you all the details of my manner of viewing it.

As to our participation in your sending of secours, I think with Mr. Moynier that it would be better that we offer our cooperation directly, when we succeed this time in founding an International Agency. As formerly in 1870 we have founded one in Basle, which has been very active and useful, and consequently if you have any substance or provisions to send, it would be better that you send directly.

Besides we shall always be at your service to help and advise you, and we shall be very glad to be kept informed what you are doing, and we shall publish your work in our trimonthly Bulletin.

I could not see again Mr. Moynier, but I know he has nothing important to add to what I say and to what he has already written to you. I believe, therefore, you have from us all the indications and information which we can give you. There remains nothing else for me, Miss Barton, than to repeat my good wishes for your useful enterprise. May you feel your physical strength to keep up and increase, as much as your moral, for the good of others and for your own satisfaction.

I have nothing more to add, and I will not put off any longer this last letter.

Accept, Miss Barton, and worthy friend, the expression of my respectful devotion,

Louis Appia, Dr.

[Rough draft of letter without date, but evidently written about July 1st, 1877]

Monsieur S. Moynier
President du Comité International de la Croix rouge My Esteemed Friend:

Permit me to thank you, as I do most sincerely, for your kind and excellent letter of June 20th, and say how happy I am to find you so fully concurring with the ideas I had advanced in relation to the action to be taken in the attempted establishment of your beautiful Order of the Red Cross in America. It is unnecessary for me to assure you that I will do all that lies in my power to accomplish this end, believing as I do most implicitly that every step taken toward softening and humanizing the conditions of war is a double step toward its extirpation from a place among the codes of nations. This proves itself by the unfailing fact that the more barbarous a nation and the more inhuman its modes of warfare, the more frequent and unmitigated its wars. This conviction, added to the strong desire which has grown within me to lessen the sufferings of those who must compose armies while they do exist among the nations of the earth, will prove a sufficient stimulus to all the powers of my nature, and I will bring to the object the fullest strength I possess, and then, if with your best aid I fail in my purpose, I must be content to submit to the inevitable.

My intelligent friend and your compatriot, Mademoiselle Kfipfer, has begged to add a letter to you, which I am most thankful for, as she can speak to you in your own tongue, and with a clearness of expression which I could not. I shall be very busy for the few coming hot weeks of August translating the many valuable pamphlets so kindly sent me, from which I hope to gather a knowledge of the action of the Society and familiarity with its spirit, which may enable me to convince my Government of the right and propriety of what we ask it to do, the wrong and absurdity of withholding it, and secure from it at least an official reply to your invitation to join the Convention.

I will not make this communication longer, excepting to repeat my thanks for your kind letter, and the generous spirit in which it was written, and assure you of the great pleasure it will afford me to be of never so small a service in a cause so noble and holy. With assurances of the highest esteem I remain,

Most honored Sir
Very truly

Clara Barton

———

Dansville, Livingston Co., N.Y Sept. 27, 1877
Monsieur Moynter President Esteemed Sir:
Your communication of the 19th August, enclosing a letter addressed to the President of the United States, arrived in due time, and my impulse was to write at once assuring you how kind and satisfactory I found them both to be. But at that moment I hoped it would be possible to see the President and present your letter very soon, and thought it better to defer my reply to you until this were accomplished, and I had some results to communicate. But you will perhaps have observed that the President and several members of his Cabinet are making very extensive travels over the country this summer, and since the arrival of your letter he has never been in Washington or acting in his official capacity in any place, long enough for me to reach him. We had expected an extra session of Congress to be convened on the 3rd of October, which would have ensured his presence in Washington, but even this being now uncertain, I feel that I must not longer delay my letter to you, with the assurance that it shall be my pleasure to present your letter to the President at the earliest moment in which I can reach him, and whenever this is done, I shall at once transmit to you the results as well as the nature of the interview.

With kind regards to Dr. Appia and sentiments of the highest esteem for yourself,
I am

Very truly

Clara Barton

———

Washington, D.C., United States January 14, 1878

Doctor Louis Appia
Geneva, Switzerland.

My Esteemed Friend:

I feel that it is time I should tell you gentlemen of Geneva what I am doing or trying to do in America with our favorite subject of the Red Cross, but, as my present letter, from the incompleteness of my work, cannot take the form of a report, I will address it, not to Monsieur Moynier, as the President of the Convention, but familiarly to you, as my friend and co-worker.

I remember to have written in the autumn that I could not get an opportunity to present the letter of Monsieur Moynier to our President until his summer journeyings were ended. But when he returned to Washington in October, I came here also, a distance of some four hundred miles, and commenced slowly and carefully my work.

I found the great difficulty to consist, not in the opposition I should meet at first, but in the facts that no one understood the subject, and there was no printed literature pertaining to it in the language familiar to the people to whom I desired to present it (with the exception of our State Department, which is, of course, conversant with all languages).

Thus my only method was to translate, write and rewrite, and explain until an understanding and interest were created. I did not think it wise to present the letter of Monsieur Moynier to President Hayes until the subject was somewhat understood by the parties to whom he would be compelled to refer it, viz., the State and War Departments, leading members of the Bar, as counsellors, and some of the prominent members of Congress. I accordingly commenced with these parties myself, explaining the subject, and doing my best to create an interest and secure cooperation whenever the matter should come up for discussion or decision. From Congress I proceeded to the heads of departments and their assistants, and, gaining an audience, explained the cause to them one by one. The interviews were frequently very long, and I have, with most of them, not only left a full translation of the Resolutions, but read them with them, hearing their queries, and explaining the practical working of the system as I had seen and known it.

When I thought I had sufficiently guarded the outposts, I ventured to ask audience of the President (this was only last week) and presented to him the letter of Monsieur Moynier and a copy of the Resolutions.

President Hayes received the letter with great respect and will refer it to the Secretary of State for decision.

I had previously found, by examination at the State Department, that the subject had once come before our Government at the time of the Convention in Paris, and been declined by President Grant, and his Secretary of State, Mr. Fish, on the ground of danger from entangling alliances, which it was a fundamental principle of our Government to avoid. This record stands in my way, and the greatest difficulty I shall have to meet and overcome will be this previous decision. If it had never been presented at all, and I had thus no former decision to reverse, I should hope for a comparatively easy task, but formalities and courtesies stand greatly in the way of reversing or setting aside the decisions of a previous authority, and especially such authority as General Grant and his popular Secretary, Mr. Fish. This adverse decision I hold to have been the result of a hasty and improper presentation of the subject without suitable explanation, and, from the lack of a full understanding of the system, it was considered wisdom on the part of our Government to let it alone.

Now, I do not despair of success in the end, for I have met only the greatest courtesy and most patient attention on the part of all officials, and I promised the President that I would wait within call, in order to be ready to make any explanations and answer any questions which he or the members of his Cabinet might desire to ask. I have no definite idea of the length of time they may hold the matter under consideration before deciding, but it is so far progressed that my own attorney can probably assist me, and he will arrive here in a day or two. This is the Honorable Judge Hale, of the State of New York, one of the best counsellors in the country, and is not only my personal attorney of many years, but also a near relative. I did not call him until I had thoroughly prepared the ground, but now that the heads of the Government understand the subject properly through my explanations, I must wait and let them make their points of law upon it and decide. One thing I am certain of, that it would have been of very little use for anyone to have presented the request in an ordinary manner, or who had not time to spend upon it, or was not willing to work for the cause. With that previous refusal in the way, it will require great care, labor, and perseverance to gain the point desired, but I shall not despair until I must. I regret that I have not in all this time a more certain progress to report, but I thought it proper to let you know what stage of the work I am in, and that all that is possible is being done. It is almost three months since I left home and came here to work for this cause. My health has not suffered, but has held firm beyond any expectation of mine. I must think this is largely due to the great kindness and friendly courtesy which has been extended to me on every hand. Every official person listens patiently to all I have to say, and asks with the greatest kindness what I would like him to do to further my wishes or aid my cause, and I know that, if in the end the Government refuses to sign, it will be only upon a strict point of law, which it feels bound not to overstep (after mature deliberation), and it will be grieved to feel compelled to disappoint either the members of the Convention or myself. The Government of so vast a country as the United States is a great body to move, and, in order to accomplish anything under it, it is necessary that one have some knowledge of it, some weight with it, and an endless patience and perseverance.

I hope it will not be another three months before I can send some more decisive information, which I shall not fail to do at the earliest moment.

My address while in this city will be in the care of that most worthy and estimable representative of your Republic, the

Honorable John Hitz, Consul-General of Switzerland, whose guest I am.

Begging pardon for so long a letter which tells so little, and hoping that this finds both you and Mrs. Appia in excellent health, and with most respectful regards to Monsieur Moynier, I remain, my esteemed friend,

With assurances of the highest esteem
Truly yours

Clara Barton

Armed with this authority, Clara Barton now undertook to secure public interest in and official recognition for the Red Cross which existed in Europe, but in America had no existence whatever excepting in her dream and hope and prayer. There still are extant a very few copies of the thin little pamphlet which she issued in 1878 addressed to the people of the United States and the Senators and Representatives in Congress. It will bear quoting entire. It contains the sum total of the knowledge which America had of the Red Cross in 1878:

THE RED CROSS OF THE GENEVA CONVENTION WHAT IT IS

By Clara Barton

To the people of the United States, Senators and Representatives in Congress:

Having had the honor conferred upon me of appointment by the Central Commission holding the Geneva Convention, to present that treaty to this Government, and to take in charge the formation of a national organization according to the plan pursued by the committees working under the treaty, it seems to me but proper, that, while I ask the Government to sign it, the people and their representatives should be made acquainted with its origin, designs, methods of work, etc. To this end I have prepared the following statement, and present it to my countrymen and women, hoping they will be led to endorse and sustain a benevolence so grand in its character, and already almost universal in its recognition and adoption by the civilized world.

Clara Barton 'Washington, D.C'

WHAT THE RED CROSS IS

A confederation of relief societies in different countries, acting under the Geneva Convention, carries on its work under the sign of the Red Cross. The aim of these societies is to ameliorate the condition of wounded soldiers in the armies in campaign on land or sea.

The societies had their rise in the conviction of certain philanthropic men that the official sanitary service in wars is usually insufficient, and that the charity of the people, which at such times exhibits itself munificently, should be organized for the best posable utilization. An international public conference was called at Geneva, Switzerland, in 1863, which, though it had not an official character, brought together representatives from a number of Governments. At this conference a treaty was drawn up, afterward remodeled and improved, which twenty-five Governments have signed.

The treaty provides for the neutrality of all sanitary supplies, ambulances, surgeons, nurses, attendants, and sick or wounded men, and their safe-conduct, when they bear the sign of the organization, viz., the Red Cross.

Although the convention which originated the organization was necessarily international, the relief societies themselves are entirely national and independent; each one governing itself and making its own laws according to the genius of its nationality and needs.

It was necessary for recognizance and safety, and for carrying out the general provisions of the treaty, that a uniform badge should be agreed upon. The Red Cross was chosen out of compliment to the Swiss Republic, where the first convention was held, and in which the Central Commission has its headquarters. The Swiss colors being a white cross on a red ground, the badge chosen was these colors reversed.

There are no "members of the Red Cross," but only members of societies whose sign it is. There is no u Order of the Red Cross." The relief societies use, each according to its convenience, whatever methods seem best suited to prepare in times of peace for the necessities of sanitary service in times of war. They gather and store gifts of money and supplies; arrange hospitals, ambulances, methods of transportation of wounded men, bureaus of information, correspondence, etc. All that the most ingenious philanthropy could devise and execute has been attempted in this direction.

In the Franco-Prussian War this was abundantly tested. That Prussia acknowledged its beneficence is proven by the fact that the Emperor affixed the Red Cross to the Iron Cross of Merit.

Although the societies are not international, there is a tacit compact between them, arising from their common origin, identity of aim, and mutual relation to the treaty. This compact embraces four principles, viz., centralization, preparation, impartiality, and solidarity.

1. Centralization. The efficiency of relief in time of war depends on unity of direction; therefore in every country the relief societies have a common central head to which they send their supplies, and which communicates for them with the seat of war or with the surgical

military authorities, and it is through this central commission they have governmental recognition.

2. Preparation. It is understood that societies working under the Red Cross shall occupy themselves with preparatory work in times of peace. This gives them a permanence they could not otherwise have.

3. Impartiality. The societies of belligerent nations cannot always carry aid to their wounded countrymen who are captured by the enemy; this is counterbalanced by the regulation that the aid of the Red Cross societies shall be extended alike to friend and foe.

4. Solidarity. This provides that the societies of nations not engaged in war may afford aid to the sick and wounded of belligerent nations without affecting any principle of noninterference to which their Governments may be pledged. This must be done through the Central Commission, and not through either of the belligerent parties; this ensures impartiality of relief.

That these principles are practical has been thoroughly tested during the fifteen years the Red Cross has existed.

The Convention of Geneva does not exist as a society, but is simply a treaty under which all the relief societies of the Red Cross are enabled to carry on their work effectually. In time of war, the members and agents of the societies who go to the seat of war are obliged to have their badges *vizéed* by the Central Commission, and by one of the belligerents—this is in order to prevent fraud. Thus the societies and the treaty complement each other. The societies find and execute the relief, the treaty affords them the immunities which enable them to execute.

And it may be further made a part of the raison d'être of these national relief societies to afford ready succor and assistance to sufferers in time of national or widespread calamities, such as plagues, cholera, yellow fever and the like, devastating fires or floods, railway disasters, mining catastrophes, etc. The readiness of organizations like those of the Red Cross to extend help at the instant of need renders the aid of quadruple value and efficiency compared with that gathered hastily and irresponsibly, in the

393

bewilderment and shock which always accompanies such calamities. The trained nurses and attendants subject to the relief societies in such cases would accompany the supplies sent and remain in action as long as needed. Organized in every State, the relief societies of the Red Cross would be ready with money, nurses, and supplies, to go on call to the instant relief of all who were overwhelmed by any of those sudden calamities which occasionally visit us. In case of yellow fever, there being an organization in every State, the nurses and attendants would be first chosen from the nearest societies, and, being acclimated, would incur far less risk to life than if sent from distant localities. It is true that the Government is always ready in these times of public need to furnish transportation, and often does much more. In the Mississippi flood, a few years ago, it ordered rations distributed under the direction of army officers; in the case of the explosion at the navy yard, it voted a relief fund, and in our recent affliction at the South, a like course was pursued. But in such cases one of the greatest difficulties is that there is no organized method of administering the relief which the Government or liberal citizens are willing to bestow, nor trained and acclimated nurses ready to give intelligent care to the sick; or, if there be organization, it is hastily formed in the time of need, and is therefore comparatively inefficient and wasteful. It would seem to be full time that, in consideration of the growth and rapidly accumulating necessities of our country, we should learn to economize our charities, and ensure from them the greatest possible practical benevolence. Although we in the United States may fondly hope to be seldom visited by the calamities of war, yet the misfortunes of other nations with which we are on terms of amity appeal to our sympathies; our southern coasts are periodically visited by the scourge of yellow fever; the valleys of the Mississippi are subject to destructive inundations; the plains of the West are devastated by insects and drought, and our cities and country are swept by consuming fires. In all such cases, to gather and dispense the profuse liberality of our people, without waste of time or material, requires the wisdom that comes of experience and permanent organization. Still more does it concern, if not our safety, at least our honor, to signify our approval of those principles of humanity acknowledged by every other civilized nation.

BIRTH OF THE AMERICAN RED CROSS

It is important that this book shall make plain, by means of all necessary emphasis, and if need be by reiteration, that the United States did not come automatically or promptly into the sisterhood of nations associated under the banner of the Red Cross. From 1864 until 1881 was a period of seventeen years. The United States was the last of the great civilized nations of the world to ratify the treaty. It is also important to make plain that the work of securing this tardy recognition of the Red Cross on the part of the United States did not devolve upon an organization in this country, or upon a group of people laboring together. If ever a great enterprise came into being as the result of the persistent, indefatigable effort of one person, that result was achieved by Clara Barton in securing the adhesion of her own country to the international agreement which included the Red Cross.

Clara Barton undertook to secure national recognition for this organization during the administration of President Rutherford B. Hayes. She had already begun work in this direction as early as 1876, and it seemed that she had every requisite for success when, in 1877, President Moynier addressed an official letter to President Hayes informing him of Miss Barton's appointment, and asking that the United States come into the agreement. But the promised success was delayed.

President Hayes received Miss Barton at the White House, and listened courteously but not enthusiastically to her story. So did the Attorney-General of the United States, the Honorable Charles Devens, to whom the President referred her, and who found no serious legal obstacle in the way of her desire. Each sent her with a note of introduction to the Secretary of State. President Hayes wrote the following little note:

Executive Mansion Washington, 4 Jany, 1878

My dear Sirs

Miss Clara Barton of New York State has some plans regarding the mitigation of the cruelties of war which she wishes to present to you. Please give her a hearing and such aid and encouragement as may be deemed by you fit.

Sincerely

R. B. Hayes

Hon. W. M. Evarts etc., etc.

But the movement encountered apathy and quiet but determined opposition, and resulted in no executive action.

In a little scratch-book I find Clara Barton's own account of this disappointment. Her narrative goes back to Civil War days and then proceeds with her experience overseas, and her service in the Franco-Prussian War:

"As I journeyed on and saw the work of the Red Cross Society, more accomplished in four months under their systematic organization than in our four years without it, no mistakes, no needless suffering, no starving, no lack of care, no waste, no confusion—all busy and at work, a whole continent marshaled under the banner of the Red Cross, working instead of weeping, nursing instead of waiting—as I saw all this and journeyed and worked with it, I said to myself, "If I live to return to my country I will try to let her people understand the Red Cross." I did more than resolve; I promised other nations I would do it. In 1873 I returned, more broken than I went. There had been years of helplessness in which I forgot how to walk; still I remembered my resolution and my promise. I came to Dansville and I brought that resolution and that promise with me. After about two years I was able to go to Washington with a letter from the International Committee of Geneva to the President of the United States asking once more that America sign the Treaty of Geneva.

"Being made the official bearer of this letter, I presented it in 1877 in person to President Hayes. He received it kindly and referred it and me to his Secretary of State, Mr. Evarts, who in his turn referred it to his Assistant Secretary, Mr. Frederick Seward, as the person who would know all about it, examine it, and report for decision. Mr. Seward had been the Assistant Secretary of his father and of Secretary Fish when it had been previously presented. He remembered this refusal and referred me to the record. He regarded it as a settled thing. I saw that it was all made to depend on one man, and that man regarded it as settled. I had nothing to hope for then, but did not press the matter to a third refusal. It waited and so did I."

Nor had she any better success in her approach to members of Congress. They were either apathetic or positively hostile. They knew nothing about the Red Cross and they cared less. The United States was not going to have anymore wars. If it ever should have any wars, this country would manage them in its own way. It did not care that anyone in Europe should tell it how to provide for the care of sick and wounded men. As for relief to be sent from America to any countries in Europe that might be in war, the American people were fully competent to create their own agencies on this side of the water, and to distribute relief through such agencies as they might select or constitute upon the other side.

Even Miss Barton's stanch friends in the Senate and in the House could give her very little aid or comfort. If she could enlist the interest of the President or of the Secretary of State, something might possibly be done. Otherwise, it was useless to try.

So far as is known, Clara Barton's little eight-page pamphlet, issued in 1878, had no more effect than Dr. Bellows's sixteen-page pamphlet in 1866. If a single newspaper had taken it up and commented favorably upon it, Clara Barton would have been practically certain to have clipped and treasured the article or editorial. There is not in her papers a single letter or newspaper clipping which indicates that any man, woman, or child in the United States responded favorably to her published letter which was quoted in the last chapter. She used her pen and her voice and her power of personal persuasion without avail. The seed of that sowing appeared to fall upon the rocks, and it took no root.

In November, 1880, James A. Garfield was elected President of the United States. Miss Barton knew him somewhat. She wrote him a letter of congratulation, to which he returned a brief but gracious reply. Soon after his inauguration she called on him at the White House and presented the following letter which nearly four years before she had brought to the attention of President Hayes:

International Committee for the Relief of Wounded Soldiers
Geneva, August 19, 1877

To the President of the United States, at Washington:

Mr. President: The International Committee of the Red Cross desires most earnestly that the United States should be associated with them in their work, and they take the liberty of addressing themselves to you, with the hope that you will second their efforts. In order that the functions of the National Society of the Red Cross be faithfully performed, it is indispensable that it should have the sympathy and protection of the Government.

It would be irrational to establish an association upon the principles of the Convention of Geneva, without the association having the assurance that the army of its own country, of which it should be an auxiliary, would be guided, should the case occur, by the same principles. It would consequently be useless for us to appeal to the people of the country, inasmuch as the United States, as a Government, has made no declaration of adhering officially to the principles laid down by the Convention of the 22d August, 1864.

Such is, then, Mr. President, the principal object of the present request. We do not doubt but this will meet with a favorable reception from you, for the United States is in advance of Europe upon the subject of war, and the celebrated "Instructions of the American Army" are a monument which does honor to the United States.

You are aware, Mr. President, that the Government of the United States was officially represented at the Conference of Geneva, in 1864, by two delegates, and this mark of approbation given to the work which was being accomplished was then considered by everyone as a precursor of a legal ratification. Until the present time, however, this confirmation has not taken place, and we think that this formality, which would have no other bearing than to express publicly the acquiescence of the United States in those humanitarian principles now admitted by all civilized people, has only been retarded because the occasion has not offered itself. We flatter ourselves with the hope that appealing directly to your generous sentiments will determine you to take the necessary measures to put an end to a situation so much to be regretted. We only wait such good news, Mr. President, in order to urge the founding of an American Society of the Red Cross.

We have already an able and devoted assistant in Miss Clara Barton, to whom we confide the care of handing to you this present request.

It would be very desirable that the projected asseveration should be under your distinguished patronage, and we hope that you will not refuse us this favor.

Receive, Mr. President, the assurance of our highest consideration.
For the International Committee:

G. Moynier, President

President Garfield heard her story with genuine cordiality. He knew her and the work she had done both in this country and abroad. He assured her of his warm personal interest and referred her to the Secretary oi State for a further discussion of the matter. His note was brief and to the point:

March 30, 1881

Executive Mansion, Washington
Will the Sec'y of State please hear Miss Barton on the subject herein referred to?

J. A. Garfield

It was several days before Clara Barton succeeded in securing an appointment with Secretary Blaine; she did not want merely to present the President's note, but to have time to tell the story of the Red Cross. Mr. Blaine agreed to see her on Monday, April 11, 1881. Her nephew, Stephen, who had come to Washington for a few days, accompanied her on this visit; and it is fully recorded in his diary. The beginning of the interview was not encouraging; for Mr. Blaine, after appointing the time, apparently forgot about it, and was occupied when they called.

The appointment had been made for 11.30 at the Department of State. Clara and Stephen waited for an hour in the Diplomatic Chamber. At the end of that time Mr. Blaine came in accompanied by Mrs. Dr. Loring, of Massachusetts. Introductions ensued, Mrs. Loring said she would "esteem it an honor to make the acquaintance of Miss Barton," and arranged for an interchange of calls. Mr. Blaine referred to Miss Barton's call at his residence, and "hoped it would not be the last." Mrs. Loring then withdrew, and Mr. Blaine apologized for having kept Miss Barton waiting. She told him the nature of her visit and presented the letter of President Garfield. Mr. Blaine told her that he knew practically nothing about the Red

Cross, and asked her to state briefly its object. He thought it would come more clearly under the supervision of the Secretary of War, but she explained the necessity for the treaty. The international aspect of the organization had not previously occurred to Mr. Blaine; he had supposed it would be purely an American Society operating under the War Department; and any encouragement given by the Secretary of State would be incidental and personal; Miss Barton replied that if he could give her time she would like to tell him in detail what was involved in the relation of the United States to the Red Cross. He replied, "Miss Barton, I can give you all the time you need."

Clara then told him the whole story from beginning to end, and Mr. Blaine listened with intent interest.

He inquired why President Hayes had not pushed the matter to a successful conclusion, and she told him of Mr. Seward's objections which went back to his father's secretaryship Civil War days, and based upon the Monroe Doctrine.

Mr. Blaine replied that "the Monroe Doctrine was not made to ward off humanity." He told her that "the grounds for Mr. Seward's objection would not stand in the way of the present administration." He assured her that he was "in full sympathy with her proposal and promised her that he "would cooperate fully with her in carrying the matter successfully through." As for the official letter from M. Moynier, he assured her that he would be prepared to reply to that letter approvingly now on the sole basis of her statement of the case; but he said that he wanted to do more than this.

She replied that she knew it would be necessary for the Senate to approve. He told her, "if it needed the action of the Senate, that could be had." The confidence with which he spoke was most reassuring. He asked her to leave her little pamphlet with him for a few days that he might become a little more familiar with the history of the movement. It was all new to him; but it was obviously a thing in which the United States should have its part with other nations; he could promise her that it would be done, and done promptly.

Mr. Blaine suggested that it would be well for Miss Barton to talk over the matter of the Red Cross with the Secretary of War. On the following day she went by appointment to see Secretary Robert T. Lincoln. Again Stephen accompanied her and made a record of it.

Miss Barton first expressed to Mr. Lincoln her appreciation of the kindness of his father. Stephen wrote, "He was much affected and very grateful."

The adhesion of the United States to the treaty was a matter for the State Department; but Robert Lincoln was greatly interested, and assured Miss Barton of his support in the operation of the Red Cross in case the Administration agreed to it.

In the next few days she made calls on other members of the Cabinet. Nowhere did she encounter opposition or apathy. The interest of President Garfield and Secretary Blaine appeared to be contagious. All official Washington seemed suddenly to have wakened to the importance of the Red Cross. She called upon several Senators and was introduced by Senator Conger, who told them of Clara Barton's work in Michigan. With this introduction and a knowledge of the President's approval, they met her with prompt and unreserved approval of her plans. Most of them had never heard of the Red Cross, but, when she told them how many other nations had approved it, and that the President and Secretary of State were ready to approve the treaty, they gave her on the spot their heartiest endorsement. She thought she understood Secretary Blaine's complete confidence that the Senate would ratify the treaty as a matter of course.

More than a month elapsed before anything else occurred. Nothing unfavorable developed. On the other hand, neither the President nor Mr. Blaine took any immediate steps. The Conkling difficulty had arisen and both Garfield and Blaine had many other things to think about. Clara Barton began to wonder whether she could induce the Senate to remind the Secretary of State of his interest in the matter.

On May 17, 1881, the Honorable Omar D. Conger, of Michigan, submitted to the United States Senate the following resolution:

Resolved, That the Secretary of State be requested to furnish to the Senate copies (translations) of the Articles of Convention signed at Geneva, Switzerland, August 22, 1864, touching the treatment of those wounded in war, together with the forms of ratification employed by the several Governments, parties thereto.

It took a little time for the Department of State to gather the documents necessary to answer the request of the Senate. But Secretary Blaine did not wait for this formality. He remembered that there was an earnest little woman awaiting some definite answer from him, and he sent her the following letter:

Department of State, Washington, May 20, 1881

Miss Clara Barton
American Representative of the Red Cross, etc.
Washington.
Dear Madam:
I have the honor to acknowledge the receipt of the letter addressed by Mr. Moynier, President of the Red Cross International Convention, to the President of the United States, bearing the date of the 19th August, 1877, and referred by President Garfield on the 30th March, 1881, to this Department.

It appears from a careful perusal of the letter that Mr. Moynier is anxious that the Government of the United States should join with other Governments of the world in this International Convention.

Will you be pleased to say to Mr. Moynier, in reply to his letter, that the President of the United States and the officers of this Government are in full sympathy with anywise measures tending toward the amelioration of the suffering incident to warfare? The Constitution of the United States has, however, lodged the entire war-making power in the Congress of the United States; and as the participation of the United States in an International Convention of this character is consequent upon and auxiliary to the war-making power of the Nation, legislation by Congress is needful to accomplish the humane end that your society has in view. It gives me, however, great pleasure to state that I shall be happy to give any measures which you may propose careful attention and consideration, and should the President, as I doubt not he will, approve of the matter, the Administration will recommend to Congress the adoption of the international treaty which you desire.

I am, madam, with very great respect, your obedient servant,

It would be interesting to know just how Clara Barton received the news. Unfortunately, her diary affords us no information. She must have gone forth from the office of the Secretary of State with wings upon her feet. There still would be months before Congress could act, but she sent the glad news at once to President Moynier and received from him an official reply which she transmitted to the Secretary of State.

Geneva, June 13, 1881

To the Honorable the Secretary of State James G. Blaine, Washington

Sir: Miss Clara Barton has just communicated to me the letter which she has had the honor to receive from you, bearing date of May 23, 1881, and I hasten to express to you how much satisfaction I have experienced from it. I do not doubt now, thanks to your favorable consideration and that of President Garfield, that the United States may soon be counted among the number of signers of the Geneva Convention, since you have been kind enough to allow me to hope that the proposition for it will be made to Congress by the Administration.

I thank you, as well as President Garfield, for having been willing to take into serious consideration the wish contained in my letter of August 19, 1877, assuredly a very natural wish, since it tended to unite your country with a work of charity and civilization for which it is one of the best qualified.

Since my letter of 1877 was written, several new governmental adhesions have been given to the Geneva Convention, and I think that these precedents will be much more encouraging to the United States from the fact that they have been given by America. It was under the influence of events of the recent war of the Pacific that Bolivia signed the treaty the 16th of October, 1879, Chili on the 15th of November, 1879, Argentine Republic on the 25th of November, 1879, and Peru on the 22d of April, 1881. This argument in favor of the adhesion of your country is the only one I can add to my request, and to the printed documents that Miss Barton has placed in your hands, to aid your judgment and that of Congress.

I now await with full confidence the final result of your sympathetic efforts, and I beg you to accept, sir, the assurance of my high consideration.

G. Moynier, President

There lies before me as I write a little pad of paper, about three by five indies in sizc, of which more than half the sheets have been used and torn off, and of the remainder all but the top six leaves are blank. Those six pages are filled with writing in pencil, and the writing is that of Clara Barton. It is just such a pad as she habitually kept by her hard and narrow cot, with a candle and a pencil at hand, so that when she woke in the night she might sit up and write the thoughts that came to her. She seldom retired before eleven o'clock, and was habitually up as early as five, but if she had waking hours between, and she often had them, she wrote down what was in her mind, put out the candle, and finished what was for her a good night's rest by sunrise or before.

"In almost any part of the world except the United States," the tablet begins, "the words Red Cross, and the emblem for which they stand, would be as familiar as are to us the words Internal Revenue or National Board of Health."

Was there ever such a time? Most of us have forgotten whether there is a National Board of Health, but "the words Red Cross, and the emblem for which they stand," have become as familiar as the Stars and Stripes.

Yet there was a time when all other countries knew of it, but in the United States we knew of Internal Revenue and of the National Board of Health, but not of the Red Cross!

The little tablet is not dated, but I have no difficulty in supplying the date. These six pages were penciled on a night between June 9 and July 1, 1881. They appear to have been intended as the basis of an article for the Associated Press, endeavoring to call a little more attention to the fact that on May 21 of that year the American Red Cross had actually been organized and that on June 9 It had elected officers. The Associated Press had sent out a paragraph announcing the organization, May 21, and this was to tell that "A subsequent meeting has been held, and the following officers elected: President, Miss Clara Barton; secretary, George Kennan," and so on. She might have told, but did not, that her own name as president was presented by President Garfield himself.

She had to explain what the Red Cross was for, although "During the last three or four years the public eye has been growing familiar with the term," through constant efforts to secure for it such recognition in America as it long had had abroad.

"Nation after nation has recognized its benign mission," the narrative runs on, "until twenty-seven countries have welcomed, received, and incorporated its humane principle into laws which govern their rules of warfare. In twenty-seven lands, wherever the national emblem is thrown to the breeze in token of war, there floats beside it this beautiful emblem of mercy, pity, justice, charity, and neutral care for the wounded, comfort for the dying, and burial for the dead. To us alone it is a stranger. For seventeen years it has knocked at our door, but our great, noisy family failed to hear."

That was her first great triumph!

So she obtained her official recognition, and then on the very next day held her meeting for organization, and that fall secured her incorporation, and the next year the treaty, and so on, and so on, one step leading to another; and when she had gotten the consent of the White House, she undertook to educate the great American Republic, and let them know what the Red Cross stood for. She hoped the time would come when the name and symbol would be as well-known in America as the words Internal Revenue or National Board of Health.

She had no publicity organization, nor press committee; but one night she sat up in bed, lighted her candle, took her little pad and pencil, and began to write:

"In almost any part of the world except the United States of America the words Red Cross, and the emblem for which it stands, would be as familiar—"and so on.

She did not finish the article in this form, though I find what use she made of it later in that year, in a pamphlet entitled "A Sketch of the History of the Red Cross." That document was reissued with added material in 1883, after the adoption of the international treaty. The two lie before me, the completed pamphlet, with the endorsement of Secretary Blaine, and the nomination, by President

Garfield himself, of Clara Barton to be president of the American Red Cross Association, and the three-cent pencil tablet on which Clara Barton began, on one night very soon after June 9, 1881, to teach the great American people what the words Red Cross and its emblem were intended to represent. She was not much given to weeping, but her tears would have wet through the little pad of paper many times before she accomplished what she undertook. But she succeeded. She lived to see the name and emblem of the Red Cross as familiar in her own country as in any of the twenty-seven that had previously adopted it. And that was what she hoped and prayed to do.

It will be noted that all these documents from the President and the Secretary of State, on the one hand, and from President Moynier and Dr. Appia on the other, are addressed to Clara Barton. So far as is now known there was no other person in America to whom they might have been properly addressed. From the time when she returned from the Franco-Prussian War until the President and the Congress of the United States had officially approved the Red Cross, and the Senate had agreed to the Treaty of Geneva, there was, so far as is known, precisely one Red Cross in the United States, and that was the one which Clara Barton had brought back from the red fields of France.

Not only so, but so far as is now known, in all those years no other voice than hers, after Dr. Bellows gave up hope, was raised on behalf of it. No one else had a vision of its possible relation to the future life of the United States. One little woman, barely recovered from her nervous prostration, trudged wearily from desk to desk in Washington, and with voice and pen pleaded in season and out of season until the American Red Cross became a fact.

Yes, the American Red Cross was now a fact. The President had consented; the Secretary of State had become an enthusiastic protagonist of the treaty; the Secretary of War heartily favored it; and the entire Senate appeared a unit in its favor. The preliminary resolution had passed the Senate without a single dissenting voice. There were certain formalities which needed to be completed before the treaty could actually be signed and ratified, but that was not worth worrying about. President Garfield and Secretary Blaine encouraged Miss Barton to go straight ahead and complete her organization.

She asked President Garfield to become the president of the American Red Cross, but he declined. She told him that in other countries kings and chief magistrates were its presidents; but President Garfield thought he knew a person to whom that honor belonged in America. When the American Red Cross was actually organized, Clara Barton was made its president on nomination of James A. Garfield, President of the United States.

On the very next day after receipt of Secretary Blaine's letter, Clara Barton held a meeting and organized a National Society of the Red Cross. The society was duly and promptly incorporated under the laws of the District of Columbia.

At a subsequent meeting, held on the 9th of June, 1881, the following officers were elected:

Miss Clara Barton, President.

Judge William Lawrence, First Vice-President.

Dr. Alexander Y. P. Garnett, Vice-President of the District of Columbia.

A. S. Solomons, Treasurer.

George Kennan, Secretary.

EXECUTIVE BOARD

Judge William Lawrence, Chairman. Miss Clara Barton.

Dr. George B. Loring. Mr. Walker Blaine.

Gen. S. D. Sturgis. Col. Richard J. Hinton.

Mrs. S. A. Martha Canfield. Mrs. F. B. Taylor.

Mr. Walter P. Phillips. Mr. Wm. F. Sliney.

Mr. John R. Van Wormer.

Gen. R. D. Mussey, Consulting Counsel of the Association.

Miss Clara Barton, Corresponding Secretary.

Nothing could have seemed more auspicious than the outlook of the American Red Cross on the day of its organization. It had the support of the President, his Cabinet, and the Senate, and its birth was hailed with satisfaction by all civilized nations. The signing and approval of the treaty appeared a trivial formality.

Just when everything was proceeding finely, President Garfield was shot by a fanatic on July 2, 1881. He lingered through the summer, and on September 19th he died.

The Red Cross Treaty had not been signed.

THE TRIALS OF A TREATY

The methods of treaty-making in the United States have varied. In a few instances the Senate has taken the initiative and asked the President's concurrent action. In at least one instance the President has negotiated the treaty without the assistance of the Senate and requested the Senate to adopt it without change. In several cases the coordinate treaty-making powers have moved together, the President concurring with the Senate's Committee on Foreign Relations. In the matter of the Red Cross Treaty, as we have seen, the President took the initiative in cooperation with the Secretary of State, and the Senate in due time requested the Secretary of State to submit the documents bearing upon the matter. This was the status when President Garfield was shot. During the weeks of his illness the Nation's interest centered in his sick-room.

It is interesting to know that the first local organization of the Red Cross was established at Dansville, New York. Clara Barton returned thither after the shooting of President Garfield, and without waiting for his death or recovery, called the people of that village together and established a local organization, the first in the United States. Some years afterward the Dansville "Express" went back over its files and found material for this brief article:

THE RED CROSS IN DANSVILLE

The First Local Society in the United States was Organised in Dansville

From the files of the Dansville *Express* of Aug. 25, 1881, we find the first local Red Cross Society in the United States was organized in this village Aug. 22d, 1881, at a meeting held in St. Paul's Lutheran Church, called for that purpose. Rev. P. A. Strobel, pastor of the church, presided and Dr. B. P. Andrews acted as secretary. Miss Clara Barton, then a resident of Dansville, explained the objects of the society.

Rev. Geo. K. Ward, Dr. J. H. Jackson, Rev. P. A. Strobel, Rev. A. P. Brush, Mrs. Mary R. Smith, and Mrs. James Faulkner, Jr., were made a committee to present a constitution, and they reported the same. Wm. Kramer and Dr. J. H. Jackson were a committee to secure names of members and 57 were recorded.

The officers elected were: President—Geo. A. Sweet; vice-president—Mrs. Fanny B. Johnson; secretary—Mrs. Mary Colvin; treasurer—Jas. Faulkner, Jr., executive board—Miss Clara Barton, Major Mark J. Bunnell, G. Bastian, Jas. H. Jackson, Major E. H. Pratt, Mrs. Geo. Hartman, Thomas E. Gallagher, Wm. Kramer, Oscar Woodruff, Mrs. Reuben Whiteman, Mrs. L. Q. Galpin.

Later, Major Bunnell was made secretary of the executive board and Hon. J. A. VanDerlip consulting counsel.

The society was active in good works for a few years and when Miss Barton moved to Washington it was allowed to die.

Soon after the inauguration of President Arthur, Clara Barton returned to Washington from a summer spent at Dansville. She was already acquainted with President Arthur; she had met him at the White House, and he had expressed interest in her undertaking. She now called on him again and reminded him that President Garfield had promised her his assistance; that there already had gone forth a letter signed by the Secretary of State, committing the United States to the Red Cross

Treaty; and that there still lay on the President's desk the official request of the Senate for information concerning the Treaty of Geneva.

President Arthur gave to Miss Barton a most cordial reception. He assured her of his own personal interest and of the obligation under which he felt to carry out every promise made by President Garfield. He promised her to call the attention of the Senate to the matter in his first address to Congress, and he kept his promise in the following paragraphs:

I cannot too strongly urge upon you my conviction that every consideration of national safety, economy, and honor imperatively demands a thorough rehabilitation of our Navy.

411

We have for many years maintained with foreign Governments the relations of honorable peace, and that such relations may be permanent is desired by every patriotic citizen of the Republic.

But if we heed the teachings of history we shall not forget that in the life of every nation emergencies may arise when a resort to arms can alone save it from dishonor.

No danger from abroad now threatens this people, nor have we any cause to distrust the friendly professions of other Governments.

But, for avoiding as well as for repelling dangers that may threaten us in the future, we must be prepared to enforce any policy which we think wise to adopt.

At its last extra session the Senate called for the text of the Geneva Convention for the relief of the wounded in war. I trust that this action foreshadows such interest in the subject as will result in the adhesion of the United States to that humane and commendable engagement.

This part of the message was immediately taken up in the Senate and referred to the Committee on Foreign Affairs, consisting of the following named gentlemen, to wit: Hon. William Windom, Minnesota; Hon. George F. Edmunds, Vermont; Hon. John Miller, California;

Hon. Thomas W. Ferry, Michigan; Hon. Elbridge G. Lapham, New York; Hon. John W. Johnston, Virginia; Hon. J. T. Morgan, Alabama; Hon. George H. Pendleton, Ohio; Hon. Benjamin H. Hill, Georgia.

The Committee on Foreign Relations opened its door wide to Clara Barton and listened with the greatest interest to her story. President Arthur followed the recommendation of his message with a special communication in response to the Senate's request of the preceding May:

(Senate Ex. Doc. No. 6, 47th Congress, 1st Session)

Message from the President of the United States, transmitting in response to Senate resolution of May 17th, 1881, a report of the

Secretary of State, with accompanying papers, touching the Geneva Convention for the relief of the wounded in war.

December 12, 1881.—Referred to the Committee on Foreign Relations and ordered to be printed.

To Senate of the United States:

I transmit herewith, in response to the resolution of the Senate of the seventeenth of May last, a report of the Secretary of State, with accompanying papers, touching the Geneva Convention for the relief of the wounded in war.

Chester A. Arthur

———

Executive Mansion Washington, December 13, 1881

To the President:

The Secretary of State, to whom was addressed a resolution of the Senate, dated the seventeenth of May, 1881, requesting him "to furnish to the Senate copies (translations) of Articles of Convention signed at Geneva, Switzerland, August 22, 1864, touching the treatment of those wounded in war, together with the forms of ratification employed by the several governments, parties thereto," has the honor to lay before the President the papers called for by the resolution.

In view of the reference made, in the annual message of the President, to the Geneva convention, the Secretary of State deems it unnecessary now to enlarge upon the advisability of the adhesion of the United States to an international compact at once so humane in its character and so universal in its application as to commend itself to the adoption of nearly all the civilized powers.

James G. Blaine

Department of State Washington, December 10, 1881

With such support from the President and the Secretary of State, and with the Senate a unit in support of the treaty, the end of the struggle appeared to be in sight. But many anxious months had yet to pass before Clara Barton's dream came true.

Even after the movement was inaugurated and recognized by Congress, very few people in America attached to it any considerable degree of importance. Among those who appreciated its full significance and hastened to give Clara Barton full credit for her splendid achievement was the man who had labored so faithfully for the organization of an American Red Cross at the close of the Civil War, Dr. Henry W. Bellows. He had labored in earlier years and had given it up, but rejoiced in the prospect of her success:

New York, 233 E. 15 Nov. 21, 1881

My dear Miss Barton:

It has been a sore disappointment and mortification to those who inaugurated the plan of organized relief, by private contributions, for sick and wounded soldiers in our late war, since so largely followed by other nations, that they should still find the United States the only great Government that refuses to join in the treaty, framed by the International Convention of Geneva, for neutralizing battle-fields after the battle, and making the persons of surgeons and nurses flying to the relief of the wounded and dying free from arrest. This great inter- national agreement for mitigating the horrors of war finds its chief defect in the conspicuous refusal of the United States Government to join in the treaty! The importance of our national concurrence with other Governments in this noble treaty has been urged upon every administration since the war, but has thus far met only the reply that our national policy did not allow us to enter into entangling alliances with other powers. I rejoice to hear from you that our late President and his chief official advisers were of a different opinion, and encouraged the hope that in the interests of mercy and humanity it might be safe to agree by treaty with all the civilized world, that we would soften to non-combatants the hateful conditions that made relief to the wounded on battle-fields a peril or forbidden act. I trust you will press this matter upon our present administration with all the weight of your well-earned influence. Having myself somewhat ignominiously failed to get any encouragement for this measure from two administrations, I leave it, in your more fortunate hands, hoping that the time is ripe for a less jealous policy than American self-isolation in international movements for extending and universalizing mercy towards the victims of war.

Yours truly

H. W. Bellows

Public sentiment in America is a strange and somewhat capricious thing. Clara Barton issued her little booklet in 1878 and it appeared to fall flat. The newspapers paid no attention to it; Congress treated it with complete indifference if not with hostility, and the President and his Cabinet ignored it. She reissued it in 1881 with added matter, and not less than three hundred newspapers and periodicals spoke kindly of it, many of them more than once, so that more than five hundred press clippings were collated as the result of that and Miss Barton's little article written for the Associated Press. Congress, that had been partly hostile and where not hostile apathetic, became suddenly and unanimously interested. The Honorable William Windom, Chairman of the Committee on Foreign Relations, and afterward a member of President Garfield's Cabinet, became a stanch friend, perhaps the first genuinely interested and largely influential friend of the movement. Senators Hoar and Wilson, of Massachusetts, and Hawley, of Connecticut, and Edmunds, of Vermont, lent to the movement intelligent and vigorous support. The Honorable Omar D. Conger, of Michigan, first in the House and afterward in the Senate, took an active part in promoting the cause. When the matter began to be discussed in Congress as the body which alone could declare war, and later came before the Foreign Relations Committee of the Senate on the proposal to ratify the Geneva Treaty, there was not a dissenting voice in either house, nor was there in the press through the country, so far as is known, a single unfavorable comment. Clara Barton's campaign of publicity had been a little handful of com upon the top of the mountains and the fruit thereof shook like the Cedars of Lebanon. The whole Nation was suddenly converted to faith in the Red Cross.

Foreign nations stood in amazement when they saw this change of sentiment. They were unable to account for it, nor could anyone else explain it to them. After eighteen years of indifference and hostility America came over to the banner of the Red Cross with wholehearted acceptance of its humane principles.

But still the question was asked why America need concern herself with an organization for war, when she was never going to have another war. The answer to this question contained one of the distinctive principles of the American Red Cross as compared with the Red Cross in other countries. In Europe, the Red Cross was organized solely for relief in time of war. In America, it was organized to meet any great public need.

As yet, however, the Red Cross was proceeding without official authority. The death of President Garfield delayed for several months the official adherence of the United States to the Treaty of Geneva. Meantime, the Red Cross was in existence, by advice of President Garfield. It had, however, only a single local organization, but it cherished national and international aims and hopes. Miss Barton herself recorded the history of the organization:

The National Red Cross of America was formed nearly a year before the accession to the treaty. This was done by the advice of President Garfield, in order to aid as far as possible the accession. "Accordingly a meeting was held in Washington, D.C., May 21, 1881, which resulted in the formation of an association to be known as the American National Association of the Red Cross."

Several years of previous illness on the part of its president had resulted in fixing her country home at Dansville, New York, the seat of the great Jackson and Austin Sanitarium and the acknowledged foundation of the hundreds of health institutions of that kind which bless the country to-day. The establishment of the National Red Cross in Washington had attracted the attention of persons outside, who, of course, knew very little of it; but among others, the people of Dansville, the home of the president, felt that if she were engaged in some public movement, they too might at least offer to aid. Accordingly, on her return to them in midsummer, they waited upon her with a request to that effect, which resulted in the formation of a society of the Red Cross, this being the first body in aid of the National Association formed in the United States. It is possible I cannot make that more clear than by giving an extract from their report of that date, which was as follows:

In reply to your request, given through the secretary of your association, that we make report to you concerning the inauguration of our society, its subsequent proceedings and present condition, the committee has the honor to submit the following statement:

Dansville, Livingston County, New York, being the country residence of Miss Clara Barton, president of the American Association of the Red Cross, its citizens, desirous of paying a compliment to her, and at the same time of doing an honor to themselves, conceived the idea of organizing in their town the first local society of the Red Cross in the United States. To this end, a general preliminary meeting was held in the Presbyterian Church, when the principles of the Treaty of Geneva and the nature of its societies were defined in a clear and practical manner by Miss Barton, who had been invited to address the meeting. Shortly after, on the twenty-second of August, 1881, a second meeting, for the purpose of organization, held in the Lutheran Church and presided over by the pastor, Rev. Dr. Strobel, was attended by the citizens generally, including nearly all the religious denominations of the town, with their respective pastors. The purpose of the meeting was explained by your president, a constitution was presented and very largely signed, and officers were elected.

Thus we are able to announce that on the eighteenth anniversary of the Treaty of Geneva, in Switzerland, August 22, 1864, was formed the first local society of the Red Cross in the United States of America.

While the Red Cross hung, like the coffin of Mohammed, between heaven and earth, a disastrous forest fire occurred in Michigan. Clara Barton at once issued, in the name of the Red Cross, an appeal for help. The first city to respond was Rochester, forty miles from Dansville, and Syracuse followed. The money was placed in the hands of the County Clerk of Livingston County, New York, who went at once to Michigan, and distributed financial help under direction of Clara Barton. She also went to Michigan, and took care of the distribution of food and clothing.

Here, in Michigan, for the first time on American soil, the banner of the Red Cross was displayed above the supply tent of Clara Barton. A part of the report of that first effort follows:

Before a month had passed, before a thought of practical application to business had arisen, we were forcibly and sadly taught again the old lemon that we need but to build the altar, God will Himself provide the sacrifice. If we did not hear the crackling of the flames, our skies grew murky and dark and our atmosphere bitter with the drifting smoke that rolled over from the Mazing fields of our neighbors of Michigan, whose living thousands fled in terror, whose dying hundreds withed in the embers, and whose dead blackened in the ashes of their hard-earned homes. Instantly we felt the help and strength of our organization, young and untried as it was. We were grateful that in this first ordeal your sympathetic president eras with us. We were deeply grateful for your prompt call to action, given through her, which rallied us to our work. Our relief rooms were instantly secured and our white banner, with its bright scarlet cross, which has never been furled since that hour, was thrown to the breeze, telling to every looker-on what we were there to do, and pointing to every generous heart an outlet for its sympathy. We had not mistaken the spirit of our people; our scarce-opened doorway was filled with men, women, and children bearing their gifts of pity and love. Tables and shelves were piled, our working committee of ladies took every article under inspection, their faithful hands made all garments whole and strong; lastly, each article received the stamp of the society and of the Red Cross, and all were carefully and quickly consigned to the firm packing-cases awaiting them. Eight large boxes were shipped at first, others followed directly, and so continued until notified by the Relief Committee of Michigan that no more were needed.

Among the fruits of Clara Barton's work in Michigan was the confidence and friendship of Senator Omar D. Conger and of Mrs. Conger, who, seeing the actual workings of the Red Cross, under direct control of Clara Barton, became its enthusiastic supporters, and her fast friends. The Michigan experience also exhibited to the Nation the value of such an organization, and showed that a country which did not intend ever to have another war might still find use for the Red Cross.

But still the treaty halted. No one was opposing it.

Every known influence was favorable to it. Its adoption and signature were the merest formality. Clara Barton was at liberty to go on with her work with the full approval of the President and his Cabinet, and wait for the adoption of the treaty which was certain to follow.

It did follow; but before it was adopted the heart of Clara Barton was well-nigh broken. She had learned the weariness and pain of working alone; she was now to learn the keener sorrow which emerges when one undertakes to work with others.

Clara Barton had succeeded; no one questioned her success. But the treaty was not yet adopted.

THE PERILS OF SUCCESS

Few people now remember that Clara Barton's success encountered any difficulties at this point in her career. Her published writings make no reference to them. Her book on the Red Cross tells the story as though events proceeded automatically through this period of transition. President Garfield became interested and referred the matter to Secretary Blaine, who became heartily enthusiastic, and he and President Garfield told her to proceed with assurance that the United States would approve the treaty. She did so, and, although President Garfield was shot, his successor made the promise good, and the Senate unanimously concurred. That would seem to have been the whole story. But, as a matter of fact the months that followed the published approval of Secretary Blaine and President Garfield, and the formal approval of the treaty, were among the most anxious and sorrowful of Clara Barton's whole life.

The nation-wide publicity which now was freely accorded the movement introduced Clara Barton to a new form of difficulty. She was well schooled in the discipline of disappointment and deferred hope. Now she came to know of the embarrassments of success. Swiftly after the Red Cross came to recognition there rose competing organizations, seeking to capitalize her success. The first day of August, 1881, saw the issue of Volume I, Number I, of "The Red Cross." It was a monthly magazine, of which there may have been no subsequent issues, the official organ of a society known as the Red Cross. It copied Clara Barton's Associated Press article, and said:

We must say it is rather late for Miss Barton, or anyone else, to talk about organizing the Red Cross.

It then proceeded to tell that this organization had been in existence since 1879:

We did not attempt to make this a national affair, as we were not in condition to do so. This country was not going to war, at any time, and the promoters first considered the propriety of getting the order on a good foundation. 'Tis true, we have not undertaken any public work as yet, but it is a very great undertaking when the territory to be gone over is taken into consideration. We have organized a body of men that no country in Europe can excel for the purpose of carrying out our objects.

The real and original Red Cross was, therefore, according to this journal, ready now to become national, and it warned Miss Clara Barton that it had the right of way. It also published a portrait of the real founder of the Red Cross, a gentleman born in England, who had come to this country when young, and engaged in "several enterprises which proved successful," none of which were named; studied law, but gave it up; studied medicine, but apparently did not practice. He was, however, according to this journal, a very great and widely known man; and his portrait showed him with so many badges and decorations upon his right breast he would surely have had difficulty in drawing his sword. He was the "Organizer and Supreme Commander." A "Grand Promenade Concert" was given in his honor in a very obscure hall in one of the American cities, with a programme which the magazine printed in full, consisting chiefly in a recitation (selected) by Miss Sadie Merryman; a song (selected) by Miss Mary C. Andrews; a reading (selected) by Miss Mary Prescott; a piano solo (selected) by Miss Mary C. Andrews; a reading (selected) by Elmer E. Prescott, and selected songs with guitar by the Misses Biederman and father. Besides these there was an "Address of Welcome," and a "Response" by the much-decorated "Organizer and Supreme Commander."

Clara Barton had a sense of humor. She could not only smile but laugh heartily at competition of this bombastic character. She collected and filed the literature, and it may be presumed that her files contain the only preserved mementoes of this organization which served notice on her that her Red Cross was an innovation.

But, nevertheless, this was a warning, and one which she had occasion to heed. For immediately a considerable number of competing organizations sprang up in several parts of the country, and some of them gave her great anxiety.

She was not superstitious, and apparently did not notice that the second Friday in January, 1882, fell on the 13th. But she recorded that it was a bad Friday for her. Two days before, she had notice that the wife of a United States Senator desired to call on her, and bring one or two other ladies with her. She had moved into her new quarters that very week, and not all her household goods were in place; so she hastened to put up her curtains and finish her unpacking; for it had rained on Monday when she expected to move, and her plans had been disarranged.

Friday afternoon the wife of the Senator came, and with her another lady.

She said she had come partly on business; that she had some months before joined a society called the "Ladies' National Red Star Association"; that this society had a meeting this week, and the question of a counter-society came up; that this counter-society was said to be called the Red Cross, and appeared to have been organized to step in and do the work which they were doing; and it was decided to adjourn the meeting for one week to inform themselves in relation to this Red Cross Society. What was it? What did it propose to do? What had it done? She said she learned near the close of the meeting that I was the head of that society, and she came to ask if it was true, and what did the Red Cross have to say for itself?

I told her I believed I was the head of the Society of which she wished to learn.

She asked what Bills we proposed to present to Congress; and I told her, None.

Why, yes, she said, they told her at the meeting that I had something before Congress.

I told her I had a treaty, which I had presented for four years.

She wanted to know what work we had done, and I told her of our work in Michigan,

She said she knew nothing about the Red Cross; had seen something about it, but thought it was some Catholic thing; where did we get our authority? Was it a national thing? Had I anything published about it?

I had a little pamphlet of two leaves, four years old. I gave her one. She said she was sorry not to get the information she came after. She left, evidently disappointed. I was sorry, also. I have no idea whether she came officially or at her own option, openly or as a spy.

Whatever the motive of the wife of the Senator who came to Miss Barton, the organization was one of which she had occasion to learn not a little. It was one that sprang up on the heels of her first success, and it crowded her hard before it was left behind and forgotten.

Clara Barton felt uneasy. The treaty was not yet ratified, and she knew not how many wives of Senators were in this rival organization, pushed by ambitious women and seeking Government approval. Not very much of such competition at that stage of the affair would be necessary to kill the treaty and the Red Cross. She went next day to see a man whose judgment she felt she could trust. She did not find him in his office, but on Sunday he called on her:

He had no special advice; was very busy. So are they all. All are busy; and I am to go on with this alone, as I plainly see. I shall make up my mind to let them all go, and I must gird myself for the work and go on with it by myself. I do not believe any member of my Society will be of any help to me in this hard work. They are all too busy.

The next day she went to the trial of Guiteau, and heard the closing pleas. She was recognized, and given a seat inside the rail, and "treated with marked attention," which gratified her. That afternoon she went to see Senator Laphamand asked him to take charge of the treaty in the Senate, and he cheerfully consented. She told him frankly that opposing organizations were already seeking recognition, but he encouraged her. A day or two later she saw Senator Windom, of the Foreign Relations Committee, on whose support she had counted; and he seemed to her to have grown sad and distant, and she felt sure he had been approached by those who were opposing her.

She found, too, that her return to Washington, with its late dinners, was not good for her. She resolved to forego heavy dinners;

to eat her last hearty meal at three o'clock, and enjoy a big red apple before going to bed. A big red apple was always a means of grace to Clara Barton. On one of the most desolate of these nights, when she came home late in the rain after a disappointing day, she gratefully records that her apple was good.

She had cheering word about her finances. Her business affairs, left in the hands of reliable New York bankers, had prospered during her absence abroad. She had used while in Europe considerably less than her income; her principal had swelled somewhat, and her annual income was more by quite a little than she had expected. About the middle of January she received her complete account, and found that she had more money than she thought; and this was a comfort. Her expenses at Dansville, though much increased by her hospitality, had kept well within her annual receipts, and she was safely provided for for life. She need never worry so far as money was concerned.

But she was worried. She began to question whether her dream of an American Red Cross would ever come true. It was bitter hard to have it fail after she had won over three Presidents, Hayes, Garfield, and Arthur; but fail she thought it must, even after it had shown in Michigan how useful it could be. She seriously thought of returning to Europe, and letting someone else take up her thankless task. She wrote: I

I am so tired. I sleep very poorly. I can only think of some good way of getting out of this country. I feel as if I should be willing to let all go, if only I could get out, and hear no more strife and bickering lies. Why should I let my life be spoiled by those who are now opposing me, and who take the joy out of my sunshine?

Why, indeed? She had money enough to live upon, in Dansville, or in Oxford, or for that matter in Washington; and she owned homes in each of those three places, and had income enough to live upon in any one of them or in Europe. Why should she expose herself longer to weariness, misrepresentation, and cruel disappointment?

It will be seen that Clara Barton had some reason to apprehend trouble growing out of the visit of the wife of the Senator. Powerful backing had already been secured for the first of the opposing organizations that gave her pain and sorrow.

But she prevailed, and the Senate at length ratified the treaty without a dissenting vote. Either the Senator's wife was more favorably impressed than Clara Barton thought, or her husband refused to be guided by her opposition.

But the opponents of Clara Barton were active to the very hour when the treaty was ratified, and there were days when it seemed that she was working at a hopeless task. She went to see influential people, only to find them out or occupied or indifferent or strangely uncommunicative. She was almost in despair.

There came a day, Monday, February 6, 1882, when her own feelings changed:

It did not seem like other days. There was either much to do or nothing to do. I knelt at my bedside, and asked earnestly, tearfully, for guidance. I only want to know my way. I feel that I can walk it, if I can be made to see it. I am so weary of all this strife, this unrest, this doubt. I am willing to let the work go into other hands. If all goes as hoped, I can call an executive committee meeting, announce the ratification of the treaty, hand in my resignation, and get out of it all. If they want the Society, they can keep it; if not, it will die if let alone and some other can be organized, or they can take the one that is now opposing me. Then I can go and rest. It has been my part to do the work of the treaty. I have tried to do it faithfully, and it has met with little moral support, even from my own committee. I will try with God's help to go on faithfully to the end, with no support but His; and if He will give it, when this is done, I shall be ready to lay the burden down, even if my enemies gain the advantage of it. This has been a day of instruction and discipline, and, I dare hope, not lost.

She went to the State Department. Mr. Adee reassured her. He did not think there would be any trouble about the treaty, or that she need fear the opposition.

She had notice of the committee meeting, and she went to the Senate. She was misdirected, and went to one or two wrong rooms, but finally found the Committee on Foreign Relations, with Senator Windom in the chair. He greeted her cordially, which surprised her after his recent apparent coldness and evasiveness. He introduced her to Senator Edmunds, but that Senator insisted upon greeting her as an old friend. They heard her with sympathy; took her little four-year-old two-leaved tract, and spoke no word about the opposition.

A few days later Senator Lapham called and told her things were not going as well as he had hoped. Senator Windom, he said, was favorable, but troubled. The matter seemed hung up at the State Department.

She told him she would go to the State Department herself and see what was the trouble.

"His good kind heart was touched, and his eyes were full."

He did not know any other way than for her to do this. And so she went.

She was admitted immediately to the Department of State, and told confidentially that it was all right. The Secretary of State had conferred with the President, and they were all ready to recommend the treaty to the Senate.

Would she like to see the treaty?

Would she? Indeed, she would!

It must be a secret; unsigned documents were not supposed to be shown; but the Secretary of State would be pleased to know whether this treaty was exactly what she wanted.

She had never seen a treaty, and did not know what it looked like. It was a volume, a kind of unbound book, of soft parchment, something like fourteen inches square. She sat down and read it, word for word, the Secretary of State watching her intermittently as he busied himself about other matters. Line by line the full significance of it came over her. It quoted in full the text of the 1864 Convention, and recited in effect the whole situation into which this would bring the United States in its relation to other nations. It was

426

a great and solemn document, such as she had never before handled; and her life and hope were bound up in it. At the very end were the formal words of ratification, with blank spaces for the signature of the President and Secretary of State, and a place for the big seal of the United States of America.

I had kept my eyes clear enough to read to the very end; but then I could hold up no longer, and how long a cry I indulged in, I do not know. But I know that it rested me; and after a while he stepped over and asked, very gently, "How does it suit you?" I told him it was all I could have hoped for, but I was ashamed to have done so badly myself. He, laughing, said that was all right. I asked him when it would be signed, and he said, "Any time, now."

At last it was done!

Why had she worried so much about it?

She worried because she knew there was reason to worry; and because there were so few to worry; and because she did not know whether her worrying; would do any good.

For it is necessary to tell a little, a very little, about why she worried.

There lie before me as I write certain letters written to Clara Barton by a woman who came to her in the latter part of her struggle to secure the recognition of the Red Cross, and who wrote to Miss Barton that to be associated with her in such work would be the crowning glory of her life:

I should think it a greater glory to be a doorkeeper in such a society as the Red Cross than to be—well, Mrs. President of the United States. If in the humblest way I can help you, I am at your service. There may be nothing for me to do. but if there is, command me.

Sadly, in after years, Clara Barton gathered up these and other documents, arranged them neatly in order, and endorsed them:

The enclosed papers will serve to show in part what the Red Cross had to meet in its incipiency before we had the treaty. This woman had been our secretary and trusted friend, but by some means became a strong competitor, and organized an opposing society.

That is all she said about it; no word of bitterness or of self-justification. But this was not the only woman who rushed to her when she first gained publicity, proclaimed that she would be a servant of the servants of Clara Barton, learned all her confidential affairs, and then betrayed her.

This volume will make no catalogue of those who ate of her bread and accepted her confidences and who proved base and ungrateful. This particular woman is mentioned because it seemed to Clara Barton that she might very possibly defeat all that Clara Barton was working for. She gained friends in high places, and she knew just whom Clara Barton counted to be her friends, and how to approach some of them.

There lie before the author, also, certain anonymous letters, received at this time, some of them written in one city and sent to other cities to be mailed. There were also some vicious newspaper articles, one of them first published in a remote Southern city, and later copied into Washington and Philadelphia papers, and these Clara Barton clipped, and labeled with the name of the person who, without any question, she believed to be their author. These and the anonymous letters and the letters of affection are all in the same package. Clara Barton arranged them, and she thought she knew.

Now, on the day that Clara Barton visited the office of the Secretary of State, she was so overjoyed that she went straight to the White House to thank the President. Mr. Arthur was not in, but her little note was accepted by his secretary, who smiled and assured her that he understood, and that the President would be glad to receive it. And she went home with a happy heart. And Senator Lapham sent her a big bouquet of roses that night.

The next Monday was the day set for Mr. Blaine to deliver the memorial address on President Garfield, and she had a seat in the gallery of the House of Representatives; which was a much-coveted honor. She rose in full expectation of going; and she went.

But at breakfast she received her mail; and there was a letter from her rival:

"It was the most abusive of all I have ever received from her. She charged me with all little meannesses, and warned me if I do not stop people's tongues, she will take redress upon me, either through the press or by law.

"It had the effect to stun or daze me until I did not want to go to the Address. But I did go."

That was one of the things that was oppressing Clara Barton in those days. That was why she was troubled when the wife of a Senator came to see her and ask whether there was such a thing as the Red Cross, and what it was, and why it was opposing another organization of which the Senator's wife was a member. That was why she was worried when the Chairman of the Committee on Foreign Relations grew strangely distant.

But she went to hear Mr. Blaine, and she met prominent people, some of whom knew her.

Two days later she had confidential tidings that the Senate Foreign Relations Committee had unanimously approved the treaty, and that it would doubtless be discussed in executive session of the Senate on the following Tuesday.

But it hung on for another month, a month through which it was hard for her to go, but through which she went bravely.

On Thursday, March 16, she felt as though hope was almost hopeless. She "had no heart to speak" that day; "had more tears than words." "It has been a sad day."

She wrote these words that evening, "weary and heartsick"; but at this point was interrupted by a note from Senator Lapham. The note will bear printing:

U.S. Senate Chamber Washington, March 16, 1882
Miss Barton:
I have the gratifying privilege of informing you of the ratification by the Senate of the Geneva Convention; of the full assent of the United States to the same, by the action of the Senate this afternoon. I had the injunction of

secrecy removed so that it could be published at once. The whole is in print, and if I get time I will send you some copies in the morning. I go home tomorrow to be gone a week.

Laus Deo!
Very truly

E. S. Lapham

It ought to have brought her joy; but she wrote:

"I had waited so long, and was so weak and broken, I could not even feel glad. I laid down the letter, and wiped my tired eyes."

Before she got to bed she had another sad tale to hear, of dissensions among those who should have been rejoicing with her, but were displeased. And she went to bed ill.

Many of the people who from this time came to Clara Barton with an earnest desire to be permitted to share in her labor were thoroughly and permanently loyal, and some of them are to this day among the foremost of those who hold her name in reverence. There were others, however, not less sincere, who were an embarrassment to her, coming in some cases with a maximum of enthusiasm and a minimum of discretion. There were still others who, after working with her long enough to gain her confidence, became fired with an ambition to organize societies of their own. There was a Blue Anchor Society, now entirely forgotten, but which caused her a great deal of anxiety. It was established by a woman whom she counted a sincere friend, who learned about the Red Cross from Clara Barton and utilized her knowledge in the formation of a rival society which at one time threatened to be more prominent in high places than the Red Cross itself. Later there was organized a White Cross Society, which gained such recognition that, in one of the Dewey parades at the end of the Spanish War, it was placed ahead of the Red Cross. It had powerful friends, and the bill for its recognition by Congress passed the Senate, but did not pass the House.

These rival organizations appear very puerile and futile now, but at the time they were a source of great anxiety to Clara Barton. It sometimes seemed to her that there were not many people whom she could trust to maintain permanently high and unselfish motives like her own. If she failed, as she was charged with failing, to share responsibility with her associates, that failure had behind it some very unhappy experiences that need not here be recorded.

Just at the point when her success, as we now view it, was practically assured, she went one Saturday to call on an influential woman whose friendship she had won in the work for the sufferers from the Michigan fires. Her heart sank within her when she found on this friend's desk the literature of an opposing organization with an invitation to join. She wondered if this friend too would desert her, and she went home greatly depressed. So far as that friend was concerned, her fears were groundless. This woman and her husband had seen her work and they remained loyal to her through life. The next day was a family anniversary, and it set her to remembering her childhood. She wrote in her diary that day:

I wish I had always remained a little girl. I did not begin like other children; did not learn how to be a child, still less how to be a young girl and woman; and so had no knowledge of the right way to get on in society. I have made only mistakes, and have always been so sensitive that I could not bear the consequences of my mistakes. The longer I live the worse it gets, until now the menacing spirits hover about my poor beset pathway, darkening it with the shadows of approaching night; there is not a ray of brightness nor even of safety; they wait like robbers to see me far enough along to set upon me and slay me outright. But there is no way but to go on; I cannot hide. I wonder if it would not have been better if I had gone, the little five-year-old girl that was snatched from death? I often revert to that sharp illness, which I can remember, as the time when perhaps it would have been better if no remedy had been found. What years of unrest, pain to myself and to others it would have wiped out, and all the world would have been as well if not better! Looking at it as calmly as I am able and with my best judgment, I can only see failure of it all. There have been no successes in my life, only attempts at success and no realization.

At such times she felt her lack of experience in social matters. The women who organized these opposing societies were able to hold parlor meetings in aristocratic homes; to organize committees with

431

long lists of names of society women as patronesses; to secure publicity, and to enlist strong political influence. She wrote in her diary:

I am very low-spirited. I am cold, alone, surrounded by harmful spirits. All the society people of the city and country seem to be arrayed in arms against me, with only my single hand, sore heart, and silent tongue to make my way against misrepresentation, malice, and selfish ambition.

These were some of the reasons why Clara Barton was not jubilant when her success finally came. She was too tired, too heart-sore to care very much. She was weary of Washington, and she thought she was ready now to go to one of her other homes and live the rest of her life in peace. The Red Cross was now an established fact; the treaty was signed and ratified. She had only to hand in her resignation and leave the work to be carried on by others; whether they were her enemies or friends, she did not greatly care, her part was done.

That was what she said in her diary, but a few days later the meeting occurred for the perfecting of the organization in its new and accredited character. She went to the meeting only partially recovered from her depression, but she returned in high spirits. "This has been a red-letter day for me," she wrote; "the meeting was largely attended." Quite a number of prominent people seemed eager to sign the constitution and become members of her organization. The cry from the flooded district along the Mississippi was loud and strong; there was work to be done immediately; it was no time for Clara Barton to resign. She wrote no more of the cruel things which she had been suffering, but went straight forward in her work of relief. It was many years before she had time to think again of resigning.

On the first day of March, 1882, the President, by his signature, gave the accession of the United States to the Treaty of Geneva of August 22, 1864, and also to that of October 20, 1868, and transmitted to the Senate the following message, declaration, and proposed adoption of the same:

Message from the President of the United States, transmitting an accession of the United States to the Convention concluded at Geneva on the twenty-second August, 1864, between various powers, for the amelioration of the wounded of armies in the field, and to the additional articles thereto, signed at Geneva on the twentieth October, 1868.

March 3, 1882.—Read; accession read the first time referred to the Committee on Foreign Relations, and, together with the message, ordered to be printed in confidence, for the use of the Senate.

March 16, 1882.—Ratified and injunction of secrecy removed therefrom.

To the Senate of the United States:
I transmit to the Senate for its action thereon, the accession of the United States to the convention concluded at Geneva on the twenty-second August, 1864, between various powers, for the amelioration of the wounded of armies in the field, and to the additional articles thereto, signed at Geneva on the twentieth of October, 1868.

Chester A. Arthur

Washington, March 3, 1882

Whereas, on the twenty-second day of August, 1864, a convention was concluded at Geneva, in Switzerland, between the Grand Duchy of Baden and the Swiss Confederation, the Kingdom of Belgium, the Kingdom of Denmark, the Kingdom of Spain, the French Empire, the Grand Duchy of Hesse, the Kingdom of Italy, the Kingdom of the Netherlands, the Kingdom of Portugal, the Kingdom of Prussia, and the Kingdom of Württemberg, for the amelioration of the wounded in armies in the field, the tenor of which convention is as follows!

[Here followed the treaty and additional articles.]

Now, therefore, the President of the United States of America, by and with the advice and consent of the Senate, hereby declares that the United States accede to the said convention of the twenty-second August, 1864, and also accede to the said convention of October 20, 1868.

Done at Washington this first day of March in the year of our Lord one thousand eight hundred and eighty-two, and of the Independence of the United States the one hundred and sixth.

(Seal) Chester A. Arthur

By the President:

Fred'k T. Frelinghuysen

Secretary of State

When the Senate finally took favorable action and President Arthur added his signature, Clara Barton did not wait for mail, but cabled the joyful news to Geneva, and received in reply the following official letter:

Geneva, March 24, 1882

Miss Clara Barton
President of the American Society of the Red Cross

Mademoiselle: At last, on the 17th instant, I received your glorious telegram. I delayed replying to it in order to communicate its contents to my colleagues of the International Committee, so as to be able to thank you in the name of all of us and to tell you of the joy it gives us. You must feel happy, too, and proud to have at last attained your object, thanks to a perseverance and a zeal which surmounted every obstacle.

Please, if opportunity offers, to be our interpreter with President Arthur and present him our warmest congratulations.

I suppose your Government will now notify the Swiss Federal Council of its decision in the matter, and the latter will then inform the other Powers which have signed the Red Cross Treaty.

Only after this formality shall have been complied with can we occupy ourselves with fixing the official international status of your society. We have, however, already considered the circular which we intend to address to all the societies of the Red Cross, and with regard thereto we have found that it will be necessary for us as a preliminary measure to be furnished with a document certifying that your society has attained the second of its objects, i.e., that it has been (officially) recognized by the American Government.

It is important that we be able to certify that your Govern meat is prepared to accept your services in case of war; that it will readily enter

434

into cooperation with you and will encourage the centralization under your direction of all the voluntary aid. We have no doubt chat you will readily obtain from the competent authorities an official declaration to that effect, and we believe that this matter will be merely a formality, but we attach the greatest importance to the fact in order to cover our responsibility, especially in view of the pretensions of rival societies which might claim to be acknowledged by us.

It is your society alone and none other that we will patronize, because it inspires us with confidence and we would be placed in a false position if you failed to obtain for it a privileged position by a formal recognizance of the Government.

We hope that you will appreciate the motives of caution which guide us in this matter, and that you may soon enable us to act in the premises.

Wishing to testify to you its gratitude for the services you have already rendered to the Red Cross, the committee decided to offer to you one of the medals which a German engraver caused to be struck off in 1870 in honor of the Red Cross. It will be sent to you in a few days. It is of very small intrinsic value indeed, but such as it is, we have no other means of recompensing the most meritorious of our assistants. Please to regard it only as a simple memorial, and as a proof of the esteem and gratitude we feel for you.

Accept, Mademoiselle, the assurance of my most distinguished sentiments,

G. Moynier
President

On the 26th of July, 1882, the following proclamation was issued by the President:

By the President of the United States of America:

A PROCLAMATION

Whereas, on the 22d day of August, 1864, a convention was concluded at Geneva, in Switzerland, between the Grand Duchy of Baden and the Swiss Confederation, the Kingdom of Belgium, the Kingdom of Denmark, the Kingdom of Spain, the French Empire, the Grand Duchy of Hesse, the Kingdom of Italy, the Kingdom of the Netherlands, the Kingdom of Portugal, the Kingdom of Prussia, and the Kingdom of Würtemberg, for the amelioration of the wounded in armies in the field, the tenor of which convention is hereinafter subjoined;

And whereas the Swiss Confederation, in virtue of the said Article IX of said Convention, has invited the United States of America to accede thereto;

And whereas on the 20th October, 1868, the following additional articles were proposed and signed at Geneva, on behalf of Great Britain, Austria, Baden, Bavaria, Belgium, Denmark, France, Italy, Netherlands, North Germany, Sweden and Norway, Switzerland, Turkey, and Würtemberg, the tenor of which additional articles is hereinafter subjoined;

And whereas the President of the United States of America, by and with the advice and consent of the Senate, did, on the first day of March, one thousand eight hundred and eighty- two, declare that the United States accede to the said Convention of the 22d of August, 1864, and also accede to the said Convention of October 20, 1868;

And whereas, on the ninth day of June, one thousand eight hundred and eighty-two, the Federal Council of the Swiss Confederation, in virtue of the final provision of a certain minute of the exchange of the ratifications of the said Convention at Berne, December 22, 1864, did, by a formal declaration, accept the said adhesion of the United States of America, as well in the name of the Swiss Confederation as in that of the other contracting states;

And whereas, furthermore, the Government of the Swiss Confederation has informed the Government of the United States that the exchange of the ratifications of the aforesaid additional articles of the 22d October, 1868, to which the United States of America have, in like manner, adhered as aforesaid, has not yet taken place between the contracting parties, and that these articles cannot be regarded as a treaty in full force and effect:

Now, therefore, be it known that I, Chester A. Arthur, President of the United States of America, have caused the said Convention of August 22, 1864, to be made public, to the end that the same and every article and clause thereof may be observed and fulfilled with good faith by the United States and the citizens thereof; reserving, however, the promulgation of the hereinbefore mentioned additional articles of October 20, 1868, notwithstanding the accession of the United States of America thereto, until the exchange of the ratifications thereof between the several contracting states shall have been effected, and the said additional articles shall have acquired full force and effect as an international treaty.

In witness whereof I have hereunto set my hand, and caused the seal of the United States to be affixed.

Done at the city of Washington, this twenty-sixth day of July, in the year of our Lord one thousand eight hundred and eighty-two, and of the Independence of the United States the one hundred and seventh.

Chester A. Arthur .

By the President:

Fred'k T. Frelinghuysen

Secretary of State

United States of America, Department of State, to all to whom these presents shall come, greeting:

I certify that the foregoing is a true copy of the original on file in the Department of State.

In testimony whereof I, John Davis, Acting Secretary of State of the United States, have hereunto subscribed my name and caused the seal of the Department of State to be affixed.

Done at the city of Washington, this 9th day of August, a.d. 1882, and of the Independence of the United States of America the one hundred and seventh.

John Davis

Thus was the American Association of the Red Cross welcomed into the fellowship of kindred associations in thirty-one other nations, the most prosperous and civilized on the globe, its position assured, and its future course made simple, direct, and untroubled.

The Official Bulletin of the International Committee also hailed the accession of the United States to the treaty in an article of characteristic caution, and of great significance. In that article the distinction was carefully pointed out between that which had already been fully agreed to, and had become invested with all the force and solemnity of international treaties, and the proposed treaty, which had been drawn up and considered with a view to ultimate adoption. This proposed treaty had received the sanction and signature of the International Committee at Geneva without ever having been formally adopted by any nation. The United States had, at the same moment, adopted both, thus becoming the thirty-second nation to adhere to the treaty of August 22, 1864, and the first to adopt that of October 20, 1868.

In the published English text, from which this version of the Additional Articles is taken, the paragraph thus marked in brackets appears in continuation of Article IX. It is not, however, found in the original French text adopted by the Geneva conference, October 20, 1868.

The Red Cross immediately effected its permanent organization; and during the next twenty years it was seldom without a task of some kind.

It will be well at this point to make plain three points which were not clearly understood at the outset, and have sometimes been misunderstood since.

The first is that Clara Barton, in establishing the Red Cross in America, was not seeking primarily to provide a place for herself. At this period she had three homes, and money enough to support herself comfortably in any one of them. We have an interesting look into the Dansville home in a letter of her brother David to his daughter, Ida Barton Riccius. He was ill, and she, not yet recovered from her own illness, took him in and nursed him back to health. He wrote:

Dansville, June 13, 1880

Clara's friends met us at the cars and rendered all necessary assistance. I was very weak and tired.

Clara lives in a very splendid old mansion, in a location unsurpassed, and a grand view of all the surroundings. Her house is filled with almost everything that adds to health, comfort, and happiness. Clara is very attentive to me. I think it came rather hard on her the first part of the time. Perhaps she will stand it a little better now that I am better and can possibly assist her a little. I have been gradually gaining since I arrived, considering how miserable I was when I came.

The living here agrees with me exceedingly well. We have plenty of good fresh milk, fresh graham bread from the bakery, fresh graham meal to make puddings, butter, cheese, applesauce, any kind of canned fruit we choose, which generally constitutes our breakfast. For dinner we have meat, fish, beans, potatoes, and things of that kind. For supper we have bread, butter, tea or coffee, cheese, and fruit of any land. This is the way we live and I enjoy it much. Clara has nearly all sorts of canned fruit in abundance, but what is best of all is plenty of nice fresh apples which I go into without mercy.

Clara Barton would have smiled a little at her brother's arrangement of her menus. She probably would have said that she

439

had a simple breakfast of graham bread, fresh butter, and fruit; a hearty midday meal of meat or fish and vegetables; and a light supper of bread, butter, cheese, and fruit, with abundance of sweet milk and an unlimited supply of good red apples.

This was the kind of home which Clara Barton left when she went to Washington to plead for the Red Cross. She often longed for it, and thought of going back there. Yet the purpose which had taken her to Dansville had been accomplished in her restored health. There was no important work for her to do there, or at Oxford. She could have a roof and red apples in either place, but she wanted to be promoting what had become the great object in life for her. That was what brought her back to Washington.

If, in all the weary months when she was fighting her lonely battles for the Red Cross, it ever occurred to her that this organization would give to her a life position, or bring to her either money or other emoluments, there is no hint of it in her diaries. So far as one may judge from these intimate self-revelations, her purpose was as genuinely altruistic as human nature is capable of becoming.

Nor is there any indication that she supposed that this would bring her additional honor. She already had more honors of certain desirable kinds than any other woman in America. Her Civil War record was known throughout the Nation. The lecture platform offered her an inviting and remunerative invitation to return if she cared to take it up. She had brought back with her from Europe official decorations such as royalty neither before nor since has ever bestowed upon an American woman.

Secretary Blaine inquired about these with interest one day, and a few days later she handed three of them to his secretary with the following letter:

Washington, D.C., Oct 31, 1881

To the Hon. Secretary of State Washington, D.C.

Dear Mr. Blaine:

After the words unintentionally dropped at the interview so kindly granted me on Saturday, it occurs to me that it is perhaps the suitable thing for me to do, possibly a duty, to explain to you, as the Head of our foreign relations, my own connection in that direction. I will with your kin] permission take the liberty to pass in, by the hand of your secretary, the accompanying "Decorations":

The "Iron Cross of Merit" issued to me in 1872 by the Emperor and Empress of Germany on the occasion of the seventy-fifth birthday of the Emperor.

The "Gold Cross of Remembrance" presented to me try the Grand Duke and Grand Duchess of Baden at the of the Franco-German War.

I am glad, Mr. Secretary, that you have seen it, as you have in the late celebration, for you will be the better able, it may be, to comprehend and excuse my persistency. Except for this constant and exhaustive occupation, I should have passed either of the last winters at Carlsruhe; but it has been sufficient to consume my entire time, strength, and spare means, and must continue to do so, until the treaty is disposed of and the Societies of the Red Cross, so indispensable to the effectiveness and utility of the treaty, are understood by the people, and measurably established throughout the country. To this end, I have at this moment in press a small work of a hundred or so pages, explaining the entire subject, its origin, history, and purposes, and of which I have ordered five thousand copies for gratuitous circulation. They will be ready at the opening of Congress or before, and I have four thoroughly formed societies, one National in this city, completed and incorporated, one Local in Dansville, New York, one in the city of Rochester, New York, for the county of Monroe, and one similarly organized in Syracuse, New York. Both Rochester and Syracuse are forming local, town societies under them, and all, in the happy absence of war, are using up their surplus energies on the burnt fields of Michigan, to which their agents have already taken thousands of dollars to the hungry, and thousands of garments to the naked.

I must beg, Mr. Blaine, that you do not misinterpret my motive in making this little revelation of foreign recognition. If the incentive had been mere personal vanity, I should probably have found a way to make the facts known, short of a decade, but it comes to me now, that it is perhaps, under the circumstances, a kind of duty that I should report to you on "Foreign Affairs."

Begging your pardon for my too long letter, I remain, Mr. Secretary, with the most grateful respect.
Very truly

Clara Barton

The next thing that should be kept clearly in mind is that she did not establish an organization dependent upon Government appropriations. In this respect her organization was quite unlike some of those that were hastily organized to oppose her. At least one of these was organized with an eye keenly intent upon one form of then existing Government service, with which it might possibly be affiliated, with an inviting prospect of salaried positions and official appointments. When the Treaty of Geneva was ratified, and not only the Senate but House of Representatives stood ready to do almost anything for Clara Barton, many of her friends in Congress assumed that the next step would be a request for a Congressional appropriation to cover the administrative expense of the Red Cross organization. To every such suggestion Clara Barton returned an emphatic negative. This was her little creed announced at the outset, and often reiterated:

The Red Cross means, not national aid for the needs of the people, but the people's aid for the needs of the Nation.

She would not accept a salary or permit any friend of hers in Congress to introduce a bill for her financial advantage.

How keenly she felt the importance of establishing the Red Cross upon this basis, and how sensitive she was to the opposition which grew formidable just before the treaty was adopted, is shown in a letter of hers to her long-time friend Frances Willard, who wrote to ask the reason why she was not moving faster in her work for the relief of the people in the flooded district along the Mississippi:

There had been no significant Mississippi flooding since 1874. During the period between January and March of 1882, the rain came down unabated. More than 235 billion cubic yards of rain fell over the Mississippi River and its tributaries. There was no way for the channel to carry such a volume of water to the Gulf without extensive inundation of the entire flood plain. There was massive destruction of property and life.

Frances Elizabeth Caroline Willard (1839–1898) was an educator, temperance reformer, and women's suffragist.

Washington,
Feby. 11, 1882

Dear Frances Willard:

Yes, I did get your letter telling me about the state of things in Mississippi and that all was lost there. I have no doubt but that it is the same the country through. It is hard and heavy and bitter, the shots of malice and detraction fall thick but I must stay at the helm and steer my ship safely into port. The Treaty of Geneva must first be secured. I have but one passage to take it through and that is lined thick on every side with guns manned by the Society ladies of the Capital of the Nation. The Red Cross, a little stranger craft from a foreign land, bearing only the banner of peace and love, and her messages of world-wide mercy begging shelter and acceptance in our capacious harbor, has chosen me for her pilot to bring her in. Besides these guns that open upon her on all sides she runs against the chains which have so long held her out—fancied Government defences of "Non-intervention," "Self-isolation," beware of "Entangling alliances," "Washington's farewell address," "Monroe Doctrine," apathy, inertia, general ignorance, national conceit, national distrust, a desire to retain the old-time barbarous privileges of privateering and piracy which we have hugged as a precious boon against every humane treaty since we began. All these my little ship has had to meet and breast and bear down, before this new and personal attack was opened upon her, so you see I cannot turn aside from my duties of a true pilot to contest a new foe. I must bring my ship through the natural dangers and anchor it safely in port though it be riddled with shot. I have thrown over all the extra weight, put on all sail, muzzled my guns, put my poor tired wounded crew to the pumps, nailed the little flag to the mast; and so you see us without other word or sign, plunging through the surf, breaking down chain after chain, through the fire and smoke, making for the shore. Never a messenger of mercy met a more inhospitable welcome, but the poor battered pilot has faith in her craft, and faith in God, and at no distant day, in spite of all, we shall throw out a sturdy old iron anchor to grapple with the reefs of the coast, and run up a little pennant beside the cross, "Treaty Ratified." After this we shall be freed from our national disgrace, relieved from the charge and duties of safe conduct for our course, and then if there is call for arbitration we will be ready.

The success of her work along the Mississippi made it evident that she must continue the direction of the Red Cross. But that did not by any means convince her that she was to give up everything else and stay in Washington. She began to look for something else to do, and something that would take her far away from the seat of government.

She rather coveted than otherwise the opportunity to show without advertising the fact that she had other and visible means of support, and that her work for the Red Cross was not undertaken for lack of other employment. Moreover, it was expected that its organization would be kept simple, and its work done promptly in times of emergency. That was why almost immediately after the Red Cross had become an actual organization, and she had been constituted its official head by Presidential nomination and international appointment, and all the opposing organizations had withered and died, she was willing to accept a salaried position in work of another kind.

About this time she had a letter from Governor Butler of Massachusetts. He knew her well and had seen much of her work during the Civil War. Out of a clear sky came his invitation to her.

Commonwealth of Massachusetts Executive Department
Boston, January 8, 1883

My dear Miss Barton:

There is a vacancy in the office of Superintendent of the Woman's Reformatory Prison of Massachusetts. It wants a woman at once of executive ability and kind-heartedness, with an honest love of the work of reformation and care of her living fellow creatures. How would that suit you? The salary is not very large. It is $ 1500.00 a year and house and expenses of living. Please let me hear from you at your earliest convenience.

Very truly yours

Benj. F. Butler

Nothing could have surprised her more than this invitation and it was four months before she decided to accept it. Even then she accepted with the stipulation that she would need to close her service in time to attend the International Convention of the Red Cross in Vienna in the following year.

Her acceptance of the position involved the giving of a bond of $10,000. With her customary independence she declined to ask anyone to sign her bond, but deposited with the State Treasurer of Massachusetts $10,000 of interest-bearing bonds and became her own guarantor.

Prison work was something of which Clara Barton knew nothing and she did not bring to it any considerable number of theories as to how it ought to be performed. In hcr first report, rendered at the end of six months, she took pains to give large credit to those who had preceded her. She disclaimed for herself either knowledge or achievement. A portion of this report will bear record here:

"With only the little experience of six months, you will readily concede that it cannot be considered my work; it would be unjust arrogance in me to assume it. The noble women and men who toiled for its existence, the faithful, tireless body of commissioners, who have watched, prayed, and labored unpaid for it, often unthanked since with its first baby breath it cried aloud. We, the women of the old Commonwealth, and more than all perhaps the two grand women who have preceded me in its charge, are entitled to consider Sherborn Prison their work. The strong brave-hearted woman, Mrs. Atkinson, who first dared to lay her hand, untried, upon that mass of chaos, and command order and law, life and reformation, to come out of it, was braver than a general. The peaceful, skillful, beloved Dr. Mosher who had the womanly courage to follow her, and strive and labor to shape still more perfectly the swelling, yeasty mass of human sin and misery till, like a wounded color-bearer she fell, bravely praying some comrade to bear them on to victory. These are the people whose work that prison is, and in their name, and theirs only, let me speak of it a moment and commend it to your loving interest and tender care.

"Last May I found, as I entered its great halls, 230 women convicts. It has at present 275 to 280 women convicts, and, with those who so kindly care for them, make up a family of something over 300. These convicts I am expected to feed, clothe, work, and govern, they in turn to be fed, clothed, to work and obey. The most comprehensive and I believe correct report I could make would be, that we all faithfully perform what is expected of us. The manner in which it is accomplished, and the causes which lead to the necessity for such accomplishment, are, then, the remaining points of importance. The causes are as various and widespread as the sins and mishaps which beset erring humanity, but if you asked me what proportion I thought would be left, after all the temptations of liquor and men were removed, I should not require a large sheet on which to write it down.

"Sherborn Reformatory is classed as a State's Prison, and is thus squared by the same rule of discipline as ordinary State Prisons for the retention of State criminals.

"And yet it is to be remembered that not a one-fourth part of these women are guilty of, or convicted of, any real crime, simply offenses—drunkenness and unseemly appearance upon the streets; and yet these poor hopeless, misguided, rum-wrecked women and night-walking girls are sentenced to the same servitude, subjected to the same code of discipline, and go out with the same brand of shame upon the brow, nay, far deeper than the clear-headed, cool, intelligent, calculating men of Concord, where every inmate is convicted of a crime. The sad conviction settles down upon me every day that the soul, brains of the crime of the Commonwealth are in Concord; the wrecks they have made are in Sherborn; and in my dealing with these women, I cannot lose sight of this fact. They are more weak than wicked, often more sinned against than sinning. This, to my mind, invites a parental, maternal system of government, and to this they are all amenable; even the most obstinate yields to a rule of kindness, firmly and steadily administered."

The records of this period are necessarily meager. Yet there have come to the author unsought testimonials of the great work which Clara Barton accomplished while there. While she never criticized her predecessors, but gave them generous praise, she stood not at all on any precedent established by them. She changed the atmosphere of the place from an institution of punishment to one of instruction and character-building. One who visited the prison while she was there has told the author of Clara Barton's power over the incorrigible; how women that were violent and untamable by the ordinary methods became docile under her direction. As for the younger women who were not hardened, and were often more sinned against than sinning, they idolized her. She established two letter-boxes in the halls, one to receive letters addressed to herself.

Any one of the three hundred inmates was at liberty to write to Miss Barton. A number of the letters which she received were preserved by her and have been read by her biographer. They were a pathetic group, some of them absurd in their requests, and others tragic in their appeal for help. The gratitude of others was quite beyond the poor power of expression possessed by these girls. In many instances these letters were followed by personal conferences very fruitful of good.

The other box was for letters of complaint addressed to the Board of Managers. Any inmate was at liberty to write a letter and place it there, assured that it would go direct, and that neither Miss Barton nor any of her assistants would read it. The first box was in constant use, the second scarcely ever contained a letter.

This was work for which Clara Barton had no natural liking. It was very far from the type of work she would have chosen. She never supposed it to be a permanent position. She accepted it because she felt that her health was sufficiently assured to justify her in undertaking some definite responsibility, and this was a place where she could go for a limited time and from it honorably retire. She was glad of a definite position in some other work than the Red Cross, yet one which did not compel her to resign her responsibilities in that organization. She found time while at Sherbom to attend a national gathering of philanthropic organizations in Denver, and deliver an address on the Red Cross. And she continued general oversight of its affairs. She retired from the work with no desire ever to see the inside of another prison; but also with a deepened interest in all work of that character, and with increased faith that in such work, as everywhere, kindness and an appeal to honor and self-respect were more effective than punishments which degrade and destroy hope.

She continued her work at Sherborn a little longer than she intended, because the term of Governor Butler was drawing to a close, and he did not wish to make a temporary appointment. She withdrew at the close of his term, and the day of her departure was a day of mourning in the prison at Sherborn.

A few months afterward an international conference was held at Saratoga and she was invited to deliver an address on prison reform. The notes of that address are preserved:

"Some steps in life are accounted unwise, some foolish, some foolhardy. Until the present hour perhaps the most foolhardy step I have ever been led to take was the temporary superintendence of a State Prison for the management, control, and reformation of women.

"Though consenting, however unwillingly, to undertake a work of which I knew nothing, and under such circumstances, I did undertake it. But, good, kind, and loving friends, in point of temerity and foolhardiness the effort of this present hour beggars that. That I, with literally no experience, no knowledge of the subject, with thoughts running always in other channels—should in any way, however tacitly, have given consent to take my place at this desk this evening beside these gentlemen who embody in themselves the experimental knowledge of the world upon this subject, and before this audience, trained to thought, the cultivated cream of the land, is to me past human comprehension. The Lord directs—let us obey.

"In May, 1883, after four months of combined importunity from the then Governor, General Butler, and all the people interested in and controlling the penal institutions of the State of Massachusetts, that I take the superintendency of Sherborn Reformatory Prison (and it was, I believe, the only point upon which the Governor and the people ever did agree), I decided to take it for six months. I remained something longer.

"I entered that prison feeling myself so ignorant of all that pertained to its line of work and methods and thought, that it seemed to me positively wicked, to waste my own time and that of the community and those who must come under me, in the strengthless, thoughtless vacancy of my attempted work—I seemed to myself a kind of empty balloon.

"At the end of eight months I went out of it, with a burden of thoughts, plans, ways and means, possible and impossible, under which my body could scarcely hold itself erect or my feet carry me away.

"I seemed more to myself like an already heavy-ladened ship, which had met another in distress and taken on shipwrecked passengers and crew, till her gunwales hugged the water and her laboring wheels wearily tugged for the land.

"So piled, so criss-crossed, so intricate, so vast, contradictory, perplexing, so vexed by customs, so hampered by foolish laws, so bound by mercenary ends, so fettered by political ambitions, aspirations, asperities and jealousies, to say nothing of the immutable laws of natural descent as related to crime—so discouraging was all this to be faced from the latter half of a busy life that I wearily and gladly turned and laid the burden down on the hands of you skilled laborers, and have mainly been content to feel and leave it there.

"The subject of prison reform seems to me to be so vast, and the methods by which it is to be attempted so varied, that it can scarcely be touched in one talk.

"The first question might be, What is meant by prison reform? and in what degree? Palliation or cure? I well remember the one question which always confronted me from visitors at Sherborn— "Miss Barton, how is it, do you really reform anyone here?" My reply was, "That depends upon what you consider reform to consist in. If you mean to ask if we take women here, badly born, worse raised, with inherited, habitual, vagrant crime in their natures, with the grogshop and the brothel for their teachers, who never lived a decent day or knew a decent night, filthy inside and out, and that by a residence of a few months here we are able to send them out to you not only good, well-behaved, industrious, cleanly, sober, orderly, honest, respectable members of society—something they never were before—infallible, proof against all the temptations and vices which you of the free community on the outside may throw in their path, so they shall never fall again; then, No, we reform no one, and our prison is a failure; but, if reform may mean that the habits which must incidentally grow up in the minds, characters, and tastes of these women during a term of two years of sober, industrious, and instructed life, in which they shall see only cleanliness and order, where the workroom shall replace the street, the quiet cell, the schoolroom, and the chapel in the place of the grogshop and the brothel, kindly spoken words of advice, prayer, praise, and song in the place of oaths and vulgarity, and a resolution at least to try to lead a better life.—if all this may be accounted In the direction of reform, then, Yes, a thousand times Yes, we reform all that come within our reach."

"The prison in itself is all well, but the danger lies beyond in the temptations, the lures, and the traps of the community into which this poor, weak creature is plunged in her first hour of regained liberty. I never saw one of these women go out with her little bundle of freedom suit, and watched the eager yet timid and half-frightened look on her face, and felt the childlike, clinging grasp upon mine, and heard the universal "Good-bye, don't forget me," that through the tears a great prayer did not rise up in my heart, "O God, strengthen her weakness—guard her from the temptations and the snares leading her down to death, of Thy virtuous and free, outside these prison walls."

"I recall once an official visit from about twenty members of the State Legislature, at Boston, for the purpose of overlooking the prison and seeing what it might need and how it could be best officially served; accordingly they appealed to me for my opinion generally—if the prison were what it should be in its appointments, if it were large enough or too large, etc., and in a general way what I would recommend to them to do; as by recent Act they had made me not only Superintendent but Treasurer and Steward as well. I replied: "This Prison is all very well—a model prison and certainly as large as it ought to be for the size of the State; and it is very probable that there is not very much that you can directly do for it at present, as an Institution; but, Gentlemen, the Institution from which you come has the making of the laws by which this Institution exists; any time when you there will find a way to make it impossible for the people of this State to get intoxicating liquors, upon which to get drunk, I will guarantee that in six months the State of Massachusetts may rent Sherborn for a shoe manufactory." I am not sure that they believed what I said, but I did and still do.

"True, crime will exist without drunkenness, but to no such extent as to require two miles of prison galleries for the women of Massachusetts.

"In this country I regard drunkenness as the great father of crime, and the mother of prisons, almshouses, asylums, and workhouses—the parent of vice and want and the instigator of murder. Whatever bears ever so little against this is to my mind "Prison Reform."

"Then follow in their mournful train the sin-bound cortege of primal and secondary causes of vice and crime and which make necessary the various methods of treatment which have been so ably discovered that no words of mine could throw a single ray of added light upon the subject. I can only concur, or perhaps express suggestively some preferences which may have presented themselves to me.

"In regard to intermediate sentences: I may not be sufficiently clear upon the technical points as presented by our good brother, but in a general way I would say I am unequivocally in favor of an unfixed term of imprisonment when the sentence is given. A fixed time of release is an independence to the prisoner beyond the power of his keepers and stands directly in the way of all reform.

"I would earnestly advocate everywhere, in all prisons, police stations, houses of detention—in short, everywhere, the placing of arrested women and women prisoners in charge of women only, and men in charge of men. It is just and right for every reason of virtue and decency; here again it is largely this contact that has destroyed; it cannot restore.

"I would, for every consideration of humanity, have the most careful, intelligent, and scientific investigation made in all prisons for any possible tendency to insanity on the part of any prisoner. The willful subjection to prison rules and penalties of those from whose benighted souls the light of reason and the power of self-control have been withdrawn is cruelty inexcusable and accursed in the sight of God and man.

451

"In the name of all mercy single these out and take them to their own place.

"Again, I would in the name of humanity lessen so far as possible the stimulating qualities of the food generally given out in prisons—more of grains, vegetables, and fruit, and less of meat. The result of this I am confident would be seen in the better temper, more tractable natures, lessened irritability, and happier frame of minds on the part of all convicts. I would have the food plentiful, but unstimulating, and the cooking wholesome. The records of the punishments in a prison could not fail in time to demonstrate the beneficial result of this course.

"Cannot this thought find somewhere and sometime a little consideration in your deliberations? In the name of humanity I suggest it.

"There remains but one subject more which I would name, and but a word of that—simply the relations and feeling to be maintained between the inmates of a prison and those in charge of them. I would recommend not only a uniform kindness and firmness of course on the part of every attendant, but a uniform politeness as well. Like begets like in spite of everything. It increases self-respect. This they have lost, and this they need to have restored so far as may be. Make punishment as rare as possible, but sure, and in all instances as light as the case will admit of. I regard undue severity of punishment as far more harmful than no correction at all. Cultivate the love of the convicts by all proper means; it is more potent than punishment.

"I believe the record of my last month at Sherborn shows not a single punishment among between three and four hundred women. They grew to feel that the only hurt of their punishment was the pain it gave me. When I met them for the last night in the chapel, and told them we should not meet again, and invited each to come and bid me good-bye, the sobs and wails that went out, and the tears that went over my hands as I held theirs for the last time, were harder for me than all the eight months work I had done among them. As I passed down the long corridors in the dark, unheard by them, at ten o'clock, and the low moans and sobs were still going out, it was too much to bear. I sought my own room—sank down, cold and shivering with the terrible thought that rushed over me— Had it not been all wrong? Was I far enough removed from them? Surely we must be too near alike, if not akin, or they would never have clung to me with that pitiful love.

"I went out from the prison walls of Sherborn next morning. I have never seen a face there since. I have never returned and I have no desire to."

THE RED CROSS IN PEACE

The Red Cross as organized in Europe, and as Clara Barton learned of it there, had no ministry except in times of war. It was one of the distinctive features of Clara Barton's plan that the American Red Cross should give service in any time of national, or possibly of international, calamity. So far as the Red Cross existed by virtue of an international treaty, its work was to care for the wounded of the battle-field; but the American Red Cross, as incorporated in the District of Columbia, and as operated under the direction of Clara Barton, offered an agency immediately available for the relief of suffering wherever the need was greater than could be met by local benefactions.

It will be remembered that the first service of the American Red Cross was in the autumn of 1881, in the forest fires of Michigan, almost a year before the official accession of the United States to the Treaty of Geneva. The report which reached Clara Barton and the Nation that half the State of Michigan was on fire, was, of course, an exaggeration, and she was not deceived by it, but she knew that the need was greater than could be met by local philanthropy. Already there had been organized a single unit of the Red Cross, at Dansville, New York. Clara Barton flung out the Red Cross flag in front of her home, and called her organization into activity. The two neighboring cities of Rochester and Syracuse came immediately to her assistance. Contributions which aggregated three thousand dollars were placed immediately at her disposal. Miss Barton's home became a center of activity, a depot for the packing and shipping of supplies. The second auxiliary of the Red Cross in the United States was organized at Rochester, with a membership of two hundred and fifty; that at Syracuse followed immediately. The total amount received and distributed by the Red Cross in money and material amounted to eighty thousand dollars.

The Michigan fires brought to Miss Barton's assistance Dr. Julian B. Hubbell. She had known him in Dansville as an instructor in the Seminary which was located there. She knew him as a man to be relied upon. When the forest fires occurred, Dr. Hubbell was a medical student in the University of Michigan. She wired him at once to proceed to the scene of the fire and give her accurate information. Dr. Hubbell reported that hundreds of people had been suffocated and burned to death in the rapid sweep of the Barnes, and that many thousands were homeless and in need of shelter, food, clothing, and medical care. Miss Barton at once commissioned Dr. Hubbell as field agent of the Red Cross. This was the beginning of a relationship which was never broken until the death of Clara Barton. Dr. Hubbell completed his medical course, and was commissioned as general field officer of the American National Red Cross. This position he occupied from 1881 until her resignation in 1904. He was with her in every one of the American fields of service; accompanied her to Turkey at the time of the Armenian massacres; went with her to Cuba at the time of the Spanish War; and was as indispensable to her as her own right hand. After the termination of her presidency of the American Red Cross, he remained near her, was with her in her last illness, and stood beside her when she died. With her nephew Stephen, he accompanied her body to the old home in Oxford and wept beside her grave. He was among the friends, and their number was not small, who were faithful to her to the very end of life.

It is not the purpose of the present author to relate in detail the story of the work of the Red Cross during the next twenty-three years. Clara Barton herself has done that in a large octavo volume of nearly seven hundred pages. To that book reference must be had for any adequate idea of her service for almost a quarter of a century. Almost every year beheld a calamity of sufficient magnitude to call for the official activity of the American Red Cross. The mere list of the fields of its service is notable:

1881, the Michigan forest fires.
1882, the Mississippi River floods.
1883, the Mississippi River floods.
1883, the tornado in Louisiana and Alabama.
1883, the Balkan War.
1884, the Ohio and Mississippi River floods.
1885, the Texas famine.

1886, the Charleston earthquake.

1888, the tornado at Mt. Vernon, Illinois.

1888, the Florida yellow-fever epidemic.

1889, the Johnstown flood.

1892, the Russian famine.

1893, the tornado at Pomeroy, Iowa.

1893 and 94, the hurricane and tidal wave in the South Carolina islands.

1896, the Armenian massacres in Turkey in Asia Minor.

1898 to 1900, the Cuban Reconcentrado relief.

1898, the Spanish-American War.

1900, the Galveston storm and tidal wave.

1904, the typhoid fever epidemic at Butler, Pennsylvania.

In almost every instance Clara Barton went in person to the held. Where she went was order, efficiency, sympathy, and comfort. In the days of the Civil War the official sign of a hospital was the yellow banner, still used in the quarantine service to designate a hospital for the treatment of contagious diseases. It was and is a respectable and worthy emblem, but there was nothing very inspiring about it. Where Clara Barton went on her missions of mercy, two flags floated, the Stars and Stripes and the beautiful white flag with its cross of blazing red.

Clara Barton loved the color red. The red rose was the flower of her family. A dash of red she almost invariably had about her clothing somewhere. It was altogether in keeping with her personal tastes that the emblem which came to symbolize her life-work was of the color which never failed to gladden her eye. In 1881 she set out, as she herself related in her first article for the Associated Press, to make the name and emblem of the Red Cross as familiar in America, as for many years it had been in almost every other civilized nation. She succeeded in doing this, not simply by a campaign of publicity, but by the practical agency of applied mercy. When fire or famine or flood devastated a region, and its victims were homeless and despairing, and local agencies for relief were overworked and working aimlessly or at cross-purposes, the unfurling of the flag of the Red Cross was the sign of hope. It meant not only human kindness and sympathy, but confidence and efficiency and success.

From every one of these twenty fields Clara Barton came back laden down with the grateful testimonials of the communities to which she had brought comfort and help.

A very brief outline of her work in these several fields may be summarized from her own reports. The work for the Michigan forest fires has already been referred to, and reference has been made to the first expedition of the Red Cross for the relief of the sufferers from the Mississippi floods. A further word should be said concerning the service of the Red Cross during the floods, and then a brief summary of the work in each of the other fields.

Mississippi and Ohio River Floods—1882-83

The spring rise of the waters of the Mississippi brought great devastation, and a cry went over the country in regard to the sufferings of the inhabitants of the Mississippi Valley. For hundreds of miles the great river was out of its bed and raging madly over the country, sweeping in its course not only the homes, but often the people, the animals, and many times the land itself. This constituted a work of the relief clearly within the bounds of the civil part of our treaty, and again we prepared for work. Again our infant organization sent its field agent, Dr. Hubbell, to the scene of disaster, where millions of acres of the richest valley, cotton and sugar lands of America, and thousands upon thousands of homes under the waters of the mightiest of rivers—where the swift-rising floods overtook alike man and beast in their flight of terror, sweeping them ruthlessly to the Gulf beyond, or leaving them clinging in famishing despair to some trembling roof or swaying tree-top till relief could reach and rescue them.

The National Association, with no general fund, sent of its personal resources what it was able to do, and so acceptable did these prove and so convincing were the beneficences of the work that the cities of Memphis, Vicksburg, and New Orleans desired to be permitted to form associate societies and work under the National Association. This was permitted, and those societies have remained until the present time, New Orleans organizing for the entire State of Louisiana. The city of Rochester, proud and grateful of its success In the disaster a few months before, again came to the front and again rendered excellent service.

In the spring of 1883 occurred the first great rise of the Ohio River; one thousand miles in extent. This river, although smaller than the Mississippi, is more rapid in its course, and its valleys hold the richest grain lands, the most cultivated farms, representing, in fact, the best farming interests of America.

The destruction of property was even greater here than m the cotton and cane lands of the Mississippi. Again our field agent was dispatched and did excellent work. The entire country was aroused, and so liberal were the contributions to the various committees of relief that when Dr. Hubbell retired from the field, having completed the work, he had still unexpended funds in hand. But they were soon needed.

The Louisiana and Mississippi Tornado of 1883

In less than a month occurred the fearful tornado of Louisiana and Mississippi, which cut a swath dear of all standing objects for thirty miles in width and several hundred miles in length, running southeast from the Mississippi River to the Gulf of Mexico.

Our special agent for the South, Colonel F. R. Southmayd, took charge of the Red Cross relief in this disaster, and so efficient was his work that societies struggled for organization under him and the Red Cross was hailed as a benediction wherever he passed. This was in May, 1883.

Our association now enjoyed for eight months a respite from active work. It was surely needed. It was the longest rest we had yet known, and afforded some small opportunity to gather up its records of past labors, organize some societies, and compile a history of the Red Cross, so much needed for the information of our people and so earnestly asked fix' by them as well as by the United States Senate.

The Ohio River Floods of 1884

The rapidly melting snows of February, 1884, brought the thousand miles of the Ohio River again out of its bed. A cry went out, all over the country for help. The Government, through Congress, took immediate action and appropriated several hundred thousand dollars for relief, to be applied through the War Department. The Red Cross agents must again repair to the field, its societies be again notified.

But its president felt that, if she were to be called every year to direct the relief work of the association in these inundations, it was incumbent upon her to visit the scene in person, to see for herself what floods were like, to learn the necessities and be able to direct with the wisdom born of actual knowledge of the subject; and accordingly, with ten hours' preparation, she joined Dr. Hubbell on his way and proceeded to Pittsburgh, the head of the Ohio River. There the societies were telegraphed that Cincinnati would be headquarters and that money and supplies should be sent there. This done, we proceeded to Cincinnati by rail.

Any description of this city upon our entrance would fall so far short of the reality as to render it useless.

The surging river had climbed up the bluffs like a devouring monster and possessed the town; large steamers could have plied along its business streets; ordinary vocations were abandoned. Bankers and merchants stood in its relief houses and fed the hungry populace, and men and women were out in boats passing baskets of food to pale, trembling hands stretched out to reach it from third-story windows of the stately blocks and warehouses of that beautiful city. Sometimes the water soaked away the foundations and the structure fell with a crash and was lost in the floods below; in one instance seven lives went out with the falling building; and this was one city, and probably the best protected and provided locality in a thousand miles of thickly populated country.

It had not been my intention to remain at the scene of disaster, but rather to see, investigate, establish an agency, and return to national headquarters at Washington, which in the haste of departure had been left imperfectly cared for. But I might almost say, in military parlance, that I was "surprised and captured."

I had made no call beyond the Red Cross societies—expected no supplies from other sources—but scarcely had news of our arrival at Cincinnati found its way to the public press when telegrams of money and checks, from all sides and sources, commenced to come in, with letters announcing the sending of material. The express office and freight depots began filling up until within two weeks we were compelled to open large supply rooms, which were generously tendered to the use of the Red Cross. A description could no more do justice to our flood of supplies than to the flood of waters which had made them necessary—cases, barrels and bales of clothing, food, household supplies, new and old; all that intelligent awakened sympathy could suggest was there in such profusion that, so far from thinking of leaving it, one must call all available help for its care and distribution.

The Government would supply the destitute people with food, tents, and army blankets, and had placed its military boats upon the river to rescue the people and issue rations until the first great need should be supplied.

The work of the Red Cross is supplemental and it sought for the special wants likely to be overlooked in this great general supply and the necessities outside the limits of governmental aid. The search was not difficult. The Government provided neither fuel nor clothing. It was but little past midwinter. A cyclone struck the lower half of the river with the water at its greatest height and whole villages were swept away in a night. The inhabitants escaped in boats, naked and homeless. Hail fell to the depth of several inches and the entire country was encased in sleet and ice. The water had filled the coal mines, so abundant in that vicinity, until no fuel could be obtained. The people were more likely to freeze than starve, and against this there was no provision.

We quickly removed our headquarters from Cincinnati to Evansville, three hundred miles below and at the head of the recent scene of disaster. A new stanch steamer of four hundred tons' burden was immediately chartered and laden to the water's edge with clothing and coal; good assistants, both men and women, were taken on board; the Red Cross flag was hoisted and, as night was setting in, after a day of intense cold—amid surging waters and crashing ice, the floating wrecks of towns and villages, great uprooted giants of the forest plunging madly to the sea, the suddenly unhoused people wandering about the river-banks, or huddled in strange houses with fireless hearths—the clear-toned bell and shrill whistle of the Josh V. Throop announced to the generous inhabitants of a noble city that from the wharves of Evansville was putting out the first Red Cross relief boat that ever floated on American waters.

The destroyed villages and hamlets lay thick on either bank, and the steamer wove its course diagonally from side to side calling the people to the boat, finding a committee to receive and distribute, and, learning as nearly as possible the number of destitute persons, put off the requisite quantity of clothing and coal, and steamed away quickly and quietly, leaving sometimes an astonished few, sometimes a multitude to gaze after and wonder who she was, whence she came, what that strange flag meant, and, most of all, to thank God with tears and prayers for what she brought.

In this manner the Red Cross proceeded to Cairo, a distance of four hundred miles, where the Ohio joins the Mississippi River, which latter at that time had not risen and was exciting no apprehension. Returning, we revisited and resupplied the destitute points. The Government boats running over the same track were genial and friendly with us, and faithful and efficient in their work.

It should be said that, notwithstanding all the material we had shipped and distributed, so abundant had been the liberality of the people that, on our return to Evansville, we found our supply greater than at any previous time.

At this moment, and most unexpectedly, commenced the great rise of the Mississippi River, and a second cry went out to the Government and the people for instant help. The strongest levees were giving way under the sudden pressure, and even the inundation of the city of New Orleans was threatened. Again the Government appropriated money, and the War Department sent out its rescue and ration boats, and again the Red Cross prepared for its supplemental work.

In an overflow of the Mississippi, owing to the level face of the country and the immense body of water, the valley is inundated at times thirty miles in width, thus rendering it impossible to get animals to a place of safety. Great numbers drown and the remainder, in a prolonged overflow, have largely starved, the Government having never included the domestic animals in its work of relief. This seemed an omission of vital importance, both humanely and economically considered, and the Red Cross prepared to go to the relief of the starving animals of the Mississippi Valley. It would also supply clothing to the destitute people whom the Government would feed.

The navigation of the Mississippi River calls for its own style of boats and pilotage, the latter being both difficult and dangerous, especially with the changed channels and yawning crevasses of a flood.

The steamer Throop was left at Evansville and the Mattie Bell chartered at St. Louis and laden with com, oats, hay, meal, and salt for cattle; clothing and cooking utensils for the destitute people; tea, coffee, rice, sugar, and medicines for the sick; and as quickly as possible followed the Government steamers leaving the same port with rations of meat and meal.

We finished the voyage of relief, having covered the Ohio River from Cincinnati to Cairo and back twice, and the Mississippi from St. Louis to New Orleans and return, occupying four months' time on the rivers, in our own chartered boats, finishing at Pittsburgh and taking rail for Washington on the first of July, having traveled over eight thousand miles, and distributed in relief , of money and estimated material, £175,000.

The Government had expended an appropriation from the Treasury on the same waters of £150,000 in money, and distributed it well. The difference was that ours was not appropriated; we gathered it as we used it.

The Texas Famine of 1885-86

Occasional rumors reached us in the years 1885 and 1886 about a drouth in Texas and consequent suffering, but they were so contradictory and widely at variance that the public took little or no heed of them. During the year of 1886 the Reverend John Brown, a North Presbyterian minister, located at Albany, Shackelford County, Texas, began making appeals by circular and oral address to the people of the Northern States, in which he asserted that there were a hundred thousand families in northwestern Texas who were utterly destitute and on the verge of starvation. He stated that since the close of the war a large number of poor families had been constantly crowding into Texas from the Southern States principally, induced thither by land agents and others, who gave glowing representations of the character of the soil for farming purposes.

These poor people, by hard labor and industry, had been generally able to make a living and nothing more. The last fall they had planted wheat and other grain quite extensively, but the rains came not and everything perished; and in the following spring and summer, too, everything put into the ground was blasted by the hot winds, so that not a thing was raised for man or beast. For fifteen months no rain had fallen, and the condition of the people was pitiable and called aloud to the charitable throughout the land for relief. They must be carried through to the next summer or they would perish. At a meeting of the citizens of Albany, Texas, they decided that the task of relieving the sufferers was greater than the well-to-do people of the State were able to undertake, and that an appeal should be made to the good-hearted people of the North for immediate aid. The Governor of Texas also published an appeal to the people of the whole land, asking for food for these people. But as there was no concerted action, and so many denials of the stories of suffering, little or nothing in the way of relief work was accomplished for some time. Spasmodic attempts were made, and some food for man and beast was contributed, but not enough to relieve a hundredth part of the needy.

The Reverend Doctor Brown went to the State Capital and endeavored to interest the Legislature in the matter, but there were seemingly so much misunderstanding and unbelief, and so many conflicting interests to reconcile, that he failed to receive any substantial assurances and left the place in disgust. When the citizens of Texas could not agree as to the necessities of their own people, it was not to be expected that the citizens of the country would take much interest in them, hence the relief movement languished from inanition.

About the middle of January, 1887, Dr. Brown came to Washington and, as solicitor and receiving agent for the committee which had issued an appeal to the country, appealed to me, as president of the American National Red Cross, asking our organization to come to the relief of the people, who were in a deplorable state, greatly needing food and clothing. I immediately shipped to Texas all the stores that were then in our warehouse, but they were no great quantity.

An appeal direct to the Red Cross required immediate attention, and I at once sought a conference with President Cleveland, who was greatly worried over the contradictory stories that were constantly printed, and was anxious to learn the truth about the matter. When I said that I should go to Texas and see for myself, he was greatly pleased, and requested me to report to him the exact situation just as soon as I had satisfied myself by personal investigation.

Dr. Hubbell and I proceeded directly to Albany, Texas, where we arrived near the end of January. We were met by the leading citizens and most heartily welcomed and accorded every privilege and attention. We began our investigations at once in a systematic way, carefully noting everything we heard and saw; and in the course of a two weeks' trip over the afflicted region, we learned the extent of the need and formulated plans for its relief.,

Making Albany our object point, we traveled by private conveyance over such territory as we thought sufficient to give a correct knowledge of the condition of the country and the people. We met large numbers of the residents, both collectively and at their homes, and learned from them personally and by actual observation their condition and what they had to depend upon during the next few months. It will be borne in mind that when we entered upon this investigation little or no relief had come from the State, and none was positively assured..

Almost no rain had fallen during a period of eighteen months; two planted crops had perished in the ground, and the seed wheat sown the previous fall gave no signs of life. The dust was rolling over the great wind-swept fields, where the people had hidden their last little forlorn hope of borrowed seed, and literally a heaven of brass looked down upon an earth of iron.

Here were twenty to forty counties, of a size commensurate with Texan dimensions, occupied by new settlers, making their first efforts in the pioneer work of developing home life in an untried country, soil, and climate. They had put their all into the new home and the little stock they could afford for its use. They had toiled faithfully, planted two and three times, as long as there was anything to plant or sow, and in most instances failed to get back their seed. Many had grown discouraged and left the country. The people were not actually starving, but they were in the direst want for many of the necessities of life, and it was only a matter of days when they would have reached the condition of the *reconcentrados* as we later found them in Cuba. Hundreds of thousands of cattle had died for the want of food and water, and their drying carcasses and bleaching bones could be seen in every direction as the eye wandered over the parched surface of the plains.

I at once saw that in the vastness of its territory and varying interests the real need of these suffering communities was not understood by the Texas people—it had not come home to them; but that once comprehending, it would be their wish to have it known and cared for by themselves and not by others outside of the State.

Assuring these poor people that their actual condition should be made known to their own people, through the authoritative means of the Red Cross, and that they should be speedily cared for, we bade them farewell and hurried away to Dallas, where we intended to send out a statement to the people of the State.

Arriving there, we sought an interview with Colonel Belo, of the Dallas "News," and laid before him the result of our observations. He placed the columns of his paper at our disposal, and through them we enlightened the people of the true status of affairs in their own State. The response was as quick as it was gratifying, and thence onward there was no further necessity for appealing to anyone outside of the State limits. Indeed, that act in the first place was the greatest mistake, as to the average Texan, feeling a genuine pride in the State's wealth and resources, it savored of frauds and imposition, and prejudiced him against the brother who would pass him by and appeal to outsiders.

The Texas Legislature appropriated one hundred thousand dollars for food, and in the meantime rain began to fall and the entire aspect of affairs began to change for the better. But there were still many needs unprovided for—clothing, fuel, seeds for gardens and fields, livestock, and many other things—and it was necessary to place these needs before the people. This the "News" took upon itself to do; and upon my suggestion it opened a popular subscription and announced that it would receive contributions of seed or cash and would publish the same from day to day and turn them over to the constituted authorities appointed to disburse them. In order to encourage the movement I inaugurated it with the first subscription, and from that time until now I do not believe anyone has heard of any need in Texas that has not been taken care of by her own people.

The Texas famine brought into sharp relief the ideals of Clara Barton in emergencies of this character. It was at first proposed to meet the situation by a Government appropriation; and a bill for such relief, passed by both houses of Congress, was promptly vetoed by President Cleveland. This veto brought severe criticism upon the President, but Clara Barton sustained him. What was needed in such an emergency, as she believed, was not to fly to Congress with appeals for an appropriation, but to call upon the people to send relief through an accredited agency that would account for the money and disburse it in systematic fashion. Her success in the Texas famine abundantly proved the wisdom of her course.

The Mount Vernon, Illinois, Tornado

On Sunday, February 19, 1888, a destructive tornado occurred at Mount Vernon, Illinois. Within three minutes after the fury of the storm had struck the town, thirty people had been killed and scores of others injured, and an immense amount of property destroyed.

To add to the horrors already wrought, fire broke out in a dozen places. Those who were uninjured quickly came to the rescue, quenching the flames and exerting themselves to relieve the unfortunate victims, who were, in most cases, pinned down under the wreckage of their houses. All night long these brave men and women worked, and when morning came the few houses that remained standing were filled with the dead and injured.

Appeals for assistance were sent out to the people of the country, but, through an improper statement of the situation, the public was misled, and, not realizing the pressing needs of the stricken community, failed to take up the matter in a business-like manner, and the town was left to suffer for a little of the great abundance that was around them. In their extremity the despairing citizens appealed to the Red Cross for aid, which responded at once.

A most deplorable situation was presented: the people were homeless and helpless, neglected, and in a state of mind bordering on insanity.

After a somewhat hasty examination of the situation, the following simple message was sent to both the Associated and the United Press:

The pitiless snow is falling on the heads of three thousand people who are without homes, without food or clothing and without money.

With only this little word to explain the needs, our generous American people responded promptly and liberally, as they always do when they fully understand what is needed.

It was unnecessary to remain longer than two weeks with these people, who, as soon as they recovered from the first shock of their great misfortune, and when they felt that kind friends were by their side, lending them moral and substantial support, manfully commenced to bring order out of chaos, to rebuild their town and resume their usual vocations. Large quantities of relief supplies of all kinds quickly came to hand, and, when we were ready to leave them, the Citizens' Committee had in its treasury a cash balance of ninety thousand dollars. And thus, with their blessings ringing in our ears, we left them.

The Yellow Fever Epidemic in Florida in 1888

During the month of August, 1888, yellow fever broke out in Jacksonville, and in September it was declared to be epidemic, the usual alarm and exodus of citizens taking place. On September 8, heroic measures to depopulate the city were taken. Every person that was still well and could leave was requested to go; very little urging was necessary. Camps were established outside of the city, where those who had not the means to go farther and get better quarters were enabled to live under medical surveillance, and away from the seat of infection.

The mayor of Jacksonville had made an appeal for doctors and nurses, which had been quickly responded to, and they were doing everything possible to attend to the rapidly increasing number of patients.

On the formation of the Red Cross Society of New Orleans in 1893, it had been carefully and wisely arranged that, in case of yellow fever becoming epidemic in any place, no unacclimated persons, or those not immune, should be sent as assistants by the Red Cross. New Orleans was the home of the famous "Old Howard Association," that had won its reputation and worn its grateful renown from the horrors of Memphis to the present time. This body freely united with the Red Cross of New Orleans, and it was arranged that the Southern States, through this society, should provide all Red Cross nurses for yellow fever, and that the northern portion of the country should raise the money to pay and provide them. We felt this to be a security, and an immediate provision which the country had never before known. Fearing that this might not, at its first inception, be fully understood, I called at once on Dr. Hamilton, then in charge of the Marine Hospital, explaining it to him, and offering all the nurses that could be required, even to hundreds, all experienced and organized for immediate action. Perhaps it was not strange that a provision, so new and so unknown in the sad history of plagues and epidemics, should have seemed Utopian, and as such been brushed aside as not only useless, but self-seeking and obtrusive. Like the entire organization of which it was a part, it had to wait and win its way against custom or even prejudice, by honest worth and stern necessity. It was the "old, old story." The world takes reform hard and slow.

As it was, however, we did what we could. Headquarters were established at the Riggs House in Washington. The good-hearted people of the North, who felt that they must go to Florida, had by some means gotten the idea that they must have a pass from the Central Committee of the Red Cross in order to go. They came to us in hundreds and were mercifully held back from a scourge for which they would have been both food and fuel, whilst the entire people of the country, in pity and horror at the reports received, were holding meetings, raising money, and pouring funds like water into the doomed city of Jacksonville, where the scourge had centered, and to which every effort was made to confine it.

Not realizing the opposition there might prove to be to our nurses, we called upon their old-time leader, Colonel F. R. Southmayd, the efficient secretary of the Red Cross Society of New Orleans, instructing him to enlist a body of nurses and take them at once to the fever district. He enlisted thirty, both men and women, white and colored, took a part with him, the remainder following next day.

Refugees who had fled from Jacksonville carried the plague to several smaller places in the surrounding country, where in some instances it acquired quite a foothold; but, owing to their obscurity and the lack of communication with the outside world, they were left alone to fight the disease as best they could. Among these places was the little town of MacClenny, where, as soon as it became known that there was a case of fever within its limits, all trains were ordered to rush through without stopping, and an armed quarantine was placed around it with orders to shoot anyone attempting to leave the town. Thus left to their fate, without doctors, nurses, or food, in any quantity, their situation was pitiable. There were a number of volunteers who had made attempts to get into MacClenny, but, owing to the unreasoning panic existing, they were not permitted to enter the place.

Colonel Southmayd had heard of these neglected people, and he succeeded while en route to Jacksonville in dropping off ten nurses so much needed at MacClenny. How he did this, I have told in a little brochure entitled "The MacClenny Nurses," that was issued at the close of the year 1888.

The fever spread during the fall to several points in Georgia, Alabama, and Mississippi, and resulted in the usual panic and flight from many places; but happily the disease got no great headway before the frost put an end to its career.

It was late in November when we closed this work; worn and disheartened as we were by both the needful and the needless hardships of the campaign, we were glad of the two or three months in which no call for action was made upon us.

The Johnstown Flood of 1889

The South Fork Dam broke after several days of extremely heavy rainfall, unleashing 20 million tons of water (18 million cubic meters) from the reservoir known as Lake Conemaugh. With a flow rate that temporarily equalled that of the Mississippi River, the flood killed 2,209 people and caused US$17 million of damage (about $425 million in 2012 dollars).

On the 30th of May, 1889, occurred the calamity of Johnstown, Pennsylvania, with all its horrors. So frightful and improbable were the reports that it required twenty-four hours to satisfy ourselves that it was not a canard.

In order to get an intelligent idea of this disaster and the terrible damage wrought by the irresistible waters, it may be well to give a short sketch of the city of Johnstown and its adjacent surroundings Before the flood there were thirty thousand people in this busy community, which embraced the city of Johnstown proper and numerous suburbs The city is situated at the junction of Stony Creek and the little Conemaugh, forming the Conemangh River. These streams are liable to sudden overflows, and, owing to the contraction of the waterway in the lower port of the city by the damping of cinders and slag from the large ironworks on the banks of the stream, and also encroachments by riparian owners, the upper portion of the city is liable to inundations About nine miles above the city a dam had been thrown across the little Conemaugh River many years ago for commercial purposes, but had been abandoned and the site with much surrounding property had been subsequently purchased by a sporting dub, whose membership embraced some of the wealthiest citizens of Pennsylvania. These gentlemen were attracted by the picturesque scenery and the hunting and fishing of the vicinity. and they spent thousands of dollars in improving and beautifying their holdings The dam was raised to a height of over seventy feet and held an immense body of water covering many acres

This large mass of water was a constant source of fear to the inhabitants of the lower valleys, who were aware of the danger that threatened them, and many protests were made against the continuance of the danger; but owing to the prominence erf the owners of the dam, and the strong social and political influence they exerted, they remained unmolested in the possession of the monster that was to break its bounds and carry death and destruction in its pitiless pathway.

A steady rainfall for several days in the latter part of May caused overflows in all the streams in western Pennsylvania, and much of the city of Johnstown was already under water to a depth of from two to ten feet, when suddenly the dam over the Little Conemaugh gave way, and its flood, resembling a moving mountain of water thirty feet high, was precipitated upon the doomed city. Numbers of the inhabitants, who had carried the fear of this disaster in their minds for years, had become so alarmed by the long-continued rains, and the floods that were already upon them, took their families and fled to the high grounds on the hillsides. But the great majority of the people, who, though fully aware of the danger, had lived with it so long that they had become careless and indifferent, took no precautions whatever. These were overwhelmed by the tide almost without warning, and before they could seek safety were swept away.

The number of lives lost will never be accurately known; but in all probability it reached in the entire valley nearly five thousand. It is said that property to the amount of twelve millions of dollars was absolutely lost.

It was at the moment of supreme affliction when we arrived at Johnstown. The waters had subsided, and those of the inhabitants who had escaped the fate of their fellows were gazing over the scene of destruction and trying to arouse themselves from the lethargy that had taken hold of them when they were stunned by the realization of all the woe that had been visited upon them. How nobly they responded to the call of duty! How much of the heroic there is in our people when it is needed! No idle murmurings of fate, but, true to the godlike instincts of manhood and fraternal love, they quickly banded together to do the best that the wisest among them could suggest.

For five weary months it was our portion to live amid these scenes of destruction, desolation, poverty, want, and woe; sometimes in tents, sometimes without; in rain and mud, and a lack of the commonest comforts, until we could build houses to shelter ourselves and those around us. Without a safe, and with a dry-goods box for a desk, we conducted financial affairs in money and material to the extent of nearly half a million dollars.

When our five months' work was completed, we had only to turn over to the hands of the leaders of the town, our warehouse with its entire remaining stock, amounting to some thousands of dollars; the care of the infirmary; one of our trained clerks, with all papers and accounts of our relief work from the day of its inception; one of our experienced working men to handle transportation—to fit up for them large, warm rooms for winter use; give them our blessing; accept theirs in fullest measure; say good-bye to them and to our faithful helpers, with heavy hearts and choking voices, and return to our home, bearing the record of a few months of faithful endeavor among a people as patient and brave as people are made, as noble and grateful as falls to the lot of human nature to be. Enterprising, industrious, and hopeful, the new Johnstown, phoenix-like, rose from its ruins more beautiful than the old, with a ceaseless throb of grateful memory for every kind act rendered, and every thought of sympathy given her in her great hour of desolation and woe. God bless her, and God bless all who helped save her!

We had employed during our sojourn in Johnstown a working force of fifty men and women, whom we had housed, fed, and paid, with the exception of the volunteers who worked for the good they could do and would accept nothing. The means which we so largely handled came from everywhere; accounts were rendered for everything, and no word of business complication ever came to us. There never has in all our work.

There was much to do in Johnstown after we left; buildings to remove and property to care for when it had served its purpose and the ground became needed. But there is always a right time for any benevolent work to cease; a time when the community is ready to resume its own burdens, and when an offered charity is an insult to the honest and independent, and a degradation to the careless and improvident, tending to pauperize and make them an added burden on their better-minded fellow citizens. And then, the moment the tradesman is able to reestablish himself, he looks with jealous eyes on any agency that diverts possible business from his channels. Thus it is not only wise, but just to all concerned to withdraw all gratuities from a people the instant they are able to gain even a meager self-support.

A rather curious circumstance, somewhat on the line of this reflection, fell to our lot after leaving Johnstown. The houses that we had built and furnished were indispensable to the tenants during the winter, when there were no other houses to be had; but in the spring the city, rejuvenated, began to build up again, and we were notified that the land on which our large houses were standing was needed by the owners, who wished to use it for their own purposes, and they requested the Red Cross to remove its buildings. We promptly sent an agent to attend to the matter, and he began the work of vacating the premises. There was no hardship involved in this, as all the tenants were by this time in condition to pay rent, the relief fund of $1,600,000 having been distributed among them in proportion to their losses, and there were houses that they m could get; in a few days our houses were empty. Then a new factor entered into the situation. When it became generally known that the Red Cross must remove these immense houses, and that a large quantity of lumber and house furnishings were to be disposed of, the self-interests of the dealers in those commodities were at once aroused, and they strongly protested against the gratuitous distribution of those articles among the people of Johnstown, asserting that the inhabitants were now prospering and had the means to buy everything they needed, and that a gift from us of any of these things would be an injustice to the honest traders who were trying to reestablish themselves.

We saw the justice of their objection and gave assurances that no injury should be done them; still, to have fully conformed to their idea and transported the entire material to some other point would have put the Red Cross to an amount of trouble and cost unjust to itself.

I am not prepared to say that our quiet field agent in charge of the work did not find resting-places for very much of this material in still needy homes, where it did no harm to anyone and for which no one but the pitiful recipients were the wiser.

Notwithstanding the fact that we took away from Johnstown as little material and furniture as was possible, after quietly disposing of the greater part of it, and this at an expense and inconvenience to ourselves which we could ill afford, there were those who could not understand why we should take anything away; and their unkind misconstruction and criticisms have scarcely ceased echoing even to this late day.

The paths of charity are over roadways of ashes; and he who would tread them must be prepared to meet opposition, misconstruction, jealousy, and calumny. Let his work be that of angels, still it will not satisfy all.

There is always an aftermath of attempted relief where none is needed, and more or less criticism of any work, for it is always so much easier to say how a thing ought to be done than it is to do it.

These little unpleasantnesses, however, cannot deprive us of the thousand memories of gratitude, appreciation, and kindnesses exchanged, which were mutually helpful; nor of the many lifelong friendships formed which will bless us all our day.

The astonishing record of the Red Cross in war and peace time continues into the twentieth century.

CLARA BARTON AT HOME AND ABROAD

Strenuous were the years of Miss Barton's administration of the American Red Cross. There was upon an average practically one disaster a year which called her organization into the field. In some instances the active work of the Red Cross upon the ground lasted only a few weeks; in other cases, as in the matter of the South Carolina Sea Islands, it consumed almost a year. The intervals between disasters were occupied by correspondence, addresses, articles for the press, and attendance to the many duties brought on by a widened acquaintance and a constantly growing interest in the work. They were years, too, in which Miss Barton was sometimes personally short of money. In no other period, as in this, do her diaries so clearly show the necessity which she felt for personal economy for the sake of the work. She declined the four-thousand-dollar salary which was suggested for her; she vetoed every proposal looking toward a Government appropriation for her personal benefit or for the work of the Red Cross. If during this long period she ever thought of the Red Cross in terms of a possible financial advantage to herself, her diaries betray no hint of it. If she ever thought of the possibility that Congress might take care of her, the innumerable letters which passed between her and the members of the two houses of Congress afford no indication of it.

The adhesion of the United States to the Treaty of Geneva did, however, take her abroad a number of times, once or more at Government expense, as one of the three official representatives of the United States at certain international congresses. The appropriations to cover the expenses of a delegate were never very large; generally two thousand dollars for the expense of three delegates. In connection with one of these journeys an interesting correspondence developed in which one of the delegates exceeded in expenditure his none too ample allowance of less than seven hundred dollars. He wrote a long letter explaining why it had been necessary for him to expend more, and desired Clara Barton to approve his request for an increase. This she declined to do either for herself or for either of the others. For her simple tastes the appropriation was ample; she lived within it and her associates had to do the same or make up the balance out of their own pockets.

Miss Barton had just returned from her arduous labor on behalf of the flood sufferers on the Ohio and Mississippi in the summer of 1884, when Secretary of State Frelinghuysen appointed her one of the three delegates to the International Conference at Geneva. Her associates were her friends Judge Joseph Sheldon, of Connecticut, and Mr. A. S. Sullivan, vice-president of the American Red Cross.

Miss Barton was so wearied with her labors in connection with the flood sufferers that she hesitated about accepting her appointment. To her great joy and to that of Dr. Hubbell, who accompanied her, the voyage proved an excellent tonic. There was not an unpleasant day, and Miss Barton was not ill an hour and did not miss a meal. Toward the close of the voyage she was called upon to address the passengers, who greeted her with great interest and listened to her with marked and reverent attention. She reached Liverpool on August 26, 1884, and had a happy and prosperous journey to Geneva where the Congress convened in December.

Four hundred distinguished delegates and representatives of the signatory powers to the treaty assembled at Geneva. There were titled rulers, distinguished representatives of nobility, eminent surgeons, noted scientists, and philanthropists whose names were known around the world.

It is not too much to say that Clara Barton was the most noted delegate to that convention and the recipient of its highest honors. There was not one among the four hundred delegates who did not know that it was she who brought the United States, last of all the great nations, to occupy a place in that gathering. Popular interest centered about her; she was pointed out and sought out as the most celebrated delegate to the congress. Not all of her associates were strangers to her; chief among the royal persons present to claim the honor of her acquaintance and introduce her as their friend were the Grand Duke of Baden, the Grand Duchess, and her imperial father, the Emperor of Germany.

It was the direct influence of Miss Barton which caused the introduction of what is known as the 11 America Amendment." This amendment was to the effect—

That the Red Cross Society engage in time of peace in humanitarian work analogous to the duties devolving upon them in periods of war, such as taking care of the sick and rendering relief in extraordinary calamities where, as in war, prompt and organized relief is demanded.

The adoption of this resolution was a high compliment to Clara Barton. She brought to the congress not only the prestige of America's accession to the treaty, but a new and notable enlargement of the sphere of Red Cross activity which she had invented, tested, and found practicable in America, and worthy of recommendation to all the world.

At Geneva she was joined by Antoinette Margot, whom she sent for as a companion and interpreter. For, though Clara Barton was fairly at home in conversation in French, she was glad of assistance at times. Antoinette had written her in the years of their separation. Her own life had been none too happy, and she had passed through a religious crisis that led her, though born a Protestant, into the Roman Catholic Church, and- later into a cloister. Even this change she credited to Clara Barton! This amused Clara, but Antoinette said that but for Clara she would have remained "a crushed-down little unhappy baby in my father's house"; Clara had given her courage and strength to face great questions and decide them:

Dear, dear Miss Barton [she wrote]: Never, never I shall forget what I owe to you. I owe you even my perfect actual happiness of being a Catholic, for, without your strong teaching, and your nerving of my heart, I could never have dared to take the step of following my convictions, when I had convictions to follow.

Clara's comment was:

Poor, simple child! It is all for the best, I think. Hers is one of those unsteady, unbalanced minds that must be controlled. She has no mastery over herself, and nothing but a priest and a confessional can make her happy.

Antoinette poured out her impulsive love in extravagant protestations of devotion. She wanted to see Miss Barton, to kiss the feet of the woman who had done so much for her, and who stood in the mind of Antoinette as the realization of the noblest ideal of womanhood.

We owe to this impulsive girl, who later entered a convent, a really fine description of Clara Barton as she stood among the representatives of all the nations that were joined in the league of the Red Cross at Geneva:

The Government of the United States has done itself no greater credit than in selecting Clara Barton to represent it among the nations abroad. During the last week I have looked on as she has sat day by day in one of the greatest and grandest assemblies of men that could be gathered—men representing the highest rank among the civilized nations of the earth; men of thought, of wisdom, of power, called together from all over the world to deliberate on great questions, of nautical import, military power, the neutrality of nations, humanity in war, wisdom in peace. In the midst of this assembly of gray-haired men, glittering with military decorations, with national honors, won and conferred, sat this one woman—calm, thoughtful, self-possessed, recognized and acknowledged as possessing every right and privilege belonging to any member of the conference; not merely permitted to be there, but there by the sovereign right of nations; not merely allowed to sit there by the courtesy due to a lady, but by the right due to a nation's representative; her vote not merely accepted as a matter of form, but expected and watched for; grave questions referred to her as the representative of a great nation, and all deference paid to her judgment: her demeanor so unobtrusive, her actions so wise, that it could not otherwise than reflect merited credit upon her and her country.

But the crowning recognition of her philanthropic labors at home and abroad was given when one of the Italian delegates, springing upon the platform, proposed to the assemblage to vote, by acclamation, that *"Mademoiselle Barton bien mérite de l'humanité."*

Even Miss Barton was moved from her usual composure by the thunders of applause. I do not know whether you in America are familiar with the peculiar significance of that phrase. It is an expression of the highest approbation, honor, and esteem that the French language can convey. It is probable that Miss Barton is the first woman in the world who has ever received such a tribute.

After her return from Geneva, Miss Barton made a journey to California, in 1886, returning by way of Charleston, South Carolina, where she had a share in the relief of that city after the earthquake.

In September, 1887, occurred another international congress of the Red Cross. This was held in Germany, at Carlsruhe, the ducal capital of Alsace and home of the Grand Duchess Louise. Here she met her friends, the Grand Duke and Duchess of Baden and the Emperor of Germany, and besides these the Empress Augusta, Bismarck, and von Moltke. Her honors here were scarcely less brilliant than they had been at Geneva, and her personal joys were more, for she was near the scenes of her labors in the Franco-Prussian War. There she was the guest of royalty; crowned heads bowed respectfully to her. From Baden Baden she wrote a letter home just after the close of the congress:

Baden Baden, Germany, Oct. 28, 1887
The International Red Cross Conference has closed. Most of the delegates have left Carlsruhe, unless, like ourselves, remaining for after-work. The Grand Duke and Grand Duchess, with their Court, have retired to Baden Baden for the customary birthday festivities of Her Majesty the Empress, and the Emperor and his suite would, as also customary, make his yearly visit in honor of the occasion, thus making that lovely and historic old town for the moment, the center of Interest for the Empire.

Dr. H. and myself were at breakfast when the hotel porter laid a telegraphic dispatch on my plate. It will be remembered, at least by personal friends, that three years ago, while in attendance at a similar international conference, the honored pleasure of a meeting with His Majesty the Emperor of Germany had been given me. This dispatch informed me that a like honor again awaited my presence in Baden Baden. Trunks were packed, adieus made, and the midday train of the following day took us in time for the appointed hour. Whoever has visited the interior of the "New Castle," the Baden Baden palace of the Grand Duke, and been shown through its tasteful apartments, rich in elegance, tradition, and history, will require no further reminder of the place where the interview would be given.

This was, as well, the birthday of the Crown Prince; and in tender paternal sympathy, for the painful affliction resting upon a life so treasured, and for the great anxiety of the German people, His Majesty the Emperor would pass a portion of the day with the beloved daughter and sister, the Grand Duchess, at the castle; and in honoring memory of the occasion, its halls were thronged with visitors who came to manifest both respect and sympathy.

At half-past one o'clock we were ushered in at the great castle doors, by their attendants in livery of "scarlet and gold," the national colors of Baden; our damp wraps removed—for it was a pouring rain—and after a half-hour sitting by a cheerful fire, among pictures which quite called one out of personal consciousness, we were escorted to the grand reception and drawing room, to the center of a magnificent apartment with no occupant but ourselves. By another door one saw the Emperor surrounded by guests, who paid formal respects. Scores of visitors with coachmen in richest livery had entered while we waited and registered titled names on the open pages.

At length His Majesty turned from the group about him, and, taking the arm of the Grand Duchess, entered our apartment. It was difficult to realize all the ninety years, as he stepped toward us with even, and steady, if no longer elastic, tread. He approached with cordially extended hand, and in his excellent French expressed satisfaction for the meeting. "In the name of humanity, he was glad to meet and welcome those who labored for it."

In recalling the earlier days of our acquaintance, Her Royal highness the Grand Duchess alluded tenderly to the winter in Strassburg of 70 and '71—which I had passed among its poor and wounded people after the siege—and, selecting two from a cluster of decorations which I had worn in honor of the present occasion, drew the attention of the Emperor to them. The one he knew; it was his own, presented upon his seventy-fifth birthday. The other he had never seen. It was the beautiful decoration of the "German Waffengenossen"—the "Warrior Brothers in arms" of Milwaukee.

It was puzzlingly familiar, and yet it was not familiar. There was again the Iron Cross of Germany, but it was on the American shield. The "American Eagle' surmounting the arms for defense; and the colors of Germany, the red, white, and black of the Empire uniting the two. His Majesty gazed upon the expressive emblem, which, with no words, said so much, and turned inquiringly to the Grand Duchess, as if to ask, "Does my daughter understand this?"

The explanation was made that it was from His Majesty's own soldiers, who, after the "German-Franco War," had gone to the United States and become citizens; and this device was designed to express, that, as by its shield they were American citizens, and true to the land of their adoption, so by its "Iron Cross," they were still German; and by the colors of the native land for which every man had offered his life, and risked it, they bound the old home to the new; and by the American Eagle and arms, surmounting all, they were ready to offer their lives again, if need be, in defense of either land.

The smile of the grand old Emperor, as he listened, had in it the "Well done" of the benignant father to a dutiful and successful son. "And they make good citizens?" he would ask. "The best that could be desired," I said; "industrious, honest, and prosperous, and, sire, they are still yours in heart, still true to the Fatherland and its Emperor."

"I am glad to hear this; they were good soldiers, and thank God, true men everywhere," was the earnest and royal response.

His Majesty continued, speaking of America, its growth, its progress, its advancement in science and humanity, its adoption and work of the Red Cross, which meant so much for mankind; and when assured that its people revered and loved the Emperor of Germany, that his life was precious to them, and that thousands of prayers went up for him in that distant land he had never seen, the touching and characteristic response betrayed the first tremor of the voice the ear had caught in its kindly tones.

"God be praised for this; for it is all from Him. I am only His. Of myself I am nothing. He made us what we are. God is over all."

We stood with bowed heads while those slowly spoken, earnest, holy words from that most revered of earthly monarchs fell upon us like a benediction.

At length His Majesty gave a hand to both Dr. H. and myself in a parting adieu, and walked a few steps away, when turning back, and again extending a hand, said, in French, "It is probably the last time," and in pleasant English, "Good-bye." And again taking the arm of the Grand Duchess walked from the room, leaving His highness the Grand Duke, one of the kindest and noblest types of manhood, to say the last words, and close the interview; one of the most impressive and memorable of a lifetime.

In another letter she told of her parting with the imperial party as follows:

Baden Baden, Oct. 24, 1887

I do not know if I have written since coming here or if my last was from Carlsruhe. We were here for the "Baden season." We were invited by the Duke and Duchess to spend a few weeks at Baden Baden, and of course all the Court proper would come. The Empress came also; and the Emperor. They will be here till next Friday, when she goes to Berlin. The Crown Prince's health is very poor. The Emperor is better than ever—bright and cheerful like a young man. We went the other evening to see him take the train for Berlin. The station reserve rooms were like a drawing-room and all the Court and royal persons were in them, to wait the coming of the Emperor, and the town. The Emperor shook hands with all, saying good-bye, made pretty gifts to some special persons, then entered the royal train, to ride all night. The day before yesterday the Empress sent for me to come to her. I spent a most delightful hour. She had a great deal to say, and made me a lovely parting gift of a ruby brooch. She insisted that we should meet again, that I should come to Europe again, and she should see me. In the p.m. the Grand Duchess sent for us to go to her and we went and spent two lovely boon. She is charming as ever. Then next evening (last evening) she sent for us to come to dine. We went and had a beautiful time. We are to go again to-morrow for a visit. After the end of this week we go to Strassburg to spend a little time. Shall most likely go to Berlin and back to Strassburg and down the French side of the Rhine to Basle, Bern, Geneva, Paris, London, Liver-pod, and then we shall be on our direct way home, but it is some little time yet before we can go home.

From her journey to attend that international congress at Carlsruhe she returned in January, 1888, and was quickly called away to Mount Vernon, Illinois, to care for the sufferers from the tornado. When she returned from this campaign, she went on a short tour delivering addresses before influential bodies. She spoke in Montclair, New Jersey, addressing a State conference of Congregational churches. She then delivered a lecture in Philadelphia, and was received with every consideration and honor. Then she went home to Washington and did her washing. This combination of her work as a world leader and a woman concerned with domestic affairs is contained in two letters to Mrs. Stafford, dated May 4 and May 8, 1888:

483

Dearest Mamie:

I had intended to write you just a line on the train to and from Philadelphia, but one was in the night—the other so full of other things and the trip so short, I did not get to it.

I can't think it was a week ago, but so it seems. The first day I met the Society on its Annual Meeting, and spoke to them a little. I attended a lunch party before the meeting and a reception after the opera at the elegant residence of Dr.-, president of the Philadelphia Red Cross. That made four things after twelve o'clock.

The next day we had informal meetings with officers of the society until two o'clock p.m. Then attended a lecture given in the regular course of the Red Cross Society. Then I gave a lecture. Then home to dress for the reception to commence at eight.

This was given in Union League Hall, very large, with a band of music. The dignitaries of the city attended in bodies. The physicians—the clergymen—the lawyers—the judges—the military army and navy in uniform. I received and shook hands with all. They left after eleven. It was a splendid reception. There was still a meeting at the hotel (The Colonnade) after our return, so we are only in bed by two o'clock next morning, got a hasty breakfast and hastened to the nine o'clock train for home; found a large mail, and I was very sleepy. I did sleep a day or two mainly, and that is what makes the week seem so short, I think.

Then just think what a washing there was on hand; had never had time to have a full wash done since our return from Mount Vernon. The Woman's Council came directly on that, and an address to write for it. Then the conference of churches at Montclair, and another address to write. Then Philadelphia, and another address to write, with all that came between. The wash went to the wall till this week, when it was taken up in its turn and put through in one day, and all ironed yesterday, and clothes put away this very minute, and I haven't left the warehouse yet, but am just dropped down at the table in front of the window, near the store (Gaby will know all about it) while Alfred brings compost from the stable alongside ready to make up some flower-beds, etc., and I direct him from the window as I scribble, to lose no time. It is just as lovely as it can be. Tell Gaby we have moved the rosebushes all down to the front of the yard, and they didn't mind it a bit, and went right on putting out buds, and he will appreciate how much better chance we had with a washing of twenty sheets, thirty pillowslips, and other things in proportion, and he knows how quickly and easily it all went out of the way, and no one got much tired, and not any sick.

I haven't time for more than a word. We are making out our foreign conference accounts for the Government and I have the report to make out directly and a bill to draw up for Congress this next week and a host of correspondence, and we are having Alfred make up our garden, in front of the warehouse, and a pretty little plot it is too. I found time one night by moonlight to plant lettuce and peppergrass and radishes, and in two days they come up and are green and pretty. Yesterday we set out two dozen tomato plants a foot high, and all of our dozen grapevines are growing; splendid varieties; and when Alfred makes up the flower-beds to-day, we shall find time to plant all the seeds I have. I have no bulbs to get, but I have a dozen nice hollyhocks, fifteen inches high, and all the rosebushes and *fleur de lys* in bloom and bud. I can't get time to hunt over the house for the little seeds we want to plant. I have nice seeds for kitchen-garden things from Dansville, but can't remember where to look for them. I want a pinch of caraway seed and twelve great sage roots and I want some catnip seed for Tommy. There is not a stalk of catnip anywhere about, and I can't get any seed. Have you some in your catnip herb bag? I like saffran, and red balm such as Julian raises; I can get plenty of elegant plants, but the old, old things are hard to find—and I have not time to look, but should so like to stick a few out in my nice beds. So here is a place for small contributions. I do hope Johny is better. Please give him all the love I can send, and try, all of you, to keep well. We are well, the Saturday work is all done up, and everything is lovely as spring can make it.

The great "Council of Women" is now over [she writes a little later]: the meetings are ended, the people are mainly leaving the city, and this hour my house has had its last visitor. Every day till now my space, and my table, has been filled to the utmost, and in addition to my full part in the "Council," its meeting, committees, and speeches.

The next morning (yesterday) I had to meet a Senate committee at the Capitol and address them at ten o'clock. Then I go with Mrs. General Logan and others to the War Department to manage business there. And now it is eight-thirty the next morning, and at ten I must be at the War Department with another committee.

Her domestic affairs attended to, she hurried to Boston to deliver an important address and attend a reception. From there she went to Wellesley and delivered an address:

485

My cold entirely left me, and I have had no trouble with it. So much for right living, and good cool blood. This is the last day of the convention. I am to speak to-night. I did say a little yesterday, and they all laughed at me; I wish you could have been here. There is to be a reception given me next Friday evening. Steve and Lizzie and Myrtie are invited. I go to the Wellesley College to take tea and speak to the five hundred girls there on Saturday evening. Some things I must miss. I get back as soon as I can, so as to go on home. I am so glad of Sunday; it was a glorious day; so good to see so many together again. I hope the children are well, that you don't wrestle too much with imaginary dirt, and are getting a little real strength.

Besides her tours abroad she had some interesting journeys in her own country, including a happy camping trip in the Yellowstone Park and the Cascade Mountains, in the autumn of 1891.

The following winter she spent in the Red Cross Headquarters in what had been the home of General Grant in Washington. It was a strenuous winter and an expensive one. She drew upon her personal resources for fuel for the large building, as well as for rent and the care of the home. She wrote to Mrs. Bullock:

Washington January 7, 1892

I have wanted to talk with you about coming to see us, but when I think how cold it is here, and how far from nice and cozy it is, I feel reluctant to invite you from a small, snug, pretty home, to this so large and, as it seems to me, less inviting one. If you did not know it, I should not dare to say you might try it, for we are having an exceptionally cold, hard winter. The ground is covered with snow, and the winds have blown an old northeaster these last days, and you will know this is not an easy house to heat. My expenses have been so heavy, and receipts so "nothing," that I cannot afford to take on more help. I am obliged to have a woman for the work and the house, a man for the fires and walk—shoveling snow and all the cold rough work—and an amanuensis as my clerk and typewriter. They are drawing steadily every month; then my rent is high and no one to help share that, and, besides this, all the world expects me to give it something if it can get through the door and get a letter to me. I have had to economize on myself.

In 1893 she was led into an experiment which caused her much anxiety and proved to have been a mistake. A man and his wife, who had been associated with her in her work along the Ohio River, expressed a desire to dedicate, as a thank offering to humanity, a tract of land more than one square mile in area, or specifically seven hundred and eighty-two acres, as a home for the American Red Cross. This offer deeply touched Miss Barton, who accepted it in the following appreciative letter addressed to the donors:

American National Red Cross
Washington, D.C., March 18, 1893

Dear Sir:

Referring to your letter of February 10th, made public February 23d, permit me to reply as follows:

In accepting the gift of land, in the State of Indiana, that you so generously dedicate to the American National Red Cross as "the almoner of humanity," and by which you have so touchingly complimented me personally, allow me to say that the friendship expressed on this and many other occasions by yourself and wife, and the personal aid you have both given of time and labor in great calamities, make me free to accept this gift without reservation, assuring you of my best endeavors to attain the humane results for which this benefaction is intended.

This land, as the property of the American National Red Cross, will be the one piece of neutral ground on the Western Hemisphere protected by international treaty against the tread of hostile feet. It is a perpetual sanctuary against invading armies, and will be so respected and held sacred by the military powers of the world. Forty nations are pledged to hold all material and stores of the Red Cross, and all its followers, neutral in war, and free to go and come as their duties require.

While its business headquarters will remain, as before, at the capital of the Nation, this gift still forms a realization of the hope so long cherished—that the National Red Cross may have a place to accumulate and produce material and stores for sudden emergencies and great calamities; and if war should come upon our land, which may God avert, we may be ready to fulfil the mission that our adhesion to the Geneva Treaty has made binding upon us.

I will direct that monuments be erected defining the boundaries of this domain, dedicated to eternal peace and humanity, upon which shall be inscribed the insignia of the Treaty of Geneva, which insignia all the nations of the earth are bound by solemn covenant to respect.

Not only our own people, but the peoples of all civilized nations will have published to their knowledge that the American National Red Cross has a home and a recognized abiding-place through all generations.

For this I have striven for years, mainly misunderstood, often misinterpreted, and it is through your clear intuition and humane thought that the clouds have been swept away and my hopes have been realized.

In accordance with views expressed by you in your letter of gift, I appoint an adviser, which I insist shall be yourself, leaving you free to appoint another to work jointly with you, knowing that in the future, as in the past, your heart will be in the work.

Clara Barton
President American National Red Cross

The gift, as it developed, was not without its conditions; the donors could not quite afford to give it outright, but would sell it for a sum very much less than its value in consideration of the philanthropic purposes to which it was to be dedicated. This seemed not unreasonable, and the deed was accepted subject to the specified conditions. It seemed to Clara Barton a beautiful achievement; there was to be one spot on the Western Hemisphere where in case of war the rights of humanity would be accepted as supreme. Located as it was in the interior of the country, and removed by rail only a few hours from the great cities of Chicago, St. Louis, Cincinnati, Louisville, Indianapolis, and Toledo, and surrounded by fertile farms, it could become in an emergency a vast storehouse of supplies, a great base hospital for the suffering.

Unfortunately, it did not prove to be all that she had anticipated. The conditions specified and implied proved to be of such a character as to render the gift unsuitable for the purposes which she had hoped to accomplish. The manager into whose hands she committed its care proved incompetent and, in the end, ungrateful. The gift had to be relinquished and the money paid toward it was written down as a total loss.

In 1896 occurred Miss Barton's experience in Constantinople, where the Red Cross had its headquarters during her memorable work for the Armenians. There she visited Scutari, and gave an address on the scene of Florence Nightingale's great work. She returned overland through Vienna, Strassburg, Paris, London, and Liverpool. She left London October 8, 1896. On her return to Washington she was given a great banquet attended by some of the most distinguished people in Washington.

The following year, 1897, she was appointed by the President to attend the International Red Cross Congress in Vienna, Austria.

In 1898 she did her notable work in connection with the Spanish-American War, and for the next two years was fully occupied with affairs at home.

In 1902 she went abroad again, this time as a delegate to the conference held in St. Petersburg, the last of the great conferences which she attended. This journey has its record in two letters, one to her niece, Mrs. Ida Barton Riccius, and the other to her nephew, Stephen E. Barton:

En route from St. Petersburg to the German Frontier
June 18, 1902

The conference is ended, Russia has been visited, and we are well, and well on the way toward home. It has been a most fortunate journey, no accidents, no illness. Attended a great and harmonious conference, royally met and cared for, with nothing to be regretted.

We went first to Havre, France, to Paris for a few days, then to Berlin a few days, then on toward Russia. At the crossing on the frontier, we were met by a Red Cross escort, and taken on, for transportation to St. Petersburg, about the 15th of May. Went into Hotel de France, where we have remained till yesterday, nearly three weeks. The conference opened on the 16th with two sittings a day, and entertainments at evening unless it was necessary to take the day for some excursion, or visit to some royal entertainment. The conference lasted about eight days: it was composed of delegates from nearly fifty nations', subjects of a humanitarian character were discussed as connected with the work of the Red Cross. In Russia everything is Red Cross, all hospital work, all emergency work, nearly all relief work, care of children, orphans, foundlings. The women are educated to do this work. They enter the schools in the hospitals at eighteen to twenty, serve one year on probation, two as novices, then they may receive and wear the Red Cross and be nurses, at a small sum in money per month, board, clothes, care if sick—a good home as long as they live. When too old, or no longer able to work, they have pensions given them and may remain in the hospital and be cared for always if they choose or if they have relatives and want to live with them they can have their pensions and go to them, and return always if they like. The hospital is always their home, if they want it, or they may marry if they choose; then they leave. They seemed so happy, looked so healthy; many of them are orphan girls who had no home; nowhere else to be. They are not Catholic, but of the Protestant Church of Russia, though I see little difference between it and the Catholic. The churches are magnificent—sock wealth of ornamentation. The bishops seem like Catholic priests. The people are very devout, but still very lively, and kind; they seem to me to be the kindest people I ever saw. All the royal persons look kind; they have good faces; but the kindest face of all is that of the Czar. He is young, handsome, looks like a mature college graduate. The Czarina is also handsome; she was the granddaughter of Queen Victoria; they have four children, are very food of them, and of end offer.

We went on an excursion to Moscow, saw the city Napoleon went to capture, and which he found trouble in getting out of. We wait to the Kremlin where he stayed; the rooms he lived in the few days while the city was burning, and the ways by which he retreated. We visited the Grand Duke, who is the Governor-General of Moscow, and whose wife is sister of the Empress, another granddaughter of Victoria, the daughter of Alice of Hesse, who died many years ago of diphtheria while nursing three children through it. The Grand Duchess is said to be the handsomest woman in Russia. I think that may be true, and after I returned to Petersburg she sent me her picture—beautiful!! Everybody was so kind to us all, but I felt they were especially kind to me. I never saw such treatment of guests; they wouldn't let you spend money. Carriages were at the disposal of all the delegates, all places of amusement free, guides provided; lunches, like dinners, provided each day at the conference, a hundred persons fed somewhere, two or three times a day, and such feeding!! Very many of the delegates were old friends of mine. I had met them in five other conferences; they were so genial and attentive.

As I am going to ask you to let Ada and Mamie read this, and Harold, too, I must tell you about the horses, the finest I have ever seen. They have two choice kinds, the "black Orlorf," and the dapple gray, good size, carriage horses, and they go like the wind. The Orlorf was brought into St. Petersburg (perhaps into Russia as well) by Count Orlorf a good many years ago. The males are not changed, kept as stallions in full strength and spirit, and, when past active or first-class service, are kept for breeding purposes. They are not allowed to be sold out of Russia, it is said. They weigh from one thousand to fourteen hundred pounds, are jet black, have glossy hair, high arching necks, step as proud as war-horses, with full even tails, trimmed at the bottom to keep them from touching the ground. The Russian harness is not half the weight of ours, and much less of it; the shafts are kept away from the body, and all horses are round and fat. I have not seen a poor horse in Russia. The grays are much like the black, only dappled, as if painted, so dark, and distinct dapples, with also the heavy beautiful tails. I asked to go through the Royal stalls—the Czar has eight hundred horses in his stud; a part are in Peterhof, ten miles away. The horses were in stalls about two thirds as wide, big stalls as Baba's, say six to seven feet, with wooden floors, a narrow crack running the whole length to keep them dry, half a foot of clean dry straw in each, a little manger for grain, a little wire rack for hay, a good blanket on each, and you have the entire outfit of this beautiful "stud of Royal horses." They were gentle and didn't mind a strange hand on them, and the gentlemanly uniformed groom encouraged it, and smiled at their quiet, good behaviour. Some of the carriages are for two, some four, and some eight horses. The gilded and gemmed carriages are especially for Coronation occasions, some of them one hundred and fifty years old, bright and beautiful as yesterday. Ordinarily the Royal people ride in common carriages and drive a great deal, to hospitals, to all houses of charity, schools, orphanages, and churches. They are the patrons of all these, and give great sums to them.

The Empress has schools of hundreds of young women and young ladies in St. Petersburg studying from the lowest to the highest branches, art and literature, which she visits every week; they are fitting themselves, not alone for society, but to go all over Russia to teach. The Russians have all the societies we have, "Prevention of Cruelty to Animals," which they don't seem to need as much as we do. I might except temperance societies, which they do not have, and probably need about as much as we, only the Russian doesn't fight and quarrel when he gets drunk; he goes to sleep.

This is an unmercifully long letter. I wish you would let it go to Ada and Mamie. If I had a typewriter I would duplicate it, and send to each, but I have none, and write all by hand. I will take this on to Berlin to post, where we shall arrive at ten to-morrow morning, for a few days' stay.

With greatest love to all,
Your always loving

Clara

This is my "howdy" to all the loved ones, from Europe.

491

Hôtel Scribe, Rue Scribe Paris, July 26, 1902

My dear Steve:

This is Saturday, and I sail to-morrow. I did not intend to write you in time for you to receive it, and perhaps feel that you must fly around to meet me in New York. I only wanted to tell you that—and when I would sail so you could calculate in what country I should most likely be. I go to Boulogne tomorrow, Sunday morning, July 27th, to catch the S.S. Pennsylvania as she steams on for New York. I expect to find Mr. Tillinghast on board, as he has arranged to finish his month's tour of southern Europe in time to take the Pennsylvania at Hamburg. Boulogne is her last point of land, and anyone knowing me would conclude I would stick to the land as long as possible.

We had a glorious conference, and were gloriously received, no kindness or courtesy, and sometimes it seemed as if no luxury, was omitted. There were no errors, and perfect harmony prevailed. We went on an excursion to Moscow for three days, returned to Petersburg, finished all up, did nothing carelessly, nor in too great haste; wrote my report of the conference, some twenty pages, sent it to President Roosevelt; made out all my accounts with the Government ready to present on my return; and when all was finished, left with Mr. Tillinghast, who took the place of secretary, for Berlin; remained a week, when Mr. Tillinghast started on his journey of sight-seeing. The other delegates had long gone, and I made for Carlsruhe for a stay of two weeks. My time was divided between the Grand Duchess and Princess Salm Salm,* who, at present, resides there. The Salm Salm was one of the old high houses of Germany, and greatly venerated for patriotic and noble qualities. The husband of the Princess you will remember historically, perhaps. Prince Felix left Germany to fight in our war; raised a regiment, became its colonel, till the close, then followed Maximilian to Mexico, stayed by him, with the Princess, till he was shot, then returned to Germany to his estates at Gravelotte. Not a bad record!

*The Princess Felix Salm Salm was an American married to a Prussian prince who served during the Civil War. She lived a remarkable life, also

492

serving during wartime. Her memoir is <u>An American Princess in the Civil War</u>.

I remained at Carlsruhe till the "close of the Court Season," was present by invitation at the closing of the Parliament, heard the Grand Duke deliver his splendid address, spent the evening after socially, and alone, with the Grand Duke and Duchess, till eleven o'clock. At two they started for the mountains, the Princess two days later; and between them I slipped off to Strassburg, then to Geneva, then via Strassburg again to Paris, to wait for my steamer. The Pennsylvania is not a quick but is a steady-going sailer, and will, D.V., get us over in about eight days, when I will quietly slip down home, as if I had never been away. No mistakes have been made, no bad luck, not a day's illness of any one that I know of. Well enough managed, it seems to me, and fortunately ended, if it does end well the rest of the way.

I didn't intend to write so much. What you haven't time to read you can put in your pocket. Love to all.

CLARA BARTON IN CUBA

For many years before the outbreak of the war with Spain, Clara Barton had been interested in the situation in Cuba. In a letter written from Washington, February 8, 1874, twenty-four years before the outbreak of the war with Spain, she said:

Spain is still fighting her only or almost sole remaining colony, Cuba. Spain had once immense colonies, but she has been so tyrannical and so careless of their welfare that she has lost nearly all. And Cuba, you know, "has an insurgent army," of so-called rebels fighting for their freedom. If she ever gets free, she must come to the United States, as she is too small to stand alone against the greed of great powers which will try to gobble her up for her riches in soil and products. The Spanish authorities have just published a new list of orders, very stringent, and they hope to crush out the Cuban insurrection in six months. You must keep watch of that, too, and see how it ends. It will be history by and by to whom Cuba belongs, and, while one has to study so hard to learn past history, it is not worth the while to let slip that which all the time is making in our own day and generation. *Comprenez vous?*

Her forecast of events proved to be reliable. The relations between Spain and Cuba grew more and more strained. A part of the Spanish policy for stamping out the rebellion in Cuba was the concentration of that portion of the civilian population believed to be hostile to the Spanish Government, in concentration camps, from which the cry of distress was continuous. Sympathy in America grew more and more pronounced, but for a long time there appeared no way in which the United States could offer relief. The difficulties of the situation were the greater because the Spanish Government believed, with some reason, that a considerable part of the American sentiment favorable to relief in Cuba was intermixed with political designs. There were, indeed, two groups of people demanding relief for Cuba. Clara Barton thus describes them:

They might have properly been classed under two distinct heads. The one, merely the friends of humanity in its simple sense; the other, friends of humanity also, but what seemed to them a broader

494

and deeper sense, far more complex. They sought to remove a cause as well as an effect, and the muffled cry of "Cuba Libre" became their watchword. Naturally, any general movement by the people in favor of the former must have the effect to diminish the contributions of the latter, too small at best for their purpose, and must be wisely discouraged. Thus, whenever an unsuspecting movement was set on foot by some good-hearted, unsophisticated body of people, and began to gain favor with the public and the press, immediately would appear most convincing counter-paragraphs to the effect that it would be useless to send relief, especially by the Red Cross:

First, it would not be permitted to land.

Next, whatever it took would be either seized outright, or "wheedled" out of hand by the Spanish authorities in Havana.

That the Spaniards would be only too glad to have the United States send food and money for the use of Havana.

Again, that the Red Cross, being international, would affiliate with Spain, and ignore the "Cuban Red Cross" already working there and here. As if poor Cuba, with no national government or treaty-making power, could have a legitimate Red Cross that other nations could recognize or work with.

Miss Barton had but recently returned from Armenia. Her experience with the Turkish Government made her keenly aware of all the obstructions which an unsympathetic government can put in the way of philanthropic relief. It was useless to attempt any assistance for the sufferers in Cuba unless Miss Barton had the full approval of the American Government, and in addition the sympathetic cooperation of the Spanish Government. But if she secured the consent of the Government of Spain, there was real danger that her work of relief would result less in the succor of the distressed people of Cuba than in the aid and comfort of the armies of their oppressors. Spain could not be expected to look with favor upon any kind of relief which promised to strengthen the Cuban rebellion. At length, however, the situation grew intolerable; it became evident that the United States must go into Cuba either with an army of occupation or an agency for the relief of suffering. As a matter of fact, the United States went in both capacities, but the Red Cross went in before the Stars and Stripes. Miss Barton herself has told the story of the invasion:

This state of things continued through the year of 1897, but as the present year of '98 opened the reports of suffering that came were not to be borne quietly, and I decided to confer with our Government and learn if it had objections to the Red Cross taking steps of its own in direct touch with the people of the country, and proposing their cooperation in the work of relief. I beg pardon for the personality of the statement which follows, but it is history I am asked to write.

Deciding to refer my inquiry to the Secretary of State, I called at his department to see him, but learned that he was with the President. This suiting my purpose, I followed to the Executive Mansion, was kindly informed that the President and Secretary were engaged on a very important matter, and had given orders not to be interrupted. As I turned to leave I was recalled with, "Wait a moment, Miss Barton, and let me present your card." Returning immediately, I entered the President's room to find these two men in a perplexed study over the very matter which had called me. Distressed by the reports of the terrible condition of things so new to us, they were seeking some remedy, and, producing their notes just taken, revealed the fact that they had decided to call me into conference.

The conference was then held. It was decided to form a committee in New York, to ask money and material of the people at large to be shipped to Cuba for the relief of the *reconcentrados* on that island. The call would be made in the name of the President, and the committee naturally known as the "President's Committee for Cuban Relief." I was courteously asked if I would go to New York and assume the oversight of that committee. I declined in favor of Mr. Stephen E. Barton, second vice-president of the National Red Cross, who, on being immediately called, accepted; and with Mr. Charles Schierenas treasurer and Mr. Louis Klopsch of the *Christian*

Herald, as the third member, the committee was at once established; since known as the "Central Cuban Relief Committee."

The committee was to solicit aid in money and material for the suffering *reconcentrados* in Cuba, and forward the same to the Consul-General at Havana for distribution. My consent was then asked by all parties to go to Cuba and aid in the distribution of the shipments of food as they should arrive. After all I had so long offered, I could not decline, and hoping my going would not be misunderstood by our authorities there, who would regard me simply as a willing assistant, I accepted. The Consul-General had asked the New York Committee to send to him an assistant to take charge of the warehouse and supplies in Havana. This request was also referred to me, and recommending Mr. J. K. Elwell, nephew of General J. J. El-well, of Cleveland, Ohio, a gentleman who had resided six years in Santiago in connection with its large shipping interests, a fine business man and speaking Spanish, I decided to accompany him, taking no member of my own staff, but going simply in the capacity of an individual helper in a work already assigned.

On Saturday, February 6, we left Washington for Cuba via Jacksonville, Tampa, and Key West.

Thus, with that simple beginning, with no thought on the part of any person but to do unobtrusively the little that could be done for the lessening of the woes of a small island of people, whom adverse circumstances, racial differences, the inevitable results of a struggle for freedom, the fate of war, and the terrible features of a system of subjugation of a people, which, if true, is too dark to name, was commenced the relief movement of 1898 which has spread not alone over the entire United States of America from Maine to California, from Vancouver to the Gulf of Mexico, but from the Indias on the west, to the Indias on the east, and uniting in its free-will offerings the gifts of one third of the best nations in the world.

Miss Barton with her cargo of supplies reached Havana on February 9, 1898. Her supplies were unloaded and stored in a convenient warehouse. She began her work of visitation and found scenes beside which, as she wrote, some which she had witnessed in

Armenia seemed humane. Six days after her arrival the Maine was blown up. The appalling news reached the United States and brought with it the practical certainty of war. The one cheering message that came as an echo of the explosion was Clara Barton's telegram, "I am with the wounded."

Miss Barton thus related the story of the sinking of the Maine, and of the work that followed:

The heavy clerical work of that fifteenth day of February held not only myself, but Mr. Elwell as well, busy at our writing-tables until late at night. The house had grown still; the noises on the streets were dying away, when suddenly the table shook from under our hands, the great glass door opening on to the veranda, facing the sea, flew open; everything in the room was in motion or out of place—the deafening roar of such a burst of thunder as perhaps one never heard before, and off to the right, out over the bay, the air was filled with a blaze of light, and this in turn filled with black specks like huge specters flying in all directions. Then it faded away. The bells rang; the whistles blew; and voices in the street were heard for a moment; then all was quiet again. I supposed it to be the bursting of some mammoth mortar or explosion of some magazine. A few hours later came the terrible news of the Maine.

Mr. Elwell was early among the wreckage, and returned to give me news.

She is destroyed. There is no room for comment, only who is lost, who has escaped, and what can be done for them? They tell us that most of the officers were dining out, and thus saved; that Captain Sigsbee is saved. It is thought that two hundred and fifty men are lost, that one hundred are wounded, but still living, some in hospital, some on small boats as picked up. The chief engineer, a quiet, resolute man, and the second officer met me as I passed out of the hotel for the hospital. The latter stopped me saying, "Miss Barton, do you remember you told me on board the Maine that the Red Cross was at our service; for whenever anything took place with that ship, either in naval action or otherwise, someone would be hurt; that she was not of a structure to take misfortune lightly?" I recalled the conversation and the impression which led to it—such strength would never go out easily.

We proceeded to the Spanish hospital San Ambrosia, to find thirty to forty wounded—bruised, cut, burned; they had been crushed by timbers, cut by iron, scorched by fire, and blown sometimes high in the air, sometimes driven down through the red-hot furnace room and out into the water, senseless, to be picked up by some boat and gotten ashore. Their wounds are all over them—heads and faces terribly cut, internal wounds, arms, legs, feet, and hands burned to the live flesh. The hair and beards are singed, showing that the bums were from fire and not steam; besides further evidence shows that the burns are where the parts were uncovered. If burned by steam, the clothing would have held the steam and burned all the deeper. As it is, it protected from the heat and the fire and saved their limbs, whilst the faces, hands, and arms are terribly burned. Both men and officers are very reticent in regard to the cause, but all declare it could not have been the result of an internal explosion. That the boilers were at the two ends of the ship, and these were the places from which all escaped who did escape. The trouble was evidently from the center of the ship, where no explosive machinery was located.

I thought to take the names as I passed among them, and, drawing near to the first in the long line, I asked his name. He gave it with his address; then peering out from among the bandages and cotton about his breast and face, he looked earnestly at me and asked: "Isn't this Miss Barton?" "Yes." "I thought it must be. I knew you were here, and thought you would come to us. I am so thankful for us all."

I asked if he wanted anything. "Yes. There is a lady to whom I was to be married. The time is up. She will be frantic if she hears of this accident and nothing more. Could you telegraph her?" "Certainly!" The dispatch went at once: "Wounded, but saved." Alas, it was only for a little; two days later, and it was all over.

I passed on from one to another, till twelve had been spoken to and the names taken. There were only two of the number who did not recognize me. Their expressions of grateful thanks, spoken under such conditions, were too much. I passed the pencil to another hand and stepped aside.

I am glad to say that every kindness was extended to them. Miss Mary Wilberforce had been at once installed as nurse, and faithful work she performed. The Spanish hospital attendants were tireless in their attentions. Still, there was boundless room for luxuries and comforts, delicate foods, grapes, oranges, wines, cordials, anything that could soothe or interest; and no opportunity was lost, or cost or pains spared, and when two days later the streets filled with hearses bearing reverently the bodies of martyred heroes; and the crape and the flowers mingled in their tributes of tenderness and beauty, and the muffled drums and tolling bells spoke all that inanimate substance could speak of sorrow and respect; and the silent marching tread of armies fell upon the listening ear—the heart grew sick in the midst of all this pageant, and the thoughts turned away to the far land, smitten with horror, and the homes wailing in bitter grief for these, so lone, so lost.

In the days after the sinking of the Maine, Miss Barton led an active life. She journeyed through the nearer provinces, established bases of supplies and returned to Havana, not only unmolested, but with every evidence of appreciation on the part of the Spanish authorities and the Cuban people. The Red Cross supplies were distributed, though in places their distribution was impeded. Miss Barton tells of a delayed distribution at Matanzas, the delay apparently having been accomplished with intent, and how well-meant private philanthropy undertook direct action:

It is not strange that from this event went out the cry of "starving Matanzas," although at that moment, in addition to our four tons of goods previously sent, the Fern lay in the harbor under the American flag, with fifty tons of American supplies, and fifty rods away lay the Bergen, under the same colors, bearing a cargo of fifty-two tons from the Philadelphia Red Cross, faithfully sent through the New York Committee, by request. So uncontrollable a thing is human excitement that these facts could not be taken in, and the charities of our whole country were called afresh to arms over "starving Matanzas," which was at that moment by far the best provided city in Cuba. The result of this was an entire train of supplies from Kansas, which, remaining there after the blockade, not being consigned to the Red Cross, was, we were informed, distributed among the Spanish soldiery by the Spanish officials. Goods bearing the mark of the Red Cross were everywhere respected, and we have no record of any of our goods having been appropriated by the Spanish authorities.

When the methods of relief had been well organized, the work of distribution went mainly to others while Clara Barton devoted her own energy to the maintenance of pleasant relations with the Spanish authorities. This she was able to do until the very end; but events far beyond her control were inevitably driving the two nations into war. Miss Barton tells the story in the following record based upon the entries in her own diary:

I met the Spanish authorities, not merely as a bearer of relief, but as the president of the American National Red Cross, with all the principles of neutrality which that implied, and received in return the unfailing courtesy which the conditions demanded. From our first interview to the last sad day when we decided that it was better to withdraw, giving up all efforts at relief, and leave those thousands of poor, dying wretches to their fate, there was never any change in the attitude of the Spanish authorities, General Blanco, or his staff, toward myself or any member of my staff. One of my last visits before the blockade was to the palace. The same kindly spirit prevailed; I was begged not to leave the island through fear of them; every protection in their power would be given, but there was no guarantee for what might occur in the exigencies of war. I recall an incident of that day: General Blanco led me to the large salon, the walls of which are covered with the portraits of the Spanish officials for generations past, and, pointing to the Spanish authorities under date of 1776, said, with a look of sadness, "When your country was in trouble, Spain was the friend of America. Now Spain is in trouble, America is her enemy." I knew no answer for this but silence, and we passed out through the corridor of guards, he handing me to my carriage with a farewell and a blessing. I could but recall my experience with the Turkish officials and Government, where I entered with such apprehension and left with such marks of cordiality.

During this interval of time important business had called me to Washington, and I only returned to Cuba sometime during the second week of April.

On April 25, 1898, Congress declared war against Spain. For two weeks it had been apparent that such a declaration was to come. American citizens were ordered by the United States Government to leave Havana some days before the outbreak of hostilities. This situation sent Miss Barton out of Cuba and quickly sent her back again. She was not, however, permitted at once to continue her relief for the distressed Cubans. The military and naval authorities of the United States were as anxious not to aid Spain as the Spanish authorities were anxious that she should not aid the rebellious Cubans. Miss Barton tells the story of her departure and return:

The order was for all American citizens to leave Havana, and the order was obeyed, but not without having laid the matter formally in council before my staff of assistants and taking their opinion and advice, which was to the effect that, while personally they would prefer to remain for the chance of the little good that might be accomplished, in view of the distress which we should give our friends at home, and, in fact, the whole country, when it should be known that we were inside that wall of fire that would confront us, with no way of extricating or reaching us, it seemed both wiser and more humane to leave. And the 9th of April saw us again on shipboard, a party of twenty, bound for Tampa. We would not, however, go beyond, but made headquarters there, remaining within easy call of any need there might be for us. Here follow the few weeks of impending war. Do we need to live them over? Do we even want to recall them? Days when the elder men of thought and memory pondered deeply and questioned much! When the mother, patriot though she were, uttered her sentiments through choking voice and tender, trembling words, and the young men, caring nothing, fearing nothing, rushed gallantly on to doom and to death! To how many households, alas, these days recall themselves in tones never to be forgotten!

Notwithstanding all this excitement and confusion and all the pressure that weighed upon him, our good President still remembered the suffering, dying *reconcentrados*, and requested that a ship be provided as quickly as possible, loaded from the warerooms of the indefatigable Cuban Relief Committee in New York, and be sent for the relief of the sufferers in Cuba whenever they could be reached. One need not say with what promptness this committee acted, and I was informed that the State of Texas, laden with fourteen hundred tons of food, would shortly leave New York en route for Key West, and it was the desire of that committee and the Government that I take command of the ship, and, with my staff and such assistants as I would select, undertake the getting of that food to its destination.

Some members of the staff were in New York, and with Dr. Hubbell in charge sailed from that port on Saturday, the 23d of April. A hasty trip from Washington, gathering up the waiting staff at Tampa, and pushing on by the earliest train brought us to Key West in time to meet the State of Texas as she arrived, board her and take charge of the snug little ship that was henceforth to take its place in American history. She was well built, but by no means new, nor handsome. Her dull black hull could in no way compare with the snow-white, green and red striped hospital ships, those heralds of relief that afterwards graced the waters of that bay. Still she was firm, sound, heavy-laden, and gave promise of some good to someone at some future day, that day being only when the great war monsters should have pealed out to the world that an entrance was made on the coast of Cuba, and we would be invited to follow.

By the authorities at Washington, the State of Texas had been consigned to the protection of the navy, and accordingly we must report our arrival. This was done to the senior officer, representing Admiral Sampson, in the port, Captain Harrington, of the monitor Puritan. This brought at once a personal call from the captain with an invitation to our entire staff to visit his beautiful ship the following day. The launch of the Puritan was sent to take us, and not only was the ship inspected, but the dainties of his elegant tea-table as well.

503

When all was over, the graceful launch returned us safely to our ship, with grateful memories on the part of the younger members of our company, who had never chanced to form an intimate acquaintance with a piece of shipping at once so beautiful and so terrible as that death-dealing engine of destruction. I record this visit and courtesy on the part of Captain Harrington as the first of an unfailing series of kindnesses extended by the navy to the Red Cross from first to last. There was no favor too great, no courtesy too high to be cheerfully rendered on every occasion.

The memories of pitiful Cuba would not leave us, and, knowing that under our decks were fourteen hundred tons of food, for the want of which its people were dying, the impulse to reach them grew very strong, and a letter was addressed to Admiral Sampson.

This brought immediately the launch of the New York to the side of our ship, and Captain Chadwick, the gallant officer whom no one forgets, stepped lightly on board to deliver the written message from the admiral, or rather to take me to the New York. Nothing could have exceeded the courtesy of the admiral, but we were acting from entirely opposite standpoints. I had been requested to take a ship, and by every means in my power get food into Cuba. He, on the other hand, had been commanded to take a fleet, and by every means in his power keep food out of Cuba. When one compared the two ships lying side by side and thought of a contest of effort between them, the situation was ludicrous, and yet the admiral did not absolutely refuse to give me a flag of truce and attempt an entrance into Havana; but he disapproved it, feared the results for me, and, acting in accordance with his highest wisdom and best judgment, I felt it to be my place to wait.

The delay which resulted was annoying but not wholly unprofitable, and there came a time when the army and navy were glad enough to have the American Red Cross in Cuba. On June 20th the Stale of Texas sailed from Key West with orders to find Admiral Sampson and report to him. They found him a few days later off Santiago, in time for their share in the stirring events which accompanied and followed the destruction of Cervera's fleet, the battle of San Juan Hill, and the surrender on July 17th of the harbor and city of Santiago.

When the city had been formally surrendered and a sufficient number of mines had been removed from the harbor to permit American vessels to enter, a very gracious compliment was paid to Clara Barton by the victorious United States Navy. The first vessel to enter the harbor was not the flagship of either of the Admirals Sampson or Schley, but the State of Texas under command of Clara Barton.

Perhaps that may be called the crowning moment of her life. Clara Barton was more than seventy-eight years old, but she stood erect on the deck of her vessel, modestly appreciative and quietly thankful, not so much for the honor that had come to her as for the opportunity of serving.

Miss Barton returned to Washington in November, 1898. The work which she went to Cuba to perform, that of relieving the Cuban *reconcentrados*, was never wholly accomplished. That relief came with the freedom of Cuba, and for this she was profoundly thankful; but she never ceased to feel sad when she thought of the people who suffered during those weeks of waiting while her vessel was packed with the supplies which the people so sorely needed. "Cuba was a hard field, full of heartbreaking memories," she wrote. "It gave the first opportunity to test the first cooperation between the United States and its supplemental hand-maiden the Red Cross."

While this cooperation was incomplete, its results were most beneficial, as many an American soldier and surgeon can testify.

At the close of the war, the Congress of the United States tendered the thanks of the Nation to Clara Barton in the following resolution which was introduced in the Senate by the venerable Senator Hoar, and unanimously adopted:

Resolved, That the thanks of Congress be presented to Clara Barton, of Massachusetts, founder of the institution of the Red Cross, and to the officers and agents of the Society of the Red Cross for their humane and beneficent service to humanity in relieving the distress of the Armenians and other suffering persons in Turkey, and in ministering to the sufferings caused by pestilence in the United States, and for the like ministration and relief given by them to both sides in the Spanish West Indies during the present war.

An even higher mark of appreciation was contained in the annual message of President McKinley:

In this connection it is a pleasure for me to mention in terms of cordial appreciation the timely and useful work of the American National Red Cross both in relief measures preparatory to the campaigns, in sanitary assistance at several of the camps of assemblage, and later, under the able and experienced leadership of the president of the society, Miss Clara Barton, on the fields of battle and in the hospitals at the front in Cuba. Working in conjunction with the governmental authorities and under their sanction and approval, and with the enthusiastic cooperation of many patriotic women and societies in the various States, the Red Cross has fully maintained its already high reputation for intense earnestness and ability to exercise the noble purposes of its international organization, thus justifying the confidence and support which it has received at the hands of the American people. To the members and officers of this society and all who aided them in their philanthropic work, the sincere and lasting gratitude of the soldiers and the public is due and is freely accorded.

In tracing these events we are constantly reminded of our obligations to the Divine Master for his watchful care over us and his safe guidance, for which the nation makes reverent acknowledgment and offers humble prayer for the continuance of his favor.

RETIREMENT FROM THE RED CROSS

It would have been well if Clara Barton had retired from the active work of the presidency of the American Red Cross at the close of the war with Spain. She had accomplished in her lifetime an almost incredible total of heroic work. She had completed seventy-eight years of service; she had created the American Red Cross and led it successfully in peace and war. On twenty different fields on both sides of the ocean she had raised its banner over areas devastated by fire, flood, famine, and pestilence. She had won the support of her Government to an enterprise till then unknown and but little regarded. She had made the Red Cross in America so useful in times of peace that the Red Cross societies of the world had widened their spheres of operation to incorporate her plans of service. She had crowned her long and arduous career with an achievement that won for her the heart of the American army and navy in Cuba, and brought to her the thanks of the Congress and of the President of the United States. She could have retired with honors such as no woman in America ever had won. If her judgment told her that this was the time for her to transfer her burden of active supervision to some younger person, her heart triumphed over her judgment.

She was eighty years of age when, on September 8, 1900, a tornado and tidal wave submerged Galveston, Texas. Five days later Clara Barton was on the ground.

Difficulties of transportation held her back for twenty-four hours or she would have been there a day sooner.

Her plea for lumber, hardware, and other materials for providing temporary shelter met with a nation-wide response, and supplies of food and clothing, as well as considerable sums of money, were placed at her disposal.

After six weeks spent in Texas, Clara Barton returned, worn out by her exertions, but bringing the grateful thanks of the people of Galveston, and, in addition, an official letter of thanks from the governor of the State of Texas and also of its legislature. The Central Relief Committee of Galveston also tendered her a series of engrossed resolutions, declaring that she deserved to be "exalted above queens," and that her achievements were "greater than the conquests of nations or the inventions of genius."

In the following year occurred the seventh International Conference of the Red Cross, already referred to, held at St. Petersburg in Russia and extending from the middle of May until near the end of June of 1902. Clara Barton headed the delegation from the United States. The conference was held under the high patronage of Her Majesty the Empress Dowager Marie Feodorovna. Miss Barton was the guest of the Emperor and Empress. No delegate to the conference was treated with greater consideration than Clara Barton. At the close of the conference she was decorated by the Emperor, who conferred upon Clara Barton the Russian decoration of the Order of the Red Cross.

Two of her letters concerning this journey have been quoted in a previous chapter. Clara Barton returned to her own land crowned with additional honors, but confronting new and wholly unexpected difficulties.

The American Red Cross had been reincorporated by Act of Congress June 6, 1900. Under the new form of organization the board and its executive committee possessed large powers. There was a feeling on the part of some members of the board that the American Red Cross was too exclusively under the direction of Clara Barton. Her work for the relief of Galveston had been undertaken almost the moment that she first learned of its great need. She had not waited to call an executive committee meeting. While her work in that field was most heartily commended, there was a feeling on the part of members of the board that the Red Cross, being now virtually a representative organ of the United States Government, its fields of service should be determined, not by the judgment of an individual, but of the governing body of the organization itself. There was further criticism growing out of the fact that, when emergencies arose by reason of any great national disaster, a considerable part of the money was sent direct to Clara Barton on the field, and expended by her without passing through the hands of the treasurer.

Miss Barton admitted that she had made these decisions at times without the formal authority of her executive committee, and that she had received and expended money according to her best judgment when the emergency was at hand. She did not desire to be bound by burdensome restrictions; she wished to be at liberty to meet the need whenever it should arrive, and in the way that seemed to be necessary.

If everything had gone well with the Red Cross during the absence of Clara Barton at St. Petersburg in 1902, it may be that she would have consented to retire on her return from that notable experience. It was hardly likely that any further honor could have come to her higher than that which she had already received. Theoretically she ought to have been training up assistants who would act effectively in her absence, and in time succeed her. It was in some respects a limitation on her part that she had not found assistants to whom she could delegate authority with confidence that it would be properly used. On the other hand, she had made some experiments in training up associates, and found reason to regret it.

While Clara Barton was on her way to St. Petersburg the disastrous Mont Pelé earthquake occurred. She had left the American Red Cross organized with a board of control which gave it authority to act in such an emergency. She returned from St. Petersburg bitterly disappointed because the American Red Cross played in that disaster, as she felt, a wholly insignificant part. It seemed to her to have displayed a complete lack of that initiative which had always characterized her action under such conditions.

Rightly or wrongly Miss Barton felt that this inability to act promptly and decisively was in some measure the result of a divided authority. She thereupon set in motion an effort to amend the by-laws so as to increase the power of the president. These changed by-laws were adopted at the annual meeting of the American Red Cross in Washington, December 9, 1902. Clara Barton was elected president for life and given the authority which she deemed requisite for effective action.

An earnest protest was made against Miss Barton's increase of power, and the disaffection increased through- out the year 1903.

On January 2, 1904, President Roosevelt notified Miss Barton that he could no longer serve as an officer of the Red Cross in the condition of unrest which had developed.

Three weeks later, on January 29th, the minority of the American Red Cross presented a memorial to Congress charging that under the new form of organization practically all power was centered in the president of the society, who was elected for life and permitted to choose her own executive committee. A committee of investigation was appointed to inquire into the affairs of the Red Cross. Of this committee Senator Redfield Proctor was chairman.

It would be difficult to describe the emotions of Clara Barton when she knew of the appointment of this committee. She was shocked and horrified. She felt as if it had been a personal disgrace; and what was worse, as she viewed it, she feared that it would result in a dissension that would ruin the American Red Cross. On the other hand, she had no mind to retire while the investigation was on. Whatever happened, she would not resign until the investigation ended.

The committee of investigation appears to have been a very sensible body. It set about gathering such material as it needed, and the examination of such witnesses as were produced by the remonstrants.

The remonstrance did not contain any charges of any dishonesty on the part of Miss Barton in the administration of the affairs of the Red Cross; or, any charge of misappropriation of any property or money by Miss Barton; or any improper act or conduct of any kind which involved any element of moral turpitude.

The charges were, in brief:

(a) That proper books of accounts were not kept at all times; and

(б) that the property and funds of the Red Cross were not at all times distributed upon the order of the treasurer of the society, as alleged to be required by the by-laws of the society; and

(c) that a certain tract of land in Lawrence County, Indiana, had been donated to the society by one Joseph Gardner; that the society was reincorporated after such donation, and such donation was never reported to the new corporation.

The reply to these charges, in brief, was that, in the main, proper books of account had been kept, but, in so far as accurate books of account had not been kept, it was due to the impossibility of keeping them while active work was in progress on the field of disaster, and, in so far as the by-laws of the society had not been complied with in the making of disbursements through the treasurer, it was impossible to do so during the stress of active relief work in the field; that so far as the Gardner donation of Indiana land was concerned, no Red Cross money had ever been invested in it; that the title to the real estate was always in the Red Cross and in the then existing corporate entity of the Red Cross, but that the land had not been found to be suited to the work of the Red Cross and the title thereto had been allowed to lapse because of the accumulation of taxes and charges for maintenance which were found to be in excess of the utility of the land to the Red Cross.

The committee of investigation held three meetings, on April 12, April 26, and May 2, 1904. Clara Barton did not attend in person, but was represented by counsel. It never became necessary for her to present her defense. At the close of the third meeting the chairman of the committee adjourned the hearing without day and the investigation came to an end. The committee never presented a report; there was no occasion to do so. The proceedings of the committee are obtainable by anyone who cares to read them, and they indicate with sufficient clearness the reasons which presumably influenced the committee in terminating the hearing after one side had been presented. There was no reason why the commit-tee needed to hear anything in defense of Clara Barton.

The investigation having ended, Clara Barton presented her resignation June 16, 1904. The resignation was accepted. The American Red Cross came under its new form of organization with the President of the United States as nominal President of the Red Cross. The committee of the opposition had proposed that Clara Barton be made honorary president for life with a salary to continue as long as she lived. She did not accept either the office or the money. She retired from the Red Cross, leaving it to the management of those who with her resignation came into its control. Her own relation with the organization ceased entirely.

Clara Barton was normally responsive to praise and abnormally sensitive to criticism. In all the years of her public life she never recovered from that supersensitiveness which had characterized her childhood. Fulsome and excessive praise disgusted her, but she enjoyed discriminating appreciation. Straightforward opposition she could meet and bear, but she shrank from criticism at the hands of those who had been her friends, and such criticism hurt her far more than anyone could imagine who beheld her self-possession and outward calm. She seemed to the world to take opposition somewhat lightly, but she bled within her armor from wounds which the world never suspected.

She retired from the Red Cross broken-hearted. Her common sense ought to have saved her from nine tenths of the suffering which she endured in that unhappy experience. She felt that she had been denationalized, repudiated by her own country, expatriated. She thought for a time that she could not continue to live in the United States, She turned her eyes toward Mexico, and thought of going there partly to escape from the sorrows which confronted her, and which she painfully exaggerated, and partly with the thought that she might there establish something corresponding to the American Red Cross. She had a friend in California, Mr. Charles S. Young, who knew much about Mexico. On January 13, 1904, after the appointment of the congressional committee and before any of its hearings, she wrote the following letter which came as near to being hysterical as anything that Clara Barton ever wrote:

You will never know how many times I have thought of you, in this last hard and dreadful year to me. I cannot tell you, I must not, and yet I must. So much of the time, under all the persecution, it has seemed to me I could not remain in this country, and have sought the range of the world for some place among strangers, and out of the way of people and mails, and longed for someone to point out a quiet place in some other land; my thoughts have fled to you, who could, at least, tell me a road to take outside of America, and who would ask the authorities of Mexico if a woman who could not live in her own country might find a home or a resting-place in theirs.

This will all sound very strange to you—you will wonder if I am "out of my mind." Let me answer—no. And if you had only a glimpse of what is put upon me to endure, you would not wonder, and in the goodness of your heart would hold open the gate to show me a mile track to some little mountain nook, where I might escape and wait in peace. Don't think this is common talk with me. I have never said it to others; and yet I think they who know me best mistrust that I cannot bear everything, and will try in some way to relieve myself.

To think of sitting here through an "investigation" by the country I have tried to serve—"in the interest of harmony" they say, when I have never spoken a discordant word in my life, meaningly, but have worked on in silence under the fire of the entire press of the United States for twelve months—forgiven all, offered friendship—and still am to be "investigated" for "inharmony," "unbusinesslike methods," and "too many years"—all of these I cannot help. I am still unanimously bidden to work on for "life," bear the burden of an organization—meet its costs myself—and am now threatened with the expense of the "investigation."

Can you wonder that I ask a bridle track? And that some other country might look inviting to me?

Mr. Young, this unhappy letter is a poor return to make for your friendly courtesy, but so long my dark thoughts have turned to you that I cannot find myself with the privilege of communicating with you, without expressing them. I cannot think where I have found the courage to do it, but I have.

I know how unwise a thing it seems, but if the pressure is too great the bands may break; that may be my case, and fearing that my better judgment might bid me put these sheets in the fire—I send them without once glancing over. You need not forget, but kindly remember, rather, that they are the wail of r an aching heart and that is all. Nature has provided a sure and final rest for all the heartaches that mortals are called to endure.

If you are in the East again, and I am here, I pray you to come to me.
Receive again my thanks and permit me to remain,
Your friend

Clara Barton

In conversation she said: "The Government which I thought I loved, and loyally tried to serve, has shut every door in my face and stared at me insultingly through its windows. What wonder I want to leave?"

In another conversation, referring to the abandonment of her dream of going to Mexico, she said: "There were but two countries where the Red Cross did not exist, China and Mexico. I did not want to go to China, but did want to go to Mexico, and fully intended to go. My friends finally dissuaded me and perhaps it was for the best, for if I had gone I probably would not have been alive now."

From this distance it is possible to view the whole situation in perspective. The present author has no hesitation in saying that the time had come for Clara Barton to retire from the active work of the administration of the American Red Cross. The organization had grown well beyond the ability of any one person to manage it in the way that Clara Barton had managed it so successfully in its earlier years. On her return either from Cuba or St. Petersburg, she ought to have retired, accepting the honorary presidency, and giving over the control and active management to younger people. The author has witnessed in not a few instances the pathetic struggle which goes on in the minds of elderly people on their prospective retirement from positions which have outgrown them. It is a situation nothing less than tragic.

A person long identified with an organization comes easily to believe, either that he cannot get on without it, or that it cannot get on without him. Clara Barton had come to believe the latter concerning the American Red Cross. She was mistaken.

There comes a time in the life of almost any organization when, if it is to prosper and enlarge, it must accept new leadership and adapt itself to changed conditions. A woman as sensible as Clara Barton was in most things should have realized this situation and not have permitted herself to be heart-broken by a change as necessary for her as it was for the Red Cross.

Nor is it necessary at this time to refer to the fact that the change might perhaps have been brought about in a kindlier spirit and with less of distress to a noble woman. If there was any lack of consideration for her, it will do no good now to remember it, nor to ascribe unworthy motives to any who had a share in it.

One thing, however, ought to be said concerning this tragic experience. If Clara Barton did not bear this sorrow like a philosopher, she bore it like a Christian. The author has searched her diaries and most intimate papers of this period without finding in any of them any spirit of personal resentment or desire for revenge. She felt that she had been deeply wronged, but she felt it not so much as a wrong done to her as an injury to the cause she loved. Her constant question was not, What will become of me? but, What will become of the Red Cross? Her books had been kept honestly and she knew it; but she also knew that, when money came to her on the field, she had been accustomed to spend it for the necessities of life for those she had come to help, and that not all of it had passed through the hands of the treasurer. She knew that no committee of Congress could find any of this money in her possession, but she also knew that her system of book-keeping had not been established with a view to a possibility of that kind of an audit. How would it affect the Red Cross if any scandal arose out of her unbusinesslike book-keeping?

She came in time to realize that she had taken this matter too seriously. She came to know the relief of lessened responsibility and to be glad that the Red Cross, with its cares and responsibilities and widening sphere of influence, had been safely transferred to other hands.

The author may be permitted to add a personal word. In his personal conversation with Clara Barton concerning these unhappy events he never heard her speak uncharitably of any of her opponents. He was not with her during the time of the actual difficulty, and has sometimes regretted that he was not there. Had he known all that he now knows from months of labor spent in the examination of her most intimate papers, he would have advised her to retire in 1898 or 1902, and to turn over all her records to her successors, and enjoy for herself a few years of unofficial honor before her long life closed. He did not at that time possess the intimate knowledge which now is in his possession, of the whole life and method of work of the American Red Cross under her administration. He is of the opinion that she ought to have accepted her retirement, not only willingly but gladly, and that she was far more troubled than she had need to be concerning the events which led to her retirement from office.

But this fact he records with sincere admiration for this noble woman, the author's friend and kinswoman, that in her conversation with him in the years that followed, and in her diaries and intimate self-revelations of her private papers, he has found no word that seems inspired by selfish ambition, by personal resentment, or by any unworthy motive.

CLARA BARTON AT HOME

Clara Barton loved a home. Although she went forth from her father's ample and generous house while still she was a young woman, and lived as school-teacher, department clerk, and humanitarian for many years, she never failed to make a home for herself if there was opportunity. Hotel life had no charms for her, and, while she enjoyed entertainment in the homes of her friends and was a gracious and appreciative guest, she always preferred a roof of her own above her head where she could be hostess rather than guest and could minister instead of being ministered unto. While she was a clerk in Washington, she had her own quarters to which she was accustomed to bring homeless women, girls who lacked friendship, and others who were in need. While she was in Europe during the Franco-Prussian War, although at times the guest of royalty, she fled from the too abundant hospitality of her friends and the excessive luxury of hotels, and lived in her own rented lodgings.

She owned, and kept until her death, a summer home in Oxford. But the home of which it is especially proper to speak is that which she erected for herself and the Red Cross, at Glen Echo, Maryland.

More than once Miss Barton had occasion to meditate on the prayer of Peter offered on the Mount of Transfiguration, that the disciples might be permitted to erect three tabernacles and remain with Jesus and the spirits of the glorified saints. "Lord, it is good to be here," is the enthusiastic cry of those who, being caught up by the spirit of a noble charity, see no reason why it should not continue permanently. Clara Barton saw to it that her work was discontinued when the need for it had passed.

When she finished her work at Johnstown, she was requested by the lumber dealers not to give away miscellaneously the material which had been used in the erection of her temporary Red Cross buildings. Times were returning to normal; there was employment at good wages for everyone who wanted to work; and there was no good reason why people should not buy their lumber or why the lumber business should be demoralized by thoughtless form of charity. Miss Barton knew that this was good sense. She learned who were the people who really needed and deserved free lumber, and these she assisted; but a portion of the lumber she shipped to Washington and erected at Glen Echo, a few miles out from the city, a permanent home for the American National Red Cross. Here she made her home during the remainder of her life. Now and then she returned for a few weeks to her summer home in Oxford, but the Red Cross Headquarters was where she lived and moved and had her being. There she dwelt and there she died.

It seemed to many to be far from an ideal home for her; it was a bare, barnlike sort of place with two tiers of rooms, the upper tier opening into a gallery as in the cabin of a steamboat. It was erected with reference to use as a possible storehouse and emergency hospital, as well as a central office building for the organization and a shelter for herself and her assistants. One might have expected that a woman who was at heart a tidy housekeeper would have preferred to put her warehouse and office building under one sufficiently ample roof, and to have erected for herself a little cottage adjacent; but Clara Barton lived and died surrounded by all that went into the daily performance of her work.

The author of this volume confesses to a certain chill and sinking of heart when he first saw the interior of the Glen Echo home. He wanted to take Clara Barton out of it and house her in a cozy little place of her own, where for a few hours of the day she could forget the Red Cross and all its cares. But Clara Barton gloried in those undecorated board walls as if they had been palatial. There she hung her diplomas and testimonials from foreign Governments as proudly as though they had been backed by glorious tapestry of cloth of gold. Her sitting-room was at the south of the house, overlooking the Potomac Canal; there she worked late at night and watched the moon as it rode over the tree-tops and reflected itself in the water. From the windows of her bedroom just above, she habitually witnessed the sunrise. Her narrow bed was a soldier's cot, and beside it was a little table with a candle, a pad of paper and a pencil. If, as often happened, she lay awake in the night, she did not fret over her insomnia, but lighted her candle, propped herself in bed, wrote down the good thoughts that came to her, and then blew out the candle and went to sleep, and was refreshed for work at five o'clock the next morning.

But there was a certain appropriateness in the construction of the Glen Echo home. One might look down from the bare walls that had seen service in Johnstown to find his feet on a rug presented by a Turkish Pasha; he searched the room in vain for relics, as such, for Clara Barton had no fondness for dust-gathering mementoes, but he could not fail to see about him inconspicuous trophies from hard-won fields of service. There was no luxury, but there was an ample, homely comfort in the air of the place. The main hall of the building was two stories high, with a gallery around the upper tier of rooms. It was a place for service, and that service was the joy and glory of her life.

Glen Echo is on the banks of a canal along the Potomac, about eight miles from the Capitol in Washington. This site she selected for herself in 1890, but did not occupy it until 1897. Her reasons for building there were that the location gave her convenient access to Washington, with ample space and freedom for outdoor life and opportunity for storage of Red Cross supplies without the excessive cost which an adequate building would have required in Washington.

At the time she erected her home, a Chautauqua Assembly was in operation in Glen Echo, and her house adjoined the grounds. Indeed, her home was almost one of the Chautauqua buildings, the front being of native stone such as was used in the construction of the large auditorium and Hall of Philosophy which stood within a stone's throw of her house. But the stone front which was the one picturesque feature of the house gave it a prison-like chill on the inside and had to be removed, and the Chautauqua Assembly itself went down and gave place to a summer amusement park. Spite of the changes in the environment, Clara Barton kept her home at Glen Echo. A Ferris wheel was erected at her front door; the roller-coaster went thundering by her window; the dancing in what had been the auditorium kept up till a late hour; and the goddess of folly with cap and bells superseded divine philosophy in the hall dedicated to the latter; but Clara Barton lived and died in her home in Glen Echo.

The inside of her house was not much more luxurious than the outside. Few homes have been erected with so little attempt at display, or with such modest provision for reasonable comfort.

In one aspect the Glen Echo home was fashioned almost like a cathedral, but in its practical arrangement much more like a ship. It had more windows than either a ship or a cathedral. They were almost as thick as they could be placed and leave any room for walls, but they were very plain windows, except that one on the stairs had a little inexpensive ornamentation and the glass in the two front doors had a red cross in each.

The front door faced north and led into a long wide hall, cool in summer, cold in winter, with an elongated oval well, railed round on the two upper floors, so that from the main deck one looked up to the upper deck and the boat deck of the ship-like building. This central three-deck cabin was ceiled with unpainted wood, not unattractive but unadorned. Doors opened on either side at regular intervals, and between the doors were deep closets where blankets, Horlick's Malted Milk, canned goods and emergency supplies of various kinds were duly stored and catalogued. If a fire or a flood broke out in any part of the country, Clara Barton was ready to start and had something with which to begin relief.

It was this attempt to combine in one a home, a storehouse, a place of refuge for the needy, and a kind of organization headquarters which struck the visitor so strangely and almost repellently. She might have built a little bungalow for herself and her offices and housed her supplies in a separate building erected for storage purposes and with emergency sleeping-rooms attached, but she wished it otherwise and she had her way.

If the reader had been privileged to visit Clara Barton there during her lifetime and had made his way down the rather long cabin to her own quarters in the south end of this ship-like cathedral, he would have found Clara Barton at home. It would have made little difference how early or how late the call was made. She was up with the sun and often before, weeding her garden, feeding her chickens, caring for her pets, and looking after her house. She rarely went to bed before midnight. Fourteen to eighteen hours a day of work she did steadily until her death.

Let us suppose that she has an important address to deliver to-morrow night. This is the way she prepares for it. She rises at five this morning and does her own room work. Her bedding is aired, her bed is made, and the carpet sweeper is rolling over her floor before six o'clock gives its warning to other members of the home-hold. She eats a simple breakfast with her household and guests and wastes no time, but still is in no haste about it. She gives no intimation that she is in a hurry, and enjoys the breakfast-table conversation, evincing a keen sense of humor and a hearty interest in all human happenings. She announces that she has attended to her most important correspondence for the morning, and excuses herself to see to the ways of her household. It is the day her curtains are to be washed, and she has to superintend affairs in the laundry and make some changes in her garden. She puts in very nearly the whole day in physical labor. She knows well how to direct the work of others, but she does not scorn to take the flatiron or the garden trowel in her own hands and show how she wants things done. Moreover, she gets things done the way she wants them. That is a habit of hers.

She lingers after the luncheon and evening meal and engages in cheerful conversation. Instrumental music has no charm for her, but good singing she enjoys if there is a distinct melody and if the words mean something. She likes to hear men sing better than she likes to hear women, and she likes the songs she knows, and is willing to hear them again and again. If among the guests is one who sings, she is a good listener. But the greater part of the evening is spent in conversation. Clara Barton was a good conversationalist. She could listen without restlessness and talk without monopolizing the privilege of talking. She was quick to see a point. She had a voice which was low, and while not sweet or musical was pleasant, and its cadences were those of the gentlewoman. Her sentences were always perfectly formed. Her grammar never needed apology; her speech was precise, but free from pedantry. Her talk was habitually cheerful. She was respectful of the opinions of others and never failed to have an opinion of her own.

After her guests have gone to bed, her light still bums. She sits in her south room, where she said it seemed as if "it was always moonlight," and in her work she enjoyed the companionship of the woods, the stars, and the many voices of the night. Even the racket of the dancing and the whirl of the merry-go-round with the joyously frightened squeals of the girls descending the roller-coaster was far less objectionable than it would have been if it had been her habit to retire early.

But she is not yet working on her address. She is taking care of the belated mail which the day has brought and which her duties in the garden and laundry have kept her from attending to, but she has been thinking about the address more or less during the day, although when midnight comes she has not written a word of it. Beside her bed, however, she places a candle, a pencil, and a pad.

Clara Barton's bed was a cot. It was not a very soft cot either. She was never a poor woman. From her father she inherited a modest patrimony, and she always had more than enough money of her own to supply her needs. She could have had a wide and soft bed if she had wanted it. She had just what she wanted, and she never cared to have people tell her that she ought to have things differently in so far as they related to her own comfort.

Do not think she was an ascetic or slept in a hard bed because she scorned bodily comfort. Comfort she had and exactly as much of it as she wanted. Luxury she did not want. She thanked no one for wasting any pity upon her. Her bed was as wide as she wished it, and as soft as she cared to have it, and in it she slept soundly and was refreshed.

Before it was light she woke and reached for her matches and her pencil, and sitting up in bed she wrote her address as fully as she cared to have it written. She rarely erased a word. Her mind was clear and her speech came to her just in the form in which she wished it. Her years of training as a school-teacher had laid well the foundations of her composition and rhetoric. She wrote, not rapidly, but accurately, and each word said exactly what she wanted to say.

Her address is finished before daylight, and she puts out the light and takes her final nap, but is up at her accustomed time, having enjoyed a good night's rest, and is out in the garden and looking after the poultry until she joins her guests at breakfast.

After breakfast she copies her address in ink. Her handwriting is like copper-plate. When it is copied, she lays it aside. The process of copying it has photographed it upon her mind. She can deliver it either with or without manuscript. Although she trembles at the sight of an audience, she has learned to face one with perfect composure and no word of her speech escapes her memory.

Perhaps she excuses herself from lunch to-day and works at her desk, but not at the speech she is to deliver. It is her habit to keep free from any needless accumulation of unfulfilled duties. She sees her guests at the table and is herself within call, but for herself she has ordered an apple, a slice of bread, and a piece of cheese. No member of her household will suggest to her that she ought to eat more, and if one of her guests feels some compunction at eating a more ample repast while her hostess dines on homely fare, it is better that she keep her compunction to herself. If the guest should rise from the table and walk into the other room, carrying some delicacy, she would meet a mild rebuke. "I asked for exactly what I wanted," Clara would say.

Outside the window at which she sits the mason wasps build their nests of mud. Woe unto the man who molests them! The sparrow finds a house and the swallow a nest in the shelter of the Lord of hosts, and the wasps are as welcome as the birds to a home at den Echo. Two or three wasps fly through the open window and light upon her half-eaten apple. She will not permit them to be driven away. There is enough for the wasps and for herself. Like Saint Francis and the birds, she is at home with every kind of gentle life, and the wasps, she maintains, are gentle if gently treated. She gently pushes them away from her apple when she is ready for another bite, cutting off a piece with her desk-knife and leaving it on the corner of her desk for the wasps. They also have a further portion in the core. They light upon her hand, her forehead, they buzz round her, but they never sting her. She and they are friends.

This is the kind of life Clara Barton lived in Glen Echo; and this is what those were privileged to see who visited her in her home.

CLARA BARTON'S RELIGION

Clara Barton was a religious woman. Her diaries, her home letters, her intimate confidences, all breathe a deeply religious spirit. But she was reserved concerning her personal religious feelings and convictions. Once, when she was abruptly asked by a stranger in a group of strangers what were her religious opinions, she answered that she could not undertake to answer so large a question in so short a time. She recorded this in her diary, with some resentment that she should have been called upon thus to stand and deliver at sight.

But sitting beside a dying soldier, she had no hesitation in praying with him, nor of telling him unreservedly her own faith in God and immortality.

She was reared a Universalist. In that faith she lived the greater part of her life. She did not, however, join the Universalist Church in her home town, and she went away quite early and never established personal relations with a church.

Her satisfaction in church-going was almost wholly in the sermon. For music she did not care, and there was nothing in ritual that appealed to her. But a well-reasoned sermon she enjoyed. Henry Ward Beecher was her favorite preacher, and she did not miss an opportunity of hearing him if she could help it. A truly great sermon or great address of any kind made a strong impression upon her; nor was it wholly intellectual. She was remarkably receptive and open to spiritual impressions. A woman of intellect and will, she was also a woman of unusually sensitive feelings and of deep, though controlled, emotions. She was ever eager to learn and had to the end of her life unshaken faith in the discovery and application of new truth.

It was reported in 1908 that Clara Barton had gone over to Christian Science. The report was not wholly correct. She became interested in Christian Science, bat she never adopted it. The minister of the Universalist Church in Oxford, the Reverend Mr. Schoppe, became a Christian Science practitioner and reader, and she was much interested through him and his wife in this change on his part.

She was interested in Mrs. [Mary Baker] Eddy. It seemed to her a notable thing for a woman, alone and against great opposition, to have accomplished what she did.

She once witnessed the wreck of a sight-seeing automobile filled with Christian Science visitors to Boston, and she was impressed by the fortitude with which they bore pain.

Moreover, she had good reason to know that there is much reckless use of medicine and much needless surgery. She had memories of years in which she suffered many things of many physicians and was nothing better, but rather worse. She saw, in war and in peace, much use of the knife that seemed to her bloody and cruel. She saw women hurrying to the operating-table, sometimes, as she believed, for no better reason than to escape the risk of motherhood, and she scorned them. She expressed herself to me in terms anything but gentle concerning married women who willingly deprive themselves of the perilous privilege of motherhood by resort to surgery. She believed that people who take medicine usually take too much; and that cheerful and wholesome living is better than medicine.

Moreover, she was always ready for a thing that was new. Her delight in the discovery of something hidden and now revealed was intense.

For all these reasons she was disposed to give Christian Science a fair hearing.

In Dr. Epler's excellent biography, free use is made of Miss Barton's correspondence with Mr. and Mrs. Schoppe, in which she expressed her interest in their new faith. My own conviction is, that while Clara Barton was thus deeply interested, those letters tend to enlarge the degree of her permanent interest. I am confident that she was less near to being a Christian Scientist than the letters themselves would indicate if taken alone. Indeed, Mr. Schoppe himself gives what I think is a wholly truthful statement, as recorded by Mr. Epler, under date of December 17, 1914:

526

Clara Barton's connecting point with Christian Science was on the positives it accented—not from its negative philosophy. She welcomed its doctrine of the Divine presence of God working with us and in us and working upon her own life—present to help. She was exceedingly grateful to Christian Science for bringing out this point of the Divine absoluteness.

Further than that she could not understand it; she could not go. She did not deny, but she believed (unlike the Christian Science negativism) in a perfectly vast realm of material and human progress. She traced it in the wonders of geological ages and historical evolution. She saw God's handiwork in a colossal complex material creation. She never could bring herself to believe the material or human creation a mortal error!

I regard this as wholly correct. She read "Science and Health' and endeavored to use the "absent treatment" of the Schoppes. The first night it seemed to do good, and the next night the effect was gone. Her effort to obtain whatever was good in Christian Science was sincere; but her experiments did not make her a Christian Scientist.

She employed physicians till the day of her death, and took medicine. But she believed that spiritual things are the real things, and that man is more than body.

The two ministers whom rite selected to have charge of her funeral in the old home in Oxford were both Congregationalists. The Reverend Percy H. Epler was chosen for his long friendship, and the Reverend William E. Barton for that and for his kinship. She did not choose, but would have been happy to have chosen, had her plans been worked out in detail, the Reverend Doctor Tyler, an aged minister of the Universalist faith, to have a share in the services. Happily, he was present, and did participate. He had baptized and buried whole generations of the Oxford Bartons, and it was a benediction to have him standing, like a patriarch, above her coffin, and speaking words of comfort and hope.

Her choice of Congregational ministers to perform this service did not imply a lack of honor for the church of her childhood. Yet, in some respects, her associations in later years were more intimate with Congregationalists than with Universalists.

I have no reason to suppose that she talked with any one more freely than she talked with me about her religion, or about her relations to the Universalist Church. I think I can represent her views essentially as they were.

She continued to believe all that was essential in the faith which she had been taught in the church of Hosea Ballou. She trusted in a God whom she believed too great and good to make an eternal hell necessary to his government. If God was infinite and also desired the salvation of all men, if He was not willing that any should perish, but that all should come unto Him and live; if Christ tasted death for every man; then, as it seemed to her, ultimately, sin must be eliminated from the moral universe and with sin must go punishment. She believed, not only with Ballou, but with Beecher, that God will not punish after punishment ceases to do good. That sin brings punishment she believed and knew, but that sin and punishment must go on eternally seemed to her to imply either that God was not wholly good or not wholly Sovereign.

Her Universalism was essentially Calvinistic; it was based on the sovereignty of God. She believed that God was great enough to

"treasure up his bright designs.
And work his sovereign will."

She believed in the divinity of Christ. She was not a Unitarian. But she held to Christ's divinity as a divinity • of preeminence and not of exclusion. She believed that Jesus became the Son of God by moral processes which are essentially within the reach of men, "that He might be the first-born among many brethren."

I think I can give a truthful impression about her feeling with regard to Universalism as an independent ecclesiastical organization. She talked freely with me about this, and expressed the definite wish that the Universalist Church and the Congregational Church might everywhere be reunited. She had something of the same feeling with regard to the Unitarian churches. She loved the memory of Theodore Parker,* whom she sometimes felt she recognized as guiding her long years after his death. She honored him, and other of the Unitarian men of his generation. She felt that both Unitarian ism and Universalism had been necessary protests against the immoral orthodoxy of the time of their origin.

Theodore Parker (1810–1860) was an American Transcendentalist and reforming minister of the Unitarian church. A reformer and abolitionist, his words and quotations later inspired speeches by Abraham Lincoln and Martin Luther King, Jr.

But she felt that that protest was no longer needed, at least to the same extent. She felt the waste of competing religious organizations. The Universalist Church was the church of her father, but the Congregational Church was the church of his fathers. She had more friends in the latter than in the former. She told me she would be glad to see the liberty of thought which Universalism had stood for sacredly preserved in a union of those denominations.

She said, "What I see in Oxford I see everywhere, a need that churches shall forget old and past disputes, and come into more compact organization, merging denominations, and preserving religious liberty."

It is a hazardous thing to repeat, after yearn have gone by, the impressions left by oral conversations. Yet I am confident that in this meager outline I give her essential faith.

She did not talk glibly about her faith. But it was very real, and very definite, and it remained with her to the end.

Concerning revivals of religion she wrote to a niece who, in the widespread religious interest awakened by Mr. Moody in the seventies, had been asked by an evangelist to take a step which, as she looked back upon it, implied more than she had intended:

Thursday night

If one acts with good intentions, believing they are doing rightly, and later, concludes it was unwise or wrong—there is a mistake somewhere, or has been. It may have been in the act, or it may be in the later conclusion, but it is only a mistake, not a sin, you poor little chick.

Another time when you are requested in prayer meeting to act on a double question, the putter of it mixing up your desire or willingness to stand up before an audience and be made a subject for public prayers with an act of personal courtesy or discourtesy to himself as to whether you want to hear him or not, once leaves you free to vote as you like, and then comes and questions your decision, and asks your reason—if you feel like answering him at all—tell him to divide his questions, put one at a time and you will act on each separately. He put two questions together, as a dodge to get all up to be prayed for, thinking and knowing it put everyone in a hard place, as all would see that it was a little impolite not to hasten to accept his offer to come and preach. Oh, how tricky.

You have done rightly in it all, my dear little girl. When he asked why you did not side with the Lord you answered that you did. That was right and all he could ask for. When he added, "Then why did you not rise and kneel," you might tell him you did not understand that request as coming from the Lord, or you should certainly have done so.

I send you a "Banner of Light" to-day. You will find two articles bearing on your subject—the one a lecture by a good sturdy Briton on Mr. Moody's sermon on "Hell." I think you will read it with interest just now, and every time you get assaulted in public prayer meeting, and followed by men, I should advise you to run home and calm your hysterical nerves by re-reading that lecture from end to end.

The other longer marked article on "Revivalism" is a fine sermon by a sound Unitarian clergyman who does not believe in special revivals of religion, as gotten up for the occasion, and to fill churches, but thinks religion, as being the best part of man's nature, will revive itself like all else in nature, and feels that God does not need to be implored to save from endless pain and loss the poor creatures He has made, but believes that if we do our best to enlighten and elevate those around us we do all we are called upon to do in the way of their salvation.

But read it well and carefully for yourself, or read it again with Ida and "reason together" about it and see if you can find in your own convictions some justification for the course you are taking with the S.S. There is much to be read, before you decide, much to learn and consider; take time and do it and don't either fall into a trap nor be driven into one.—Selah!

She retained to the end of her life a high regard for the church of her fathers, the Universalist Church. Of it she wrote to Mrs. Jennie S. M. Vinton at Oxford:

I am glad to learn by your valued letter of September 5th that the old church of our fathers is about to be refitted and I thank you for the information. It is thoughtful of you to name the facts of the early history of the church which I am happy to corroborate, both by tradition and recollection. My father was present at the ordination sermon of Hosea Ballou (a white-headed boy he seemed). He was one of the pillars of the church. His family came over the hills of extreme North Oxford, five miles every Sunday, to sit in its high pews. When I was a grown young woman it was decided to build the present church, and no body of church people ever worked harder than we. We held fairs, public and home, begged, and gave all but the clothes we wore; we cleaned windows and scrubbed paint after workmen, bought and nailed down carpets, fitted up the parsonage, and received the bride of the Reverend Albert Barnes, our first settled pastor. And I carried their first baby to the christening.

There are few people there who have memories of harder church work and better church love than I.

Think this over, dear sister, and remember that I have never lost my love for the old church of my fathers, my family, and my childhood.

She believed whole-heartedly in immortality. Not only so, but she believed that her friends were near. She never recovered from the impression that came to her, after the death of her brother Stephen, that he was an influence, a living influence, for good in her life. That influence was exerted directly. As she woke in the morning while it was yet dark, and faced the duties of the day, she was able to think and plan with such clarity of vision that she felt that she was helped by the presence of those whom she had loved and who had counseled her in life. Through Stephen she felt the influence of her mother, as she believed, and, less directly, that of her father. She said, "I do not believe I am a Spiritualist," but she could not shake off, and did not desire to shake off, the conviction that those whom she had loved were near her.

The latest, and in some respects the most satisfactory, statement of her faith, was written a year before her death, to Judge A. W. Terrell, of Austin, Texas:

I suppose I am not what the world denominates a church woman. I lay no claim to it. I was born to liberal views, and have lived a liberal creed. I firmly believe in the divinity of Jesus Christ, the Jesus of Nazareth; in His life and death of suffering to save the world from sin, so far as in His power to do. But it would be difficult for me to stop there and believe that this spark of divinity was accorded to none other of God's creation, who, like the Master, took on the living form, and, like him, lived the human life.

THE PERSONALITY OF CLARA BARTON

At the beginning of her public career, Clara Barton was short of stature and slender as she was short. Her form rounded out in middle life, but she never exhibited any approach to stoutness. She was so well proportioned as to give the impression of being taller than she was. When she spoke in public, if she stood beside a presiding officer, it was seen that she was small of stature, but when she stood alone, she gave the impression of being, and was often described as being, above medium height. Her maximum height, attained in adolescence, was five feet two inches in moderately high-heeled shoes. The author measured her in her later years, and she was exactly five feet tall without her shoes.

Her carriage was erect, except for a slight stoop in the shoulders. There never came any sag in her person, any letting down of her erect standing. Her spine below the shoulders was carried to the end of her life as erect as in youth. As she stood or sat, she never had the bearing of an old person. When seated, she commonly kept her back well away from the back of the chair, depending upon nothing external to assist her in maintaining her erect bearing.

She walked quietly, deliberately, and flat-footedly. She put her whole foot down at once. There was a certain firmness in her gait which indicated strength of character and resolute purpose. She did not dart or rush or drift or flutter; she walked, and her walk was of moderate speed and of marked decision.

Her hair was brown, and in her younger days she had great wealth of it. She took good care of it; and, while there was less of it in her later years, it retained its fine texture, its soft silky wave, and its rich brown color. The writer asked her once if she had a single gray hair. She replied that she thought she had one, but had forgotten just where it was.

Her eyes were brown, and in some lights appeared black. I find at least one description of her as she appeared on the lecture platform in which she was described as tall, with hair and eyes black as the raven's wing. The reporter is not to be blamed for his departure from truth. She looked tall when she stood alone, and her eyes and hair appeared as he described them, when seen in some lights.

Her features were regular. Her nose was prominent and straight. Her mouth was large, and very expressive. Her features were remarkably mobile. Her forehead was both high and wide, and in her middle life she wore her hair so that its full breadth and height appeared beneath the graceful parting of the hair. In her later years her hair was combed down over the temples on either side, and remained parted in the middle. Her chin was a very firm chin. It did not protrude, neither did it recede. There was not the slightest suggestion of a lantern-jaw; but there was a clear-cut prominence of the chin that suggested a firm decision and a tenacious purpose. She said to the writer, "Every true Barton knows how to possess an open mind and teachable disposition with a firmness that can be obstinate if necessary, and no one can be more obstinate than a Barton." Obstinate she certainly could be, but she was reasonable to a marked degree. No one who saw her shut her mouth when she had made a decision could cherish any doubt of ho tenacity of purpose; and her chin was anything but a weak one.

She did not stare, but she had a habit of fixing her eyes upon an object or a person which did not put arrogance or pretense at ease. She could, on occasion, look through a person as if she discerned his inmost thoughts. But ordinarily her look into one's face was gentle and companionable and sympathetic.

Clara Barton affected none of the arts by which women advanced in years attempt to appear young. On the other hand, she had no intention of growing old. She said to me that she did not see why people should be so curious about anybody's age; what did it matter? So far as she was concerned, there was no secret about it; but when people had learned the date of her birth, how could they know whether she was old or young?

She did not greatly like to be asked for her "latest photograph." The photograph which she liked best, the one which she had framed and which the author has just as it stood on her desk, was the familiar Civil War portrait.

On December 30, 1910, she wrote in her diary, concerning her friend, Julia Ward Howe, whose death she mourned, and whose biography she had read through with keen interest:

I notice a strife over the placing of Mrs. Howe's portrait in Faneuil Hall. The art committee object to it, but the people demand that it be placed there. No reasons on the part of the art committee are yet given. The painting is by Mr. Elliott, husband of Maude. I wonder at the idea of people having their pictures taken after time and age have robbed them of all their characteristic features. I regard this as a mistake. I want the last picture of the friends I love to show them in their strength and at their best. Mrs. Howe's picture as now painted would have shocked even herself in strong middle life. Why not show the world the writer of the "Battle Hymn of the Republic" as she was when she wrote it? Is it the rush of the curious for the "latest photo"? I think the idea wrong. I wish the art committee would insist on a picture of Mrs. Howe at the age of forty years.

When Clara Barton was in her eighties, she often, as was her custom, would sit upon the floor, & la Turk, with her work spread around her. When her work was finished, she would rise, with the suppleness of a girl, without touching her hands to the floor.

She had an almost morbid shrinking from the infliction of pain, or from the taking of life. She was not strictly a vegetarian. If she was at another's table and meat was offered her, she ate it sparingly.

She carried through life a pulse ten beats slower to the minute than that of an ordinary woman of her years, but her pulse beat steadily and reliably. A half-cup of coffee stimulated her almost to the point of intoxication, and a child's close of medicine was too much for her. So simply did she live that when she died at the age of ninety-one there was not a physical lesion, not a diseased organ in her body. Her physician, who for thirty years had been her almost daily companion, Dr. J. B. Hub-bell, declared that, barring accident, or some acute attack, such as that which actually caused her death, she could easily have lived to be one hundred years of age and still not have been technically old.

There was nothing about her voice or manner that suggested a really aged person. Senility was farther removed from her at ninety than horn most women at sixty. A California octogenarian was compiling a book of personal testimonies by aged people and wrote to her asking for the secret of her long life. Her answer was contained in four words, "Low fare, hard work." If to this she had added anything, it should have been a self-forgetful purpose, a serene spirit, and an upholding faith.

From her father Clara Barton inherited a spirit of broad philanthropy and wide human interest. From her mother she inherited a warm heart and a very hot temper. It was this temper that gave her self-control. She kept it perfectly under her bidding, and that lowered voice was the sign of mighty resolution and smouldering passion under the control of a conquering will.

Clara Barton was a lifelong believer in woman's suffrage. She was a close friend and a warm admirer of Susan B. Anthony, and shared her aims and hopes for her sex. She believed in women receiving the same wages as men for the same work. She was never as militant an advocate of the rights of women as Miss Anthony, however. Temperamentally she was of quite another disposition. In her later years she saw with marked disapproval what she regarded as the unwomanly efforts of women to advance their cause. This she believed hurt the cause more than it helped it, and whether it helped or hurt she did not like it.

A lady who was about to undertake a long journey by rail spoke to Clara Barton of her dread of it. Railway travel, she said, always tired her out and made her sick. Miss Barton said, "Travel rests me."

Her friend asked her how she managed it. She replied:

"I delegate to the conductor and the engineer the full responsibility for the running of the train. I do not overeat, nor take with me candy or other needless food to upset my digestion just when I am getting less than my usual exercise. I carry with me a book and a note-book. When I think of something that I want to remember, I jot it down; when I see something that interests me, I make note of it. I read as long as I enjoy reading; and when I grow tired of that, I close my eyes and rest, and let the train go on."

Her friend replied, "That all sounds very simple; I will try it."

She returned from her journey, reporting that she had had a delightful time, and that she had alighted from the train at each end of the trip less weary than when she started.

The directions which Clara Barton gave were those which she herself had tested.

Clara Barton lived long, and her life had many changes. Account has been given of certain episodes in her young womanhood in which she was loved and did not return the affection of the men who loved her. The question has been asked and should be answered whether in her later years she had any experience which made up for the lack of love in her youth. Some stories, nearly or quite apocryphal, have been told concerning the men who are supposed to have loved her and whom she loved, but whom she refused because she loved her work more.

The lovers of her youth were all good, worthy men, as good as the average New Englander. There is nothing to be said concerning any one of them that is not to his credit; but no one of them was the equal of Clara Barton. There was no tragedy about her experience, neither was there any consciousness of the ecstasy of a love completely possessing her. These affairs left her something of loneliness, but no memory of bitter grief or cruel disappointment. She could write, and did once write, some tender, sentimental verses about a sad parting, but the sadness did not break her heart, nor permanently cloud that of any of her lovers.

The time came when all this was changed. She lived in Washington, amid a wide circle of friends, among them men of every station in life. No longer was she possessed of ambition beyond that of any man of her age and acquaintance. There were men whom she knew and men whom she liked, who had ambitions equal to her own and ideals with which her own had much in common. During the Civil War she might have chosen any one of scores of grateful men, as her husband. But she seems hardly to have given matrimony a thought in those years. After she became famous, she was less readily accessible to any multitude of lovers, but at least one man to whom she had been kind sought to reward her with his heart and hand, and, after she had returned from Europe, at least one man whom she met abroad pressed upon her his ardent and unrewarded affections. If she had married any one, she would have married an American. No offer of matrimony from a man not of her own land would seem to have made any appeal to her. This offer of marriage she regarded rather with amusement than with serious consideration. It was honorable, but in her judgment most unsuitable, and she refused with a smile—not the smile of contempt, but of good-humor and healthy merriment.

Among other friends in middle life there were two whom she would seem to have considered in the aspect of possible lovers.

In the days during and following the Civil War, she came to know intimately an American professor of wide repute, who at that time was pursuing extended researches in Washington. He was a widower of about her own age, a profound scholar, and he became a dear and trusted friend. For several months their paths were thrown together and for a time they boarded at the same table. She was interested, not only in his work, but in himself. The ardor and enthusiasm with which he worked impressed her. Like herself, he was little bound by precedent, and was engaged in a task which he confidently believed would increase the sum of human learning. There was something in a task of this character that made a direct appeal to Clara Barton. Much as she prized any kind of useful knowledge, she especially admired the spirit of the pioneer, and honored the man who blazed new paths and widened the horizons of learning. Such a man was this friend of hers. He read to her in many evenings the results of his investigation, and she shared his enthusiasm for his task. Her two nephews, Bernard and Sam, then in Washington, were wont to poke quiet fun at him and to joke their aunt about the possibility of his becoming an uncle of theirs and swamping the family with his knowledge of subjects which the boys cared little about. She took their raillery in good part. But one day, when she thought it had gone a little too far, she reproved her nephews and made a spirited defense of the professor. She said, "You need not wonder that, notwithstanding all your attempts to make fun of him, I admire a man of his profound learning and high character." Her nephews then believed that their respect for each other had merged into affection, but, as the years went by and he and Clara gradually lost sight of each other, they came to think that they might have been mistaken, that the two were good friends and nothing more. So far as the author is aware, there exists no evidence from which an answer can be had to the question of how much they really cared for each other, or, if they cared, why they did not marry. The author has his own conjecture, and it is only a conjecture, but it is this: Both he and she were at that time at the beginnings of a great work. How long either one would need to continue to labor and sacrifice before success was won, neither could determine.

The last and in some respects the most interesting, as certainly the most distinguished, among Clara Barton's matrimonial possibilities, came to her late in life. During the Civil War she became acquainted with a man who even then was held in high regard, and was attracting the attention of his own State and to some extent of the Nation. Rising largely by his own exertions to a position of eminence, he became one of the leading men of the generation. Through all the years when she was pursuing her war relief work, with scant appropriation for postage, he cheerfully loaned her his frank and was her friend. Through many long years they knew each other and always held each other in esteem. He was in Washington and so was she, and there was little need of interchange of letters between them; nor is there in the letters that are preserved any indication of personal affection. Those letters grew out of particular events when one or the other of them was away from Washington, and for the most part they had no significance as indicating the extent to which they may have cared for each other.

But there came a time when his work and her work brought them into close and more constant relations. They were both at the zenith of their respective careers. At that time he was a widower. Both were free and they could have married without the sacrifice of any important interest. The home which they might have established would have been a congenial one.

At that time Clara Barton took a brief vacation and went to Oxford where she prepared a new wardrobe, including a white satin dress. To her niece Mamie she confided that an occasion of unusual significance was in prospect, and that more would be known of it later.

Just at this time this distinguished statesman died. His death was a great shock to Clara Barton. She made no public lamentation; she never hinted even to those who were nearest to her that her grief was other than that which she might properly feel for an honored friend of many years. Her nieces believed that his death prevented their marriage. Her nephew, Stephen, says:

Their friendship was long and intimate, and it would not have been strange if they had cared for each other. In many respects their lives would have been well adapted to each other. But if their regard for each other ever expressed itself in terms of love, or approached the prospect of marriage, I do not know it. It may have seemed to either or both of them a pleasant possibility, but they were mature people, each with a great work to do; and if his death cut short what was growing from friendship into love, I do not know it. Such a feeling either one of them might very worthily have held toward the other. I know that she held him as a dear and trusted and honored friend, and he esteemed her likewise.

If Clara Barton loved this able and good man, she bore her disappointment as she was accustomed to bear her disappointments, in self-restrained and dignified silence. Her silence shall remain unbroken. If they loved, it was a love worthy of them both; if they were good friends and only good friends, it was a friendship honorable to both.

So far as the author has been able to learn from those who were closest to Clara Barton during her lifetime, and so far as it is disclosed by her diary and letters, this is all there is to be known concerning the love affairs of Clara Barton.

There were times when Clara Barton felt keenly her isolation. But, in 1911, she recorded in her diary some of the domestic trials of some of her friends, and added, "After all, Aloneness is not the worst thing in the world."

While extremely modest, Clara Barton was far from being a prude. She was never terrified by appeals to respectability, nor could she be frightened by any warning concerning men or women whom gossip condemned.

In 1884, when she was on her steamboat, *Joseph V. Throop*, assisting in the Ohio River floods, the boat one night tied up at a landing, and a goodly number of people came on board. Among the rest were two young women. One of the prominent ladies of the town found opportunity to whisper to her that these were young women whose social standing was not above question. "Then they will need help all the more," she said; and she gave those two girls an hour of her evening. Such warnings she often received, and, far from accepting them as her basis of discrimination, she invariably reacted in the other direction.

She never undertook any work without first carefully thinking it through in an effort to discover just where it was to end and how it was to be provided for. She had no sympathy with people who start good movements for other people to support when their well-meant but poorly reckoned endeavor fails. "They get hold of a log they can't lift," she said, "and they make a great call for someone to come and lift it for them." That was never the way in which she did things. She thought them through in advance.

Clara Barton worked slowly. While she formed her decisions promptly in emergencies, she formulated them carefully and with painful precision. It was not by doing things easily she accomplished so much, but by rising early and working late and keeping constantly at the thing she wanted to do. She attempted to use stenographic assistance, but with only moderate success. She had to work out her letters and addresses in her own way. A certain kind of routine work her secretaries did for her, to her great relief, but her real work she had to do herself.

She coveted the ability to work more rapidly. She admired that ability, and perhaps overvalued it, in others. She once wrote to me: "Where do you find time to do so many things? One of the griefs of my life is to see other persons getting things done—really done—and I accomplish so little. I don't see how they do it."

No more could they see how she did it; but she did it by working with an industry and devotion that never found an easy way of accomplishing results.

A friend of hers was deeply interested in a movement for which he wished the endorsement of Clara Barton. She believed in the work he was doing, and was willing to commend it; but she wanted to know a little more about it, and then she wanted time to think out what she wanted to say about it. He became very desirous of having her commendation in time for a particular use; and his wife invited Clara Barton to their home to dine. She willingly accepted, and enjoyed the visit. She knew the family, and held them in high esteem. After dinner, and some conversation, the man produced a typewritten statement of some length which he had prepared, endorsing his work. This he read to her, and she liked it. But when she understood that he had prepared this for her to sign, she was shocked. She refused to sign it.

Her friend could not at first understand her scruples. Did she not believe in this work? She did. Had she not expressed to him her approval and signified her willingness to furnish him a statement which he would be at liberty to publish? She had. Had she not listened to his reading of this very statement with expressions of hearty approval? She had. Was there anything in it she would like to change? If so, she was at liberty to make any erasure or interlineation she desired. No; there was nothing she cared to change, except that she cared to change everything in it.

He assured her that he was asking nothing of her which' men of the highest honor did not do constantly; that in a busy world people had to avail themselves of assistance such as he offered her; that his own standards of honor were high, and he would never think of asking her to sign a statement which did not fully express her own convictions.

All this she understood, and she did not censure him. But she could not do what he asked of her. The statement which he had prepared was not hers. The opinions expressed were in full accord with her own, and the language was as good as any she could have chosen, and there was nothing in the document to which she could object; but it was not hers.

Her idea of a document which she could sign as her own was one which she should have thought out on first wakening, perhaps in the middle of the night, and sketched in pencil on the pages of the little pad at the head of her bed, and then thoughtfully copied in her own hand with careful weighing of each word and phrase. That would have been her own.

Certainly that was a needlessly narrow conception of the extent to which she might honorably have employed the minds and willing hands of others in her own too heavy toil. But it was a conception grounded in the highest possible conviction of honor.

Clara Barton was a self-willed woman. So was Mother Bickerdyke. So was Dorothea Dix. So, most emphatically and uncomfortably for those who withstood her, was Florence Nightingale. If comparisons were in order, which they certainly are not, she was not the least considerate of the four of other people's opinion, nor most reluctant to admit herself in the wrong. Like Florence Nightingale, she had opportunities of marriage in her youth, and resolutely turned to other work under force of a strong conviction, and that conviction had mighty impelling power. Lytton Strachey, in his remarkably penetrating sketch, says: Everyone knows the popular conception of Florence Nightingale. The saintly, self-sacrificing woman, the delicate maiden of high degree who threw aside the pleasures of a life of ease to succor the afflicted, the Lady with the Lamp, going through the horrors of the hospital at Scutari, and consecrating with the radiance of her goodness, the dying soldier's couch—the vision is familiar to all. But the truth was different. The Miss Nightingale of fact was not as facile as fancy painted her. She worked in another fashion, and toward another end; she moved under the stress of an impetus which finds no place in the popular imagination. A Demon possessed her. Now demons, whatever else they may be, are full of interest. And so it happens that in the real Miss Nightingale there was more that was interesting than in the legendary one; there was also less that was agreeable.

The disposition of Florence Nightingale lacked much of being angelic. When she encountered the stupidity of official red-tape or the brutality and indifference of army surgeons, her words blistered. She hurled invectives and she employed sarcastic nicknames, and she denounced everything and everybody who opposed her. But when she arrived in Scutari forty-two wounded men out of every hundred were dying, and when she left them her hospitals showed a death-rate of twenty-two out of every thousand. Clara Barton had a tongue less sharp than Florence Nightingale's, but she had a will no less inflexible. Both women had soft voices, which they never raised. Men fled from the soft tones and vitriolic words of Florence Nightingale. When Clara Barton grew angry, she lowered her voice. Instead of a woman's shrill falsetto, men heard a deep and determined tone quietly affirming that the thing was to be done in this way and in no other. Few men withstood that tone.

Some readers of this book, I am sure, have been shocked to read the opinion of Dr. Bellows of the Sanitary Commission concerning the uselessness and worse of the ordinary woman nurse in war hospitals. That opinion was shared by Dorothea Dix, by Clara Barton, and to an even greater degree by Florence Nightingale.

Not very long after Florence Nightingale had reached Scutari with her thirty-eight nurses, and about the time when she was having to ship some of them back, her official friends in England thought to win her eternal gratitude by sending to her forty-six additional nurses, under the personal direction of her old friend, Miss Stanley. But she refused to accept them, and sent in her resignation. She would not have these "women scampering through the wards" and upsetting all her regulations. "They are like troublesome children," she said. Even the religious ones were given to what she called "spiritual flirtations" with the soldiers; and, as for those who had not the fear of God or the dread of hell-fire, there were drunken orderlies and dissolute officers and unmarried chaplains to be considered.

I have wondered what Dorothea Dix would have said if forty-six nurses not of her selection had been suddenly dumped upon her; I think she would have gone into hysterics and shipped them all back. Clara Barton, I believe, would have set them to emptying slops and scrubbing floors till she found the few out of whom she could make nurses. She would not have written the kind of letters about them which Florence Nightingale wrote. She would have scolded a little in her diary, and have written the committee who had sent them a letter of thanks, requesting them not to send anymore until she asked for them, and meantime to send her some bandages and some lemons. But she would have felt much as Florence Nightingale felt. They were both self-willed women. They needed all their will-power. It was well they had it.

Many interesting parallels suggest themselves between the work of Clara Barton and that of Florence Nightingale.

They were contemporary in a remarkable degree. Florence Nightingale was a few months the alder and died a few months sooner than Clara Barton, bat both lived to be more than ninety years of age. Miss Nightingale was born May 12, 1820, and died August 13, 1910; Clara Barton was born December 25, 1821, and died April 12, 1912. They faced the question of marriage in much the same fashion, and each one gave herself in much the same spirit to her life-task. They were not unlike in their religious faith and in its practical expression. The long, confidential letters of Florence Nightingale, written painfully when she ought to have been in bed, remind us of the detailed epistles which Clara Barton found time to write, mostly late at night. Each had a love of humor which stood her in good stead; Miss Barton's had less sting in it than that of Miss Nightingale, but otherwise it was not unlike, and it was a great help to both of them. Each had a gentle voice, and each knew how to use it effectively without raising it. Each protested to the end of her life that her real work was not that of the popular imagination, that of personally ministering to any considerable number of side or wounded soldiers, but a work of direction and organization; and neither succeeded in making the public believe it. Not long before her death, Clara Barton relieved her mind in her diary concerning

545

the sort of newspaper article which invented fairy-tales of this sort: "Oh, these women reporters!" she said in her diary. "They never get anything right. They are forever telling and inventing the same old kind of gush!" Florence Nightingale also had a profound distrust of the limitations of members of her own sex; but also she knew, as did Clara Barton, the brutality, the stupidity, and the inefficiency of men. Miss Nightingale often wondered if there were in all the army enough officers of sympathy and conscience to have saved Sodom. Sometimes she doubted if there was one.

All the women who went to the battle-front and were worth their carfare were women of strong will. Mother Bickerdyke, in her rough and great-hearted way, was a lady; but when she faced an incompetent surgeon and drove him out of the hospital and he appealed to General Sherman, the General confessed himself powerless: "She ranks me," he said. Dorothea Dix was a lady to the very depth of her sensitive soul, a devoted, consecrated Christian lady; but she could be very properly disagreeable on occasion, and she brooked no interference with her authority. Florence Nightingale was a lady, born and bred; but vitriol was mild compared to some of her outbursts. Clara Barton was a lady to her very finger-tips; and she had had enough of experience in Washington among officials and men of influence so that she knew how on occasion to be much more diplomatic and gracious than most other women with her responsibilities. Moreover, she shrank from giving pain, and was careful of her words. But she had as strong a will as had Florence Nightingale, and, while she was as a rule more amiable than that lady in her more violent moods, she got things done. People sometimes found her arbitrary, impatient, and obstinate; had she been less so, it had gone hard with the interests which she cherished. She was capable of being arbitrary, impatient, and obstinate, and the same is true of each of the other women whom her name calls to mind. But among them she was not the least gentle, considerate, and self-forgetful. She required that things should move, and move in the direction of her decision; but she was at heart, and on most occasions in her demeanor, quiet, gentle, affectionate, and calm.

Clara Barton had many devoted and loyal friends. They were held by her in warm and enduring affection; and some of them, for ho sake and her work's sake, made generous sacrifices. She had other friends who came to her in bursts of generous enthusiasm. These also were in good part sincere, and if some of them found her habits so simple and her task so heavy as to afford them smaller share than they had hoped in personal association with her, they were none the less generally firm in their friendship. It was not to be expected that everyone could live permanently on her high plane of single-mindedness. Some of her friends were a trial to her, for it was not easy for her to understand why, when they once knew the task she was working at, they did not manifest stability of purpose and perseverance in well-doing. But these she counted her friends. When one of these left her roof because the fare was too plain, Clara Barton said, "She is not willing to wash herself seven times in Jordan."

There were others—and in the course of her long life there were a number of them—who came to her with ardent protestations of affection and of devotion to her cause, who in time wearied of the strain, or resented her strong hand in management, or who came to believe that they themselves could do better the work which she had undertaken. Some of them betrayed her most sacred confidences, and returned her evil for good.

Few women were so ill-fitted by nature to bear this kind of disappointment as Clara Barton. She was morbidly sensitive, and given to self-accusation. How unworthy she must be, she thought, if these persons did not continue to love her. The wounds of their defection went unhealed. Yet here was one of the finest triumphs of her nature. She never cherished permanent resentment.

One time a friend of hers recalled to her a peculiarly cruel thing that had been done to her some years previous, and Clara Barton did not seem to understand what she was talking about.

"Don't you remember the wrong that was done you?" she was asked.

Thoughtfully and calmly she answered, "No; I distinctly remember forgetting that."

Friends deserted Clara Barton, but she never deserted a friend. If a friend of hers was evil-spoken against, that only increased her loyalty. She would not believe evil unless compelled to do so, and, if compelled, she interpreted the wrong, if possible, in terms of charity. Only baseness and treachery and betrayal of trust won her scorn.

At one time, in connection with her relief work on the rivers, a man who had acted as her local agent was arrested for burglary. She was at a distance and wires were down. She refused to believe him guilty. When later details made it impossible to doubt that he had done essentially the deed with which he was charged, she still believed that there must be some explanation. Later it developed that the offense was technical, and grew out of a dispute as to the ownership of certain premises which he had entered, and the other claimant, instead of suing him for trespass, sought to do him the greater injury by having him arrested for burglary. How the question of the ownership of the property was ultimately settled, I do not know, but her confidence in the man as one incapable of willful crime was justified.

Consul-General Hitz, of Switzerland, long her friend, became a banker in Washington. Apparently he had little talent for the banking business, and undertook to finance the Swedenborgian Church, of which he was a member, out of the revenues of the bank. Of his guilt before the law there appears to have been no question; as to his essential honesty Clara Barton had no doubt. She did not condone the offense, nor question that the amount taken must be made good; but she did not believe that so good a man and so true a friend ought to remain in prison. After high influence had been exercised unavailingly on his behalf, she persisted, and he was released.

Her voice has already been mentioned. Its key was about the average pitch of a woman's treble voice. In conversation it was flexible, and very pleasant. On the platform it was clear and penetrating. Her tones were not musical, but were distinctly agreeable. Her inflections were those of the gentlewoman of the old school. There was a soothing, conciliatory, almost caressing quality in her voice. It had no harsh notes. It was diametrically opposite to all that was harsh and strident. It was gentle, winsome, and in every accent suggestive of courtesy and good-breeding. When she lived abroad, no one accused her of a high, harsh, nasal American voice. It was a New England voice, but as soft as that of any Southern lady of the old days.

But when Clara Barton grew very much in earnest, her voice changed. That change was one of the most remarkable things about her. It did not rise. It did not grow harsh or self-asserting. It dropped a half octave or, as it sometimes seemed, a full octave. It was a deep, full voice. It was almost bass. Her eyes darkened as her voice went down, and flashed lightning to her tones' quiet thunder. She had a temper, which she kept well under control, but when she spoke in a low tone, those who heard her knew that its fires were red.

She was modest in her dress, but she had an eye for bright colors. In her youth she was a painter, and she learned how to mix colors on her palette. She never felt so sure of her good taste in the matter of dress as she did of her ability to make pleasing contrasts on canvas. She trusted much to the good judgment of her friend, Annie Childs. When she followed her own judgment, she inclined to green, which she loved to set off with red. Red was her color, and she said, the Barton rose was the Red Rose, all the way from the Wars of the Roses down. She loved red roses. She loved red apples. She liked to wear red ribbons and trimmings. With a background of green, red was always safe. In her youth and young womanhood she often determined to vary her costume, and repeatedly went to the stores determined to buy something beside green. Her nieces said, "If Aunt Clara says she is going to town to buy a brown dress, we know that she will buy a brown dress; for Aunt Clara invariably does exactly what she says she will do. So we know that she will select and pay for a brown dress. But we also know that by the time she gets it home the color will have changed; when she opens the package, it is sure to have become green."

In later years, dressmakers took her in hand, and widened the range of her choice. But she seldom appeared in any gown that did not lend itself to a little dash of red; and when she wore just what delighted her own eyes, her dress was green, with a complementary dash of red.

Something must be said about her habit of economy, and it must be said with some care lest it give a very wrong impression. Clara Barton was economical to a very marked degree. If a list of her actual economies were here given, it would produce on many minds the impression that she was stingy. This would be wide of the truth. If a valid distinction may be made between two words that are nearly synonymous, she was parsimonious, but was not penurious.

She was reared in a community and in a family where want was unknown, but where money was earned by hard work, and capital was accumulated by thrift and economy. It was part of her birthright and of her being. There was about her nothing that inclined her to waste or even extravagance.

She entered into life early as a teacher, at first at a small salary. She had opportunity to save, and she did save. Her necessary expenses were small, and she began at the outset to save money. She continued to save money. She had good business judgment, and, excepting for a few times when she permitted her sympathies or her friendships to get the better of that judgment, her investments, conservatively made, were remunerative.

When she first went abroad in 1869, she knew that she had money enough to support her as long as she lived. If she recovered her health, the lecture platform was still open to her, and she could earn and save above all expenses from four thousand dollars to six thousand dollars a year. If she returned an invalid, she had the income on about thirty thousand dollars, which was more than she needed. In no year of her life, probably, did she spend upon herself as much as eighteen hundred dollars. Even when she traveled abroad, her expenses were moderate, and she never drew on her principal for her own support. But eighteen hundred dollars or two thousand dollars a year, which was about what her investments brought her, did not invite reckless extravagance. She knew that she must exercise reasonable economy, and her tastes were such that this was no hardship.

When, therefore, she sat up at night rather than take a sleeping-car, it was not wholly that she was unwilling to pay for the price of the berth. She had been accustomed to doing so until an attempt was made to rob her, after which she was greatly disinclined to the use of the sleeper. Her prime reason for sitting up was that she disliked sleepers after that night. But she was not at all averse to saving two dollars. She slept few hours in the night, and was accustomed to sleeping under un- favorable conditions. She thought she rested quite as well sitting in a corner of her seat as lying in a stuffy and dark berth.

Her lunch at home was often a few crackers and a red apple, and the more nearly she regulated her diet when journeying in accordance with her custom at home, the better life went with her. So her bag often contained a little package of the kind of crackers which she liked, and one or more big red apples. If she sat in her seat and ate these, it was not primarily because she was unwilling to pay a dollar for her lunch; she had the dollar, and she had no ambition to leave any considerable sum of money behind her when she died. On the other hand, she was not unmindful of the good she could do with the dollar in some other way. And she did that good with it. She was parsimonious with herself; she was generous toward others.

To enumerate her economies would misrepresent her. It would seem that she was niggardly. The contrary was true. She abhorred waste. She could not tolerate extravagance. But she could draw her last dollar, and did draw her last dollar from investment, to put into her search for missing soldiers, and she could do it and did do it without whining and without fear. Even the possibility that she might die a pauper did not terrify her or win from her in her diary any more than a half-mirthful recognition. She economized in things she did not greatly care for that she might do the things that were to her of supreme importance.

She did not hoard money. The amount which she had at the end of her lecturing career, she did not greatly increase, nor, until she got deep into the work of the Red

Cross, did it materially diminish. In order to support the Red Cross work in its earlier stages, she drew upon her principal, and she did not to the end of her life restore it to what it had been before. But she never complained of this, nor did it in the least worry her. Year by year she had sufficient income, with reasonable economy, to supply all her needs. Now and then she delivered an address and received a hundred dollars. Occasionally she replied to a request of newspaper or magazine for an article, and received a check in return. For a year she received a salary from the State of Massachusetts as matron of the Reformatory for Women at Sherborn. The annuity paid to her by the Massachusetts General Hospital gave her a little more margin. She was free from worry as to her own finances. I have not found in her diary or her letters a single sentence in which she expressed anxiety about her own financial future. There were several times when she was not sure what she ought to do next, and in her decisions she was not unmindful of financial necessities. But she did not keep in constant thought her own need of saving money for herself. She saved, because it was natural for her to save, and because she had causes at heart which she wished to save for.

Careful in her expenditures upon herself, Clara Barton lavished her love upon others. She cherished her friends, and there was little that she was not willing to do for them. More than once she jeopardized plans of her own for the sake of unselfish ministry to others, some of whom had little claim upon her. She received under her own roof, fed at her table, sheltered at her fireside, and assisted from her purse not a few people who later proved ungrateful; indeed, those who wrought her most pain were those whom she had befriended and of whom she later learned that they sought not her. but hers.

Yet it would not be fair to give any impression that the number of ingrates among her companions was large. Relatively, it was small, Those who loved her loved with a fervent loyalty; and there are few things more beautiful than the adoring and grateful affection which those bestow upon her memory who knew her longest and best. A strong individualist, she inspired in those who came to know her well that perfect confidence and grateful devotion which are the crowning test of leadership. There were those, who, for her sake and that of any cause which she held dear, would have gone with her singing to the stake, and she would never have permitted one of them to go there unless she went first.

The author was her relative, her friend of many years. He loved her and admired her; but he has felt his own praises weaken and pale and disappear in the presence of those who, working in intimate association with her through the years, proclaimed to him her virtues in terms that but for their sincerity and the knowledge of those who spoke would have seemed extravagant. The surest proof of her genuine goodness is the unfaltering devotion of those who knew her best, and for that reason loved her most.

Clara Barton was a woman of tact. She needed all the tact she had and more. In every field in which she labored, she was flooded with volunteer workers who wanted to help. Some of them were competent; more were -not. I recently talked with my long-time friend. Father Field, sometime head of the Cowley Fathers, and learned that he was at the Johnstown flood, and saw much of Clara Barton. They rode together in a buggy over a road filled with trees and house-roofs and he feared she would be thrown out, but she told him to drive on; she had driven over worse roads, and with bullets besides. He said that her greatest difficulty as he saw it there was the number of people of good impulse but little discretion who rushed into Johnstown to help. Dr. Bellows said a blunt word about the women who made their journey to the battle-field, that most of them were in the way. This was unfortunately true of many of the well-meaning people who rushed to the assistance of Clara Barton in time of flood or fire. Assistance she must have, and must take what was offered. But the handling of this untrained force was a matter which called for the greatest tact as well as executive ability.

Not only so, but, when the work in a particular field was over, there were always those who had come as volunteer workers who insisted on bestowing themselves upon Clara Barton to make Red Cross work their life-work. Some of them were competent, and she was glad of them. But in the course of her years of experience she accumulated a series of misfit volunteer assistants, some of whom it was not easy afterward to get rid of.

She had little love of music. She did not sing or play any musical instrument. When traveling abroad, if forced to attend the opera, she saved the time from utter waste by writing a home letter while singers of world-wide repute performed and sang before her. Having a low and soft voice, she disliked the high notes of women's voices. Good, melodious quartet music she heard with mild enjoyment, and if she can be said to have liked any music it was that of male voices. A chorus of men always pleased her. Some of the war songs always thrilled her, though more for the associations than the music. There was one song, popular during the later years of the Civil War, which she never heard often enough. It was the song of an old slave, who, dying years before the war, had believed that he would rise on the day when freedom came to his race. The author also remembers it, as it was taught to him almost before he could walk:

Nicodemus the slave was of African birth.
He was bought for a bagful of gold;
He was reckoned as part of the salt of the earth,
And be died years ago, very old.
T was the last word he said as we laid him away
In the stump of an old hollow tree—
"Wake me up," was his charge, "at the first break of day.
Wake me up for the great jubilee."
Chorus:
Then run and tell Elijah to hurry up, Pomp,
To meet us at the gum-tree down in the swamp.
To wake Nicodemus to-day.

It was sung at the minstrel shows after the Emancipation Proclamation; but it was not as a minstrel show song that Clara Barton enjoyed it. There was a solemn dignity about the old slave's faith that inspired her; and the authoritative tones of the words "Wake Nicodemus" thrilled her through and through.

Her lack of love of music reached its climax in her abhorrence of piano-drumming. For piano music she had some little love, but not enough to compensate for the annoyance for having a piano where it could be pounded by any visitor, skilled or unskilled. For many years she refused to have a piano in her house. At last she permitted one to be procured, and she gave it house-room, and sometimes heard it played with satisfaction. But when she was hard at work and wanted to concentrate her thought, she found no joy in the thoughtless hammering which an open piano seemed to invite. There was a time for all things, even for piano-playing, and in its proper time and place she could permit it and enjoy a part of it; but she did not want the menace of it from early morn till dewy eve and several hours thereafter. Her home was a very open place of entertainment, and she could not well inquire, before admitting a person who needed shelter, what were his or her habits and ability with respect to the torture of piano keys. So she would have preferred a home with only such music as was brought in where and when it was wanted. But she accepted the piano as in some sort inevitable, and it did not annoy her as much as she had expected.

If Clara Barton did not care for music, she did dearly love poetry. From her earliest childhood she was reading it, committing it to memory, copying it, and writing original lines of her own. There lies before me, as I write, her first copy-book. The strokes and curves she learned to imitate are there, then the letters, lower case and capitals, then the first words, "thoughtful," "Nation," and "National," and the sentence, chosen perhaps for its varied arrangement of letters with the simplest stem and curve, and partly because it was not well for a New England child at school to begin life with any illusion about its essential character, "Man was made to mourn."

Later she procured a bound volume, and in it she copied her favorite poems, and wrote others of her own, in her most careful and painstaking hand. Her "copper-plate" penmanship was never more exquisite than in this volume, in which her own poems and the poems she loved are written in order as she found or composed them.

No quality in Clara Barton was more marked than the breadth of her sympathies. She shuddered at the thought of needless pain. I have a crude little picture, a page out of a child's book, which she found in her childhood and preserved to the end of her life. It is entitled "What came of firing a gun." A dead bird lies on the ground, and is approached on the one side by a boy with a gun in his hand and on the other by a horrified girl. It is not a great work of art, but it tells its story and conveys its lesson.

She never gave needless pain. She regarded all life as akin to the life of God, and sacred with the imprint of God's own image. She looked upon all life that can suffer or enjoy, the life of bird and beast and fish, as something on which it is a sin to inflict needless pain.

From the time she saw, in her little girlhood, the killing of an ox, and felt that the blow that struck and crushed its skull had struck her own head, she never saw pain without feeling it. She could have said with Whitman of the suffering she saw—

> My wounds on me grow livid as I lean
> Upon my staff and look.

She did not merely sympathize with suffering; she suffered. She not only was glad of other people's joy; it was her joy. She rejoiced with those that did rejoice and wept with those that wept. Not often do her diaries record her weeping; and the tears she records as having shed are oftener for others' sorrows than for her own. Her sympathy was genuine, and of the sort which can truly be called vicarious. She took it upon herself.

Her sympathies were so strong that she would have been useless in the presence of danger and pain but for her remarkable self-control. I asked her once how she acquired this, and she said it was simply by forgetting herself. She saw something that needed to be done, and went about the doing of it so promptly, so completely absorbed by the necessity of it, that she forgot to be horrified by the sight of blood, forgot to faint as timid females were supposed to do. Days and weeks and months and years of it she would endure and never once give way. Then would come a revulsion and a horror and a weakness and a collapse. Again and again she held herself in hand through nervous strain that would have crushed most women or men, and when it was all over went nervously to pieces.

It appears a pity that, being capable of maintaining her self-control till the end of the crisis, she could not still have maintained it when the need was over. But it was a part of her delicately strung organism to bear any manner of strain while the need lasted, and then to snap. The remarkable fact is, not that she ultimately gave way, but that she endured so long and so much.

Clara Barton was a woman to her finger-tips. Nothing that she saw or suffered ever coarsened her or made her oblivious to the finer things of life. Nothing that came of her association with men—and rough men at that—made her anything less than a woman and a lady. She was distinctly feminine. She had her own way of ignoring any incident occurring in her presence at which she might have been expected to be shocked, but of stickling at any trivial act which implied that she was indifferent to proprieties. Teamsters, with their wagons deep to the hubs in mud, might swear at their mules and she would never hear it; but at night by the camp-fire she could rebuke with a quiet and effective word or look the slightest approach to impropriety of word or deed. She was no prude when she had a duty to perform, and conventionalities meant little to her in the presence of human need. But on her return to home life, she was gentle, ladylike, and a stickler for proprieties.

She had no love for the mannish woman. She was much in the society of men. In many respects she preferred the society of men to that of women. She entered into their joys and experiences appreciatively. But in it all she was distinctly feminine. She was a woman always, a lady always. People who expected to meet in her a big, aggressive female, with a long stride and a heavy voice and a domineering attitude, were amazed. She was a little, undemonstrative gentlewoman of the old school.

One of Clara Barton's most outstanding qualities was her almost complete disregard of precedent. The fact that a thing had always been done in a given way was evidence to her that it could be done again in that fashion, but was of almost no value to her as proving that that was the best way to do it. She always had faith in the possibility of something better. It irritated her to be told how things always had been done. She knew that a very large proportion of things that have been done since the creation have been blunderingly done, and she was always ready to listen to suggestions of better ways. Having once decided upon a course that defied the tyranny of precedent, she held true to her declaration of independence, and saw her experiment through.

In this she was not reckless or iconoclastic. She simply forbade herself the cheap luxury of a closed mind. If no better way presented itself, she was content with the old way of doing. But she was eager for any new thing that might improve upon the past. Here was preeminently a forward-looking mind and a soul with face ever toward the sunrise.

CLARA BARTON'S LAST YEARS

Clara Barton lived for eight years after her retirement from the Red Cross. After her first disappointment and the giving-up of her dream of exile in Mexico, her heart turned to a form of work which already had been much upon her mind. In establishing the American Red Cross, she had determined from the outset that it should be of use in peace as well as in war. The conviction grew upon her that it should be broadened still further so that its activities should not be confined to periods of calamity, but that there should be established under its direction various forms of community service. Particularly did she desire that in every community there should be organizations for home nursing and first aid to the injured.

Before her retirement from the Red Cross, she had proposed to her associates the addition of a First Aid Department as a part of its activities. This did not seem to her board of control an advisable field for the Red Cross to enter at that time. After her resignation from the presidency of the American Red Cross, she organized the "National First Aid Association of America," which was incorporated under the laws of the District of Columbia and had its general office in Boston. The plan included a large sustaining membership with a nominal fee of a dollar a year, and an active membership composed of those in every community who attended a course of lectures and passed a physical examination.

The plan of this new organization, as originally planned by her for the Red Cross, was fully set forth in a brief manuscript which she prepared:

During the entire period of the present differences among sections of the members of the American National Red Cross, I have never once felt that it was the desire of the American people that I should personally enter within the circle of disturbance, and I have consequently remained a silent and sorrowful spectator of a controversy that appeared to me to be leading where no true, loyal friend of the Red Cross would care to follow.

Every effort I have ever made on behalf of the people of the United States, during the long years of my work, has been met with friendly approval or thoughtful response. These efforts have always been made on behalf of suffering humanity, in times of dire distress and peril, and I have administered with a free but careful hand the benefactions of whatever nature that have been entrusted to me; and as freely I have given of all I possessed of strength, health, and private means.

Never once have I made a suggestion on behalf of myself or my difficulties, and I have therefore had the confidence to feel that nothing was expected of me but a straightforward advance along the natural path of my life-work. So certain have I been of this, and so confident in the firm loyalty, safe counsel, and moral support of the eminent help surrounding me, that I have felt free to devote my energies during the past months to perfecting a plan for so broadening and strengthening the organization of the Red Cross that it may enter on a new field of useful activity—on a work that will appeal directly to the people everywhere, and prepare them, in these times of peaceful well-being, to meet intelligently and successfully any emergency or disaster that may occur, either nationally or individually. It is my desire that this new work shall be the means of creating ample funds to meet any great national calamity, and that the Red Cross may hereafter enter the field fully equipped at the instant the call may come.

In times past urgent calls have come to us and precious time has been lost through lack of funds and suitable equipment. It is most desirable that this condition should be remedied, and it is to this end that I am making an appeal to the American people—not for their money nor their substance, but that they cooperate with me earnestly in this new work: this effort to benefit themselves, that I am endeavoring to inaugurate. It will be borne in mind that, in the twenty years of its existence, the American National Red Cross has never appealed, never asked for, or sought the control of, a dollar even for relief; but has, as it seeks to do in this, left the people free in the exercise of their own choice and intelligence. The only apparent suspension of this method took place during the active service of the

Spanish-American War, when the great committees, formed at the instance of President McKinley, raised money for relief, in the name of the Red Cross, and applied it; the society itself holding its normal position under the attorneyship of the noble Cuban Relief Committee, which did honor to itself and the Nation.

Can it be too much to expect that this one appeal will meet a ready response at the hands of the people?

We are actively organizing a new branch of the Red Cross, to be known as "The First Aid Department" of the American National Red Cross, which department will be largely educational and will concern itself in instructing the people everywhere throughout the United States in the best modem methods of first aid treatment, in all cases of accident and emergency.

There will be two distinct branches of this work. For the first an emergency case, similar to that in use in England, Germany, and other Red Cross Treaty Nations, and this has been adapted to Red Cross needs and methods under the direct supervision of the Medical Board of the Red Cross Hospital. It contains material and surgical dressings of the best class known to modern surgery. A most valuable part of the permanent equipment of this emergency case is a series of emergency charts, arranged for instantaneous reference, giving simple brief instructions for dealing with every conceivable case of accident, pending the arrival of the doctor. This chart is the combined work of a committee of eminent physicians and surgeons; and, apart from the admirable manner of its arrangement, may be regarded as the highest standard of authority upon first aid methods of treatment known to the world.

The other branch of the department will undertake the formation of first aid emergency classes in every city in the country. Ambulance corps will be formed among the employees of mills and factories, industrial corporations, railroad employees, the police, and employees of public departments. These employees will be drilled and instructed in first aid methods, and, apart from the value of the knowledge they will obtain for local use and service, they will form an efficient force to draw from as helpers in great national calamities.

These methods are in no way experimental. In many European countries, as Germany, Russia, and even Asiatic Japan, they form one of the strongest features of the Red Cross. They are also in perfect accord with its first principles, viz., the voluntary help of the people for the Government, if in need, and the organized help of the people for each other in misfortune.

This practical work in the united hands of the whole American people should raise the organization far above the need of charitable gifts for its support. The Red Cross belongs to the people; they should be their own almoners and administer their own charities.

The intelligent thought of the philanthropists of the world is behind these methods; tried, well assured, and successful. Do we need to know more?

I make a strong appeal for the formation of local committees everywhere; to cooperate with the headquarters staff of the First Aid Department in the formation of classes. I appeal earnestly to physicians in every town in the United States to render their aid. Next to the stricken victim and immediate friends will the kind-hearted doctor appreciate this timely and intelligent help.

I appeal to every employer of labor throughout the country on behalf of this movement. I need not remind him that it is a duty, for his own kind heart will call him with a tender care to the welfare and safety of those whom circumstances and conditions have, for the time being, made his own. Their well-being is his, and protection from the inevitable dangers surrounding them will be his first care. My own convictions assure me that this appeal will be heard and responded to. I have known my country people—their good judgment, good hearts, and generous natures—too well to permit a moment's doubt.

We have established headquarters for this department at 31 East 17th Street (Union Square), New York City, where all inquiries relative to the Red Cross Emergency Corps and the formation of classes should be addressed to the General Superintendent.

The plan of organization includes the formation of a finance committee, consisting of men of national reputation, who shall have entire charge of the funds of the Red Cross. This course is made necessary by the increased scope of the work contemplated, and also because it is desirable, when one returns, worn and weary, from a field of work, that no question shall arise as to the proper distribution of funds.

I offer no excuse for making this appeal, beyond the vast importance of the work and the strong, ever-present desire to see that work which has been a part of my life grow into a great beneficent institution that shall be worthy of this country and its people; to see the Red Cross a badge of honor and distinction, and to know that the time will come when the active members of the American Red Cross will form the Legion d'Honneur of the United States.

This peace-time and year-round activity of the Red Cross was a part of Clara Barton's programme from the first. It was a distinctive feature of the American Red Cross, as she planned it, that its operation should not be limited to the battle-field. Her work in time of great calamity was taken over by European organizations, which in time went beyond the development of the Red Cross in America, and exhibited the full practicability of what she from the outset had believed. When she retired from the Red Cross, she took up this work as a separate activity; and she lived long enough to see the Red Cross, no longer under her direction, taking up a plan which she had long advocated. She made a little smiling comment upon it in her diary, and wished it success.

It would have gratified Clara Barton exceedingly could she have known that during and after the Great World War there would be organized throughout America, under the direction of the American Red Cross, classes for the training of people, especially women, in these and kindred lines of service. It is one more illustration of the wisdom and prevision of Clara Barton.

The years following her retirement found her active in the work of the Woman's Relief Corps, of which she had long served as national chaplain. She was also a guest of honor at two or more National Grand Army encampments, and was everywhere hailed as the friend of the soldier. During these years she seemed to grow younger rather than older. When she was past eighty-four, a newspaper reporter described her as "a middle-aged woman."

She made two visits to Chicago in her last years, and the visits did not greatly weary her. The last of these visits was in May, 1910. She was guest at a continuous round erf engagements. At the May Festival of the Social Economics Club, she shook hands with nearly two thousand people. She attended a breakfast with eleven hundred guests and shook hands with nearly all of them.

The author of this volume holds this visit in happy memory. It occupied three weeks, one of which Miss Barton spent in the home of her cousin, the author. He accompanied her to a reception given in her honor at Abraham Lincoln Center, and saw her safely on her way to a number of other engagements which she had promised to attend. She met innumerable friends, many of whom called at the house to see her, and she answered scores of letters. She rose very early in the morning and sat at her desk until late at night, and was always calm, strong, and resolute.

She had promised to speak to the young people at their meeting on Sunday evening; but when this arrangement became known there was a demand for a wider hearing. She cheerfully consented to speak in the large auditorium of the church on Sunday evening. Her voice was clear, and filled the great room; every person present heard distinctly, although she was almost ninety years of age. Nor did she forget to tease her cousin a little over the fact that she spoke to more people in the evening than he in the morning; though his morning congregation was not a small one.

Between her engagements were frequent opportunities during that week for visits with her. She talked calmly about all her experiences. She reviewed her work on the battle-field during the Civil War, and spoke with deep interest of her experiences in Constantinople where she had been near to the scene of the earlier work of Florence Nightingale. She talked of her religious convictions, and of the faith with which she was facing the future. She spoke in detail about the American Red Cross. It is only just to her memory to record that in all her conversation there was no word of bitterness or resentment, or any approach to jealousy as she saw that organization moving forward under the direction of others.

She was happy, full of fun, gracious, considerate, and interested in all that was going on in the world. When she sat in her chair at the end of a strenuous day's work, she rarely leaned back to touch the back of the seat; she had a back of her own, she said.

If the author could give to his readers a truthful impression of that visit, it would be the best possible insight into the character of Clara Barton. She combined in the rarest possible degree self-reliance and modesty. She knew that the work which she had done was a great work, but it confused her when any one told her so. She responded to every suggestion of appreciation, but she grew shy whenever she heard herself praised. Throughout the whole visit she manifested the finest quality of the cultured gentlewoman.

One thing she deeply regretted, and that was that her retirement had not yet brought her sufficient leisure to sort her papers and prepare for the writing of her biography. That such a book would be written she fully realized, and she cared much who wrote it. She was perfectly well in body and clear in mind, and what she hoped to do was to go through a vast accumulation of manuscripts and make the task of writing an easier one.

The author urged her to write the book herself, and she hoped to continue the work which she had begun and to write the story of her life in short sections. One such section she wrote and it is quoted in the first volume of this present work. But she found too much to do in helping the lives of others to pay very much attention to the record of her own life.

So the years went by and her life-work was completed and her biography remained unwritten. She was always thinking of another thing that needed to be accomplished, and saying concerning it, "Until that work is done, I cannot go to heaven."

DEATH AND RESURRECTION

Clara Barton died young. Even to those who were near her, she never seemed to grow old. At ninety there was no mark of physical infirmity upon her, nor was there any slightest slackening in the interest of the object for which so long she had cared. On her ninetieth birthday she wrote to the Reverend Percy H. Hepler:

Notwithstanding the much and more that has been said of "age" and all the stress laid upon it, I could never see and have never been able to understand how it came to be any business of ours. We have surely no control over its beginning, and, unless criminally, none over its ending. We can neither hasten nor arrest it, and how it is a matter of individual commendation I have never been able to see. I have been able to see painfully that the persistent marking of dates and adding one milestone to every year has a tendency to increase the burden of "age" and encourages a feeling of helplessness and release from activities which might be a pleasure to the possessor. I have given the exact age as recorded, lest I be suspected of trying to conceal it, but I have never, since a child, kept a "birthday" or thought of it only as a reminder by others.

Somehow it has come to me to consider strength and activity, aided so far as possible by right habits of life, as forming a more correct line of limitations than the mere passing of years.

Something similar to this she said to the author. She had no pride in her great age; she did not like to be thought of as an old lady. Years were to her merely opportunities of service, not measures of life. Notwithstanding this attitude, which prolonged her life and kept her young in spirit, Clara Barton was nearing the end of life's journey. She had a heavy cold in the winter of 1908 and 1909, but fully recovered, and never seemed better in health than in the summer of 1910 when she made her journey to Chicago referred to in the last chapter. Unfortunately, she reached New England in a cold summer storm, which seemed almost like sleet, and her exposure seriously weakened her.

She returned to Glen Echo in August, but did not fully recover her strength. That winter she had double pneumonia, and her physician told her she had but one chance of life. "I will take that chance," she said calmly. She took that chance and recovered.

But she did not grow strong again. The news of the death of her niece, Mrs. Riccius, was a great shock to her. Her heart almost ceased to beat. Always her concern for those whom she loved affected her more than anything that could happen to her.

In the summer of 1911 she made her last visit to Oxford. She made the journey with no ill effects, but the summer did not bring her permanent improvement. Long years of constant work and the serious illness of the winter had caused a slight weakness in the muscular action of the heart. Otherwise, her physicians could find no organic ailment.

When she was at work in Galveston in 1900, she was seriously ill. Her physician whispered to her nephew, Stephen, that she could live only a few hours. She overheard the word, and calling Stephen to her whispered to him, "I shall not die; don't let them frighten you." In that spirit she had met the numerous predictions of her death in the various illnesses of the years.

But it was not so after the summer of 1911. She went back to Glen Echo without her usual invigoration from her weeks in New England.

Still she did not give up. She had periods of old-time vigor. Here is an entry in her diary for Friday and Saturday, February 11 and 12, 1910:

At night I fold the wash of Monday for ironing to-morrow. Up at six: commenced ironing and continued till all was done, at one o'clock. At night took the clothes from the frames and put them in place, and felt that for once one thing was done as it should be. 'Twas finished before leaving.

She commented on the bad behavior of the Suffragettes, whom she believed to be injuring their cause by unwomanly conduct.

A week later:

We moved the large desk to my chambers from the dining room below. A spacious desk it makes. One should be able to write a History of the World with such accommodations.

She was concerned for her old and faithful horse, Baba; and, when one night he was out in pasture and it turned somewhat cold, she could not sleep, but got up at four o'clock in the morning, fed Baba a full feed of corn, and some fruit from the table, and went back to bed.

Her diaries of 1907 had been neglected. She tried to bring them up to date from her pencil notes:

It seems to have been a hard year for me. It makes me tired to read it.

That spring she trimmed the rosebushes and set out flowers. A fire broke out in her room; the floor grew hot from the burning-out of the soot in a sheet-iron drum; and she got water and wet the floor till the chimney and pipe had burned out.

She mourned over the death of Mark Twain:

We have lost something very precious in his rich van of humor. There are losses that are never made good. We have not another Whittier, or another Mark Twain.

The diary for 1911 begins with the multitude of Christmas greetings received and sent. The process took her several days and left her very weary. This led her to reflect that she was kept so busy with inconsequential writing that she had no time to do the writing she so much wanted to do, her Life and the story of her work.

She had an invitation from the "Review of Reviews" to write an article on "Hospitals and Hospital Nurses of the Civil War." She declined, on the ground that she knew nothing about the subject! She had not been a nurse, and did not pretend to write as if she had been.

This was in January, 1911, and in February she had pneumonia, but recovered.

That summer she had two or more visits from a man who expressed himself with great emphasis on the subject of the immodesty of woman's dress; she agreed with him, but felt it was hardly fair to talk to her as if she were to blame or needed to be convinced. "But really, he is not without provocation. Huge hats, dangerous hatpins, hobble and harem skirts, and the conduct of the Suffragettes are hard to defend."

Most of her visitors just ran in from Washington, and ran away, hurrying back to the city. One day an old friend came and spent the afternoon and the night:

This day has been extremely social. It is really refreshing to see a man who has a little time, and not always in a rush with a watch in his hand to catch the next train. I fail to believe that these nervous persons accomplish the most, or are actually the best business men. Hurry is a habit with them. They make everyone uncomfortable with their own selfish plans, and all are relieved to get them off and see them go.

In April she began to feel that she could take up and finish her History of the Red Cross.

In that month, Dr. Hubbell was grafting trees. She had always coveted the learning of that art; so she took lessons in tree-grafting. Also, she began to learn the use of the typewriter, at the age of eighty-nine.

She was interested in the trial of the Los Angeles dynamiters; in the activity of Mr. Bryan, whom she wished the Democrats might have sense enough to nominate; and, if a Democrat had to be elected, she, a Republican, wished it might be he.

She read a "Life" of the Bronte sisters. She read in good English translations "The Apology" of Socrates, the address of Xenophon to his army, some of the orations of Demosthenes, and other good old literature. She read the daily papers, and commented on all important current happenings.

She provided a final home for Baba, eighty miles away in Virginia, bade him a fond farewell, and sent money regularly to keep him well fed.

In May she wrote her will; the same will that was probated a few months later.

She commented on the great Suffrage parade in London, with satisfaction that the cause of Woman Suffrage was gaining, but with rather sad reflection that, fallible as men were, she had found women even more so; and she thought suffrage would be a blessing, but not an unmixed blessing.

She salted down eggs in early summer, and in the late fall they were candled and found good. She oversaw the management of her household, and part of the time she did her own cooking, in this, her last summer.

These citations are given, not because they are important in themselves, but because they give little glimpses of her life in her last few months. Certainly she did not permit herself to rust out in mind or body. A physical examination after her recovery from pneumonia in 1911 found her with every bodily organ sound, but with a pulse somewhat easily disturbed.

On Christmas, 1911, her ninetieth birthday, she sent to the world through the press this message:

Please deliver for me a message of peace and good-will to all the world for Christmas. I am feeling much better to-day, and have every hope of spending a pleasant and joyful Christmas, my ninetieth birthday.

Her hope was fulfilled and she celebrated her ninetieth Christmas with quiet but cheerful festivities.

As the rigor of winter came on, she was taken again with double pneumonia. In the weeks that followed, hope alternated with fear, until, on April 12, 1912, at nine o'clock in the morning, she cried out, "Let me go; let me go," and the earthly life of Clara Barton came to its close.

A few days before she died, she talked with her nephew, Stephen, concerning her funeral, and chose for herself the principal speakers. She desired that her long-time and trusted friend, Mrs. John Λ. Logan, should say the principal words in a preliminary service to be held in Glen Echo, and that at the main funeral service to be held in Oxford, the chief speakers should be her friend the Reverend Percy Epler, and her cousin, the Reverend

William E. Barton. She mentioned others as those whom she would be glad to have share in the services, and her wishes were carried out.

On Sunday afternoon a brief service was held at Glen Echo. The Reverend John Van Schaick, Jr., pastor of the "Church of our Father," Universalist, of Washington, read the Scripture and offered prayer.

The Reverend W. W. Curry, a veteran of the Civil War, paid her a brief and heartfelt tribute, which was followed by three addresses, by Chaplain Coudon, of the House of Representatives, Mrs. John A. Logan, and the Honorable Peter V. De Graw.

The body reached Oxford in the early morning of April 16th, accompanied by Mr. and Mrs. Stephen E. Barton; Francis Atwater, of Meriden, Connecticut; Dr. Eugene Underhill, President of the Nurses' College of Philadelphia; and Dr. Julian B. Hubbell. It had long since become apparent that no church in Oxford would contain the congregation. The service was held in Memorial Hall, which was filled to overflowing, and it was estimated that as many as five hundred people were unable to secure admission. Delegations were present from many cities, and representatives of various patriotic organizations were in attendance. Floral tributes had been received from many parts of the Nation, and a magnificent wreath was sent by the Grand Duchess of Baden. The casket was almost hidden with flowers. Above it was a great red cross made of carnations, and upon the casket was a large bouquet of red roses, the flowers which all her life she most had loved and which had belonged to her family since the days of the Wars of the Roses.

Appropriate music was rendered by the Schumann Quartet of Boston, who sang sympathetically Tennyson's "Crossing the Bar." The opening words of Scripture, "I am the Resurrection and the Life," and of the comforting sentences, "Let not your heart be troubled," were recited by the Reverend William E. Barton.

The Reverend John P. Marvin read the Bible lesson. Mrs. Allen L. Joslyn read a beautiful tribute from the Town of Oxford, and Mr. J. Brainard Hall, of Worcester, a veteran of the Civil War, represented the Woman's Relief Corps in a tribute which included the placing of a silk flag upon her breast as she lay in the casket.

The two formal addresses were then delivered by the ministers whom she had chosen, the Reverend Percy E. Epler, pastor of the Adams Square Congregational Church of Worcester, and the Reverend William E. Barton, of Oak Park, Illinois.

For an hour after the service, the people filed through the hall and past the casket for a last look at her face.

The body was then borne to the hearse, escorted by a guard of the Grand Army of the Republic, its chaplain, H. A. Philbrook, and the color sergeant leading the procession.

The North Oxford Cemetery has a beautiful and sightly elevation, containing the largest lot in the enclosure where for generations the Bartons have been buried. There her body was laid to rest, the hands of old soldiers lowering it to its last resting-place.

It was a glorious day in the spring. The services had begun at one o'clock, and, as the procession entered the cemetery, the sun was near its setting. The cemetery was thronged with people, the crowd containing many who had been unable to secure admission to the hall. The music in the hall had been rendered by a male quartet. Clara Barton had never cared greatly for music, but the music that she liked best was that rendered by male voices or sung heartily by a congregation. In the cemetery one hymn was sung, "Nearer, my God, to Thee," the whole great congregation joining in the singing.

A prayer was offered by a blind soldier, Chaplain Simmons, of Worcester.

The closing scene can hardly be described. Dr. Barton took his place at the head of the grave, holding in his hand a large bunch of red roses, and the place at the foot of the grave was taken by the Reverend Doctor Tyler, "Father Tyler," a venerable and saintly man, who had buried the fathers and mothers of the Barton family in Oxford. He stood with his long white beard and silver hair irradiated by the sunset; and, in a voice tender, and reverent and comforting, spoke the following words:

In the few words with which I am to close this service, I shall indulge in no repetition of what has been said, and so well said, by the principal speakers on this occasion, eulogistic of the life and the life-work of the most celebrated woman of the world, whose mortal remains we have here deposited in the resting-place of her choice, among the beloved of her family. My thought will lead you in another direction, which has hardly been alluded to, if at all, in the eloquent addresses to which we have listened.

As we look into the grave and bid farewell to the mortal remains of Clara Barton, we instinctively are led to ask ourselves, "Where is Clara Barton who for more than ninety years made them the agencies of her great work in the world?" The life, the spirit, the soul—has that been destroyed by death? Does utter annihilation follow the development and growth of such a life?

As a Christian minister I feel I give a voice to the scriptural revelation of life and immortality when I say emphatically, "No!" She still lives! She has entered the pearly gates of die Holy City and is now walking the golden streets of the New Jerusalem! She has been born again into the newer life, as Christ taught the inquiring Pharisee, and oar aged friend is now among the youngest of the Immortal!

I feel that while the Nation mourns because of her going, all heaven is rejoicing because of her coming! This great gathering of friends who sorrowfully bid her good-bye is but typical of the greater multitude of friends who have gone before her, and who, with smiling faces and extended hands, have given her a heavenly welcome. In a little while, after the pain of our grief has softened, we shall be glad, and bless God that He has taken her to Himself.

Now we know nothing, or but little, of the vocations and employments of the eternal life; except concerning the angels as "ministering spirits" they are nowhere revealed; but reasoning from analogy I am convinced that as doing is necessary to our happiness here, so a busy activity must be essential to the happiness of Heaven. In this regard we may be assured that Clara Barton will not be found wanting.

And so by faith beholding her as a happy spirit in the glorious life to which she has been promoted, we may all join in giving to these relics of her earthly life, as they peacefully rest for always in their last home, a heartfelt, loving

Good-Bye!

At the close of this brief and touching address, Dr. Barton spoke the words of committal; and, as he uttered, "Dust to dust, ashes to ashes," dropped upon the lowered casket the large red roses, and pronounced the benediction.

Just then a mother stepped up and whispered, "My little girl was born in Clara Barton's birthplace; in the very room where she was born. Will you baptize her, and will you do it now?"

"Bring her to me," said the minister, "and I will christen her 'Clara Barton.'"

So the name was bestowed in that hour upon another little girl, whose parents sought that the spirit that had lived in Clara Barton might live again in the life of their own daughter.

Two years from the following summer, the world witnessed a desolating war, and the months that followed wrought their inevitable destiny by plunging America into the seething conflict. Long before America formally entered the fight, the American Red Cross was active in measures of relief for the sorrowing nations of Europe. When, at length, the United States itself entered the war, the Red Cross blazed forth in every community between the oceans. Churches and town halls and private homes became depots where supplies were collected, bandages rolled, and workers trained. Hospitals, in our own country and along the battle-front, were erected and equipped. To them went thousands of American young women, each one of them wearing, on her arm or cap, the symbol which Clara Barton brought back to her own land after the close of the Franco-Prussian War. In their heroism and their deeds of mercy, Clara Barton lived again.

THE END

Discover more lost history from BIG BYTE BOOKS

Made in the USA
Columbia, SC
24 January 2022